American Musicological Society-Music Library Association Reprint Series

The American Musicological Society and the Music Library Association have undertaken to sponsor the republication of a series of scholarly works now out of print, translations of important studies, essays, etc. An editorial committee representing both organizations has been appointed to plan and supervise the series, in cooperation with Dover Publications, Inc., of New York.

Sir John Hawkins, *A General History of the Science and Practice of Music*
W. H., A. F., and A. E. Hill, *Antonio Stradivari, His Life and Work*
Curt Sachs, *Real-Lexikon der Musikinstrumente,* new revised, enlarged edition
The Complete Works of Franz Schubert (19 volumes), the Breitkopf & Härtel Critical Edition of 1884-1897 *(Franz Schubert's Werke. Kritisch durchgesehene Gesammtausgabe.)*
Charles Read Baskervill, *The Elizabethan Jig and Related Song Drama*
George Ashdown Audsley, *The Art of Organ-Building,* corrected edition
Emanuel Winternitz, *Musical Autographs from Monteverdi to Hindemith,* corrected edition
William Chappell, *Popular Music of the Olden Time,* 1859 edition
The Breitkopf Thematic Catalogue
Otto Kinkeldey, *The Organ and Clavier in the Music of the 16th Century*
Andreas Ornithoparcus, *Musice active micrologus,* together with John Dowland's translation, *A. O. his Micrologus, or Introduction, Containing the Art of Singing*
O. G. T. Sonneck, *Early Concert-life in America (1731-1800)*
Giambattista Mancini, *Practical Reflections on the Figurative Art of Singing* (translation by Pietro Buzzi)

A.M.S. - M.L.A. JOINT REPRINT COMMITTEE

Sydney Beck, The New York Public Library, Chairman
Barry S. Brook, Queens College
Hans Lenneberg, University of Chicago
Nino Pirrotta, Harvard University
Gustave Reese, New York University

THE
ELIZABETHAN
JIG

RICHARD TARLTON
(From Harl. MS 3885, fol. 19)

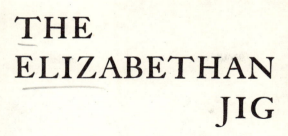

THE ELIZABETHAN JIG

AND RELATED SONG DRAMA

By CHARLES READ BASKERVILL

DOVER PUBLICATIONS, INC.
NEW YORK

This Dover edition, first published in 1965, is an unabridged and unaltered republication of the work first published by the University of Chicago Press, Chicago, Illinois, in 1929.

Library of Congress Catalog Card Number 65-12255

Manufactured in the United States of America

Dover Publications, Inc.
180 Varick Street
New York 14, N.Y.

PREFACE

THIS study of the stage jig has been in progress inter-
mittently for fifteen years. In 1913 I wrote a paper
on "Extant Elizabethan Jigs," supplementing on the
English side what Bolte had done on the Continental in his
*Singspiele der englischen Komödianten und ihrer Nachfolger in
Deutschland, Holland und Skandinavien.* The article was with-
held until I could consult the ballad collections in England, but
a summary of its more important aspects was published in the
Program of the Meeting of the Modern Language Association
for 1913 (see *Publications of the Modern Language Association*,
Vol. XXIX, Appendix, p. xxvii). The texts of the ballads and
a large body of the notes from which this survey has been made
were secured in the summer of 1914. Unfortunately for my
peace of mind, it was the less tangible problems of the jig that
proved especially interesting, and other studies in which I was
engaged—dealing with folk drama, the minor dramatic forms
of strollers and comedians, and other literary types reflecting
popular taste—promised to give a better understanding of its
art even if they did not throw definite light on its history. Some
of these studies have been published and are cited from time to
time here; some I hope to complete ultimately. These and other
tasks, serious interruptions to my work, and the sheer burden of
preparing the text of this volume have delayed its publication
until now. In many respects the final results of my labor have
been disappointing. The gaps in the records are innumerable,
and the evidence for many a point is tantalizingly vague and
indirect. But even such material as I have been able to gather
gives, I believe, a fairly correct general view of the rise, vogue,
and decline of the jig, of its background, its art, and its influence. Though much of this material lacks literary significance,
the mass of it contributes its share to an understanding of the
poetic and dramatic activities of a whole age—one that resulted
in the greatest creative outburst in the history of English
literature.

The number of references required is so large that I have
felt it necessary to reduce bibliographical detail in the notes as
far as possible. In particular, editions of plays are not often
specified. For most of the important dramatists including
Shakespeare, modern texts with act and scene division have
been used, supplemented in the case of Jonson by the folios.
Scattering plays are sometimes cited by line, especially those
printed by the Malone Society, and sometimes by signature,
either from the originals or from the Farmer facsimiles. In general I have used modernized forms for titles of the better known
works, and of books, plays, pamphlets, and ballads frequently
cited here, in many cases following the original spelling only for
the first occurrence of the title. The policy of using quotation
marks for the titles of the jigs and singspiele, which vary from
very brief songs to pieces of considerable length, has led to some
illogicalities that seem unavoidable. Ballad entries on the
Stationers' Register are cited in roman with quotation marks,
except that where both roman and italic occur in the same
entry in Arber's *Transcript*, the distinction has been kept at
least in my first citation. The spelling of words with majus-
cules has been avoided both in titles taken from the Register
and elsewhere. For the late Restoration period, I have usually
not attempted to differentiate the type of various styles and
sizes which is used in the complicated titles of many songs and
ballads from plays and songbooks.

It is a pleasure to thank those who have helped in the work.
The publication of my first study in outline caused three students of the jig to offer material. The late Thornton S. Graves
turned over to me a considerable number of allusions collected by 1914, some of which have not been noted by other
students. Soon afterward W. J. Lawrence also sent me a
small collection of references. In 1917 Hyder E. Rollins, learning of my work, put into my hands an excellent paper on the
farce jig which he had prepared for publication, and later added
some notes. Beyond this acknowledgment and the list of earlier
discussions in the field which is given at the opening of the
first chapter, it has not seemed feasible to indicate in detail all
of my indebtedness to individuals or to printed sources. In
fact, I do not know in many cases whether my first acquaintance

with a particular passage came from my own reading, from other students, or from older works on the drama. Further, the material both of Mr. Lawrence and of Mr. Rollins has since been supplemented and published by them, and their discussions are cited in my text. An article on "The Elizabethan Stage Jig" by Mr. Lawrence, which shows a clearer understanding of the subject than his earlier writings, has appeared in his *Pre-Restoration Stage Studies* since my text was completed. In another phase of the work—the effort to decipher some of the blurred passages in the foreign pieces published here—Archer Taylor and Leonard Bloomfield have given generous assistance.

I am under great obligation to Stephen Gaselee, former librarian of the Pepys Library, who in 1913 went through the Pepys Collection of Broadsides in search of jigs, sending me copies of some of the ballads, and in 1914 made it possible for me to work through the collection during his vacation. The present librarian of the Pepys Library has kindly permitted the copying of a number of ballads and given me an opportunity to consult the collection again in 1924. To the authorities of the British Museum, of the Bodleian, and of the Cambridge University Library also, my thanks are due for many courtesies shown while I was at work in these libraries and for permission to have various rotographs made. I am indebted to the staff of the University of Chicago Library—and through them to the officials of other libraries, particularly the Dulwich College Library and the Berlin Library—for securing rotographs of several important texts printed in Part II. The librarian of All Souls College, Oxford, was instrumental in obtaining permission for me to have a part of MS 155 rotographed. To the officials of the University of Chicago Press I am indebted for help at various stages in the publication of this book—for securing a special subsidy for publication, for advice in regard to form, for much pains in the effort to reproduce old texts, and so forth. My thanks must be expressed also to the American Council of Learned Societies, which granted a subvention to meet in part the expense of rotographing and of preparing copy.

My great debt in this, as in all of my work, has been to my

wife, Catharine Q. Baskervill. In searching for and copying
material, in weighing its significance, in organizing the book and
revising it, and in verifying references, she has aided me
steadily. I have had to rely on her particularly in discussions
of music and dance.

C. R. B.

UNIVERSITY OF CHICAGO
July 1, 1928

CONTENTS

PART I. THE HISTORY OF THE JIG

PART II. TEXTS

PART I
THE HISTORY OF THE JIG

CHAPTER I

THE BACKGROUND OF THE JIG

FROM the era of Tarlton to the end of the reign of James I or even later, contemporary allusions go to show that the jig enjoyed an enormous popularity with London playgoers. This fact has been generally recognized since the time of Malone, and various editors and historians of the drama have written brief accounts of the type.[1] When the greatness of the vogue is taken into consideration, the amount of material that remains for a study of the jig seems meager, but the *genre* never rose to the dignity of literature. The jig was the darling of the groundlings, not the *literati*. Even the allusions come largely from satirists and moralists. Yet enough definite information can be assembled to warrant a fuller survey of the field than has so far been attempted.

The surviving pieces that can be identified as jigs furnish a natural point of departure. Clearly the characteristic stage jig of the period was an afterpiece in the form of a brief farce which was sung and accompanied by dancing. The extant English dialogues that would correspond to this description are "Attowell's Jig," "Rowland's Godson," "Singing Simpkin," "The Blackman," and a piece which occurs without title in a Dulwich College manuscript and is called throughout this volume "The Wooing of Nan." To these may be added "The Cheaters

---

[1] See Malone, *Prolegomena* to the *Plays of Shakespeare* (1803), III, 142–49; Dilke, *Old English Plays*, VI (1815), 326–31; Collier, *History of English Dramatic Poetry* (1831), III, 378–81; *ibid.* (1879), III, 338–40; Collier, *New Facts regarding the Life of Shakespeare* (1835), pp. 17–20; Halliwell-Phillipps, *Tarlton's Jests*, Shakespeare Society, pp. xviii–xxvi; Hazlitt, *Bibliographical Collections and Notes*, 2d Ser., p. 20; Bolte, *Singspiele der englischen Komödianten und ihrer Nachfolger in Deutschland, Holland und Skandinavien* (1893), dealing with the jig on the Continent; Hönig, *Anzeiger für deutsches Altertum*, XXII (1896), 296–319, a review of the preceding; Creizenach, *English Drama in the Age of Shakespeare*, pp. 312–14; *Works of Behn*, edited by Summers, III, 477–78, an extended note based on material furnished by W. J. Lawrence; Greg, *Henslowe's Diary*, II, 189; Lawrence, "He's for a Jig or ——," *Times Literary Supplement*, July 3, 1919; Rollins, *Pepysian Garland*, pp. xiv–xx; Chambers, *Elizabethan Stage*, II, 551–53.

Cheated" by Thomas Jordan, though it was written in the second half of the seventeenth century and not for the theater. The jig was also featured by English actors on foreign tours, and in consequence a great deal of Continental material bears on the English form. Over thirty German, Dutch, and even Swedish "singspiele" have been preserved, representing more or less closely the art of the English jig. They include, for example, the most famous of all the jigs, "Rowland," which has not survived in English. These pieces, both English and foreign, have at least three characters and develop a certain complication of plot. There is, too, a jig of "Simon and Susan," a wooing dialogue with four characters and a naïve attempt at plot, which according to the title was designed for country pastimes. The name jig is also attached to four ballads that are simple dialogues of two characters: "A New Northern Jig" and "The Soldier's Farewell to his Love," both sentimental; "Kit and Pegge," a comic dialogue of lovers; and "Clod's Carol," which satirizes the follies and vices of women. A vulgar dialogue with a narrative opening and a few narrative phrases, "The Soldier's Delight in the North," which was registered in 1640, is described as "A New North-countrey Jigge." The ballad jig printed in *A Quest of Enquirie* late in the sixteenth century is for one singer. After the Restoration six extant ballads that are of various types but in no case of pure dialogue form were published with the word jig in the title. There remain a large number of jigs of a simpler and more lyric nature, which are discussed chiefly in this and the following chapter. They range from medieval lyrics of a few lines to contemporary songs of several stanzas, and dialogue form is no more characteristic in them than in the mass of popular songs generally. From the point of view of origins, the jigs of this class are to my mind of the greatest significance.

So far, only those pieces have been taken into account which in one way or another are definitely recognized as jigs. The field at its narrowest, however, cannot be limited in this way. Even after the term had become firmly fixed in professional and literary usage, songs for jigs, like other songs, must usually have taken their titles from their content; and when the first novelty of the stage vogue had worn off, they were probably not often designated jigs in their titles. Otherwise we should undoubtedly be able to identify a much larger number of jigs. In the case of the lost "ballad of *a newe northerne Dialogue betwene Will, Sone, and the warriner, and howe Reynold Peares gott faire Nannye to his Loue*," licensed in August, 1591, the title happens to be full enough to show that the ballad was a song drama requiring a cast of several singers. Nashe attributes to Deloney a jig of "John for the King," which is presumably the lost piece of that name entered on the Register merely as a ballad.[1] Only three out of the six farce jigs in English are anywhere called jigs, but the farce specimens are recognizable by their form even when the term is lacking. To judge from the ballads called jigs which are dialogues of two singers, the jig of this type is not distinguishable, however, in form, in theme, or in tone from a mass of dialogue ballads printed in the sixteenth and seventeenth centuries, the term apparently having to do with the method of performance only. A dialogue entered on the Register as a ballad with the opening words "Margarett my sweetest" for title, and printed as a broadside under the name "The Souldiers Farewel to his love" survives also in a form in the Percy Folio Manuscript without title and is there called simply a jig. Except for this fact, the piece would have no more significance for the student of the jig than scores of other dialogues that strew the ballad literature of the time. Probably a number of such dialogues were written especially as jigs, and perhaps others were so regularly sung with dance as to be recognized jigs. But presumably any ballad that commended itself to the performers might be presented with dance and was accordingly a jig. In the same way, on the basis of the various brief songs, usually not even in dialogue, which go under the name of jig, a tremendous number of miscellaneous songs belonging to the sixteenth and seventeenth centuries might well have been jigs. Nashe, in fact, gives a conception of "jig" as merely one of the recognized terms for lyric when he mentions together at the end of *A Countercuffe giuen to Martin Iunior* "certaine Hayes, Iigges, Rimes, Roundelayes, and Madrigals."

The prominence of the word jig in the vocabulary of London at the end of the sixteenth century is of course due to the spec-

[1] See p. 295 below.

tacular success of song-and-dance drama in the hands of professionals. But the fact that the vogue of the word coincided with a great expansion of song and dance on the stage does not mean that the jig originated there. According to my own theory—based on the evidence of this study as a whole—by the middle of the sixteenth century a variety of dance or song-and-dance acts were current among the people, taking the name jig from the type of dance most characteristic in them; these were exploited by the comedians during an era when song and dance were generally popular on the stage and folk elements introduced in a spirit of antimasque were in especial favor; finally, with the natural tendency to feature terminal song and dance in the theater, the jig became primarily an afterpiece. A special development of a professional sort naturally followed. Yet throughout the history of the stage jig, its popular origin had a marked influence on both material and tone.

The difficulty in defining the field of the jig is thus a much more general one than that of simply identifying certain songs as jigs. Before the term became current in literature, and afterward as well, a similar art was frequently covered not only by the word ballad but by such broad terms as dance, song, and game. This is a point that needs to be strongly enforced from the beginning in any attempt to deal with the background of the stage jig. The professional jig, in fact, is of far less significance as a fad of the London populace when Elizabethan drama was at the peak than it is as an expression and a development of a general art of song-with-dance which was very prevalent in England during the sixteenth century.

To understand the prevalence of this art we need to go back to medieval pastimes, where dance was commonly accompanied by song and frequently by pantomime or mimesis. During the Middle Ages and the Renaissance a great variety of sports and pastimes were popular with all classes. The occasion might be a simple gathering on the village green of a summer afternoon or in the hall on a winter night. It might be a marriage feast, a harvest supper, or a local wake or fair. More likely it was one of the great festivals celebrated pretty generally throughout Western Europe, as those of Easter, May, Whitsuntide, Midsummer, or the Christmas season. The nature of the festivities depended partly on the occasion celebrated, so that the same group varied its pastimes at Christmas, May Day, Midsummer, or Harvest. Often the chief feature was some modification of ancient pagan ritual, but even here the different parishes had their special customs. Different groups also claimed some particular festival which they observed with special rites—the school boys Innocents' Day, the school girls St. Catherine's Day, and so on. In the towns the organized trades celebrated their own feasts with song and dance and the great festival occasions with pageants, processions, and often formal plays. The milkmaids had their merrymakings,[1] the Londoners their feasts at taverns and guildhalls, and the courtly their disguisings and masques.

Of course such revelry was often of the most informal sort; but the general tendency, especially on the great festival occasions, was to organize it under leaders, usually a lord and a lady or a king and a queen, with attendants who paralleled the functionaries of a castle or a royal court. The leaders presided over the pastimes and often played a prominent part in them. No doubt the celebrants generally engaged in social dancing, in the pastimes that have survived as singing games of children, and in sports and contests of various sorts, the festival king or queen awarding prizes in contests or dispensing punishments in forfeit games. But there was a special group of entertainers representing the talent of the community. Some of these prepared a group dance like the morris, or a mummers' play, or perhaps even a dramatic performance of some sort drawn from a more sophisticated source. Much of the entertainment, however, seems to have been of a simpler type, consisting of comic speeches or of special dances and songs by one or two characters. At least one disard in the rôle of fool or daemon commonly took a conspicuous part in the procedure, at times as leader. After the local celebration the whole organization was often carried to the neighboring villages, and troupes from villages in the same general region exchanged visits. Groups of performers also frequently went on rounds of visits to the castles of neighboring lords and to the more important towns during their

[1] For milkmaids' festivals and songs, see Brand, *Popular Antiquities* (1849), I, 214, 217, 252; Chappell, *Popular Music of the Olden Time*, I, 282, 296.

holidays, becoming for the time bodies of strolling players. To the whole procedure of the organized group various names were applied, like revels, disguising, interlude, or game. The most comprehensive term from the time of Chaucer till the middle of the sixteenth century was game. In default then of a better general term, the word game is often used in the ensuing pages with the meaning it bore around 1500.

There is of course no occasion for a detailed discussion of the games here,[1] but in view of the importance of shepherd pastimes in the literary allusions to the jig, some of the evidence for pastoral games in the sixteenth and seventeenth centuries may not be out of place.[2] The references to shepherd pastimes taken collectively can hardly represent a mere literary convention. Barnes in Ode 11 of his *Parthenophil and Parthenophe* pictures the May game of shepherds with the crowning of the chosen nymph as queen. In an account of pastimes at the end of Book I of *Arcadia*, Sidney describes two groups of shepherds as dancing and singing responsively a song of requited and of unrequited love. A wooing dialogue with an opening very similar to that of "The Wooing of Nan" is sung by a shepherd and a shepherdess in Browne's *Britannia's Pastorals* (Bk. I, Song 3, ll. 241–82). A poem by Chester in which a shepherd introduces pastoral pastimes of "A merrimt of christmas"[3] at Lleweny ends with the words:

A homely cuntry hornepipe we will daunce
A sheapheards prety Gigg to make him sport
and sing A madringall or roundelay
to please our Lordlike sheapheard lord of vs
take hands take hands our hartes lett vs Advaunce
and strive to please his humour with A daunce.

[1] See *Studies in Philology*, XVII (1920), 19–87, for my survey of the dramatic games in vogue in the Middle Ages. Records are of course fuller in the fifteenth and sixteenth centuries, but it can hardly be doubted that there was an actual expansion of the games with an increasing influence of professional art. Their importance in the artistic and social life of the folk during the sixteenth century is indicated clearly enough even in the records of song and dance at feast, bridal, wake, and fair which are cited in this and the following chapter.

[2] See *Modern Philology*, XIV, 237–39, 242–44, for pastoral figures like Robin and Wat in the Middle Ages.

[3] See *Poems by Salusbury and Chester*, ed. Brown, pp. 19–20.

In *The Winter's Tale* (IV, iv) Perdita speaks in a general way of those who play in Whitsun pastorals. Indications are that summer games with pastoral features prevailed in the Cotswold region at least from the latter part of the sixteenth century till the middle of the seventeenth. About 1592 a shepherd game, with a king and a queen and a clown who sang, was presented before Elizabeth at Sudeley. Drayton in his ninth eclogue pictures the Cotswold shepherds as gathered for their annual game. One feature is a dialogue song about love—with queries somewhat after the manner of the popular romantic song "Walsingham"—which was sung at the command of the "clownish" shepherd king. During the first half of the seventeenth century the Cotswold games were highly developed and seem to have furnished pastime for the Stuart kings.[1] The courtly interest in this type of game may account in part for the number of references scattered through the madrigals to shepherds' pastimes with their queens, their processions, their songs and dances.[2]

The vital union of song with festival dance during the Middle Ages is generally recognized.[3] By the beginning of the sixteenth century, instrumental music was rapidly replacing song for the social dance among the cultured, and the simple carols were to some extent losing their hold. Among the folk also there was probably a growth away from the art of the singing game—a process which finally relegated song for social dance to the singing games of children. Yet throughout the sixteenth century the combination of song with dance remained a living and creative force. Elyot, for example, giving the names of special dances, refers to those "taken as they be nowe . . . . of the firste wordes of the dittie, whiche the songe comprehendeth wherof the daunse was made."[4] In 1576 Gascoigne speaks of music of the voice for dancing;[5] and at the same period Northbrooke represents his contemporaries as dancing "with dis-

[1] For these various details in regard to the Cotswold games see *Modern Philology*, XIV, 244-47.

[2] See, for example, Fellowes, *English Madrigal Verse*, pp. 121, 136, 147, 195, 218, 223, 248-49.

[3] For some illustrations, see Chambers, *Mediaeval Stage*, I, 160-71.

[4] *Governour*, Everyman's Library, p. 93.

[5] *Works*, ed. Cunliffe, II, 553.

ordinate gestures, and with monstrous thumping of the feete, to pleasant soundes, to wanton songs, to dishonest verses."[1] In the *Discourse of English Poetrie* (1586) Webbe comments on the general impulse toward the production of song for dance in his day:

neither is there anie tune or stroke which may be sung or plaide on instruments, which hath not some poetical ditties framed according to the numbers thereof, some to Rogero, some to Trenchmore, to downe right Squire, to Galliardes, to Pauines, to Iygges, to Brawles, to all manner of tunes which euerie Fidler knowes better then my selfe.[2]

While Webbe does not say that the ditties are for dance, he mentions only dances. The first three represent popular native dance tunes; the galliard, the pavan, and the brawl are courtly dances. The process which Webbe describes is illustrated in Gascoigne's *Adventures of Master F. J.*: Ferdinand, "calling the musitions, caused them softly to sounde the Tynternall, when he clearing his voyce did *Alla Napolitana* applie these verses following, unto the measure."[3] The performance is called a "singing daunce, or daunsing song." The connection is implied in Florio's translation of *chiarantana* as a "kinde of Caroll or song full of leapings like a Scotish gigge." It is important to keep constantly in mind the conventionality of dance with song, for the surviving songs themselves can only rarely be expected to show a connection with dance, and more rarely still is the method of performance described.

This conventional union explains the large number of terms that were used interchangeably for song and for dance. "Carol," "round" or "roundel," and "ballet" or "ballad" came out of the Middle Ages, and they remained in use for both song and dance in spite of the change in meaning that "ballad" underwent in the sixteenth century. "Barginet," which in the form "bargaret" is found in *The Flower and the Leaf* (l. 348), is the

[1] *Treatise against Dicing, Dancing*, etc., Shakespeare Society, p. 171.

[2] See Gregory Smith, *Elizabethan Critical Essays*, I, 272.

[3] See *Works of Gascoigne*, ed. Cunliffe, I, 398–400. For directions for dancing a tinternel, see Rawlinson Poet. MS 108, fol. 10.

name of a dance mentioned in *The Adventures of Master F. J.*[1]
and of a song by Lodge in *England's Helicon*. "Bransle" or
"brawl," introduced into England as the name of a dance, remained distinctively a dance term, but in the lines from *The
Faerie Queene* (III, x, 8),

> Now making layes of love and lovers paine,
> Bransles, ballads, virelayes, and verses vaine,

we find Spenser late in the sixteenth century extending "bransle" to cover "love song." It is natural enough that the name
of a dance should come to include the song that accompanied
it and finally to be applicable to the song itself. This I take to
be the case with "jig," like "ballad" commonly used for both
song and dance.

The earliest use of "jig" for song or dance which has been
traced occurs slightly after the middle of the sixteenth century,
though the term might easily have been current among the
people for generations before that time.[2] Alexander Scott's
"Ballat maid to the Derisioun and Scorne of wantoun Wemen"
contains the lines:

> Sum luvis new cum to toun
> With jeigis to mak thame joly;
> Sum luvis dance vp and doun
> To meiss thair malancoly;
> Sum luvis lang trollie lolly.[3]

Grattan Flood in his *History of Irish Music* (p. 160) calls attention to a letter of Sir Henry Sidney to Queen Elizabeth in
1569 in which reference is made to the dancing of jigs by the
Anglo-Irish ladies of Galway. Perhaps the first definite use of
the word for song which has survived occurs in the second edition of Foxe's *Acts and Monuments* in 1570, where certain lyrics
are called "Scottishe Gigges and rymes" (I, 470). *Misogonus*,
variously dated from 1560 to 1580, contains in II, ii, a play on

---

[1] See *Works of Gascoigne*, ed. Cunliffe, I, 398.

[2] Pulver declares that, to judge from its musical character, the jig "was danced in
England long before it was named." "Many authorities," he adds, "mention an early
fourteenth century tune which, they say, is virtually a Jig, but I have not been able to
locate and examine it" (*Proceedings of the Musical Association*, XL, 80).

[3] See *Bannatyne Manuscript*, Hunterian Club, I, 363. Cited in *New English Dictionary*.

the word jig as dance.[1] By 1581 the jig was established among the social dances of the upper classes, to judge from the first Preface of Riche's *Farewell to Militarie profession*, and in the following year Gosson includes the dancing of jigs among the common devices of the stage.[2]

Several of the examples cited in the preceding paragraph refer to the jig as Scottish, and the earliest entry on the Stationers' Register under the name jig is that of "A New Northern Jig," licensed in January, 1591. The adjectives Scottish or northern are, in fact, so frequently linked with the word jig in its earlier occurrences as to suggest that the attention of the London public was first attracted by a type of song with dance which came out of the north.[3] The Scottish jig evidently had a distinctive musical form and was characterized by especially vigorous dance action.[4] Possibly some quality of quaintness or vigor in the northern jig made an unusual appeal to the London theatergoer and started the vogue. On the other hand, it is far more likely that this popularity was only one phase of a general vogue of northern song. Songs were constantly being advertised in their titles as northern or Scottish or as sung to northern or Scottish tunes.[5] To the metropolis these terms probably meant little more than rustic or provincial ordinarily. There are, however, some later ballad dialogues discussed in chapter vi that may have come from Scotland.

---

[1] The large number of vulgar puns on "jig" in the Renaissance suggests that the word had in some form a sexual connotation among the people, though the popular expansion of the term in connection with dance would doubtless be a sufficient explanation. See Dunbar, *Poems*, ed. Schipper, p. 194, note on l. 79; *Cynthia's Revels*, IV, i, 159–60; *Roxburghe Ballads*, IV, 369, VII, 229, 327, and IX, 685. Compare "gig" for a light woman in *NED* and Bradley-Stratmann.

[2] *Playes Confuted in fiue Actions*, Sig. G. See *Publications of the Modern Language Association*, XLI (1926), 673, for a passage from Bright's *Treatise of Melancholy* (1586): "euery serious thing for a time, is turned into a iest, & tragedies into comedies, and lamentation into gigges and daunces."

[3] For a few additional allusions to the Scottish jig, see *Entertainments at Elvetham* (1591), *Works of Lyly*, ed. Bond, I, 441 (here used of instrumental music); Induction to *James IV*; *Westward Hoe*, V, iii; *The Fleire*, III, i.

[4] See pp. 358, 359, below.

[5] For a few early examples of entries on the Register, see Arber's *Transcript*, II, 294, 347, 376, 384, 399, 454; for a few examples from the broadsides, see *Roxburghe Ballads*, I, 24; II, 229, 312, 476, 565, 639.

Certainly the jig in the period under consideration was not characteristically Scottish or northern. The term seems to have been a common one for country or festival dance or song. A shepherd lad in *Ould Facioned Love* by "T. T. Gent" (1594) mentions among the "countrie secrets" taught him by the friendly shepherds,

> To sing in time, as sometimes shepards use,
> To daunce our jiggs on pasture grac'd with flowrs.[1]

Breton's *Mothers blessing* (1602) contains the lines,

> Make not thy musique of a country Iigge,
> But leaue the Lout, to tread the Morris-daunce.[2]

At the wedding with which *The Woman Killed with Kindness* opens, country lads and maidens dance "all their country measures, rounds, and jigs." Dekker has in *A Knights Coniuring* a burlesque of the Orpheus legend in which that "most cleare throated singing man" is represented as a strolling fiddler paying for his wife with "jigs and countrey daunces."[3] Swains in *Comus* (l. 952) with "jigs and rural dance resort." The general association of "jig" with country song is seen in Florio's definition of *strambótti* in 1598 as "countrie gigs, rounds, catches or songs, virelaies,"[4] and in Cotgrave's definition of *strambot* in 1611 as "A Jyg, Round, Catch, countrey Song." It was probably from a use in country festival that "jig" came to have the meaning of the medieval term carol as applied to dance lyric. In Marlowe's *Edward II* (II, ii) a song which, according to Fabyan's *Chronicles*, was sung "in daunces, in carolis of ye maydens & mynstrellys of Scotlande"[5] is called a jig. The ballad "Clod's Carol" has the secondary title "A proper new Iigg."[6]

"Jig" was frequently used of shepherds' songs, and it was taken over into the literary vocabulary of London as synony-

[1] See Beloe, *Anecdotes of Literature*, II, 71.

[2] Ed. Grosart, p. 7.   [3] Percy Society, pp. 24–25.

[4] See also *strambottino*, "a short fine gig, round or catch," and the similar definitions of *strambóttare* and *strambottiere*.

[5] Ed. Ellis, p. 420. See p. 42 below for Molle's use of the word jig in translating a Latin account of festival song with dance.

[6] See Text 6.

mous with the term roundelay so much affected by Spenser and
other pastoral writers. Two sophisticated examples of the
shepherd's song called a jig were printed in *England's Helicon*.
One is "Doron's Jig" taken from Greene's *Menaphon* (1589). It
is there introduced with the statement that the shepherd Doron
desired his companion to sound a roundelay while he sang a
song "which he carolled to this effect." The other is John
Wootton's "Damaetas' Jig in Praise of his Love." Barnfield
in *The Shepheards Content* (1594) pictures the shepherd as returning to his cot at night "singing a Iigge or merry Roundelay." In a poem from Weelkes's *Madrigals* (1597) a shepherd
declares, "all our merry gigs are quite forgot."[1] "A sheapheards
prety Gigg" has already been cited as belonging to the pastoral
pastimes of "A merrimt of christmas"[2] at Lleweny. In translating Du Bartas (1605), Sylvester uses "jig" for a shepherd's
song in the passage,

> If neere vnto the *Eleusinian* Spring,
> Som sport-full Iig som wanton Shepheard sing,
> The Ravisht Fountaine falls to daunce and bound.[3]

Probably the singing and dancing of jigs was no more characteristic of shepherd pastimes than of country pastimes generally,
but the pastoral cult served to bring the jig rather prominently
into the literary allusions of the time.

The word itself is of doubtful origin. The authorities of the
New English Dictionary are unable to offer any satisfactory theory, though they suggest several possibilities. To the first—that
"jig" is related to the Old French *gigue*, the name of a medieval
musical instrument of the fiddle type—the objection is that Old
French *gigue* did not develop the meanings of "jig" and that it
was obsolete before the English word appeared, the modern
French *gigue* being taken over from English. The theory that
the substantive jig is related to the obsolete French *giguer*, "to
leap or frolic," is rejected for lack of any convincing link be-

[1] No. ii. See *Palaestra*, XXIX, 132.

[2] *Poems by Salusbury and Chester*, ed. Brown, p. 20. For the association of "jig" with "roundelay" and "canzons" in another connection, see Nichols, *Progresses of James I*, I, 572.

[3] See *Diuine Weekes and Workes* (ed. of 1621), p. 52.

tween the two. In connection with the verb jig it is pointed out that similarity in the meaning of these two words may be "accidental, or due to parallel onomatopoeic influence, the large number of words into which *jig-* enters indicating that it has been felt to be a natural expression of a jerking or alternating motion." A number of the examples cited, like "jig-a-jog" or "jig-a-jig" and the expression "to jig it up and down," used of dance, make such a derivation seem possible. No effort is made to connect "jig" with "gig," though an onomatopoeic source is suggested for both.[1] Danckert and Pulver, who have dealt with the jig as a musical form, both accept the word as of English origin. Danckert sees an onomatopoeic influence in "jig" as in "jog" and "jag."[2] Pulver concludes that "jig" is a doublet of "gig"—"meaning anything round or revolving"—which he derives from Icelandic *geiga*. Having in mind the definition of "jig" given by Halliwell in his dictionary, "a ludicrous metrical composition, often in rhyme, which was sung by the clown, who occasionally danced," Pulver asks, "What is more natural than to suppose that a word meaning 'to revolve' should have been taken to designate the verses with a constantly-recurring refrain (*à la* Rondo), and that such a set of verses being 'sung by the clown' should have lent its name to the dance in which the said clown afterwards indulged?"[3]

My own conjecture is that "jig" as a doublet of "gig" was applied to a type of dance in which whirling or turning on the toe was a conspicuous feature. Whatever the origin of "gig," its most ordinary Elizabethan meaning is a top. Though little is left by way of actual description of the jig as dance, there are references to the jig dancer's turning like a top, turning like a globe, turning o' the toe, dancing like a whirligig, and wheeling until giddy.[4] Such a conjecture is of course at variance with Pulver's opinion that the dance ballad gave the name to the

---

[1] In two cases cited in the *NED* the two words are evidently confused as a result of the vagaries of an older spelling. See pp. 75–76, 94, below for "gigge of a geering, gibing wit" and "new gigges for a countrie clowne" instanced in the *NED* under "gig" meaning "fancy, joke, whim."

[2] *Geschichte der Gigue*, p. 9.   [3] *Proceedings of the Musical Association*, XL, 78.

[4] See pp. 357–58 below. This, however, was a feature of the rapid, vigorous dancing in general for which the Elizabethans showed such a passion.

dance. I judge, however, that the jig was primarily a dance distinct in kind and in musical form.

Allusions to the jig merely as dance are seldom taken into account in this study, but they are very numerous, beginning earlier than the stage jig of song and dance can be traced, and continuing to the present day. Two early examples from *Misogonus* and Riche's *Farewell* have been mentioned. Thomas Morley, the earliest writer on music from whom we might expect notice of the jig as dance, after discussing the musical form of the chief courtly dances and the country dance—the rhythm, the number of strains, the number of semibreves in a strain—adds, "There bee also many other kindes of daunces (as *hornepypes Iygges* and infinite more) which I cannot nominate vnto you."[1] Though he fails to describe the hornpipe and the jig, Morley slightly later in his treatise (p. 182) scores the tribe of descanters who are not able to compose even a Scottish jig properly. It seems easier to explain the related uses of "jig" as extensions of dance than to suppose that the songs called jigs, as varied in form as the extant ones happen to be, brought about the use of the word for a distinct type of dance.

The jig, moreover, like the hornpipe, the country dance, and the morris, belonged primarily to the folk, and all of these dances were still accompanied by song in the folk festival. But both the typical ritual dances—the morris and the sword dance —and the typical social dance of the folk—the country dance— are "figure" dances. They involve groups of performers and employ figures that call for interaction. The simple song-and-dance of one or perhaps two or three performers singing in turn would require, on the other hand, a form of dance that is essentially individual—in other words, a step dance. The typical step dance of the folk in the period studied here seems to have been the jig. My theory is, then, that as a result "jig" became a generic term for popular song with dance.

Apparently when the jig was taken up by professionals, the early name held its own while a rapid development of the art of song and dance in the theater led to a wide extension of its meaning. A frequent uncertainty as to the meaning of the word is in fact one of the great difficulties in dealing with the field. It is sometimes impossible to determine whether "jig" refers to a

[1] *Plaine and Easie Introduction to Practicall Musicke* (1597), p. 181.

particular form of dance or to song for dance or to song-and-dance. Deloney calls one of the songs in *Thomas of Reading* a country jig, though those who sing it are seated. For a time the farce form of the jig probably determined the most distinctive meaning of the word. Yet the passion for the stage jig seems to have given the term not only much of the popularity but also much of the looseness of meaning characteristic of slang. In the choruses of *James IV*, "jig" is repeatedly applied to parts of the play. Elsewhere I point out the tendency to use the term for any popular type of composition and for odd or comic action[1]— meanings that probably grew out of the farcical situations so common in the stage jig.

If the jig is to be regarded as an outgrowth of the song with dance characteristic of popular pastimes, its immediate background must be sought in the song of the people, especially that which seems to have had a more or less dramatic function. I have no doubt that by the end of the sixteenth century both the popular jig and popular song generally showed the widest variety of themes, but the same two lines of interest are important in both—the love motive and satire. In the non-professional jig, particularly at an early period, the love motive was probably in the ascendant. So far as the nature of the shepherd jigs is indicated, they are love songs. The two examples in *England's Helicon* belong to this class, and Wootton's jig contains the lines:

> In every jig, in every lay
> Both sing and say, "Love lasts for aye."

In the poem cited from Weelkes's *Madrigals* (No. ii) a shepherd complains:

> all our merry gigs are quite forgot,
> all my Ladies love is lost, god wot.

The jig is associated with love song in a poem which was introduced into *Greene's Vision* of 1592:

> such wanton laies,
> Are not worthie to haue praise.
> Iigges and ditties of fond loues,
> Youth to mickle follie mooues.[2]

---

[1] See pp. 139, 147 n. 1, below. [2] *Works of Greene*, ed. Grosart, XII, 199.

In *The Anatomy of Melancholy* Burton speaks of the "light *Inamorata*" or "idle phantastick" who "thinks of nothing else but how to make Jigs, Sonnets, Madrigals, in commendation of his Mistress."[1] A sophisticated love song called a jig is introduced in Hemings's *Fatal Contract*, IV, iii.[2] Among the ballad dialogues designated jigs, "A New Northern Jig" and "The Soldier's Farewell to his Love," as well as the country jig of "Simon and Susan," follow the tradition of the jig as love song.

In social pastimes as well as in seasonal festivals, it was probably a common thing to enact the wooing or marriage. This is suggested by the pervasiveness of the love motive in the children's games of all countries. The simplest form may have been a pantomime dance. Barclay refers to the "volage amorous" of the old wooer in a dance, and Nashe to the fool in a burlesque May game as dancing around Maid Marian to "court" her; Arbeau for France describes the wooing as enacted by two groups of dancers.[3] But song must have been usual with the wooing dance.[4] An early description of a lover's expressing his passion in pantomime accompanied by music and song as he dances with his lady, while she expresses her love and shyness in the same way, is preserved in *Ruodlieb*.[5] From the twelfth century comes the story of the priest who, having heard *choreae* sung all night about the church, was unable to keep the refrain

---

[1] Ed. Shilleto, II, 136.

[2] A white-letter ballad printed by John White at Newcastle, "A Godly Ballad, intituled, *I will go seek my Saviour; and let the World be*" (Roxburghe Collection, III, 694, 695), opens with a very late reference to jigs of the type:
"Those Poets vain who think no Shame
    To make those Jigs of Love;
    God's holy Word they do prophane."

[3] For these passages see Barclay, *Mirrour of Good Maners*, Spenser Society, p. 4 (the passage is quoted in chapter iv); *Works of Nashe*, ed. McKerrow, I, 83; Arbeau, *Orchesographie*, fol. 66. For a pantomime wooing dance of French shepherds, see Bédier, *Revue des deux Mondes*, January, 1906, pp. 411–12.

[4] See Chambers, *Mediaeval Stage*, I, 161, n. 3, for a few of the early ecclesiastical prohibitions against pagan singing and dancing on festival occasions. The term *chorea* is used a number of times, and love songs are specified in several cases. What Chambers calls "the only dance prohibition of possible A.-S. *provenance*" of which he knows (from *Judicium Clementis*) forbids on pain of excommunication that anyone either dance or sing "orationes amatorias" at the church.

[5] Ed. Seiler, IX, 38–57.

"Swete lamman dhin are" out of his service.[1] The group performance characteristic of the *choreae* would be the primitive method even where the song is appropriate for the individual lover—as in the choruses of the widespread children's game "Here come three Dukes" (or "Lords of Spain"). The Elizabethan "Cushion Dance" is apparently a survival of an actual folk game with distribution of mates. In this dance a dialogue is sung by the musician and each of the dancers in turn as cushion-bearer—alternately a man and a woman—with the refrain sung by the two. The cushion-bearer appeals to the musician because of the reluctance of the mate chosen, and the musician commands that "Joan" or "John" enter the dance.[2] Other songs and dances involving the choice of mates, especially garland dances, are discussed in chapter viii. Nashe indicates the use of love song with dance in connection with the late sixteenth century morris when he complains in the Preface to *Astrophel and Stella* that his style "cannot daunce trip and goe so liuely, with oh my loue, ah my loue, all my loues gone, as other Sheepheards that haue beene fooles in the Morris time out of minde."[3]

Popular love songs in a variety of types are very numerous. Of the simple dialogue wooings, one of the finest is the song current in the time of Henry VIII which opens "Hey, troly loly lo, maid, whither go you," and represents a knight as wooing a milkmaid as she goes to milk her cow.[4] It follows of course a typical pastourelle tradition. Variants of this song are very popular among modern folk singers, and one form is a singing game in dialogue.[5] A frequent convention in wooing song is the

[1] Giraldus Cambrensis, *Gemma Ecclesiastica*, I, 43 (see Rolls Series, II, 120, or Chambers and Sidgwick, *Early English Lyrics*, pp. 329–30).

[2] See Gomme, *Traditional Games*, I, 87–94; Chappell, *Popular Music*, I, 153–56.

[3] The words "Hay my loue, O my loue"—perhaps from some well-known song used by the shepherds in their dances, perhaps from a similar song—are quoted in *The Case is Altered*, IV, vii, as if conventionally connected with wooing. A song or round in Ravenscroft's *Deuteromelia*, No. 23, may illustrate the type of song to which Nashe refers:

"My loue, lou'st thou mee?
then quickly come and saue him that dyes for thee."

[4] Add. MS 31922. See Chambers and Sidgwick, *op. cit.*, pp. 62–63. For two other early dialogues, "Mi hartys lust and all my plesure" and "Bewar my lytyl fynger," the latter of a rollicking character, see *Anglia*, XII, 596–97, 590–91.

[5] See *Modern Philology*, XIV, 238.

offer of gifts to win a maid to marriage. It is found in dialogues like "The Keys of Canterbury" and "I will give to you a paper of pins," which are still favorites among the folk, and is burlesqued in a number of sixteenth and seventeenth century ballads.[1] The prevalence of dialogue form in early love song is suggested by various titles in which the lover addresses the lady with terms of endearment, an invitation, or a plea for a kiss. One of the many tunes to which the shepherds of *Colkelbie Sow* dance is called "My deir derling" (l. 356). "And let us daunce *Herk my Lady*" occurs in an early lyric printed by Rimbault in his *Little Book of Songs and Ballads* (p. 30). Here again the convention seems to be reflected in a number of parodies or burlesques.[2] The popularity of the invitation song goes back at least to the time of *The Canterbury Tales*, for the Pardoner is described in the Prologue (ll. 672–73) as singing full loud, "Com hider, love, to me," while the Summoner bears the burden. There is a dialogue song of the fifteenth century which opens with the invitation, "Come over the woodes fair and green,/ Thou goodly maid."[3] The folk dialogue "Come over the bourne, Bessie, to me," frequently mentioned, is known only in an adaptation representing England as the wooer of Elizabeth.[4] Marlowe's "Come live with me and be my love" furnishes a famous literary example of the type. The invitation "Dainty, come thou to me" occurs in the refrain of "A New Northern Jig." The plea for a kiss illustrated in the jig of "Kit and Pegge" is represented in two fifteenth century dialogues which were probably song dramas. In the one beginning "I pray you come kyss me/ My lytle prety mopse," the lover is mocked though he wins the kiss.[5] The other, "Lende me yowre praty mouth, madame," is ascribed to Charles of Orleans.[6] The song "Bais-

[1] See Sharp, *One Hundred English Folksongs*, pp. xxxiv–xxxv, 148–49; Newell, *Games and Songs of American Children*, pp. 51–55; pp. 191–93, 196–97, below.

[2] See Dunbar, "Brash of Wooing," *Poems*, ed. Laing, II, 28–30, and II, 406–8 (a note on this poem calling attention to the related "I said to hir, My darling deir," in the Bannatyne MS); Bale, *Three Laws*, ll. 475–78; *Roxburghe Ballads*, IX, 600, 846.

[3] See Chambers and Sidgwick, *op. cit.*, pp. 64–67.

[4] See Rimbault, *Little Book of Songs and Ballads*, pp. 71–76; Dick, *Notes on Scottish Songs by Burns*, pp. 18, 88.

[5] See *Hist. MSS Com.*, V, 458; *Bagford Ballads*, I, 519.

[6] See Ritson, *Ancient Songs and Ballads*, ed. Hazlitt, pp. lviii–lix.

sons nous belle" accompanies a sixteenth century French galliard described by Arbeau in his *Orchesographie* (fol. 54). In
England a song of "Joan, come kiss me now," which from its
opening may have been a dialogue, had considerable popularity
in the sixteenth and seventeenth centuries. It was often moralized or parodied, and furnished the name of a popular dance
tune.[1] In a ballad medley of the seventeenth century, one line
reads, "Come hither, sweet, and take a kisse."[2] One of the songs
in Ramsay's *Tea-Table Miscellany* of 1724[3] is sung to the tune
"Come kiss with me, come clap with me." The convention is
burlesqued in the dialogue song "Come smack me, come smack
me, I long for a smouch," quoted in chapter ii from *Promos and
Cassandra*, Part I. Another conventional motive was that of
the rejected or forsaken lover. At marriages, and perhaps in
seasonal games, it was the custom for unsuccessful lovers to
wear the willow garland and sing of their woe.[4] Of the many
sophisticated willow songs, the best known is the sixteenth
century ballad parts of which are sung by Desdemona in *Othello*,
IV, iii. Probably the shepherd's song "All my loues gone" mentioned by Nashe belonged to this general class. The great vogue
of songs dealing with the parting of lovers is noticed in chapter
vi in connection with "A New Northern Jig" and "The Soldier's
Farewell to his Love," both of which use the theme.

The evidence for satiric song as jig among the folk is fuller
and more definite than that for love song, perhaps because the
bitter animosities of the sixteenth and seventeenth centuries
brought popular satire into considerable prominence. There
are, in fact, so many allusions to satiric jigs which could have
no connection with the stage that the subject is reserved for
discussion in the next chapter with a view to illustrating more
fully the relation of the folk and the professional jig to popular

---

[1] See Medwall, *Nature*, Part II, l. 150 ("Com kys me Johan gramercy Ione");
Ravenscroft, *Pammelia*, No. 22; Naylor, *Elizabethan Virginal Book*, pp. 90–92; Chappell, *Popular Music*, I, 147–48, 218; II, 771 ("John, come kiss me now"); Dick, *Songs of
Burns*, pp. 188, 422–23; Betterton, *Revenge* (1680), end of Act II, where a character
leaves the stage singing "*John* come kiss me, *&c.*" and dancing.

[2] *Roxburghe Ballads*, I, 58.

[3] Ed. of 1871, I, 60–61.

[4] See Brand, *Popular Antiquities*, I, 121–24, and p. 254 below. For broadsides see
Roxburghe Ballads, VII, 352–60.

song. It may be pointed out here, however, in a general way that the element of satire was strong in popular pastimes, especially in feasts of misrule. Lords of misrule under various names were common in the castles, colleges, and villages of England in the period around Christmas; presided in London over the revels of kings and nobles, students at the inns of court, and sheriffs; and were not infrequent in spring and summer games.[1] Throughout the sixteenth century, religious forms continued to be parodied in the ceremonies of boy bishops, and legal forms in the revels of the inns of court. Both in clerical feasts and in the festivities more typical of the folk, there were goblin-like figures, scapegoats, and fools[2] who seem to have served primarily as a mouthpiece for satire and burlesque. In translating the *Apophthegmes* of Erasmus, Udall explains that he renders "*Fescennina carmina*, or *Fescennini rhythmi*, or *Versus*" as "(accordyng to our Englyshe prouerbe) a ragmans rewe, or, a bible. For so dooe we call a longe ieste that railleth on any persone by name, or toucheth a bodyes honestee somewhat nere" (fol. 245); and in another connection he tells of the custom at English feasts of having "some iestyng feloe, that maye scoff and iest vpon the geastes, as they sitten at the table" (fol. 34). "*Immoderate* and *Disordinate Ioy*," says Lodge in one of his character sketches, "became incorporate in the bodie of a ieaster . . . . his studie is to coine bitter ieasts, or to show antique motions, or to sing baudie sonnets and ballads." And Lodge adds that, given a little wine, he "hath all the feats of a Lord of misrule in the countrie."[3] The term ragman used by Udall is frequently met in connection with satire, and a whole series of satiric sketches under the name of ragman's roll was apparently

---

[1] See Chambers, *Mediaeval Stage*, I, 173, 403–19; Index to Machyn's *Diary*, Camden Society, under "Misrule"; Index to Feuillerat's *Revels of Edward and Mary* under "Lord of Misrule."

[2] For payments made by the king to boy bishops and their devils and ruffys, or ruffins (a type of goblin), at Edinburgh around 1500, see *Accounts of the Lord High Treasurer of Scotland*, I, 68, 239; II, 128, 350, 410; III, 175, 176; IV, 87, 89, 180; etc. For references by Scottish poets of the same period to leading Billy Blind, a similar figure of traditional ballads, see Gomme, *Traditional Games*, I, 39–40. For Friar Rush and Robin Goodfellow in Christmas games of England around 1600, see Jonson, *Love Restored*; Maxwell in *Studies in Philology*, XIX, 232; Kittredge in *PMLA*, XV (1900), 426, n. 1.

[3] *Wits Miserie* (1596), p. 84.

not unusual. A literary development is found in the fifteenth century poem "Ragman Roll," a series of satiric sketches of women which are represented as drawn by lot at the command of King Ragman Holly, obviously a Christmas festival leader presiding over the medieval game of fortune-drawing known as Ragman's Roll.[1] Such satiric and burlesque features and the disards of whom they were characteristic belonged primarily to the Christmas season. There was, however, at least one comic figure of the ragman type in the spring games—Jack-a-Lent, who was vegetation daemon and scapegoat. Machyn records a procession of March 17, 1553, with the shriving of Jack-a-Lent. He was probably executed, like the Fool of the Revesby Play, who makes a burlesque testament. In the adaptation of game features for satiric ballads and dramatic "toys," Jack-a-Lent became a popular mouthpiece for satire.[2] Moreover, his characteristic songs were more than probably accompanied by dance. At least the words from Baron's *Pocula Castalia* (1650), "no Jack-a Lent danc'd such a way,"[3] suggest that his prowess as a dancer was recognized. One of the dances in Playford's *Dancing Master* is called "Jack a Lent." On the satiric features of the early revels was modeled a wealth of song, especially in monologue form, of a sort appropriate for fool or clown. Some phases of it are illustrated in the next chapter.

Comic and farcical jigs, if they existed among the masses, would be less likely, I think, to come into literary notice than the wooing or the satiric type. Yet the jig, which fell into the hands of the clown when it reached the stage, may already have been associated with coarse or comic song, the actors merely placing the emphasis on the type best suited to their purpose. The country jig printed in Deloney's *Thomas of Reading* as a part of his depiction of country life is a humorous dialogue in which Cuthbert and the hostess of Bosom's Inn lay their plans to cuckold the host. Comic and farcical themes must have been common in popular song. Udall vouches for the use of jests in songs for marriage and other festivals. In discussing Fescennine

[1] See Wright, *Anecdota Literaria*, pp. 74–88; *Studies in Philology*, XVII, 38; *PMLA*, XXIII (1908), 486.

[2] See pp. 46–47 below for the balladry associated with his name.

[3] See Brydges, *Censura Literaria*, I, 170.

verse in the *Apophthegmes* (fol. 245), he refers to "syngyng merie songes and rymes for makyng laughter and sporte at marryages, euen like as is nowe vsed to syng songes of the Frere and the Nunne, with other sembleable merie iestes, at weddynges, and other feastynges." "The Friar and the Nun" is another of Playford's dances.[1] In *The Christen state of Matrimonye* (fol. li) Coverdale, deploring the obscene dancing and revelry at weddings, speaks of the songs with which the bridal pair were sung to bed. Songs dealing with intrigue would be especially appropriate to wedding festivities, to which burlesque of the marriage relation in songs of the *mal mariée* type belonged.[2] Perhaps the repertory of the wedding feast influenced that of the games generally. But it is likely that comic and farcical ballads of various kinds were numerous by the middle of the sixteenth century. In 1572 Whitgift likens Cartwright to the curst wife who, while beating her husband, cried out as if he were beating her, and to the thief of Erasmus' *Colloquies*, who ran away with the priest's purse, all the while crying out on the priest. Cartwright in reply mocks him for making his readers merry with the

bagpipe or country mirth, not with the harp or lute, which the learned were wont to handle. For he hath packed up together the old tale of the curst wife, and of the thief that took away the priest's purse, very familiar and homely gear. It might peradventure make M. Doctor hop about the house; but the learned and the wise cannot dance by this instrument.[3]

The passage shows the prevalence of such jests in country pastime, and implies their use in song for dance. The popularity of robbery as a motive in pantomime dance is noticed later (pp. 138, 294). The incident of the thief who cried out against his victim is found not only in Erasmus' "Fabulous Feast" but in *Mery Tales and Quicke Answeres*, No. xx, and is at least suitable for ballad treatment whether or not it ever

[1] For the popularity of the tune, see Chappel, *Popular Music*, I, 145-46.

[2] See Brome, *English Moor*, II, i, for the singing of old songs at the window of the bridal chamber in the seventeenth century, and I, ii, and IV, v, for other songs and for burlesque dance in celebration of a marriage. See pp. 262-66 below for songs on the old man as lover.

[3] See *Works of Whitgift*, Parker Society, III, 320, 322.

took ballad form. The story of the curst wife is preserved as a narrative ballad in a manuscript of about 1578.[1]

In regard to form, there remains a wide gap between the developed farce jigs of the theater and the early songs, predominantly lyric, which can be identified as jigs of the people. It is not necessary to assume, however, either that a more dramatic type did not exist among the folk or that the simple type was not represented on the stage, though when the writing of jigs for professionals began, the natural tendency was toward dramatic form. Probably in the beginning of the vogue the simplest and briefest sort of jig was often sung and danced incidentally during plays as well as at the end. Even in 1610, with the farce jig in full swing, there is a very suggestive association of terms in Daborne's *Christian turn'd Turke* when one of the characters advises that a tragedy be digested with "a gig, a catch."[2]

Ballad jigs for two singers also were probably used by both folk and professionals. "Kit and Pegge" with its broad burlesque of the conventions of wooing song and "The Soldier's Delight in the North" with its bawdry are distinctly in the vein of comic stage song, but a jig like "The Soldier's Farewell to his Love" with its naïve and sentimental tone seems appropriate to popular pastimes rather than the theater. Certainly there is no reason to doubt that song drama was common from an early period. The record in 1447 of a payment to "ij ludentibus Joly Wat and Malkyn" suggests to me a simple song drama of the pastourelle type.[3] Attention has already been called from time to time to the dialogue form of songs used in pastimes, as in "The Cushion Dance." In "The Nutbrown Maid" we have an early song very suitable for performance, and the opening stanzas explain the purpose to present it dramatically. The general popularity of the dialogue ballad in the sixteenth century can be judged not only from the number that have survived, some of them very dramatic in method, but from the stress put on dialogue form in the titles of the Register from an early period. The

---

[1] Cotton. Vesp. A. 25. See *Jahrbuch für rom. und engl. Sprache und Literatur*, Neue Folge, II, 82, 219–23.

[2] Ll. 836–37 (*Anglia*, XX, 215).

[3] See Toulmin Smith, *York Plays*, p. xxxviii; *Modern Philology*, XIV, 238.

best evidence for the dramatic nature of such pieces is the fact
that records of a much later era show the folk performing in
their festivals a number of dialogue songs and ballads that were
published in the sixteenth and seventeenth centuries without
evidence of performance. While in some cases such songs may
have passed into the folk repertory through the influence of the
professional jig on folk performance, almost certainly on the
whole they represent song drama of the older festival. At any
rate I have used them freely in chapter vi as indicating a dramatic tradition among the people.

Moreover, whether or not song drama analogous to the farce
jig was current with the folk before the era of the stage jig, a
type of interlude more dramatic than the simple dialogue of
two characters had pretty clearly developed as festival drama
in the fifteenth and sixteenth centuries. The Robin Hood plays,
three of which survive from this period, furnish definite examples. To judge from the evidence left, the plays as a whole must
have retained many song and dance features illustrative of
festival practice. The morris was conventionally associated
with them; and the close of the one complete play left, "Robin
Hood and the Friar," is an introduction to a dance. The ballad
nature of the early fragment on Robin Hood and the Knight
may reflect singing. Bellenden in translating Boece's *History of
Scotland* records: "About this tyme was yᵉ waithman Robert
hode with his fallow litil Johne, of quho*m* ar mony fabillis &
mery sportis sou*n*g amang the vulgar pepyll" (fol. 102; Bk.
xiii). Certainly the dominance of the pastourelle figure Marian
in the Robin Hood cycle[1] would argue for song drama. Probably,
too, some of the plays were more farcical than the extant specimens would suggest. In *The Downfall of Robert Earl of Huntington* (IV, ii) the Friar in defending the Robin Hood material
of the play declares:

> For merry jests they have been shown before,
> As how the friar fell into the well
> For love of Jenny, that fair bonny belle;
> How Greenleaf robb'd the Shrieve of Nottingham,
> And other mirthful matter full of game.

[1] See Chambers, *Mediaeval Stage*, I, 171–76.

This may be an allusion to lost literary drama, but more likely it concerns the Robin Hood cycle of folk plays. No trace of a play on the Friar's escapade remains, but a seventeenth century narrative ballad on the subject seems to have had a great vogue, and there are allusions to the story from the time of Skelton to the time of Playford, who included in his *Dancing Master* the tune "The Maid peept out at the Window, or (The Frier in the Well.).".[1] Other favorite jests might easily have assumed dramatic form among the people before the use of the farce jig in the theater.

It is very difficult to enforce the relation which I believe to have existed between the jig and popular song generally. One thing that obscures it is the dominance of the broadside ballad over other forms of song in the period. The jigs of one large class were undoubtedly typical dialogue ballads except for their emphasis on plot. They represent, however, only one phase of the development. The jigs discussed in chapter viii taken as a whole show in a number of features—in material, in the use of song and dance elements, in variety of form including lyric measures—a close kinship to the more formal festival drama of the period so far as it can be reconstructed from the best evidence available. The kinship cannot be proved, however, since popular forms of the Middle Ages and the Renaissance have perished almost completely in England. Even the record of the games belongs chiefly to the eighteenth and nineteenth centuries, when they had greatly declined, whereas they were at their height just before the rise of the jig. Though spoken dialogue prevails in the plays of the modern mummers, such specimens as those published in *Modern Philology*, XXI, 241–72, indicate the extent to which song and dance must have been utilized in the older games in connection with drama. It is possible, then, that in some of the extant jigs of the Elizabethan stage we have our nearest approach to the art of ancient popular drama. The jigs of this class, however, had less chance to survive than typical ballad jigs suitable for broadside publication.

A type that may be regarded as offering a courtly parallel

[1]See Chappell, *Popular Music*, I, 273–75, and *Roxburghe Ballads*, VII, 222–24.

to the popular jig is found in the sixteenth century English masque, which also points to the importance of song and dance in dramatic forms of the Middle Ages. Medieval records of games, as in the case of the thirteenth century song-and-dance "Jeu du Chapelet" discussed by Bédier,[1] frequently belong to the courtly. In pastimes described in *The Flower and the Leaf* (ll. 161–353) a queen leads the dance of the ladies of the Leaf, singing a roundel, to which the company all "answer." Afterward the knights join them, and the group, each knight paired with a lady, sing songs of love as they dance around a laurel tree. Then the leader in the company of the Flower sings a bargaret in praise of the daisy, the rest answering her. Sophistication of such simple forms in the Middle Ages is indicated in numerous records of disguisings, but it was toward the beginning of the sixteenth century that the love of song, dance, and drama among the courtly flowered in an elaborate type of disguising and masque, with emphasis on the spectacular and scenic, which was too difficult and complicated except for formal occasions and well-trained performers. Literary material influenced the content, but the masque always remained primarily a dramatic dance introduced by song. The antic dance and the antimasque, arising later out of the popular and comic elements of both folk and courtly disguisings, drew again directly from folk dances, but the traditional union of song and dance remained vital. The masque reveals a serious tone and an interest in the spectacular forms of staging, costuming, and action; the antimasque, both in its strange figures and in its type of dance, reveals a love of the bizarre. But the dramatic jig, like farce, reflects the realistic—the coarse, odd, and comic—aspects of life, with an element of burlesque.

So far I have emphasized the conception of the stage jig as merely a professional offshoot of the folk art of song with dance in the sixteenth century and have tried to show its relation to the general field of popular song. Its relation to the ballad calls for special notice, however, because in the era of the stage jig the ballad of broadside type was the prevailing form of popular song. The process by which this came about is difficult to follow. There was, of course, a decided shift in the meaning of

[1] *Revue des deux Mondes*, January, 1906, pp. 402–6.

the word ballad itself during the sixteenth century. While "carol" and "roundelay" were passing from a popular to a somewhat restricted and even literary use about 1500, the process was reversed in the case of "ballad." The courtly association of the word is indicated as late as *The Four Elements* (about 1520) when Ignorance refuses to sing "some lusty balet" because he scorns the subtleties of pricksong, but offers to sing a song of Robin Hood, the "best that ever was made," and actually sings a nonsense song (ll. 1389 ff.). Early in the century, however, the term was being applied to all manner of lyrics and festival songs.[1] In many cases it evidently covers the medieval type of lyric, as in Woodville's "Balet," or complaint on his imprisonment (1483);[2] the ballads of "Passe tyme wyth goodde cumpanye" and "I love unlovydde" mentioned in 1521;[3] and most of the songs referred to by Copland about 1525 in the Prologue of *The seuen sorowes that women haue when theyr husbandes be deade:*

> Haue ye the balade called maugh murre
> Or bony wenche, or els go from my durre
> Col to me, or hey downe dery dery
> Or a my hert, or I pray you be mery.

But the process by which the term was extended to include a long, formal festival song or a narrative song must already have been under way. Perhaps the folk while retaining the word ballet for their dance songs were using varied types more elaborate than the early lyric, including narrative and comic songs, *débats*, and dialogues belonging to the pastourelle con-

[1] See Wright and Halliwell, *Reliquiæ Antiquæ*, II, 27 ("lewde balettes, rondelettes, or virolais"); *Accounts of the Lord High Treasurer of Scotland*, I, 184, January 2, 1491[-2] (a ballad sung to the king); Medwall's *Nature* (direction at the end of the second part for singing "some goodly ballet," evidently religious or moral); *Letters and Papers of Henry VIII*, III, 1099 ("divers baletts, &c." sung before the princess on Christmas Day, 1522); Douglas, Prologue to *Aeneid*, Bk. XII; Lyndsay, Prologue to *Testament and Complaynt of the Papyngo*, stanza 5; *Rede me and be nott wrothe*, ed. Arber, pp. 66–69 (the term used for a ballad-like song of fifteen stanzas with a refrain. See also pp. 114–16); Skelton, *Dyuers Balettys and Dyties solacyous deuysyd by Master Skelton, Laureat*, and *Garland of Laurel* (*Works*, ed. Dyce, II, 221, 225); More, *Dialogue* in *Works* (1557), p. 177; *Maid Emlyn*, l. 34; Elyot, *Governour*, Everyman's Library, p. 86.

[2] Ritson, *Ancient Songs and Ballads*, ed. Hazlitt, p. 149.

[3] *Letters and Papers of Henry VIII*, III, 447.

vention, though the term ballad to designate such songs cannot be traced until later. But on the basis of the evidence known to me, it seems likely that the late sixteenth century meaning of "ballad" sprang from the use of the French *balade* on festival occasions. In England Lydgate was employing the *balade* in his masques as a type of descriptive or explanatory song during the early part of the fifteenth century.[1] The practice probably continued, but by the end of the century the English had ceased to follow the rules for the formal *balade* even in the numerous court lyrics of the early Tudor period. Among the folk generally, the meters that have become traditional in the ballad were already in constant use for narrative songs—as in "The Battle of Otterburn," "St. Stephen and Herod," "Adam Bell," "A Gest of Robyn Hode," and "Robin Hood and the Monk"—long before the actual records of the term ballad for such songs begin. This use of the word was established by the middle of the sixteenth century, however. The Stationers' Register leaves no reasonable room for doubt. Almost from the beginning, narratives were freely entered for broadside publication as ballads. While the name at first designated also songs of merely lyric nature, these became increasingly subordinate. The development by the end of the century of a number of compounds like "balladry," "balladize," and "balladmonger," applicable chiefly to the field of the broadside ballad, shows the change in meaning as practically complete.[2] Shorter songs of a carol type continued, however, to appear at times as broadside ballads, and in the Restoration "ballads" and "songs" representing the two classes are difficult to distinguish.

The literary men of London who around the middle of the century were interesting themselves in the new lyric and the new drama contributed also to the development of the ballad. Surrey's use of long lines akin to ballad meters, which has never been explained, may have been due to an interest in native forms like the traditional ballad. The large group of poets who followed him used the poulter's measure and ballad lines freely. Many of their songs, moreover, were of such stanzaic forms

---

[1] Brotanek, *Die engl. Maskenspiele*, pp. 306–25. See Withington, *English Pageantry*, I, 164, for the use of a "balet" in an entertainment in 1498.

[2] See *NED* for examples.

and such length as the conventional broadsides of the period. Redford, Edwards, Gascoigne, and Turberville produced these virtual ballads. Some of the songs included in *Tottel's Miscellany* and a number of those in Robinson's *Handefull of pleasant delites* were printed separately as ballads.[1] Robinson's miscellany, published apparently in 1566 and again in 1584, is described on the title page as a collection of "sonets" and "histories." These were common terms for the ballads of the cultured which represented conventional love poetry and classic themes. During the sixties a large number of entries on the Register vouch for the vogue of classical stories cast in ballad form.[2] Several manuscript collections of songs composed largely of ballads were also made during the period between 1560 and 1580.[3] The interest of the cultured in the type of poem to which they had contributed had waned by 1580. The school of the sixties was apparently degenerating into a "rakehellye route of our ragged rymers" when Ascham made his protest against the barbarity of rhyme in the *Scholemaster* of 1570, and native poetry clearly languished until the time of Spenser. Attacks of the Puritans hastened the separation. Defenders of poetic art declared that the only legitimate ground for objection lay in the abuse of poetry, and singled out the popular rhymes of untrained men, especially the ballad makers, as the cause of the poor esteem in which poetry was held. From this time on, "ballad" was regarded as a term of contempt. For a while poets followed classic and Continental models carefully, leaving the popular field to the balladmonger and the populace.

Of the passion for the ballad among the people there can be

[1] For the first, see *Tottel's Miscellany*, ed. Arber, pp. 137–38 (Canand?), 163–64 (Heywood), 205–7; *Ancient Songs and Broadsides*, Philobiblon Society, pp. 217–19, 437; Rollins, *Old English Ballads*, p. xxix; Rollins, *PMLA*, XXXIV (1919), 276. For the second, see the notes of Rollins's edition of 1924.

[2] In 1565–6, for instance, the following ballads were licensed: "kynge Pollicente" (*Transcript*, ed. Arber, I, 298); "history of Troilus" (I, 300); "tow [*i.e.* two] lamentable songes Pithias and Damon" (I, 304); "history of Alexander Campaspes and Appelles" (I, 306); "a songe of Appelles" (I, 307); "Appelles and Pygmalyne" (I, 312); "the goddes Diana" (I, 313). There was also a "Dytty" of "Orpheous and his wyf" (I, 312).

[3] Ashmol. 48 (ed. Wright, *Songs and Ballads*, Roxburghe Club); Sloane 1896 (Rollins, *Old English Ballads*, pp. xxx–xxxi); Cotton. Vesp. A. 25 (Böddeker, *Jahrbuch für rom. und engl. Sprache und Literatur*, Neue Folge, II, 81–105, 210–39, 347–67; III, 92–129).

no doubt. In *Kindheart's Dream*[1] of 1592 Chettle makes an extensive attack on the professional ballad singer, who has infected all of London and extended his efforts to the neighboring shires. The profession, he protests, should belong to the old or crippled with no means of livelihood except beggary, but able men have taken it up. Other pictures of the ballad peddler, like Autolycus of *Winter's Tale* or Nightingale of *Bartholomew Fair*, are drawn in contemporary literature. Autolycus has a passing merry ballad, the beginning of which he sings in dialogue with the two country girls Mopsa and Dorcas, with the comment, "There's scarce a maid westward but she sings it" (IV, iv). In *A Strange Metamorphosis of Man transformed into a Wildernesse* (1634) one of the satiric sketches—No. 15, on the Goose—contains the passage: "if there be any that seeme to have a smatch in that generous Science [poetry], he arrives no higher then the stile of a Ballet, wherin they have a reasonable facultie; especially at a WAKE, when they assemble themselves together at a Towne-greene, for then they sing their Ballets, and lay out such throats as the countrey Fidlers cannot bee heard." Butler speaks in his *Principles of Musik*[2] (1636) of the influence exerted on the pastimes of "unstable yunkers" by ballad makers and dance makers, "the on with obscene and filthy woords, the other with immodest and shameles gestures," and he blames the ballad makers more because they spread their pestilent merchandise "not onely at such publik Merriments; but also in privat houses, yea & openly in the streets, and market-places, where they have their Factors, who vent it boldly without any blushing." Mercenary minstrels, says Butler, publish the filthy songs of the one and teach the filthy fashions of the other. But he rejoices in what he believes to be at present an improvement in taste both in song and in dance.

A great deal of this ballad singing must have been accom-

[1] Ed. Rimbault, Percy Society, pp. 13–20. Whatever "balet" meant in 1543, it is the term used by Coverdale in *The Christen state of Matrimonye*, fol. li, for the songs sung in wedding festivities. Alley in 1565 declares in his *Poor Man's Library*, fol. 63, that for "ballet makers, and enditers of wanton songes, no reuengement, but rewardes are largelye payd." Lodge's reference to the jester who studies "to sing baudie sonnets and ballads" has just been quoted from *Wits Miserie* (p. 84).

[2] Pp. 130–31. See Herrick, *Hesperides*, No. 405, for what I take to be a list of ballad themes popular at this time.

panied by dance. It is impossible to say how early the word
ballad may be taken to mean a song of the broadside type, but
throughout its changing history its close association with dance
is indicated. Dunbar in *The Goldyn Targe* (ll. 129–30) speaks
of the singing of ballads as ladies danced. In discussing music,
Ascham combines "these balades and roundes, these galiardes,
pauanes and daunces"[1]—all dance terms. The name of a dance
gives the title to a ballad entered on the Register in 1561–2 as
the "balled intituled *hay the gye*."[2] After deriving "ballad" from
the Italian *ballare*, "to dance," Gascoigne in *Certain Notes of
Instruction* (1575) adds, "And in deed those kinds of rimes
serve beste for daunces or light matters." In *Christs Teares*
(1593) occurs the passage: "that the young-men in their merry-
running Madrigals and sportiue Base-bidding Roundelayes, for
thee should haue honoured mee: That the Virgins on theyr
loude tinternelling Timbrils, and Ballad-singing daunces, should
haue descanted on my prayses."[3] In 1636, with the newer
meaning of "ballad" fully established, Butler refers in his *Principles of Musik* (p. 8) to the "infinite multitude of Balads (set
to sundry pleasant and delightfull tunes, by cunning and witti
Composers) with Country-dances fitted unto them."

The songs used for dance in the late sixteenth and early
seventeenth century doubtless varied from the medieval type
of lyric[4] to long narrative ballads. Many were probably what
might be called "ballets"[5]—carols, pastourelles, freeman's
songs, wooing dialogues. So much may be inferred from the
scattering evidence in regard to the nature of the songs—largely
lost—which gave names to sixteenth century dances, from the
music discussed in Chappell's *Popular Music of the Olden Time*,
from songs for dance in plays, and from a number of dances in
the various editions of Playford's *Dancing Master* whose names

[1] *Toxophilus* (1545), ed. Arber, p. 39.

[2] *Transcript*, I, 178, 185.

[3] *Works of Nashe*, ed. McKerrow, II, 73. A marginal note reads, "A Ballade in
French is any song that is sunge dauncing."

[4] See Fellowes, *English Madrigal Verse*, pp. 176, 186–87, 195, 215, for very brief
songs from the madrigal books which seem to be for dancing.

[5] See *NED* under "ballad" and *English Dialect Dictionary* under "ballet" and
"ballant."

are derived from late ballads of a lyric quality.[1] The longer narrative or dialogue ballads, however, must have been used freely
during the sixteenth and seventeenth centuries for many country and stage dances. As early as 1542, Udall in translating a
passage of Erasmus adds a parenthesis which I take to mean
that such narratives as the Robin Hood ballads were then regarded as appropriate to dance: "he [Diogenes] begoonne to
syng suche an other foolyshe song, (as Robyn hood, in barnes-
dale stood &c.) & sembleed as though he would daunce withall."[2]
In *A Handefull of pleasant delites* (1584), which has been mentioned as important in the development of the ballad, many of
the tunes are suggestive of dance: "Cecilia Pavan," "Quarter
Brawls," "Black Almain," and "New Almain"—all names of
courtly dances—besides such popular native dance tunes as
"Greensleeves," "All in a Garden Green," and "Lusty Gallant." It is noticeable that numbers of the broadside songs
were written to be sung to dance tunes,[3] and conversely that
names of dance tunes frequently show, or at least suggest, a
connection with the broadside type of song,[4] like "The Maid
peept out at the Window, or (The Frier in the Well.)" and
"Gelding of the Divel" in Playford's *Dancing Master*. Such
titles probably became associated with dance through the use
of song for dancing.

It is in keeping with what has been said of the jig as popular
song that at the period when the ballad was in the ascendant
the jig was commonly regarded simply as a ballad. I have mentioned several cases of songs entered on the Register merely as
ballads and elsewhere identified as jigs. Those entered as jigs
were frequently also designated ballads: "a ballad of *Cuttinge
George, and his hostis* beinge a Jigge," "a ballad intituled *A
plesant newe Jigge of the broome-man*," "a ballad, of master
Kempe*s Newe Jigge of the kitchen stuffe woman*," "a ballad

[1] See pp. 211, 213 n. 2, 214 n. 3, 279 n. 2, below.

[2] *Apophthegmes*, fol. 75. But see p. 29 above for a medley song in *The Four Elements*
with these words as the opening line.

[3] See for example Wooldridge-Chappell, *Old English Popular Music*, Vol. I, *passim*,
especially pp. 232–36, 251–60.

[4] *Ibid.*, I, 286, 289, 296, 297, 304, 311; II, 17.

called Kemp*s newe Jygge* betwixt, a souldiour and a Miser and Sym the clown." Even so elaborate a piece as "Attowell's Jig," with its four characters, four scenes, and four tunes, was printed simply as a broadside ballad.

The free interchange of the two terms in connection with the non-professional jig carries with it, I think, the implication that the ballad singer's performance was very commonly a jig. Chettle, for example, in his complaint against the fraternity of ballad singers speaks twice of their "jigging vanities."[1] *A Quest of Enquirie*, which is discussed in chapter ii, repeatedly illustrates the point, as when reference is made to the "jygging rymes" of the ballad singers or it is proposed that they sing a new jig at the bride's window. Kemp at the end of his *Nine Days' Wonder* tells of inquiring what jigmonger had made ballads on him. In *The Anatomy of the English Nunnery at Lisbon* (1622) Thomas Robinson says of the nuns: "at sundry times, playing vpon their instruments for their fathers recreation, they sing him ribaldrous Songs and jigs, as that of *Bonny Nell*, and such other obscene and scurrilous Ballads, as would make a chaste eare to glow at the hearing of them" (p. 13). The same connection is made in Hemings's *Fatal Contract* (IV, iii), written probably about 1630:

> Wee'l hear your jigg,
> How is your Ballad titl'd?

In Ford's *Love's Sacrifice* (III, i) Nibrassa tells the disgraced Julia, "make thy moan to ballad-singers and rhymers; they'll jig out thy wretchedness and abominations to new tunes." The probability is, then, that the general allusions to ballad singing among the people cover many actual jig performances, and that in their use of the ballad jig the comedians were merely giving a professional turn to what was common enough in everyday life. I believe that at least from the middle of the sixteenth century to the end of the seventeenth, jigs were being performed in the streets, in tavern gatherings and feasts, in games, at fairs, and at entertainments of various sorts—a belief based upon the universal passion for balladry, dance, and dramatic "toys" on

---

[1] *Kindheart's Dream*, ed. Rimbault, pp. 16, 19.

such occasions[1] as well as upon the definite allusions to jigs during that period.

A concluding word on the background of the jig may be said in regard to song and dance acts based on popular dance which developed on the Continent into entertainments of a type somewhat analogous to the jig. Dramatic dance in Italy perhaps best illustrates the point. Social dances, about which treatises were written as early as the fifteenth century, were a passion in Italy as in other European countries at the end of the sixteenth century. But even those of the cultured were apparently still the old dramatic dances of the games oftener here than in England. Gascoigne speaks of a song with dance as being "Alla Napolitana," and Morley mentions a class of Italian ballets "commonly called *fa las* . . . . as I take it deuised to

[1] In addition to the varied examples given elsewhere in this study it is needless to cite more than a few of the many definite illustrations. See *Malone Society Collections*, I, 160, for an indictment of one of a riotous crowd for "singing in the churche vpon Childermas day/fallantida dillie &c" in 1583—a performance probably belonging to Christmas misrule; the opening of *Greene's Tu Quoque* for an invitation to supper in a brothel where there would be "good company, a noise of choice Fidlers, a fine boy with an excellent voice, very good songs and bawdy"; Jonson's Epigrams CXV and CXXX for mimus performances and *The Devil is an Ass*, I, i, for the vice at a sheriff's dinner; *Social England Illustrated*, New English Garner, p. 400, for a passage from Peacham's *Worth of a Penny* referring to a period about 1620, which tells of one Godfrey Colton, "by trade, a tailor: but a merry companion with his tabour and pipe, and for singing of all manner of *Northern Songs* before Nobles and Gentlemen, who much delighted in his company; besides, he was Lord of Stourbridge Fair and all the misorders there"; Robinson, *Anatomy of the English Nunnery at Lisbon*, p. 17, for a description of the reveling of the Confessor: "And when he is merrily disposed (as that is not seldom) then must his dearling *Kate Knightley* play him a merry fit, and Sister *Mary Brooke*, or some other of his last-come Wags must sing him one bawdy song or other to digest his meat." Robinson's statement that the nuns were accustomed to sing ribaldrous songs and jigs to amuse the father (p. 13) has already been quoted. In a list of the nuns on p. 32 the two mentioned above are described as "merry singing wagges." Customs in the seventeenth century are evident from such general allusions as Prynne's in 1633 to song and dance in bridals, wakes, etc. (*Histrio-Mastix*, pp. 222, 236, 252–53, 268–69), and especially to "ribaldrous, amorous Songs: (which now are *too to rife, not onely in Stage-playes, but even at private Christians Feasts, and other Taverne-meetings*" (*ibid.*, p. 263); Playford's reference to "light and effeminate Musick, as pleasant *Amorous Songs, Corants, Sarabands*, and *Jiggs*, used for honest mirth and delight at Feasts and other Merriments" (*An Introduction to the Skill of Musick* [11th ed., 1687], p. 52); and the claim which the Office of the Revels made in 1663 to jurisdiction over the "rurall feasts commonly called Wakes, where there is constantly revelling and musick," and also over "nocturnall feasts and banquettings in publique houses, when attended with minstrelsy, singing & Dancing" (Adams, *Dramatic Records of Sir Henry Herbert*, pp. 132–33; see also p. 134).

be danced to voices."[1] In Scipio Bargagli's *Trattenimenti; dove da vaghe donne, e da giouani Huomini rappresentati sono honesti, e diletteuoli giuochi: narrate novelle; e cantate alcune amorose Canzonette*, published at Venice in 1587, which purports to describe certain pastimes of gentlefolk in Siena about the middle of the century, one feature is a typical medieval carol or round dance— "ballo tondo, o ballo a canzoni, tanto in usanza di tutti i nostri paesi, & contrade. & però, accioche da noi in questi tre solennissimi giorni del potente Carnouale, sì fatta colpa non si commetta." The dancers are foreleaders in turn, each singing and having his words repeated in chorus by the circle of dancers (pp. 284–87). In another game, called "Dialogo di Ninfe, & di Pastori," the participants in guise of shepherds and nymphs sing and act their parts (pp. 124–29). Songs for use in pageants and pastimes which have survived in Italy from the middle of the sixteenth century include also specimens for burlesque and farcical rôles.[2] Late in the century Morley in his *Plaine and Easie Introduction to Practicall Musicke* (1597) describes dramatic entertainments accompanied by the galliard: "The Italians make their galliardes (which they tearme *saltarelli*) plaine, and frame ditties to them, which in their *mascaradoes* they sing and daunce, and manie times without any instrumentes at all, but in steed of instrumentes they haue Curtisans disguised in mens apparell, who sing and daunce to their owne songes" (p. 181). Throughout the sixteenth century, songs accompanied by dance were exceptionally popular in Italian plays, especially as *intermezzi*, and late in the seventeenth century Menestrier gives an account of ballets in the *intermèdes* of Italian comedies and tragedies with the dancing of *entrées* to the accompaniment of song.[3]

A number of passages from Arbeau's *Orchesographie* which

---

[1] *Works of Gascoigne*, ed. Cunliffe, I, 398; *Plaine and Easie Introduction to Practicall Musicke*, p. 180.

[2] See Altrocchi, *PMLA*, XXXVI, 476 ff.

[3] See Prölss, *Geschichte des neueren Dramas*, Vol. I, Part 2, pp. 197, 271, 305–6; Solerti, *Gli Albori del melodramma*, Vols. I–III; Menestrier, *Des Ballets anciens et modernes selon les règles du Théâtre* (1682), pp. 280–94. See also Lambranzi, *Nuoua e Curiosa Scuola de' Balli Theatrali*, Nuremberg edition (1716), for music, for cuts of the characters in a hundred stage dances, usually by two or three comic characters, and for descriptions of the first fifty dances.

are cited in chapter x show the dramatic character of much of
the popular dancing in France. According to Charles de Bour-
gueville, in certain feasts at Caen early in the sixteenth century
"l'on faisoit des danses aux Colleges que l'on appeloit Choreas,
là où l'on iouoit des Farces et Comedies."[1] Numerous song and
dance features are indicated in the texts of French farces, especially of the sixteenth century, and dialogues and dramatic
chants are frequent in the ballets of the seventeenth.[2] For
Spain it is said that from the earliest times no *auto* was performed without music and dance. Disguised dances to song
were popular also in pageants and games.[3] At the end of the
sixteenth century, according to Rennert,[4] dances called

bayles, and short interludes, called *entremeses*, were inseparable from
the comedia. . . . . Of the nature of these *bayles* we know very little,
except that many of them were *deshonestos*. They were always accompanied by words or by singing; the three or four most celebrated
bayles, at least, having each its particular air, to which the later ones
were often sung. They were frequently of such a loose and licentious
nature that they caused great scandal and obliged the authorities to
intervene and suppress them.

In the same way the jigs became a byword for their coarseness
and obscenity, and often passed their tunes on to others. Rennert says that "the most famous as well as the most voluptuous
and indecent [of the *bayles*], it seems, was the *Zarabanda*,"
which is first heard of about 1588. Many of the "ancient"
bayles took their names from the ordinary dances that had a
social vogue throughout Europe—the galliard, pavan, almain,
tordion, or canaries. Some of the names like "Las gambetas"
seem to be descriptive terms; some like "La carretería" (compare "The Carman's Whistle") and "La gorrona" (cock dance?)
suggest folk dances; others like "Madama Orliens" and "Pésame
dello" apparently represent the subject or the opening words of
the song.

In all the countries of Western Europe both professional

[1] *Les Recherches et Antiquitez de la Ville et Uniuersité de Caen* (1588, reprint of 1833),
p. 337.

[2] See Gérold, *L'Art du chant en France au XVIIe siècle*, pp. 53–64, 167–78.

[3] See Rennert, *The Spanish Stage in the Time of Lope de Vega*, pp. 62–68.

[4] *Ibid.*, pp. 69–75. See also Marín, *El Loaysa de "El Celoso Extremeño*," pp. 256 ff.

dances and those current among the people have doubtless been subjected in every age to foreign influences, as is indicated by the prevalence of the term *morisca* throughout Europe from the Middle Ages or the popularity of the strongly dramatic French brawl in England and Scotland during the sixteenth century. Yet I have been unable to find evidence of much extraneous influence on the English comedians during the ascendancy of the jig. The spread of such dances as the pavan, the galliard, or the canaries over Europe seems to belong primarily to an earlier development of social dancing. On the other hand, the vogue of the Italian Harlequin dance and of Spanish dances like the saraband and the chaconne among English comedians came after the decline of the stage jig in England. Apparently a medieval tradition was carried on independently in England and in Continental countries, with a marked dramatic development as a distinguishing feature of the jig.

CHAPTER II

THE SCOPE OF THE JIG AS ILLUSTRATED IN POLITICAL, RELIGIOUS, AND PERSONAL SATIRE

THE purpose of this chapter is to illustrate as thoroughly as possible from a single field the conception of the jig which I have tried to present in the preceding chapter—its folk origin, its character as popular song, its range from very simple to fairly complex types and from an informal use among the folk to a great professional vogue. Here the whole period during which I have conjectured that the jig was in popular use is taken into account, whereas in the first chapter emphasis was laid on the early period because of its importance for origins. The field chosen is that of political, religious, and personal satire. In the first place, jigs of this class do not come up for discussion later because, though a number of allusions establish the fact that they found their way into the theater, no certain specimen, either in the dialogue ballad or in farce form, is known to survive. In the second place, the evidence for their non-professional use is particularly full. The jig was beyond doubt an important form of satire in the period, a fact that seems to have been rather completely overlooked.

Among the political songs which the Elizabethans designated jigs, a number belong to an era long before the word emerges. Throughout the Middle Ages the conflict of races and parties in Great Britain produced a large body of song. Something of its extent can be judged from the political songs edited by Wright for the Camden Society and the Rolls Series. During the thirteenth and fourteenth centuries, for example, the hostility between the English and the Scots bred a multitude of short mocking lyrics. Fabyan[1] records that when the Scots had successfully defended Berwick, "in derysyon of the kynge" they made a "mokkysshe ryme" by which Edward was "somdeale

[1] For the passages cited from Fabyan, see *Chronicles*, ed. Ellis, pp. 398, 420, 440.

amouyd." This rhyme of five lines is quoted, and also one of six with which the English retaliated when the tables were turned at Dunbar. Bannockburn was commemorated by the Scots in the song:

> Maydens of Englonde, sore maye ye morne,
> For your lemmans ye haue loste at Bannockisborne,
>   With heue a lowe.
> What wenyth the kynge of Englonde,
> So soone to haue wonne Scotlande
>   With rumbylowe.

"This songe," the chronicler adds, "was after many dayes sungyn, in daunces, in carolis of ye maydens & mynstrellys of Scotlande, to the reproofe and dysdayne of Englysshe men, w^t dyuerse other whiche I ouer passe." The same song is quoted in Marlowe's *Edward II* (II, ii) and called a jig. Under the year 1327–28, again, Fabyan records that the Scots in mockery of the English "made dyuerse truffys, roundys, & songys, of the which one is specially remembryd as folowyth.

> Longe beerdys hartles,
> Paynted hoodys wytles,
> Gay cotis graceles
> Makyth Englande thryfteles."

In 1570 when Foxe gives an account of these events, he says merely, "the Scottishe Gigges and rymes were these," and quotes the one beginning "Longe beerdys hartles."[1] In the picture of the same conflict which is given in *Edward III*, the Countess of Salisbury declares (I, ii) that the Scots, if victorious,

> will deride vs in the North,
> And, in their vild, vnseuill, skipping giggs,
> Bray foorth their Conquest and our ouerthrow
> Euen in the barraine, bleake, and fruitlesse aire.

The passage found near the opening of *John a Kent and John a Cumber*,

> Our cowardise, to our eternall shame,
> In England, Wales, and Scotland, shall be sung
> By every jygging mate our foes among,

---

[1] *Acts and Monuments*, I, 470.

shows again the Elizabethan conception of early satiric song as jig.

Exultation over victory rather than derision of the enemy is stressed in several songs called jigs by Molle in his *Living Librarie* (1621), translated from the Latin of Camerarius. The story is told of how the Emperor Aurelian in a certain war killed so many of his enemies with his own hand that "in praise of him certaine jygges were made which the yong lads vsed to sing vpon festiuall daies" (p. 322). The original here reads: "adeo vt etiam balistea pueri & saltatiunculas in Aurelianum tales componerent, qui diebus festis militariter saltitarent."[1] The "foot of them was this," says Molle, and gives two specimens of six lines each. A third follows immediately as the "burden" of a "song"—in the Latin *cantilena*—made on another occasion.

A very interesting use of the word jig occurs near the beginning of Heywood's *Edward IV*, Part II (1599). Scales reports to the king in regard to a French count from whom the English have been expecting aid:

> My Lord he lies, and reuelles at S. Quintens,
> And laughes at *Edwardes* comming into France,
> There Dominering with his drunken crue,
> Make Jigges of vs, and in their slauering Jestes,
> Tell how like Rogues we lie here in the field,
> Then comes a slaue one of those drunken sottes,
> In with a Tauerne reckoning for a supplication,
> Disguised with a cushion on his head,
> A Drawers Apron for a Heraldes Coate,
> And tels the Count, the king of England craues
> One of his worthy honors Dog-kennels,
> To be his lodging for a day or two.
> With some such other Tauerne foolerie:
> With that this filthy rascall greasie rout,
> Brast out in laughter at this worthy iest,
> Neighing like horses.

This may be taken as representing English custom rather than any actual French incident. It is probable that jigs were often

---

[1] See *Operae Horarum Subcisiuarum siue Meditationes Historicae* (Frankfort, 1602), p. 378.

hastily written to fit such occasions. If, however, the last part of the passage is a description of a jig, the performance may have been an improvised burlesque, such as was perhaps not infrequent in feasts and tavern gatherings. In I *Henry IV* (II, iv) Hal and Falstaff play the Prince and the King at the Boar's Head tavern, Falstaff with a cushion on his head for a crown; and in *The Famous Victories of Henry the fifth* (B 4) John Cobbler and Derick enact an encounter of the Prince and the Chief Justice.

In both England and Scotland satire on contemporary events during the sixteenth and seventeenth centuries was chiefly inspired by movements that were religious as well as political. Three waves of satire and polemics spent themselves in the struggle of Protestant and Catholic, of Anglican and Puritan, and of Puritan and Cavalier. The first two were primarily religious, but with Cavalier and Puritan in the seventeenth century, the previously subordinated political point of view became all important. From first to last an enormous mass of satiric song was produced. In the two later movements there is record of the satiric jig, and the lack of a similar record in connection with the Reformation is probably due to the fact that the word had not come into common literary use before the intensity of the struggle died down. At any rate, we have seen that the reformer Foxe, when he comes to deal with satiric lyrics of an earlier epoch, recognizes them as jigs.

Several phases of the satire connected with the English Reformation[1] are at least worth attention in connection with the jig—its popular features, the emphasis on song, and the use made of the stage. Henry's "act for the aduauncement of true

---

[1] See Germann, *Luke Shepherd* (Augsburg, 1911), for a survey of the poetical pamphlets; Chambers, *Mediaeval Stage*, II, 217-24, for a summary of the struggle in the field of drama; Rollins, *Old English Ballads, 1553-1625*, pp. xi-xviii, for an account of it with special reference to the ballad. The vogue of the polemical ballad at least was fully as great in Scotland as in England. See Rollins, *op. cit.*, p. x, for a complaint of Henry VIII to the Scottish king in 1537 against ballads attacking him and his religion; *Extracts from the Records of the Burgh of Edinburgh*, II, 252, for a ban put upon anti-Catholic "ballettis and rymes" by Mary Queen of Scots in 1558; *Bagford Ballads*, I, xxv and n. 3, for the narrow escape of one ballad maker from the gallows and the hanging of two for satirical ballads in 1579, with the passage of an act slightly later suppressing "songsters." Much of this balladry is preserved. See *Satirical Poems of the Reformation*, Scottish Text Society (2 vols.), and *Roxburghe Ballads*, VIII, 361-92.

religion, and for the abolishment of the contrary" (1543) complains of the perversion of truth not only "by wordes, sermons,
disputacions, and argumentes, but also by prynted bokes,
prynted balades, playes, rymes, songes, and other phantasies."
Penalties are provided for those who "plaie in interludes sing
or ryme any matier contrarye to the saide doctrine" as well as
for those who offend in print. But it is lawful to "sette forth
songes playes and enterludes" to rebuke vice and foster virtue
provided they do not meddle with interpretations of Scripture
contrary to what is authorized. Edward's proclamation of 1549
regulating the drama as a means against sedition specifies not
only interlude and play but "Dialogue or other matter set forthe
in form of Plaie." Mary, in turn, finds sedition nourished by
"playinge of Interludes and pryntynge false fonde bookes,
ballettes, rymes, and other lewde treatises in the englyshe
tonge," as well as by more direct teaching.[1] Toward the end of
Mary's reign the government seems to have been struggling
with an unusual outburst of dramatic satire. The Privy Council on April 30, 1556, inquired into the case of a company of six
or seven calling themselves Sir Francis Lake's Men, who performed seditious plays and interludes in "the north parts." The
result was an order to officers not to suffer "any playes, enterludes, songes, or any such like pastimes . . . . under any color
or pretense."[2] In 1557 players were arrested in London and
Canterbury, in one case in connection with a piece called the
"Sacke full of Newes," and rigid orders were promulgated for
the censorship of London plays and the suppression of plays
outside the city during the summer.[3] In the same year Pole's
"Articles touching the Lay-people" during visitations in the
diocese of Canterbury include an inquiry as to "whether anye
Mynstrels, or anye other persones dooe vse to syng any songes
agaynst the holye Sacramentes, or anye other the rites and
ceremonies of the churche."[4] After the accession of Elizabeth,

---

[1] See Hazlitt, *English Drama and Stage*, pp. 4–5, 8, 16–17, for these passages except
the one from the act of 1543 providing for penalties, which is omitted by him and cited
here from the complete act in *Statutes of the Realm*, III (1817), 894–97.

[2] See Strype, *Ecclesiastical Memorials*, VI, 413–14.

[3] *Acts of the Privy Council*, 1556–58, pp. 102, 110, 119, 168–69.

[4] Foxe, *Acts and Monuments* (1563), p. 1561.

the Venetian Papers reflect a fresh outburst—this time of "squibs and lampoons, or ballads" abusing Catholics and of plays apparently bringing prominent Romanists on the stage.[1] One order of 1559 mentions certain anti-Catholic plays as "usually performed daily in the hostels and taverns," and another forbids "in future the performance in the hostels and taverns of certain plays and games on holidays" in abuse of the Catholic religion.[2]

While a great deal has survived in the way of sober and more or less dreary polemics, there is little to indicate the lines along which the more popular and telling satire of the singer and stage player developed. Luke Shepherd in *A Pore Helpe*[3] (ll. 198–206) represents the Catholics as complaining

> Agaynst these men of newe facion,
> That stryue agaynst the holy nacion
> And Jest of them in playes,
> In tauerns and hye wayes,
> . . . .
> And synge, pype mery annot,
> And play of wyll not cannot.

The practice of adapting familiar song to various uses was common in the sixteenth century, and current popular songs were often parodied in the interest of religious satire. The complaint that the Protestants sing "pype mery annot" and "play of wyll not cannot" evidently refers to such a parody, and a stage use of it seems to me indicated in the passage. In *Ralph Roister Doister* (I, iii) the three maids, one of them named Annot, sing a song of four stanzas beginning "Pipe, mery Annot, etc.," which represents a contest of the workers and ends with their rebellion:

> I will not! I can not! No more can I!
> Then giue we all ouer, and there let it lye.

[1] See *Cal. State Papers, Venetian*, 1558–1580, pp. 27, 53, 80–81, etc. See *Cal. State Papers, Spanish*, 1558–1567, p. 247, for the complaint of the ambassador in 1562 about "the constant writing of books, farces and songs prejudicial to other princes."

[2] *Cal. State Papers, Venetian*, 1558–1580, pp. 71, 65.

[3] See Hazlitt, *Early Popular Poetry of England*, III, 251–66. For the authorship of this piece, see Bale, *Index Britanniae Scriptorum*, ed. Poole and Bateson, p. 283.

Possibly the song to which Shepherd refers was a mockery of the failure of the Catholics in England.[1]

Another attack on the Catholics based on popular song is William Keith's "Ballet declaringe the fal of the whore of babylon intytuled Tye thy mare tom boye w[t] other," presumably of Mary's reign.[2] The Catholic church figures here as an unmanageable mare. Harleian MS 7578 contains a spirited ballad, which has also been ascribed to Keith, with the same stanzaic form and virtually the same refrain, in which instructions for controlling a mare are applied to a woman.[3] The music given for it is by Robert Johnson, a composer of Henry VIII's time. The refrain runs:

> Ty the mare, Tom boy, ty the mare, Tom boy,
>> Lest she stray
>> From the awaye,
> Now ty the mare, Tom boy.

This, with slight change, is the burden of a song in *Tom Tyler* representing Tom's shrewish wife as a mare. In 1609 Rowlands refers to some version of "Tie the mare, Tom boy" in his *Crew of kind Gossips:*[4]

> *Ile tye my Mare in thy ground* a new way,
> Worse then the Players sing it in the Play.

Evidently this song or group of songs was affected on the stage during a long period.

The satirists also took advantage of many conventions that seem especially appropriate to the rôle of clown or vice. Jack-a-Lent, whose connection with dance and whose place in the spring games of London in 1553 were mentioned in chapter i, was naturally a favorite figure in the popular satire of the Reformation. In a letter written to Somerset in 1547, Gardiner

---

[1] The lines "Haue in than at a dash,/With swash myry annet swash," which occur in Bale's *Three Laws* (ll. 392–93), may represent some other burlesque of the song.

[2] See Collier, *Bibliographical Account*, I, 424–27, for this and for another ballad by Keith, which attacks the Catholics under the figure of Misrule.

[3] See Ritson, *Ancient Songs and Ballads*, ed. Hazlitt, pp. 175–77.

[4] Hunterian Club, p. 19.

complains of the rhymes "sette fourth to depraue Lent" and of the money the people pay for them. Lent is "buried in rime," he declares, "and Steuen Stockfish bequeathed, not to me, though my name be noted." In reply Somerset reminds Gardiner that in Henry's time "there were that wrote such leude rimes, and plaies as you speke of," and he marvels that Gardiner should take "iack of lents leud balade" so much to heart. "The people bieth those foolish ballats of Jack a lent, So bought they in times past, pardones, and carroles, and Robbin hoodes tales. . . . . Lent remayneth still . . . . although some light and leud men do bury him in writing." In his next letter Gardiner reports that "Jack of lentes testament" has been openly sold in Winchester market.[1] Possibly some of this ballad stuff had been used in the spring games, for the exchange of letters took place in May and June. The testament was a favorite form of legal parody. Burlesque of religious forms is represented in the "Recantacion of Jacke Lent late vicare generall to the mooste cruell Antichriste of Rome," published by Day in 1548.[2] Two lost ballads of a later period that possibly dealt in social satire are "how the worlde ys well amended quod lettle Jack of Lente &c," licensed in 1562–3,[3] and "a shorte and sweete memorye of Jack a Lentes honestie," licensed February 14, 1578. "Honest Jack of Lent" claims to be the author as well as the singer of an elaborate song of 1625 called "Jack of Lent's Ballat," which satirizes in part the follies of the time, including those of the Catholics and the Puritans.[4]

Another conventional comic figure and type of satire is found in the early ballad "An old Song of John Nobody." Here "Little John Nobody" attacks reformers and their doctrines

---

[1] For these passages, see Foxe, *Acts and Monuments* (1563), pp. 734, 735–36, 739.

[2] See Hazlitt, *Handbook*, p. 476. Elderton's famous ballad "Lenton stuff" mentions Jack-a-Lent as preaching repentance (Wright, *Songs and Ballads*, Roxburghe Club, p. 191).

[3] Arber's *Transcript*, I, 205.

[4] See *Choyce Drollery*, ed. Ebsworth, pp. 20–30. The song celebrates the coming of the new Queen Henrietta Maria from France. See also Taylor's "Jack a Lente: his Beginning and Entertainment."

while pretending that he "durst not speak."[1] This is probably the ballad entered on the Register on August 1, 1586, as "Nobodies Complaint," along with a large group of ballads, doubtless most of them old. *The Fitzwilliam Virginal Book* contains a "Nobodyes Gigge" (No. CXLIX) under the name of Richard Farnaby, and this air appears in Continental versions with the title "Pickelhering"[2]—a fact which pretty obviously means that it was used by English comedians abroad. The conventionality of the news motive in satire and especially in satiric song is pointed out later in this chapter. The "Sacke full of Newes," for which players were arrested in 1557, is called a play, but Foxe records what is possibly a characteristic use of the news motive in song for religious satire. In the second year of Mary's reign, the prentice of a minstrel at Colchester was tortured because he "chaunced to sing a song called Newes out of London, which tended agaynst the Masse and against the Queenes misproceadinges."[3] The satirical list typical of the ragman's roll is illustrated in a ballad from the Frank manuscripts, an account of which is given in *Historical Manuscripts Commission* (VI, 457). The ballad attacks prominent Protestants individually with the victims' names written in the margin. It may be the work mentioned in the record of an inquiry directed against the ownership of "popish books, including one called *A knacke to knowe a knave*,"[4] for the author's declared purpose is to teach "how to discerne who is a very Knave."

[1] See Strype, *Mem. of Cranmer* (1853), II, 383–84; Percy, *Reliques*, Bk. V, No. iii. In England the figure was often represented with breeches reaching from the neck (see the title-page of *Nobody and Somebody*, Jonson's *Entertainment at Althorpe*, and Greene's *Quip*), and the satire was ironically spoken by Nobody or directed at Nobody (Baskervill, *English Elements in Jonson's Early Comedy*, p. 11 n.). See "The welspoken Nobody" in Collmann, *Ballads and Broadsides*, Roxburghe Club, No. 91. For a full discussion of the Continental material especially, see Bolte's article in *Shakespeare Jahrbuch*, XXIX, 8–27.

[2] Danckert, *Geschichte der Gigue*, pp. 30–31; see also pp. 11, 14, 26. "Nobody's Jig" is included in the later editions of Playford's *Dancing Master*. See *Catalogue of Manuscript Music in the British Museum*, II, 200, for "No Body's Jigg."

[3] *Acts and Monuments* (1570), II, 2287.

[4] *Hist. MSS Com.*, XI, App. VII, p. 281. See also II, App., p. 155. Perhaps, however, several pieces bore the same proverbial title that was given at the end of the century to a play dealing with manners. The line "And knauish knackes are there deuisde" occurs in Satire VI of Hake's *Newes out of Powles Churchyarde* (1579), where

Probably there was a mass of drama almost or quite as formal as Bale's, sufficient in itself to account for the stress laid upon the stage in efforts to root out heresy. Yet, when the royal proclamation of 1549 in an attempt to be comprehensive adds to the words play and interlude the words "Dialogue or other matter set forthe in form of Plaie," and when the Privy Council meets a campaign of players with an injunction not only against plays and interludes but against songs and "any such like pastimes," there is reasonable ground for believing that the controversy was carried on not only in non-dramatic song but in brief interlude, ballad debate, song drama, and other more or less dramatic types dear to the populace. How early the polemic dialogues characteristic of the Reformation[1] began to take on ballad form it would be impossible to say. There is an approach to ballad meter in "A Goodly Dyalogue betwene Knowledge and Symplicitie," published by Scoloker and Seres, in which Knowledge attacks the mass and other phases of Catholic doctrine while Simplicity defends them at first but is converted in the end. We can begin to trace the polemic ballad in dialogue, however, soon after the inception of the Register. In 1561–2 a ballad was licensed "intituled Rusticus and Sapyence."[2] For March 23, 1588, again, there is an

---

the writer is attacking the Catholics—with the marginal annotation, "Haue you not seene the knacke to knowe knaues by, compiled by many knaues?" A ballad "wherein is shewed a knacke howe to knowe an honest man from a knaue" was licensed November 5, 1594. See also p. 74 below.

[1] *Rede me and be nott wrothe* by Roy and Barlow, called in the introductory epistle a dialogue or brief interlude, and Shepherd's *John Bon and Mast Parson* both have Lutheran dialogues as their exemplars (Herford, *Literary Relations of England and Germany in the Sixteenth Century*, pp. 39–43, 51–55), but the English color is very strong. The first is a news dialogue giving an account of the death of the Mass; the second, representing the popular motive of the droll clown victorious over the man of learning or rank, glorifies the plowman. See also Hazlitt, *Handbook*, p. 473, for "A goodly Dialogue and Dysputation between Pyers Ploweman and a Popist Preest, concernynge the Supper of the Lord." The fragmentary "Overthrowe of the Abbyes, A Tale of Robin Hoode" is a verse allegory in dialogue based on the material of the May game, one shepherd telling another a story symbolizing in Robin Hood a bishop, and so on (Furnivall, *Ballads from Manuscripts*, I, 295–98). See Chambers, *Mediaeval Stage*, II, 221 n. 4, for the interesting proposal made to Henry VIII near the end of his reign that Robin Hood plays should be abolished in order to substitute for them plays memorializing the expulsion of the Bishop of Rome from England, as the annual Hock Tuesday play celebrated the destruction of the Danes.

[2] *Transcript*, I, 178.

entry of a "proper newe ballade dyaloguewyse betwene Syncerytie and Wilfull Ignorance." An extant ballad with a very similar title—"A pleasant Dialogue betweene plaine *Truth*, and blind *Ignorance*"—is in method probably so typical of a popular form of ballad satire as to deserve a brief description.

This dialogue is preserved in Deloney's *Garland of Good Will*,[1] and Mann assumes, unnecessarily I think, that Deloney wrote it.[2] The *Garland* might easily have included old favorites, perhaps retouched by him. The ballad may have been an early effort of Deloney's, however, and if so, it is very likely one of the jigs on which his reputation as a jig maker was founded.[3] It opens with Truth's encountering an aged father Ignorance and asking why he gazes so sadly on "this decaied place." Ignorance replies,

> Chill tell thee by my vazonne
>   that sometime che haue knowne
> A vaire and goodly Abbey,
>   stand here of brick and stone:
> And many holy Friers,
>   as ich may zay to thee:
> Within these goodly Cloysters
>   che did full often zee.

According to the aged father, it was a merry world before the friars went, with everything plentiful and cheap—forty new eggs to be had for a penny. The Bible, he says, is "too big to be true," and nothing it holds is worth the "pretty prayers" of the old days. But of course he gives over in the end and resolves to be done forever with the subtle papists. The sprightliness of this dialogue, its quaint turns, its rustic dialect, and its vivid indication of the scene would make it effective for presentation as song drama.

It is more difficult to suggest possible developments of satire along somewhat more dramatic lines. Some kind of mummery on the part of players from Cambridge directed against Bonner and others was performed at Hinchinbrook in August, 1564.

---

[1] *Works*, ed. Mann, pp. 351–55. Mann takes it for granted that the ballad is the one registered in 1588 (p. 576).

[2] *Ibid.*, pp. xxxvii, xl, etc.   [3] See pp. 108–9 below.

Guzman reports: "The actors came in dressed as some of the imprisoned Bishops. First came the bishop of London [*i.e.* Bonner] carrying a lamb in his hands as if he were eating it as he walked along, and then others with different devices, one being in the figure of a dog with the Host in his mouth."[1] Two elaborate satires on Bonner are in the vein of burlesques designed for feasts of misrule, like *Gesta Grayorum* and *The Christmas Prince*. *A Commemoration or Dirige of Bastarde Edmonde Boner, alias Sauage, vsurped Bisshoppe of London* (1569), said to be "compiled by Lemeke Auale," contains a confession by Bonner, a mock dirge, with nine lessons and responses mixed with Latin from the Catholic service, a mock pedigree in verse, and so on. In the following year appeared *A recantation of famous Pasquin of Rome* with such features as a petition to the Pope and a mass for Bonner. Parody of this sort could have been presented very effectively. A kindred piece which was almost certainly intended for use in festival revelry is Elderton's *A New merry News*,[2] with its news of taverns and drinkers, its calling of a parliament of lovers of wine, its mock arms and mock oaths.

Hard on the Anglican victory followed an era of militant Puritanism. In particular the Puritans showed a growing hostility toward drama and folk game. In the next chapter a passage is quoted indicating that their attitude called forth stage satire from Tarlton. Shortly after his death the more uncompromising and fanatical sentiment of the Puritans came to a focus in the Marprelate controversy of 1588–89. The series of pamphlets in which Martin arraigned the bishops expresses fully this hostility toward the stage and folk pastime, his enemies being repeatedly mocked in terms of popular amusements. In *Hay any Worke for Cooper*, for example, one Glibbery of Halstead, a priest, is represented as having been a vice in a play, leaving the pulpit to join "a Summer Lord with his May-game, or Robin Hood with his Morris Dance"; and in *The Just Censure and Reproofe*, Anderson, parson of Stepney, is charged with

[1] *Cal. of State Papers, Spanish*, 1558–1567, p. 375. See Chambers, *Elizabethan Stage*, I, 128.

[2] Printed about 1576. See Hazlitt, *Fugitive Tracts*, 2d Ser., No. IX; *Studies in Philology*, XVII, 217-20.

having played the potter's part in a morris dance.[1] The opponents of Martin took his cue. In *The Returne of Pasquill*, a proposed work called the "May-game of Martinisme" is described, in which Martin is to play Maid Marian, and other well-known Puritans other rôles.[2] *Martins Months minde* contains the repentance, confession, and testament of Martin, who among other things repents of the "foolery" that he "learned in Alehouses, and at the Theater of Lanam and his fellowes," and in his will disposes of his equipment as fool—his coat, hood, coxcomb, and bauble.[3]

Twice in the tracts the jig is mentioned in connection with this satire. At the end of *A Countercuffe* Pasquil promises Martin Junior: "You shall shortlie haue a Glosse and a Commentarie vppon your Epilogue, with certaine Hayes, Iigges, Rimes, Roundelayes, and Madrigals, seruing for Epitaphes to your Fathers Hearse, to make the world laughe out the long Winters nights." It would be hazardous to infer from the passage anything about the use of jigs against Martin, but a passage from *Martins Months minde* shows conclusively that the jig was a common form of satire on Martin and that it was used on the stage. "For what face soeuer they set on the matter," says the author of the tract, "these Iigges and Rimes, haue nipt the father [Martin] in the head & kild him cleane, seeing that hee is ouertaken in his own *foolerie*. And this hath made the yong youthes his sonnes, to chafe and fret aboue measure, especiallie with the Plaiers," who are mentioned as "hir Maiesties men."[4] The Queen's Men were particularly active in the campaign of the players against Martin. John Laneham, from whom Martin professed to have learned foolery at the Theatre, was a prominent member of the company and apparently a leader in the movement.[5] The line from Lyly's *A Whip for an Ape*, "And let old *Lanam* lash him [Martin] with his rimes,"[6] suggests that Laneham was the author as well as the actor of jigs.

---

[1] See Pierce, *Marprelate Tracts*, pp. 226–27, 369–70.

[2] *Works of Nashe*, ed. McKerrow, I, 82–83.

[3] *Works of Nashe*, ed. Grosart, I, 180, 191.

[4] See *Works of Nashe*, ed. Grosart, I, 166.

[5] For his connection with the Queen's Men and for their use of the Theatre, see Murray, *English Dramatic Companies*, I, 7, 32, 33.

[6] See *Works of Lyly*, ed. Bond, III, 421.

None of the jigs of the Marprelate controversy seem to have survived. Not even ordinary ballads especially appropriate for the purpose have been preserved. Two pretended ballad titles, however, which are mentioned in *Pappe with an hatchet*, may show something of the spirit of the treatment:

I was once determined to write a proper newe Ballet, entituled *Martin and his Maukin*, to no tune, because *Martin* was out of all tune. *Elderton* swore hee had rimes lying a steepe in ale, which shoulde marre all your reasons: there is an olde hacker that shall take order for to print them. O how heele cut it, when his ballets come out of the lungs of the licour. They shall bee better than those of *Bonner*, or the ierkes for a Iesuit. The first begins, Come tit me come tat me, come throw a halter at me.[1]

It is probable, however, that dramatic jigs as well as ordinary ballads were sung by the comedians. While the author of *Martins Months minde* in speaking of "Iigges and Rimes" as having killed Martin possibly uses the two terms to cover one idea, he may on the other hand have in mind contrasted types of satire and may refer to actual dramatic jigs.[2] There is no reason why in the year following Tarlton's death stage jigs should not have had dramatic form, and evidence enough exists for the players' interest in a variety of dramatic skits against Martin.

McKerrow, in a valuable note on the activity of the players and the efforts of the authorities to suppress it, suggests that the dramatic attacks on Martin could perhaps be called shows more appropriately than plays.[3] Indeed it seems much less likely that the regular play was frequently concerned with Martin than that a dramatic skit lampooning him was frequently given in addition to the regular play. Several of these dramatic satires are described or mentioned in the Marprelate tracts. In the opening paragraph of *A Countercuffe giuen to Martin Iunior*, reference is made to the "Anotamie latelie taken of him [Martin], the blood and the humors that were taken from him, by

[1] See *Works of Lyly*, III, 398. A "Ballad Intituled *A gentle Jyrke for the Jesuit*" was licensed February 13, 1581. "Come tit me," etc., sounds like a parody. The passage seems at least to identify Elderton with the controversy.

[2] See Pierce, *op. cit.*, pp. 328, 412, for allusions in the *Theses* and the *Protestatyon* to the satire of "rimers and stage-players."

[3] See *Works of Nashe*, IV, 44-45.

launcing and worming him at *London* vpon the common Stage."
Two passages from *The Returne of Pasquill* use the term *Vetus
Comoedia* in connection with performances satirizing Martin.
The first reads:

Me thought *Vetus Comædia* beganne to pricke him at London in
the right vaine, when shee brought foorth *Diuinitie* wyth a scratcht
face, holding of her hart as if she were sicke, because *Martin* would
haue forced her, but myssing of his purpose, he left the print of his
nayles vppon her cheekes, and poysoned her with a vomit which he
ministered vnto her, to make her cast vppe her dignities and promo-
tions.

In the second passage *Vetus Comoedia* is said to have "called in
a counsell of Phisitians about *Martin,* and found by the sharpnes
of his humour, when they had opened the vaine that feedes his
head, that hee would spit out his lunges within one yere."[1] The
author of *Martins Months minde* declares that Martin was

sundrie waies verie curstlie handled; as first *drie beaten,* & therby his
bones broken, then whipt that made him winse, then wormd and
launced, that he took verie grieuouslie, to be made a *Maygame* vpon
the Stage, and so bangd, both with prose and rime on euerie side, as
he knewe not which way to turne himselfe and at length cleane
Marde.

And he adds that "euerie stage Plaier made a iest of him, and
put him cleane out of countenance."[2] One of the marginal gloss-
es here, evidently on "whipt," is "A whip for an Ape." Bond in
an introductory note to the verse tract "A Whip for an Ape,"
usually ascribed to Lyly, takes it for granted that the reference
in *Martins Months minde* is to this piece. But there may have
been a dramatic satire with the same title. A passage in *An
Almond for a Parrat* refers to Martin "as he was attired like an
Ape on ye stage."[3] It would have been a characteristic bit of
satire to introduce Martin as a trained ape on the string of a
juggler. In the Induction to *Bartholomew Fair* Jonson mentions

[1] For these two passages see *Works of Nashe,* ed. McKerrow, I, 92, 100. In a note
on the first, McKerrow points out that *Vetus Comoedia* would imply a show, perhaps
in the nature of an interlude, rather than a regular play (IV, 60).

[2] *Works of Nashe,* ed. Grosart, I, 175–76.

[3] *Works of Nashe,* ed. McKerrow, III, 354.

as one of the old attractions of the Fair "a Iugler with a wel-educated Ape to come ouer the chaine, for the *King* of *England*, and backe againe for the *Prince*, and sit still on his arse for the *Pope*, and the *King* of *Spaine*." Martin's performance may well have featured an ape's dance, for about 1612 baboon dances seem to have been a stage fad and scandal.[1] The various accounts of the players' attacks on Martin which have been brought together here suggest to me brief farces rather than formal dramas. Whether any of them were song and dance dramas is another question.

During the period of comparative quiet that followed on the Marprelate controversy, the spirit which appears in *The Alchemist, Bartholomew Fair, Fucus Histriomastix, The Muses' Looking-Glass,* and other plays probably ran through much popular satire now lost. On the eve of the Commonwealth, however, as Puritans and Cavaliers girded themselves for their great contest, a new violence of feeling expressed itself in a fresh outburst of pamphleteering and balladry of a controversial sort. In the satiric tracts all the old forms and conventions of satire were again pressed into service. Even Martin was revived.[2] Some of the tracts, like *Pigges Corantoe or Newes from the North* (1642), with its broad nonsense satirizing conditions in England, utilized the news motive. In the mercuries, or news sheets, as well as in the pamphlets generally, there was a conspicuous use of such features as satiric songs and ballads—particularly parodies of popular songs—and burlesque accounts of plays and folk games. The issue of *Mercurius Democritus* for April 20–28, 1652, will illustrate the trend. It contains a droll description of proposed May games of citizens with a masque and bear-baiting, and closes with "a very pretty Dittie" in dialogue sung by "a Scotch Presbyter, and a Green-land Cavaliere" as part of entertainments at a "Musick House at the Globe in Charter-house Lane." In two of the pamphlets, spec-

---

[1] See p. 117 below. For trained apes and imitations in the drama of the period, see *Modern Language Notes*, XXXII, 215–21; XXXV, 248–49.

[2] *A Dialogue. Wherin is plainly layd open the tyrannicall dealing of Lord Bishopps . . . . by Dr. M. Mar-Prelat,* printed in 1589, was reprinted in 1640. *The Araignement of Mr. Persecution . . . . by Yongue Martin Mar-Priest* and probably *Martin's Eccho: or A Remonstrance from His Holinesse Young reverend Martin Mar-Priest* appeared in 1645. Another is mentioned on the next page.

imens of the jig are printed also, and these probably follow an older tradition as closely as do other features of this seventeenth century satire.

The more interesting of the two pamphlets is called *Vox Borealis, or the Northern Discoverie: by Way of Dialogue between Jamie and Willie. Amidst the Babylonians, Printed by Margery Mar-Prelat, in Thwackcoat-Lane, at the Signe of the Crab-tree Cudgell; without any priviledge of the Cater-Caps, the yeare coming on*, 1641.[1] This is a news dialogue containing among other things a mocking account of plays by the prelates, a satiric ballad and a fragment of another ballad parodying the old song of "John Dory,"[2] a burlesque testament, and a jig. The Governor of Edinburgh Castle, says one of the interlocutors (C 4-D 1),

keeps a couple of false Knaves, to laugh at the Lords (a Foole and a Fidler) and when he and they are almost drunke, then they goe to singing of *Scots ijgges*, in a jearing manner, at the *Covenanters*, for surrendring up their Castles.

The Fidler he flings out his his heels and Dances and Sings

> *Put up thy Dagger* Jamie,
>   *and all things shall be mended*,
> *Bishops shall fall, no not at all*
>   *when the Parliament is ended*,

Then the Foole he flirts out his folly and whilst the Fidler playes he sings

> *Which never was intended*,
>   *but onely for to flam thee:*
> *We have gotten the game*,
>   *wee'll keep the same*,
> *Put up thy Dagger* Jamie.

The jig may have been written especially for the tract, but it is hardly more than an adaptation of an old song, for a tune under the name of the Elizabethan composer Giles Farnaby is given in the manuscript *Fitzwilliam Virginal Book* with the title "Put up thy Dagger, Jemy."[3] What is quoted here probably represents only the opening of the jig.

The account of this performance helps greatly to enforce

[1] Reprinted in *Harleian Miscellany*, IV (1809), 422–41.

[2] See Chappell, *Popular Music*, I, 67–68, 359ª.

[3] Ed. Maitland and Squire, No. CXXVII.

the idea of the jig as originally simply popular song accompanied by dance. Customarily, we are told, when the Governor of the Castle of Edinburgh and his household are in their cups, two semiprofessional entertainers perform jigs. An example is given which, like "Pipe mery annot" and "Tie the mare, Tom boy," seems to parody popular song. Even if the song was newly written by the pamphleteer and was not actually a current jig, it still illustrates the type, and it does not differ essentially from a multitude of other satiric songs and ballads not called jigs. Like most of them, it is not in dialogue, though the alternate singing gives a dialogue effect. Vigorous dancing accompanies it. There seems to be no reason why any other mocking song to a tune suitable for lively dancing might not have been a jig. Songs of political satire were probably performed as jigs in great numbers in camps and castles, in taverns and other places of informal gathering during the period—a custom which is reflected in the picture of an older epoch drawn in the passage quoted earlier from Heywood's *Edward IV*.

Undoubtedly there was an abundance of material for such performances. The vogue of popular ballad and song is reflected throughout the satiric tracts, as I have said. In the words of a song at the end of the tract called the *Resolution of the Round-heads* (1642):

> Your Wit abounded,
> Gentle Round-head,
> When you abus'd the Bishops in a Ditty,
> When as you sanged,
> They must be hanged,
> A Timpinee of malice made you witty.

The Cavaliers, however, were still more given to turning their wit against the Roundheads in ballad and catch. An interesting early record of the use of satiric song on both sides is found in *Vox Borealis* again (B 2):

There was a poore man (and ye ken *povertie is the badge of Poetry*) who to get a little money, made a Song of all the Capps in the King-dome, and at every verse end concludes thus,

> *Of all the Capps that ever I see,*
> *Either great or small, Blew Cappe for me.*[1]

[1] This song was probably modeled directly on the popular ballad the "Song of the Caps" or "Ballad of the Caps," in which different caps stand for classes and types of

But his *mirth* was quickly turned to *mourning,* for he was clapt up in the *Clinke* for his boldnesse, to meddle with any such matters. One *Parker,* the Prelats Poet, who made many base Ballads against the *Scots,* sped but *little better,* for he, and his *Antipodes* were like to have tasted of Justice *Longs liberalitie:* and hardly he escaped his Powdering-Tubb, which the vulgar people calls a Prison.[1]

The second tract containing a jig is *A New Play Called Canterburie His Change of Diot* (1641),[2] a brief satire on Laud in the form of a burlesque play. To complete the idea the play ends with the following jig:

The Gig betweene a Paritor *and the* Foole.

*P*Aritor,	*W*hat newes sir, what newes, I pray you know you,
Foole,	Correction doth waite sir, to catch up his due.
Par.	His due sir, whats that, I pray you tell me,
Foole,	not blew cap, nor red cap, but cap of the See,
Par.	What caps are these pray you, shall I never know,

---

citizens. See *Sportive Wit,* pp. 23 ff.; *Choyce Drollery,* ed. Ebsworth, pp. 135–38, 319–20; D'Urfey, *Pills to Purge Melancholy,* IV, 157–59. Collier, *Book of Roxburghe Ballads,* pp. 172–76, gives a version as printed for the early seventeenth century printer Trundle. Similar use of the cap is frequent in the literature of the period, as in II *Honest Whore,* I, iii. In the Civil War there was, of course, much symbolism of caps as representing political parties, the blue cap standing for the Scots. A reference to Cater-Caps occurs in the title of *Vox Borealis* itself, and different kinds of caps are used symbolically in the jig to be quoted from *Canterburie His Change of Diot.* A ballad intitled "Blew Capp" was entered on the Register March 22, 1634. The ballad "Blew Cap for me" is preserved in the Roxburghe Collection (*Roxburghe Ballads,* I, 74–79) and in *Choyce Drollery* (ed. Ebsworth, pp. 133–35, 317–19; dated by Ebsworth 1633–48), but the refrain is different from that given in *Vox Borealis.* The tune "Blew Cap for me" appears in Playford's *Dancing Master.*

[1] Parker is known to have written ballads against the Scots though he denied being the prelates' poet. See Rollins in *Modern Philology,* XVI, 457–63. The passage seems to imply that "Antipodes" was a ballad, but it was entered on the Register, July 18, 1638, under the vague term book. The characterization of the times as topsyturvy was conventional. See for example *Pigges Corantoe,* p. 7, for the complaint: "But now the world is turned upside downe, and all are acting the Antipodes, young boyes command old Souldiers, wise men stand cap in hand to fine fooles, maidens woe widowes, married women rule their husbands. . . . . It was not so in *Temporibus Noah,* ah no"; *Catalogue of a Collection of English Ballads,* Bibliotheca Lindesiana (cited later as the Crawford Collection), No. 458, for a ballad of about 1640 to 1650 with the title "A Cheat in all Trads, Or the World turned upsid down"; and *Rump,* I, 135–36, for a song opening "The world is now turn'd upside-down," with a refrain "And alas poor Parliament now, now, now."

[2] See Ashbee's *Occasional Fac-simile Reprints,* No. XV.

Foole,   The caps that would us, and our Church overthrow,
They both sing,   O wellady, wellady, what shall wee doe thene
    Weel weare tippet foole caps, and never undoe men.

Paritor,   Did you never heare pray, of Lambeth great Faire:
Where white puddings were sold for two shillings a paire.
Foole,   Yes Sir I tell you I heard it and wept,
I thinke you are broke e're since it was kept,
Par.   Broke I am not, you foole I am poore.[1]
Foole,   your master is sicke you are turned out of doore,
They both sing,   O wellady, wellady, &c.

Parator,   I might have beene Iester once as well as you,
Foole)   you Iested too much, which now you doe rue,
Par.   wherein have I jested, like a foole in place,
Foole,   to worke projects for such, who practise disgrace,
Par.   you foole will not profit make any thing done,
Foole,   such profit make fooles, soone after to runne,
Both together,   O wellady, wellady, &c.

While the play itself is the crudest sort of burlesque, this after-piece was undoubtedly modeled on current jigs and may have been a typical stage jig of a late period. It has a number of popular features—in its use of the news motive for satire and of caps as distinguishing parties, in the presence of the fool with his mocking answers, and in the ancient refrain of "Welladay" sung by the pair together. The rapid dialogue, too, is characteristic of many of the jigs, as will be seen later.[2]

The device of casting satire in the form of news, which has already been encountered several times and comes into frequent notice later, seems to me important enough for the background of the jig to call for some comment here. Apparently Nashe refers to news pieces as satiric jigs when he says in *Pierce Penilesse* (1592): "Looke to it, you Booksellers and Stationers, and let not your shops be infected with any such goose gyblets or stinking garbadge, as the Iygs of newsmongers."[3] Moreover,

---

[1] *am poore* is printed as one word.

[2] For a tune called the "Parrator," see *Roxburghe Ballads*, I, 504; II, 353. For "A new ballad of the Parrator and the Divell," see *Shirburn Ballads*, No. LXXV. A ballad "Devill and the pariter" was entered on the Register December 14, 1624, and "The Paritour" June 1, 1629.

[3] *Works*, ed. McKerrow, I, 239.

the fact that the author of *Canterburie His Change of Diot* chooses a news dialogue to serve as jig for his burlesque play suggests that the formula would at least be recognized as typical of the jig.

The device reflects the passion for sensation and gossip at which Breton glances in his mock litany of *Pasquils Passe* (1600) when he prays to be delivered from "a delight in hunting after newes." Satire was so frequently given this form by "Rymesters, Play-patchers, Jig-makers, Ballad-mongers, and Pamphlet-stitchers"[1] that the presence of the word news in titles is usually significant of a burlesque or satirical treatment. The motive runs extensively through ballads and songs, and will be illustrated later from this field. In Dialogue VII of the *Arte of Flatterie* (1579) Fulwell indicates the use of news satire on the stage when he pictures the fool as the mouthpiece of stage satire and puts satiric news in his mouth, though not in the form of song. He who would school folly by means of the stage, says Fulwell,

Best welcome is when he resines, the Scaffold to the foole.
Lo now the foole is come in place, though not with patcht pyde coate,
To tell such newes as earst hee saw within Cocklorels bote,

and the shipload of flatterers and climbers is then described.[2] Stage song in the form of satiric news is suggested by Fenton, however, when he condemns the magistrate for not suppressing "these Players, whether they bee Minstrels, or Enterludours, who, on a scaffold" babble "vaine newes to the sclander of the world, put there in scoffing the vertues of honest men."[3]

The news song is usually a monologue addressed to an audience, but the colloquy of neighbors or those who meet by the way is also common. Sometimes the news is mere nonsense and burlesque. An excellent specimen of this kind, which is fairly

---

[1] These are the classes that the author of the satiric *News from Gravesend* claims in the Epistle Dedicatory to have summoned (Collier, *Bibliographical Account*, II, 24). For pamphlets with news titles, see Hazlitt, *Handbook*, pp. 417–19.

[2] See also *Hyckescorner*, ll. 326–89.

[3] *A forme of Christian pollicie gathered out of French* (1574), p. 144. The passage is added to the original.

early, opens with droll and homely details of a thoroughly conventional type:[1]

> Newes! newes! newes! newes!
> Ye never herd so many newes!
>
> A . . . . vpon a strawe,
> Gudlyng of my cowe,
> Ther came to me jake-dawe,
> Newes! newes!
>
> Our dame mylked the mares talle,
> The cate was lykyng the potte;
> Our mayd came out wit a flayle,
> And layd hor vnder fotte.
> Newes! newes!

Ballads in which neighbors were characterized by the coarseness or drollery of their gossip evidently developed early. The
ballad licensed in 1562–3 as "go[o]d morowe to you good syster
Jone"[2] and a second licensed September 18, 1579, as "Jo[a]ne
came ouer London bridge and told me all this geere" were apparently of this type. What is probably a variant of the first is
a monologue preserved in D'Urfey's *Pills to Purge Melancholy*
(VI, 315–16), opening "Good morrow Gossip *Joan*." It tells
of such incidents as,

> I've lost my Wedding-Ring,
>   That was made of Silver gilt;
> I had Drink would please a King,
>   And the whorish Cat has spill'd it.

This song was probably popular through a long period.[3] In a
poem called "Newes" which was published in *Prince d'Amour*

---

[1] See Böddeker, *Jahrbuch für rom. u. engl. Sprache u. Literatur*, Neue Folge, II, 90.
Böddeker dates the manuscript in which it is preserved before 1579. Halliwell (Wright
and Halliwell, *Reliquiæ Antiquæ*, I, 239–40) assigns the song to the reign of Henry VIII.
One line in a medley of the same period (*Anglia*, XII, 596 n. 3), "yesterday was owr
dame kow broght to grase," must have been taken from a similar song.

[2] *Transcript*, I, 200. See also p. 96 for the ballad "be mery good Jone" (1558–9).

[3] See *Modern Philology*, XXIII, 124. For the tune, which was used in several
ballad operas, see Chappell, *Popular Music*, II, 672–73. The song has survived in folk
lore to the present day (Williams, *Folk-Songs of the Upper Thames*, pp. 41–42), and
others of the type survived until the eighteenth and nineteenth centuries. Herd col-

(1660), nonsense is combined with definite satire on the abuses of the day. Beginning with a promise of "strange news," it tells of a time when "Charing-cross was a pretty little boy" or it snowed pease and bacon, and contains thrusts at such classes as lawyers, landlords, brokers, and shrewish wives.[1] Another song with the same title appeared in *Merry Drollery*[2] the following year. The first stanza is typical:

> White Bears are lately come to Town,
>   That's no news;
> And Cuckolds Dogs shall pull them down,
>   That's no news
> Ten Dozen of Capons sold for a Crown,
>   Hey ho, that's news indeed.

This seems to be a monologue, but a second character might have sung the alternate lines. In the ballad dialogue "Newes good and new," which is discussed in chapter vi, nonsense news yields completely to ironic satire on the ills of society.

It is probable that news songs were commonly sung by disards like the fool or clown of game or stage and by grotesques like Robin Goodfellow. They must have been especially prevalent in Christmas pastimes, where the spirit of parody and burlesque ruled. Characteristic comic figures are found in Nashe's *Pierce Penilesse*, in which a minor devil tells the news to the clown, and in a similar prose satire, *Tell-Trothes New-yeares Gift* (1593), reporting a conversation between Robin Goodfellow, just come from hell, and Tom Tell Troth, a clown in whose mouth nonsense and satire of the news type were placed.[3] The presentation of satire as news from hell or heaven

---

lected an example turned to the purpose of political satire, which opens "O wow, Marget, are ye in?" (Hecht, *Songs from Herd's Manuscripts*, pp. 214–15, 322). See also Cromek, *Remains of Nithsdale and Galloway Song*, pp. 112–13, for "What news to me, Carlin?"

[1] Printed also in *Merry Drollery* (1661) with the title "Nonsence" (ed. Ebsworth, pp. 29–30, 366).

[2] Ed. Ebsworth, pp. 159–61, 378.

[3] Published by the New Shakspere Society. Entered on the Register December 16, 1592. See *NED* under "Tom"[7] for early occurrences of the name Tell Troth, and Cheyney, *History of England*, I, 93, for an abusive letter signed "Tom Tell Troth." A ballad called "Tom Tell Truth" was licensed in 1564–5 (*Transcript*, I, 270), which

with devil, goblin, or ghost as spokesman is frequently found in the news tracts[1] and ballads. The first recorded ballad of the type seems to be that entered in 1561–2 as "newes out of heaven and hell."[2] On August 9, 1583, again a ballad was licensed with the title "A message of Newes sent from the highe courte of heaven sent latelie by Lazalus [i.e. Lazarus] prince of povertie vnto all his lovinge freindes the poore distressed people here on earth &c." In all probability the news features of religious polemics were borrowed from the games at the time when numerous popular conventions—like the satire of Jack-a-Lent—were being adapted to the purposes of the Reformation. A few Restoration ballads of the type are cited below.[3]

Following the era of *Vox Borealis* and *Canterburie His Change of Diot* there came a long period during which plays and ballads were under ban, and the Cavaliers, who produced the bulk of the satire after 1642, were not in a position to indulge freely in ridicule of the Puritans. But if it was difficult to control players and printers, it was still more difficult to control the writers and singers of ballads. The production of satiric song went merrily on, and presumably the singing and dancing of it. The activity in this field may be judged by the mass of satiric balladry which appeared in broadsides and particularly in collections after the Restoration. *The Rump*, for example, which came out in 1662, is described on the title-page as a collection of the "Choycest Poems and Songs relating to the Late

---

was possibly the same one published in the Restoration as "Tom Tell-Truth . . . . to the Tune of, *Tanta ra ra ra, Tantivee*," beginning "I killed a man . . . . run . . . . without a head" and continuing with such nonsense as "I see *Paul's* steeple run upon wheels" (*Roxburghe Ballads*, VIII, 425).

[1] Early examples of titles are *News out of hell: a dialogue betwene Charon and Zebul, a deuil*, 1536; Basille, *Newes out of heauen*, 1541 (Ames, *Typographical Antiquities*, ed. Herbert, I, 486, 496); *Newes come from Hell of loue vnto all her welbeloued frendes*, a tract licensed to Copland in 1565–6 (Arber's *Transcript*, I, 296; Collier, *Bibliographical Account*, II, 22–23).

[2] *Transcript*, I, 181. The account in "The Dead Man's Song," printed for F. Coules, is called at the end "the newes from heaven and hell" (*Roxburghe Ballads*, I, 223–29). The ballad was entered March 1, 1675, under the printed title.

[3] Apparently the influence of the convention is to be seen in the Epilogue of Dryden's *Tyrannic Love*, where Valeria (acted by Nell Gwynn), who has killed herself in the play, appears as the "Ghost of poor departed Nelly . . . . a little harmless Devil," to tell "strange news."

Times. By the most Eminent Wits, from *Anno* 1639. to *Anno* 1661," and the Epistle to the Reader declares that they were written to do his majesty service during a time when it was unsafe to own the authorship.

I have not found the name jig attached to satiric ballads of the Restoration, though numbers of them in lively and burlesque vein might have been effectively performed as jigs. The news device continues popular,[1] and religious forms are parodied in the litanies which had an unusual vogue through the Restoration period.[2] The Puritan leaders are also satirized as the Nine Worthies.[3] Ballads modeled on the songs of trades celebrate Cromwell as a brewer,[4] and a series of songs on the cobbler, especially on Hewson, who rose to such prominence under Cromwell, carry on the tradition of the cobbler in religious polemics.[5] Chappell mentions the ballads "A Hymn to the Gentle Craft; or, Hewson's Lamentation" and "The Cobbler's Last Will and Testament; Or, the Lord Hewson's Translation" in connection with the tune "My Name is Old Hewson the Cobbler," used for several ballad operas and evidently derived from a ballad of the same sort.[6]

By way of dialogue there is "A Choice and Diverting Dialogue between Hughson the Cobler and Margery his Wife; which Happened about Twelve o'Clock, at his arrival Home from the Ale-house," opening,

> So you old sot, is this an hour
> To be hearde rapping at your door?[7]

[1] See Wright, *Political Ballads published in England during the Commonwealth*, Percy Society, pp. 219–22, for "News from Hell," in which a ghost brings news of the devil's discomfiture over the dissolution of Parliament, and pp. 126–31, 139–45, 146–63 (this with ragman's roll also), 205–14, for other news ballads, in some cases with the introduction of the devil. See also *Roxburghe Ballads*, IX, xix,* for the title "The Case is Altered; or, Dreadfull News from Hell" (1660).

[2] See *Rump*, I, 160–65; II, 115–19, 183–88; Wright, *Political Ballads*, pp. 135–38, 261–65. See Wright, pp. 242–48, for a passing use of legal parody also, in "Hugh Peters Last Will and Testament: or, The Haltering of the Divell."

[3] *Roxburghe Ballads*, VII, 658–60; *Rump*, II, 104–6; Wright, *Political Ballads*, pp. 188–94.

[4] *Merry Drollery*, ed. Ebsworth, pp. 221–25, 252–54, 387, 392. See also pp. 255–57.

[5] See p. 102 below.   [6] *Popular Music*, II, 450–51.

[7] See Douce Penny Histories, Vol. V (Bodl. Douce PP. 180 [14]). The first two stanzas are quoted in Halliwell's *Fugitive Tracts*, Percy Society, p. 95.

The influence of this satire on Hewson is apparent in a "Dialogue between a Cobler and his Wife,"[1] a song of six stanzas which seems particularly suited for performance as jig. Joan opens the altercation:

> Go, go, you vile sot!
> Quit your pipe and your pot;
> Get home to your stall and be doing:
> You puzzle your pate
> With whimsies of state,
> And play with edge-tools to your ruin.

She reproaches Kit for giving up his Bible and psalter to "riot and roar/ For *Babylon's* whore." Kit, however, is fired with political ambitions:

> I'll new vamp the state;
> The church I'll translate:
> Old shoes are no more worth the mending.

Both this dialogue and the one between Hewson and his wife follow closely the model of the conjugal brawls to be studied in chapter vi,[2] especially those in which the wife accuses the husband of drunkenness and lack of thrift. Some evidence for the dramatic presentation of the type is given there.

Though the name jig is not associated with any of these songs, the large number of the mocking allusions to the jig indicates its importance in the period. Presbyterian Whigs are said to have been the first to teach Scottish jigs.[3] Cleveland in

---

[1] See *The Hive* (2d ed., 1724), I, 35–36 (and also *Vocal Miscellany* [3d ed., 1738], I, 66–67), where the dialogue was probably shortened for miscellany publication. I have not run across an earlier form, but the piece seems to be at least early enough to reflect the resurgence of Catholic hopes in the reign of James II. It was probably written before 1682, for Hickes's *Grammatical Drollery* of that year contains a song (pp. 37–38) that offers a coarse parallel. A prose piece called "A New and Diverting Dialogue Both Serious and Comical that passed the other day between a noted Shoemaker & his Wife" (Brit. Mus. 1077. g. 36 [5] and 11621. b. 31 [5]; see also Halliwell, *op. cit.*, p. 96), with a landlord for a third character, was popular as a chapbook at the end of the eighteenth century and the opening of the nineteenth. It resembles the prose brawls of the Commonwealth.

[2] See pp. 171–74 below. See D'urfey, *Pills*, II, 265–66, for "A Comical Dialogue Between blunt English Johnny, and his Wife Scotch Gibby, about Modern Affairs," which is introduced by a short prose dialogue.

[3] See *Roxburghe Ballads*, V, 23. Similarly Jack Presbyter, a term modeled on Jack Pudding, is a popular one for the Presbyterians (*ibid.*, IV, 596, 648–49; V, 34, 40).

his "Mixed Assembly" describes the Puritan leaders as advancing in couples to dance a jig. The account is in the burlesque vein of Nashe's May game of Martinism. In late editions of Playford's *Dancing Master* a tune is given called "Old Noll's Jig."[1] In many cases the allusions are to dance, for the folk jig as dance was enormously popular in the Restoration. On the other hand, the charge brought against one of the loyal clergy during the Commonwealth was that he "had rather hear *a Pair of Organs*, than the singing of *Hopkins's* Psalms, which he called *Hopkins's Jiggs*,"[2] and we hear of Geneva jigs as well as of Geneva ballads.[3]

Personal satire was exceedingly common among the people.[4] Individuals were of course constantly being held up to ridicule in songs and ballads that were secretly posted or sometimes printed and spread broadcast;[5] and throughout the period, to be made the hero of comic ballads hawked and sung about the streets and byways was regarded as the natural penalty of becoming ridiculous or notorious.[6] A few of the more interesting phases of this personal satire need to be illustrated before its relation to the jig is taken up.

A very crude form of mockery is reflected in the record of an Oxfordshire investigation of 1584 into the singing of a libelous song:

Anne Wrigglesworth of Islip cited, negat "that ever she made any ryme, but she said a certeyne ryme and for goodwill she told the same to Goodwife Willyams and her daughter, and to the Goodwife Cadman and her daughter, *becaus she thought it was made to there dis-*

[1] See Chappell, *Popular Music*, II, 449–50. See p. 414 for an account of how soldiers under Cromwell celebrated their vandalism at Peterborough by piping "lascivious jigs" about the marketplace "on two pair of organs" while their comrades danced.

[2] See Walker, *An Attempt to Recover the Numbers and Sufferings of the Clergy* (1714), p. 9.

[3] See *The Transproser Rehears'd: or the Fifth Act of Mr. Bayes's Play* (1673), p. 17: "Now having had our *Geneva* Jigg, let us advance to our more serious Councils." For a "Geneva Ballad" satirizing the Puritans, see *Bagford Ballads*, II, 649.

[4] For a general statement, see Cheyney, *History of England*, I, 92–93.

[5] See Hartshorne, *Ancient Metrical Tales*, pp. 225–26, for an early example.

[6] For a few of the well-nigh innumerable passages showing this, see Chappell, *Popular Music*, I, 253; II, 422–23.

creditt, and she hard it as she came to the markett to Oxford abowte Christmes last of one Robert Nevell who did singe it by the way and the ryme is this viz

> Yf I had as faire a face as John Willms
> his daughter Elzabeth hasse,
> Then wold I were a taudrie lace as Goodman
> bolts daughter Marie dosse;
> And if I had as mutche money in my pursse
> as Cadmans daughter Margaret hasse,
> Then wold I haue a basterd lesse
> Then Butlers mayde Helen hasse."[1]

This is apparently a formula into which any names could be fitted. Such formulas for singing at fairs and general meeting places were probably prevalent among the vulgar. They are known even at the present day. Another account with a number of droll details belongs to the proceedings of the Star Chamber for 1632,[2] when several defendants were heavily fined for making falsely a scurrilous song defaming a certain Martha Osmonton and a man of the "holie Brotherhood." The song was begun in Rymes alehouse by a servant of one Martin; Turpin gave a quart of wine to a scribe to write it down; Martin and two others set it to "the tune of the Watch Currants and Tom of Bedlam"; and Turpin showed it to three people, including the widow Palmer when he went to buy sugar in her shop. No names were called, but it was generally understood who were meant, partly from the description of Martha, "Her face is long, her browes are black, her high woodden heeles they are in the fault."

A specimen in dialogue which uses the device of news is found in "A dialogue betwene a serving man and a Clowne of the state of Oxn" from a manuscript of All Souls College (155, fols. 242–45). This ballad of over forty stanzas heaps the most scurrilous abuse upon a number of individuals, with plays upon their names, the names being written in the margin of the manuscript. It opens:

[1] Quoted from *Bagford Ballads*, I, xviii–xix, where *Historical Collections for Oxfordshire*, MSS. XIV. *Eccles. Records*, fol. 263, at the Bodleian is cited as the source. The verse is printed in italic.

[2] See *Reports of Cases in the Courts of Star Chamber and High Commission*, ed. Gardiner, Camden Society, pp. 149–53.

Ser::   Howe, nowe, John a dogg*es* what newes a broad?

Clo: And thinke yo^w I haue nought abode
        because I seeme a carelesse clowne
        I ride and heare the newes abroade
        I sit and see the trickes in towne./

        The devill is dead in devonshire late
[*Ser.*]   an happie tale if it be true:
[*Clo.*]   wch gives the checke and not the mate
[*Ser.*]   and are you dead S^r devill adewe:/

I judge that this ballad in its present form belongs to the early part of the seventeenth century, but its framework is evidently old. Brydges in his *Censura Literaria* (II, 242–43) gives an account of a ballad written by Thomas Buckley, an Oxonian of the early part of Elizabeth's reign, entitled "Ho, ho, John of Dogs, what news?" Brydges prints only the first stanza, which is substantially the same as the one above beginning "The devill is dead." The opening of these two news ballads is probably highly conventional. A round from Ravenscroft's *Pammelia* (No. 56) begins "Iacke boy, ho boy newes," and the first words are quoted by Grumio in *The Taming of the Shrew*, IV, i, when Curtis asks him for the news. The lines,

> The devil is dead, for there I was;
> Iwis it is full true,

occur in an old nonsense song[1] similar in material to the old nonsense news song already discussed.

It may be that the form of personal abuse known as flyting simply reflects life among the uninhibited masses, but certainly it was popular enough in the sixteenth and seventeenth centuries and at times took on the color of recognized pastime. Flyting was repeatedly forbidden at Edinburgh during the sixteenth century. It was decreed in 1548, for example, that

---

[1] See Chambers and Sidgwick, *Early English Lyrics*, p. 254. See Brit. Mus. *Cat. of MS Music*, II, 208, for a "Scot[c]h Jigg," or "ye D'ls Dead." For the phrase as a proverb, see Skelton, *Colin Clout*, ll. 36–37; Heywood, *Three hundred Epigrammes, vpon proverbes*, No. 98. Compare the reiterated "Le diable est mort" of Denys in *The Cloister and the Hearth*.

"na maner of wemen within this burgh speciallie the frute sellares be fund on the hie gaitt flyting with vthers or with the officeris of the burgh or vsing of ony maner of bairdrie."[1] The proverbial profanity and abuse of the fishwives of the Billingsgate region of London may have arisen from decades of practice in flyting. Lupton says of the tavern gatherings of the fish-women, "when they haue done their Faire, they meet in mirth, singing, dancing, and in the middle as a *Parenthesis*, they vse scolding, but they doe vse to take and put vp words, and end not till either their money or wit, or credit be cleane spent out."[2] A prose dialogue of a later period between "two fishwives, in *Newgate Market*, upon a market-day, where they had store of audience"[3] has the appearance of picturing realistically the scurrilous tradeswomen of the day. But a passage in Davenant's *Wits* (1636) referring to the amount of noise made by apple-wives who wrangle for a sieve (I, i) suggests the organized flyting with a prize to the winner. *Mercurius Democritus* for December 22–29, 1652, makes a burlesque announcement of a "Tryal of Skill" to take place between a fishwoman and a kitchen-stuff woman with such weapons as "Tooth and Naile, Long tongue & Taile, Thou Whore, and thou Whore"; and *Mercurius Fumigosus* for February 7–14, 1655, tells of a contest between "a Shee-Dragon in Popping-hole Alley" and a "Billings-gate Fish-woman," with kitchen-stuff women acting as judges. "Now I had thought," says the author of *The Transproser Rehears'd* (1673), "that in a Controversie betwixt the Oyster-women and the Opponent *Tankard-bearers*, the cause had ever been carried with confidence & Noise, and that the Rabble adjudg'd the Victory on their side, who manag'd the dispute with the greatest clamour, prosecuting the baffled Scold, that is the *modester*, with stones & hooting" (p. 31).

The influence of tradition is perhaps to be seen, then, in certain seventeenth century ballads which are mere railing

---

[1] *Extracts from the Records of the Burgh of Edinburgh*, II, 141. See also I, 97; II, 73.

[2] *London and the Countrey Carbonadoed*, Aungervyle Society, p. 29.

[3] From *Vinegar and Mustard or Worm-wood Lectures for Every Day in the Week .... Taken verbatim in short writing by J. W.* (1673), reprinted in Hindley's *Old Book Collector's Miscellany*, Vol. III, No. 29.

matches.[1] Their nature is clear from such titles as "The Bloody Battle at Billingsgate, Beginning with a Scolding bout between two young Fish-women, Doll and Kate," and "The Unthankful Servant: Or, A Scolding Match betwen Two Cracks of the Town, Margery Merry thought, and Nancy her Mistress."[2] The type is illustrated in the ballad flyting called "A new Dialogue between Alice and Betrice, As they met at the Market one Morning early,"[3] opening "Good Neighbour, why d'ye look awry." Beatrice accuses Alice of trying to ensnare her husband:

> You smack, you smick, you wash, you lick,
>   you smirk, you swear, you grin,
> You nod, you wink, and in your Drink,
>   you strive for to draw him in.
>
> *Alice.* You Lye you Punk, you're almost Drunk,
>   and now you Scold and make a Strife,
> With running in the Score, and playing the Wh . . . ,
>   you lead him a weary Life.
>
> *Bet.* Tell me so once again, you Dirty Quean,
>   and I'll pull you by the Coif.

This dialogue would seem highly appropriate to the pastimes of the fishwomen whom Lupton speaks of as singing, dancing, and scolding at the alehouses in the evenings. A shortened redaction of it in which the two husbands take part at the end was actually sung on the stage—in Ravenscroft's *Canterbury Guests* of 1695.[4] D'Urfey in his use of jig conventions toward the end of the century introduced a ballad of this type into his *Massaniello*, Part I, in a fashion that suggests a dramatic vogue. In V, i, a satirical picture of a citizens' feast is presented, with "a comical Entertainment of Singing and Dancing." The song

---

[1] Smith and Gray, Camell and Churchyard, waged their warfare in a series of ballads (Collmann, *Ballads and Broadsides*, Roxburghe Club, Nos. 19–30; Hazlitt, *Fugitive Tracts*, Ser. I, Nos. VI–XII). The famous literary flytings of Scotland between Dunbar and Kennedy and between Montgomery and Polwart, as well as those of Skelton in England, were in verse.

[2] See Pepys Collection of Ballads, IV, 289, and Brit. Mus. C 39. k. 6, No. 8. The first has narrative stanzas introducing and closing the dialogue.

[3] See *Bagford Ballads*, I, 67–70. The copy, licensed by Pocock, dates between 1685 and 1688. The dialogue is printed in D'Urfey's *Pills to Purge Melancholy*, V, 73–74, simply as "A Song."

[4] III, v. The stage form was set to music by Purcell (*Works*, Purcell Society, XVI, xiii–xv, 87–94). The tune called for in the broadside is "Mopsaphil."

is "A Dialogue between two Fish-Wives" very similar in tone and language to those printed on broadsides.

Popular devices of a more or less dramatic character also were used to satirize individuals, apparently tradesmen in particular. According to the report of the Manuscripts Commission, the Bridgewater manuscripts under date of 1609 contain

Notes about a case brought by John Hole, a clothier of Wells, employing about 500 poor people weekly, against Stephen Milward and a great many other persons (including the mayor of Wells) for libellous plays acted on Sundays in May and June 1607: including, minstrels, for playing at cards and drinking in time of divine service, "actors of the shewe, wherein the plaintiff and other tradesmen were deciphered, and acted by their persons and trades," one Will Gamage, author of a first libel, and "who acted the holing game[1] with pictures, in the lewd manner described in the bill," painters of the pictures, &c.; William Williams, *alias* Morgan, who invented the second libel, with others who sent the first one to London to be printed; and various persons who in the Common Council voted money from the town-stock and church-stock to maintain the suit against the plaintiff. With a letter from the Earl of Hertford to Lord Ellesmere, dated at Littleton, 13 Nov. 1609, asking for favour to be shown to the Recorder of Wells, as being near to him, and to the mayor's son, as being his household servant. Notes of precedents for the prosecutions for similar libels, viz., for a libel by one Colmer against Thos. Smalebrooke, a mercer in Bremingham, for his manner of buying and selling, usury, &c., which ended thus,

"Read now my frindes who this catchpoole should be,
The steward of the towne in plaine tearmes tys hee,
Smalebrooke by name, a Brooke that yeldes no fish,
But froggs and toads, and that's no deynty dishe";
for which Colmer in 5 Ja. I was pilloried and fined; libel against three tradesmen of Gloucester and their wives; &c.[2]

This type of attack on tradespeople is recorded in Exeter as early as the middle of the fourteenth century, and had doubtless never ceased in England.[3]

---

[1] This may have repeated an old device or been based on one, for on December 23, 1587, Wolf entered on the Register "a small thinge called *the game at the hole, otherwyse, yf you be not pleased, you shalbe eased.*"

[2] *Hist. MSS Com.*, XI, App. VII, p. 161. An account of satire on the Earl of Lincoln in a play that was apparently part of a May game in 1610, is also given here.

[3] See Chambers, *Mediaeval Stage*, II, 190.

It is clear enough from general allusions both in the sixteenth and in the seventeenth century that songs of a personal type, whether of abuse or of flattery, were constantly used as jigs. One of the most interesting allusions occurs in Nashe's *Strange Newes, Of the intercepting certaine Letters* (1592): "*Hay gee* (Gentlemen) comes in with his Plowmans whistle in prayse of *Peter Scurfe* the penne-man, and *Turlery ginkes*, in a light foote Iigge, libels in commendation of little witte very loftily."[1] Whatever this may mean by way of satire on Harvey, the reference is to song and dance of countrymen. In *A Pil to purge Melancholie*, written about 1599, there is an epistle signed "Snuffe," in which the one addressed is accused of presuming "to call my vnstayned name in question, with thy scattring papers like halfe penny gigges"; and the answer, signed "Snipsnap," states, "I do perseuere in my scuruie louzie meaning, to beray & betray the world with my flattring papers like sixe pennie gigges."[2] Taylor in *Superbiae Flagellum* denounces libelers who "rime and Iigge on others detriment," and Fennor in his *Defence* declares that he lives to

> Make Iigges and Ballads of thy apish toyes,
> For to be sung by thred-bare Fidlers boyes.[3]

At the end of his *Nine Days' Wonder* Kemp pays his respects to the "impudent generation of Ballad-makers," whom he accuses of having filled the country with "lies of his never-done acts" in connection with his morris dance from London to Norwich. "I have made a privy search," he says, "what private Jig-monger of your jolly number hath been the Author of these abominable Ballets written of me."

Nowhere is the relation of jig to popular song more clearly seen than in *A Quest of Enquirie, by women to know, Whether the Tripe-wife were trimmed by Doll yea or no. Gathered by Oliuer Oat-meale*[4] (1595), with its broadly burlesque treatment of Lon-

---

[1] *Works*, ed. McKerrow, I, 296.

[2] See Brydges, *British Bibliographer*, I, 149–50.

[3] Taylor, *Works* (1630), Sigs. E and Oo.

[4] See *Elizabethan England* in Grosart's Occasional Issues. This mock inquiry was based on an actual legal investigation, an account of which is given in the tract *The Brideling, Sadling and Ryding, of a rich Churle in Hampshire, by the subtill practice of*

don low life. This tract has much to do with the jig and ballad of personal mockery, and the two terms are again and again used interchangeably. Anne Tripewife, who has newly acquired a second husband, Nicholas Tricks, is made the target of ballad and jig makers when it becomes known that she has been cozened by a "cunning woman." In a mock eclogue between the pair, Tricks complains of those who jest at them "with Ballads and with Iigs," and the bride in anger expresses the wish,

> All helplesly gainst jygging rymes complaine,
> Let euerie Ballad-singer beare thee downe.

The introductory epistle contains the passage: "He sweares that where he hath been a mortall enimie to all Ballad singers, he will neuer inuaigh against them more, if they will sing at your windowes a new Jigge, termed *Anne Tripes*." But Anne has professed sympathizers in the fraternity of balladmongers as well as detractors. Master Jeffrey Kexon, friend of Tricks, represents himself as coming to the rescue in a "Dittie" defending the wife and applauding the husband's rare conquest in marrying her. The author of the tract presents this "Iigge for the Ballad-mongers to sing . . . . to giue a good morrow to the Tripe-wife" with the request that those who read it will not go about the streets singing it nor chant it at the bride's door. The jig, which parodies closely the opening of "Rowland," is printed in full as Text 1. In it the point is made not only that the tripe-wife is derided generally in ballads but that her "trimming" at the hands of Doll is likely to be sung by players on the stage. While this statement may be only a bit of drollery, it is possible that a good deal of such personal satire as was sung about the streets was of a sort to hit the humor of the playhouse public in the form of jigs.

---

one Iudeth Philips, a professed cunning woman, or Fortune teller. With a true discourse of her vnwomanly vsing of a Trypewife, a widow, lately dwelling on the back side of S. Nicholas shambles in London, whom she with her conferates, likewise cosoned (1595). Josias Parnell on February 25, 1595, entered on the Register three works that seem to have been different: "ij bookes the One intituled *a trew Discoverye of ij notable villanyes practised by One Judith Phillips the wyfe of John Phillips of Crowne Allye in Bishopsgate strete/* and the other entituled *the notorious cousenages of Dorothie Phillips otherwise called Dol Pope,*" and "a ballad thereof."

In particular I suspect that jigs on the well-known characters of the London underworld were commonly sung both among the people and on the stage. In a passage from Chettle's *Kindheart's Dream*, an old bawd protests that the players lay bare "our crosse-biting, our conny-catching, our traines, our traps, our gins, our snares, our subtilties: for no sooner haue we a tricke of deceipt, but they make it common, singing jigs and making iests of vs, that euerie boy can point out our houses as they passe by."[1] The first part of this seems to refer to dramatic or pantomimic jigs depicting roguery, but the second part shows at least that particular rogues were impersonated on the stage in mockery. Evidently the notorious women of the day were favorite subjects with the jigmonger. The author of *The Passionate Morrice* (1593) declares that "it is great pittie wee should not haue many knackes to knowe knaues by, and as many Iigges to gird garish girles with."[2] In satirizing roaring girls, chiefly for their swaggering and their aping of men, Taylor says in *Superbiae Flagellum*,

> But these things haue so well bin bang'd and firk'd,
> And Epigram'd and Satyr'd, whip'd and Ierk'd,
> Cudgeld and bastinadoed at the Court,
> And Comically stag'de to make men sport,
> Iyg'd, and (with all reason) mock'd in Rime,
> And made the onely scornefull theame of Time;
> And Ballad-mongers had so great a taske,
> (As if their muses all had got the laske.)
> That no more time therein my paines I'le spend,
> But freely leaue them to amend, or end.[3]

Both passages may refer merely to general satire on the class, but they suggest to me attacks on individuals.[4]

Though no specimens are preserved, there is some evidence that the clown's jests and witticisms were developed into a simple type of dialogue jig having some kinship with the flyting. In the farce jigs studied later, the clown's mockery of other characters is common. About the middle of the seventeenth century Gayton in his *Festivous Notes upon Don Quixot* implies

---

[1] Ed. Rimbault, pp. 37-38.

[2] New Shakspere Society, p. 91.   [3] Folio of 1630, D 4*v*.

[4] See pp. 137-38 below for further discussion of the passages cited here.

that the jibing contest was a conventional form of the jig: "Our
Tragedy is chang'd into pure Comedie, and instead of a Prize,
we are like to have a jigge of two principall Clownes, each gibing
the other, they are now at the Ti-hee, and without tickling,
laugh till their sides ake."[1] The end of "The Gig betweene a
Paritor and the Foole" quoted above is evidently of the type.
Possibly the lost "pleasant Jigge betwene a tincker and a
Clowne" entered on February 4, 1595, belonged to the same
class.[2]

The jigs discussed in this chapter have shown a wide range.
Foxe uses the term for a brief lyric sung in dances and carols of
the maidens and minstrels of medieval Scotland; the author of
Martins Months minde, for songs by the players ridiculing Martin Marprelate; the author of *A Quest of Enquirie*, for a ballad
without dialogue belittling a tripewife; Heywood in *Edward IV*,
for burlesques by drunken soldiers in tavern revelry; Taylor,
for songs on the absurdities of roistering females; Molle again,
for song and dance of youths on festival occasions; the author
of *Vox Borealis*, for the song and dance of a fiddler and a fool in
the drunken revelry of Edinburgh Castle; the author of *Canterburie His Change of Diot*, for a short dialogue following a burlesque play; Gayton, for the raillery of professional clowns.
There is a suggestive association of terms in Wither's

> a Rime,
> A Curtaine Iigge, a Libell, or a Ballet,
> For Fidlers, or some Rogues with staffe and wallet
> To sing at doores.[3]

The delight of the people in the performance of abusive jigs is
seen in a question which Daniel Rogers asks his readers in

[1] Ed. of 1654, p. 108.

[2] The ballad of "The Courtiour and the Carter" entered on the Register in 1565–6
(*Transcript*, I, 310) may have dealt with an early jest of a courtier's mocking a clown
and receiving a discomfiting retort. At least the ballad keeps practically the title of
such a jest in *A Hundred Merry Tales*, "Of the courtear and the carter" (No. liii). A
similar jest is found in *Scoggins Jests* (*Shakespeare Jest-Books*, II, 106–7). Perhaps some
such jig inspired Ayrer's elaborate singspiel "Von etlichen närrischen Reden des Claus
Narrn vnd anderer, zusammen colligirt," with the exchange of witticisms between
Prince Friedrich and Claus. The first part suggests jibing jigs. Ayrer's direct sources,
however, as Bolte points out, seem to have been German (*Singspiele*, pp. 14–15).

[3] *Abuses Stript and Whipt*, Bk. II, Satire 3.

Naaman the Syrian His Disease and Cure (1642), making it the touchstone of spirituality: "Canst thou relish a bargaine, a game at cardes and dice, any base talke of the world, (though never so long) any idle tale, or gigge of a geering, gibing wit, or any merry conceit and discourse, or matters of the belly, backe, purse and commodity" (p. 204). Foxe's reference to satiric songs as jigs in 1570 has already been mentioned as apparently the earliest certain use of the word for song, and in the Prologue to *Amphitryon* Dryden makes the accusation,

> Yet in Lampoons, you Libel one another.
> The first produces still, a second Jig;
> You whip 'em out, like School-boys, till they gig,

at a time—in 1691—when the jig, except as dance, had all but disappeared from contemporary allusions.

CHAPTER III

THE RISE OF THE STAGE JIG

PERHAPS the best approach that can be made to the subject of the stage jig before Tarlton's death is through certain general phases of the actor's art, for records of the jig are few in this period and none of the extant specimens can with certainty be dated so early. Naturally, then, much of what is said here is conjectural so far as its direct bearing on the jig is concerned.

A general consideration that undoubtedly has its interest for the rise of the stage jig is the importance of song and dance in the art of the sixteenth century actor. Regular provision for music with plays is suggested in some early records of musicians and minstrels performing in connection with actors. References to hearing the melody in addition to seeing the play, which occur several times in the accounts of the Shrewsbury Corporation, might refer to instrumental music only, but the word *cantilenae* used in at least one of these cases in connection with *histriones* can mean only songs.[1] The amount of song and dance in early sixteenth century plays must have varied with the type of company and of drama. Such features would naturally be most abundant in performances by the children's companies, for example, and in romantic plays, especially those written for the festivals of the upper classes. It is recorded of the *Golden Arbor* of 1511 that two gentlemen of the Chapel Royal dressed as shipmen sang and that there were "diuers fresh songes."[2] *The Arraignment of Paris, Summer's Last Will and Testament,* and *Midsummer Night's Dream* are late examples

---

[1] See Chambers, *Mediaeval Stage*, II, 252–53, under the years 1520, 1525, 1533, 1535; *Hist. MSS Com.*, XV, App. X, pp. 31–34. For other records see Chambers, *op. cit.*, II, 247–49. For chanting and dancing in Basque and Breton plays, apparently a survival of medieval art like that in the mummers' plays, see *Modern Philology*, XIV, 505–6. In his colloquy "Diversoria" (*Opera Omnia* [1703], I, 717) Erasmus uses the phrase "quemadmodum solent actores fabularum, qui scenis admiscent choros."

[2] *Letters and Papers of Henry VIII*, II, 1495–96; Hall, *Henry VIII* (1548), fol. x.

of the same influence. On the other hand, some of the early moralities, especially those that seem to have been written for adult actors, have practically no dancing or singing. Yet even here no law can be laid down, for *The Four Elements* is crowded with song and dance acts. Of the later plays, it is necessary to mention only *Like Will to Like* or *Tom Tyler* in the farcical field, and *Bugbears, Promos and Cassandra*, or *Patient Grissell* in the romantic field, to illustrate the prevalence of song and dance in connection with sixteenth century drama.

From the beginning of the Renaissance until after the Restoration there is a certain general resemblance in the types of song and dance employed in plays. Lyrics, catches, group dances, and other forms with an art apparently different from that of the stage jig continued to be popular within the plays. In music, the part singing of the trained musicians of the time no doubt predominated over the simpler art that formed the basis for game song. Some of the plays—notably the lost plays of Cornish—were the work of men distinguished as musicians. In the manuscript in which Redford's *Wit and Science* occurs, there is a group of songs probably written by such men for the use of choir boys.[1] From the point of view of literature the situation is similar. The songs incorporated in the texts of the plays were written by dramatists who professed generally an uncompromising contempt for the taste of the folk.

Yet the popular influence was strong in sixteenth century drama, possibly because plays were still largely festival performances. Adaptations of processions and disguisings are frequent. In the second part of *Promos and Cassandra* (I, ix) the citizens receive their king, a group on a stage welcoming him in song. A procession with a song of harvestmen is found in *Old Wives Tale* (ll. 303–11). In *Bugbears* (II, iv) a group of revelers in guise of devils, wearing visards and using squibs, sing a chorus ending, "syng hegh hoe Iolye heygh hoe a sprityng go we," to a song of the foreleader descriptive of their performance. A "crewe of Clownes" including a Moor and a Maid Marian furnish "countrey merriment" in *John a Kent and John a Cumber*, appearing on the stage at intervals to present an oration to the visiting lords, to rouse the brides and bridegrooms with song on

---

[1] See *Modern Philology*, XXIV, 499.

the wedding day, and to perform a morris dance. The processions of *Summer's Last Will and Testament*, in their mixture of popular and sophisticated elements, are doubtless more typical of the stage. To the representation of the seasons by various groups is added the drollery of clownish, mythological, or abstract figures, and the song and dance of morris men, reapers, satyrs, and wood nymphs.

This popular influence resulted in an unmistakable vogue of festival or folk dance on the stage. In a passage to be quoted shortly, Gosson mentions morrises and hobbyhorses as well as the dancing of jigs among the devil's enticements in the theater. Both the jig and the hornpipe appear among the incidental dances of *James IV*. Country dance is called for in *Misogonus* (II, iv) and is elaborately featured in *The Woman Killed with Kindness* (I, ii). The morris provides an antic element at the beginning of *Summer's Last Will and Testament* and in *John a Kent and John a Cumber* (Act IV), *Jack Drum's Entertainment* (I, i), *Two Noble Kinsmen* (III, v), *Women Pleased* (IV, i), and so forth. Harington's expression in *The Metamorphosis of Ajax* (1596), "Such as I haue seene in stage playes when they daunce Machachinas" (L ij), is evidence for the common use of the sword dance on the stage.[1] The figure dances of the folk were utilized also in masques, as in the *Mask of the Four Seasons*,[2] Jonson's *Entertainment at Althorpe* and *Metamorphosed Gipsies*, and *The Masque of the Inner Temple and Gray's Inn*.

The case for popular song is not so clear. Songs not organically connected with the plays must have been used, however, in cases where stage directions call for songs that are not specified. Such pieces were probably selected in many instances from current popular song. The early morality *Wealth and Health* opens with a stage direction: "Here entreth Welth, and Helth, synging together a balet of two partes." This may refer to "ballad" in the medieval sense and to part singing. In *The*

---

[1] "Matachin" was used for the sword dance in Great Britain as on the Continent. See *NED* and Reyher, *Les Masques Anglais*, p. 458. Arbeau applies this term and "buffon" to the pyrrhic dance which he describes in *Orchesographie*, fols. 97–104. In *The Complaint of Scotland*, EETS, p. 66, the name buffons is given to a folk dance. Cotgrave defines the word as a morris.

[2] See *Inigo Jones and Five Court Masks*, Shakespeare Society. See also Reyher, *Les Masques Anglais*, p. 458, for several pyrrhic dances in masques.

Three Lords and Three Ladies of London (Sig. C), however, Simplicity "sings first, and Wit after, dialoguewise, both to musicke if ye will"; and while the song is not indicated, it is of a popular type, for the pair have just been discussing the ballads which Simplicity has for sale—"chipping *Norton* a mile from Chappell othe heath, A lamentable ballad of burning the Popes dog: The sweet Ballade of the *Lincoln*-shire bagpipes, And *Peggy* and *Willy*." Their song is spoken of later as a ballad. In *The Arraignment of Paris* (l. 785) there is a stage direction for singing an "old songe called the woing of Colman."

Popular influence at least colored strongly many of the songs written into the context of plays. Few of them are of broadside length, and it is doubtful whether ballads would ever have been used freely on the stage without the complete detachment from the play which the afterpiece afforded. Two dialogue songs that are interesting, however, because of their ballad form in spite of their literary tone and their wealth of classical allusion are found in *Patient Grissell* (ll. 840-75) and *Horestes* (ll. 538-601), both belonging to the period when ballads had a vogue among the courtly. The first is sung to the ballad tune "Malkin" and has the refrain "Heigh hoaw, my true loue," etc. It was entered on the Register separately in 1565-6 as a ballad with the title the "sonnge of pacyente Gressell vnto hyr make."[1] The second takes its tune and its refrain of "Lady, Lady" from Elderton's famous ballad "Pangs of Love."

Many of the briefer songs in plays seem to reflect the influence of festival practice. Of these the most dramatic are representations of the wooing.[2] In the singing of the dialogue by two choral groups or by a foresinger and chorus, songs in Redford's *Wit and Science* and Wilson's *Three Ladies of London* resemble the children's game "Here come three Dukes." In Redford's

---

[1] See Arber, *Transcript*, I, 296. The songs in this play include also a love song (ll. 969-78) to a dance tune ("the latter Almain") and a spinning song (ll. 219-66) with a refrain "Singe danderlie Distaffe, & danderlie," etc. "Danderly Dyscaffe" is given as the title of a ballad licensed in 1565-6 (*Transcript*, I, 302).

[2] The old song in *The Arraignment of Paris* accompanies an elaborate pantomime wooing. Venus "singeth an old songe called the woing of Colman. A foule croked Churle enters, & Thestilis a faire lasse wooeth him. he crabedly refuzeth her, and goethe out of place. She tarieth behinde." Thestilis then sings a complaint and farewell, while shepherds "reply" in chorus.

play (ll. 935 ff.) Wit and his three companions sing to Science and her three companions:

> O ladye deere,
> Be ye so neare
>   To be knowne?
> My hart yow cheere
> Your voyce to here;
>   Wellcum, myne owne!

The ladies reply agreeing to be their own, and the other stanzas elaborate the motive. In *The Three Ladies* (A iiii) five suitors for favor sing a song beginning "Good Ladyes take pittie and graunt our desire." Conscience answers for the ladies, and after several speeches sung alternately rejects the suitors. Iniquity, Ismael, and Delila of *Nice Wanton* (ll. 141–45) sing a short dialogue with a chorus like that of the song in *Wit and Science:*

> *Iniq.* Lo! lo! here I bryng her.
> *Ism.* What is she, nowe ye haue her?
> *Dal.* I, lusty mynyon louer?
> *Iniq.* For no golde wyl I gyue her.
> *All together.* Welcome my hony ay.

A simple dialogue song in which the lover is accepted with the words, "I am thy owne, behold," is found in *The Marriage of Wit and Wisdom* (sc.x). Such songs might well be adaptations of old game songs similar to those found in modern singing games of children.

Much of the song and dance in the plays embodies the spirit of burlesque, satire, and drollery which also belonged to popular revelry. In some burlesques of the wooing, the comic tone that pervades the song drama of the period is found. A dialogue song of sixteen lines between Cantalupo and Squartacantino in *Bugbears* (I, iii) parodies the terms of endearment and the exclamations conventional in wooing songs. The wooing of the maid Dalia by the country clown Grimball in *Promos and Cassandra* (Part I, IV, vii) burlesques particularly the type of song in which a kiss is begged:

> *Gri.* Come smack me, come smack me, I long for a smouch,
> *Da.* Go pack thee, go pack thee, thou filthie fine slouch.

> *Gri.* Leard howe I loue thee,
> *Da.* This can not moue mee:
> *Gri.* Why pretie Pygsney, my harte, and my honny?
> *Da.* Because goodman Hogsface, you woe without mony.
> *Gri.* I lacke mony, chy graunt,
> *Da.* Then *Grimball* auaunt.
> *Gri.* Cham yong sweete hart, and feate, come kysse me for loue,
> *Da.* Crokeshanke, your Jowle is to great, such lyking to moue.
> *Gri.* What meane you by this?
> *Da.* To leaue thee by gys.
> *Gri.* First smack me, first smack, I dye for a smouch,
> *Da.* Go pack thee, go pack thee, thou filthy foul slouch.

In beginning this song, Dalia bids Grimball sing, and he replies that he will "Both syng, spring, fight and playe, the dewl and all." If this is intended to describe the action, as it seems, the song was sung in dialogue, danced, and acted. A scene in *Ralph Roister Doister* which seems to echo features of the wooing game[1] calls for a dance accompanying a comic song on the duty of the husband to be subservient to the wife. Delila and Iniquity of *Nice Wanton* (ll. 194–205) also sing a mocking dialogue of the *mal mariée* type. In *Tom Tyler* (ll. 469–91) the stanzas of a song, "Go tie the mare Tomboy," in which Tom's shrewish wife is represented as a restive mare, are sung alternately by Taylor and Tyler. Squartacantino's song on his master in *Bugbears* (III, i) satirizes the old man as lover.

The use of song and dance is a common device for the depiction of comic types in the plays. Mariners appear as conventional rogues to sing in *Common Conditions* (l. 995) and *The Marriage of Wit and Wisdom* (sc. iii). Ravenscroft gives a song suitable for such a group in *Deuteromelia*, No. 6. The three tippling gossips of *Tom Tyler* sing several songs, apparently with dance. Triads are very common in such songs. Three tinkers sing in *Common Conditions* (ll. 211–42); three beggars in *The Three Ladies of London* (E iii); three rogues in *The Tide Tarrieth no Man* (D iiii); three rascals in *King Darius* (ll. 568–86); the vice, the devil, and the collier, and later the vice and two rogues, in

---

[1] I, iv. The promise of a "peck of argent" is similar to constant offers in children's wooing games (Newell, *Games and Songs of American Children*, pp. 42, 45, 55), and the list of possessions that follows suggests the burlesque treatment of the motive in "The Wowing of Jok and Jynny" and related ballads (see pp. 191–93, 196–97, below).

Like Will to Like;[1] and so on. Songs by peddlers of wares in plays come up for notice later in connection with jigs exploiting these characters of the London streets (pp. 289–93). In the drunken Hankin, who enters singing a Dutch song in *Wealth and Health* (l. 386), we have the foreigner with his comic patter. Hance of *Like Will to Like* also enters singing and a little later dances a drunken dance "as evil-favoured as may be demised."[2] The promise in *Thersytes* of "minstrelsy that shall pype hankyn boby" (C iii) probably refers to a characteristic performance of a Hankin as a fool.[3]

Sometimes the comic song simply expresses the spirit of revelry, reaching a climax in cries like "care away," "huffa," and "heigh o," as in *Misogonus*, II, ii; the opening of *The Trial of Treasure*; *Promos and Cassandra*, Part I, I, ii, and III, vi; *Respublica*, V, viii. Similar in spirit are such songs as that of Simplicity in *The Three Ladies of London* (D iii) with its refrain "Sing downe adowne." Some of the songs are made up of topsy-turvy nonsense. The vice Nichol Newfangle sings a nonsense song in *Like Will to Like*.[4] A variant is found in the medleys. *The Longer thou Livest* opens with the entry of Moros "Synging the foote of many Songes, as fooles were wont," and a later song of his "hangeth together like fethers in the winde" (D ii). Ignorance in *The Four Elements* (ll. 1410–33) sings several stanzas composed of snatches of various songs, including bits of nonsense of the type noticed under the news songs. The medleys in the song collections of the sixteenth century show the vogue.[5]

Dance accompanies many of the songs already mentioned. Frequently a stage direction will call for a dance or the context will prepare for one. When the devil, the vice, and the collier agree to dance in *Like Will to Like*, a direction reads: "Nichol Newfangle must have a gittern or some other instrument (if it may be); but if he have not, they must dance about the place

---

[1] Ed. Farmer, pp. 10, 33–34.   [2] *Ibid.*, pp. 21, 23.

[3] See Gomme, *Traditional Games*, I, 355–56, for a version of a children's singing game with the refrain "Hinkumbooby round about," and pp. 360–61 for the grotesque action of the accompanying dance.

[4] Ed. Farmer, pp. 27–28.

[5] See Herrig's *Archiv*, CVII, 59–61; Chambers and Sidgwick, *Early English Lyrics*, pp. 254–55; *Anglia*, XII, 596 n. 3.

all three, and sing this song that followeth, which must be done also, although they have an instrument."[1] Sometimes the song is merely descriptive of the dance action. One of the most interesting examples of this is found in *The Four Elements* (ll. 1320 ff.). A troupe of dancers without the hall and two of the rioters within sing responsively. When the dancers have entered, Sensual Appetite "syngeth this song and dauncyth with all and evermore maketh countenaunce accordyng to the mater and all the other aunswer lyke wyse." I omit the repeated parts of the song:

> Daunce we
> Praunce we
> So merely let us daunce ey
> And I can daunce it gyngerly
> And I can fote it by and by
> And I can pranke it properly
> And I can countenaunse comely
> And I can kroke it curtesly
> And I can lepe it lustly
> And I can torn it trymly
> And I can fryske it freshly
> And I can loke it lordly.

Sometimes when dance is not expressly called for, the content of the song seems to indicate it. The vice in *Like Will to Like* apparently dances to his nonsense song, for the second stanza opens, "And now will I dance, and now will I prance." The words "Caper then" in a comic song in *Midas*, III, ii, suggest accompanying dance, though dance does not seem to be featured in Lyly's plays. It is possible, in fact, that dance so commonly accompanied song, especially comic song, on the stage that it is to be taken for granted in many cases where directions are lacking. The situation found in *Tom Tyler* is probably typical. When the three gossips first meet and drink, Tipple suggests, "Nay fall to singing, and let us go dance"; whereupon Strife says, "I will bring you in," and she sings the first stanza of "Tom Tyler," the other two singing in turn (ll. 214–37). In "The Mill a," the next song in the drinking bout, the line "Let us trip, and let us skip" suggests accompanying dance. When

[1] Ed. Farmer, p. 10.

the trio meet later to celebrate the conquest of Tyler, a song is
introduced by Strife's statement that she is ready to dance or
sing (l. 680). At the end of the play, Patience proposes:

> Then take hands, and take chance,
> And I will lead the dance.
> And sing after me, and look we agree,

and the whole group join in a song. The impression is that dancing accompanies the singing of the play generally.

Comic song and dance was naturally the special province of
the fool, clown, or vice.[1] His pre-eminence, if it needed illustration, would be clear enough from the examples already cited.
Like Moros of *The Longer thou Livest*, he has "songes good
stoare" (Sig. D). According to an early account of the acting of
Lyndsay's *Ane Satyre of the thrie Estaitis*, the office of the vice
Solace was "but to make mery, sing ballettes with his fellowes,
and drinke at the interluydes of the play."[2] The author of *The
Arte of English Poesie* (Bk. II, chap. ix) speaks in 1589 of "Carols and rounds and such light or lasciuious Poemes, which are
commonly more commodiously vttered by these buffons or
vices in playes then by any other person."

The tendency to detach song and dance features from the
context of the play and use them as intermean or afterpiece is
especially significant. In *James IV*, for example, the Induction,
Acts I, II, and IV, and scene iii in Act IV are brought to a close
with song or dance or a combination of the two. But the tradition of ending plays with such features was of course old long
before the rise of the stage jig. Dance is called for after the
Digby *Killing of the Children* and Lyndsay's *Satire of the Three
Estates*. Hymns after religious plays like the Chester *Antichrist*,
The Play of the Sacrament, and *The Conversion of Saint Paul*
probably furnished models for the pious songs after such sixteenth century plays as Bale's *Three Laws* and *John the Baptist*.
Prayers for Elizabeth are sung after *Ralph Roister Doister* and
Damon and Pithias. Possibly the requests for prayers for the
sovereign at the end of other early plays are directions for song.

---

[1] See pp. 355–57 below for the pre-eminence of the fool as a dancer in folk games.

[2] Printed by Halliwell in his edition of *The Marriage of Wit and Wisdom*,
Shakespeare Society, p. 66.

After *Appius and Virginia* a song on Elizabeth's fame is indicated. Stage directions or concluding lines call for "some goodly ballet" after *Nature*, "Remembre me" after *Wit and Science*, and a "heauenly song" after *The Pedlers Prophecie*. *David and Bethsabe* ends with the line, "Now may old Israel and his daughters sing." Moral songs for the conclusion are included in the text of *Nice Wanton* and *King Darius;* while similar songs are printed after *The Disobedient Child*, *Like Will to Like*, and *The Trial of Treasure* without directions for singing. The nature of the song is not indicated in the stage direction "The second Song" after *New Custom* or "Cantent" after *Respublica*. Secular songs, however, round out *Bugbears*, *Midas*, and *Histriomastix*, and songs of the type not connected with the theme of the play follow some early interludes. A comic song for a group dance as well as a serious song appears at the end of *Tom Tyler*. In the manuscript that contains *Wit and Science* the final fragment of a play by Redford is given along with direction for a song opening "Hey nony nonye," which followed it.[1] The convention continued in simple songs and dances at the end of plays throughout the vogue of the jig. There is dance after *Henry IV*, Part II, song after *Twelfth Night*, song and dance at the end of *Sir Giles Goosecappe*, choral chant at the end of *The Birth of Hercules*, and the classical chorus after plays like *Virtuous Octavia* and *The Tragedy of Mariam*. A favorite device was the introduction of dance at the close by means of a betrothal or marriage celebration, as in *Sir Giles Goosecappe* and *Much Ado*. At least in the plays of Shakespeare mentioned here, we have pieces performed during the zenith of the professional jig and by the very company most prominent in fostering it.

In connection with the song and dance specialties of the clown it is worth remembering that the art of the old mimus was very highly developed in the Renaissance. Comic descriptive and narrative pieces are frequently broken by dialogue in *dits*, *sermons joyeux*, etc.[2] The device survives in the monologues of vices in English moralities, and reaches its finest development in the two monologues of Launce on his "Curre" in *Two Gentlemen of Verona* (II,iii;IV,iv). Probably dialogue songs

[1] See *Wyt and Science*, Shakespeare Society, p. 55.
[2] See Faral, *Mimes français du XIII* siècle*, pp. viii–xv.

were often presented by one singer with skilful impersonation. In singing the fine dialogue of Henry VIII's time, "A Robyn Joly Robyn/tell me how thy leman doeth,"[1] the actor who played the part of Feste in *Twelfth Night* (IV, ii) may have attempted two voices as he had just done in the incident in which he impersonated the parson. In his journal for 1582 Richard Madox records a curious performance: he went to the theater, he says, "to see a scurvy play set out all by one virgin, which there proved 'a fyemarten' without voice, so that we stayed not the matter."[2] Apparently one actor recited or sang—to judge from the emphasis on voice—a dramatic piece impersonating a number of characters. That solo song with dance might be presented in a very dramatic manner is seen in Moth's account of the brawl in *Love's Labour's Lost* (III, i), but Davies describes in his *Orchestra* the impersonation of a man and a woman by a single dancer who changes from one side to the other as he changes character.[3] This art of the mimus may not have exerted any very direct influence on the jig, for clearly after the fully developed dramatic form gained the ascendancy the rôles were sung by different actors. Even in the early stage jig, performance by one actor may not have been the rule. Yet I think it highly probable not only that the monologue sung by the chief clown was the commonest type on the stage at first but that the range of its art was fairly wide.[4]

There are many indications, however, that minor dramatic types were current among players in greater variety than the student who focuses on formal drama is likely to realize. Some

---

[1] See *Anglia*, XII, 241–42, 272; XVIII, 487–88. For one singer's representing two voices in modern folk song, see *Journal of the Folk-Song Society*, II, 58.

[2] *Cal. of State Papers, Colonial Series, East Indies*, 1513–1616, p. 86. Halliwell-Phillipps, *Outlines of the Life of Shakespeare* (1890), I, 363, notes the passage. Graves, *South Atlantic Quarterly*, XIV, 144, considers "without voice" to indicate a dumb woman.

[3] Stanzas 82–83. The passage is added to material taken from Lucian (Bullen, *Some Longer Elizabethan Poems*, New English Garner, pp. viii–ix), and is not, I think, to be regarded as representing merely Davies' conception of Greek pantomime.

[4] Performance by one actor may have remained one method of presenting the dramatic jig, though not the usual one. See Hönig, *Anzeiger für deutsches Altertum*, XXII, 303–4, for a record of one person's singing "Rowland" in Germany. The tune, however, was widely used on the Continent, and the reference may be to some song other than the dramatic jig.

evidence for their use in the satire of the Reformation and the Marprelate controversy has already been given. Chambers in his *Elizabethan Stage* (II, 455) quotes in translation a German's account of a bear-baiting at London in 1584, with the comment, "It is interesting to observe that the baiting proper was supplemented with fireworks and an entertainment, which must have been of the nature of a jig." The traveler reports, "The next was that a number of men and women came forward from a separate compartment, dancing, conversing and fighting with each other." There is, too, an interesting variety of terms for the devices of comedians in the period, and while they often refer only to comic parts of formal drama, at the same time they point to the prevalence of more or less dramatic skits. "Merriment," for example, we have seen applied to a shepherds' game at Christmas with song and dance (p. 8). Nashe declares in *Pierce Penilesse* that the enemies of plays when they are dead shall be brought upon the stage "in a merriment of the Vsurer and the Diuel,"[1] and the term is used for the comic action of both Tarlton and Kemp.[2] "Toy," again, was a favorite term among the cultured to designate any slight or unworthy composition, but it was also employed in a somewhat more specific way for frivolous dramatic devices, very much as Marlowe, Shakespeare, and Jonson use "jig." The author of *The Wars of Cyrus* assures his audience,

<blockquote>
toies
Or needlesse antickes imitations,
Or shewes, or new deuices sprung a late,
we haue exilde them from our Tragicke stage.[3]
</blockquote>

---

[1] *Works*, ed. McKerrow, I, 213.

[2] See Nashe, *Works*, I, 188 (the story of a justice—"hauing a play presented before him and his Towneship by *Tarlton* and the rest of his fellowes, her Maiesties seruants, and they were now entring into their first merriment [as they call it], the people began exceedingly to laugh, when *Tarlton* first peept out his head"); I, 287 ("*Will Kempe*, I mistrust it will fall to thy lot for a merriment, one of these dayes"); title-page to *A Knacke to knowe a Knaue* ("With Kemps applauded Merrimentes of the men of Goteham").

[3] C 3. See also Medwall, *Fulgens and Lucres*, Part II, ll. 22–31, where scenes of clownish wooing in the play are called "toyes" inserted for those who care only for such "tryfles and Iapys"; Tyndale, *An aunswere vnto Syr Thomas Mores Dialogue* (1530), p. 249, "disguisings & toyes wherof we know no meanyng"; Prologue to *Tom Tyler*, in which the play with its wealth of song, dance, and farcical features is described by the

A lost work of Tarlton's was entered on the Register December 10, 1576, as "a newe booke in Englishe verse intituled Tarltons *Toyes*." Indeed the term seems to be applied to the whole range of the great comedian's art when Nashe in the address to the "Goodman Reader" of *The Terrors of the Night* speaks of the "first yere of the reigne of Tarltons toies." It was also applicable to music, especially for dance. The comic ballad "Shall I wed an aged man" has "Trentam's Toy" for its tune,[1] and *The Fitzwilliam Virginal Book* contains several brief "toys."

Cases in which several terms are used, apparently in order to distinguish various types—as in the passage just quoted from *The Wars of Cyrus*—are especially interesting. In the Prologue to *The Testament and Complaynt of the Papyngo* (l. 41) Lyndsay speaks of the excellence of Sir James Inglis in "ballattis, farses, and in plesand playis." Attention has already been called to a proclamation of Edward's reign which sought to regulate not only play and interlude but "Dialogue or other matter set forthe in form of Plaie." Foxe says of an Oxford preacher, Hubberdin, that his "doynges and pageants if they might be described at large, it were as good as any enterlude for the reader to behold"; and he mentions Hubberdin's "forged tales and fables, dialogues, dreames, dauncinges, hoppinges and leapinges, with other lyke histrionical toyes and gestures vsed in the pulpit" against heretics.[2]

---

term "merrie toyes"; Gascoigne, Prologue to *The Glass of Government*, with the warning to the audience that the play will not please as well as "Bellsavage fayre" one who wishes to "heare a worthie Jest" or "feede his eye with vayne delight," and that the author is not writing a comic interlude or "*Italian* toyes" full of "pleasaunt sporte"; Fulwell, Prologue to *Like Will to Like*, in which the claim is made that the author includes no "lascivious toys" among his matters of mirth; Northbrooke, *Treatise against Dicing, Dancing*, etc., Shakespeare Society, p. 104, where one of the conditions laid down for rendering plays tolerable in the schools is that they shall not be "mixte with vaine and wanton toyes of loue."

[1] See *Shirburn Ballads*, ed. Clark, p. 269. For other examples of "toy" see *NED*; Medwall, *Nature*, Part I, ll. 786, 1001; Rastell, *Four Elements*, ll. 1311–12:
"Disportis as daunsynge syngynge
Toys tryfuls laughynge gestynge."

[2] *Acts and Monuments* (1570), II, 1912. One performance is described in detail in which the divine, summoning Christ and the apostles, various church worthies, and certain heretics, makes them "euery one (after his dialogue maner) by name to aunswere to his call, and to sing after his tune for the probation of the Sacrament." After they sing he also has them dance "after his pype," and carries the performance through with such zest that the pulpit gives way.

Clear evidence for song drama among the "histrionical toyes" of the time is lacking. There seems, however, to have been an early tendency to associate "interlude" with the minstrel's art. In translating William of Malmesbury's statement that Alfred with an attendant entered the camp of the Danes as a mimus, Fabyan expands it thus: "he dyd on hym ye abyt of a mynstrell, & with his instrument of musyke he entred the tentes & pauylyons of the Danys, & in shewynge there his enterludes & songes," etc.[1] Bale in 1544 refers to "baudy songes" as sung by "poore minstrels, and players of enterludes."[2] In *A forme of Christian pollicie gathered out of French* (1574) Fenton adds to his original a passage protesting that the magistrate should put a stop to the objectionable performance of "these Players, whether they bee Minstrels, or Enterludours, who, on a scaffold," babble "vaine newes," etc. (p. 144). Song drama used on the stage might easily have been included under the term ballad. Lyndsay's praise of Inglis in ballads, farces, and plays at least carries with it a suggestion that ballads too were a dramatic form.[3] When Breton at the beginning of the seventeenth century, speaking of ballads, says in his *Dialogue full of pithe and pleasure*, "Indeed they are most in vse with Players, and Musitians, for else they goe downe the world for imployment,"[4] he probably has in mind the typical jig in the case of players.

A general phase of comic art in the period which seems to me especially significant in relation to the jig is the evolution of clownish types toward the close of the sixteenth century. The popularity of such comic figures as the foreigner, the sailor, the collier, the peddler, or the rogue, especially in connection with song or dance, has been pointed out already. In the adaptation of Roman comedy; in the importation of masques, far-

---

[1] *Chronicles*, ed. Ellis, p. 167. For the original, see *Gesta regum Anglorum*, ed. Hardy, I, 181.

[2] See Chambers, *Mediaeval Stage*, II, 446–47.

[3] See *DNB* for a payment of 10s to Hawes for a ballad which might well, I think, have been in the nature of song drama for court performance. In Scotland three men sang a ballad to the king on January 2, 1492, and two women sang on several occasions (*Accts. L. H. Treas. Scotland*, I, 184, 275, 279; III, 162, 331, 383). See *ibid.*, I, 329, for singing by a man and a woman in 1497. These accounts suggest the possibility of dialogue singing with dance.

[4] Ed. Grosart, p. 6.

ces, *commedia dell'arte*, Latin school drama, and other forms of comedy from various Continental countries; and in the dramatization of novella, folk book, and jest, there was ample opportunity to extend the range.[1] Apparently, however, little interest was felt in strictly new figures on the part of the populace. Throughout his career Jonson was satirizing the taste of the people for old favorites like the devil and the vice, and such types as Harlequin and Scaramouche did not gain a hold in England until late in the seventeenth century. In spite of the occurrence of fresh and individual rôles, comic figures in sixteenth century plays are on the whole cast in a few general molds. In his allegorical attack on players in *A Mirrour of Monsters* (1587), William Rankins describes and classifies them as follows: "some trans-formed themselues to Roges, other to Ruffians, some other to Clownes, a fourth to fooles, in the fift place Louers and Leachers . . . . . The Roges were ready, the Ruffians were rude, theyr Clownes cladde as well with Country condition, as in Ruffe russet, theyr Fooles as fonde as might be, theyr Louers and Leachers leude" (fol. 7).

There was a foundation of realism, however, in the treatment of these conventional characters—of the older devil and vice as well as of ruffian, rogue, clown, or fool. They gave the color of everyday life to their comic patter, their clownish tricks, their swagger, and their rascality. Some of the oddest figures that had a vogue reflected social conditions of the era. The foreigner with his jargon, represented by the drunken Hankin of *Wealth and Health* and by the lustful wooer of *Jack Drum's Entertainment*, must have amused Londoners in actual life. The collier, the tinker, the broom-man, are actual types,

[1] The interest of the courtly during the sixteenth century in odd and comic types in dance is indicated by such groups as the following named in the records of masques: "reysters," "huffkyns," "Swarte Rutters," "frowees," "babions," marketwives, fishwives, fishermen, clowns, peddlers, drunkards, shipmen, mariners, friars, Tartars, Moors, Turks, Almains, Irishmen, and Hungarians (see *Letters and Papers of Henry VIII*, II, 1490, 1517; III, 1550–56; and the Indexes of Feuillerat's *Revels of Edward and Mary* and *Revels of Queen Elizabeth*). For the masses there are such records as those of friars and nuns in masques at a London wedding in 1562 (Machyn, *Diary*, p. 288), of minstrels at Ipswich in 1569 "playing the Fooles in the Halle" (*Hist. MSS Com.*, IX, 249), of "certen Spanyards and Ytalyans who dawnsyd antycks & played dyvrse other feets" in the Hall at Norwich in 1546–47, and of players of an "antycke" at Plymouth in 1547–48 (Murray, *English Dramatic Companies*, II, 363, 381).

however much their traits may be heightened. It is possible that this trend resulted in part from the vogue of ballad and jig among the comedians. In the ballad, which stood for popular taste, the drift toward realism was far-reaching from an early period. Not only are realistic rogues, ruffians, and vagabonds favorites as in drama, but lovers, husbands, wives, and neighbors are pictured more consistently as droll clowns, artisans, and tradespeople. Moreover the small gentry and other representatives of the prosperous classes are less sharply differentiated from the lower social orders in ballad than in drama. In the eighties, after the interest of literary men in the form had waned, comic and vulgar ballads increased in number.

While the conventional comic types in both ballad and play remain sufficiently distinct in fundamental traits, they show a tendency to shade into each other—figures like vices, devils, and goblins crossing with rogues, ruffians, vagabonds, and clowns. Robin Goodfellow, primarily a goblin of folk game, appears in *Grim the Collier of Croyden* as a clownish goblin and in *Wily Beguiled* as a fully evolved clown. In particular, comic types generally tend to take on the color of the clown. The genuine clowns, few in the earlier period, become numerous, and their traits are elaborated. By the time the stage jig reached its fullest development, this shift had made clownish figures of the chief comic characters in Shakespeare's early romantic plays.

On the whole, moreover, the clownish rôles employed by the comedians were probably made to conform to country types. Rankins, in the classification of actors just cited, describes the clowns as not only dressed in russet, the characteristic garb of the country, but "cladde as well with Country condition." As I shall show a little later, Tarlton seems to have been a typical country clown distinguished by his russet garb. Not only the realistic country clown, however, but the grotesques of pastimes generally—the goblin, scapegoat, and fool—probably had a strong influence on the clownish rôles of the comedians. An early popular conception of the goblin as clown is preserved in the names Hobgoblin and Hodgepoke and is suggested in the game "Hobman's Blind." Of the same family is Robin Goodfellow, whose treatment in plays has just been mentioned. The fact that the ragged garb indicated for daemonic figures at an early period in the term ragman was used in Shakespeare's time for both rogue and goblin is evident from Forman's description of Autolycus as "the Rog. that cam in all tottered like coll pixci."[1] A number of symbolic names seem to have developed from customs of the seasonal games. The conception of the fish clowns probably owed much to the mummery of the spring or Lenten games—in which fish insignia were at least frequently used symbolically.[2] Fish names were given to two of the most important clownish figures developed by the English comedians abroad[3]—Stockfish and Pickleherring—and Pickle Herring is one of the two chief clowns in the Revesby Sword Play. Similar names in formal English drama are Cob of *Every Man in his Humour* and Pilcher of *Blurt, Master Constable*. John Posset, another outstanding clown of the English troupes on foreign tours, doubtless derived his name from the Christmas drink. The use of kindred names in festival celebrations is suggested by the appearance of Wassail in Jonson's *Masque of Christmas* along with the clownish Baby-cake, "drest like a Boy, in a fine long Coat, Biggin, Bib, Muckender, and a little Dagger."[4] The English clown was also introduced on the Continent under the names John Conget, John Clam, John Panser, and John Grundo, so that "English John" is used by Ayrer as a generic term for the clown. The Johns and Jacks belong to a series of stock figures who, like the Toms,[5] were popular in song, ballad, and game. Typical sixteenth century

---

[1] See *New Shakspere Society Transactions*, 1875–76, p. 416.

[2] See *Records of the City of Norwich*, ed. Hudson and Tingey, I, 345–46, for Lenten, clothed "in white with redde herrings skinnes," who followed the king of Christmas at Shrovetide in 1443; Creizenach, *Schauspiele der engl Komödianten*, p. xciv n., for the fool's cap adorned with herring in Holland during the fifteenth century; Elderton's ballad "Lenton stuff" for Jack-a-Lent's coming in with the "hedpeece of a herynge" to say "repent yowe," etc. (Wright, *Songs and Ballads*, Roxburghe Club, p. 191). See p. 47 above for the name Steven Stockfish in early balladry.

[3] For the English clown abroad, see Creizenach, *Schauspiele*, pp. xciii–xcvi.

[4] See Maxwell, *Studies in Philology*, XIX, 232, for the Knave of Clubs as featured in Christmas games in the sixteenth century. A related figure is found in Post-and-Pair, one of the characters in Jonson's *Masque of Christmas*. A speech or song suitable for the latter character occurs in Egerton MS 923, fol. 49 (see *Enterlude of Youth*, ed. Bang and McKerrow, pp. 97–98).

[5] See Chambers, *Mediaeval Stage*, I, 192–93.

figures are Jack-a-Lent and Jack Pudding; and Jacks and Johnny Jacks with various characteristics of clown, vagabond, and goblin survive in modern mummers' plays.[1] According to a statement of Humphrey King, to be quoted shortly, Tarlton loved the May pole with his heart. His bent is seen also in his constant use of the pipe and tabor, the instruments most characteristic of folk game and country mirth. In the passage from *Pasquils Mad-cappe*,

> Tell country Players, that old paltry iests
> Pronouncèd in a painted motley coate,
> Filles all the world so full of cuckoes nests,
> That nightingales can scarcely sing a note,[2]

Breton may reflect the invasion of the professional stage by the clownage of the folk game.

This whole development probably reached its height in the jig. Tarlton's jig to which reference is made in the title of *Tarltons Newes* is called in the title of *The Cobler of Canterburie* a clown's jig. Marlowe in the Prologue to *Tamburlaine* associates

> jigging veins of rhyming mother wits
> And such conceits as clownage keeps in pay.

Not only was the clown the conventional mouthpiece of the jig, but apparently the country clown was the conventional type. In the words of a poem prefixed to the second part of Greene's *Never too Late* (1590), "A Carters ligge is fittest for a Clowne." Lane in *Tom Tel-Troths Message* (ll. 215–16) represents every ballad maker as striving

> to weare a lawrell Crowne
> By penning new gigges for a countrie clowne.

Lane's work appeared in 1600, the year of Breton's complaint to country players and during the period when the jig reached its zenith in professional hands.

My conjecture is that the country jig in various types first appeared on the stage as part of the general vogue of song and

---

[1] See 2 *Notes and Queries*, XI, 272; XII, 487–88; *Folk-Lore Journal*, II, 7; IV, 355–56; *Folk-Lore*, X, 192; *Wiltshire Archaeological Magazine*, I, 81; XXVII, 313–14; XXIX, 142–43; *Antiquary*, XLIV, 380; Ditchfield, *Old English Customs*, pp. 310–23.

[2] Ed. Grosart, p. 11.

dance in the theater. The fact that it was a relief element would account in part for the spirited tone, the coarse humor, and the narrative interest which prevailed over the lyric quality that had associated the word with "carol," "roundelay," and "catch." The usual atmosphere given to country scenes by the Londoner, moreover, was not that of poetic pastoral but of farce. It was the tendency to treat in burlesque fashion whatever came from the country. The convention of terminal song and dance, by freeing the jig from any connection with the play, made possible the use of more elaborate types than could be employed incidentally. The result was a relatively formal dramatic *genre* adapted to professional use and to the taste of the London playgoer. Almost certainly the pre-eminence of the broadside ballad as popular song contributed to the development of the characteristic farce jig since it offered the jigmonger a form admirably suited to the representation of jest and tale in dialogue song.

The earliest known bit of definite evidence for the jig on the stage is found in *Playes Confuted in fiue Actions*, published in 1582. Gosson says:

For the eye beeside the beautie of the houses, and the Stages, hee [the Devil] sendeth in Gearish apparell maskes, vauting, tumbling, daunsing of gigges, galiardes, morisces, hobbihorses; showing of iudgeling castes, nothing forgot, that might serue to set out the matter, with pompe, or rauish the beholders with varietie of pleasure [Sig. G].

The next allusions concern Tarlton. At the end of *Tarltons Newes* the dead actor is made to declare: "they appointed that I should sit and play jigs al day on my tabor to the ghosts without cesing, which hath brought me into such use, that I now play far better than when I was alive," and he starts piping. Cittern, recorder, and bass viol parts for a "Tarltons Jigge" are to be found in the music manuscripts of the Cambridge University Library.[1] All of these records might be taken as referring to music or dance only, but there are two titles that clearly connect Tarlton with the jig embodying a comic plot: *Tarltons Newes out of Purgatorie. Onelye such a jest as his Jigge, fit for Gentlemen to laugh at an houre, &c.* and, in direct answer to this,

[1] Dd. XIV. 24, fol. 17; Dd. V. 21, fol. 5; Dd. V. 20, fol. 5.

The Cobler of Canterburie. Or An inuectiue against Tarltons Newes out of Purgatorie. A merrier Iest then a Clownes Iigge, and fitter for Gentlemens humors. Apparently, then, the rise of the professional jig belongs to "the reigne of Tarltons toies." Beyond these allusions nothing is known of its history until after his day, but such evidence as remains in regard to his art and repertory as a clown may throw some light on the art of the jig.

Tarlton was the first English actor to achieve a fame that lived and to exert an influence that was recognized for generations.[1] According to Bastard, without precedent Tarlton made folly excellent and was extolled for that which all despise.[2] John Davies of Hereford in *Wits Bedlam* proclaims Dick Tarlton lord of mirth, and declares that all clowns since have been his apes.[3] In the Dedication to *An Almond for a Parrat*, which appeared the second year after Tarlton's death, Kemp is addressed as "Jestmonger and Vice-gerent generall to the Ghost of Dicke Tarlton." According to the jest "How Tarlton made Armin his adopted sonne, to succeed him," Armin too learned his art from seeing Tarlton act. Richard Baker's verdict about the middle of the seventeenth century was that Tarlton "for the Part called the Clowns part, never had his match, never will have."[4] In 1651 the author of *An Excellent Comedy, Called, the Prince of Priggs Revels* commends his work in the title as "Repleat with various Conceits, and Tarltonian Mirth."[5]

It is possible that Tarlton's importance in the early history of the stage jig accounts in part for the trend toward clownish drollery implied in the allusions quoted. Halliwell (pp. xxvi-xxvii) cites Nashe, Peacham, and Fuller to show that Tarlton's power lay in his voice, his facial expression, his action rather than in his lines. Both Nashe and Peacham tell of the laughter that arose the instant he thrust his face into view of the audience. Fuller adds: "Indeed the self-same words, spoken by another, would hardly move a merry man to smile; which, uttered by him, would force a sad soul to laughter."[6] This is the

---

[1] See Halliwell's Introduction to his edition of *Tarlton's Jests and News out of Purgatory*, cited below as *Jests.*

[2] *Chrestoleros*, Bk. VI, Epigram 39.

[3] See *Jests*, p. xv. [5] See Bodleian Old Plays, Malone 230 (2).

[4] See *Jests*, p. xxvii n. [6] *Worthies* (1840), III, 140; *Jests*, p. xxvii.

essence of clownage in any age of course, but evidently Tarlton excelled at it. In view of his activity as a writer and his interest in the ballad, it is safe to assume that he wrote many of his jigs, and in them he doubtless made the most of an art of which he was peculiarly master.[1]

Tarlton's equipment as a clown is several times described or pictured. In the Preface to *Tarltons Newes* the ghost of the actor is represented as appearing to the author "attired in russet, with a buttond cap on his head, a great bag by his side, and a strong bat in his hand, so artificially attired for a clowne as I began to call Tarltons woonted shape to remembrance." Chettle's Kindheart in recounting his dream tells how he recognized Tarlton "by his sute of russet, his buttond cap, his taber, his standing on the toe, and other tricks."[2] In the Prologue to Percy's *Cuck-Queanes and Cuckolds Errants*, Tarlton's Ghost refers to "My drum, my Cap my Slop, my Shooe." These are all conspicuous features of the portrait from Harl. MS 3885, fol. 19, that serves as frontispiece to the present volume, and verses attached to it mention his "cote of russet hew" and his start-ups.[3] In the portrait he is piping and beating his tabor. Wilson in *The Commendation of Cockes and Cock-fighting* tells of "a cocke called Tarleton, who was so intituled because he alwayes came to the fight like a drummer, making a thundering noyse with his winges,"[4] a passage which suggests that Tarlton made his entries beating his drum. The picture is rather consistently drawn. It may represent Tarlton in some famous single rôle or some typical rôle of formal drama, but it is more likely that the whole equipment was characteristic of him in stage specialties. Presumably rôles in formal drama would have differed considerably. It is at least hardly probable that they would typically have permitted his entrance with the pipe and tabor, which are characteristic of the country dancer. But these instruments are directly connected with Tarlton's jigs in the pas-

---

[1] See p. 137 below for later jigs in relation to this type of clown.

[2] *Kindheart's Dream*, ed. Rimbault, p. 10.

[3] See *Jests*, pp. xliv–xlv. According to Halliwell (p. 3), the portrait accompanying the early editions of the *Jests* is substantially the same. See also p. xliii for references to other cuts.

[4] *Jests*, p. xxxiv.

sage quoted from the end of the *Newes* which tells of his playing jigs for his fellow ghosts.

Of the few rôles mentioned as Tarlton's, one at least belonged to formal drama—his "part of the clowne" in "a play of Henry the fift" described in the *Jests* and seemingly identified as that of Derick in *The Famous Victories of Henry the fifth*.[1] Other jests refer to his traveling with his company and acting in plays, but particulars are usually lacking. Peacham in *The Truth of our Times* (pp. 103–5) records having seen Tarlton act the part of a third son in what would seem to have been a short interlude founded on the jest of a father's bequeathing his property to two older sons, who piously express the hope that he will live long to enjoy it, and then bequeathing the halter to his graceless third son, who immediately expresses the same wish.[2] A reputation for the rôle of drunkard is suggested by the author of *Machivells Dogge* when he mentions the swaggering of "captaine Tospot with his Tarleton's cut,"[3] and also in the first of the jests, "How Tarlton plaid the drunkard before the Queene." Several of the jests tell of his entertaining the Queen, especially as she dined, and in one case his "clownes apparell" is mentioned (p. 7). A scrap of paper probably written just before Tarlton's death contains the words:

How Tarlton played the God Luz with a flitch of bacon at his back, and how the Queen bade them take away the knave for making her laugh so excessively, as he fought against her little dog, Perrico de Faldas, with his sword and long staffe, and bade the Queen take off her mastie; and what my Lord Sussex and Tarlton said to one another. The three things that make a woman lovely.[4]

The last part seems to refer to a court-of-love debate. The fight with a small dog is likely a burlesque of a popular pantomimic

[1] Pp. 24–25. See Morgan, *Some Problems of Shakespeare's 'Henry the Fourth'*, pp. 4–13, for the difficulty in explaining this account on the basis of the extant text of *The Famous Victories*, presumably a form of the Tarlton play. Jonson in the Induction of *Bartholomew Fair* apparently gives an account of Derick scenes which are in part lost, for he describes a typical rôle of Tarlton as one in which the clown is cozened by Adams the rogue and the two are arrested by the watch with mistaking words.

[2] If this was a type of prodigal son play, as Graves conjectured (*Modern Philology*, XVIII, 495–96), there may be an allusion to it in the *Jests*, p. 14, in an account of one occasion when "Tarlton's part was to travell" and he kneeled "to aske his father blessing."

[3] See *Jests*, p. xxxiii.   [4] *Cal. of State Papers, Dom.*, 1581–90, p. 541.

trick of strolling performers. According to *The two Maids of More-clacke* (1609), a tinker must have his "wench, staffe and dogge," and fighting with a "Masty" is mentioned among the performances of the tinker in the play.[1] But I am unable to offer any suggestions as to the God Luz with a flitch of bacon. The conjecture that Tarlton played a goblin rôle as Robin Goodfellow or, what is more likely, that the two appeared together in some famous dramatic skit seems justified by the frequent connection of the two names after Tarlton's death. *Tarltons Newes*, according to its title, was "Published by an old companion of his, Robin Goodfellow," and in Robin Goodfellow's Epistle, which follows that of the Cobbler in *The Cobler of Canterburie*, Robin says, "Why, see you not how cranke the Cobler is, that will forsooth correct *Dick Tarltons* doings, a man famous in his life for merrie conceites, and especially for a booke of my publishing?" This seems to allude to the *Newes*, but that work was issued after Tarlton's death, so that Robin's reference may be to some genuine work of Tarlton's published during his life. If so, a reminiscence of it is evidently to be found not only in the title of the *Newes* but also in the ballad entered August 20, 1590, as "a pleasant Dyttye Dialogue wise betwene Tarltons ghost and Robyn Good Fellowe."

Indications of Tarlton's interests in the field of song should have an especially close bearing on the jig. He was of course famous for extemporal verse, and it seems to have been his custom to show his skill in it *at the end of the play*. One of the jests (p. 28) gives an account of such a performance "at a play in the country, where, as Tarlton's use was, the play being done, every one so pleased to throw up his theame." Some of the verse quoted in the *Jests* and elsewhere seems unsuited for song or dance, but much of his extemporizing evidently took the form of song. According to another of the jests, "While the queenes players lay in Worcester city to get money, it was his custome for to sing extempore of theames given him."[2] "*A sorowfull newe sonnette*, Intituled *Tarltons Recantacon vppon this theame gyven him by a gentleman at the Bel[le]savage without Lud-*

---

[1] C 3. For jests of the mastiff tearing a man masquerading as a devil, see *Conceits of Old Hobson*, No. 7, and *Knave of Clubs*, Percy Society, pp. 15–17.

[2] P. 27. See also p. 40; *Kindheart's Dream*, ed. Rimbault, p. 39; Harvey, *Works*, ed. Grosart, I, 168 ("piperly Extemporizing, and Tarletonizing").

gate (*nowe or ells never*) *beinge the last theame he songe*" was licensed August 2, 1589. Its genuineness is open to question, but the title suggests one direction in which Tarlton's fame as an extemporizer lay. I suspect that songs extemporized in part and following in the main a set formula were not infrequent in the period and that the "Recantation" was of this sort.

For the most part, however, Tarlton's songs were no doubt set pieces. Two lost ballads—"Tarlton*s farewell*," licensed September 23, 1588; and, evidently in answer, "Tarlton*s, repentance of his farewell to his frendes in his sicknes a little before his deathe*," licensed October 16, 1589—as in the case of the "Recantation," are perhaps less likely to have been written by Tarlton himself than by others who took advantage of the special interest aroused by his death. But a ballad on his death called "Willie and Peggie," in which the lament takes the form of the farewell, must, it seems to me, get its point from some song either written or performed by Tarlton; else the name Willie apparently applied to him here and in Spenser's *Tears of the Muses*, and the ascription of the ballad to Tarlton, cannot be explained.[1] Indeed, in Cambridge MS Dd. IV. 23, fol. 25, music for "Tarltons Willy" is preserved. "Willie and Peggie" was sung to the tune of "Tarlton's Carol,"[2] possibly another sentimental song connected with the comedian. The ballad of actual news also is a form to which he may have been attracted. "Qd. Richard Tarlton" appears at the end of a long narrative ballad called "A very lamentable and wofull discours of the fierce fluds whiche lately flowed in Bedfordshire, in Lincolnshire, and in many other places. . . . the 5. of October, 1570."[3] "Tarlton*s Devise vpon this vnlooked for great snowe*,"

[1] See *Shirburn Ballads*, ed. Clark, pp. 351–53; Rollins in *Journal of American Folk-Lore*, XXX, 376–77. The vogue of farewell songs before the death of Tarlton is noted in chapter vi. See *Roxburghe Ballads*, II, 228–34, for "A pleasant new Northerne Song, called The two Yorkshire Lovers. To a pleasant new Court tune; or, the tune of *Willy*," printed for John Wright. It is a pastoral ballad, partly narrative, in the vein of Marlowe's "Come live with me," representing the wooing of Willy.

[2] See *Ballads from Manuscripts*, II, 92, or Herrig's *Archiv*, CXIV, 344, for another ballad to this tune.

[3] See *Tarlton's Jests and News*, ed. Halliwell, pp. 125–31. For its entry on the Register, see Arber's *Transcript*, I, 440 (see also I, 441). The "tru Reporte of the newes in Heryfordshyre" was entered the same year (I, 443). See also I, 181, for the ballad entitled "newes out of Kent" (1561–2), and II, 340, for "A ballat begynnynge *heighe*

however, which was licensed February 7, 1579, was from its designation as a device apparently dramatic in form, whether it was a ballad or a prose dialogue.[1]

Undoubtedly Tarlton's forte was comic and satiric song. He evidently carried on the tradition of the medley as the clown's song, for Martin Parker wrote two medleys to be sung to the tune of "Tarleton's Medley."[2] In *Greenes Newes both from Heauen and Hell*, the ghost of Greene reports that an assembly called by Lucifer for serious discussion was broken up by Dick Tarlton's appearing "apparrelled like a Clowne, and singing this peece of an olde song.

> *If this be trewe as true it is,*
>   *Ladie Ladie:*
> *God send her life may mende the misse,*
>   *Most deere Ladie.*"[3]

This is an adaptation of lines in Elderton's "Pangs of Love" (1559), and apparently satirizes a vogue of the refrain in wooing songs.[4] Parodies of legal and religious forms such as we have seen associated with figures like Jack-a-Lent were probably favorites with Tarlton. The extemporal "Recantation" entered on the Register, if really Tarlton's, was likely of this type.

---

hoe my hart is heavye to write the pitifull newes in euery plac[e]" (1578). The lost "Diolige of the Rufull burr[n]ynge of Powles," which was licensed as a ballad in 1562–3 (*Transcript*, I, 202), furnishes an early example of the dialogue ballad dealing with current happenings.

[1] The "ballat of *a northerne mans reporte of the wonderfull greate snowe in the southerne partes but most specially of many mervailous monsters yat he sawe in London with other Mischances &c*," entered February 14, 1579, was probably an immediate imitation of Tarlton's device. Some idea of the method of reporting these snows is possibly to be had from two prose dialogues, *The Great Frost* of 1608 (*Social England Illustrated*, New English Garner, pp. 163–85) and *The Cold Yeare, 1614* (*Miscellanea Antiqua Anglicana*). The second follows the other often verbatim. In both, the effects of the cold year in city and country are discussed between a London shopkeeper and a countryman from the north, who has come to London to see the marvels of the great frost; and both show the crossing of news of actual events with comment on social conditions.

[2] *Roxburghe Ballads*, I, 52; II, 240.

[3] Ed. McKerrow, pp. 58, 91–92.

[4] See the wooing dialogue in *Horestes*, ll. 538–601; *Trial of Treasure*, Percy Society, p. 36; *Handful of Pleasant Delights*, ed. Rollins, pp. 29–31, 96–97; *Twelfth Night*, II, iii, 83–84, with the notes of commentators. Collier, *Bibliographical Account*, I, 454, notes a reference in *Laugh and lie downe* (1605) to the tune "Lady, Lady, my faire Lady."

There are several allusions to his use of the burlesque testament,[1] though not in a form suitable for song. In 1642 the following fragment, either modeled on a folk rhyme or giving rise to one, was quoted in *Pigges Corantoe* as Tarlton's:

> The King of France with forty thousand men,
> Went up a Hill, and so came downe agen.

If the ascription is just, we here have Tarlton in the rôle of political satirist.[2] It is pretty certain that he carried the propaganda against the Puritans into the theater. Humphrey King in *An Halfe-penny-worth of Wit* (p. 21) characterizes "merry Tarlton" as one

> That lou'd a May-pole with his heart.
> His humour was to please all them
> That seeme no Gods, but mortall men,
> For (saith he) in these our daies,
> The Cobler now his Last downe laies,
> And if he can but reade, (God wot)
> Hee talkes and prates he knowes not what,
> Of May-poles, and of merriments
> That haue no spot of ill pretence.

The author of *Mar-Martine* after speaking of the railing and libeling that marked the Marprelate controversy adds:

> These tinkers termes, and barbers iestes first *Tarleton* on the stage,
> Then *Martin* in his bookes of lies, hath put in euery page.[3]

Within a year of Tarlton's death Laneham and his fellows of the Queen's company were performing jigs at the Theatre in ridicule of the Martinists, and it is reasonable enough to suppose that Tarlton's satire on the zealots of his day took the form of jigs for stage use.

One fine satiric piece signed with the initials R. T. is ex-

---

[1] See the end of Harington's *Ulysses upon Ajax* and *Jests*, pp. 35–36.

[2] See Bohun, *The Character of Queen Elizabeth* (1693), p. 353, for an account of "a pleasant Play" by Tarlton in which he offended the Queen by satirizing the power of Leicester and saying, as he pointed at Raleigh, "See the Knave commands the Queen."

[3] *Works of Lyly*, ed. Bond, III, 426. In *The Elizabethan Stage*, I, 294, Chambers states, "Tarlton is said himself to have satirized the existing ecclesiastical order in a mock discovery of Simony 'in Don John of Londons cellar.'"

tant—"The Crowe sits vpon the wall," a ballad of seventeen stanzas in the nature of a ragman's roll dealing in social satire.[1] It opens:

> Please one and please all,
> Be they great, be they small,
> Be they little, be they lowe,—
> So pypeth the crowe,
> Sitting vpon a wall,—
> Please one and please all,
> Please one and please all.
>
> Be they white, be they black,
> Haue they a smock on their back,
> Or a kircher on their head,
> Whether they spin silke or thred,
> Whatsoeuer they them call,—
> Please one and please all,
> Please one and please all.

Professor Raleigh in his *Shakespeare* (p. 100) calls this ballad one of Tarlton's jigs, "wherein each of the short verses was satirically directed at this or that member of the audience," and he points out the fact that Malvolio is probably quoting the refrain when he says in *Twelfth Night* (III, iv), "it is with me as the very true sonnet is, 'Please one, and please all.' "

A somewhat similar piece is the "Jigge of a horse loade of Fooles," which Collier assigned to Tarlton and pronounced the only extant jig.[2] It may have been sung and danced by Tarlton, for it is a good example of the conventional ragman's roll with its list of the various classes of fools—the player fool, the Puritan fool, the fool of state, the poet fool, and so on. Bits of satire resembling this "jig" in one way or another are found in an early disard's song[3] with satiric speeches seemingly directed at typical persons in an audience; in many old lists or orders of fools and vagabonds;[4] and in numerous seventeenth

---

[1] See *Ancient Ballads and Broadsides*, Philobiblon Society, pp. 377–82.

[2] *New Facts regarding the Life of Shakespeare*, pp. 17–20; *Tarlton's Jests and News*, ed. Halliwell, pp. xix–xxvi.

[3] See *Anglia*, XXVI, 280–81.

[4] See *PMLA*, XVI (1908), 491 n.; *Cambridge History Eng. Lit.*, III, 550.

century ballads satirizing various classes, such as "A Fooles Bolt is soone shot."[1] There is a strong probability, however, that the "Jigge of a horse loade of Fooles" is one of Collier's forgeries.

Our best clue to the character of the Tarltonian farce jig lies in the two titles already quoted—*Tarltons Newes out of Purgatorie. Onelye such a jest as his Jigge, fit for Gentlemen to laugh at an houre* and *The Cobler of Canterburie . . . . A merrier Iest then a Clownes Iigge, and fitter for Gentlemens humors*. In both cases "jest" and "jig" are singular. Yet "jest" can hardly be taken as applying to the framework of these collections alone. The first title would seem to mean either that some jig of Tarlton's bore a resemblance to one of the stories in the *Newes*, or more probably, that the same sort of plot was characteristic in Tarlton's jigs. The tales of the *Newes* are of the novella and jest type, and at the beginning of *The Cobler* one of the company is reported as saying that most of them were "stolne out of *Boccace Decameron*." On the other hand, the stories of *The Cobler*, which are here so favorably contrasted with the "Clownes Iigge," are themselves of the same stuff as the novelle. Those in both collections belong to the general type of farce from which jigs were often derived later. In fact, in several cases the situations on which they turn are found in extant jig or singspiel. Three of the tales in the *Newes* are merely droll jests that might have come from the Wise Men of Gotham: "The Tale of the Cooke," drawn from *Decameron*, VI, 4, with its explanation of the crane's having only one leg; "The Tale of the Vickar of Bergamo" with its account of the substitution of coals for the Vicar's feather of the angel Gabriel; and "The Painter of Doncaster," in which the painter who spoils the rood is paid because he failed for lack of practice. "The Three Cuckolds" is a series of satiric studies, and *The Cobler* matches it with eight "orders of Cuckolds." There were many ballads on cuckolds, as well as a popular dance tune in the seventeenth century called "Cuckolds all a Row."[2] "The Tale of Pope Boni-

[1] See Rollins, *Pepysian Garland*, pp. 316–22.

[2] For some of the ballads see *Roxburghe Ballads*, IX, cxxxii*–cxxxiii*, clxiv*–clxv*, 603–4, 605; for the dance tune, see Chappell, *Popular Music of the Olden Time*, I, 340–42. See the end of Wycherley's *Country Wife* for a dance of cuckolds.

face" is a prose riddle story similar to the well-known traditional ballad "King John and the Abbot of Canterbury," which is printed as No. 45 in Child's collection of ballads. Such riddles have been popular in every literature, and there is evidence for their use in song drama and farce.[1] Of the three novella tales in the *Newes*, "The Tale of Friar Onyon" is founded on *Decameron*, IV, 2, a story used also by the German dramatist Ayrer for one of his jigs, "Der verlarft Franciscus"; "The Gentlewoman of Lyons," a version of the story found in *Decameron*, VII, 6, has the same plot as the jig "Singing Simpkin"; and incidents in "The Two Lovers of Pisa," a version of a story told by Straparola, are paralleled in the English jig surviving in German as "Pückelherings Dill dill dill."

The evidence with regard to Tarlton's jigs seems slight, but in comparison with the definite evidence for his part in formal drama it is neither small nor indefinite when the ephemeral nature of the jig is taken into account. His performance of jigs doubtless contributed much to his general fame as a comic artist. This is indicated not only by the records of his jigs but by the relative emphasis on song in the whole body of material that concerns him. It is possible that the stage jig emerges during the career of Tarlton simply because he is the first actor around whose name anecdote and allusion gathered. It is much more probable, however, that finding the jig at the beginning of his career merely one of a number of incidental attractions on the stage, he saw in it a medium especially suited to his talents, and developed its varied possibilities to such a point that at his death the foundation was already laid for its astonishing popularity during the next two or three decades.

[1] See *Modern Philology*, XIV, 497–98.

CHAPTER IV

A GENERAL ACCOUNT OF THE STAGE JIG
AFTER TARLTON'S DEATH

SHORTLY after Tarlton's death the fuller and more definite records of the stage jig begin. From this time on, there are a number of unquestioned specimens, some titles of lost jigs, entries on the Register, and a large body of general allusions as evidence in regard to both the art of the jig and its history as a stage form. The texts of the jigs themselves are printed in full in the second part of this volume, and in the later chapters of the first part there is some discussion of their history, their sources, and particularly their literary affiliations. In the present chapter I wish to give merely a brief general survey of the field based on the more definite evidence in regard to the stage jig.

The custom of the afterpiece was firmly established before the end of the sixteenth century. As early as 1592 Nashe refers at the end of *Pierce Penilesse* to

> the queint Comædians of our time
> That when their Play is doone do fal to ryme.

A few years later Davies in Epigram XVII shows that an afterpiece of dance and song could be taken for granted at the theaters generally:

> For as we see at all the playhouse doors,
> When ended is the play, the dance and song,
> A thousand townsmen, gentlemen, and whores,
> Porters and serving-men together throng.

The foreigner Platter, who attended a performance of *Julius Caesar* on September 21, 1599, reports: "zu endt der Comedien dantzeten sie ihrem gebrauch nach gar vberausz zierlich, ye zwen in mannes vndt 2 in weiber kleideren angethan, wunderbahrlich mitt einanderen."[1] Of a performance slightly later, he writes, "Zu endt dantzeten sie auch auf Englisch vnndt Irlend-

[1] See *Anglia*, XXII, 458–59.

isch gar zierlich." At the same period Hentzner comments on
the many plays performed in the theaters, "quas varijs etiam
saltationibus, suavissimâ adhibitâ Musicâ, magno cum populi
applausu finire solent."[1] Neither of these foreigners mentions
song, and Platter at least is chiefly impressed with the dancing.
The second record quoted from him suggests to me disguised
dances. No doubt the widest variety of forms prevailed in the
afterpiece from such dances as that of the epilogue speaker in
II *Henry IV* to the more elaborate farce jigs. But the passage
from Jonson's *Every Man out of his Humour* (1599), "a thing
studied, and rehearst as ordinarily at his comming from hawk-
ing or hunting, as a jigge after a Play" (II, i), and one from *Jack
Drum's Entertainment* (1600), "As the Iigge is cal'd for when the
Play is done" (Act I),[2] lead to the conclusion that by the end of
the century a typical jig was regularly performed.[3]

In 1591 began the licensing of certain pieces under the name
jig, and by the end of 1595 the following entries had been made
on the Register:

a newe Northerne Jigge
the Seconde parte of the gigge betwene Rowland and the Sexton [evi-
dently the lost "Rowland," extant in a German form, was one part]

[1] *Itinerarium* (1612), p. 132 ("Anno 1598").

[2] Collier conjectures from this passage that the jig was perhaps not "advertised in
the bills, nor performed, unless it were 'called for' by the audience" (*Hist. Eng. Dram.
Poetry* [1879], III, 182). Shirley in *Changes* (IV, ii) speaks of gentlemen of the period
as not being able with honor to call for a jig after the play. These passages may mean
simply that, the play over, the spectators expressed their impatience for the more
popular part of the performance by calling aloud for the jig to be brought on. It is
probable too that the audience frequently called aloud for a favorite jig, since a dramatic
company might easily have had a considerable repertory of jigs most of which could be
produced almost at a moment's notice. With the other evidence at hand, the passage
from *Jack Drum's Entertainment* can hardly be taken to mean that at this particular
era the jig was performed only when especially demanded. As for advertising jigs in
bills, there seems to be no evidence that the title of the jig for a given occasion was
announced beforehand unless "The Ship" was a jig. See Field's *Amends for Ladies*
(1611) for a reference to "Long Meg and the Ship at the Fortune" (II, i). The Nuremberg playbill printed in facsimile at the end of Cohn's *Shakespeare in Germany*, after
announcing the title of the play, says merely, "Nach der Comoedi soll præsentirt
werden ein schön Ballet vnd lächerliches Possenspiel."

[3] The word may of course have been used for the afterpiece without any attempt
at fine distinctions, but in *Every Woman in her Humour* of 1609, Terentia does make a
distinction when she refers to the comedian's scenes of civil war as followed by "a
clapping conclusion, perhappes a Iigge" (Sig. D).

the Thirde and last parte of Kempes *Jigge*
a merrie new Jigge betwene Jenkin the Collier and Nansie
a ballad of *Cutting George, and his hostis* beinge a Jigge
a pleasant Jigge betwene a tincker and a Clowne
A plesant newe Jigge of the Broome-man [called in the margin "Kempes"]
master Kemps *Newe Jigge of the kitchen stuffe woman*
Phillips *his gigg of the slyppers*
A pretie newe J[i]gge betwene ffrancis the gentleman Richard the farmer and theire wyves ["Attowell's Jig"]
Kemps *newe Jygge betwixt, a souldiour and a Miser and Sym the clown* ["Singing Simpkin"]

The first is a non-dramatic dialogue, and the last two are elaborate farce jigs. The second belonged at least to the farce type. The remainder have been lost. The use of an actor's name identifies four other entries as representing stage jigs, however. There is little ground for conjecture as to the nature of the remaining three, but the titles feature characteristic figures of contemporary farce.

Two additional farce jigs are extant that can be assigned to the period before 1600—"Rowland's Godson" and "The Wooing of Nan." The lost piece licensed in August, 1591, as a "ballad of *a newe northerne Dialogue betwene Will, Sone, and the warriner, and howe Reynold Peares gott faire Nannye to his Loue*" was evidently dramatic. Deloney's lost jig of "John for the King" is mentioned by Nashe in 1596.[1] This is the extent of the definite material for a study of the sixteenth century stage jig outside of some singspiele based on early jigs that are no longer extant.

Deloney is the only ballad writer of the period whose connection with the jig is recorded. Besides Nashe's mockery of him as the author of "John for the King," Kemp in an address to ballad makers at the end of the *Nine Days' Wonder* declares, "I have made a privy search, what private Jigmonger of your jolly number hath been the Author of these abominable Ballets written of me," and he adds, "I was told, it was the great Balladmaker T. D., *alias* THOMAS DELONEY." Deloney's interest in song drama is seen in the country jig woven into his *Thomas of*

[1] *Works*, ed. McKerrow, III, 84.

Reading and in the satiric ballad called "A pleasant Dialogue betweene plaine Truth and blind Ignorance," which has already been discussed in chapter ii as a probable jig. The authorship of jigs, however, was apparently of no more significance than that of other ballads, for the jig had no standing as literature at any period of its career. Even Henslowe fails to give names when he makes an entry in his *Diary* of 6s. 8d. "Layd owt for ij gyges for shawe & his company to ij yonge men the 12 of desemb3 1597."[1] In the old days Tarlton and Laneham, both of whom seem to have been writers of verse as well as actors, probably wrote some of the jigs which they performed; but Kemp more likely had his name associated with particular jigs through his acting.[2] The reputation that attached to the individual jig naturally belonged to the actor who made it a success, for the appeal of song and dance drama more than of other dramatic types depended on the effectiveness with which it was performed.

But in spite of a Marlowe's contemptuous attitude to the jigging veins of rhyming mother wits, the outstanding dramatic company of England, the Chamberlain's, was featuring the jig during the last decade of the sixteenth century, and the foremost comedian was content to win fame in it. If the development of the stage jig is to be associated with the name of Tarlton, the era of its glory must be linked with the name of Kemp. My reasons for believing that Kemp introduced "Rowland" on the Continent before 1589 are stated in connection with that jig. If I am right, he is, more than any other single actor, responsible for starting the vogue of the singspiele, for "Rowland" was by all odds the most influential of the jigs on the Continent. The licensing of the "Thirde and last parte of Kempes Jigge" in 1591 at least presupposes two earlier jigs with his stamp. As we have just seen, three other jigs were licensed under his name later. One of them, "Singing Simpkin," is second only to "Rowland" in importance. By 1598 the popular enthusiasm for Kemp's performances was so great that it drew the fire of the satirists. "The orbs celestiall," says Marston in

[1] Ed. Greg, I, 70, 82.

[2] Kemp attributes to another the verse parts of his *Nine Days' Wonder* except for four lines which might have been quoted.

The Scourge of Villanie, Satire XI, "Will daunce Kemps jigge";[1]
and Guilpin in *Skialetheia*,[2] Satire V, protests that

> Whores, Bedles, bawdes, and Sergeants filthily
> Chaunt *Kemps* Iigge.

In 1600 Kemp prefaced his *Nine Days' Wonder* with an address
in which he describes himself as one "that hath spent his life in
mad jigs and merry jests." Lute music for "Kemps Jiggs" is
preserved in Cambridge MS Dd. II. 11, fol. 99*v*; and a jig bearing Kemp's name was printed in Playford's *Dancing Master*.[3]

[1] *Works of Marston*, ed. Halliwell, III, 301.

[2] Ed. Grosart, Occasional Issues, p. 56.

[3] Danckert (*Geschichte der Gigue*, p. 12) gives the following transcription of the air
from the Cambridge lute book, which he attributes to Naylor:

See *Geschichte der Gigue*, pp. 30–31, for the influence of the tune on Continental music.
The following version of the "Kemp's Jigge" found in *The Dancing Master* is from the
first edition (1651):

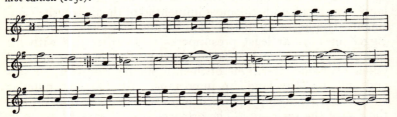

Danckert prints these two tunes—the second (p. 15) from the 1686 edition of *The Dancing Master*—as illustrating two different types of the true jig music. Here again, as in
the case of Tarlton, we may have merely dance music, but the connection with Kemp's
name makes it highly probable that the tunes belonged to farce jigs.

But Kemp was probably only the most conspicuous of a number of prominent comedians who were attracted to the field in the same period. The name of George Attowell, which is attached to "Attowell's Jig," figures several times in the annals of the dramatic companies.[1] The Phillips of "The Jig of the Slippers" was presumably Augustine Phillips, for so long an important member of the Chamberlain's company. When Henslowe paid for two jigs for Shaw and his company in 1597, Shaw was prominent in the affairs of the Admiral's Men. It may be assumed, I think, that at the end of the sixteenth century the leading English comedians at home as well as abroad were regularly dancers and singers of jigs, and that the chief English companies kept a group of actors skilled in the performance of song and dance specialties. The activity in this line on the Continent is discussed later.

With the opening of the seventeenth century a less tolerant attitude is discernible. In the extensive satire of the dramatists on popular taste, "jig" is conspicuous as a term of contempt. Hamlet takes revenge for Polonius's criticism of the players by saying, "he's for a jig or a tale of bawdry, or he sleeps" (II, ii). In the Dedication of *Catiline* Jonson praises the Earl of Pembroke that he should dare in "these Iig-giuen times, to countenance a legitimate Poeme," and both in the Epistle accompanying the quarto of *The Alchemist* published in 1612 and in the Induction to *Bartholomew Fair* he satirizes "the concupiscence of jigs and dances" which reigns.[2] The Dedication of Massinger's *Roman Actor*, licensed in 1626, contains the defiance: "If the gravity and height of the subject distaste such as are only affected with jigs and ribaldry, (as I presume it will,) their condemnation of me and my poem can no way offend me: my reason teaching me, such malicious and ignorant detractors deserve rather contempt than satisfaction."

The jig fell into disrepute not only because of its low art but chiefly because of its obscenity, an objection that may have

[1] See p. 240 below.

[2] The copy of the 1612 quarto of *The Alchemist* used by Gifford has "concupiscence of dances and of antics," a natural variant at the time.

grown out of its action as well as its subject matter.[1] Already in 1598 Guilpin seems to have had indecent jigs in mind when writing a passage of the Satyre Preludium in his *Skialetheia*. In classifying base poets who "melt true valour with lewd ballad stuffe," he makes one class consist of those whose "Lady Muse is comicall, / *Thalia* to the back, nay back and all." He continues:

> And she with many a salt *La volto* iest
> Edgeth some blunted teeth, and fires the brest
> Of many an old cold gray-beard Cittizen,
> *Medea* like making him young againe;
> Who comming from the Curtaine sneaketh in,
> To some odde garden noted house of sinne.

In his *Strange Horse-Race* of 1613, Dekker says of the jig performance:

> Now, as after the cleare streame hath glided away in his owne current, the bottome is muddy and troubled. And as I haue often seene, after the finishing of some worthy Tragedy, or Catastrophe in the open Theaters, that the Sceane after the Epilogue hath beene more blacke (about a nasty bawdy Iigge) then the most horrid Sceane in the Play was: The stinkards speaking all things, yet no man vnderstanding any thing; a mutiny being amongst them, yet none in danger: no tumult, and yet no quietnesse; no mischifs begotten, and yet mischiefe borne: the swiftnesse of such a torrent, the more it ouerwhelmes, breeding the more pleasure.[2]

[1] Objections to the wantonness of dance usually, but not always, come from the Puritans. In 1586 the author of *The Praise of Musicke* (p. 79), while defending music and dancing, admits that "obscenity may bring the stage in suspicion of vnchastnes and incontinency, make dauncing disfauorable & odious." Guilpin refers to his Muse as haply being accused of "dauncing this Iigge so lasciuiously" (*Skialetheia*, Epigram 69). See also Mangold's description of the English dancer in 1597 (Herz, *Englische Schauspieler*, p. 35). One of the clearest statements in regard to the obscenity of stage action is found in a discussion of stage abuses in *This Worlds Folly. Or A Warning-Peece discharged vpon the Wickednesse thereof* by I. H. (1615), in the same general connection in which an attack is made upon the extreme lewdness of jigs. In the midst of much that might be taken as referring to subject matter, the author says: "these are they, who by their wantonizing Stage-gestures, can ingle and seduce men to heaue vp their heartes and affections, as a voluntary sacrifice to that exulcerated Fiend *Asmodeus* [in the margin here "The spirit of Lechery"], and all other abhominable Idoll-sinnes, obstinately alienating and tearing their selues and soules from the spirit of Grace; and by howe much more exact these are in their mimicke venerean action, by so much more highly are they seated in the Monster-headed *Multitudes* estimation" (B 2).

[2] *Non-Dramatic Works*, ed. Grosart, III, 340. See *Review of English Studies*, I, 186, for an unruly audience at the Curtain in the same period.

The lost jig of "Garlic" was notorious for its bawdry, and an extreme picture of the obscenity of jigs is drawn when Haddit, the jig maker portrayed in the first act of Tailor's *Hog hath Lost his Pearl* (printed in 1614), promises that his jig "Who buys my four ropes of hard onions?" shall contain "more whores than e'er garlic had." Haddit is able to command four angels for this piece, a price that is undoubtedly exorbitant enough to give point to the satire on the grossness of popular taste, for Henslowe paid only 6s. 8d. for two jigs in 1597. In 1615 the author of *This Worlds Folly* deplores the popular obsession with "obscæne and light Iigges, stuft with loathsome and vnheard-of Ribauldry, suckt from the poysonous dugs of Sinne-sweld Theaters" (Sig. B).

Little is left on which to base a definite estimate of the jig at this period. From 1595 until 1623 the word does not occur on the Stationers' Register. On September 3, 1623, *A Booke of Jiggs conteyning three bookes or partes* was entered to Francis Grove, but no trace of it is left. The book may well have been a collection of dance music. Possibly from the time when jigs became a great drawing-card until after the stage vogue began to decline, an effort was made to keep them out of print. A more important point is that an extremely low moral tone in an age of growing Puritan sentiment would tend to prevent the licensing of such jigs as seem to have held the boards. Moreover, as the interest in plot increased, the jigs—still considered ballads—probably outgrew the modest limits of a broadside and became an anomaly so far as publication was concerned. The three extant farce jigs printed in the seventeenth century appeared in collections after 1650. That a developed farce form was typical in the period seems to be indicated in one of the meanings which Cotgrave gives for "farce"—"the Iyg at the end of an Enterlude, wherein some pretie knauerie is acted"— and also in the statement of Knolles in 1606 that nowadays a comedy or jig is put at the end of every tragedy.[1]

Not a single farce jig is extant that can certainly be assigned to the first half of the seventeenth century, though "The Blackman" and some of the singspiele probably represent the art of the English jig at this time. Of the lost jigs, only one certain title remains from the period, that of "Garlic." There is, besides, the

[1] See Chambers, *Elizabethan Stage*, II, 551, n. 4.

possibility that the titles "The Ship" and "Shankes Ordinary" discussed in chapter ix represent lost jigs. The only name positively identified with the history of the early seventeenth century jig is that of the actor John Shank, or Shanks, who wrote the "Ordinary." A satiric poem, "On the Time-Poets," celebrates the fame of "Basse for a Ballad, *John Shank* for a Jig."[1] Since the poem deals only with writers, the allusion is evidently to Shank as author of jigs.

For the seventeenth century the evidence seems to indicate a divergence of practice in regard to the jig corresponding to a divergence in tone and ideals with the different classes of theaters. The jig came into its own when there was no distinction of private as against public houses, and the company that perfected it was the best in England. After 1600 the policy of the private houses probably tended to discredit the jig and to throw it more definitely into the hands of the companies that catered to the populace. The fact that by 1600 Kemp had left the Chamberlain's Men and by 1602 had joined Worcester's may reflect a shift in attitude on the part of his old company.

Lawrence claims that jigs never had a place in "the economy of the private theatre,"[2] and he is perhaps right as regards the farce type, in spite of the fact that Knolles in 1606 speaks of *every* tragedy as followed by a comedy or jig.[3] In art and in tone the seventeenth century jig was presumably alien to the taste of the discriminating audiences at the private houses. Bacon, who would represent the extreme attitude of the cultured, may be glancing at jigs when he says in his essay "Of Masques and Triumphs": "Acting in song, especially in dialogues, hath an extreme good grace: I say acting, not dancing (for that is a mean and vulgar thing)." In a passage which has been quoted from Dekker's *Strange Horse-Race*, a picture is drawn of the commotion attendant on the jig "after some worthy Tragedy,

[1] See *Choyce Drollery*, ed. Ebsworth, pp. 7, 271. The piece was printed in 1656, but Ebsworth dates it between 1620 and 1636, the year in which Shank died. The other allusion is to William Bass, his name being printed in the margin.

[2] *Elizabethan Playhouse and Other Studies*, Ser. I, p. 80.

[3] See Chambers, *Elizabethan Stage*, II, 551, n. 4: "R. Knolles, *Six Bookes of a Commonweal* (1606), 645, 'Now adayes they put at the end of euerie Tragedie (as poyson into meat) a comedie or jigge' (translating Bodin's 'obscoena quadam fabula turpissimis ac sordissimis narrationibus condita')."

or Catastrophe in the open Theaters"—a phrase which, if taken literally, would mean the public theaters. The Prologue of *The Fair Maid of the Inn*, licensed in 1626 and performed at Blackfriars, complains of the hostility which some really worthy play is likely to encounter, while

> A jig shall be clapt at, and every rhyme
> Praised and applauded by a clamorous chime.

But the author rejoices that to his house

> Come nobler judgments, and to those the strain
> Of our invention is not bent in vain.

In the Praeludium to *The Careless Shepherdess*, acted at the private Salisbury Court after 1629, the thrifty citizen is made to declare:

> And I will hasten to the money Box,
> And take my shilling out again, for now
> I have considered that it is too much;
> I'le go to th'Bull, or Fortune, and there see
> A Play for two pense, with a Jig to boot.

The Prologue written for a performance of Shirley's *Doubtful Heir* at the Globe about 1640 shows at least what was understood to be the difference in the general requirements of that house and Blackfriars. Shirley excuses the absence of shews and dance, target fighting, bawdry and ballads, clown, squibs, and devil because the play had been written for Blackfriars.

Among the public theaters it is noticeable that the only houses mentioned by name in connection with the jig are those to the north of the city—the Curtain, the Fortune, and the Red Bull. Guilpin's reference in 1598 to "*La volto* iest" and the evil influence exerted by this type of performance belongs to the Curtain. Wither in *Abuses Stript and Whipt* (1613) raps those

> base fellowes, whom meere time
> Hath made sufficient to bring forth a Rime,
> A Curtaine Iigge, a Libell, or a Ballet,
> For Fidlers, or some Rogues with staffe and wallet
> To sing at doores.
> —Book II, Satire 3.

The Fortune seems to have been the most notorious of the theaters that figure in the history of the jig. It was here that "Garlic" was produced. In 1612 jigs were drawing such disorderly crowds to the Fortune that on October 1 "An Order for suppressinge of Jigges att the ende of Playes" was issued at the General Session of the Peace at Westminster:

Whereas Complaynte have (*sic*) beene made at this last Generall Sessions that by reason of certayne lewde Jigges songes and daunces vsed and accustomed at the play-house called the Fortune in Goulding-lane divers cutt-purses and other lewde and ill disposed persons in greate multitudes doe resorte thither at th'end of euerye playe many tymes causinge tumultes and outrages wherebye His Majesties peace is often broke and much mischiefe like to ensue thereby, Itt was hereuppon expresselye commaunded and ordered by the Justices of the said benche That all Actors of euerye playehouse within this cittye and liberties thereof and in the Countye of Middlesex that they and euerie of them utterlye abolishe all Jigges Rymes and Daunces after their playes And not to tollerate permitt or suffer anye of them to be used vpon payne of ymprisonment and puttinge downe and suppressinge of theire playes.[1]

Instructions are added to apprehend any players who "do persiste and contynewe their sayd Jiggs daunces or songes" or any persons attempting outrages. Evidently after the play additional audiences of the vulgar poured into the Fortune to be entertained with such jigs as "Garlic." The public theaters that would be especially affected by this order covering Middlesex County are the Fortune, the Curtain, and the Red Bull.

In denouncing the immorality of the stage, I. H., author of *This Worlds Folly*, printed in 1615, apparently had these three theaters particularly in mind, and though the attack is general, he seems to be making a special point of the jig. After his denunciation of "obscæne and light Iigges" already quoted, he goes on almost immediately (B 2) to flay "*Fortune*-fatted fooles, and Times Ideots" for the filth which they discharge in the face of the city, mentioning specifically only "Garlic." The passage is quoted more fully in connection with the discussion of that jig in chapter ix. He then turns his attention to Thomas Greene, leader of the Queen's Men and a prominent figure of the period

---

[1] See Jeaffreson, *Middlesex County Records*, II, 83-84. Dekker's picture of the tumult at jig performances in "the open Theaters" belongs to the following year.

in clown's rôles, who was at the Red Bull from 1610 until his death in 1612:[1] "*Vos quoque, and you also, who with Scylla-barking, Stentor-throated bellowings flash choaking[2] squibbes of absurd vanities into the nosthrils of your spectators; barbarously diuerting Nature, and defacing Gods owne image, by metamorphising humane *shape into bestiall forme." In the margin "Or, Tu quoque" is printed opposite Vos quoque, and "Greenes Baboone" opposite "shape."[3] Apparently the whole passage, except the play on the famous Greene's Tu Quoque, refers to a bizarre rôle of the comedian's as baboon, and this, I believe, was in the form of a dance. Early in the year following Greene's death, a He-Baboon and a She-Baboon appeared in the Second Antimasque of Beaumont's Masque of the Inner Temple and Gray's Inn. Probably about the same time, a bavian, or baboon, "with long tayle and eke long toole," was introduced—in addition to the clown—for a morris dance in The Two Noble Kinsmen, III, v. The pedant instructs him,

> carry your taile without offence
> Or scandall to the Ladies; and be sure
> You tumble with audacity and manhood;
> And when you barke, doe it with judgement.

Possibly in these cases we have an imitation of a famous stage dance of the comedian lately dead. I. H. speaks of his barking, and the passage in The Two Noble Kinsmen with less indignation suggests other disreputable aspects of such a performance. It is more than probable that Jonson is referring to other imitations of the rôle when he says of Mime in Epigram CXXX, published in 1616,

> Whil'st thou dost raise some Player from the grave,
> Out-dance the Babion, or out-boast the Brave.[4]

[1] See Adams, Shakespearean Playhouses, pp. 298–99.

[2] flash choaking is printed as one word

[3] See p. 295 below for a passage from Parrot's Springs for Wood-cocks in which Greene's Tu Quoque and "Garlicke Iigs" are associated, and pp. 313–16 below for the use of squibs in Dutch jigs.

[4] In his essay "Of Masques and Triumphs" Bacon mentions the baboon among the figures common in antimasques. See p. 54 above for the use of the ape in the Marprelate controversy, and the Induction to Bartholomew Fair for Jonson's satire on the device. In Ram-Alley (1611) the ape's tricks are imitated in one scene (G 1-2). In an

Having touched on what he evidently regards as the high lights in the depravity of the Fortune and the Bull, I. H. now turns to the Curtain: "Those also stand within the stroke of my penne, who were wont to *Curtaine* ouer their defects with knauish con-ueyances, and scum off the froth of all wanton vanity, to quali-fie the eager appetite of their slapping Fauorites," a description which is at least more applicable to the jig of the period than to the regular drama. Then follows immediately the passage al-ready quoted in which the author arraigns the players for their wanton gesture and "mimicke venerean action."

The same three houses are noticed about 1613 in a stanza of William Turner's "Dish of Lentten stuffe," which at least bears on the jig and which gives our best clue to the comedians who were probably its chief exponents in the reign of James:

That's the fat foole of the Curtin,
    and the leane foole of the Bull:
Since *Shanke* did leaue to sing his rimes,
    he is counted but a gull.
The players of the Banke side,
    the round Globe and the Swan,
Will teach you idle trickes of loue,
    but the Bull will play the man.[1]

There are records establishing the fact that in 1610 and at the beginning of 1613 Shank was a regular member of the company which occupied the Fortune.[2] It is reasonable to suppose, then, that he was a leading spirit at that house when "Garlic" and "The Ship" were performed and when the turbulence of the audience caused the order forbidding the afterpiece. The pas-

earlier scene (Sig. B) the jest about the newest tricks of the baboons may indicate some performance like Greene's. One woman in *Every Woman in her Humour* (1609) says, "I have seen the *Babones* already" (Sig. H). See Brit. Mus. *Cat. MS Music*, III, 174–75, for "The Babboon's Dance" and "The Ape's Dance at the Temple" in Add. MS. 10444, and *Oxford Hist. Music*, III, 213–16, for Mathew Locke's music for an apes' dance.

[1] See Rollins, *Pepysian Garland*, p. 35. Collier, *A Book of Roxburghe Ballads*, p. 207, conjectures that this ballad may have been sung by Turner as a stage jig.

[2] See Murray, *English Dramatic Companies*, I, 209, 211. This company, under the patronage of Prince Henry until his death in 1612, and then under that of the Palsgrave, played at the Fortune, old and new, from almost the beginning of James's reign until a number of years after his death.

sage from Turner seems to refer to that prohibition.[1] It also shows that Shank's reputation as an actor rested largely on his performance of jigs. He may very well have had the leading rôle in "Garlic" and even have been the author. It is fitting that three outstanding clowns should be pictured as attractions of the three houses which seem to have been making a specialty of the jig. Fleay identifies Thomas Greene as the lean fool and William Rowley as the fat fool.[2] Attention has just been called to Greene's connection with the Bull. The Curtain also seems to have been controlled by his company about 1612, but was let to others.[3] Murray thinks that Prince Charles's Men moved into the Curtain late in 1609 or early in 1610.[4] It is then possible that the fat fool was William Rowley, as Fleay assumes, for Rowley, whose name appears in a list of the Prince's players in 1610, was a prominent member of this organization for many years.

The second half of the stanza from Turner, if read out of its connection, would naturally be taken as opposing the romantic comedies of the Bankside houses—like Beaumont and Fletcher's plays or Shakespeare's later comedies—to the chronicle and adventure plays which continued popular at the Red Bull, with such heroes as Guy of Warwick, Tamburlaine, and the Four Sons of Boulogne (Heywood's *Four Prentices*). But when the passage is taken as a whole, it seems at least possible that the author had jigs in mind throughout and was contrasting the lusty farcical pieces at the Bull with a more refined type pre-

---

[1] See Maxwell, *Philological Quarterly*, V, 299–305, for evidence that Shank probably joined the King's Men not long after the final appearance of his name in a list of the Palsgrave's players in 1613. If this is true, the prohibition of jigs may have had something to do with the change. It is perhaps possible, too, that "leaue to sing his rimes" reflects the change from a company that featured him prominently in jigs to one in which the jig was at least relatively neglected.

[2] See *Chronicle History of the London Stage* (1890), p. 375 n.: "The 'lean fool' is Thomas Greene, the Queen Anne's player at the Bull. The 'fat fool' is William Rowley, the player in Prince Henry's company at the Curtain who acted Plum Porridge in the Inner Temple Mask, and in it 'moved like one of the great porridge tubs going to the Counter.' Shank's rhymes were acted as 'Shank's Ordinary' after he moved to the King's Company, c. 1623."

[3] Adams, *Shakespearean Playhouses*, p. 88.

[4] *Eng. Dram. Companies*, I, 230.

vailing on the Bankside.[1] While it is highly improbable that conventions of the jig were entirely distinct in the two classes of public theaters, the Bankside houses apparently escaped the notoriety of the others in connection with the jig. They may have featured less dramatic and less objectionable types. The passage from Turner, at any rate, draws a contrast between the general policies of the two groups of houses.

After 1612 the history of the stage jig is very obscure. Allusions are plentiful, but with the lack of evidence as to the nature of the jigs involved and with the variety of meanings possible to the word, generalizations are hazardous. It is a question how effective the order of 1612 proved. For a time interact performance of jigs may have resulted. "Many gentlemen," says one of the characters in Shirley's *Changes* (IV, ii), produced at Salisbury Court in 1632,

> Are not, as in the days of understanding,
> Now satisfied without a jig, which since
> They cannot, with their honour, call for after
> The play, they look to be serv'd up in the middle.

It is possible that Shirley has in mind not so much the formal farce jig as the simpler types which belonged to the general stream of comic stage song and dance. Indeed, he may mean only that the type of jig which was conventionally "serv'd up in the middle" was recognized as appropriate for the gentlemanly audiences of the private house. On the other hand, he may refer to the prohibition of 1612 and to the kind of jig then performed after plays. But whatever the character of the jigs or their position on the program, the indications are that about the beginning of the reign of Charles I patrons of the better houses were demanding jigs. It is evident from the Dedication of *The Roman Actor* that in 1626 Massinger was feeling the pressure of a public which preferred jigs and ribaldry to such plays as his, and the Prologue of *The Fair Maid of the Inn* seems gratuitous unless the author was trying to turn the flank of an audience actually favorable to jigs.[2]

[1] If "Shankes Ordinary" was a jig, however, its being licensed for the King's Men in 1624 would imply the use of formal jigs at the Globe.

[2] Similar devices were used earlier in the century in inductions and prologues to check the custom of sitting on the stage. See *Modern Philology*, VIII, 581–89.

The jig as afterpiece was in use again by 1632 at least. In *London and the Countrey Carbonadoed* of that year Lupton says that "most commonly when the play is done, you shall haue a Jigge or dance of al trads,"[1] and in the same period the author of *The Careless Shepherdess* satirizes the taste of the citizen who would leave Salisbury Court and go to the Fortune or the Bull in order to see a play and a jig to boot. Allusions to the afterpiece continue until after the closing of the theaters. The issue of *Mercurius Anti-Britannicus* for August 11, 1645, refers to the "Iigge, which shuts up the scene with mirth," and in 1654 Gayton speaks of riotous holiday audiences as going to the Bankside and providing themselves with "the Horse and Jack-an-Apes for a jigge."[2] Both passages imply the ordinary use of jigs after plays. Moreover, the formal farce jig was still current. As we shall see, at least two old farce pieces helped to console audiences at the Bull for the lack of plays during the Commonwealth, and at the end of the period Jordan composed an elaborate specimen for a civic entertainment. In *Glossographia* of 1656 Blount uses the phrase "in the nature of *Farces* or Gigs."[3]

Yet the allusions after the first quarter of the century indicate on the whole a changing convention. The dance of the trades, which Lupton mentions as an alternative to the jig, represents one kind of performance that encroached on the typical farce jig. In 1635 when a country jig is called for in Glapthorne's *Lady Mother*, II, i, apparently a group dance is performed to the accompaniment of instrumental music, and one of the characters remarks in reminiscence, "Oh those playes that I have seene of youre, with their Jiggs ith tayles of them like your French forces!" In the Prologue to Davenant's *Un-*

---

[1] Aungervyle Society, p. 27.

[2] See *Festivous Notes upon Don Quixot* (1654), pp. 271–72. See also p. 108 for a reference to a "jigge of two principall Clownes."

[3] Under "Opera" (commenting on false types). See p. 152 below for a passage from Corey in 1672 in which "Plot of Gigg" occurs. The phrase sounds like a reference to the farce jig except that it is difficult to imagine the newer generation of 1672 as reverting to a form which had its heyday about the beginning of the century. Still the fact that Ravenscroft uses a number of plots of old farce jigs in *London Cuckolds*, his satire on the London populace, suggests to me the probable currency of those jigs among the "citizens" in 1682. See p. 243 n. below.

fortunate Lovers (1638) it is said of the *previous generations* of theatergoers,

> Good easy judging souls, with what delight
> They would expect a jig, or Target fight.

The burlesque play *Canterburie His Change of Diot* of 1641 ends with a brief non-dramatic song in dialogue called a jig, and this, as I have said, may have been in form a characteristic stage jig of its period. Probably typical farce jigs continued to be used as afterpieces to some extent until the closing of the theaters at least, especially in the houses that had featured them. But it is clear both that the word jig was applied to other types oftener than to the farce type and that the development of stage song and dance in the period was leading toward masque and opera.

The history of the jig goes on for a long time, however, outside of its function as formal afterpiece. After 1642, the ban put upon plays naturally heightened the interest of the public in minor dramatic types.[1] In the Preface to the 1673 edition of *The Wits, or, Sport upon Sport*, a collection of skits representative of drama in the Commonwealth period, Francis Kirkman makes the following comment:

then all that we could divert our selves with were these humours and pieces of Plays, which . . . . were only allowed us, and that but by stealth too, and under pretence of Rope-dancing, or the like; and these being all that was permitted us, great was the confluence of the Auditors; and these small things were as profitable, and as great get-pennies to the Actors as any of our late famed Plays. I have seen the Red Bull Play-House, which was a large one, so full, that as many went back for want of room as had entred; and as meanly as you may now think of these Drols, they were then Acted by the best Comedians then and now in being.

The conventional form was the droll, or prose farce, which, as Kirkman implies, was frequently revamped from humorous or

---

[1] I suspect, however, that by the second quarter of the seventeenth century jigs had found a place among the miscellaneous shows like fencing matches or exhibitions of rope dancers and tumblers which frequently made up the program at the regular houses. See Adams, *Dramatic Records of Sir Henry Herbert*, pp. 46–47, 48, 81, 106–7, 123–24, for records of such shows, in some cases even at the Globe and Blackfriars. When the Fortune and the Bull enlarged their quarters about 1625, they were recognized as catering to the "meaner sort of people" with a very popular type of entertainment. See Adams, *Shakespearean Playhouses*, pp. 302–3.

telling scenes of old plays. The farce jig shared to some extent in the vogue however. Kemp's "Singing Simpkin" at least was included in a volume published without date under the title *Actæon and Diana, with a Pastorall Story of the Nymph Oenone; Followed By the several conceited humors of Bumpkin, the Huntsman. Hobbinal, the Shepherd. Singing Simpkin. And John Swabber, the Sea-man Printed at London by T. Newcomb, for the use of the Author Robert Cox.* According to the title-page of the second edition (1656), these pieces had been acted at the Red Bull with great applause. The enlarged edition of *The Wits* which appeared in 1673 contains thirty-seven pieces, including those of Cox's volume. In addition to "Singing Simpkin," Kirkman prints "The Blackman." In his Preface he characterizes Cox as the principal actor and contriver[1] of these pieces and tells of the great enthusiasm of audiences when he appeared in a favorite rôle as bumpkin.[2] Cox's then is the last important name connected with the acting of jigs.

According to Kirkman again, the material of his collection, including its two famous old jigs, had been appropriated as well by the itinerant showmen whose great activity in the seventeenth century is reflected in numbers of records for the towns and villages of England.[3] The title-page of *The Wits* advertises

[1] Kirkman's term "contriver" is a better one than "author," which is found on the title-page of Cox's volume. Unless "Singing Simpkin" has been wrongly identified on the Register, it had been on the boards at least since 1595. In Kirkman's *Wits* "John Swabber," instead of the usual argument, has the statement, "Argument is needless, It being an ancient Farce, and generally known." See Bolte, *Danziger Theater,* pp. 229-30, for the influence of this farce in Holland earlier in the century. In Kirkman's volume both the "Humour of Simpleton" and the "Humour of Bumpkin" are called "thorow" farces and described as "very well known." The actors of the period evidently used a great deal of old farce material.

[2] An account of one performance and of the arrest of Cox in the "Suburbs," possibly at the Red Bull, is given in *Mercurius Democritus* for June 22-29, 1653: "The Rope dancers having impl[o]yed one Mr. *Cox* an *Actor* . . . . to present a modest and ha[r]mless jigge, called *Swobber*, yet two of his own quallity, envying their poor brother should get a little bread for his Children, basely and unworthily betrayed him to the Souldie[r]s," etc. "John Swabber" is, in fact, a prose farce. Rollins, *Pepysian Garland,* p. xix, n. 6, states that the performance was at the Bull, but there is no positive evidence of this.

[3] See Murray, *Eng. Dram. Companies,* II, 251-54, 313, 342, 351, 354, 355, 357, 359, 374, 411, and Adams, *Dram. Records of Sir Henry Herbert,* pp. 47, 125, for the issuing of licenses for performances of tumblers or rope walkers, for exhibitions of rare animals or monstrosities, for "Italian motions," and for dramatic shows. In connection with the

the selections as having been "sundry times Acted In Publique, and Private, In *London* at *Bartholomew* In the Countrey at other Faires. In Halls and Taverns. On several Mountebancks Stages, At *Charing-Cross*, *Lincolns-Inn-Fields*, and other places. By Several Stroleing Players, Fools, and Fidlers, And the Mountebancks Zanies. With loud Laughter, and great Applause."[1] In character sketches written after the Restoration, Butler too says of the mountebank, "He bails the Place with a Jigg, draws the Rabble together, and then throws his Hook among them."[2] Jigs were probably a drawing-card with itinerant players from a much earlier period, however.

It is likely also that the older jigs of the theaters influenced the more formal feasts of citizens. "The Cheaters Cheated" was written about 1660 for a sheriff's dinner. Moxon may allude to this type of farce in his *Mechanick Exercises* of 1683 when he describes the revelry at the annual feast of printers: "This Ceremony being over, such as will go their ways; but others that stay, are Diverted with Musick, Songs, Dancing, Farcing, &c."[3] At the end of the seventeenth century, dramatists in a number of cases wrote into their plays festival entertainments, especially of citizens, with song and dance. The songs belong to a rather dramatic type of dialogue ballad.[4] Several are brawls, and one may be a version of a jig licensed in 1595. The fashion is illustrated in records of ballads performed at civic feasts following the Restoration.[5]

Though I have tried to show that jigs were performed among the people before they were taken up by professionals, and con-

---

fair at Bristol in 1663, instructions were sent from the Office of the Revels to the mayor of the town in regard to "musick, Cockfightings, maskings, prizes, Stage players, tumblers, vaulters, dancers on the ropes, such as act, sett forth, shew or present any play, shew, motion, feats of actiuity, or sights whatsoever" (Adams, *ibid.*, pp. 123–24).

[1] In the Preface, Kirkman commends his work to these various classes in the words: "As for those Players who intend to wander and go a stroleing, this very Book, and a few ordinary properties is enough to set them up, and get money in any Town in England. And Fidlers purchacing of the Book have a sufficient stock for all Feasts and Entertainments. And if the Mountebanck will but carry this Book, and three or four young Fellows to Act what is here set down for them, it will most certainly draw in Auditors enough, who must needs purch[a]ce their Drugs, Potions, and Balsoms."

[2] *Genuine Remains*, II, 306.
[3] See Arber's *Transcript*, III, 25.
[4] See p. 70 above and pp. 173–74, 203, below.
[5] See pp. 177–79 below.

tinued to have an independent hold straight through the stage vogue, it is undoubtedly true that the professional use of the jig stimulated tremendously the popular interest in the form, and from the sixteenth century influenced the non-professional repertory. In 1598 according to Guilpin's *Skialetheia* (Satire V), whores, beadles, bawds, and sergeants were chanting Kemp's jig, and in 1615 the author of *This Worlds Folly* pictures his contemporaries as "squeaking out" on the streets objectionable jigs drawn from the theaters (Sig. B). It is probable but not certain that in a passage already quoted from Wither (p. 115) a Curtain jig is included with a ballad as sung "at doores" by fiddlers and vagabonds. Long after the jig as a professional form was forgot, stage material was kept alive as song drama among the people. What is apparently the final record of the jig in England shows the rural folk late in the eighteenth century still carrying on the traditions of Cox and the strolling players of Kirkman's day.

The account is found in a long note written by Dilke in his *Old English Plays* (VI, 326–31), which was published in 1815. It reads in part:

These *jigs*, it is certain, continued to be represented in the North of England during the Christmas festivals by young men for the amusement of their friends, long after they had ceased to be so on any regular theatre: and I remember in my early youth to have very frequently been entertained with an account of the dramatic exploits of a very respectable old gentleman, who had been a leading personage on these occasions, had enacted Achilles in Heywood's "Iron Age," and figured in several other dramas. He had also been a performer in two or three *jigs*, and occasionally repeated and sung portions of the plays and *jigs* in which he had performed.

Dilke himself could remember the performance of a jig taken from *The Merchant of Venice*, which ended:

> *Bassanio.* Here's a health to thee, Antonio.
> *Antonio.* Thank thee heartily, *Bassanio*.
> *Chorus.* In liquor, love, and unity,
>   We'll spend this evening merrily.

From the old gentleman comes an account of another jig, seemingly derived from Fletcher's *Coxcomb*, and very similar in style to the brawls noted in the sixth chapter. He reports that a tri-fling sum was offered him to make a jig out of scenes from a certain play. It is not clear from the fragments given how dramatic these pieces may have been, but they were probably not merely brief songs. The admission fee for one of them was half as much as for a play performed by the same actors.

Before the jig is considered in relation to the general movements in stage song and dance which developed in the seventeenth century, song drama on the Continent must be taken into account. Early in its history the jig was carried abroad by English troupes. In consequence there is much Continental material which has a close bearing on the English jig in its prime. No effort is made here to follow the history of the form abroad. I wish merely to show the close relationship between the foreign and the English material which is the basis for accepting the singspiele as indicating to a considerable extent the range of conventions and types in the farce jigs so largely lost in English.

A word needs to be said first of the general activities of the traveling troupes[1]—activities that correspond roughly in time to the great vogue of the farce jig at home. "Will the Lord of Leicester's jesting player"—presumably Kemp himself—was in Holland in 1585. In 1586 Kemp, his boy, and five English actors are on record as being at the court of Friedrich II of Denmark for a time. In the fall of that year Kemp's five companions visited Germany at the solicitation of Christian I of Saxony, in whose service they remained for nearly a year; and there is also some reason to believe that they played at Danzig. In 1590 Robert Browne, formerly of Worcester's company, received payment for a performance at Leyden. He soon returned to England, however, and in 1592 was granted a passport to travel abroad with John Bradstreet, Thomas Sackville, and Richard Jones. Cohn and Herz have conjectured that this troupe, which traveled through Germany in 1592 and 1593, came at the invitation of Count Heinrich Julius of Brunswick.

---

[1] The latest general treatment of these companies is Herz's *Englische Schauspieler und englisches Schauspiel zur Zeit Shakespeares in Deutschland*. See also Cohn, *Shakespeare in Germany*; Creizenach, *Schauspiele der englischen Komödianten*; Meissner, *Die englischen Comödianten zur Zeit Shakespeares in Oesterreich*. Chambers, *Elizabethan Stage*, II, 270–92, gives a concise summary with bibliography.

Though the art of the English comedians had gained fame before the appearance of Browne, their complete conquest of Germany was probably due to his activities. For about thirty years Browne crossed to the Continent at intervals with troupes of players. Moreover, the earlier companies that entered the service of German princes or traveled through the country were under the direction of the chief men in Browne's early troupes, various combinations of original members with recruits being traceable. Sackville, for example, who remained in Germany when Browne apparently returned to England after 1593, soon headed a very successful company of his own, and retired early in the seventeenth century as a prosperous citizen of Frankfort. Webster, John Green, Kingman, Machin, Reeve, Blackwood, Thayer, and Reynolds were all at one time or another associated with Browne. But independent troupes visited various parts of the Continent, including Germany, and one of them with John Spencer in command won fame in the Low Countries and Germany from about 1604, when it was playing at Leyden.

The repertory of the English actors had a powerful influence in Germany especially. It included not only tragedies, histories, and romantic comedies, but prose farces, jigs, and special musical, dance, and acrobatic features. Much of their earlier material was translated and extensively imitated. The plays of Count Heinrich Julius published in 1593–94 are said to show clearly the influence of the English comedians.[1] A few years later Jakob Ayrer of Nuremberg imitated very freely the whole range of their art, translating romantic plays, adapting English farces, and writing singspiele in which the art of the jig was adapted to his own stage. There is reason to believe that a considerable number of his comic scenes in singspiele, farces, and plays were derived from English jigs and farces now lost.[2]

The chief comic rôles of the traveling troupes popularized on the German stage the conventional clownish figures of the English stage. It was Sackville who made John Bouset, or Posset, a famous clown, and we hear of other "English Johns" before 1600. The name Stockfish is associated with Spencer. In the late singspiele the stock clown is Pickleherring, introduced

[1] See Herz, pp. 8–10.
[2] See Wodick, *Jakob Ayrers Dramen*, pp. 44 ff.

Creizenach thinks by Reynolds.[1] Pickleherring sometimes appears in pieces not connected with the English comedians, but he seems to belong to them primarily. While in England little can be said of the comic art of the actors who are associated with the jig, except perhaps Tarlton, with the crystallization of the clowns into certain types abroad it is possible to get some conception of the typical clowns of the singspiele from scattered descriptions and also from the treatment of them in the general repertory of the actors. Creizenach has made a study of "Die lustige Person" of the English troupes—names, costumes, traditional jokes, and tricks.[2] Undoubtedly much of his stock in trade was the common property of the clown, but he is constantly reminiscent of Tarlton's art. The "John" of Sackville's troupe, which is presumably the one described by Mangold in his *Markschiffs Nachen* (1597),[3] would be John Bouset, or Posset. Jan is a master at jests and clownish tricks, says Mangold; he can distort his face so that he doesn't look like a man, is in no danger of being pinched by his shoes, has room for one more in his breeches, wears a jacket that would make a clown of him, and withal thinks himself a fine fellow. Creizenach adds other points based on the works of Count Heinrich Julius and of Ayrer, who used the English clowns a number of times, especially John Bouset. John Bouset often carries a pipe and sometimes, like other English clowns, a drum. He raises a laugh by looks and actions without speaking a word. A favorite trick is to stick his head out first, and he is likely to appear laughing or crying, looking stupid, or swaggering. He strokes his beard, slaps his knee, trembles with comic terror. The last recalls Tarlton's making Elizabeth laugh excessively at his fear of her little dog. Like the all-licensed fool from the time of the early moralities, John Bouset takes the audience into his confidence, asking a bystander a question or jesting at a fellow actor. Most of these characteristics appear from time to time in the other Johns. Pickleherring, who figures in several singspiele and is the Simpkin of the German version of "Singing Simpkin," is variously pictured, the flat shoes being the chief feature that persists. He boasts that he can give his face a thousand forms

[1] *Schauspiele*, pp. xciii–xcv.

[2] *Ibid.*, pp. xciii–cviii.   [3] See the extract given by Herz, pp. 34–36.

and never fails to get his laugh from the audience. On the side of farce the immediate and rather complete penetration of the English influence may be due to the fact that these droll figures and their farcical performances have much in common with the characters and tricks of early German jests and farces. But the English influence is direct and unmistakable.

Particularly in the earliest records the English comedians are called simply musicians or dancers or jumpers.[1] Kemp appears in the court records of Denmark as an instrumentalist, and his companions, who included Thomas Pope and George Bryan, afterward of some prominence in the Chamberlain's company, are termed "instrumentister och springere." The Duke of Saxony employed them as fiddlers and instrumentalists whose duty it was to entertain him with their music, their leaping, and other pleasing things. This practice is explained by Cohn as due to the fact that, the professional actor being unknown in Germany, such general terms as player were not current (p. xxvi). But in many later records in which the acting of plays is especially mentioned, or the players are called comedians, stress is laid on other features of their art.[2] Browne's group of 1592 was permitted to travel to show skill in music and "agility" as well as in comedies, tragedies, and histories. As I have said, Mangold presumably has Sackville's troupe in mind when he tells in his *Markschiffs Nachen* of his intention to see the English act. He describes only three performers—the clowns John and Wursthänsel and a dancer—and he adds that it isn't always the play itself which attracts the people but the fool's jokes and the dancer's tight hose. Cohn (pp. cxxxiv–cxxxv) quotes from the Chronicle of Röchell an account of an English troupe at Münster in 1599. Eleven actors performed five comedies in the English tongue on successive days. They had various instruments— lutes, citterns, fiddles, pipes, and the like—and at the beginning and end of their comedies they danced many new and strange dances not current in that land. There was a rogue of a clown who, between acts while the performers were changing their costumes, made the people laugh with his clownage and his

---

[1] See for example Bolte, *Shakespeare Jahrbuch*, XXIII, 99–101.

[2] See for example *Shakespeare Jahrbuch*, XXIII, 103, 104; Cohn, p. xxxi; *Archiv für Litteraturgeschichte*, XIII, 316; Meissner, pp. 41, 84.

quips in German. The activities of an English company playing in Frankfort in 1607 consisted in making music, springing,
dancing, and various other forms of droll amusement.[1] In 1611
Spencer's troupe comprised nineteen actors and sixteen musicians.[2] According to a record of 1612, the repertory of a company visiting Nuremberg included comedies and tragedies, excellent music, and various foreign dances; and in 1613 there were
tragedies and comedies along with "Zierlichen täntzen, lieblicher
musica vnd anderer lustbarkeit."[3] From Amsterdam comes the
following, translated by Cohn (p. xc) from Brederode's *Moortje*,
III, iv (1615):

> Heard you the English and other strangers sing?
> Saw you their jolly dance, their lusty spring?
> How like a top they spin, and twirl and turn?

Handicapped at first by ignorance of the vernacular, the
English actors might be expected to fall back for their best effects on such features as music, dance, acrobatic performances,
and action of a rather broadly farcical sort. But the evidence
for great activity along these lines persists long after they adopted the vernacular. Such phases of their art probably always
played a larger part in their performances abroad than at
home. On the other hand, the practice of the comedians abroad
suggests a much more extensive use of song and dance specialties at home than the extant records indicate.

In the jig the traveling troupes introduced an entirely new
genre, which made a tremendous impression. Doubtless many
of the enthusiastic references to the singing and dancing of the
comedians are chiefly tributes to the jig, but it is even more difficult to separate jig from other song and dance on the Continent than in England since there was no single foreign term
corresponding to jig. The number and distribution of the extant pieces, however, shows the popularity of the singspiele
throughout Germany and the Low Countries and among the
Scandinavian peoples. A great many more English jigs have

---

[1] See Herz, p. 133.

[2] See Cohn, pp. lxxxiv–lxxxv. Fourteen instrumentalists were employed in a Turk-
ish play which they performed.

[3] *Archiv für Litteraturgeschichte*, XIV, 126–28.

survived abroad than in England itself, and the allusions to individual singspiele are much more numerous. The Continental vogue seems to have been even greater in the seventeenth century than in the sixteenth. Certainly in its pure form the farce jig lived longer abroad than at home, and the position of the singspiel was evidently one of comparative dignity on the Continent long after the decline of the jig in England.

The earliest recorded collection containing jigs has apparently been lost—Michael Praetorius' *Musarum Aoniarum tertia Erato. Darinnen 44 ausserlesene teutsche weltliche Lieder begriffen, beneben etlichen Englischen Comedien mit vier Stimmen* (Hamburg, 1611).[1] In 1620 there appeared at Leipzig the still extant *Engelische Comedien vnd Tragedien. Das ist: Sehr Schöne, herrliche vnd ausserlesene, geist- vnd weltliche Comedi vnd Tragedi Spiel*, with five singspiele included. A second edition was published in 1624. *Liebeskampff Oder Ander Theil Der Engelischen Comoedien vnd Tragoedien* came out in 1630 with two singspiele at the end. Other pieces have been preserved in manuscript or in print in various ways. Of the five English farce jigs belonging to the sixteenth or early seventeenth century, there are foreign versions of three. "Rowland," which in spite of its influence has not survived in English, is known in several German forms. "Pückelherings Dill dill dill," representing fairly definitely a lost English jig, is preserved in German, Dutch, and Swedish. Even the singspiele not certainly of English origin may be regarded as modeled more or less closely on the English type, and some pieces that clearly draw on German sources may have been suggested by lost English jigs dealing with similar jests or incidents.

The fullest treatment of the texts of the singspiele is that of Bolte in *Die Singspiele der englischen Komödianten und ihrer Nachfolger in Deutschland, Holland und Skandinavien*.[2] Bolte lists thirty-two pieces as extant (some of them with several variants), giving bibliographical details and information as to subject matter, form, tunes, and so forth, and publishing much of the music used with them. Twelve of the texts, representing

[1] See Bolte, *Singspiele*, p. 5.

[2] See also Herz, *Englische Schauspieler und englisches Schauspiel zur Zeit Shakespeares in Deutschland.*

five different singspiele,[1] he prints in full. For the sake of completeness the thirty-two singspiele are listed below, but in a different order from Bolte's since they are here grouped on the basis of their relation to the English field. The number which Bolte gives a singspiel is indicated in brackets except where the two lists agree. He has supplied titles for most of the singspiele in the first three groups, and with two exceptions his titles are used in this book.

I. Relatively early single singspiele closely connected with the English field:

    1. "Der engelländische Roland"

    2. "Von den Männern," a companion piece to "Rowland," called by Bolte "Jan, der ungetreue Ehemann"

    3 [13]. "Die streitenden Liebhaber"

    4 [21]. "Die tugendhafte Bäurin," a version of "Attowell's Jig"

    5 [25abcd]. "Pückelherings Dill dill dill," called by Bolte "Die Müllerin und ihre drei Liebhaber," with variants

    6 [23b]. B. Fonteyn, "Monsieur Sullemans Soete Vryagi," an expanded Dutch version of "The Blackman" [23a]

II. Singspiele printed in *Engelische Comedien und Tragedien:*

    7 [14bcd]. "Pickelhering in der Kiste," a translation of "Singing Simpkin" [14a], with variants

    8 [15]. "Der Narr als Reitpferd"

    9 [16]. "Der Windelwäscher"

    10 [17]. "Studentenglück"

    11 [18]. "Der Pferdekauf des Edelmannes"

III. Singspiele printed in *Liebeskampff:*

    12 [19]. "Der Mönch im Sacke"

    13 [20]. "Der alte und der junge Freier"

IV. Singspiele of Jakob Ayrer:

    14 [3]. "Von dreyen bösen Weibern, denen weder Gott noch jhre Männer recht können thun"

    15 [4]. "Der verlarft Franciscus mit der venedischen jungen Wittfrauen"

    16 [5]. "Der Münch im Kesskorb"

    17 [6]. "Eulenspiegel mit dem Kauffmann und Pfeiffenmacher"

---

[1] Nos. 5, 6, 7, 24, and 28 in my list which follows.

18 [7]. "Der engelendische Jann Posset, wie er sich in seinen Dinsten verhalten"

19 [8]. "Von etlichen närrischen Reden des Claus Narrn vnd anderer zusammen colligirt"

20 [9]. "Der Wittenbergisch Magister in der Narrenkappen"

21 [10]. "Der Forster im Schmaltzkübel"

22 [11]. "Knörren Cüntzlein"

23 [12]. "Von einem ungerechten Juristen, der ein Münch worden"

V. Singspiele presumably of Dutch composition:
24. J. van Arp, "Droncke Goosen"
25 [22]. J. J. Starter, "Der betrogene Freier"

VI. Late elaborated forms of singspiele (printed in 1673 or later):
26. "Die seltzame Metamorphosis der Sutorischen in eine Magistrale Person"
27. "Der viesierliche Exorcist"
28 [28ab]. "Harlequins Hochzeit," extant in German and Danish
29 [29ab]. a) "Harlequins frühzeitiger und unverhoffter Kindtauffen-Schmaus," a continuation of the preceding; b) a different continuation by Reuter
30. "Lustige Nacht-Comoedia"
31. "Harlequin, Der ungedultig, hernach aber mit Gewalt gedultig gemachte Hahnrey"
32. "Der Offizier im Nonnenkloster"

All the singspiele in the first three groups—but not all the variants—are reprinted in this volume except the foreign forms of "The Blackman" and "Singing Simpkin," all of which Bolte has printed along with their English originals. "Die tugendhafte Bäurin," omitted by Bolte, is included here in connection with its original, "Attowell's Jig," in order to give further evidence of how closely many of the singspiele may represent lost English jigs. The evidence that the singspiele of the first group were translated from or based on English jigs is definite except in the case of "Die streitenden Liebhaber," and there is no reason to doubt the English origin of this simple early piece. In *Engelische Comedien und Tragedien* and *Liebeskampff* we have specimens from the repertory of the English comedians. The English basis of the former is scarcely to be

questioned. While the plays of *Liebeskampff* seem to have been
written under the primary influence of new trends in German
drama, the indications are that the two singspiele in the volume
follow the old traditions of the jig. No source has been discovered for either, but both have material that was conventional in
the popular literature of England. So far as I know, the singspiele of these two volumes have never been reprinted with the
exception of "Pickelhering in der Kiste." It has seemed worth
while to print also the Dutch singspiele of van Arp and Starter,
which make up the fifth group. Both may be ultimately English, just as Fonteyn's "Monsieur Sullemans Soete Vryagi" is
English; and they are of a type not represented among the jigs
or elsewhere among the singspiele. "Der betrogene Freier," besides, is not easily accessible. The remaining pieces—in the
fourth and sixth groups—are merely discussed in chapter ix.
Ayrer's singspiele were written in avowed imitation of the English jig, and on the whole their value for our purpose is considerable, though they probably vary widely as to the extent of
their debt to the English prototype. Except for Ayrer there is
no convincing evidence that Continental dramatists created
original singspiele before the end of the seventeenth century.
Of the late seventeenth century singspiele listed, however, the
first three continue the conventions of the early farce jig in
characters, incidents, and much of their technique, and were
possibly expansions or adaptations of early English song drama.

Indications are that on the Continent jigs were more frequently performed as intermeans than as afterpieces. The Nuremberg playbill which Cohn reproduces at the end of his
Shakespeare in Germany announces that after the comedy "ein
schön Ballet vnd lächerliches Possenspiel" will be presented.
But the group of singspiele in *Engelische Comedien und Tragedi-
en* is introduced with the direction that they may be performed
at will between the comedies. Some version of "Rowland" was
performed after the third act of a play in 1617, and Bolte conjectures that an interact piece of 1618 was "Der Mönch im
Sacke."[1] Hönig attributes this change from English custom
to the influence of Ayrer, whose singspiele, he points out, are
long and fall easily into several parts suited for performance be-

---

[1] See *Singspiele*, pp. 9, 13, for these items.

tween the acts of a play, after the manner of the prose *Pickel-heringspiele*.[1] The use of extraneous farce material as intermeans probably goes back to a general medieval tradition, which is traceable in Great Britain as early as Lyndsay's *Satire of the Three Estates*. Both Ayrer's version of Machin's *Dumb Knight* and an apparently independent Danzig version are accompanied by an entirely separate prose "Zwischenspiel vom wunder-thätigen Stein" divided for interact performance.[2] Evidence as to interact material in England, however, is very inconclusive until after the Restoration.[3]

To the brief survey of the field which has been made, something should perhaps be added in regard to the general art of the farce jig. This is not to ignore the fact that pieces belonging to all the classes to which the term jig was applicable in the period were undoubtedly performed on the stage, or that after-pieces of many kinds were in use. A study of the jig naturally centers, however, in the farce type, which made the stage jig the sensational success that it proved both at home and abroad.

The extant jigs and singspiele show a considerable range in form, in tone, and in theme. "Rowland" and "The Wooing of Nan" have only seventy-two lines, but most of them run to several hundred—"The Cheaters Cheated" to more than five hundred and "Der Mönch im Sacke" to over six hundred. In several cases one scene would suffice for the action, but frequently more are implied or indicated. In the number of characters the pieces vary from three in "Rowland's Godson" to six or seven in "The Wooing of Nan" and even more in some of the late singspiele. One noticeable feature of the technique is the frequent approach to the naturalness of spoken dialogue through the rapid alternation of singers and the irregularity in the length of the "speeches." Occasionally a character will sing only a few words out of a stanza, and not infrequently he takes up his part in the middle of a line. Short speeches, usually of a line, are characteristic in asides and mocking dialogue. The early jigs seem to have been written in the ordinary meters of the narrative ballad, and the majority of the extant pieces, both English

[1] See *Anzeiger für deutsches Altertum*, XXII, 309-10.

[2] Bolte, *Danziger Theater*, pp. 222-25, 268-79.

[3] See pp. 150-51, 154, below.

and Continental, are of this type. Sometimes a single verse form continues throughout, but the use of several meters is more common. In general there seems to have been a tendency toward expansion and toward complexity of form. "Pückel-herings Dill dill dill" and "The Blackman," for example, show an admixture of lyric measures and choral parts with ballad verse. Both contain some prose also, and the former some verse that is spoken instead of being sung. Evidently the ballad farce was modified by the developing influences in stage song and dance—antic and medley dance, country and disards' song, etc. In "Der Exorcist," a redaction of a lost English piece, the numerous songs interspersed in the prose dialogue show the drift of the late singspiele toward comic opera.

In the jigs and singspiele taken as a whole, intrigue is the chief theme, coarseness and mockery the dominant elements. Shrewish and sensual women, duped husbands, swaggering gallants, intriguing monks, mocking clowns, furnish the farcical humor. In the English pieces taken alone, however, neither bawdry nor clownage plays the part that one might expect from the attacks on the jig. "The Wooing of Nan," which presents a country festival with a dance contest, opens with the suggestion of a country idyl, though it closes with the usual coarseness of farce. "Attowell's Jig" deals with a common intrigue motive, but it depicts a faithful wife and has at times the poetic note of a humble muse. Even of "Rowland's Godson" it has justly been said, "Granted the situation, the ballad steers clear of further offence."[1] Presumably the type of jig that called forth such indignant protest from the better element has not managed to survive in English. "Rowland," too, and its companion piece are entirely inoffensive, as well as a few other foreign pieces known to be English in origin. The element of bawdry and vulgarity is better represented in the singspiele, "Der Pferdekauf des Edelmannes" and "Der betrogene Freier" being two good examples. As for clownage, the country clown, for whom Lane pictures every ballad maker as writing jigs in 1600,[2] appears in triumph at the end of "The Wooing of Nan," written probably in the last decade of the sixteenth century. He is a

[1] See *Shirburn Ballads*, ed. Clark, p. 354.
[2] See *Tom Tel-Troths Message*, ll. 215–16.

prominent figure in "The Blackman" and the hero of the rather elaborate plot in "Cheaters Cheated" written about 1660. But the distinctly droll clown with a mixture of knavery and naïveté or of stupidity and blundering uncouthness is not fully developed in these examples from the English jigs, though he is exploited in a number of English plays at the close of the sixteenth century—in Derick of *The Famous Victories*, in Adam of *A Looking Glass for London and England*, in Strumbo of *Locrine*, in Mouse of *Mucedorus*, and in Shakespeare's Launce and Launcelot, for instance. The type is fairly well represented, however, in the clowns of some Continental jigs, notably in Jan of Ayrer's "Von dem engelendischen Jann Posset" and in Jan Pint of "Die Metamorphosis." Both of these "Johns" show some of the traits that gave Tarlton his fame as a clown. Properly speaking, there is no clown in "Rowland's Godson," "Von den Männern," and several other pieces that are clearly English in origin, and "Attowell's Jig" lacks even a comic character. Usually, however, some comic figure has the function of making mocking comment on characters and action, chiefly in brief asides.

From first to last, the number of individual jigs produced must have been very large, even with due allowance for repeated performances of favorite pieces. In fact, the few remaining specimens can hardly be regarded as representative in view of the allusions to whole classes of jigs that have disappeared. The lost jigs used by the Queen's Men in the Marprelate controversy form a distinct group that could have had only a brief vogue. But the author of *The Passionate Morrice* in 1593 and Taylor in *Superbiae Flagellum* much later both speak of roistering women as the subject of jigs.[1] According to Taylor, they had been comically staged, jigged, and belabored by balladmongers so much that they were hardly worth a satirist's shafts. The cosenage and intrigue of the London underworld was commonly featured in jigs at a period shortly after Tarlton's death, for in Chettle's *Kindheart's Dream* (1592) the bawd is represented as complaining to Tarlton—who symbolizes the drama in the tract —that players "open our crosse-biting, our conny-catching, our traines, our traps, our gins, our snares, our subtilties: for no

[1] See p. 74 above.

sooner haue we a tricke of deceipt, but they make it common, singing jigs and making iests of vs, that euerie boy can point out our houses as they passe by."[1] In "Droncke Goosen," the tavern keeper and his wife rob the drunken clown. But "The Cheaters Cheated," written considerably more than half a century after the era of Chettle's allusion, is the only extant jig to illustrate the art of coney-catching in London. There is evidence enough, however, for the popularity of robbery as a motive in connection with antic or mimetic dance.[2] Later (p. 203) the conjecture is made that the lost jig of "Cutting George and his Hostess," entered in 1595, was a simple dialogue of two singers, but it might easily have been a farce jig dealing with some escapade of the cutter, or swaggerer. Chettle's allusion to jigs as laying bare the sharp practices of rogues so that every boy could point out their houses opens up all the possibilities of jigs on individuals of the class. There was a strong tendency to exploit in drama and ballad such of these figures as captured the popular imagination.[3] Again, when Randolph expresses his

---

[1] Ed. Rimbault, pp. 37–38.

[2] See *Cal. of State Papers, Venetian,* 1558–80, p. 27, for "a double mummery" at court in which "one set of mummers rifled the Queen's ladies, and the other set, with wooden swords and bucklers, recovered the spoil"; *James IV,* IV, iii, for the dance of antics around the clown Slipper while the rogue Andrew robs him of his purse; *Honest Lawyer,* G 2–3, for a trio who, entering like "Fairies, dancing antickes," bind and rob Gripe; Jonson's *Metamorphosed Gipsies,* in which the group of gipsies pick the pockets of a group of country youths and maids during country dances; Shirley's *Triumph of Peace* for directions for two dances—"The Maquerelle, Wenches, Gentlemen . . . . dance together; the Gallants are cheated; and left to dance in, with a drunken repentance" and "enter a Merchant, a' Horseback with his portmanteau; two Thieves set upon him and rob him: these by a Constable and Officers are apprehended and carried off." In 1699 Ward saw at Bartholomew Fair "a Dance in imitation of a *Foot-Pad's Robbery;* and he that acted the Thief, I protest, did it so much like a Rogue, that had he not often committed the same thing in Earnest, I am very apt to believe he could never have made such a Jest on't; Firing the Pistol, Stripping his Victim, and Searching his Pockets, with so much Natural Humour, seeming Satisfaction and Dexterity, that he shew'd himself an absolute Master of what he pretended to" (Morley, *Memoirs of Bartholomew Fair* [1859], p. 348, quoted from *The London Spy*).

[3] Among the actual cutters of the sixteenth century the most famous apparently was Cutting Dick (Heywood, *Wise Woman of Hogsden,* II, i; Kemp, *Nine Days' Wonder,* in *Social England Illustrated,* ed. Lang, p. 153; Wither, *Abuses Stript and Whipt,* Book II, Satire 2; *Cal. of State Papers, Dom.,* 1601–3, p. 136). See *Henslowe's Diary,* ed. Greg, II, 231, for payment for additions made to *Cutting Dick,* an old play of Worcester's Men, in 1602. Desperate Dick, who is the subject of a ballad entered in 1568–9 (*Transcript,* I, 387) and whose name is mentioned by Nashe (*Works,* ed. McKerrow, III, 5;

contempt for those who study the base in order to write, learning

> the nonsense of the constables.
> Such jig-like flim-flams being got to make
> The rabble laugh, and nut-cracking forsake,[1]

he may have in mind a popular type of actual jig in which constables furnished the humor as they do in several plays. In fact,
I think that the large number of passages in which "jig" seems
to mean merely humorous incident, trick, affair, may reflect the
variety of farcical motives typical in the stage jigs.[2]

In regard to music, tunes are specified only for "Rowland's
Godson" and "Attowell's Jig" among the English farce pieces.
It is in keeping with the popular nature of the jig that "Loth to
depart," to which "Rowland's Godson" is sung, and "Walsingham" and "Go from my window"—two of the tunes used in

---

IV, 303), was likely a different person. Nashe also mentions ballads on the death of
Cutting Ball (*ibid.*, III, 55). See *Fair Maid of the West*, Part I, III, i, for an allusion to
roisterers in which Little Davy is joined with Cutting Dick. In the Induction of
Bartholomew Fair the Stagekeeper comments on Jonson's failure to give his public such
features as "a little *Dauy*, to take toll o'the Bawds" and "a *Kind-heart*, if any bodies
teeth should chance to ake," the tooth-drawer also being apparently an actual person
(Chettle, *Kindheart's Dream*, ed. Rimbault, pp. xv–xvi). Of the roistering females, Meg
of Westminster was the subject of ballads entered August 27, 1590, and March 14, 1595,
and of a play for which performances are recorded from 1595 until 1597 (*Henslowe's
Diary*, ed. Greg, II, 174)—all during the first great vogue of the jig. See also Field,
Amends for Ladies (1611), II, i, for reference to this play or to some other dramatic
piece celebrating her deeds. Haddit, near the beginning of Tailor's *Hog hath Lost his
Pearl*, declares of his jig which was to rival "Garlic" that it is worth Meg of Westminster. Middleton and Dekker drew an idealized picture of Roaring Moll in *The
Roaring Girl*, and the lost ballads and plays on these characters may often have been
in the same spirit. In the Epilogue of 1611, however, the authors complain of a book—
possibly Day's lost work on Moll entered August 7, 1610—setting forth "base tricks,"

> "Foul as his brains they flowed from, of cutpurses,
> Of nips and foists, nasty, obscene discourses,"

a passage which is more in keeping with the spirit of the passage from Chettle. According to her own statement in 1605, Moll was present at a play at the Fortune when she
sat on the stage "in mans apparel and played upon her lute and sange a song"
(*Review of English Studies*, I, 78).

[1] *Works*, ed. Hazlitt, II, 514.

[2] See *NED* under "jig"[5]; Heywood, *Edward IV*, Part I, Sig. F; *Greene's Tu Quoque*,
Sig. K; Fletcher, *Humourous Lieutenant*, IV, iv, near end; Shirley, *Bird in a Cage*, V,
i, and *Coronation*, V, i; Sylvester, *Du Bartas* (1621), p. 1196; Nichols, *Progresses of
James I*, I, 263 n. 3; Birch, *Court and Times of James I*, II, 167.

"Attowell's Jig"—are among the oldest of the ballad airs. The Dutch version of "The Blackman" calls also for "Fortune my foe" and, at two different points, for "Sir Edward Nowell's delight." There was an evident tendency to repeat tunes that proved effective. In "The Blackman" the lines which parody "Walsingham" must have been sung to the tune of that ballad. The air most widely used in jigs was that of "Rowland," which was taken over for "Die streitenden Liebhaber" as well as for five of Ayrer's pieces. The tune for the early part of "Singing Simpkin" accompanies also a part of "Der betrogene Freier" and "Droncke Goosen." It is a question whether this "Engelsche Fa la la" and the tune "Rowland" were written for the jigs or were already familiar.[1] "Rowland" is found in England and on the Continent under various names. In the singspiele the tunes are usually specified. In *Engelische Comedien und Tragedien* and *Liebeskampff* most of them are printed along with the text. Though the influence of English music is of course considerable in the singspiele, a great deal of Continental music came to be used also, as Bolte's summaries of the tunes show.

A frequent change of meter involving a change of tune has already been mentioned as one phase of the effort to give variety to the farce jig. Among the English pieces "Rowland's Godson" alone requires but one tune; "Attowell's Jig" designates four tunes for its four brief scenes; and in "The Cheaters Cheated" there are directions for nine changes of tune, so that this jig with the Song on the Companies at the end would call for eleven tunes. A number of early singspiele—"Rowland," "Von den Männern," "Die streitenden Liebhaber," and Ayrer's pieces —are sung to one tune. Except for an inserted song which is indicated but not given, the long "Mönch im Sacke" also requires but one tune. On the other hand, "Droncke Goosen" of only a hundred and fifty lines has three tunes, and "Der betrogene Freier" with about three hundred lines has nine. Five are printed for "Der alte und der junge Freier," and eight for the second edition of the Dutch "Blackman." The principle seems to be stated by Moth in *Love's Labour's Lost* (III, i) when he says in describing the French brawl, "keep not too long in

[1] See pp. 236–37, 313, and 224, 227–28, 230–31, below.

one tune, but a snip and away." The result was sometimes a fairly elaborate type of ballad operetta.

Only one record as to the instrumental music used with the farce jigs is known to me. The title of the edition of "Rowland" printed in 1599 calls for "allerley Instrumenten." This fits in with the evidence already cited in regard to the large number of musicians attached to the English troupes abroad and the many instruments used. At home the jig was doubtless accompanied by playhouse musicians, who were needed for songs, "strains" of music, processions, and so forth in plays, even when interact music was not furnished. Tarlton mentions the pipe and tabor in the account given at the end of the *Newes* of how he diverted the inhabitants of purgatory with jigs, but he could not have piped and sung at the same time. At any rate, the music accompanying the jig probably passed as far beyond the pipe and tabor as the professional jig did beyond the country jig.

The most difficult phase of the jig is dance. Even as a professional form the jig belonged to the popular field, so that detailed descriptions of the method of performance are not given as in the case of some of the masques in which literary men and masters of the dance collaborated. In both the jigs and the singspiele, indications as to dance are few and seldom or never definite. It is natural to suppose that each actor danced as he sang his part. This was almost certainly the method in the brief jigs of the people, and it is perhaps implied in some references to the stage jig. Of two satirical allusions to Kemp, one is to the dancing and the other to the chanting of his jig.[1] "Rowland" is described in the title as "Gar kurtzweilig zusingen vnd zu Dantzen." In 1632, according to Lupton, "most commonly when the play is done, you shal haue a Jigge or dance of al trads, they [the players] meane to put their legs to it as well as their tongs."[2] But as the jigs expanded into song dramas of several hundred lines, the dancing was scarcely kept up during the singing of the entire dialogue. "The Cheaters Cheated" probably indicates the direction of the development. At stanza 24, after Moll has

---

[1] See Marston, *Scourge of Villanie*, Satire XI; Guilpin, *Skialetheia*, Satire V.

[2] *London and the Countrey Carbonadoed*, Aungervyle Society, p. 27.

sung several stanzas, a stage direction reads, "Tune changeth, she singeth and danceth," and at stanza 35 there is another in regard to Moll and Wat, "Both dance to their own singing." Music is given for a special duet of the lovers in "Der alte und der junge Freier" with the word "Tantz" at two different points in the staff, showing that dance did not accompany the whole song. Occasionally a bit of song descriptive of vigorous action seems to be inserted for the sake of introducing a dance.[1] Not only do spoken parts intervene in some cases, but the action called for often makes dancing impossible. In part of "Singing Simpkin," for example, the clown sings from a chest. There are also traces of a system of pauses for dance such as we find in the mummers' plays. In "The Wooing of Nan" the word "daunsing" is inserted between the fourth and fifth stanzas; and later, after the dialogue has prepared for the contest of two village youths, there is a direction, "They daunce." When the turn of the gallant comes, he asks Nan to dance with him, and "daunce againe" is written after the stanza. Terminal dance also would be a particularly effective feature for the whole group of dancers here and in other pieces. The courant printed on a separate page at the end of "Der Pferdekauf des Edelmannes," which is given in addition to the tunes used for the dialogue, suggests terminal dance.

Hentzner testifies to the variety of dances with which plays were concluded in England at the end of the sixteenth century; and according to several of the German records quoted, the dances of the comedians on the Continent were many. The ballad and dance airs used for the English jigs and the music that Bolte prints at the end of his *Singspiele* as connected with the jig abroad will illustrate the variety of types. In the individual pieces, so far as the dialogue was accompanied by dance, changes of tune and of meter and stanzaic form may be taken as standing for changes in dance also. Certainly in the jigs where dances were introduced incidentally, variety would be the rule. In "The Wooing of Nan," for example, the two village youths dancing in competition on the green would naturally perform a folk dance, not unlikely a morris jig. The Gentleman would be distinguished from them by his courtly dancing as well

[1] See pp. 479–81, 505–6, below. See also p. 84 above.

as by his dress and manner, for the difference in "estate" now becomes the point of the rivalry.

Probably the folk origin of the stage jig influenced its dances strongly in the beginning. It may have been usual in the early simple forms for the actors to dance the ordinary folk jig as they sang their parts in turn. I have already suggested, however, that among the people the word jig had early come to be used generically for song-and-dance, even when the dance was not actually a jig. At the end of the *Newes*, Tarlton declares that he has played jigs for the ghosts until his technique is now better than when he was alive. For proof, he adds, "thou shalt hear a hornpipe." This may refer to music for an actual jig dance, but it may also refer to music for a hornpipe to be danced in a jig. The picture here and the allusion to Tarlton's love of the May pole associate him strongly with folk dance in general. Kemp, too, was a famous morris dancer. If the country clown was as conventionally the jig hero as Lane implies, folk dance must at least have held its own through the height of the stage vogue. Even the figure dances of the folk become of conceivable interest for the farce jig when we take into consideration the pieces with incidental or terminal dance in which the whole group might join. In a number of the jigs and singspiele the group is large enough for such dances, and country dance, morris, and sword dance were popular in masques[1] as well as in plays.

But other types of dances, including the courtly dances in favor, were also used by the comedians.[2] In *Old Meg of Herefordshire* (1609) there is an allusion to "a Galliard on a common stage, at the end of an old dead Comedie,"[3] as if the word galliard too had acquired the special meaning which "jig" developed earlier. When Guilpin, in the Satyre Preludium of *Skialetheia*, speaks of "many a salt *La volto* iest" by which the old

[1] See p. 79 above.

[2] The dances in the song-and-dance acts called *bayles* in Spain, which have already been compared with the stage jig, were, on the evidence of the titles, often the ordinary social dances—the galliard, pavan, tordion, almain, canaries, and so on (Rennert, *Spanish Stage in the Time of Lope de Vega*, p. 74). According to Morley, the Italians framed ditties to their galliards, which they sang and danced in their *mascaradoes* (*Plaine and Easie Introduction*, p. 181).

[3] *Miscellanea Antiqua Anglicana*, p. 10.

citizen is so fired that, leaving the Curtain, he seeks the stews, the reference is possibly to jigs featuring the dance called the volte, since the author is dealing with the comic phases of lascivious balladry. One of the tunes in "Der betrogene Freier" is entitled simply "Courante Serbande"; and the courant at the end of "Der Pferdekauf des Edelmannes" is almost certainly for dance. But in addition to the current dances, either of the folk or of the courtly, the comedians must have developed many interesting and effective dances for particular rôles—like that of the drunken clown in "Droncke Goosen"—following the tradition of comic, droll, and antic dance for fool, vice, and clown. Indeed, the attention paid to antic dancing in the seventeenth century probably contributed to the waning of interest in the dialogue jig among professionals.

In general character, stage dancing must have catered to the contemporary craze for spectacular dance. Marston in *The Scourge of Villanie*, Satire XI, expresses the fear that the orbs celestial will undertake to dance Kemp's jig, reveling "with neate jumps," and he begs them not to fall to capering. The vigor of the comedians' dancing evidently produced a sensation abroad. Mangold dwells on the leapings of the dancer. The account of the English actors in Nuremberg in 1612 already cited goes into detail in regard to the dancing only. There were various foreign dances with wonderful turns, hops, leaps backward and forward, "vberworffen," and other odd movements droll to see. Brederode mentions the lusty spring, the spinning, twirling, and turning of the English. In the Renaissance, vigorous dancing was considered appropriate to the wooing,[1] and it would seem still more suitable to the drollery and mockery of the satiric jig or the lively and comic action of the farce jig. The dancing of clever professionals in comic rôles would easily be subject to exaggeration, and it was probably influenced by the

---

[1] An early example is from Barclay's *Mirrour of Good Maners*, Spenser Society, p. 4:
"Not well presentith he [an old man] the wower in a daunce,
   But very ill he playeth the volage amorous,
   which fetered in a gine woulde gambalde leape & praunce,
   Attached to a chayne of linkes ponderous."
Since Barclay adds all the details to the Latin "non benè saltantis personam sustiner ille," the passage must be based on English practice.

"feats of agility" which were exhibited by the tumblers and acrobatic performers of the day.[1]

[1] For an account of an Italian tumbler who performed before Elizabeth at Kenilworth, see *Laneham's Letter*, ed. Furnivall, pp. 18–19. Laneham is moved to wonder whether the Italian is man or spirit: "such feats of agilitiee, in goinges, turninges, tumblinges, castinges, hops, iumps, leaps, skips, springs, gambaud, soomersauts, caprettiez and flights: forward, backward, syde wize, a doownward, vpward, and with sundry windings, gyrings, and circumflexions: allso lightly, and with such easines, az by mee in feaw words it iz not expressibl by pen or speech, I tell yoo plain." Tumbling is demanded by the Citizen's Wife in connection with the jig "Fa-ding" in *The Knight of the Burning Pestle*, III, v. See also p. 95 above and p. 368 below.

CHAPTER V

THE AFTERMATH OF THE JIG

APPARENTLY the distinctly dramatic jig which had arisen at the end of the sixteenth century out of the mass of song and dance entertainments in pastimes, feasts, and stage acts, began in the early part of the seventeenth century to sink into a subordinate place in the body of song and dance material on the better London stages. The continued popularity of stage song and dance is expressed in the romantic masque, the antic masque and dance, country dance and song, and the dance and song of droll characters and conventional disard types. Most of these elements had in the first place contributed to the dramatic jig, which they now reabsorbed in their larger confines. The farce jig, however, probably gave to the song and dance of the stage generally a more decided bent toward the use of farce motives and droll or comic characters with appropriate mimetic action. Indeed, in comic types and seemingly in comic dance action a large body of the miscellaneous operatic material on the stage is allied with the conventions of the farce jig. But a shift in taste fairly early in the century is unmistakable. Feltham may have had it in mind when he claimed in *Jonsonus Virbius* that Jonson—who himself used much popular and jig-like material—had reformed the stage, presenting

> Thalia that had skipt
> Before, but like a maygame girl, now stript
> Of all her mimic jigs.

The interest in plot and dialogue singing characteristic of the farce jig becomes subordinate to the interest in drollery and variety of action, and in picturesqueness of characters, costuming, and scenery for stage song and dance.

Though the farce form probably determined the most typical meaning of the word jig for a few decades, in the seventeenth century "jig" meant all that it had meant earlier, and more.[1] Folk dancing became the passion of the courtly,[2] and the jig had its full share in the fad, so that perhaps the majority of the references to jig in the seventeenth century are to dance alone. On the stage the jig was sometimes merely dance, as in the case of "Fa-ding" in *The Knight of the Burning Pestle* (III, v) or the country jig in *The Lady Mother* (II, i). Indeed, after the Restoration an outstanding form of stage dance seems to have been the jig.[3] Again, simple brief songs were sung on the stage under the name jig. Some of them may represent satire on the type, but they testify to its existence. In *The Staple of News* (IV, ii) Jonson applies the terms madrigal, saraband, and jig to two amorous lyrics which inspire a reveling group with the spirit of dance. A love song in Hemings's *Fatal Contract* (IV, iii) is called both a jig and a ballad. After a brief song in *The Sun's Darling* (III, i) Raybright protests against having his ears poisoned with "nasty jigs." When Daborne refers in *A Christian turn'd Turke* (ll. 836–37) to digesting a tragedy with "a gig, a catch," he probably has in mind catch-like songs used as afterpieces around 1610. All but two of the simple ballads identified as jigs were printed in the seventeenth century, some of them late. They vary in type and keep pace with the changing styles in balladry. But in addition to these earlier meanings

[1] In fact, it seems to have been extended to any popular type of composition. See Address "To the Gentlemen Readers" prefacing *The Life of Long Meg of Westminster* (1635) for the statement, "many men haue made many pleasant jigges, as the Iests of Robin-hood, and Beuis of South-hampton, and such others, as serue to procure mirth, and driue away melancholy"; p. 123 n. 2 above for reference to the prose farce "John Swabber" as a jig; and p. 319 below for two of Brome's plays as jigs in the mind of the country gentleman. The use of the word for odd or comic incident has already been noticed.

[2] See pp. 365–66 below.

[3] See Davenant, *Playhouse to be Let*, Act II (by a buffoon) and Act III (by four men); Howard, *Committee*, IV, i (an Irish jig by two dancers); Dryden, *Secret Love, or The Maiden Queen*, V, i (by Nell Gwynn as Florimel), and *Sir Martin Mar-all*, V, iii (by Tony); Lacy, *Old Troop*, at end; Shadwell, *Humorists*, Act IV; Mrs. Pix, *Spanish Wives*, II, iii (followed by a dialogue song). Pepys saw Mary Davis dance a jig "after the end" of *The English Princess* on March 7, 1667, and another on May 31, 1668. In *The Coronation of Queen Elizabeth* (1680), besides an "Antick Jigg" of the Cook (III, ii), a woman danced a jig at the end (Morley, *Bartholomew Fair*, pp. 275, 279). At the end of Shadwell's *Sullen Lovers* a boy sits down and then dances a jig. "A Jig called Macbeth" is printed in *Musick's Delight*, No. 65, and the same tune as the "Dance in the Play of Macbeth" in *Apollo's Banquet* (1690), Part I, No. 11. A few jigs bear the names of great actors, as "Tom Nokes' Jigg" (Chappell, *Popular Music*, II, 505).

"jig" was evidently used for such features as dance entertainments of an antic and farcical nature or scenes of drollery and farce in plays, especially plays in which comic figures of the sort found in the older jigs were presented with song and dance. This development connects the jig with the newer fashions in seventeenth century song and dance, and it may be the change which justified the gallants of Shirley's day in their insistence on jigs.

In the first half of the century "jig" is a number of times associated with "antic." Apparently even Shakespeare's antic material presenting chiefly daemonic figures is classed with jigs in the Induction of *Bartholomew Fair*. The Scrivener reports Jonson's attitude:

If there bee neuer a *Seruant-monster* i'the *Fayre;* who can helpe it? he sayes; nor a nest of *Antiques?* Hee is loth to make Nature afraid in his Playes, like those that beget *Tales, Tempests,* and such like *Drolleries,* to mix his head with other mens heeles; let the concupisence of *Iigges* and *Dances,* raigne as strong as it will amongst you. . . . .[1]

In some verses which William Browne prefixed to Massinger's *Bondman* of 1624, the claim is made:

> Here are no gipsy jigs, no drumming stuff,
> Dances, or other trumpery to delight,
> Or take, by common way, the common sight.

Whatever "jig" taken alone may mean here, these lines evidently refer to gipsy material in some other play. Most likely the play was Middleton's *Spanish Gipsy,*[2] produced the preceding

---

[1] See also p. 111 above for the alternation of "antic" and "jig" in the Epistle prefixed to the *Alchemist*.

[2] See III, i, for a lively song of one gipsy, apparently for a group dance; III, ii, for a marching song of the group with chorus, and a catch-like song with chorus followed by a dance; IV, i, for a song with dialogue effect and choral passages accompanied by dance, in which a recruit is initiated, and a spirited solo song of the gipsy's life. Actual dances of Spanish gipsies may have influenced these dances. See *Harleian Miscellany,* II (1809), 548–49, 556, for Treswell's account in 1605 of the Earl of Nottingham's embassy to Spain, with the description of a group of "gypsies (as they termed them) men and women dancing and tumbling, much after the Morisco fashion"; a "company of gypsies likewise, singing and dancing, playing, and shewing divers feats of activity" by the way; and "morrice-dancers, in manner of gypsies" in Madrid. The gipsies in *Metamorphosed Gipsies* "should be Morris-dancers by their gingle" but the napkins and the supernumeraries are lacking.

year, though Browne may also have had in mind the same dramatist's *More Dissemblers besides Women* (IV, i) of 1623 and
Jonson's *Metamorphosed Gipsies* of 1621.[1] In a passage found in
the manuscript of Day's *Parliament of Bees* a servant declares,
playing upon the term jig, that the poet shall be received

> with Jack droms Intertaiment, he shall dance
> the Jigg calld beggers bushe.[2]

While the first phrase gives the second an obvious meaning, the
term jig was probably suggested by the vogue of beggar song
and dance in the period. This vogue is seen to best advantage
in Brome's *Jovial Crew: or, The Merry Beggars;*[3] but there are
also a large number of beggar ballads,[4] many of which may have
been accompanied by dance, and *The Dancing Master* contains
a dance tune called "The Begger Boy." Again, Ford in *Perkin
Warbeck* (III, ii) apparently speaks of songs for antic dance as

---

[1] The gipsy was a popular figure in song and dance, however. For Egyptians in
masques of the mid-sixteenth century, see Feuillerat, *Revels of Edward and Mary*, pp.
16, 19, 190–92. For other instances in seventeenth century drama, see Carew, *Coelum
Britannicum*, fifth antimasque; Davenant, *Playhouse to be Let*, Act V; Newcastle,
Triumphant Widow, Act II; Crowne, *Calisto*, end of Act III; etc. Byrd composed a
"Gipseis Round" (*Fitzwilliam Virginal Book*, No. CCXVI), and the ballad "The
brave English Jipsie" (*Roxburghe Ballads*, III, 328–33), printed by Trundle before 1626,
was sung to the tune of "The Spanish Jipsie," the name of a country dance tune in
The Dancing Master.

[2] Ed. Bullen, p. 33.

[3] See Act I, for a beggars' song of the joy of their life, with a dance following, and a
wandering song of the group; Act II, for a canting festival song of the group, the Mort's
song, and a dance of the group; IV, ii, for the droll epithalamium of an ancient couple,
followed by a group dance with the old couple hobbling in the midst. See *Bagford
Ballads*, I, 216–18, for a ballad called "The Beggars Chorus In the Jovial Crew," which
is not found in the 1652 edition of Brome's play. Cartwright's *Royal Slave* (IV, iii),
Shirley's *Triumph of Peace*, and Nabbes' *Spring's Glory* call for beggars' dance. See
Fletcher's *Beggar's Bush*, II, i, and III, i, for a number of songs by the beggars, though
most of them are not typical of the life.

[4] See *Bagford Ballads*, I, 195–99 ("The Jovial Crew; Or, Beggars-Bush," beginning
"A Beggar, a Beggar,/A Beggar I'le bee"); II, 872–77 ("The Beggars' Wedding, or
The Jovial Crew"); II, 877–79 ("The Jovial Beggars Merry Crew"); II, 877 (reference
to "The Jovial Crew," beginning "Come, let's to the Tavern"); *Roxburghe Ballads*, I,
136–41 ("The cunning Northerne Begger"); III, 322–28 ("The Begger-boy of the
North"); *Wit and Drollery* (1682), pp. 71–74 ("The Jovial Crew," beginning "Good
People give ear"), pp. 74–79 ("The Blind Beggar"), and pp. 252–54 ("A Beggar");
Pills to Purge Melancholy, IV, 142–44 ("The Beggar's Delight"); Douce Collection, I,
96a ("Hey for our Town. But a Fig for Zommersetshire. Or, The Beggars delight, and
Hey for the Boozing Ken"); etc.

jigs. In connection with the preparation for a dance of "Four Scotch Antics" and "Four Wild Irish" in the masque, Huntley asks,

> Is not this fine, I trow, to see the gambols,
> To hear the jigs, observe the frisks, be enchanted
> With the rare discord of bells, pipes, and tabors,
> Hotch-potch of Scotch and Irish twingle-twangles,
> Like to so many quiristers of Bedlam
> Trolling a catch!

In Randolph's *Amyntas* (I, iii) Jocastus, who is slightly later hailed as "president of the jigs," plans to entertain the fairy court with an "anti-masque of fleas" dancing corantoes, and "a jig of pismires."[1]

"Jig" and "antic" are joined also in a satiric pamphlet of the year 1651, cast in burlesque dramatic form with the title *The Joviall Crew, or The Devill turn'd Ranter . . . . A Comedie Containing A true Discovery of the Cursed Conversations, prodigious Pranks . . . . of a Sect . . . . called Ranters*. The Devil calls for a merry jig, and eleven characters enter "singing in *Chorus* & dancing." Two-line parts are sung by different characters, one being,

> About, about, ye Joviall rout,
> Dance antick like Hob-gobblins.

In Cleveland's "Mixed Assembly" the burlesque account of a jig danced by a group of Puritans opens with the line, "A Jigg, a Jig, and in this antick dance." It is evident that in spite of changing modes "jig" remained an accepted general term for dance song.

The system of intermeans and of interspersed song and dance to which Shirley seems to refer grew in importance from the sixteenth century.[2] In 1617, the Italian Busino wrote an

---

[1] The foolish Mopsus suggests also a masque of birds who are to dance a morris in the air. The figures are on a scale suited to the fairy world, but I suspect that Randolph was satirizing the vogue of animal antics. See pp. 54–55, 117, above for baboon or ape dances. A bear dance occurs in Jonson's *Masque of Augurs*, and the ballad used with it was in part taken over in *The Drinking Academy* (III, ii), which is reprinted by Rollins in *PMLA*, XXXIX, 837–71.

[2] See pp. 77–86 above for a discussion of song and dance in sixteenth century plays. Interact material has been studied by Graves in *Studies in Philology*, XII (1915), 110–24, and by Lawrence in his *Elizabethan Playhouse and Other Studies*, Ser. I, pp. 81–83. See also Wright, "Extraneous Song in Elizabethan Drama" in *Studies in Philology*, XXIV, 261–74.

account of visiting a London theater, where he failed to understand the play but was diverted by "the various interludes of
instrumental music and dancing and singing."[1] The system did
not reach full development, however, until the reign of Charles
I at least. Prynne in his *Histrio-Mastix* of 1633 bases three
formal sections of the argument against the stage (pp. 220–90)
on the fact that dances, songs, and music are "concomitants or
circumstances of Stage-playes." He declares that plays are
regularly attended with dancing (p. 221) and accompanied by
"Pastorals, Songs and Poems" (p. 273). Apparently interact
performances are meant chiefly, for he says that there is "nothing more frequent, in all our Stage-playes . . . . then amorous
Pastorals, or obscene lascivious Love-songs, most melodiously
chanted out upon the Stage betweene each seuerall Action,"
both to fill in the interim and to give the hearers pleasure
(p. 262). Beyond Prynne's insistence on pastoral stuff, it is difficult to determine the nature of this interact material. Carew's
"Four Songs, By Way of Chorus to a Play"[2] is probably an
example of the "Love-songs" to which Prynne refers. To some
extent ballads were being introduced into plays and masques,[3]
and they would lend themselves much more readily to interact
performance. Probably non-dramatic ballad jigs and even the
less elaborate farce jigs were used both as intermeans and as
afterpieces. The *intermèdes* of the lost pastoral play *Florimene*
acted in 1635 seem to have been in the nature of masques.[4] But
the evidence in regard to extraneous song and dance is largely
indirect, being based on indications as to the comic song and
dance and balladry that appealed to the courtly classes of the
period. On the whole the songs preserved within the plays before the closing of the theaters are relatively simple, chiefly of a
lyric and catch type, though they are often organized into more
formal operatic acts in masque scenes.

[1] See Adams, *Shakespearean Playhouses*, pp. 279–80. Adams accepts the evidence
that the house was the Fortune. If so, its notorious farce jigs may have been going on
as interact performances.

[2] *Poems*, ed. Vincent, pp. 83–87.

[3] See Heywood's *Rape of Lucrece*, *The Mountebank's Masque*, and Jonson's *Bartholomew Fair* (III, i), *Metamorphosed Gipsies*, and *Masque of Augurs*, for comic ballads as monologue or choral songs.

[4] See *Designs by Inigo Jones*, Walpole and Malone Societies, pp. 98-101.

After the Restoration there is a tremendous amount of satire on the passion for song and dance and other more or less extraneous features on the stage, and the term jig is not infrequently met. Howard in the Preface to *The Women's Conquest* (1671) declares that in serious plays the auditors are "diverted by Scenes, Machins, Habits, Jiggs, and Dances," and in the First Prologue he burlesques contemporary taste in the statement, "we are to act a Farce to day, that hath sixteen Mimicks in it, several Jack-Puddings, and Punchinellos, never presented before, with two and thirty Dances and Jiggs *a-la-mode* besides." In the Prologue of *The Generous Enemies* (1672) Corey, condemning the new generation, declares that their fathers had enjoyed serious plays,

> But you, their wiser Off-spring, do advance
> To Plot of Gigg; and to Dramatique Dance.

In the Folio of Davenant's works, published in 1673, a "Prologue spoken at the Duke's Theater" with *The Wits* contains the lines,

> So Country Jigs and Farces mixt among
> Heroique Scenes make Plays continue long.

Buckingham takes his fling in *The Rehearsal* (1671) at song and dance acts along with other extravagances of drama.[1] The campaign of burlesque was continued by Duffet, who parodied Settle's *Emperor of Morocco* in his *Empress of Morocco* (1674), the Davenant revisions of *Macbeth* and *The Tempest* in the same musical farce and in *The Mock Tempest* (1675), and Shadwell's *Psyche* in *Psyche Debauch'd* (1678). D'Urfey, destined himself to be the chief proponent of comic song including old ballads largely in dialogue, accuses the audience in the Prologue of *The Siege of Memphis* (1676),

> you'd laugh to hear, Old *Cole* of *Windsor*,
> A bawdy Ballad, though with non sence cram'd,
> Will please ye when a serious Play is damn'd.

---

[1] See Summers' edition, pp. 112, 145.

In the Epilogue[1] of *The Injured Princess* (1682) he complains:

> The way to please you is easie if we knew't,
> A Jigg, a Song, a Rhyme or two will do't,
> When you'r i'th' vein.

The attack on song and dance in connection with drama continues for generations in satires, prefaces, and prologues of plays, but the field is too broad to be significant for specific jig types.

For the present study the evidence in regard to song and dance on the stage is more interesting after the Restoration than earlier in the century, because the adaptation of song and ballad related to the older jig field is clearer. Stage directions record the constant introduction of dances during the course of the action, both alone and in connection with songs, especially after songs or in entertainments and masques. Songs by characters of every class, but particularly comic characters, abound in monologue, dialogue, and choral form. Masques multiply in plays of all types. In addition there are scenes of reveling at weddings, in summer games, and in feasts and entertainments, which permit the introduction of song and dance and farcical action, sometimes small in amount but often considerable. Most of this material is very loosely connected with the action. As the Critic says in the Praelude to Ravenscroft's *Italian Husband* (1698), poets "bring in their Musick by head and shoulders, and [it] may serve in one Play as well as another." In a number of cases songs were printed, not in the texts of the plays, but at the beginning or at the end[2]—as in the edition of Heywood's *Lucrece* which came out in 1638. Some of the song and dance acts coming at the very close of the play are virtually afterpieces. In many plays there are directions for a

---

[1] Printed anonymously in *Covent Garden Drollery* (1672), p. 34.

[2] See the end of Dryden's *Duke of Guise* (1683), Crowne's *Sir Courtly Nice* (1685), D'Urfey's *Fool's Preferment* (1688), and Southerne's *Sir Anthony Love* (1691). Three songs, one a dialogue, are printed at the beginning of D'Urfey's *Richmond Heiress* (1693); and two dialogues (by D'Urfey and Motteux) at the beginning of Mrs. Pix's *Deceiver Deceived* (1698). Interact operatic pieces printed with plays are noticed just below.

dance at or near the end,[1] and song with dance or in dialogue closes others.[2] Masques, antic entertainments, or country revels introduced at the end, particularly for weddings, continue, as in some of the earlier plays, to furnish excellent substitutes for the old jigs.[3] A number of operatic pieces were performed independently between acts or as afterpieces,[4] and similar use was probably made of a great deal of material that is not recorded.

The farce jig at the end of the sixteenth century was an expression of the naïve and racy taste of the common man. From an early period in the seventeenth century it was the cavalier who more and more completely set the tone of theatrical performances, and the progressive coarsening of his taste is doubtless responsible for the more farcical spirit shown in the songs and dances of plays. While the material is often similar to that of the jig, the approach is different. The taste of the courtly in song and dance is perhaps best revealed in their informal

[1] See Lacy's *Sauney the Scot* and *Old Troop;* Porter's *Carnival;* Sedley's *Mulberry-Garden;* Dryden's *Evening's Love;* Shadwell's *Humorists, Miser, Epsom Wells, Squire of Alsatia, Bury Fair,* and *Volunteers;* Ravenscroft's *Careless Lovers* and *Mamamouchi;* Etherege's *Man of Mode;* Mrs. Behn's *Dutch Lover* and *Rover,* Part I; Wycherley's *Love in a Wood* and *Country Wife.* Pepys mentions dances at the end of *The Scornful Lady,* September 16, 1667, and *The Sea Voyage,* September 25, 1667. Final dance is frequent in plays written around 1700 also.

[2] See Lacy's *Dumb Lady,* Mrs. Pix's *Spanish Wives,* and Craufurd's *Courtship A-la-mode* for dance songs. *The Husband His own Cuckold* (1696) by John Dryden, Jr., closes with a comic dialogue beginning "Why so Coy, and so Strange?" a brawl of husband and wife with emphasis on jealousy and sensuality (see pp. 171–74 below). D'Urfey has at the end of *Don Quixote,* Part III (1696), "A Dialogue Sung between Lisis and Altisidora, a Boy and a Girl, suppos'd to be Brother and Sister," beginning "Ah my Dearest Celide," which represents sensual children. "An Epilogue. For Mrs. Lucas" in *Pills,* II, 342, prepares for her singing with Bourdon after a play "the last new Dialogue." Neither the play nor the song is named.

[3] See D'Urfey's *Massaniello,* Part II, and *Cinthia and Endimion; Fairy-Queen;* Betterton's *Prophetess;* Settle's *World in the Moon;* Vanbrugh's *Aesop;* etc. For examples in earlier seventeenth century plays, see Beaumont and Fletcher's *Women Pleased,* Cartwright's *Lady-Errant* and *Royal Slave,* and Brome's *Court Beggar* and *Love-sick Court.*

[4] Examples are the masque-like pastoral scenes performed at the beginning and end and between the acts of Crowne's *Calisto,* the simpler pastoral dialogues between acts of Powell's *Cornish Comedy,* Motteux's burlesque *Loves of Mars and Venus* between acts of Ravenscroft's *Anatomist,* and *The Four Seasons* performed at the end of Motteux's *Island Princess.* Pepys tells of a farce at the performance of *Horace* on January 19, 1669: "Lacy hath made a farce of several dances—between each act, one: but his words are but silly, and invention not extraordinary as to the dances; only some Dutchmen come out of the mouth and tail of a Hamburgh sow."

revelry, which was strongly influenced by the pastimes of the folk. In the entertainments of the court or gentry, game and dance and song characteristic of the folk[1] and sometimes involving coarse mimetic action were utilized in a spirit approaching more or less closely to burlesque. Entertainments for the progresses of James I included songs and dances of various types, some distinctly vulgar. In 1617 among sports shown before the king in Lancashire were the "dancing the Huckler, Tom Bedlo, and the Cowp Justice of Peace."[2] In 1618 the "marriage of the son of a farmer" with the dance at his wedding was presented at Enfield and then at Theobalds,[3] and a play or masque of "Tom of Bedlam the Tinker, and such other mad stuff" at Theobalds[4]. In *The Entertainment at Althorpe*, *The Metamorphosed Gipsies*, and *The King's Entertainment at Welbeck*, Jonson organized the sports of country festivities into formal masques. One scene in *The King and Queen's Entertainment at Richmond* (1636), which was printed in Kirkman's *Wits* as a separate droll under the title "Wiltshire Tom," presents much rustic drollery in prose, with a country dance and a wooing dialogue of a shepherd and a shepherdess. For something like forty years before 1638 the courtiers held annual celebrations in the Cotswold Hills, with "games, sports, plays, and Chivalrie." The nature of them is obscure, but there are allusions to much pastoral material, and a long wooing dialogue purporting to have been used in these

[1] For Arabella Stuart's account of games in 1603, see Nichols, *Progresses of James I*, IV, 1060–61. In Brome's *Jovial Crew*, Act II, a squire's daughter longs for the pleasures that she and her sister were wont to enjoy—"to see my Ghossips cock to day; mould Cocklebread; daunce clutterdepouch; and Hannykin booby; binde barrels." For "Hannykin booby," see p. 83 above. For "Clutterdepouch," a vulgar dance, see Randolph, *Hey for Honesty*, III, iii. For sports, including "Clapperdepouch" and "Saw you my cock to-day," see Lacy, *Sir Hercules Buffoon*, II, ii.

[2] See *Journal of Nicholas Assheton*, Chetham Society, p. 45.

[3] See Sullivan, *Court Masques of James I*, pp. 107–8.

[4] See Reyher, *Les Masques Anglais*, p. 524; *Progresses of James I*, III, 465. Birch, *Court and Times of James I*, II, 57–58, prints in full a letter of Chamberlain calling the last entertainment "beastly gear," which displeased "specially by reason of a certain song, sung by Sir John Finett, wherein the rest bear the burden, of such scurrilous and base stuff, that it put the king out of his good humour, and all the rest that heard it." See Fellowes, *English Madrigal Verse*, pp. 553–58, for songs sung in another entertainment of 1618, at Brougham Castle in Westmoreland. They include two in dialogue, a ballad, and a dance lyric with a conventional picture of rustic reveling.

games has survived.[1] A pamphlet of 1646 in the British Museum called *The King Found at Southwell, and the Oxford Gigg playd, and Sung at Witney Wakes: With the Masque shewed before divers Courtiers, and Cavaliers, that went thither from Oxford, and severall Ketches and Songs at the said Wakes*, by Lloyd, has nothing to do with the King or Southwell, being simply an account of reveling at the wakes. "Oxford Gigg" seems to be the general title applied to the whole. A morris group sang and danced with foolery of the clown; a fiddler and his boy played and sang; and there were performances on the pipe and tabor, the bagpipe, and the harp, besides the catches sung by the group of celebrants. As a satire on this type of pastime, Aubrey planned about 1670 "The Country Revell" at Alford, which was to picture intriguing and rioting esquires, a rout of country people, shepherds, constables, gipsies, a ballad singer, a dairy maid, a sow-gelder, and a "Lady of the Maypole,"[2] most of them types fully exploited in the collections of drollery and in the plays of the late seventeenth century. The *Huntington Divertisements*, an actual "Enterlude for the Generall Entertainment at the County-Feast, Held at Merchant-Taylors Hall, June 20, 1678," with its rustic drollery has an even more extensive range of characters, songs, and dances in the current modes of the Restoration. Apparently citizens and courtiers joined in the dances.

As a result of the whole movement, not only folk dances but the varied types of song used for country dance and for antic and droll dancing became increasingly popular among the courtly, and the long discredited ballad once more found favor with the cavalier class. In *Hyde Park* (IV, iii), licensed in 1632, when Venture warns Lord Bonvile that his song is "a very ballad, my lord, and a coarse tune," his lordship replies,

> The better; why, does any tune become
> A gentleman so well as a ballad?

By 1639 Monsieur Device of Newcastle's *Country Captain* could say of the ballad, "the greatest witt lyes that way now" (Act II).

[1] See p. 209 n. 5 below.

[2] See Marks, *English Pastoral Drama*, pp. 180–82; *Roxburghe Ballads*, IX, lxxxix*–xc*, 569. Some of the features were a song of a justice, "But give me a buxome Country Lasse"; a ballad, "Downe lay the Sheapheard Swayne"; "An Amorous Colloquiae" of Phyllis and Damon; and "A Morris Dance."

The incursion of the ballad into the pastimes of the courtly took a number of forms. As a result of the religious and political conflicts of the seventeenth century surveyed in chapter ii, an outstanding form was satiric balladry with its numerous parodies and burlesques. The frequent use of satiric song as jig has been shown. In their love of burlesque, antic, drollery, and country pastimes, however, the gallants of the age utilized most of the types of London balladry and country song, and perhaps helped to create new ones. The comic genius of the age expended itself in the portrayal of the traits, appearance, and droll action of country clowns, citizens, vagabonds, swaggerers, foreigners—in comic ballad and song as well as in antimasque and comedy. The pastoral fad of the age also had its influence, and innumerable songs of shepherds and haymakers, of country clowns and naïve country maids, of swaggering and sensual northern or Scottish characters, allowed the courtly, especially after the Restoration, to carry on an artistic pose, at the same time indulging their love of drollery and their court wit. From the first, many pieces called ballads were catches or songs, and the lyric element increased as the courtiers turned to country song rather than the stricter balladry that had prevailed in satire.

This balladry of the courtiers had a marked effect on the broadside. Certain types of popular ballads continued to be printed in broadsides for the folk alone, but courtly drolls and pastorals in ballad form also appeared as broadsides. While a naïveté of tone distinguishes certain types of ballads as popular, and others picture common life with a heightening of burlesque and drollery to a point that separates courtly song from the kindred ballads of the folk, the broadsides generally increase in coarseness and in drollery and in sophisticated bawdry. The two types often meet. Indeed, while the cavaliers and their dramatists and ballad writers continued to satirize the citizens of London, the distinctions of class were becoming less sharp as the wealthy merchant rose into power; and this fact is nowhere more clearly indicated than in the evidence that before the middle of the century all classes were using in their pastimes the plebeian ballad and country dance.

Not only does this balladry increase in volume after the

Restoration, but its importance from the point of view of presentation can be shown. A few of the specimens are still called jigs. A number were printed in plays or in connection with plays. But the best evidence comes from the collection of a mass of such songs in the many drolleries and songbooks which appeared from the end of the Commonwealth and reached a climax in the six volumes of D'Urfey's *Wit and Mirth: or Pills to Purge Melancholy*. According to the title-pages of a number of these song collections, the pieces in them had been performed in theaters, at court, or at feasts,[1] so that the function of the bulk of them is clear though only a small proportion of the individual songs can be identified as sung in plays. These Restoration ballads, exploiting chiefly the drollery and sensuality of roguish and clownish characters, range from lyrics of ballad material and tone to songs of broadside type. In songs woven into plays, the tendency is to the more lyric form. But the extraneous songs printed along with plays and a number of songs used in entertainments and masques introduced into plays are nearer to the strict ballad form. The drolleries and songbooks of the period contain a mass of balladry of this last type, rather long for singing as an interruption to the dialogue of a play. Doubtless the songs were performed between acts or at the end. In the early eighteenth century, when theatrical performances began to be advertised, plays were already buried under supplementary material partly of this nature, and the development was hardly a new one.

If the jig of two singers bears the relation to the field of the comic dialogue ballad that I try to indicate in the next chapter, there was an extensive revival of the art of the simple jig in the Restoration. In any case, a kindred art is found in the dialogue songs of the plays which are so frequently comic or sensual wooings, in the revival of ballad dialogues in many types by D'Urfey and others, especially for the presentation of citizens' entertainments and country revels, and in a few dramatic dialogues de-

---

[1] See for example *Westminster Drolleries* (1671, 1672), *Covent Garden Drollery* (1672), *Methinks the Poor Town has been troubled too long, or, A Collection of all the New Songs*, etc. (1673), *A Perfect Collection Of the Several Songs Now in Mode Either at the Court or, Theatres* (1675), Playford's *Choice Ayres*, Books I–V (1675, 1679, 1681, 1683, 1684), *The Newest Collection of the Choicest Songs, As they are Sung at Court, Theatre*, etc. (1683), and Playford's *Banquet of Musick* (1688).

picting brawls and intrigues which found a place in the popular burlesque masques with a Lucianic tone.[1] Shortly after 1700 some evidence for the continued stage use of such dialogue songs is to be had in the collections of sheet music in the British Museum, like that in H. 1601 or the one made by Walsh about 1715 with the title "A Collection of the Choicest Songs and Dialogues Composd By the most Eminent Masters of the Age" (G. 151). In both collections some dialogues are included with titles stating what actors sang them and usually what plays they were performed in or with. In the advertisements of plays early in the eighteenth century, especially in *The Daily Courant*, "comical dialogues" are not infrequently recorded as additional entertainments. Among these records there is one of the dancing of a specific dialogue song which gives, I think, definite evidence that the art of the jig survived into the eighteenth century. In *The Daily Courant* for June 11 and 12, 1712, "Blouza-Bella by Mr. Prince, and Mrs. Bicknell" is advertised among "Entertainments of Dancing" to be performed on the twelfth at Drury Lane. The song is presumably D'Urfey's burlesque "Italian Song, Call'd Pastorella; made into an English Dialogue," opening "*Blowzabella* my bouncing Doxie," which was published in *Pills to Purge Melancholy* (I, 190–95). It is a dialogue of two vagabonds, a piper and a toy-peddling doxie, debating about their trades somewhat in the jealous manner of the Tinker and Joan in "A merry discourse" (Text 17), though here the song is colored by coarseness and bawdry as in "The Souldiers delight in the North Or, A New North-country Jigge betwixt a Man and his Wife" (Text 7). During the great vogue of song and dance on the stage in the early eighteenth century, new fashions arose, of course, but old traditions of dialogue ballads and songs reaching back often to the early seventeenth century play a surprisingly large part. Probably dance traditions were equally significant, and the connection of dance and song still vital. At any rate, folk dances including jigs had lost none of their popularity by 1700.

A development in the larger field of song and dance which calls for recognition here in connection with the jig was that of

[1] See, for example, Motteux's *Loves of Mars and Venus*, Acts I and II, and *Presumptuous Love*, cited on p. 174 below.

the distinctly English types of opera, with song and dance set in spoken dialogue. Whereas the jig tended to exploit dialogue and even farcical story in song, in English opera dialogue and story are largely left to spoken parts, the emphasis in both song and dance being laid on the expression of character and attitude. Perhaps the courtly masque furnished the most significant contribution to this opera, especially through the common use of masques in plays. From the masque came particularly the picturesque scenery that contributed so much to the success of seventeenth century opera. For comic opera considerable importance attaches to the large "antic" element in masques and the related disguisings, which readily combined with popular forms of song and dance both of comedians and of the folk. Many of the less formal masques of the court throughout the sixteenth century were disguisings for group dances in which appeared both comic or odd human figures and supernatural figures like satyrs. Similar types were represented also in pageants and disguisings of the masses.

A number of the more popular figures in the earlier disguisings passed into those of the seventeenth century, came to be important in antimasques and antic dances of the stage, had a place in the comic scenes, or "drollery," of pageants and feasts, and seemingly appeared at times not only in ballad and song but—if the titles are significant—in the more dramatic country dances as well. Typical figures are Scotchmen, Irishmen, Dutchmen, sailors, cooks, shepherds, clowns, peddlers, rogues, drunkards, beggars, and gipsies.[1] The vogue of gipsies and beggars in song and dance has been mentioned in connection with the relation of antic and jig. Comic or antic dances of drunkards as well as of rogues and wooers are noticed elsewhere in connection with the conventions of farce jigs (pp. 83, 138, 248). One of the interesting figures in the general field of antic was the madman. Madmen dance in *The Duchess of Malfi* (IV, ii), *The Changeling* (IV, iii), and Campion's *Lords' Masque*. A mad girl sings numerous snatches of song in *Hamlet* and *The Two Noble Kinsmen*. Tom a Bedlam, cited above as appearing in revels before the king, and similar mimus figures were frequently the mouthpiece

[1] See pp. 90–91 above for the sixteenth century; and Reyher, *Les Masques Anglais*, passim, and Brotanek, *Die englischen Maskenspiele*, passim, for the seventeenth.

of song and ballad.[1] In *The Figure of Nine* the "madmans Morris" is mentioned among the "sorts of common Dances alwayes used,"[2] and "the Lancashire witches" and "the drunkards antick" among "pretty sports." Dances and songs of witches occur in *Macbeth*, Jonson's *Masque of Queens*, Middleton's *Witch*, and Heywood's *Lancashire Witches*. In Fletcher's *Nice Valour* (V, i) fools led by Cupid perform a posture dance, and in Jonson's *Love Freed from Ignorance and Folly* there is a dance of she-fools.[3] It is needless to extend the types.

The elaboration of such song and dance material transformed a play into an operatic piece. In the romantic field, for example, the series of songs and dances recorded for the lost *Alba*,[4] performed at Oxford in 1605, suggests pastoral opera, and the regularly placed masque scenes and antic dances in Cartwright's *Royal Slave* of 1636 foreshadow heroic opera with its elaborate scenery. Comic opera is approached through the enlargement of the song element in the rôles of the merry men in *The Knight of the Burning Pestle* and *The Rape of Lucrece*. Song and dance in *The Spanish Gipsy* and *The Jovial Crew*, probably given the name jig in passages already quoted, furnish a form of comic operetta. To such material the spectacular element of scenery is added in Heywood's *Love's Mistress*. Through the multiplication of operatic features in drama, Restoration plays developed into operas of several types. No doubt Davenant's introduction of foreign opera stimulated the movement, but English conventions of the sort surveyed in this volume seem to have been most influential until the eighteenth century. For opera

[1] For one such song, see *London Mercury*, VII, 518–24; VIII, 79–80, 188–89, 303, 414. For records or texts of others, see Brydges, *Restituta*, III, 430; Chappell, *Popular Music*, I, 328–36; II, 512, 778–79; *Westminster Drolleries*, ed. Ebsworth, App., pp. xlviii-l; *Roxburghe Ballads*, II, 256–61; D'Urfey, *Pills*, I, 1–3, 76; III, 43–44; IV, 189–90; V, 32–34. These include play songs, catches, and ballads. For a dialogue song of the type sung in D'Urfey's *Richmond Heiress*, Act II, see *Pills*, I, 73–75.

[2] See *Roxburghe Ballads*, II, 153–58; VI, 542, for the ballad "The Mad Man's Morrice" by Crouch, picturing love madness. It was published as a broadside and in several drolleries. Compare "Lunaticus Inamoratus; Or, The Mad Lover," given in part in *Bagford Ballads*, II, 888.

[3] See Morley, *Memoirs of Bartholomew Fair*, p. 289, for Southwell's allusion in a letter of 1685 to performers "acting fools, drunkards, and madmen" as typical of Bartholomew Fair.

[4] *Malone Society Collections*, I, 247–59.

in the native tradition, Restoration writers, including Dryden, formulated a theory of an "English Opera," defending spoken dialogue to introduce song and dance as superior to recitative.[1] A number of heroic operas continued the traditions of the romantic masque with its spectacular scenes and of the pastoral with its idyllic setting.[2] Usually, however, varied combinations of song, dance, entertainment, drollery, and masque furnish the operatic element, whether in new plays or in revised forms of early plays like *Macbeth* and *The Tempest* in which older material was supplemented. Moreover, any play of any type could readily be given an operatic cast—as was often done, especially to furnish comic relief—by the addition of extraneous song and dance or by the use of supplementary entertainment. The comic and antic elements increased in all types of operatic plays, and many of those produced toward the end of the century are almost pure farce exploiting antic or clownish characters with their appropriate song and dance acts. Even in heroic opera there was a far-reaching influence of antic and country song and dance. Whether the antic devices went much farther toward comedy than the representation of the strange and marvelous, or country scenes departed more than slightly from the idyllic, they exist because of the interest in such forms of song and dance, and they tend to overshadow the heroic element. But the antic was often comic, and the pastoral burlesque. In keeping with the spirit of burlesque, of drollery, and of bawdy suggestiveness that prevailed in the late seventeenth century, opera became largely comic and farcical.

If much of this opera was almost as formless as earlier plays with their sporadic song and dance, there was a growth toward definite types of comic opera in the passion for certain conventional forms of song and dance associated with conventional farce characters. The ground was clearly laid in the seventeenth century for the distinct types of comic opera belonging to the eighteenth. Antimasque, drollery, and burlesque developed into the comic masque of the seventeenth and eighteenth centuries. Various antic and pantomimic acts of single disards or of

[1] See the passages cited by Reyher, *Les Masques Anglais*, pp. 480–82.

[2] See *ibid.*, pp. 465–86, for an excellent discussion of the subject.

groups, with the constant increment of similar foreign material, prepared the way for the pantomimes of the eighteenth century. Finally, all the material needed for the development of ballad opera was furnished by the droll catches, ballads, and dances of robbers, rogues, vagabonds, country clowns, and similar figures that had been featured in jigs, antic dances, and scenes of plays for more than a century.

Though the great vogue of the true farce jig was not long-lived, it doubtless increased the popular demand for song and dance on the stage and helped to fix the popularity of many farcical characters in song and dance acts. Moreover, the farce jig was itself a distinct form of comic opera, and it survived until after the more definite movement toward opera began with Davenant. In the long run it may have been responsible in no small measure for the complete triumph of English comic opera in the form of ballad opera. Among the later jigs "The Blackman," for example, shows a variety of effects in its interspersed prose, its street cries that were probably chanted, and its shifting verse forms for dialogue, including lyric measures. It seems certain that "Der Exorcist" with its prose dialogue and its numerous songs not in dialogue is an outgrowth of the farce jig, and it is fairly probable that the piece appeared in England in something like its present form before 1642. The singspiel belongs to a type of operatic farce akin both to the sixteenth century play *Tom Tyler*—significantly republished in 1661— and to the later ballad opera. It cannot be claimed that comic opera attained maturity in the farce jig, but the possibilities so fully developed at the end of the seventeenth century and the beginning of the eighteenth were at least conceived and tested during the career of the farce jig.

CHAPTER VI

THE SIMPLE BALLAD AS JIG

IN THIS chapter an attempt is made to deal with the field of the simple ballad from the point of view of the probable range in the types used as jigs in the London area. I have considered the designation jig for a ballad as the most significant indication of its dramatic function. But the use of the term seems to have been more or less fortuitous, and a number of other ballads on one score or another give evidence of dramatic presentation. All of the pieces that call for special consideration here evidently belong to popular types of balladry, and I have tried to illustrate the vogue by noting some of the more interesting specimens in each type. It has already been pointed out that the pieces called jigs have no common quality to distinguish them from the general mass of ballads. On the basis of them the number of potential jigs in the balladry of the period would be enormous. Again, it is not practicable to attempt a distinction between ballads performed by professional actors and by other classes. In the long career of the stage jig, the actors probably did not neglect any type. Especially at the beginning of the vogue, as naïvely sentimental a ballad as "A New Northern Jig" or as soberly satirical a ballad as "Clod's Carol" might have proved very acceptable on the stage. There is, however, no record for stage performance of any of the simple ballads published as jigs.

The stage jig must frequently have been a solo performance. Even among the early broadsides, where comic ballads are relatively few, there are many that would have made particularly effective jigs for individual clowns—nonsense songs, strings of impossibilities, prophecies, ragman's rolls, jests in narrative form reporting brisk conversation, street cries, medleys, parodies, and the like. Miscellaneous songs in sixteenth century plays and the monologue rôles of Tarlton have given some evidence for performances of this type. Further evidence is found in the satiric jigs of chapter ii. The importance of such rôles in the part played by the disard in games or the entertainer in feasts would point to their use by the clown who was adapting popular song and dance for the stage. Comic dances and droll or satiric songs of individuals were a favorite type of performance. This is a phase of the subject that receives relatively little attention in the present survey, however, because the significant development in the sixteenth century stage jig was so clearly toward the use of dialogue and plot. Moreover, until well into the seventeenth century, the extant broadsides called jigs are dialogues.

In the treatment of the dialogue ballad, songs that fall just short of true dialogue form have in the main been disregarded. Yet many of these clearly call for two singers. It is evident that the interjected "quoth he," the explanatory prologue, the brief narrative close, or even a bridge of narration introduced into the middle of a song, was not regarded as interfering with dialogue form. These parts were simply sung by one performer or the other. "The Nutbrown Maid" and "The Country-man's Delight; Or, The Happy Wooing" discussed later, are old examples. A number of seventeenth century ballads were printed as dialogues with speakers' names although the dialogue is interspersed with narrative and descriptive lines of the author.[1] Some of these at least were with little doubt presented dramatically. A special type is furnished by dialogue ballads and songs with a *chanson d'aventure* opening. This form became usual in the Middle Ages and has remained popular ever since. Among the seventeenth century songs of the type are two late ballads called jigs. A traditional ballad, "Old Moll," very similar to a number of the comic wooing dialogues noticed later, will illustrate the use of such forms in song drama. "Old Moll" has been incorporated in part in the texts of two mummers' wooing plays, and has been collected as an independent song dialogue in two versions.[2] One is a pure dialogue beginning "Good morning, Moll, where art thou going?" and the other

---

[1] See, for example, "Love in a Maze" (*Roxburghe Ballads*, II, 42–48) and "The Crafty Maid" (*ibid.*, III, 652–55).

[2] For the passages in mummers' plays, see *Modern Philology*, XXI, 271–72, and for the songs, Williams, *Folk-Songs of the Upper Thames*, pp. 95–98.

opens with a conventional narrative stanza—"As I was walking all along," etc.[1]—and has a "chorus" not related to the dialogue. Again, some of the broadsides in which dialogue and narrative are mixed seem to be versions of songs that were originally pure dialogues. Popular "playhouse" dialogues, for instance, were sometimes expanded with narrative parts to give the length desirable for broadside publication. On the other hand, longer and more dramatic forms—typical stage jigs, in fact—may sometimes have been reduced to the limits of the broadside.[2] Traces of a similar laxness of form are found even in the extant dramatic jigs. In "Pückelherings Dill dill dill," Don Jansa according to a stage direction enters and sings to his attendant, but his speech opens as narrative.

I have tried to indicate whenever possible the date of publication for individual ballads and the periods during which there is evidence for the frequent publication of certain types. It is doubtful, however, whether the attempt has much value. Many ballads do not seem to have been entered at all. Others may have been entered only after a long career as broadsides. At times ballads were licensed in great numbers, no doubt because successful publishers were forced to give an accounting. In 1586, 1624, 1656, and 1675 there were wholesale entries of ballads, many of which must have been published long before. Several pieces mentioned in this chapter were re-entered after a period amounting to as much as fifty years, and many old pieces may have been re-entered after long intervals under changed names. Since ballads, particularly the early ones, perished in great numbers, it is possible that many of the late broadsides are exemplars of much earlier texts. In particular, the coarser ballads from which the early bawdy jigs were probably drawn, could not be printed until after the Restoration, except surreptitiously. Though D'Urfey's *Pills* was not published until late in the seventeenth century, it includes some songs from the early part of the century and even from the sixteenth.

Ballads in the nature of debates and brawls may be discussed

---

[1] See *Catalogue* of the Crawford Collection, Nos. 86–140, for a considerable number of seventeenth century dialogues with similar openings. For the sixteenth century especially, see the list of songs beginning "As I" in the Index of Chappell's *Popular Music*.

[2] See pp. 176–77 below.

first because they so frequently deal with droll characters similar to those found in the farce jigs and the singspiele. These ballads are of many kinds. Some in the nature of religious debates and flytings were mentioned in chapter ii. A number of others present neighbors or gossips discussing such topics as women and marriage. An early example of this kind is a "Dialogue betwene the Comen Secretary and Jelowsy, touching the Unstableness of Harlottes," printed by John King about the middle of the sixteenth century.[1] Jealousy, desiring to marry "yf y^t I durst," questions the Secretary, who from a wide knowledge of women expounds their vices. The following question and answer are typical:

> Jelowsy.
> Than thus: she that hath a rollynge eye,
> And doth convey it well and wysely,
> And therto hath a waverynge thought,
> Trowe you that this trull wyll not be bought?
> Secretary.
> Yes; but take hede by the pryce ye have no losse:
> A mad marchaunt that wyll gyve V marke for a gose.
> Beware a rollynge eye w^t waverynge thought, marke that,
> And for suche stuffe passe not a dantyprat.

This ragman's roll of satiric sketches of women continues through twenty-four stanzas, with the woman who loves much dallying, one who is "light of credence," one given to idleness, one who cannot keep counsel, and so on—the questions of Jealousy suggesting the sharp answers of the Secretary.

A similar pessimism about women is expressed in the one ballad of this general class which is called a jig—"*Clods Carroll: or,* A proper new Iigg, to be sung Dialogue wise, of a man and a woman that would needs be married." It is printed here as Text 6. The fact that the broadside was printed for Henry Gosson dates the copy between 1603 and 1641.[2] The title is

---

[1] Beloe, *Anecdotes of Literature*, I, 388–93, prints the dialogue in full. The two stanzas quoted here are from Collier's account in *Bibliographical Account* (1865), I, 398–400. A version without the Secretary's comments, apparently early, is found in Rawl. MS C. 813, fols. 31–32, reprinted in *Anglia*, XXXI, 352–53.

[2] In giving the dates for the various ballad publishers here and later, I follow the lists in Arber's *Transcript*, V, lxxxi–cxi, 216–77; in the *Catalogue* of the Crawford Collection, pp. 535–45; and in *Roxburghe Ballads*, I, xvii–xxiii.

misleading, for the interlocutors are a man that would needs be married and a woman into whose mouth are put the conventional warnings against her sex.[1] In the second part, the man, now married, admits that the advice given him was sound.

Good and bad qualities in wives or husbands are treated in a number of other dialogues between acquaintances, sometimes with the naïve and amusing aspects of village gossip rather skilfully presented. The ballad entered on the Register in 1565–6 as "a Dialoge betwene a mayde of the Cetye and a mayde of the Cuntrye a bowte chosyng of husboundes"[2] probably belonged to this general class. Howell's "Dialogue touching the matrimoniall degree," printed in *Newe Sonets, and pretie Pamphlets* (entered on the Register in 1567–8),[3] is a ballad debate of two men, one praising marriage and the other the bachelor's state.[4] A "ballett intituled *the prayse and Dysprayse of Women very fruthfull to the Well Dyspoysed mynde*" was licensed in 1563–4.[5] The same phrase occurs in the title of a ballad printed in the second half of the seventeenth century as "A Merry Dialogue between Thomas and John. In the praise, and dispraise of Women, and Wine," which begins "Some Women are like to the Wine."[6] It is sung to the tune "Women and Wine," described in the title as "a gallant delightful new Tune, well known amongst Musitioners, and in Play-houses." The long continuance of the theme in popular song is indicated by a modern dialogue, "A Single and a Married Life,"[7] in which the married man praises women and the single man expresses his doubt. Martin Parker wrote several dialogues on marriage that illustrate both the range of themes and the use of old conventions. In "Man's Felicity and Misery" he portrays the qualities of the

[1] See Erk and Böhme, *Deutscher Liederhort*, No. 836, for a similar ballad of about 1650, in which the man's adviser is his mother, with the outcome related in a narrative part.

[2] *Transcript*, I, 315.

[3] *Ibid.*, I, 358.   [4] Ed. Grosart, pp. 30–31.

[5] See *Transcript*, I, 234. For a song "In Praise and Dispraise of Women," beginning "Women to praise who taketh in hand," see Johnson's *Crowne-Garland of Goulden Roses* (1612), Percy Society, pp. 52–54.

[6] *Roxburghe Ballads*, VII, 149–50.

[7] See Gould and Sheppard, *Songs and Ballads of the West*, No. 88.

good wife and the bad in a dialogue between Edmund and his
cousin David, one of them claiming the best wife that ever man
had, and the other the worst.[1] In "Household Talke, or; Good
Councell for a Married Man. Delivered in a Prittie Dialogue,
By Roger a Batchelor, to Simon, a (Jealous) Married-man,"
Simon tells the details of his misery as a husband, with the refrain, "My Cosen makes a Cuckold of me"; and Roger offers
him consolation with the ironic refrain, "A Cuckold is a good
man's fellow."[2] Its opening, "Neighbour Roger, woe is me!"
paraphrases the opening of "Rowland." Parker's "Well met,
Neighbour; Or, A dainty discourse betwixt Nell and Sisse" is a
brisk dialogue dealing with men "that doe use their wives
amisse."[3] The two gossips, meeting as Nell goes in haste to
"Margeryes labour," give each other news of all the scandal
touching the husbands of the community. "Have among you!
good Women," licensed April 17, 1634, is a companion piece
exposing the wives.[4] It is described as a highway discourse between two men going to Maidstone market. "The cunning
Age," written by John Cart and printed for John Trundle
(1603–26), presents the evils of husbands in a dialogue of three
gossips, "a re-married Woman, a Widdow, and a young Wife."[5]

The shrewish wife is the theme of many ballads,[6] and some
of them presenting jests may have been precursors of the farce
jigs. Two such ballads at least were perhaps used by the come-

---

[1] *Roxburghe Ballads*, II, 182–88. Entered July 16, 1632, and March 1, 1675. A
catch-like song with a "Reply" and "Chorus" for each stanza was published in *Merry
Drollery* (ed. Ebsworth, pp. 302–4) with the title "Of a Good Wife and a Bad" and in
D'Urfey's *Pills*, IV, 181–82, but its interest is solely in the bad. In the quaint "John,
come kiss me now" (see Naylor, *Elizabethan Virginal Book*, pp. 90–92), John has a long
list of grievances against wives.

[2] *Roxburghe Ballads*, I, 440–46.   [4] *Ibid.*, I, 434–40.

[3] *Ibid.*, III, 98–103.   [5] Rollins, *Pepysian Garland*, pp. 239–43.

[6] Note such early ballad titles on the Register as "a commyssion vnto all those
whose wyves be thayre masters &c," 1564–5 (*Transcript*, I, 269); "a breffe [a]brygement
of maryage and so what Jogges the Wyves geves on the elbowe," 1565–6 (I, 294);
"shewyng how maryage ys bothe parydice and also purgatory &," 1565–6 (I, 311);
"my wyfe she wyll do all she can take mastrye as better hande &c," 1566–7 (I, 328);
"I will say as I do fynde my wyf to me ys nothynge kynde," 1566–7 (I, 333); "a yonge
womans skyll/and how she became mistress and Ruled at hyr Wyll &c," 1567–8 (I,
358); "yf a Weked Wyfe may have hyr Will &c," 1567–8 (I, 362); "a lamentacon of a
poore man troubled with a brawlinge wife," August 15, 1586; "The grief and vexacon

dians. "Get up and bar the Door,"[1] with its jest going back to Italian novella and French farce, was probably carried to Germany in some form of farce.[2] "A merry new Song. Wherein is shewed the sorowful Cudgelling of the Cobler of Colchester, and the great fault he committed against his wife, for the which he suffered hard penance. To a pleasant new tune called Trill lill"[3] may have been sung and danced by Kemp. At the opening of his *Nine Days' Wonder* Kemp calls himself *"Cavaliero* KEMP, Head Master of Morrice dancers, High Headborough of heighs, and only tricker of your Trill-lilles, and best bell-shangles." The connection indicates that "tricker of your Trill-lilles" refers to dancing. I have not been able to trace the tune "Trill lill" outside of the ballad on the cobbler of Colchester, which also uses the words for a refrain.[4] The ballad is a narrative by a spectator, who gives an account of the wife's beating the cobbler for eating a pie and a custard. The explanations which the husband and wife make to the spectators are repeated, with

---

that comes by a Scolde" November 27, 1588; "A merye newe ieste of a wife that threst her husband with a ffealle," August 15, 1590; "a pleasant ballad of a combat betwene a man and his wyfe for the breches," August 27, 1591. The piece entered as "the Colliers misdowtinge of forder strife, made his excuse to Annet his wief," April 17, 1591, is not called a ballad. See *Ancient Ballads and Broadsides*, Philobiblon Society, pp. 189–93, for the early "Mery balade, how a wife entreated her husband to haue her owne wyll," which is practically a dialogue. "A merry Jest of John Tomson and Jakaman his wife" (*Roxburghe Ballads*, II, 137–42), entered August 1, 1586, presents the jealous scold. Spirited narrative and monologue ballads dealing with the shrewish wife and with other types discussed in this section are numerous in the various collections of broadsides. Many are printed in the *Roxburghe Ballads*.

[1] Child, *Popular Ballads*, No. 275.

[2] The motive, combined with another, is found in a prose farce published in *Engelische Comedien und Tragedien*. There are a number of different German forms of this farce in the first half of the seventeenth century. One was used by Ayrer before 1605 for interact performance in his *König in Cypern*, an adaptation of Machin's *Dumb Knight*. See Tittmann, *Die Schauspiele der engl. Komödianten*, pp. liv–lv, and Bolte, *Das Danziger Theater*, pp. 225 ff. Wodick, *Jakob Ayrers Dramen*, p. 61, argues for a German origin for the farce, however.

[3] Printed in Lemon's *Catalogue of Broadsides of The Society of Antiquaries of London*, pp. 29–32.

[4] As a drinking term "trill-lill" is used in *Old Wives Tale*, l. 632; *Looking Glass for London and England*, l. 1688 (IV, v); *James IV*, l. 1204; and Nashe's *Lenten Stuffe* (*Works*, ed. McKerrow, III, 194, 265; IV, 403). See *NED* under "trillil." "Trim-trillilles" is applied to dice in *Bacchus Bountie* of 1593 (*Harl. Misc.*, II [1809], 273).

the wife's threat against anyone who dares to interfere. She
administers abuse with blows:

> Gwyp with a murrain, sir, she saide,
>   Must your old choppes be fed
> With custards and with apple pyes;
>   A rope come stretch your head.
> I'le teach you take the Rye brown loafe
>   and know the Essex cheese
> Is fitter for your rotten teeth
>   then any one of these.

But her revenge goes a step farther:

> And though, quoth she, indifferent well
>   thy carkasse I did bumme,
> Yet from thy carnion greedy guts
>   I'll fetch out every crumme.
> With that she did a feather take,
>   and in his throate it thruste,
> Then up he cast the apple Pye
>   and laid it in the dust.
> The Dog, quoth she, shall eat it free
>   ere that thy guts shall fill,
> And ever she cried as on him she flyed
>   Have with you my harts trill lill.

A first-class comedian could have done a great deal with this
dramatic narrative, and the material may also have had a more
dramatic form. In its group of characters and its situation the
ballad is akin to the singspiel of the English comedians, "Der
Windelwäscher."

There is a fairly extensive group of dialogue ballads in the
nature of conjugal brawls or flytings. A Scotch example, "Dame,
do the thing whilk I desire," probably an old piece, survives
in Sloane MS 1489 of the time of Charles I, with the words "a
Scotch brawle" written in the margin (fol. 18). In it the dame
meets all her goodman's pleas for a more thrifty housewifery
with the defiance, "I'll do but what I will mysell."[1] "A merry

---

[1] See Chambers, *Songs of Scotland prior to Burns*, pp. 115–18. See pp. 112–15 for
a monologue of a husband who does not wish to obey his wife and wear his old cloak, a
symbol of the homelier virtues, but insists upon being "girded gallantlie." A stanza is
sung in *Othello*, II, iii.

Dialogue betwixt a married man and his wife, concerning the affaires of this carefull life,"[1] printed in the early decades of the seventeenth century, is a spirited debate as to the relative burdens of husband and wife. The woman ends by threatening her husband with a three-legged stool, and he concludes that it is hopeless to expect a woman to yield in anything. From the point of view of presentation, one of the best of these brawls is "A pleasant new Ballad, both merry and witty,/That sheweth the humours, of the wiues in the City," in Pepys Collection, I, 376. As Henry Gosson was the publisher, it is earlier than 1641. An abusive wife finds her husband meek and compliant under her demands for luxuries and lovers, but she goes so far that he suddenly turns on her and makes her agree to light the candles at the wrong end and pin the basket. She even offers to stoop to his shoe. This ballad in a form typical of the late seventeenth century was included in several drolleries.[2] The Pepys Collection contains also a very coarse specimen of the domestic brawl in "A Dialogue Between A Baker and his Wife" (IV, 147). The wife opens the attack with "Where have you been, you drunken Dog?" Edward Ford, whose activities, like those of Martin Parker, began as the stage jig declined, wrote a dialogue with a similar opening which was almost certainly designed for singing dramatically. The quick shifting of tunes found here was not a convention of the ordinary ballad but is a frequent device in the jig. The main title of the piece is cut away. The secondary title, "A merry discourse, twixt him and his *Ioane*," etc., introduces us to the drunken tinker Jack and his wife, a kitchen-stuff woman.[3] The ballad is printed as Text 17. Though the wife rails at Jack in the early part, she is won by his promise of reformation.

---

[1] *Roxburghe Ballads*, II, 158–63. A ballad entitled "the Comonycation betwene the husbounde and the wyf and Dyscommodytes of maryage" was licensed in 1566–7 (*Transcript*, I, 338), and another called "A triall of Skill betwixt man and wife," on August 27, 1633.

[2] See *Westminster Drollery* (1671), ed. Ebsworth, pp. 44–47, "The kind Husband, but imperious Wife"; Hickes's *Grammatical Drollery* (1682), pp. 109–10, "The Patient Man, and the Scolding Wife"; *Oxford Drollery* (1671), pp. 148–52, "The old scolding Wife." The ballad in the Pepys Collection has been printed by Rollins in his *Pepysian Garland*, pp. 207–11.

[3] *Roxburghe Ballads*, I, 248–53. Compare Kemp's lost "Jig of the Kitchen-stuff Woman."

The domestic debate enjoyed a great popularity after the Restoration. In "The Curtain Lecture," opening "Of all Comforts I miscarried,/When I play'd the Sot and married," the drinking, roistering husband refuses to mend his ways. Like several other pieces noticed here, this song found a place in D'Urfey's *Pills* (II, 136–38). Many of these domestic dialogues are closer than "The Curtain Lecture" to the "Dialogue between a Cobler and his Wife," cited in chapter ii, in that they turn the argument between husband and wife into satire on contemporary conditions or picture the clownish husband as ambitious to leave his plow and try a more "princely vocation."[1] In the latter part of the seventeenth century and the early part of the eighteenth, abusive dialogues between husbands and wives were often introduced into plays, sometimes with an amount of stage direction that shows how dramatically the type was performed. In almost every case these dialogues belong to representations of citizens' feasts in plays. A song beginning "Since Times are so bad, I must tell thee, Sweet-heart," in which the clown Colin finally promises his wife to stick to the plow while she sticks to her distaff, is presented in an "Entertainment . . . . of Singing and Dancing" at a banquet in D'Urfey's *Don Quixote*, Part II (IV, iii).[2] In a similar song from *The Wonders in the Sun, Or, The Kingdom of the Birds* (III, i), which opens "Pray now *John* let *Jug* prevail," "three or four Brats" also play a part. The wife fails to dissuade a husband who is determined to give up the flail and go to the wars. He orders her to mind her spinning, her linen, her cheese, pigs, and geese, and threatens to thump her if she tries his patience further. When she reminds him that she is good at thumping too,

[1] See p. 65 above. In connection with these songs see *Choyce Drollery*, ed. Ebsworth, pp. 57–59, and Ashmolean MS 36, 37, No. 126, "Hods bodekins chil warke no more," in which the clown expresses his intention to become a soldier.

[2] Printed also in *Pills*, I, 88–90, where attention is called to the fact that it was set to music by Purcell. See *Works of Purcell*, XVI, xxv–xxviii, 167–77. The success of the type of song is partly indicated by the number of printed forms in which some of the specimens can be found. I have not attempted to list these, but this song from *Don Quixote* is found in Purcell, *Orpheus Britannicus*, I (1698), 168–74; Walsh's *Collection of the Choicest Songs and Dialogues*, Brit. Mus. G. 151, about 1715; Brit. Mus. H. 1601, No. 384; *Vocal Miscellany*, I, 100–101 (with the heading "Go, go, you vile Sot," the opening words of the "Dialogue between a Cobler and his Wife"); Ramsay, *Tea-Table Miscellany*, II, 43–45; *Journal of American Folk-Lore*, XXXV, 408–10 (traditional).

"they stand in a Posture of Fighting till the Brats Squawling round 'em, she crys and begins again." He ends by running off the stage and the others run after him. So far as dramatic quality is concerned, the text published in the play gives an entirely different impression from the one published in *Pills* (I, 139–42), where stage directions are lacking and the presence of the "Brats" is not indicated. In *The Island Princess* (1699), largely the work of Motteux, a dialogue opening "Hold, *John*, e're you leave me" is sung in the fourth act by Leveridge and Pate as a clown and his wife, with directions for the wife's weeping, threatening, wheedling, crying, and kissing the husband. This song was popular enough to be advertised by title in 1710 as an interact piece at Haymarket by Doggett and Leveridge, with *The Old Bachelor* on July 6, and with *Hamlet* on July 26.[1] Motteux had introduced a somewhat similar dialogue into his *Love's a Jest* of 1696 (Act II). The short operatic piece *Presumptuous Love* (1716), with its mythological characters, has a dialogue sung by the clown Damon and his wife Mopsa which is very much like the "Dialogue between a Cobler and his Wife." Mopsa, however, yields to the ambitious Damon when she hears that "King" Ixion has promised to make him a landlord if he successfully plays the pander between Ixion and Juno.

Evidence for the use of the domestic brawl as drama among the folk is furnished by a traditional survival in Lancashire, which can be traced to the eighteenth century. This is a dialogue called "The Droylsden Wakes Song" printed by Harland in *Ballads and Songs of Lancashire* (pp. 201–5). It represents a quarrel between husband and wife over which is the better spinner. A man dressed as a woman takes the part of the wife. The pair are described as "engaged with spinning-wheels, spinning flax in the olden style, and conducting a rustic dialogue in limping verse, and gathering contributions from spectators." Recently Williams has published a dramatic dialogue sung by two strollers, "The Struggle for the Breeches," which is a series of complaints and recriminations of a husband and wife in speeches of one line.[2]

The colloquies both of husband and wife and of two neigh-

---

[1] I am indebted to Professor Sherburn for these items from *The Daily Courant*.

[2] *Folk-Songs of the Upper Thames*, pp. 268–71.

bors or gossips not infrequently become serious discourses on the problems of humble life. A few of the more effective dialogues of this type may have been stage songs, but the majority, to judge from their tone, were probably sung only among the people. For example, the comic treatment of the scolding wife disappears and a frankly didactic tone is adopted in a number of dialogues between husband and wife (or even a betrothed pair) which are exhortations to a more honorable or thrifty life, discussions of domestic responsibilities and cares, or efforts of one to cheer the other.[1] Dramatic use seems more probable in the case of a few dialogues that survey the evils of society in the vein of "Nobody's Complaint" and the satiric news pieces.[2] An effective early seventeenth century ballad of this type is "Newes good and new" from the Pepys Collection (I, 210), printed for John Trundle.[3] It opens:

> *Iohn.* Now welcome neighbour *Rowland*,
>   From London welcome home,
> What newes is there I pray you?
>   From thence I heare you come.
> *Row.* The best that ere you heard,
>   Youle say't when I you shew.
> *Iohn.* I hardly can beleeue it,
>   Tis too good to be true.

[1] See, for example, in *Roxburghe Ballads*, "A new Ballad, Containing a communication between the carefull Wife and the comfortable Hus[band,] touching the common cares and charges of House-hold" (I, 122–25), licensed January 2, 1579, and December 14, 1624; "The Housholder's New Yeere's-Gift, containing a pleasant Dialogue betwixt the Husband and Wife, pleasant to be regarded" (I, 125–28), licensed January 14, 1598; "Robin and Kate; or, A bad husband converted by a good wife, in a dialogue betweene Robin and Kate" by Parker (II, 413–18), licensed May 9, 1634; "The Carefull Wife's Good Counsel; Or, The Husband's firm resolution to Reform his Life, and to lay up something against a Rainy Day" (III, 478–80); "The Chearful Husband: or, The Despairing Wife. In a Dialogue between a loving couple, about the Cares and Crosses of these troublesome times" (III, 514–17); "A Dainty new Dialogue between Henry and Elizabeth" (III, 663–66). The ballad licensed September 22, 1592, as "a pleasant communicacon betwene a yonge man a howseholder, and his love hee woed for his wief" was probably an early example of the type.

[2] One indication of the interest in such material is found in the Fool's prophecy in *King Lear*, at the end of III, ii, which seems to be a bit of interact drollery that has crept into the text of the play.

[3] Printed by Bolte, *Jahrbuch des Vereins f. nd. Sprachf.*, XIII, 66–68, and Rollins, *Pepysian Garland*, pp. 217–21.

Row. The Lawyer in his pleading
    to gaine giues no respect,
Though Clients haue no mony,
    he doth not them neglect:
But truly pleades their cause,
    of these there be not few.
Iohn. I neuer will beleeue it,
    Tis too good to be true.

Rowland continues with his marvels of reformed lords, ladies, clergy, usurers, tradesmen, brokers, and landlords, picturing at the end a city in which there are no more drunkards, thieves, or whores, and the prisons stand empty. In spite of its sober manner, this news dialogue was not improbably written especially for performance as a jig. Like several of the jigs, it borrows the name Rowland. It is also written in the meter of "Rowland," though the tune called for is "Twenty pound a yeere." More bitterly satiric still is "A Dialogue betweene Master Guesright and poore neighbour Needy,"[1] licensed July 16, 1634, and signed with the initials of Ed Ford. Here the honors fall to Master Guesright, who argues that money is the one motive power in life, and to prove it cites the greed of those in the various trades and professions down to that of the hangman.

Ford was the author also of a curious ballad called "A merry Discourse betweene Norfolke Thomas and Sisly Standtoo't his Wife,"[2] in which the simplicity and friendliness of country life are set over against the confusion and heartlessness of London life. In spite of a narrative opening and two other narrative passages of some length, the ballad is printed throughout as dialogue with speakers' names. Its form suggests to me an adaptation of a dramatic piece for broadside publication. In the first part Thomas and Cicely have left their straw-thatched cottage in Norfolk and have come to London, where they walk the streets marveling at the wonders and vices of the great city. "Now you must by this time suppose them about the Exchange," is a direction at the end of Part I. In the second scene they knock at the door of a brother but are not hospitably received.

[1] *Roxburghe Ballads,* I, 230–33.
[2] *Ibid.,* II, 169–77. The ballad was entered March 29, 1638.

A narrative passage given to Thomas tells how the pair fare no better with two other relatives. The old man vows that they will go back to Norfolk and enjoy their dog. The ballad is sung to a dance tune, "The Spanish Pavan."

Some ballad colloquies picturing men of different social rank as discussing their problems seem to be distinctly popular *débats*. "A merry and pleasant Discourse Betwixt Simple-wit, the Tennant, And *Mr*. Money-love, the Landlord,"[1] a dialogue contrasting the luxury of the upper classes and the straitened life of the poor, has the same interlocutors as "A Song called Landlord and Tennant" given as an afterpiece with the Plowboys' Play at Revesby in 1779.[2] Another ballad, printed in 1686[3] and apparently already traditional, "A Dialogue between the Husband-man and Serving-man," which contrasts the toil of the one class with the ease of the other, has been recorded as a song drama among the modern folk,[4] and furnishes the final scene of some mummers' plays.[5]

A sophisticated development of such ballad debates is found

[1] Rawlinson Collection 566, No. 146. It was printed at the end of the seventeenth century by Thackeray and Whitwood but was doubtless much older, for the refrain—"Oh, then, good Landlord, do not raise my Rent"—was apparently used by Parker in l. 55 of his "New Medley; Or, A Messe of All-together" (*Roxburghe Ballads*, II, 239-45).

[2] See *Folk-Lore Journal*, VII, 338, 354-56.

[3] In *Loyal Garland* (5th ed.), ed. Halliwell, Percy Society, pp. 66-69. C[limsell]'s "A Pleasant new Dialogue; Or, The discourse between the Serving-man and the Husband-man" (*Roxburghe Ballads*, I, 299-305), of the first half of the century, seems to be a sophisticated adaptation, and the broadside "God speed the Plow, and bless the Corn-Mow" (*ibid.*, VI, 520-25) is a half-narrative form of the traditional text. In "The Contention, between a Countryman & a Citizen, For a beauteous London Lass" (Pepys Collection, III, 255), beginning "There is a Lass of London City," the plowman, who is scoffed at by his rival, is presented as the successful wooer. Though this dialogue ballad was printed by Brooksby late in the seventeenth century and was sung to "O Mother Roger," a tune popular at the time, it may have been entered September 18, 1579, as "a pretye disputacon betwene a citizen and a cuntreman." At least the clown's contrasting his "Felt and Frieze" and "Leather breeches" with the Citizen's "Cloth & Beaver" suggests Greene's *Quip* and its source.

[4] See Dixon, *Ancient Poems, Ballads, and Songs*, Percy Society, pp. 42-46; *Jour. Brit. Arch. Assn.*, XLII, 320-21; Broadwood and Maitland, *English County Songs*, pp. 144-45; Sharp and Marson, *Folk Songs from Somerset*, No. 71; Williams, *Folk-Songs of the Upper Thames*, pp. 112-15; etc.

[5] See *Folk-Lore Record*, III, Part I, 91-102, and *Notes and Queries for Somerset and Dorset*, IX, 9-19.

in a considerable number of pieces sung in London civic feasts, especially in the second half of the seventeenth century, with interlocutors representing different social classes or various races united in support of the monarchy.[1] Such a dialogue with a "chorus" was sung before Monk at Drapers' Hall on March 28, 1660, "A Dialogue Betwixt Tom and Dick. The former a Country-man, The other a Citizen."[2] Another is "The new Medley of the Country man, Citizen, and Soldier," printed in *Merry Drollery* in 1661. It was doubtless written by Jordan for a feast, since a form with few variations from that in *Merry Drollery* was used in a mayor's feast of 1671 and printed with Jordan's *London's Resurrection to Joy and Triumph*. While much of the material, like the agreement of all three to support the Crown, marks it as an occasional piece, the ballad suggests the stage jig strongly enough to justify its inclusion as Text 18. Jordan was the great exploiter of ballad drama for civic feasts, as D'Urfey was for the stage later. Another dramatic droll used at the feast of 1671 was written by Jordan—"A Countryman, A Citizen, and Sedition, An old Instrument of Oliver's Faction,"[3] with a conventional portrayal of the clown Tom Hoyden including his whipping of Sedition as the Countryman whips the Citizen in "The new Medley." Jordan's "Musical interlude presented by three persons; Crab, a west-countryman; Swab, a seaman: and Self a Citizen,"[4] performed at the Lord Mayor's

---

[1] A great number of the songs for feasts, however, were not dialogues but so-called medleys, a succession of speeches sung to different tunes. An example is "A Short Representation," with final chorus, said to have been sung for Monk on April 11, 1660, in which an Englishman, a Welshman, and a Scot take part (Fairholt, *Civic Garland*, Percy Society, pp. 24–30). For a medley of 1689 see Brit. Mus. C 20. f. 2, No. 180, and *Musical Miscellany*, III (1730), 36–41. For various examples of unrecorded date, see *Merry Drollery*, ed. Ebsworth, pp. 127–30, 138–40 (also in *Roxburghe Ballads*, VI, 489–92), 333–37; *Rump*, I, 252–53, 323–26; *A Choice Coll. of 180 Loyal Songs* (1685), pp. 300–301 (also in *Pills*, II, 152–56)—with the fifth strain headed "Jigg." Several medleys of 1660 have not been reprinted. For the speeches and songs of that year, see *Roxburghe Ballads*, VII, 656–84, and IX, ix*–xvi*; Crawford Collection, Nos. 806–18; Hazlitt's *Manual* under "Speech"; etc. For records of songs sung at lord mayors' feasts, see Fairholt, *Lord Mayors' Pageants*, Part I, *passim*, and Withington, *English Pageantry*, Vol. II, *passim*. For an early example of political songs in plays, see the dialogue in Davenant's *Playhouse to be Let*, Act III, between two soldiers and two seamen, followed by a jig danced by the four singers.

[2] See Brit. Mus. C 20. f. 2, No. 38; *Roxburghe Ballads*, VII, 672–74; etc.

[3] See Fairholt, *Lord Mayors' Pageants*, II, 127–36.

[4] *Ibid.*, pp. 169–76, in the reprint of *The Triumphs of London*.

feast in 1678, includes a dance of the clown to song and an allusion to the picking of his pockets by rogues—both reminiscent of "The Cheaters Cheated." In the changes of tune and the use of a type of clown with dialect for all three of these pieces, Jordan has continued features of his art shown in "The Cheaters Cheated," but the political element does not overshadow the comic in his farce jig as it does in the simpler ballad pieces.

A majority of the dialogue ballads deal with the love motive, whether in romantic, comic, or bawdy vein. It has already been pointed out that the first occurrence of the word jig on the Stationers' Register is in an entry for January 5, 1591, when William Wright paid sixpence for permission to print "*A merrye and plesant newe ballad.* Intituled *alas the poore Tynker.*/ and *a newe Northerne Jigge.*" Apparently two ballads were intended for printing on one broadside, a proceeding not unusual in the period. Again on December 10, 1638, a ballad called "A new Northerne Jigg" was licensed, this time to Thomas Lambert. In spite of its lack of distinctiveness, the title would hardly have been used on the Register for two different ballads except by oversight. This colorless title was probably firmly associated with the popular old ballad which was printed, seemingly without entry, by the assigns of Thomas Symcocke (1618–29)[1] as "A new Northeren Iigge, called, Daintie come thou to me," and is here reprinted as Text 2. The ballad is not too long for one of the two columns in an ordinary broadside. No speakers' names are indicated, and the song may be simply a lover's address to his lady, but I judge that the stanzas were sung by the two alternately, both probably singing the refrain.[2] The second title, "Daintie come thou to me," taken from the last line of the refrain, is modeled on the invitation song, whose long-continued popularity has already been shown (p. 20). What is evidently a moralization of "A New Northern Jig" is found in a ballad beginning "Jesu, my loving spouse," which has a refrain "Jesu, come thou to me" and is sung to the tune "Dainty, come thou

---

[1] See McKerrow, *Dictionary of Printers and Booksellers*, pp. 261–62.

[2] According to Collier, who included the jig in *Twenty-five Old Ballads* (pp. 51–54), the woman sings stanzas ten and eleven and joins in the final chorus. Chappell in printing it in *Roxburghe Ballads*, I, 628–31, makes no attempt to assign the speeches.

to me."[1] The words "Dainty, come thou to me" are quoted in *Two Maids of More-clacke* (C 4) and twice in Brome's *New Exchange* (II, i; III, ii). Miles uses the tune in *The Famous Historie of Fryer Bacon* for one of the songs that he sings as he watches for the brazen head to speak, and it was popular with the ballad writers.[2] That it was considered suited for a very vigorous type of dancing is to be gathered from Taylor's reference in *A Navy of Land Ships* to "a Morrisca or Trenchmore of forty miles long, to the Tune of *Dusty my deare, Dirty come thou to me, Dun out of the mire,* or *I wayle in woe and plunge in paine.*[3] The tune of "A New Northern Jig" is clearly parodied in the second one named.

The farewell, which calls forth the passionate vows of love in "A New Northern Jig," was a favorite motive in courtly and popular song, especially during the sixteenth century, with some constantly recurring phrases like "needs be gone." In the "caterwauling" of *Twelfth Night* (II, iii) Sir Toby and the clown sing in dialogue parts of a song beginning "Farewell, dear heart, since I must needs be gone," which occurs as a pastoral in Jones's *First Booke of Songes & Ayres* (1600).[4] Among the snatches of old songs which Merrythought sings in *The Knight of the Burning Pestle* are the last two lines of this song (II, viii) and parts of other songs of the type known only from the frag-

---

[1] See *Shirburn Ballads*, No. XVIII, and Rollins, *Old English Ballads*, pp. 198–202. Rollins identifies this with the ballad licensed in 1568-9 (*Transcript*, I, 380) as "A tru invocation of God in the name of Christe Jesus." I see no basis for the identification, but if it could be made, it would establish an early date for "A New Northern Jig" or some forerunner. A song published in *Merry Drollery* (1661), opening "Come hither, my own sweet duck," seems to parody loosely a few phrases from the jig (see *Choyce Drollery*, ed. Ebsworth, pp. 247–53, 367).

[2] See, for example, *Roxburghe Ballads*, II, 465, VI, 682, and VII, 582; *Shirburn Ballads*, No. LXXIII; Rollins, *Old English Ballads*, pp. 71, 88; Rollins, *Pepysian Garland*, p. 78 n. Chappell, *Popular Music*, II, 517, gives evidence for the identity of the tune with that of "Whittington." Bass viol and recorder parts for "A northern Jigge" are found in Cambridge University MS Dd. V. 20, fol. 8, and Dd. V. 21, fol. 7.

[3] Folio of 1630, Sig. I*v*.

[4] No. xii, "Corydon's Farewell to Phillis" (Fellowes, *English Madrigal Verse*, p. 494). It is found also in *The Golden Garland of Princely Delights* (Percy's *Reliques*, Bk. II, No. x). See also *Mucedorus*, III, i, for the clown's song ending "shepheard, begon; shepheard, begon; begon, begon," etc., and the answer of Mucedorus, "And must I goe, and must I needs depart?" For similar phrasing in the madrigals, see Fellowes, pp. 13, 122, 410, 506.

ments he gives.[1] Two English tunes current on the Continent are called "Farewell" and "Warumb willtu wegziehen," the latter being the title of a version of the "Rowland" tune.[2] A song of four stanzas with a woman's parting address to a faithless lover, "And wilt thow be gone, my Deare?" is included among the Shirburn Ballads (No. XIX), though it has a kinship to the madrigals. In *The Tide Tarrieth no Man* (1576) Wapull apparently burlesques the formulas of such songs when the Vice answers the Courtier's "cursed Corage adue" with the words (Sig. E):

> And in fayth will you needes begon,
> . . . .
> Farewell frost, will you needes be gone,
> Adue since that you will needes away.

There are a number of other early passages that seem to be burlesques of the vogue, especially by comic actors.[3]

One parting song which may have been a stage jig achieved great popularity at the end of the sixteenth century. It was licensed to Richard Jones on August 6, 1584, as "A Ballat of. *O swete Olyuer Leaue me not behind the*[e]." Just two weeks later "the answeare of 'O sweete Olyuer' " was entered to Henry Carr. On August 1, 1586, when Edward White received at one time permission to print thirty-six ballads, evidently not all of them new, " 'O sweete Olyuer' altered to ye scriptures" was one of the

---

[1] In I, iv, "But yet, or ere you part (oh, cruel!)/ Kiss me, kiss me, sweeting, mine own dear jewel!" and "Heigh-ho, farewell, Nan." Balurdo in *Antonio's Revenge*, III, iv, takes his leave with a stanza beginning "Farewell, adieu: Saith thy loue true."

[2] See Bolte, *Singspiele*, pp. 4, 168. An air with the title "Then wilt thou goe and leaue me her" is preserved in an early seventeenth century manuscript of the Advocates Library of Edinburgh (Dauney, *Ancient Scotish Melodies*, p. 9). "A northerne songe of 'Ile awaie' " was entered August 15, 1586. For a song by Cooper, a musician of Henry VIII's time, called "Farewell my Joy and my swete hart," see Flügel, *Neuenglisches Lesebuch*, p. 136.

[3] See *Wealth and Health*, l. 429 ("Is he gone, farewel") and l. 779 ("Is he gon"); *Misogonus*, I, iii, near the end; and *Mother Bombie*, II, iii, at the end. For the stock expression "Farewell, frost" in several of these passages, see *Works of Nashe*, ed. McKerrow, I, 360; IV, 203. Several references to "Farewell, gentle Jeffrey" suggest either an old comic song or a burlesque of a parting song (*Mankind*, ed. Brandl in *Quellen*, ll. 149–52; *Bugbears*, I, i, 69–70; Heywood's *Proverbs and Epigrams*, Spenser Society, p. 29). See *Ancient Ballads and Broadsides*, Philobiblon Society, pp. 330–31, for a ballad printed by Griffith in 1569 which begins, "Adewe, sweete harte, adewe!/ Syth we must parte!" but takes on a mocking tone after the first stanza.

titles. The fullest quotation from the song that remains is given in *As You Like It*, III, iii. On leaving Sir Oliver Martext, Touchstone sings,

> Farewell, good Master Oliver; not,—
> > O sweet Oliver,
> > O brave Oliver,
> Leave me not behind thee:
> but,—
> > Wind away,
> > Begone, I say,
> I will not to wedding with thee.

The three lines beginning "O sweet Oliver" are clearly the opening of the original song. The other three probably represent Oliver's reply, but the difference in tone may mean that they come from the "answeare of 'O sweete Olyuer' " or from a related song in a burlesque or comic vein. They suggest that the song was a true dialogue, not a mere plea. The popularity of the original ballad can be judged from these entries and from the many allusions to it. In Harleian MS 7578 there is a medley, probably of the sixteenth century, with the lines—

> then came peres of pelton/Jenken and daway
> Sade olywer/abyde abyde/and I vil bere/yow company.[1]

Breton opens the ninth letter in his *Poste with a Packet of Mad Letters*, Part II, with "O Braue *Oliver*, leaue me not behind you." The epithet "sweet" is frequently used with Oliver,[2] and even where the reference is clearly to Charlemagne's peer, the old song is probably responsible for the adjective. The tune "Soet Olivier" is included in a collection of music made by Thysius at Leyden early in the seventeenth century, along with the Rowland tune and a number of other English dance and ballad airs,[3] and Land has pointed out its identity with "The Hunt is

[1] Herrig's *Archiv*, CVII, 60.

[2] See *Works of Nashe*, ed. McKerrow, III, 225 ("if you be *boni socij* and sweete Oliuers"); Dekker, *Honest Whore*, Part I, II, i ("this sweet Oliver will eat mutton till he be ready to burst"); Jonson, *Every Man in his Humour*, III, vii, near end ("Sweet OLIVER, would I could doe thee any good" and "Doe not stinke, sweet OLIVER, you shall not goe"); Jonson, "Execration upon Vulcan," in *Underwoods* ("All the madde *Rolands*, and sweet *Oliveer's*"). "O brave Oliver" was frequently used in ballad satires on Cromwell (see the ballads cited by Rollins, *Cavalier and Puritan*, p. 221).

[3] See Bolte, *Singspiele*, p. 4.

up."[1] A number of circumstances taken together lead me to believe that "O sweet Oliver" was a jig, which English actors carried abroad. The allusions to the piece at home indicate an interest in it beyond that in the ordinary ballad, and the fact that so old and popular a tune as "The Hunt is up" was known in the Low Countries not under its own name but under the name "Soet Olivier" implies an especial importance for the ballad abroad. Moreover, "O sweet Oliver" was licensed and evidently had a vogue not long before Kemp's visit to the Netherlands with Leicester's expedition. Its possible connection with one of the Rowland jigs is argued elsewhere (p. 224).

The treatment of the farewell in these parting dialogues follows various lines,[2] but the mass of them in the seventeenth century picture with the frankest expression of emotion the farewell of the soldier or sailor who is forced to leave. Most of them are in the spirit of popular song, and perhaps few reached the stage. On December 14, 1624, "Margarett my sweetest" was licensed along with a hundred and twenty-seven other ballads, many of them old. These are the opening words of a broadside in the Pepys Collection bearing the title "The Souldiers Farewel to his love" (Text 3). With some slight variation in phrasing, the same dialogue appears in the Percy Folio Manuscript under the simple title "A Iigge."[3] The ballad is strongly

[1] See *Tijdschrift v. noordnederl. Muziekgesch.*, I, 222. He also calls attention to Starter's variant of the tune under the title "Een ronden-dans om de Bruydt te bedde te dansen." See *Athenaeum*, June 4, 1881, for Reginald Poole's comment on the relation of "Sweet Oliver" and "The Hunt is up" to the effect that the Dutch tune is "a dance tune, a branle," which "has only lost the sprightliness of the English by a change into 'common' time." For the English tune, see Chappell, *Popular Music*, I, 60–62, where attention is called to the fact that in *The Complaint of Scotland* the tune is mentioned for dancing, "for which, from its lively character, it seems peculiarly suited."

[2] Martin Parker (*Roxburghe Ballads*, II, 316–22) tried his hand with the theme in "A Paire of Turtle Doves; Or, A dainty new Scotch Dialogue between a Yong-man and his Mistresse, both correspondent in affection," in which it is the lady who must leave. As in "A New Northern Jig," the lovers protest their constancy in extravagant terms and vow to remain faithful until various impossibilities come to pass. In "A Conscionable Couple" (*ibid.*, III, 560–63), entered on the Register March 29, 1656, the lover is forced to leave his native land for religion's sake, and the maid resolves to go with him. The dialogue printed in *Merry Drollery* (1661), beginning "My Mistris, whom in heart I loved long," represents a man as testing a seemingly indifferent mistress with the pretense that he is leaving for a journey full of danger (see edition of 1691, ed. Ebsworth, pp. 113–15).

[3] Hales and Furnivall in their edition of the manuscript quote (II, 334 n.) a note by Percy on the Pepys version and on the relation of the song to "The Nutbrown Maid."

influenced by the theme of "The Nutbrown Maid." A soldier, supposedly leaving for the wars, subjects his sweetheart to a test like that of the Nutbrown Maid, with a happy outcome.

An example of this type of song which is certainly Elizabethan—since a feminine pronoun is used in alluding to the sovereign—is found in *Shirburn Ballads* (No. LVIII) with much of the conventional phraseology. It opens with a soldier's "My deare, adewe! my sweet loue, farewell." The woman pleads,

> Wilt thow forsake me? and wilt thow leaue mee,
> my sweet loue, and be gone?

But the lover "must needs be gone" to fight in his country's cause. The ballad shows a courtly touch and was set to music by Orlando Gibbons. The title is missing, but as sonnet was an old literary term for ballad, this may be the "Sonnet betwene a Souldiour and his love," entered on the Register August 20, 1590. A ballad called "The Souldier and his Loue" was licensed July 17, 1640. We may have here a re-entry of the old ballad, but in view of the date, it is more likely that the piece is "The Discourse betweene A Souldier and his Loue"[1] found in the Pepys Collection (I, 296), which was printed for "F. Coules." The soldier of this ballad bids his Peg adieu, but she has no mind to be left. He tells her of the dangers and difficulties to be met, ending with the warning refrain,

> And doe not kilt thy Coat,
> to goe along with me.

But Peg, in the manner of the Nutbrown Maid and the Margaret of the jig, is willing to endure whatever befalls, and so will "kilt" her coat and go along with her lover.[2] In a somewhat similar Restoration ballad, with sprightly refrains, the invitation of popular song is stressed rather than the parting. This is "The Loyal Soldiers Courtship; or Constant Peggy's Kind

---

[1] See *Bagford Ballads*, II, 546–47, for a dialogue printed by Blare in 1689, called "A Dialogue between a Souldier and his Love, at his taking his leave," beginning "Dearest Love, I now must leave thee."

[2] A ballad "Of the soldier and Peggy" was licensed March 13, 1656, and "A new ballad of the soldier & Peggy," March 1, 1675. But see *Roxburghe Ballads*, II, 475–79, for a narrative ballad with a different treatment called "A new Ballad of the Souldier and Peggy."

Answer" in the Pepys Collection (IV, 207), beginning "Upon the Banks of Ireland,/ when first we Landed there." It pictures an English soldier as wooing an Irish lass to go with him back to his native land. The lover overcomes her fear of her parents' frowns and of his own inconstancy—a frequent note—and she consents to share all the hardships of his soldier's life.

An early example of the ballad with the sailor's farewell as its theme is "The Seamans leave taken of his sweetest *Margerie*," probably printed not long after 1626.[1] "Sweet *Margery* I am prest to the Sea," the Seaman tells her, and she answers, "But wilt thou be gone my Hony sweet." He protests that he "must needs be gone," and vows not unlike those of "A New Northern Jig" follow. Specimens in the Pepys Collection are "The Constant Seaman And his Faithful Love" (IV, 189), opening "Farewel my dearest Dear/ for needs I must away"; "The two Lymas Lovers, Thomas and Betty" (IV, 166); and "The Marriners Delight" (IV, 165, 171), opening "Farewel my Dearest Dear,/ for thee and I must part." "The Saylor's Departure from his dearest Love" in the *Roxburghe Ballads* (VII, 534–36), to be sung to the tune "Adieu, my pretty one," opens "Now I am bound to the Seas, and from my love must part." It was licensed March 26, 1656. Three interlocutors appear in the dialogue called "The Seaman's Adieu to his Dear," in which a sailor who has been pressed into service comes to bid his sweetheart farewell. She pleads in vain with the captain, even offering him money for her lover's release.[2] There are a number of comple-

---

[1] In the Collection of the Manchester Free Reference Library, I, 17, printed by J. H. for Francis Coules in the Old Bailey. A copy in the Pepys Collection (IV, 158) was printed for Wright, Clarke, Thackeray, and Passenger, about 1675. One stanza of the ballad is incorporated in a song included in Ramsay's *Tea-Table Miscellany* (I, 180):

> "If I had wisht before I had kist
> that love had bin so deare to win,
> My heart I would, have clos'd in gold.
> and pin'd it with a Silver pin."

Lines like these or "I have seven Ships upon the Sea"—which seems out of keeping with the general situation—suggest the traditional ballad.

[2] *Roxburghe Ballads*, VII, 523–26. Charon is the third interlocutor in a curious ballad called "The True Lover's Joy; Or, A Dialogue between a Seaman and his Love" (*ibid.*, VII, 521–22). The maid appeals to Charon to take her with him, since her lover is indifferent and is leaving, but the lover recalls her and protests his affection. For dialogues in courtly song of Charon and a man or woman desiring to join a departed lover, forsake a cold mistress, etc., and for Italian and French forerunners, see Gérold,

mentary dialogues of a conventional sort depicting the girl as welcoming a sailor home.[1]

The dialogues of parting lovers seem to have had a strong appeal both for the London public and for the English folk up to modern times. They are to be found in white-letter ballads around 1700,[2] in the songbooks sold by chapmen a century later,[3] and to a considerable extent in the traditional songs of the modern folk.[4] A very interesting form of one traditional song, sung as a dialogue by a Scotch woman and her husband who immigrated to America, carries us back to "The Soldier's

---

L'Art du chant en France au XVIIe siècle, pp. 54–56; *Modern Philology*, VII, 45–46; Herrick, *Works*, ed. Pollard, II, 58–59, 270–72, 282–83; *Select Musicall Ayres, and Dialogues* (1652), Part II, pp. 14, 18; Fletcher, *Mad Lover*, IV, i; *Roxburghe Ballads*, VI, 24–25; etc. Dialogues with Charon were popular in other forms.

[1] For a particularly good example of this type, see *Roxburghe Ballads*, II, 469–75, "A pleasant new Song betwixt the Saylor and his Love," with the refrain "kisse and bid me welcome home." The vows of constancy follow the usual formulas. A ballad with the refrain of this song as title was licensed on December 14, 1624, and one with the title, "A pleasant song betweene a Saylor & his love," on March 1, 1675. See Pepys Collection, IV, 157, for "A dainty new Ditty of a Saylor and his Love" with the first line "My only love, thour't welcome to the shore," in which the sailor pretends to prefer the sea to the harbor of his sweetheart's arms, but is only putting her to the conventional test. A ballad was licensed under this title July 18, 1637, and with the "dainty" omitted, March 26, 1656. See also "The Seamans Return to his Sweetheart; or The Constant Lovers happy Agreement" (Pepys Collection, IV, 175) and "A new Dialogue Call'd Billy, the Midship-man's Welcome home" in *The Midship-Man's Garland* about 1700 (*Bagford Ballads*, I, 108, 112–14).

[2] See Pepys Collection, V, 363, "The Dover Lovers: or, A pleasant Dialogue," etc. (opening "Fare you well, adieu my Dear"); V, 364, "The Undaunted Marriner; or, The Stout Seaman's Valliant Resolution, in a Dialogue," etc. (opening "Farewel my Dearest *Nancy*"); and *Roxburghe Ballads*, VII, 552, "The Unkind Parents; Or, The Languishing Lamentation of Two Loyal Lovers" (beginning "Now fare thou well, my Dearest Dear").

[3] See *The Linnet* for "Jemmy, the Sailor's Adieu," beginning "Adieu my dearest Nancy, once more I must away"; and Batchelar's *Pleasing Songster* for "William and Nancys parting," beginning "Farewel my dearest Nancy,/Now i must go to sea," full of the conventional phrases found in similar seventeenth century ballads. Both these songbooks are in Douce Popular Songs, Bodleian PP. 163. See *Bagford Ballads*, I, 111–12, for two soldier's parting songs belonging to the period of the American Revolution.

[4] See, for example, Sharp, *One Hundred English Folksongs*, No. 30, for a sailor's farewell to his "dearest Nancy," who wishes to follow him; No. 55, "The True Lover's Farewell," a lament in dialogue form with the lovers' vows to remain constant till day turns to night, rivers run dry, and rocks melt with the sun; and No. 56, "High Germany," in which the lover urges the girl to go to the wars. See *ibid.*, pp. xxviii–xxix, xxxiii, for Sharp's notice of other broadside and traditional versions of these songs.

Farewell to his Love" and to "The Nutbrown Maid." This song, beginning "When ye gang awa, Jamie," represents a lover as about to cross the sea to Germany. Jeanie begs to go with him, but he tells her, falsely, that he already has a wife and children. Convinced of her devotion, he ends by offering himself and all his bowers in true ballad fashion.[1]

A dialogue of lovers that stands somewhat in a class to itself is "A Country new Iigge betweene *Simon* and *Susan*, to be sung in merry pastime by Bachelors and Maydes," the only one of the simpler ballad jigs whose purpose is indicated. The ballad is scarcely a typical broadside, for four characters take part entering at different times, but there is no complication of plot. Simon and Susan express their love and in successive scenes receive the consent of her mother and of her father to their marriage. The phraseology at least was probably influenced by older song.[2] Two broadside versions of the jig, differing only

[1] A copy of the dialogue was furnished to me by Professor A. H. Tolman, who had also heard of a performance of it by two singers in a public concert in Wisconsin some thirty years ago. The ballad was published by Such about the middle of the nineteenth century (see the Crampton Collection, IV, 32, in the British Museum). See Child, *English and Scottish Popular Ballads*, IV, 299–300, for another version of the dialogue.

[2] "Simon and Susan" and the second part of "This Maide would giue tenne Shillings for a Kisse" (Rollins, *Pepysian Garland*, pp. 78–83) call for the tune "I can, nor will no longer lye alone," a title taken from the ballad "A Maiden's Lamentation for a Bedfellow. Or, I can, nor will no longer lye alone. As it hath been often sung at the Court. To the tune of *I will give thee kisses, one, two, or three*." The tune had evidently belonged to some earlier ballad, which probably had a refrain "I will give thee kisses, one, two, or three," and this ballad influenced both "Simon and Susan" and "This Maide would giue tenne Shillings for a Kisse." In the second part of the latter, the lover promises the maid who longs for a kiss,

> "Nay thou shalt haue a hundred one two or three,
> More sweeter then the hunny that comes from the Bee,"

and in the next stanza,

> Nay thou shalt haue a hundred one two or three,
> More sweter then the blossomes from the Tree."

See also the end of the sixth and the last stanza in this part. In "Simon and Susan" the first stanza ends,

> "That I may giue you kisses,
>   one, two, or three,
> More sweeter then the hunny,
>   that comes from the Bee."

The refrain throughout is a variation on the last two lines here or on the ending of the next stanza,

> "And fresher then the Blossomes,
>   that bloomes vpon the Tree."

in slight details, are known—one printed for Henry Gosson, and the other by W. I., probably one of the two printers named William Jones, whose activities extend from 1589 to 1618 and from 1601 to 1626 respectively. The second is chosen for reprinting as Text 4 because on the ground of spelling I judge that it is the earlier.

There are many sentimental wooing ballads with two interlocutors. Probably they were composed chiefly for the broadside trade, though as a rule they would be no more ineffectual as song drama than "A New Northern Jig." A broadside, for example, entered March 12, 1656, "Come turn to mee, thou pretty little one; and I will turn to thee,"[1] which derives its title from the first form of the refrain, has in spite of many lofty poetic figures, a lyric quality along with simple terms of endearment suggestive of old songs. Many of these dialogues are little more than lovers' pleas.[2] The wooer's offer of his wealth with phrases reminiscent of folk song, as in "house and land" and "at thy command," are found in "A Serious Discourse between two Lovers," beginning "My pretty little Rogue, do but come hither," written by John Wade, and in "The West-Country Wooing; Or, The Merry-conceited Couple," beginning "My Joy and

---

The earlier song which furnished the tune for "A Maiden's Lamentation" and influenced the other two ballads mentioned was perhaps older than "The Carman's Whistle," which ends "ile give thee kisses three." See p. 227 for a date about 1590 for the manuscript containing "The Carman's Whistle."

[1] *Roxburghe Ballads*, VI, 276–78.

[2] See *Roxburghe Ballads*, III, 551–53, "The Constant Country-Man; Or, A Loving Dialogue between honest Thomas and his True-Love Nancy" ("Pritty Nancy, my love"); IV, 344–46, Bowne's "The Doubting Virgin, And the Constant Young Man" ("Oh, my dearest, do not slight me"); IV, 375–78, Bowne's "Doubtful Robin; Or, Constant Nanny" ("Dearest, *Nanny* prithee tell me"); VI, 256–58, Blunden's "The Faithful Lovers of the West" ("Why should I thus complain on thee?"); VI, 296–98, "The Passionate Lover; Or, The Damsel's Grief Crown'd with Comforts" ("Sighs and groans, and melancholly moans"); VII, 289–91, "The Loving Lad and Coy Lass" ("All haile, thou bright and bonny Lass! my joy and onely sweeting"). See also Pepys Collection, III, 26, "True Love Indeed. Being the Courtship of *William* —— of *Portsmouth*, to his Sweet-Heart *Betty*" ("Come hither, my dear Betty, and sit thou down by me"); III, 64, "The true Lovers Good-morrow" ("In the month of February"), a Valentine wooing; III, 214, "The true Lovers Conquest, or, The scornful maiden overcome by true Love and Loyalty" ("Fair Nymph! those sparkling eyes of thine"); IV, 57, "The true Lovers Happiness, Or, Nothing Venture, nothing have" ("Oh my dearest come away"), entered July 1, 1678. Wooing dialogues with a *chanson d'aventure* opening are especially numerous.

only Dear, come sit down by me," a dialogue with a few narrative phrases, which Ebsworth conjectures is Wade's.[1]

Many of the wooing dialogues develop a point of interest or of tension through some such feature as the scorn of the girl or the wantonness of the wooer, and so pass the line into the classes of comic or vulgar ballads to be treated next. This tendency is illustrated in a German song "Schön Anna, Hertzallerliebste mein." Bolte has given space to this dialogue in his *Singspiele* (pp. 22–24) on the ground that, though it is not properly dramatic nor definitely identified with the stage, it shows the influence of the song dramas of the English comedians. "Schön Anna" has survived on a broadside along with two other songs which from other sources can be dated at least as early as 1615 and 1614. It is a wooing dialogue of ten stanzas, quite as dramatic as the simple English jigs, and, with its short speeches and quick thrust, much in the manner of some of the jigs. The tone of the piece is sentimental except for the sharp and jeering replies of the girl. She pretends at first to believe that the youth is mocking her, and then accuses him of betraying other maidens. He woos ardently, and she suddenly capitulates with the promise that only death shall part them. This song may easily be a German version of an English jig.[2]

The bent of the known stage jigs was so persistently toward the farcical and the droll that we may be sure the jig dealt with love less often romantically than in burlesque or vulgar fashion. The pert and scornful maiden and the clownish or the wanton wooer are stock figures in popular ballads, many of which are pure dialogues well suited for performance as jigs. Among the English ballads giving a humorous turn to the wooing dialogue is included "A mery new Iigge. Or, the pleasant wooing betwixt *Kit* and *Pegge*," printed as Text 5, in which the rustic lover woos Peg and is flouted by her. The plea for a kiss, popular in early wooing song,[3] and the use of the tune "Strawberry leaves make

---

[1] *Roxburghe Ballads*, VII, 254–55, 252–53. For folk song, see p. 215 below.

[2] See *Handful of Pleasant Delights*, ed. Rollins, pp. 39–42, 100–101, for "A proper Sonet, Intituled, Maid, wil you marrie. To the Blacke Almaine," an early Elizabethan dialogue to a dance tune, in which the lover scorns and mocks the maid as fickle because she has chosen another.

[3] See pp. 20–21 above.

maidens fair,"[1] suggest the influence of early popular song. The name of the author, Valentine Hamdultun (Hamilton?), is otherwise unknown to me. Probably a lost jig entered January 14, 1592, to John Charlewood as "a merrie newe Jigge betwene Jenkin the Collier and Nansie" belonged to the same general class. There is a possibility, however, that Jenkin and the collier were two different characters[2] and the piece a farce jig.

"Kit and Pegge" has so many conventional features that to find it called a jig opens up a wide range of possibilities. Similar motives were developed in a large number of ballad dialogues throughout the seventeenth century, with varying emphasis and varying degrees of coarseness and burlesque. Unlike the jig, however, these ballads pretty consistently picture the scornful lady as suffering a sudden change of heart rather than lose the chance of a husband. With "Kit and Pegge" may be compared "A mad kinde of wooing, Or, a Dialogue betweene *Will* the simple, and *Nan* the subtill," beginning "Sweet *Nancie* I doe loue thee deare."[3] Both were printed for Gosson (1603-41), so that they are relatively early. In "A mad kinde of wooing" Will resents with vigor Nan's mockery of him as a clown, and she accepts him after he has answered promptly and boldly her queries as to whether he can use a wife rightly and maintain her well. The occurrence of similar phrasing in mummers' plays perhaps indicates the currency of the piece as song drama.[4] With a stanza given to the speakers in turn, the dialogue lacks the swift give-and-take of "Kit and Pegge" with its rapid alternation of speakers, but the tune used is that of "the new dance at the Red Bull Play-house."[5] "The Louers Guilt, Or a Fairing for

---

[1] See Sharp, *One Hundred English Folksongs*, pp. xxxi, 100-101, for the use of this refrain in a very popular traditional song akin to the early pastoral dialogue "Hey, troly loly lo, maid, whither go you" (see p. 19 above).

[2] The collier on the Elizabethan stage was a fairly definite figure to whom the name Grim was recognized as appropriate. See *Like Will to Like, Damon and Pithias*, and *Grim the Collier*. Jenkin might have been used for the collier conceived in a somewhat new rôle, but names had a good deal of significance in the ballad field, and Jenkin suggests a sporting type of citizen or prentice, as Nancy suggests the village maid.

[3] Pepys Collection, I, 276. The exemplar in *Roxburghe Ballads*, II, 121-26, was printed by the assigns of Symcocke, 1618-29.

[4] See *Modern Philology*, XXI, 235 ff.

[5] "Red Bull" is the name of a tune in Playford's *Dancing Master* (1698), and the same air occurs in *Apollo's Banquet* as "The Damsell's Dance" (Chappell, *Popular Music*, I, 294).

Maides: Being a Dialogue betweene *Edmund* and *Priscilly*,"[1]
which opens "My Loue she is faire,/ surpassing compare," was
printed for John Trundle (1603–26). Priscilly ridicules her lover's appearance and his "rusticall wordes" but is brought to
accept him in the end. A final stanza is added by "Author."
In "A most pleasant Dialogue: Or A merry greeting betweene
two louers,"[2] beginning "Good morrow faire Nansie, whither
so fast," the abusive female is conventionally but skilfully presented, the lovers coming to an understanding in the usual
fashion. This ballad, entered May 24, 1632, was printed for
H[enry] G[osson] and signed "C. R." Part I of "A delicate new
Song, Entituled, Sweetheart, I loue thee,"[3] also printed for
H. G., is a dialogue in which a country lover woos a London lass.
But she would have a city swaggerer instead of one whose great
breeches betray the country clown. She scornfully advises him
to seek some country Kate or Nell, and he proceeds on her advice. In the second part she has discovered her mistake
and gives warning to other city dames. There is a probability
that some at least of the clownish wooings printed for the
early stationers close on the great vogue of the stage jig were
primarily for stage use.

The conventions of these ballads were continued in later
dialogues. Except for two quite unnecessary narrative stanzas
at the close, Price's ballad "The two Jeering Lovers: Or, A
pleasant New Dialogue between Dick Down-right of the Country, and pretty witty Nancy of the Citie,"[4] which opens "Come
hither sweet *Nancy*,/and sit down by me," would have delighted the groundlings as a stage piece. In answer to Dick's wooing,
Nancy calls him Sir Lobcock and refuses his offers of such feminine finery as a "Taffety Apron" and a "brave Holland
Smock." She describes in coarse detail his uncouth figure and
unkempt garb, telling him to find some country Joan. When
he is about to take her at her word, she calls him back and
promises to be constant to him all the days of her life. In
another of Price's ballads, "The Maiden's Delight; or, A Dainty New Dialogue," opening "I am a Jovial Batchelor, and free

[1] Pepys Collection, I, 250–51.

[2] *Ibid.*, I, 310–11.   [3] *Ibid.*, I, 262.

[4] See Rollins, *Cavalier and Puritan*, pp. 414–19. Probably this is "The two feering lovers, &c" licensed May 15, 1656.

from care and strife," it is the prodigal gallant whom the girl scorns in favor of the tradesman.[1] The piece is related to a folk wooing dialogue with offers of gifts and to some mummers' plays.[2] The comic feature of "The Faithful Farmer: Or, The Down-right Wooing betwixt Robin and Nancy," beginning "My little, pritty youthful *Nancy*," is the clown's catalogue of his worldly goods, as in

> Love, I do protest and vow,
> I have got a Cart and Plow,
> Seven Pigs, besides a Sow,
> Dearest, can you love me now?[3]

Instead of being contemptuous of him, Nancy fears she is too mean a bride for one with so much to commend him. A somewhat coarser ballad with emphasis on the rustic's possessions is "The Down-Right Wooing Of Country *William* and his pretty *Peggy*," opening "Come, prethy *Peggy*, let's imbrace."[4] Abuse of the wooer as a clown appears again in "The Scornful Maid and the Constant Young-Man"[5] by T. R[obins] and in "The Merry Discourse between Two Lovers: Or the Joyful meeting betwixt *John* and *Betty*," beginning "My dearest come hither and listen to me."[6] A few comic wooing dialogues of the late Restoration period have become traditional songs. "Young Roger of the Vale" represents a plowman's wooing of Bonny Nell, who will be satisfied with nothing less than a farmer's son, until Roger is about to leave to marry "buxom Joan." As a pure dialogue this ballad has been incorporated in a mummers' wooing play, and versions with a few narrative phrases were printed in many song collections and have survived as traditional songs.[7] A similar but more sentimental song is "The Farmer's

---

[1] *Roxburghe Ballads*, VIII, 94–95. The ballad was licensed September 24, 1656.

[2] See *Modern Philology*, XXI, 236–37. For other parallels to this folk dialogue, "The Handsom' Woman," see pp. 188–89 above and p. 215 below.

[3] *Roxburghe Ballads*, IV, 371–75.

[4] *Ibid.*, VII, 262–64.   [5] *Ibid.*, IX, 867–68.

[6] Wood Collection E. 25, No. 77. Licensed March 1, 1675.

[7] See *Modern Philology*, XXI, 266. The title of No. 126 in the Crawford Collection sounds as if the ballad were modeled on "Young Roger." A fragment also of a wooing song in D'Urfey's *Wonders in the Sun* (1706), III, i, beginning "Oh Love, if a God thou wilt be" (reprinted in *Pills*, I, 100–102, and Ramsay's *Tea-Table Miscellany*, II, 16–18), is found in a mummers' play (*Modern Philology*, XXI, 255). This is one of the many old types of dramatic ballad that D'Urfey introduced into his plays around 1700.

Son" of the end of the seventeenth century. It was printed in various forms and has been popular among the folk as a traditional song.[1] The air was also used in ballad opera. The amount of variation in the early printed versions suggests that they were based on traditional forms of the seventeenth century.

In some of the songs already mentioned, the burlesque of the clown is fairly broad. The type of song probably goes back to the Middle Ages. The clown's boasting of his rustic wealth as an inducement to his Mawkin to smile on his suit is found in medieval farce and in the early Scotch "Wowing of Jok and Jynny" with its mixed narrative and dialogue.[2] In Howell's *Arbor of Amitie* (1568) there is a poem in ballad meter, "Iacke showes his qualities and great good will to Ione," in which a clown offers the future inheritance of his father's calf and cow, sow and "viftene Pigges," and "newe wheelbarro," and boasts of his prowess with the flail and in the dance.[3] A still earlier ballad of a similar John and Joan has a long history that is perhaps fairly representative of a number of old songs whose career cannot be so easily traced.

A manuscript said to date from the early part of Henry VIII's reign contains the music for the ballad, accompanied by the words of one stanza:

> Ioan, q^d Iohn, when will this be?
> Tell me, when wilt thow marrie me?
> My cowe and eke my calf, and rents,
> My lands and all my tenements!
> Saie Ioan, said Iohn, what wilt thow doe?
> *I cannot come every daie to woe.*[4]

[1] For printed forms, see Pepys Collection, V, 216 (white-letter, for Blare), "The Conquer'd Lady: Or, The Country Wooing between *Robin*, the rich Farmer's Son, and Madam *Nelly*, a Nobleman's Daughter"; *The Country Farmer's Garland* (Brit. Mus. 11621. b. 60), "The Farmer's Courtship to a beautiful young Lady"; Ramsay, *Tea-Table Miscellany* (1871), II, 172–74, "The Farmer's Son"; *Musical Miscellany*, I (1729), 130–32; *Vocal Miscellany* (1738), I, 76–77; *Merry Companion* (1739), pp. 178–79. For use among the folk, see Dixon, *Ancient Poems, Ballads, and Songs*, Percy Society, pp. 171–73. For some additional versions, for the air, and for the use in ballad opera, see Chappell, *Popular Music*, II, 656–57.

[2] See *Rex Viole* (Zingerle, *Sterzinger Spiele*, No. XI) and Laing, *Early Popular Poetry of Scotland*, ed. Hazlitt, II, 24–27. Compare the ballad in *Deutscher Liederhort*, No. 855.

[3] Ed. Grosart, pp. 89–91.

[4] See *Roxburghe Ballads*, III, 590–92, where Chappell gives most of the details in the history of the song.

The downrightness of the final line, evidently a refrain, caught the popular fancy. The author of *The Arte of English Poesie* (1589) gives an account of an interlude he had written which used this line and the same theme.[1] The refrain was quoted or was adapted in ballads from the end of the sixteenth century.[2] On January 18, 1592, permission was given to print "a newe Ballad of *John wooinge of Jo[a]ne &c.*" This new ballad was probably an adaptation of the old one, and not unlikely an early jig of the country clown. Music for the song survives in a manuscript dating after 1597.[3] Only one stanza has been preserved from the sixteenth century, but this stanza forms the opening of two seventeenth century ballads in dialogue. What is evidently the older ballad, extant in two different broadside editions, has the title "The Country-man's Delight; Or, The Happy Wooing. Being The successful Love of John the Serving-man, in his courting of Joan the Dary-maid."[4] It is sung to a "New play-house tune; *or, Dolly and Molly.*" John's boast that he was free-born harks back, as Chappell says, to a society earlier than that of the first manuscript music. A monologue consisting of the first three stanzas of this ballad and a different fourth stanza was printed in D'Urfey's *Pills* (III, 114–15). According to Chappell, the redaction was the work of D'Urfey, who sang the shortened song before Charles II and included it in his *New Collection of Songs and Poems* in 1683. The same four stanzas form the opening of "The North Country lovers" in the Pepys Collection very different from the ballad that has just been cited. The Pepys broadside is described as a "Pleasant new Song," has a new tune, and is said to have been sung at court. Perhaps

[1] Ed. Arber, pp. 212–13. Perhaps the ballad entered in 1562–3 (*Transcript*, I, 211) as "the Daperest Country man that came to the Couurte to wooy" was similar.

[2] By Petruchio in *Taming of the Shrew*, II, i, 116; in "A Wooing Song of a Yeoman of Kent's Son" published in Ravenscroft's *Melismata* (1611); in "The Ingenious Brag-gadocia" (*Roxburghe Ballads*, IX, 600); and in "The Faithful Farmer," which has just been noticed. For the use of the line in a traditional song, see Hecht, *Songs from Herd's Manuscripts*, p. 103.

[3] Brit. Mus. Add. 36526. The tune here differs from that given in the old manu-script, but the one stanza of the song accompanying it is practically the same.

[4] *Roxburghe Ballads*, III, 593–96, printed from a copy from which the printer's name is missing. Another edition in the Roxburghe Collection (IV, 37) was printed for Brooksby.

D'Urfey simply used the first four stanzas of this ballad. On the other hand, he or some other balladist of the period may have lengthened the short song in a new way to make the second ballad. The piece is printed here (Text 16) as a specimen of the ballad dialogue known to have been sung at court.[1]

The clown's dialect is a comic feature in a number of these songs, as in the one from Howell's *Arbor of Amitie*. It is exaggerated in the broadly burlesque "Merry Wooing of Robin and Joan" (Text 15), which has three singers. Robin talks to his mother about his plan to put on his fine attire and woo Joan Gromball again. She advises him to take a napkin and wipe his nose. Meeting Joan, he boasts of his apparel and possessions, and is mocked as a fool. The ballad was published in *Wit Restored* (1658), and by Conyers as a broadside in the last quarter of the seventeenth century with two additional stanzas in which the girl conventionally changes her mind. Its broad dialect and its inclusion in *Wit and Drollery* (1682) as well as *Wit Restored* suggest presentation before a courtly audience as a bit of drollery.[2] This "Merry Wooing" may, like the "Happy Wooing" of John and Joan, be a reworking of an old song. Its tune, "The Beginning of the World," or "Sellenger's Round," is that of a sixteenth century country dance, and the name Grimball is used for the clown in the broadly burlesque wooing song of *Promos and Cassandra*, Part I, IV, vii. More significant is the evidence for a vogue of the ballad in a slightly different form. A Scottish traditional version given by Herd, which is largely narrative, corresponds to the droll in its first twenty-eight lines except that the clown addresses himself instead of his mother. The conclusion of the piece tells of the clown's retreat, his blubbering at the marriage of Joan, and his mother's hitting him with a dishclout.[3] There is also indication that some ballad of the type was current at the beginning of the seventeenth century. In representing the wooing of Luce by Hum-

[1] Long, *Dictionary of the Isle of Wight Dialect*, pp. 120–21, 124, gives a traditional version of the monologue in five stanzas.

[2] See *Roxburghe Ballads*, VII, 311, for Ebsworth's note on the versions. He records also a late appearance in Dryden's *Miscellany Poems* (1716).

[3] See Hecht, *Songs from Herd's Manuscripts*, pp. 216–18, 323–24. Ebsworth, *loc. cit.*, unjustly calls this a rank plagiarism.

phrey in *The Knight of the Burning Pestle*, Beaumont, who no doubt burlesques popular drama in this feature as in the rest of the play, puts in the clown's mouth a first address to his lady which in droll lilt and language seems to be modeled on the similar address of Robin to Joan:

> Fair Mistress Luce, how do you do? Are you well?
> Give me your hand, and then I pray you tell
> How doth your little sister and your brother;
> And whether you love me or any other.
> —I, ii, 44–47

In the Scottish version, Robin says,

> And how do you do, my little wi Nan,
> My lamb and slibrikin mouse?
> And how does your father and mother do,
> And a' the good fok i' the house?

The corresponding passage in "The Merry Wooing of Robin and Joan" reads:

> Good morrow my honey my sugger-candy,
>   My litle pretty mouse,
> Cha hopes thy vather and mother be well,
>   At home at thine own house.[1]

These passages suggest Beaumont's knowledge of a version of "Robin and Joan" somewhat similar to the traditional version and perhaps a survival of an early burlesque of the clown.

A white-letter broadside in the Roxburghe Collection (III, 499) without printer's name, "A Dialogue Between Jack and his Mother," beginning "Jack met his Mother all alone," resembles "Robin and Joan" in the clown's statement to his mother that he will don his "Roast-meat Cloths" and woo Joan. In reworking the Robin and Joan situation, the balladist selected the conventional features of the comic wooing dialogues —the offer of gifts, the list of the mother's possessions, the clown's declaration that he can marry Doll or Kate, and the change of the girl's mockery to acceptance. "Roben's Cöortèn,"[2] a traditional ballad partly narrative, in which the mother advises

---

[1] For the endearing epithets see pp. 20, 82, above.

[2] See Udal, *Dorsetshire Folk-lore*, pp. 315–16. Less significant is the kindred song in Williams, *Folk-Songs of the Upper Thames*, pp. 171–72.

Robin to put on his best clothes and seek a wife, preserves the opening situation and the burlesque tone of "Robin and Joan." A brother is the adviser in "The West-Country Dialogue: Or, A Pleasant Ditty between *Anniseed-Robin* the Miller, and his Brother *Jack* the Plough-man, concerning *Joan,* poor *Robin's* unkind Lover," with the opening line "Well met, my loving Brother *Jack*."[1] Jack advises Robin to marry Joan, but Robin declares that he has already appeared before her in his best apparel, including his grandfather's hat, has made a congee down to his toes, has offered her his cow and calf, and has told her that he was his father's heir. But she has only shown a disposition to batter his snout and kick him about the floor. Jack insists that he go at it again, and Robin resolves to spend a whole shilling in presents of custards, cakes, and ale. If he doesn't win her with all this, he'll quit her utterly. A John plays the part of adviser to his master in the traditional song "My Man John," which was once used in Yorkshire as a song drama.[2] The adviser figures also in several farce jigs.

There is no reason to suppose that Lane's reference in 1600 to all the balladmongers as making jigs for country clowns applies to the farce jig any more than to the simpler form. The number of the clownish wooing dialogues, their dramatic possibilities, and their comic quality all point to their use as jigs. While the complete ballad dialogues noticed here are chiefly preserved in Restoration broadsides, the type has been shown to go back to a period long before the era of the jig. The burlesque treatment in jigs of this class would commend them to the gallants who insisted upon having jigs served up to them. The interest of the courtly classes in burlesques of the countryman's wooing is traceable in the songbooks during the early part of the century. I have already mentioned Ravenscroft's "A Wooing Song of a Yeoman of Kent's Son." In the same author's *Briefe Discourse* (1614), Hodge Trillindle successfully woos Malkin in a dialogue, both using the broadest dialect (Nos.

---

[1] *Roxburghe Ballads,* VII, 260–61. See Rollins, *Modern Philology,* XIX, 77–79, for a character called Anniseed-water Robin about the middle of the century. One of Playford's dances is "The Irish Lady, or Anniseed-water-Robin."

[2] For the song, see Sharp, *One Hundred English Folksongs,* No. 67. For dramatic use, see Mrs. Gutch, *Printed Folk-Lore Concerning the North Riding of Yorkshire, County Folk-Lore,* II, 258.

xvii–xix); and in No. x of Corkine's *First Book of Airs* (1610), a clown protests to his sweetheart against her forsaking him after he has given her "rings and things and geare" and has bought his "kerzie wedding briche." After the middle of the century the country clown is presented in some of Cox's drolls and in a number of plays. The clown from Taunton Dean was especially famous. Tom Hoyden of Taunton Dean is a character in Brome's *Sparagus Garden*. Jordan's use of such figures has been noticed above.[1]

There was also a goodly amount of sheer vulgarity and pornography in the ballads of the sixteenth and seventeenth centuries. Attacks on the obscenity of the ballad cannot be taken at face value of course; but Chettle, for instance, in his arraignment of the sellers and singers of lewd, unlicensed ballads at the end of the sixteenth century has forestalled a charge of mere puritanism by mentioning four examples, two of which are known—"Mother Watkin's Ale" and "The Carman's Whistle."[2] In view of the emphasis laid on the obscenity of the jig, it seems probable that many of the stage jigs were drawn from dialogue ballads of the sort which Chettle deplores. Presumably it was not the farce jig only which set the moralists of the era by the ears. The worst of the ballads pretty certainly have not survived. If they were printed at all, it was doubtless irregularly. Enough have been preserved, however, in broadsides and songbooks to suggest some of the time-honored veins of bawdry that the simple jig of the early seventeenth century probably utilized. Much of the material of these jigs must have lived on in stage tradition, to emerge in such collections as D'Urfey's *Pills to Purge Melancholy*, made up in no small part of stage stuff.

Of the English songs dealing with intrigue, a relatively un-

[1] See *Roxburghe Ballads*, VIII, 205–6, for "The Taunton-Dean Damosel." See also p. 206 for part of "The Somersetshire Clown," beginning "Go, vind the Vicar of *Taunton-Dean*," which gives the clown's complaint over Joan's desertion of him. For the complete song and the statement that the words are by D'Urfey, see the early music sheet Brit. Mus. H. 1601, No. 166 (also in *Merry Companion* [1739], pp. 269–70). A traditional song, "Richard of Taunton Dean," describing how Richard, dressed in his country best, went to woo the parson's daughter Jean, seems to go back to the eighteenth century (Dixon, *Ancient Poems, Ballads, and Songs*, pp. 201–3, 247–49; Broadwood and Maitland, *English County Songs*, pp. 166–67; etc.). See also pp. 318–19 below.

[2] See *Kindheart's Dream*, ed. Rimbault, pp. 13–20. Attention has already been called to the fact that Chettle twice refers to this balladry as "jigging vanity."

objectionable group consists of folk songs, both in lyric and in ballad form, which seem to be based on a pagan custom of allowing a youth secret access to his mate before marriage.[1] In them the lover pleads for admission and is usually, though not invariably, allowed to enter after the girl has expressed a conventional reluctance. All those mentioned here are dialogues or show a strong influence of dialogue form. Two of them, now lost —"Open the door" and "Go from my window"—were popular in the sixteenth century. A closely related comic dialogue of four stanzas beginning "Arise, arise, my Juggy, my Puggy," in which the girl at last yields to the lover's plea, is one of two songs printed at the end of the 1638 edition of Heywood's *Rape of Lucrece* with the statement to the Gentle Reader that they "were added by the stranger that lately acted Valerius his part." This is probably a stage modification and perhaps illustrates the insertion of jigs into plays to which Shirley refers.[2] Two dialogues with the refrain "Go from my window" have comic and mocking material that suggests other adaptations by comedians. One is an early sixteenth century piece found on a mutilated sheet of Selden MS B 24, fol. 230, in which the wooer is mocked for lack of courage.[3] The other is a widespread song that tells of a wife's assignation, of her husband's unexpected return home, and of the warning which she gives in the form of a lullaby to her child when the lover comes seeking admittance. Many ballads were modeled on these songs. Two seventeenth century broadsides picturing the visit of the lover are dialogues except for a narrative close—"Loves Return, Or, The Maydens Joy," beginning "Arise from thy bed,/ my Turtle and dear," and "John's Earnest Request," beginning "Come open the Door, sweet *Betty*."[4] Of the seventeenth century ballads on this theme, perhaps the most interesting as comic song drama

---

[1] I have dealt with this group in *PMLA*, XXXVI, 565–614. See particularly pp. 571–76, 580–83. In one type, the "hunts-up," the parting motive is used.

[2] See p. 120 above. For a burlesque form, see D'Urfey, *Pills*, IV, 44.

[3] Professor Carleton Brown called my attention to this fragment.

[4] For the first, see Rollins, *Cavalier and Puritan*, pp. 471–76, and for the second, *Roxburghe Ballads*, VI, 202–3. "The Secret Lover; Or, The Jealous Father beguil'd" (*Roxburghe Ballads*, VI, 205–6) has a dialogue core of eight stanzas in which the father enters as a third character.

is "The Repulsive Maid," beginning "Sweet, open the door, and let me come in,/ For to be a Wooer I now begin."[1] The girl's refusal brings a quarrel, with charges and countercharges, and she dismisses the wooer in a final stanza,

> "Walk Knave!" is a Parrot's note,
> And if the Hang-man don't get your coat,
> I'le met you at *Holborn-hill* in a Boat,
>   If ever I love you more.

Among the sensual wooings of a conventional type that appear in the late broadsides, one of the sprightliest is "The New Way of Marriage; Or, A Pleasant Contract between *John* and *Kate*,"[2] which opens "Dearest do! You easily may,/ The place is agreeing to't." John insists that marriage is not the mode and can only lead to boredom. His plan is to "Love and lye without a tye, yet still be true," and Kate proves not to be old-fashioned. "The Young Mans Joys Compleated, or, The Coy Damsel Conquered by his pure Love and Loyalty,"[3] with a first line "Now to my true Lover Betty," elaborates the girl's talk of the treachery of men, but a narrative close tells of her yielding to his urgency. In "A way to Woo a Witty Wench,"[4] opening "O My dearest, do not grieve," the maid manages to keep the situation in her own hands. The ballad has an effective refrain. In "The Deluded Lasse's Lamentation; Or, The False Youth's Unkindness to his Beloved Mistress," to the tune "Is she gone, let her go," when the lass reproaches the youth for betraying her with false promises, he taunts her for yielding to him. As in the case of some jigs, the first lines—here a whole four-line stanza—seem to be drawn from some other song which furnished the tune.[5]

A vulgar dialogue that seems to me of especial significance

---

[1] *Roxburghe Ballads*, VI, 208–11. "The repulsiue Maid" was entered on the Register July 17, 1640, and "Sweet open the doore," July 26, 1658.

[2] *Roxburghe Ballads*, VII, 158–59.   [3] Douce Collection, II, 263a.

[4] *Roxburghe Ballads*, VII, 244–46. This may be the ballad entered July 26, 1658, as "A way to woo a pretty wench."

[5] For the ballad, see *Roxburghe Ballads*, IV, 22–25. The first stanza is almost the same as one which opens a short song in *Westminster Drollery*, ed. Ebsworth, Part I, p. 81, in which a youth mocks a girl whom he has betrayed. A mummers' play incorporates the stanza from the ballad apparently (*Modern Philology*, XXI, 254).

because of its early date and its connection with stage conventions has been preserved without title in Rawlinson Poet. MS 108, usually dated about 1570.[1] It is printed as Text 14. This dialogue, in which a Spaniard with his broken English makes an assignation with an Englishwoman, may with some confidence be identified as the one entered on the Register to Edward Alde on August 1, 1586, as a ballad "betwene a Spanishe gent[leman] and an English gentlewoman." Obviously there was some movement at the period to check the irregular publication of ballads, for between August 1 and 15, over two hundred were licensed, a hundred and twenty-three at one time to Jones without the formality of entering separate titles. Many of these pieces must have been older than the entries. A hint of the foreign woman in comic wooing dialogue is found in the entry on the Register of a ballad "and ever I ffayth I tanke you" in 1569–70.[2] Use was made of the comic foreigner in drama as early as *Wealth and Health*.[3] The Spaniard appears as comic or lustful wooer in the three Spanish lords of *Three Lords and Three Ladies of London*, Don Armado of *Love's Labour's Lost*, Torquattus of *Hispanus*, Pharamond of *Philaster*, etc. The lost jig of "John for the King" and its probable relation both to our ballad dialogue and to *Jack Drum's Entertainment* are discussed in chapter ix. A suggestion that such sham gallants as Segnior Domegro of the ballad were popular figures in jigs is possibly to be found in the use of Monsieur and Cavalier for Kemp and Monsieur for the clownish wooer in "Singing Simpkin."[4]

[1] See Brydges, *British Bibliographer*, II, 609.

[2] *Transcript*, I, 407. Arber has supplied an *h* in brackets, and the omission may of course be accidental. "Yes forsooth and I thanck you too" was licensed April 3, 1640. Practically these words are used for a refrain or for the title of the tune in several later ballads of the eager maid. See *Roxburghe Ballads*, VII, 112, 116–17; *Bagford Ballads*, I, 462, 466–68, 477*, 542*. See Chappell, *Popular Music*, II, 584–85, for the air.

[3] See Holthausen's edition, pp. xvii–xviii, for a date before 1519. See ll. 833–40 for some Spanish patter, and l. 386 for a drunken Dutchman's singing. Snatches of a drinking song that appear in plays especially at the end of the sixteenth century, with Monsieur Mingo, Domingo, etc., in the refrain, may represent the Spaniard as a drunkard. See *Summer's Last Will and Testament*, ll. 968–1115, and McKerrow's note, *Works of Nashe*, IV, 433; *Returne from Parnassus*, Part I, l. 1469; II *Henry IV*, V, iii. A play called *Myngo* or *Myngs* was performed at Bristol in 1577 (Chambers, *Elizabethan Stage*, II, 89).

[4] See pp. 226, 244, 332, below.

The name jig is given to a brief dialogue song dealing with intrigue which was introduced into Deloney's *Thomas of Reading* just at the close of the sixteenth century. Cuthbert says to the hostess of Bosoms Inn, "Nay sit downe by my side, and I will sing thee one of my country Iigges to make thee merry," to which she replies, "if you fall a singing I will sing with you." Their song runs:

Man. Long haue I lou'd this bonny Lasse,
          Yet durst not shew the same.
Wom. There in you proue your selfe an Asse,
Man. I was the more to blame.
          Yet still will I remaine to thee,
          Trang dilly do, trang dilly:
          Thy friend and louer secretly,
Wom. Thou art my owne sweet bully.

Man. But when shall I enioy thee,
          delight of thy faire loue?
Wom. Euen when thou seest that fortune doth,
          all manner lets remoue.
Man. O, I will fold thee in my armes,
          Trang dilly do, trang dilly,
          And keepe thee so from sudden harmes,
Wom. Thou art my owne sweet bully.

Wom. My husband he is gone from home,
          you know it very well.
Man. But when will he returne againe?
Wom. In truth I cannot tell.
          If long he keepe him out of sight,
          Trang dilly do, trang dilly,
          Be sure thou shalt haue thy delight.
Man. Thou art my bonny lassie.[1]

Deloney evidently devised this jig to fit the particular situation of his story, but he doubtless conformed to the conventions of the country jig. The lyric cast and the refrain suggest early song rather than the ballad. The jig is not danced since the singers are seated.

A lost ballad jig that may have had some kinship with De-

[1] *Works of Deloney*, ed. Mann, pp. 229-30.

loney's country jig, in theme at least, was entered to Thomas Gosson on February 17, 1595, as "a ballad of *Cuttinge George, and his hostis* beinge a Jigge." This may have been a formal farce jig of course, but my surmise is that an adaptation of it survives in the ballad in D'Urfey's *Pills* (I, 270–75) entitled "A Dialogue between a Town Sharper and his Hostess, Sung by Mr. Leveridge and Mr. Pate; in the first Part. Set by Mr. Daniel Purcell." The song is one of a series reprinted from D'Urfey's *Massaniello*, but the reference should be to Part II (1699), Act II, scene ii. In this scene there is a satiric picture of city manners, and the dialogue, like a number of those noticed above, probably represents faithfully enough actual song and dance acts in city entertainments. The title is close to that of the jig, for the sharper at the end of the seventeenth century corresponds to the cutter or swaggering rogue at the end of the sixteenth.[1] The bawdry of the piece is thinly covered by plays on words of a type popular in many ballads like "Mother Watkin's Ale" and "The Soldier's Delight in the North." Before the last stanza there is a stage direction for a dance of the two. The refrain "Fa la la" suggests another link with early jigs.[2]

In the reign of James I a song called "Bonny Nell" is mentioned in the general class of "ribaldrous Songs and jigs."[3] A probable clue to its nature is given in a passage from Massinger's *Old Law* (IV, i) when one of the characters says of Helen of Troy, "As long as she tarried with her husband, she was Ellen; but after she came to Troy, she was Nell of Troy, or Bonny Nell." This suggests the wanton woman or unfaithful wife as Bonny Nell's rôle. There are a number of other allusions to Bonny Nell, but their connection with the song is questionable at least.[4]

[1] See pp. 137–38 above for the portrayal of rogues in the early jigs.
[2] See pp. 236–37, 313, 315, below.   [3] See p. 35 above.
[4] See "The Country Man's Delight" (D'Urfey, *Pills*, IV, 122–26) where, in an account of country frolicking, a contrast is drawn between the heroine of the folk and of the courtiers:

> "Tho' bonny *Nell* do bear the Bell,
>   'Mongst Gallants gay and gaudy;
> Our *Margery*'s as light as she,
>   And yet she is not Baudy."

In "Young Roger of the Vale," noted above, the girl announces herself as "Bonny Nell." "Nell's Courtship or a Dialogue Between Hasty Nell and Fainthearted Johnny"

The ballad printed as Text 10—"A Pleasant Jigg Betwixt
Jack and his Mistress: Or, The Young Carman's Courage cool'd
by the suddain approach, of his Master, who found him too
kind to his Mistress"—has a mixture of dialogue and narrative
parts. The term jig may identify this ballad as a dance song,
but it may have merely a sexual meaning.[1] The broadside was
printed at the end of the seventeenth century. Intrigue between
mistress and prentice is developed in the farce jig "Rowland's
Godson," where John and his master's wife trick the husband
into so complete a faith in them that they have freedom for
their amour. In the broadside printed for Brooksby with the
title "An Amourous Dialogue between John and his Mistris.
Being a compleat and true relation of some merry passages between the Mistris and her Apprentice; who pleased her so well,
that she rewarded him with fifty broad pieces for his pains,"[2]
there is no development of plot, but the piece is a pure dialogue.
"A Merry Discourse between Billy and his Mistris,"[3] opening
"Come sit thee down, *Billy*, I have something to say," is a similar dialogue, somewhat confused at the end, and completed
with a narrative section. It has a two-line refrain. Another
side of the domestic picture is given in the vulgar "Merry Dialogue between a Maid and her Master, Or, All covet all Loose."[4]
A narrative close of several stanzas is apparently added to
stretch the piece for broadside publication.

(Pepys Collection, IV, 67), a commonplace wooing ballad partly narrative, begins
"As bonny Nell went to the Mill." In *Westminster Drollery*, ed. Ebsworth, Part I, pp.
59–60, the expression "she simpered smooth like Bonny bell" in "Corydon's Song"
from Lodge's *Rosalynde* is changed to "much like bonny *Nell*." For the tune "Bonny
Nell," see Chappell, *Popular Music*, II, 501–2.

[1] See *Roxburghe Ballads*, VII, 327. Of the songs in a collection in the British
Museum, H. 1601, No. 331, "The Irish Jig: Or, The Night Ramble" (also in *Pills*,
V, 109) uses the term a number of times in an account of sexual intercourse; and No.
346, "A Jigg Danc'd in the Schoole of Venus, or the 3-Penny Hops Burlesq'd by M[r].
John Vernham" is similar.

[2] *Roxburghe Ballads*, III, 395–98. Probably entered September 5, 1681, as "John
and his mistresse."

[3] *Bagford Ballads*, II, 502–5. Published about 1684.

[4] Rawlinson Collection 566, No. 42. With the tune and refrain "Fill her belly full,
full," compare what may be the name of a dance in *Colkelbie Sow* of the fifteenth
century—"Full of bellis fulfull" (ll. 297, 340).

A ballad and farce motive popular in Europe from the six-teenth century at least[1] was the frank or bold sensuality of a girl often young and naïve, as in the representation of the girl's delight in "The Carman's Whistle"[2] or her longing in "Cory-don's Song" from *Rosalynde*, "A Maiden's Lamentation for a Bedfellow. Or, I can, nor will no longer lye alone,"[3] and many later pieces. The monologue is usual.[4] One late ballad on the theme is called a jig, "The West-Country Jigg: Or, Love in Due Season" (printed as Text 11). The ballad relates, with some interspersed dialogue, an eager girl's lamentation, the appear-ance of a young man, and their quick agreement. Its lyric meas-ure and the mixture of prettiness of speech with bawdry indi-cate the work of a Restoration wit. The theme appears in some songs that are to my mind more suggestive of the stage jig. "Faine wold I change my maiden liffe" is a short dialogue with chorus, sung by two maids.[5] In "The Young Farmer's Answer To his Sweetheart Nanny," a dialogue except for two needless narrative stanzas at the close, Frank assures Nanny "For the burden of thy maiden-hood no longer thou shalt bear."[6] One form the motive takes is the discussion between mother and

[1] See Zingerle, *Sterzinger Spiele*, No. XVIII, end. The development of the motive through talk of mother and daughter is found in Keller, *Fastnachtspiele*, No. 97, *Der Wittwen und Tochter Vasnacht*, and *Deutscher Liederhort*, Nos. 833, 834, 837.

[2] See Herrig's *Archiv*, CXIV, 353-54.

[3] See p. 187 n. 2 above.

[4] See "This Maide would giue tenne Shillings for a Kisse" of the early seventeenth century (Rollins, *Pepysian Garland*, pp. 78-83, especially p. 82); "Hey ho, for a Hus-band. Or, the willing Maids wants made known" (Pepys Collection, IV, 9), opening "You maidens that are fair and young"—with a title that suggests Beatrice's "I may sit in a corner and cry 'Heigh-ho for a husband' "; "The Maidens sad Complaint for want of a Hus-band," opening "O when shall I be married,/hogh be married?" (Wood Collection E. 25, No. 57), entered July 1, 1678; the short song beginning "Can any one tell what I ayle?" with the refrain, "I can, nor will, noe longer lye alone" (*Percy Folio Manuscript*, IV, 55); *Roxburghe Ballads*, III, 585-87; VI, 238-39, 246-47; VII, 116, 141-42, 374; VIII, 435; IX, clxxii*-clxxiv*, 693; Chappell, *Popular Music*, II, 454-55, 462.

[5] See *Percy Folio Manuscript*, II, 46-47.

[6] *Roxburghe Ballads*, VIII, 207-8. See Rawlinson Collection 566, No. 30, for "The Controversie between Robin and Dolls House-keeping," beginning "Robin thou said'st thoud'st love me long," which shows a mixture of motives but opens with the girl's insistence on immediate marriage and has the refrain "and then I can cry have at it, have at it." There is one narrative stanza at the end.

daughter.[1] In Cox's prose droll "Simpleton the Smith," Young Simpleton sings a dialogue song, "Oh! Mother let me have a Husband kind." In a broadside with the title "Modesty Amazed; Or, The *Dorsetshire* Damosel importunate with her Mother, to know *Roger's* meaning in Wooing,"[2] a naïvely sensual girl begins her account of Roger's wooing with "Oh, Mother! *Roger* with his kisses/Almost stops my breath, I vow," and is warned to tarry until marriage. A narrative close tells how Roger overhears and offers to wed the maid at once. The ballad is a variant of a shorter song which was included in *The Loyal Garland* of 1686, and is reprinted by Ebsworth in connection with the broadside version. The tune evidently had some vogue.[3] The sensual girl of a less innocent type is presented in the dialogue "The Mother and Daughter," opening "Why how,

[1] See Fellowes, *English Madrigal Verse*, p. 198, for the short monologue of a girl, beginning "Mother, I will have a husband,/And I will have him out of hand," taken from Vautor's *Songs of diuers Ayres and Natures* (1619). Two broadsides, in dialogue except for slight narrative parts, are "The Hasty Virgin: or, The Daughters desire for a Husband," beginning "Mother, I have a desire to wed" (Pepys Collection, III, 175), and "The Maulsters Daughter of *Marlborough*," beginning "Mother, let me marry" (Pepys Collection, III, 70; see *Roxburghe Ballads*, VIII, 207 n.). A fairly formal song drama with mother and daughter as interlocutors has been recorded by Tweddell as performed in Yorkshire Mell suppers, with the opening lines "Mudher, Ah'll hev a man,/If there be yan to be had" (quoted by Mrs. Gutch in *Printed Folk-Lore concerning the North Riding of Yorkshire, County Folk-Lore*, II, 257–58). The mother's desire that the daughter marry a wealthier man than the one of her choice relates the dialogue to a number of songs that are merely debates about the class from which a daughter shall choose. See, for example, the mid-sixteenth century ballad "The Fermorar and his Dochter" (Laing, *Early Popular Poetry of Scotland*, ed. Hazlitt, I, 112–15), possibly licensed in 1557–8 as the ballad "betwene a Ryche farmer and his Dougther" (*Transcript*, I, 75); "The Ploughman's Praise" (*Roxburghe Ballads*, IX, 681–83); "The Mothers Kindness, Conquer'd by her Daughters Vindication of Valiant and Renowned Seamen" (Pepys Collection, IV, 212).

[2] *Roxburghe Ballads*, VIII, 200–202. See *ibid.*, pp. 205–6, for a similar ballad, partly narrative.

[3] See *Roxburghe Ballads*, VIII, 200, for its use by Playford and D'Urfey, and IV, 372, 418; IX, 603, 607, for its use with broadside ballads. The ballad may have been licensed April 29, 1686, as "The innocent country girle, or the maid's question to her mother." For the vulgar innocence of the very young girl in late songs, see a dialogue of a boy and a girl, "Celemene, pray tell me" (*Works of Purcell*, XXI, v–vi, 38–43; *Pills*, I, 109–10), said to have been sung in Southerne's *Oroonoko* (1695) and, according to another copy, in Dryden's *Conquest of Granada;* the dialogue of a brother and sister in D'Urfey's *Don Quixote*, Part III (1696), V, ii; and a song printed at the beginning of Mrs. Pix's *Deceiver Deceived* (1698) with the title "A Dialogue in the fifth Aact, between a Boy and a Girl, and an Old Man. Written by Mr. Motteux."

Nan! what is the reason, that you look so pale and wan?"[1] The mother draws from the girl the story of her relations with handsome George and threatens to beat her for being with child. The daughter in return is circumstantial about some of the mother's escapades, with the refrain "O Mother, I've mump'd you now!" and the mother has to pay for her silence.[2] This may have been the ballad licensed June 22, 1629, as the "Daughter rebukes her mother," but the situation is not unusual in ballads.

On August 1, 1586, the day on which "A Spanish gentleman and an English gentlewoman" was licensed, permission was given Edward White to print thirty-six ballads. Two of the titles are "An exhortation for goinge to bed" and "An answere to 'goo to bed swete harte.' "[3] This theme is mentioned here because of its long-continued popularity and its use for stage song. In Cowley's *Guardian* of 1641 (V, vi) and the later version *The Cutter of Coleman Street* (V, vi), the cutter sings a short song "Come to my bed, my dear." "Oh! to bed to me," etc., is used in the refrain of several related narrative ballads in the seventeenth century.[4] "The Hasty Bridegroom,"[5] opening "Come from the Temple away to the Bed," was entered on the Register June 17, 1656, and March 1, 1675. It consists of a long speech by the man and a compliant answer by the woman, with a narrative close. In D'Urfey's *Pills* (VI, 198–200) a shortened version of the song appears in the form of the man's simple address to the bride. This is another case of D'Urfey's revival of old ballad motives. He includes also in his *Choice New Songs* of 1684 (pp. 12–13)[6] a song called "The Wedding. A Dialogue between John and Jug," which is said to have been sung by Mr. Reading and Mrs. Norris in *The Cheats of Scapin.* It opens "Come *Jug,*

---

[1] *Roxburghe Ballads,* VIII, 203–4. In the narrative ballad "Mother Watkin's Ale," about 1590 (Herrig's *Archiv,* CXIV, 346–47), there is a short passage between mother and daughter about the girl's pregnancy.

[2] For a variation on the motive in stage song, see the dialogue in D'Urfey's *Massaniello,* Part II, II, ii, in which a chimney-sweeper's boy, accused of theft by a cook-maid, silences her and is given food when he reveals his knowledge of her relations with the coachman.

[3] Compare "goo to rest &c," entered on November 7, 1586.

[4] See *Roxburghe Ballads,* VII, 461–65.

[5] *Ibid.,* pp. 458–61.   [6] In *Pills,* I, 292–93; compare IV, 133–35.

my Honey, let's to bed," and uses also the comic device of listing the husband's possessions.[1]

Two types of the ballads dealing with the love motive have been reserved for separate notice because they are so distinctive in characters and settings. They consist, first, of pastoral songs and, somewhat later, songs of haymakers; and second, of the songs of provincial and Scottish characters. Their vogue was due to the cultured classes, but they passed into a body of broadsides. Among the Scottish ballads there are several called jigs. But though the pastoral was used in the seventeenth century for the portrayal of clownish as well as of idyllic country life, no specimen of the period is extant under the name jig. The pastoral love song deserves attention, however, because as I have shown, it was a well authenticated type of country jig at least,[2] and because it remained a favorite form with the song writers throughout the seventeenth century.

The early use of pastoral dialogue in entertainments is illustrated in "A Dialogue betweene two Shepherds, utterd in a pastorall shew, at Wilton"[3] among Sidney's miscellaneous pieces, in which the sadness of one shepherd and the questions of the other suggest the talk of country friends in some of the broadsides cited. On the visit of the king of Denmark to England in 1606, a shepherd's wooing of a shepherdess was represented at the conduit in Fleet Street.[4] She mocked him, declaring that she would love him when certain impossibilities came to pass such as the peaceful presence of two kings in one kingdom. The shepherd's claim to the maiden because of the fulfilment of this con-

---

[1] See Brit. Mus. H. 1601, No. 361, for a music sheet with "A Dialogue in the Mad Lover between Mr Bowman and Mr Dogget in Womens Cloaths," beginning "Proud Woman I scorn you" and ending with a series of variants on "let us go to Bed." Somewhat similar is a dialogue beginning "Hark you, Madam, can't I move you?" sung in Act IV of Motteux's *Love's a Jest* (1696). The two songs are specimens of the sensual brawls of lovers and married folk (see pp. 154 n. 2, 159, above, and the dialogue in *Pills*, II, 118–20).

[2] See pp. 13–14 above. Two literary examples have been cited from *England's Helicon*.

[3] *Works*, ed. Feuillerat, II, 323–24. See also *ibid.*, pp. 333–34, for a singing contest in his *Lady of May;* Davidson, *Poetical Rhapsody*, ed. Bullen, I, 40–42, for the Countess of Pembroke's pastoral for Elizabeth, "A Dialogue between two Shepherds, Thenot and Piers," etc.; pp. 8–9 above for song in shepherds' pastimes.

[4] See Nichols, *Progresses of James I*, II, 68, 73 n. 1; IV, 1074–75.

dition fits the song to the occasion, but the theme of impossibilities is another convention of the ballad. One roundelay preserved in the *Alleyn Papers*,[1] "It fell upon a sollem holledaye,"
which is sung by a man and a boy, may be a stage song. The
man's bombastic narrative of being shot by Cupid and the boy's
mocking refrains show a kinship to features of certain farce
jigs.[2] In the works of Jonson, Herrick, and other poets slightly
later, there are a number of pastoral dialogues with titles indicating the occasions on which they were sung at court. The
scene from *The King and Queen's Entertainment at Richmond*
(1636) which presents country sports contains a dialogue "Did
not you once, Lucinda, vow," sung by two rustics.[3] Collections
of these pastoral dialogues are found in songbooks also, as in
the various volumes of "Ayres and Dialogues" published by
John Playford in 1652, 1653, 1655, 1658, 1659, and 1669 from
the works of Lawes and others. Prynne gives ample evidence
of the stage vogue when he deplores the "amorous Pastorals, or
obscene lascivious Love-songs, most melodiously chanted out
upon the Stage betweene each seuerall Action," and declares
that plays are regularly accompanied by "Pastorals, Songs and
Poems."[4] The pastoral enjoyed especial favor in the reign of
Charles I, probably under the influence of his French queen.

After the Restoration, pastoral songs continued to be popular on the stage and in entertainments,[5] and they were expanded

[1] Ed. Collier, pp. 29–30. For other examples of the early pastoral song in dialogue,
see *Works of Deloney*, ed. Mann, pp. 344–46, "A pastorall Song" in *The Garland of Good
Will*, which is a complaint of Phillis against shepherds and a defence of them by
Amaryllis, with an undersong of three shepherds; Johnson, *A Crowne-Garland of Goulden
Roses* (1612), Percy Society, pp. 63–65, "Coridon and Phillida," a wooing dialogue;
Chappell, *Popular Music*, I, 377, "The Shepherd's Dialogue of Love between Willy
and Cuddy," a complaint of the forsaken Cuddy, from *The Golden Garland of Princely
Delights* (3d ed.; 1620).

[2] See pp. 237, 242, 244, 261, 281, below.

[3] The dialogue appears in Add. MS 22582, fol. 15, probably older than the *Enter-
tainment* (see Bang and Brotanek's edition, pp. v–vi); in Playford's *Select Musicall
Ayres and Dialogues* (1652), Part II, p. 12, and his *Select Ayres, and Dialogues* (1659),
Book II, p. 72; and in *The Loyal Garland* (5th ed., 1686), Percy Society, pp. 62–63.

[4] *Histrio-Mastix*, pp. 262, 273.

[5] For dialogues in plays, see Tate, *Dido and Aeneas*, Prol. (*Works of Purcell*, III,
2–3); Betterton, *Prophetess*, V, i (*Works of Purcell*, IX, xvi–xvii, 120–27); Dryden, *An
Evening's Love*, Act V, *Duke of Guise*, Act V, and *Amphitryon*, Act IV; etc. See Chappell,
Popular Music, II, 525–30, for the history of the pastoral lyric beginning "My lodging

or imitated in many broadsides, frequently with their play-house origin indicated.[1] Besides the more or less sentimental dialogues, a number of a vulgar type, usually produced in plays, were printed in drolleries or on broadsides. In "The Kind Lad & scornful Lass: or, A Comical Dialogue between *Corydon* and *Mopsa*,"[2] beginning "Now *Mopsa* now we are alone," the girl will take no risks with her holiday dress. "An Excellent New Song: or, No Kissing at all. In a Dialogue between *Coridon* and *Mopsiphil*, as it was sung in a late Opera in the Theatre Royal"[3] represents the girl as refusing to kiss before marriage. D'Urfey of course wrote similar ballads—for example, "A Dialogue between Solon and Berenice," beginning "*Damon*, if I should receive your Addresses," and "A Dialogue betwixt Alexis and Sylvia," beginning "Sit down my dear *Sylvia*.[4]

---

it is on the cold ground," sung by a shepherdess in Davenant's *Rivals*, V, i. It was printed in songbooks and miscellanies until the nineteenth century and was made the basis of many ballads. The air, too, was popular in ballads and ballad opera. For pastoral dialogues in entertainments, see Mrs. Behn, *Miscellany. Being a Collection of Poems* (1685), pp. 26–35, 206–11—"Damon and Thyrsis. A Pastoral on the Earl of Pembroke's Wedding" and "Selinda and Cloris. Made in an Entertainment at Court." See *Folly in Print* (1667), pp. 1–3, for a wooing dialogue in ballad form, "The Cotsal Sheapheards," which was apparently used in the sports of the Cotswold Hills. For the pastoral dialogue in droll and pageant, see Cox's *Oenone* and Jordan's *London in Luster* (1679), p. 17.

[1] Among the broadsides that are not pure dialogues are "The Kind Lovers. . . . . A most pleasant new play song" (Pepys Collection, III, 228); "Coridon and Parthenia," described as a "New Play Song" (*Roxburghe Ballads*, III, 568–71); "Love's Triumph over Bashfulness. . . . . Being a pleasant New Play-Song, by way of Dialogue between *Celia* and *Strephon*" (*ibid.*, VII, 442–44). Pastoral dialogue ballads are "The Loves of Damon and Sappho: Or, The Shepherd Crown'd with good Success. . . . . A Pleasant new Play-house Song" (*ibid.*, VI, 153–54); "Strephon and Cloris: Or, The Coy Shepherd and Kind Shepherdess. . . . . To a pleasant New Play-house Tune" (*ibid.*, VI, 127–30; D'Urfey's *Pills*, IV, 313–16; etc.); "The Jolly *Shepherd*, and Jovial *Shepherdess; or*, A Pastoral Dialogue Between Alexis and Celia" (Douce Collection, I, 105*a*); "Good Luck at last: or, The Art of Scorning discovered" (*ibid.*, I, 89*b*); "The Love-sick Shepherd Cured. Or, The Longing Shepherdess joy compleated" (Pepys Collection, V, 330); etc.

[2] Pepys Collection, V, 188, for C. Bates.

[3] That is, in *The Fairy-Queen*, Act III. See Purcell, *Orpheus Britannicus*, I (1698), 232–36, and *Works of Purcell*, XII, xvi–xvii, 83–89. For the ballad, see Pepys Collection, V, 190. It begins "Now the maids and the men are making of hay," and was printed for Deacon. See *Bagford Ballads*, I, 537*–38*.

[4] For the first, see *Marriage-Hater Match'd*, IV, i; for the second, *Third Collection of New Songs* (1685), pp. 22–26, and *Pills*, II, 61. See *Methinks the Poor Town has been troubled too long. . . . . New Songs . . . . at the Court or Theatres* (1673), p. 30, for a coarse dialogue "An Old Shepheard Courts a young Nymph."

There is evidence that from about 1640 new types of Scottish or pseudo-Scottish songs with spirited movement and lively refrains enjoyed a growing popularity. They are, in my opinion, distinctly dance songs and belong to the craze for folk dance in the seventeenth century. Probably the interest in them was stimulated by the Scottish contacts resulting from the civil wars. The trend shows itself first in scattering ballads different from the earlier northern songs, but in the Restoration the Scotch pieces appear as lyrics in plays and drolleries, and many of the late ballads bear evidence of expansion from these or from other lyrics. A small number were probably adapted from traditional songs, but the bulk of them seem to be imitations of a few folk or popular songs.

The earliest of these pieces with the word jig in the title is "The Souldiers delight in the North Or, A New North-countrey Jigge betwixt a Man and his Wife," printed as Text 7. It was apparently entered to Mrs. Griffin on April 24, 1640, under the first part of the title. The ballad is a coarse portrayal of a wife's sensuality, with a rather belated rebuke from the husband. Here and in the next group of pieces, the *chanson d'aventure* opening scarcely detracts from the effectiveness of the dialogue. There are two spirited four-line refrains, one used by the woman and one by the man.

Four related ballads of the Restoration, two of them called jigs and two courants, clearly get their designation from their character as dance songs. They are all brief songs dealing with the sensual wooer. The first of the group, and the most interesting, is "The New Scotch-Jigg: Or, The Bonny Cravat" (Text 8), with a four-line refrain, "*Jenny* come tye my," etc., which furnished the name of the tune. According to Ebsworth,[1] the ballad was printed about 1670–77. Except for the two narrative stanzas of the opening, it is a pure dialogue with conventional features of wooing dialogues like the girl's reproach, the man's offer of gifts and his list of possessions, the girl's objections, and her consent to tie his cravat again on promise of marriage. The tune "Jenny, come tye my Cravat" was published in Henry Playford's *Apollo's Banquet*[2] and in *The Compleat Dancing Mas-*

---

[1] *Roxburghe Ballads*, VIII, 467. See *Choyce Drollery* (1656), pp. 45–47, for a narrative song "The Maid of Tottenham," which turns on the tying of the girl's garter.

[2] Sixth ed. (1690), p. 48.

ter. This ballad was imitated in the other three of the group. "The Second Part of the new Scotch Jigg: Or, *Jenny's* Reply, To *Johnny's* Cravat" (Text 9) is similar in structure but with more pretense at sentimentality. The tune is the same, and the refrain has become Jenny's plea to Johnny to tie her kirtle. The third ballad, written by John Wade, "The Scotch Currant; Or, The Tying of Johnny's Cravant," to the tune "Jenny, come tye my bonny Cravat; or, Give me the Lass,"[1] is more like the first and has a good deal of conventional phraseology. Ebsworth points out a passage that is apparently imitated in "The Second Part of the new Scotch Jigg." Of the four ballads, the most spirited is a sequel to Wade's, with the title "The New Corant; Or the merry wooing of Jonney and Jenny. . . . . To a new Tune call'd Up goes aly aly," beginning "Here is a fine new ditty/ If you will but draw near."[2] The man woos with an unusually droll account of what he possesses and what he will inherit from various members of his family—and, in answer to the girl's charge of inconstancy, there is a still droller passage about sleeping with four and twenty maids who went over the lea. The lively refrain is in keeping:

> Then up goes aly aly
> up goes Mary & Nan
> Johnney was courting of Jenny
> and so they went merrily on.

Another group of Scottish wooings, without the name jig, is characterized by the barbarous bluntness of the man and by a series of short speeches cast in the same refrain-like mold. "Jenny, Jenny; Or, The False-hearted Knight and Kind-hearted Lass,"[3] largely in dialogue, represents the wanton wooer as replying to the reluctant maid with "*Lig all the blame upon my*

[1] *Roxburghe Ballads*, VIII, 463–65. It opens "As *Johnny* met *Jenny* on a Summer's day."

[2] Pepys Collection, III, 293. Printed for Coles, Vere, Wright, and Clark (1655–80). For the tune "Up went Aily" see Brit. Mus. *Cat. MS. Music*, II, 207. For a sixteenth century "Wowing of Jok and Jynny" with its list of rustic possessions, see p. 193 above; for a Jockey and Jenny ballad with a hornpipe dance, see p. 360 below. "A Ballad of Jockey and Jenney" was entered December 9, 1615.

[3] *Roxburghe Ballads*, VII, 350–51. It opens "There was a Lass in our Town." This was one of the large number of ballads entered March 1, 1675.

back, Jenny, Jenny!", "*Then down to yonder Green-wood go,
Jenny, Jenny!*", etc. After her betrayal he answers her request
for a boon with mockery. He will not buy her an ambling mare;
she may ride on her spinning-wheel. He will not buy her a pair
of shoes; the next that rides her may shoe her. Ramsay printed
a song with a number of passages found in this ballad but with a
variant address of "Janet, Janet," "My jo Janet," etc.[1] In
Newcastle's *Triumphant Widow* (1677) there is a bit of purer
dialogue with one echo of these songs and with similar brisk
lines, which is professedly taken from a "ballet" with a picture
(I, i). A traditional Scottish song " 'I'll go to the greenwood,'
Quo' Nansy, quo' Nansy," has forthright speeches of both the
girl and the man.[2] Among other songs with the movement, one
in Hickes's *Grammatical Drollery*, beginning "My *Nanny*, quoth
he: Why *Janny*, quoth she," is called "A new Song, to the new
Jig-tune."[3]

An old song somewhat different in theme but similar in
method was entered on the Register June 1, 1629, as a ballad of
"Nicoll a Cod." The broadside version is lost, but the song has
been preserved in a number of traditional versions.[4] One collected by Herd opens:

> "Whan'll we be marry'd
> My ain dear Nicol o' Cod?"
> "We'll be marry'd o' Monday,
> An' is na the reason gude?"

[1] *Tea-Table Miscellany*, I, 57–59. See Dick, *Songs of Burns*, pp. 194, 427–28, for
Burns's use of the song and for various forms of the song and tune.

[2] See Hecht, *Songs from Herd's Manuscripts*, pp. 155–58, 301. See *Roxburghe Ballads*, IX, 692, for a version combined with a seventeenth century song and refrain,
"Laddy, lye near me." The tune "Lad[d]y lye near me" is given in *The Dancing Master*
of 1651, etc. See Dick, *Songs of Burns*, pp. 164, 413–14, for "Who but I, quoth Finlay,"
and for Burns's adaptation.

[3] Pp. 60–61. See also pp. 39–41, for "A Song called the Hasty Wedding," beginning
"I'm in love, says *Noll*: Indeed, says *Doll*"; and pp. 75–76, for a song with offers of
gifts and the refrain "My Mother does tell me I munnot, I munnot," etc. Compare
Anderson's "The Dawtie" in 3 *N. and Q.*, IV, 35.

[4] See Hecht, *Songs from Herd's Manuscripts*, pp. 159–60; 4 *N. and Q.*, II, 154, 187,
283; Long, *Dictionary of the Isle of Wight Dialect*, pp. 154–55; Williams, *Folk-Songs
of the Upper Thames*, pp. 168–69.

"Will we be marry'd nae sooner,
My own dear Nicol o' Cod?"
"Wad ye be marry'd o' Sunday?
I think the auld runt be gane mad."

In the same fashion Nicol decides on the guests and wedding feast. The refrain, "My own sweet Nichol a Cod," is the name of the tune used for "Joans Victory"[1] about the middle of the century, an indication that the ballad has not changed greatly. The similarity of "Nicoll a Cod" to a German song of about 1570,[2] the apparent adaptation of a related song with a refrain "I mun be maried a Sunday"[3] in *Ralph Roister Doister* (III, iii), and the kinship of "Nicoll a Cod" with certain broadside ballads[4] and also with some modern Scottish folk songs[5] suggest that in "Nicoll a Cod," and possibly in other pieces with a similar

[1] Crawford Collection, No. 616. See Rollins, *Analytical Index*, p. 169, for this use of the tune and for an allusion to "mine owne S. *Nichol.* a Cod" in 1648; *Roxburghe Ballads*, I, 54, for the line "O when shall we be married" in "An excellent new Medley" by Parker.

[2] See Uhland, *Niederdeutsche Volkslieder* (1845), II, 713, 1029, for the song beginning "Mein man der ist in krieg zogen" (No. 276).

[3] Petruchio in *Taming of the Shrew*, II, i, 326, declares, "we will be married o' Sunday," and a traditional song with the refrain can be traced from about 1700 (see *Shakespeare Society's Papers*, I, 80–82). See Sharp, *One Hundred English Folksongs*, pp. xxx, 88–89, for a country dance tune "I mun be marry'd a Tuesday" printed in 1708 and in the edition of *The Dancing Master* in 1719, and for a modern folk song with a kindred refrain.

[4] In "Susan's Courtship: or, Sweet *William* Woo'd by the *Farmer's* Daughter of *Devonshire*," beginning "Sweet William, prithee tell me, wilt thou wed," the man in brisk replies mentions the lack of a hat, neckcloth, coat, shirt, breeches, and ring, yielding at last (Pepys Collection, III, 24). "The Wife's Resolution to find her Husband full Employment," beginning "O Now, dear wife, I am marry'd to you" (Roxburghe Collection, III, 603), has refrain-like commands of the wife and reports of the husband resembling a children's singing game with incremental repetitions. In "The Jealous Old Dotard; or, The Discovery of Cuckoldry," beginning "Whither art thou going, my old man?" about 1674, the wife's queries and the husband's crisp replies calling her slut, etc., concern his return, his supper, and his cuckoldry (*Roxburghe Ballads*, VIII, 198).

[5] "Reckle Mahudie" (Hecht, *Songs from Herd's Manuscripts*, pp. 161–62) is a dialogue between a mother and son arranging a wedding, with the same form and meter as "Nicoll a Cod." "The shepherd's wife cries o'er the lee" (*ibid.*, pp. 163–66, 302), with the husband's queries "What will ye gie me to my supper," the list of dishes, and his refusal to come until he is offered the privilege of the bed, may be an old game song. See *Modern Philology*, XXI, 249, 257, 268, for the narrative ballad "The Scotch Wedding" with its droll list of dishes and for similar passages in mummers' plays. This ballad began to appear in miscellanies at the opening of the eighteenth century.

technique, we have a revival of old popular song, probably song and dance drama of the folk.

In another group of Scotch songs, usually picturing the sensual wooer and the canny girl who demands marriage, a lyric quality is characteristic instead of the drollery of rapidly exchanged speeches. One of these, and possibly the earliest, is "The Bonny Scottish Lad and the Yielding Lass,"[1] which opens:

> [*Lad.*] Bonny Lass I love thee well,
> [*Lass.*]   bonny Lad I love thee better,
> [*Lad.*] Wilt thou pull off thy Hose and Shoon,
>   and wend with me to *Liggan* Water?
>
> [*Lass.*] *Liggan* Water is so deep,
>   and I am loath to wet my feet.
>   But if you'll promise to marry me,
>   I'll put off my Shoon and follow thee.
>
> [*Lad.*] I have House, and I have Land,
>   I have all things at command,
>   I have a thing that you ne'er see,
>   Bonny Lass wilt thou Mow with me?

The six stanzas of the first part, in pure dialogue, seem a complete unit and show a strong influence of folk material not only in tone but in the suggestion of the vagabond wooer[2] with his invitation, in the offer of inducements, and in a number of verbal echoes of game songs. The third stanza especially is close to a stanza of the traditional wooing dialogue "The Handsom' Woman" already noticed (p. 192). Almost certainly we have here a folk song molded to the Scottish pattern, perhaps an Irish song, as "Liggan Waters" suggests.[3] The second

---

[1] See *Roxburghe Ballads*, III, 475–77. The tune, "Liggan Waters," described as new, had a wide vogue in ballad opera, as Chappell points out. The stanzas quoted here are taken directly from Roxburghe Collection, II, 41.

[2] See pp. 274–76 below.

[3] Compare "A Scotch Song made to the Irish Jigg, and sung to the King at Whitehall" in D'Urfey's *Choice New Songs* (1684), pp. 14–15, and *Pills*, V, 44–45. This narrative piece with an intermixture of dialogue is a cross between the political brawl and the vulgar wooing. Moggy spurns Jockey's wooing with a refrain "for no sneaking Rebel shall lift a Leg o're me" until he agrees to fight not "For the dull Commonweal" but "for true Monarchy."

part is decidedly inferior and was probably added to make the song long enough for a broadside. Chappell surmises that the short song was a stage duet.

Another ballad which bears the mark of a dramatic piece lengthened for broadside publication is "Chastities Conquest; Or, No trusting before Marriage,"[1] opening,

> [*Lad.*]   Canst thou not weave bone-lace?
> [*Lass.*]   Yea, by 'lady, that I can.

What may be a short court song of the type is found in Playford's *Banquet of Musick: or, A Collection of the newest and best Songs sung at Court, and at Publick Theatres*,[2] beginning,

> *Jockey.*   Fairest *Jenny!* thou mun love me;
> *Jenny.*   Troth, my bonny Lad, I do.

The speeches are longer in "A Dialogue by *Jockey* and *Jenny*," opening "*Jenny*, gin you can love," which was included in the group of songs printed separately with the music after D'Urfey's *Fool's Preferment* (1688), and described as "A *Scotch* Song sung in the 4th Act." All three of these songs are dialogues of the brutally direct wooer who will not consider wedding and of the girl who will not yield except in marriage. The number of other Scotch pieces in plays and drolleries indicates the increasing vogue in the seventeenth century. In some cases the Scotch wooers are shepherds. Like the late pastorals, these Scottish wooing songs furnished opportunity for a combination typical of much courtly song—that of sentimentality and lyric measures with sensuality and droll characterization—and again, like the pastorals, the shorter songs frequently served as the basis for expansion in ballads.[3]

---

[1] *Roxburghe Ballads*, III, 496–99. Here again Chappell deals with the popularity of the tune, named from the first line. The tune is found in *The Dancing Master* under the title "A Trip to Marrowbone."

[2] Bk. VI (1692), No. I; also in *Pills*, III, 229.

[3] See Chappell, *Roxburghe Ballads*, III, 536–46, for the drollery versions of "Tell me, Jenny, tell me roundly" and the expansion in the dialogue ballads "Come to it at Last; Or, The Successful Adventurer" and "Coy Jenny and Constant Jemmy; Or, True Love Rewarded with Kindness. . . . . To a new play-house tune; or, *Tell me, Jenny, etc.*" To this group may be added "The Love sports of Wanton Jemmy and Simpering Jenny; or the Servingman and his Mistris the Chamber-maid" (Douce Collection, II,

Two ballads with the word jig in the title remain to be noticed, neither of them in dialogue. The first is "The West-Country Jigg: Or, A *Trenchmore* Galliard," printed for Brooksby (Text 12). The tune is "Up with Aley Aley" belonging to "The New Corant; Or the merry wooing of Jonney and Jenny," which has just been discussed. The ballad gives a vivid description of the drinking, dancing, and revelry of a group of villagers including the parson, and ends with a wedding. Possibly the title is merely descriptive,[1] the dance performed by the revelers being a west country jig or a trenchmore galliard. But presumably this "West-Country Jigg," like the one with a secondary title "Love in Due Season," was a dance song. Narrative ballads describing dancing and merrymaking are numerous after the Restoration, especially in D'Urfey's *Pills*,[2] and they were probably used in pastimes and in plays for singing with romp-

---

140). From "Sit thee down by me, mine own Joy" (*Pills*, III, 256–57) comes "The Bonny Scottish Lovers: To a pretty yet common, Northern Tune" (Rawlinson 566, No. 110). "Dear *Jockey*'s gone to the woods," found in several miscellanies, was used for "The Scotch Wooing; or, Jockey of the Lough, and Jenny of the Lee" with a sequel (*Roxburghe Ballads*, VII, 305–6, 348–49). "Ah, *Jenny*, gen your Eyes do kill," from Mrs. Behn's *City Heiress*, III, i, was published in several miscellanies, furnished the tune for a score of ballads, and was expanded in "The Loves of Jockey and Jenny: Or, The Scotch Wedding" and in "Jockey's Lamentation turn'd to Joy; Or, Jenny yields at Last" (*Roxburghe Ballads*, VI, 176–83). D'Urfey's "The bonny grey-ey'd Morn began to peep," said by Ebsworth to have been sung in *A Fond Husband* (1676), was used in "An excellent new Play-House Song, call'd The bonny Grey-Ey'd Morn; Or, Jockey Rous'd with Love," a monologue (*Roxburghe Ballads*, VII, 302–3); and "In January last," found in the same play (I, i), was used in "The Scotch Wedding; Or, A Short and Pretty Way of Wooing," with narrative phrases (*ibid.*, VIII, 456–61).

[1] This is suggested by the cuts on the broadside—of a bagpiper and of a circle of dancers.

[2] See I, 91–95, "Come all, great, small" from *Don Quixote* (wedding frolic with stoolball); II, 19–20, "*Andrew* and *Maudlin*, *Rebecca* and *Will*" (festival dance, etc.); II, 46–48, "Gillian of Croyden, a New Ballad," beginning "One Holiday last summer" (rioting, drinking, and political gossip); II, 68–69, "The Country Sheep-Shearing: Made to the Watermens Dance," beginning "*Jenney* and *Molly*, and *Dolly*" (merry-making); II, 218–19, "A Song made upon a New Country Dance at Richmond," beginning "Strike up drowsie Gut-scrapers" (movements of the dance described with a direction in the midst "The Dance"); III, 162–63, "Thus all our lives long we're Frolick and gay" (games, dances, love-making); III, 300–301, "You Lasses and Lads" (May-pole dance and courtship); IV, 26–28, "The Green-Gown" (running at barleybreak); IV, 122–26, "The Country Man's Delight," beginning "In Summer time" (dancing of country youths); IV, 145–47, "*Joan* to the *May-pole* away let's run" (dance); IV, 196–97, "The Country Wake" (haymakers' revelry). See also p. 360 below.

ing dances. A similar ballad found in D'Urfey's *Several New Songs* (1684) and other miscellanies and also in broadsides is "The Winchester Wedding. . . . To a new Country Dance; or, *The King's Jigg*."[1] The wedding of Arthur o' Bradley was the subject of four different but related songs,[2] one of which—a ballad beginning "See you not *Peirce* the Piper"—was used at the end of Lacy's *Dumb Lady*. They all have a lilting refrain of "O rare Arthur o' Bradley," etc.

Finally, there is in the Pepys Collection (V, 68) a ballad of 1691 entitled "The Soldiers Catch: Or, The Salisbury Jigg, Lately Sung at Court," which is printed here as Text 13. Though its interest from the point of view of the stage jig is not great, it serves to illustrate the variety of song regarded as jig. A group of soldiers sing the jig, and apparently dance it, as the opening line is a demand for "Room boys, room." Its content is political.

[1] *Roxburghe Ballads*, VII, 208–9. See Chappell, *Popular Music*, II, 495–96, 784, for the air. Under the name "The King's Jig" or "Winchester Wedding," the tune was included in the editions of *The Dancing Master* of 1686 and after.

[2] See *Roxburghe Ballads*, VII, 312–19. Ebsworth prints three of these songs and mentions the fact that the fourth—from Douce Collection, IV, 18, 19—was sung by the comic actor Taylor in London between 1816 and 1822. Dixon includes the last in his *Ancient Poems, Ballads, and Songs*, pp. 160–67, and Williams has collected the same version among the folk (*Folk-Songs of the Upper Thames*, pp. 271–74). Arthur o' Bradley is heard of in *The Marriage of Wit and Wisdom* (sc. vi, l. 4) and is the subject of frequent allusions in the seventeenth century. See Ebsworth's list.

CHAPTER VII

JESTS AND NOVELLA PLOTS IN THE BALLAD JIG

IN ADDITION to the character or attitude of the singers, which has furnished the interest in the simple pieces so far studied, the true farce jig has the appeal of plot, though often in the most elementary form. The safest basis for a study of the farce jig at the height of the vogue is found in the five extant English jigs belonging to the sixteenth century or the early part of the seventeenth, along with the nine singspiele which on reasonable grounds can be accepted as English or which were published as part of the repertory of the English comedians. On the basis of certain differences in theme and technique I have divided these pieces into the two groups discussed in this chapter and the next. The line of cleavage, however, is far from clearcut. The group dealt with here includes the jigs and singspiele in which stories ranging from a simple jest to a somewhat complex fabliau or novella plot are dramatized in a rather pure ballad form.

Discussion of the ballad jig naturally begins with "Rowland." Apparently there was a series of Rowland jigs. On December 16, 1591, Thomas Gosson entered "the Seconde parte of the gigge betwene Rowland and the Sexton," and twelve days later "the Thirde and last parte of Kempes Jigge." The connection of the two ballads seems reasonably certain. It would be a strange thing for the same publisher to enter the second part of one jig and the third part of another at approximately the same time without entries for the other parts, and there is nothing in the Register to indicate forerunners of either. More probably the two belonged to a series of Rowland jigs associated with Kemp's name. In the English originals these are all lost, but one, probably two, are preserved in German.

The only song of the series about which anything definite can be said was printed in 1599 with the title "Roland genandt. Ein Fewr new Lied/der Engellendisch Tantz genandt/zugebrauchen auff allerley Instrumenten/&c. Gar kurtzweilig zu-singen vnd zu Dantzen: In seiner eignen Melodey."[1] A second edition without speakers' names appeared at Magdeburg about 1600 in "Zwey Schöne Newe Lieder. Das Erste. O Nachbar Rupert/Mein Hertz ist voller Pein/etc. Im Thon. Mein Hertz ist mir verwundet/etc." A third edition was printed apparently at Augsburg as the second song of a pamphlet, without date, entitled "Zwey Schone newe Lieder/genanndt der Rolandt/von der Männer vnd Weyber vntrew."[2] There are also two early manuscript forms, one with the air in Hainhofer's lute books dated 1603, and a second in a song collection from the Tyrol dated 1600-1603.[3] A final version is printed as No. 148 in Uhland's *Niederdeutsche Volkslieder* of 1883 (*Niederdeutsch Liederbuch*, No. 134). Although there are a number of variations in the wording of these texts, all seem to have been based on the same translation of the English original. Hainhofer's text opens "O Nachbaur, lieber Robert" and refers to the sexton as "Glöckner"; the others open "O Nachbar Robert" and use "Küster" for the sexton. But in general the variations seem to be such as might result from loose transcribing or oral trans-mission.

Though the German text of the edition of 1599 is printed in full later (Text 25), a fairly literal translation is given here be-cause the phraseology of the jig was influential and its technique of short speeches and numerous asides, especially in mockery, is carried much farther in some later jigs.

> *Rowland.* O neighbor, neighbor Robert,
>   My heart is full of woe.
> *Robert.*   O neighbor, neighbor Rowland,
>   And why should it be so?

[1] See Bolte, *Singspiele*, pp. 8-9, for a discussion of the various forms listed here.

[2] The two singspiele of this pamphlet, the first of which is discussed just below, have been reprinted by Keller in *Fastnachtspiele*, II, 1013-25, and by Kopp in Herrig's *Archiv*, CXVII, 8-12. Kopp gives the variant readings of "Rowland" from the 1599 edition.

[3] The first is printed by Böhme, *Altdeutsches Liederbuch*, No. 85, and by Erk and Böhme, *Deutscher Liederhort*, No. 488. It is said to be clearly a copy of a printed form (*Liederhort*, II, 310). The second is included in Heintz's manuscript collection of folk songs in the library of the University of Bonn, S 504 (see Bolte in *Jahrbuch des Vereins f. nd. Sprachforsch.*, XIII, 65).

Row.	John Sexton woos my Peggie, And that has brought me pain.
Rob.	Content you, jolly Rowland, In sooth she does but feign.
Row.	The two are in the churchyard.
Rob.	Fie! fie! what harm in that?
Row.	They juggle there, I fear me, And do I know not what.
Rob.	Be patient, honest Rowland, And do as I shall say.
Row.	See, there they come together; Alas! my heart they slay.
Rob.	Lie down, thyself concealing, And hear what they may say.
Row.	Nay, rather I'll be standing, And chase them far away.
Rob.	Then I'll forsake thee, Rowland.
Row.	But what hast thou in mind?
Rob.	My craft shall serve to help thee.
Row.	I'll strike the sexton blind.
Sexton.	My Margaret, what ails thee? Why cast strange looks on me?
Margaret.	In truth, because thou lovest Not me as I love thee.
Sex.	Hast thou forsaken Rowland?
Marg.	That happened long ago.
Sex.	Then shall I now possess thee.
Row.	Here lies one who says no.
Rob.	God save thee, pretty Peggie, I bring thee tidings drear.
Marg.	And what is that, good Robert? Thou hast not made it clear.
Rob.	Thy Rowland's life is ended.
Marg.	O Robert, is it so?
Rob.	Because thou lov'st the sexton.
Sex.	Forever let him go.
Rob.	O thou, hard-hearted Peggie, Thy Rowland broughtst to death.
Sex.	O sweetest love, forget him.
Row.	I'll rob thee of thy breath.

Marg.	O Robert, much it grieves me.
Rob.	From thee it brings a mock.
Sex.	Turn now to me and choose me.
Row.	The sexton will I knock.

Rob.	But see where he is lying
	That chose to love thee well.
Marg.	Forgive me, bonny Rowland;
	My pain no one can tell.
Sex.	In vain is all thy sorrow;
	Come, Margaret, with me.
Marg.	Tears cannot now help Rowland;
	Sexton, I'll go with thee.

Sex.	Straight shall my wedding follow.
Marg.	I wish it to be so.
Row.	But hear me, neighbor Sexton,
	A word before you go.
Marg.	Lives still my lovely Rowland?
Sex.	This wears my heart away.
Row.	Go hence and ring the church bells;
	This is my wedding day.

Marg.	I love none but my Rowland.
Row.	Now, Sexton, go thy way.
Sex.	Will Margaret forsake me?
Marg.	Thou art a stupid jay.
Sex.	Ne'er trust a fickle maiden.
Row.	Go dig the sexton's grave,
	For Margaret is Rowland's;
	So get thee hence, thou knave.

In "Zwey Schone newe Lieder, genanndt der Rolandt, von der Männer vnd Weyber vntrew," "Rowland" appears as "Von den Weybern" and a companion piece slightly longer as "Von den Männern." Though the general title apparently gives the name "Rolandt" to the two singspiele jointly, Rowland does not figure in "Von den Männern." There is no question that the new piece was an early English jig. In the title of "Von etlichen närrischen Reden des Claus Narrn," one of Ayrer's singspiele written in 1598, the tune called for is "Last vns ein weil bey einander bleiben," and in a Dresden manuscript version the phrase "wie man das engelländische Spill singt" precedes.[1] This is only a slight variation on "Ein weyl last vns beysamen bleybn," the first line of "Von den Männern." "Von den Weybern" and "Von den Männern" are as closely related as the complementary titles indicate, and conventional phrases of the latter like "O Nachbar Jan" and "Ach lieber Jan" emphasize the relation. At the opening of "Von den Männern" three gossips are about to part so that two of them may hasten home to their husbands. Because of their remarks about the devotion of their husbands, Agnes is led to declare the superiority of her man Jan to all under heaven. The others mock her and finally persuade her to feign death in order to test him. When Jan sees his wife's body, he first protests that he will die with her and then that he will never marry again. But as the other women are leaving, he calls Clar back and declares his love. In attempting to win her over, he displays the utmost contempt for his dead wife. The wife, having meanwhile expressed her indignation in asides, leaps up and beats him; and Jan follows meekly after her, admitting that "the gray mares are the best nags." Clar and Cat, left behind, rejoice at the victory of woman and moralize on the necessity that all wives know the rascality of their husbands. In developing the comic possibilities in the disloyal husband and the shrewish wife, this ballad makes a nearer approach to pure farce than "Rowland." It is printed as Text 26.

I have assumed that the singspiel dealing with Rowland and the Sexton which is preserved in so many German texts represents the original jig that created a sensation in England as "Rowland," and the name "Rowland" is used for it throughout this volume. There are at least several English parodies or quotations which correspond closely to the wording of the first stanza in the singspiel. The entry of "the Seconde parte of the gigge betwene Rowland and the Sexton" indicates, however, another jig in which the two figure, for "Rowland" seems too short to have been divided for printing as two separate broadsides. The wording of the entry "the Thirde and last parte of Kempes Jigge" suggests a third part joined with the other two by virtue of its nature and of Kemp's connection with the series.

[1] See Bolte, *Singspiele*, p. 14.

"Von den Männern" might easily have been this third part, for it bears a close relation to "Rowland," and yet the absence of Rowland himself would give a reason for the change of title.

Outside of the Register there seems to be no definite trace of the lost jig on Rowland and the Sexton. Both in Germany and in the Low Countries, however, titles of the Rowland air are found in which Rowland is addressed instead of Robert—"O Roland lieber Roland" and "O Nachbar Roland, mein Hertz ist voller Pein" in Germany, and "Nabuer Roelant" and "Brande Roelant" in song collections of Amsterdam and Brussels.[1] Possibly Rowland was sometimes substituted for Robert because the song and air were widely known as "Rowland," but the titles hint at a companion piece to "Rowland" sung to the same tune, with an opening address to Rowland corresponding to that to Robert in "Rowland" itself. If there is anything in this conjecture, both of the Rowland songs may have been influenced by the opening of the old ballad "O sweet Oliver, O brave Oliver" already discussed as probably an early jig (pp. 181–83), or vice versa. This is suggested by "lieber" in "O Roland lieber Roland" and especially by the "Brande Roelant" mentioned above, as well as by the phrase "lieber Robert" in Hainhofer's text of "Rowland" and by the fact that the tune is given in several Dutch song collections as "Soet Robbertgen."[2] An early jig on Rowland might very appropriately have been written to match one on Oliver. It would not be surprising if the first part of "Rowland and the Sexton," like "O sweet Oliver," followed to some extent the model of the old parting song and dealt in comic or mocking fashion with the parting of Rowland and Margaret. When the Sexton asks Margaret in the extant song if she has forsaken Rowland, she answers, "Das ist schon lang geschehen." The difficulty about this conjecture, however, is that it would make "Rowland" the second in the series, whereas it is natural to suppose that the fame which we

[1] For the first two, see Erk and Böhme, *Deutscher Liederhort*, II, 308, 312. Compare the opening of "Newes good and new" (p. 175 above)—"Now welcome neighbour *Rowland*." For the last two, see Bolte, *Singspiele*, p. 10. Mangold says in 1596, "Einer sang: O Nachbawr Ruland" (*ibid.*, p. 9).

[2] See Bolte, *Singspiele*, p. 10.

know attached to the extant piece led to the writing of the later
jigs in the series.[1]

There are also some allusions to cuckoldry in connection
with Rowland, and it seems to me possible that in the second
part of the jig Rowland was cuckolded by the Sexton. In *Eastward Hoe*, V, v, Security sings:

> A Maister Touchstone,
>> My heart is full of woe:
> Alasse, I am a cuckold!
> And why should it be so?

Parker's "Household Talke,"[2] cited in chapter vi, opens:

> *Simon.*
> Neighbour Roger, woe is me!
> I am sorely discontented;
> . . . .
> My Cosen makes a Cuckold of me.
>> *Roger.*
> Neighbour Simon, be not sad.

If these passages are anything more than imitations of the
wording of a popular jig, they suggest a ballad on the cuckoldry
of Rowland, with an opening similar to that of "Rowland." In
"An excellent new Medly" the line "Sir Rouland for a refuge
tooke/Horne-Castle" is, of course, a parody of the famous line
quoted by Shakespeare, but it may also glance at a Rowland
jig.[3]

[1] The situation is puzzling nevertheless. If the first part in Gosson's series had
been printed by someone else or by Gosson himself without permission, he would hardly
have advertised it by entering his ballad as a second part. The most plausible reason for
his failure to enter the first part would be the refusal of license because the ballad was
found objectionable. The extant "Rowland" is entirely innocuous, however.

[2] See *Roxburghe Ballads*, I, 440–46.

[3] See *Roxburghe Ballads*, I, 56–61. Chappell suggests that the initials F. D. in a
Pepys copy of the ballad are a misprint for those of Deloney. The parody quoted in the
text follows the lines,
> "Boyes rings the bels and make good cheere,
> When Kempe returnes from Rome."
Though there may be no connection between the two, the allusion to Kemp at least
indicates a date early enough for a hit at a Rowland jig to be included appropriately in
a medley of current songs. The ballad also contains the lines,

There is some reason for believing that the Rowland jigs were several years old at the time of the licensing in 1591. The two entries to Gosson are followed by the identical proviso of the clerk, "so it apperteyne not to anie other." Since the proprietorship of ballads and literary work in general seems to have been determined in the Stationers' Company by the entries on the Register, the proviso suggests that the clerk was doubtful whether the jigs had not previously been entered to someone else and consequently that he had reason to believe they were old pieces.[1] If Gosson's entries are taken as evidence that the Rowland jigs were Kemp's, and if Kemp rather than some other English actor introduced them on the Continent, it is highly probable that he carried them with him when he went abroad in 1585. The fact that he was in the Low Countries with Leicester in 1585 and in Denmark in 1586 has been mentioned. Between this time and 1588 or 1589, when his connection was probably made with the newly organized Strange's Men,[2] Kemp returned from the Continent. In 1590 the dedication of *An Almond for a Parrat* to "Caualeire Monsieur du Kempe, Iestmonger and Vice-gerent generall to the Ghost of Dicke Tarlton" gives evidence of his success on the English stage as Tarlton's successor. His recent Continental fame is also indicated in the same connection in the statement that Harlicken inquired at Bergamo about Kemp, of whose "pleasance" he had heard report. A series of records from this time until after "Rowland" began to be recorded on the Continent in 1596, show considerable activity and popularity for Kemp in England, and make

----

"Iohn Sexton play'd the arrand knaue
To digge a coarse out of the grave
and steal the sheet away."

The sexton was possibly a popular character in farces and jigs. An interest in the type is no doubt indicated by the grave-digger and his old song in *Hamlet*, a scene used later as a droll (Kirkman, *Wits, or, Sport upon Sport* [1672], pp. 56–61).

[1] So far as there seems to be any basis for my conjecture that the Rowland jigs had some relation to "O sweet Oliver," the theory of an early date is strengthened. The songs dealing with Oliver were licensed in 1584 and 1586, and whether "O sweet Oliver" or the Rowland jigs came first, the presumption is that in the case of a very popular ballad, imitation would not be long delayed.

[2] See Greg, *Henslowe's Diary*, II, 69–72.

it rather improbable that he was abroad again during the period.[1]

The tune of "Rowland" can be traced in England earlier than the song itself. When Lord Willoughby, Leicester's successor in the Low Countries, returned to England in 1589, a ballad was written celebrating the event.[2] The air, which was called from the ballad itself "Lord Willobies Welcome Home," is the same as that of "Rowland." Bolte conjectures that Leicester's players paid tribute to their patron by using later for their song drama the tune associated with a ballad celebrating the successful return of his expedition,[3] but it is more probable that the ballad on Lord Willoughby took the air already made famous by the players who went out with the expedition. The tune for "The Carman's Whistle" as given in Rawlinson Poet. MS 185 is "neighbor Roberte." Both Bolle and Clark assign this manuscript to 1589–90.[4] If they are right, the date of "Rowland" is set back at least a year or two earlier than the entry on the Register. It is very significant, I think, that the use of the tune under a title which harmonizes with the names it bore abroad is recorded so early in a manuscript collection of popular ballads. The ballad "Jasper Cunningham" also calls for the tune "O neighbour Robert" both in the exemplar printed for Thomas Millington (1593–1603)[5] and in the much later one printed for Coles, Wright, Vere, and Gilbertson.[6] It is my theory that the air was known as "Lord Willoughby" after 1589 in accordance with the custom of naming a tune from the latest

[1] As we have just seen, a third part of Kemp's jig was licensed at the end of 1591; his name was included among the chief players of Strange's Men on May 6, 1593, when the company was granted a license to act outside of London (Murray, *Eng. Dram. Companies*, I, 87–88); his "Applauded Merriments" in *A Knack to Know a Knave* was licensed at the beginning of 1594—January 7; he performed at court at the end of 1594 (Chambers, *Elizabethan Stage*, II, 194); and jigs with his name attached were licensed again in January, May, and October, 1595. Pretty certainly during this period he was playing Peter in the newly revised *Romeo and Juliet*.

[2] Chappell, *Popular Music*, I, 114–16.   [3] *Singspiele*, p. 10.

[4] See Herrig's *Archiv*, CXIV, 327–28, and *Shirburn Ballads*, ed. Clark, p. 334.

[5] See Newton, *Catalogue of Old Ballads of Fred. Ouvry*, p. 4; *Roxburghe Ballads*, III, 104.

[6] Wood Collection, 402, fol. 56.

popular ballad with which it was associated. In a seventeenth century edition of "The Carman's Whistle" the tune
is given as *"The Carman's Whistle; or Lord Willoughby's
March."*[1] In many collections of music, it is called "Lord Willoughby," probably because these works were designed for the
cultured and the name had dignified associations.[2] The air appears, however, in the *Fitzwilliam Virginal Book* about 1620
under the name "Rowland" as arranged by Byrd (No. CLX),
and in Add. MS 30485, fol. 115, under the name "O neighboure
Robart."[3]

No source for the simple plot of "Rowland" has been found.
In the famous Widow of Ephesus story, the inconsolable widow
quickly forsakes her self-immolation with the body of her husband and takes a lover, allowing her husband's corpse to be
hung in the place of a stolen one in order to protect the lover.[4]
One Renaissance jest tells how a newly made widow rebukes her
father for saying that he has a better man selected for her, but
within a few hours of the burial inquires about the prospective
husband.[5] In another, when a husband pretends death to test
a wife, she leaves the body neglected while she prepares and
consumes a heavy meal, beginning her clamors only upon the
arrival of a neighbor.[6] "Rowland" adapts the pretended death

[1] Chappell, *Popular Music*, I, 139-40. For music of "The Carman's Whistle"
distinct from the Rowland air, see *My Ladye Nevells Booke*, ed. Andrews, p. 189.

[2] See Cambridge MS Dd. II. 11, fol. 58 ("my L. Williaghby Tune. J. D[owland]"),
after 1588; *Lady Neville's Virginal Book* of 1591 (an arrangement by Byrd); Robinson's *School of Music*, 1603 (Chappell, *Popular Music*, I, 114); Egerton MS 2046, Nos.
28 and 53 (arrangements by Byrd and Dowland; *Catalogue of MS Music in British
Museum*, III, 67); *Forster's Virginal Book*, 1624; Paris MS 18586, fol. 64v (*My Ladye
Nevells Booke*, ed. Andrews, p. xliii).

[3] See Brit. Mus. *Cat. MS Music*, III, 106. The manuscript is said to have been
written in the sixteenth and seventeenth centuries.

[4] See Campbell, *Seven Sages of Rome*, pp. ci-cviii, for the versions.

[5] *Mery Tales and Quicke Answeres*, No. x; *Pasquils Jests* in Hazlitt's *Shakespeare
Jest-Books*, III, 44.

[6] *Mery Tales and Quicke Answeres*, No. lxxxii; *Pasquils Jests*, Hazlitt's *Shakespeare
Jest-Books*, III, 21; Poggio, *Facetiae*, No. cxvi; Pauli, *Schimpf und Ernst*, ed. Bolte,
No. 144 (see II, 297); etc. See Erk and Böhme, *Deutscher Liederhort*, No. 910, for a traditional dialogue song, "Der Weltlauf," in which a wife will not return home for the
sickness or death of her husband but comes for wooers. See also No. 913, a song of about
1530 in which a husband prays for the death of his wife, buries her with joy, and returns
to the maid; and No. 914, a version of a modern song of the type. See Taylor in *Modern*

and the woman's shallow grief to a plot depicting the rivalry of wooers. In "Von den Männern" the same plot is used with a change of sex in the corresponding characters, so that the story becomes a satire on the loyalty of men to their wives.

Judged merely on the merits of the text, it is somewhat difficult to understand the impression that "Rowland" made both in England and abroad. Parodies or echoes of the jig in *A Quest of Enquirie*, *Eastward Hoe*, and Parker's "Household Talke" have already been cited. As Peter in *Romeo and Juliet* (IV, v) Kemp is made to quote the second line of "Rowland"—"My heart is full of woe," in German, "mein hertz ist voller Pein." Commentators on the passage have referred the line to "A pleasant new Ballad of two Lovers,"[1] but in both cases the words evidently go back to the jig. In *Haue with you to Saffron-walden* (1596) Nashe makes a burlesque statement about the dramatic works to be written on Gabriel Harvey, including one with "a Iigge at the latter ende in English Hexameters of *O neighbour Gabriell, and his wooing of Kate Cotton*."[2] The influence of "Rowland" is probably reflected also in the title "Rowland's Godson" for a jig in which the name does not occur, and in the use of the name for a character in both "The Wooing of Nan" and the dialogue ballad "Newes good and new" already discussed (p. 176). There is a temptation to carry the point farther, but after all, Rowland was a common name in the period. The plot of the jig was apparently utilized for an English farce preserved in *Engelische Comedien und Tragedien* under the title "Ein lustig Pickelheringspiel von der schönen Maria und dem alten Hahnrey." In this piece an old husband, at the advice of a neighbor, feigns death as a test of his wife. The wife proposes to bury him under the gallows tree, Pickleherring

---

Philology, XV, 226-27, for the widespread story in which a husband deceives his wife by pretending blindness and slays her paramour. The adventures of the corpse in stories like the last, and the mutilations of it in versions of the Widow of Ephesus story, sometimes take a comic turn that suggests the mockery of the corpse in "Von den Männern" or the liberties taken with it in "Von der schönen Maria," a farce related to "Rowland." In *Heptameron*, No. 71, and in a tale of Whetstone's *Heptameron of Ciuill Discourses*, a wife about to die revives when she sees her husband kiss the maid, a situation resembling that in "Von den Männern."

[1] See *Shakespeare Society's Papers*, I, 12-15; *Roxburghe Ballads*, II, 304-7.

[2] *Works*, ed. McKerrow, III, 114.

makes merry with the body, and the supposed widow summons her lover. When confronted by her husband on the way to her betrothal, she pretends that her actions have been a retaliatory jest.[1] This story seems to have influenced one important play, Chapman's *Widow's Tears*, drawn from the Widow of Ephesus story, which has been changed so that the death of the husband becomes a pretense of death, and the wife, after accepting her disguised husband as a lover, pretends to have been aware of his deceit.[2] The extraordinary vogue of the "Rowland" tune with the great musicians of the time as shown in their numerous adaptations of it has already been noticed.

For the Continent most of the evidence is given by Bolte.[3] The various versions of "Rowland" and the allusions to performances cited by him show the spread of the jig to many regions of Germany—Frankfort, where it seems to have been performed in 1596, Magdeburg, Augsburg, Hamburg, and Jaufen in the Tyrol. A stage direction after the third act of Heinrich Kielmann's *Tetzelocramia* (1617) reads: "*Hic inseratur interscenium* Der Roland, ein Tantz von Vier Persohnen, Roland, Rubbert, Münch, Grietha."[4] Six other singspiele, five of them by Ayrer, are sung to the tune of "Rowland." There are also at least eight versions of the air in German songbooks of the seventeenth century, and more than a dozen other songs and ballads call for the tune. The use of the title "Soet Robbertgen" for four versions of the tune in the Low Countries is pointed out by Bolte. In addition I have noticed in Cambridge MS Dd. VI. 49, fol. 41, a song to the tune of "Soet Robbertge" in a group of

---

[1] Ayrer apparently borrowed from the farce the similar scenes of Act V of his *Comedia von einem alten Buler vnnd Wucherer*.

[2] In Beaumont and Fletcher's *Tamer Tamed*, Rowland appears as a lover and there is a pretended death as a test without any evident connection with the jig. In Middleton's *Michaelmas Term* the husband's pretended death results in the loss of his wife to the lover. In Marston's *What you Will* and Armin's *Two Maids of More-clacke* a supposedly dead husband returns in time to interrupt the wedding of the wife. Feigned deaths are of course frequent in Elizabethan drama in plots of a different type.

[3] *Singspiele*, pp. 8–11. See also Erk and Böhme, *Deutscher Liederhort*, II, 310–12, and Bolte, *Jahrbuch des Vereins f. nd. Sprachforsch.*, XIII, 64–68.

[4] The appearance of "Münch" instead of the sexton suggests a version different from any that have survived.

Dutch "Chansons" dated 1599. A lost Dutch translation beginning with these words seems to be indicated. Bolte also cites
what is apparently a late allusion to "Rowland" on the part of
the Dutch dramatist Vos. Forms of the tune under other titles
have already been mentioned for the Netherlands. Finally,
about 1640 the air is recorded for a Danish song.

In view of the importance of the "Rowland" tune and the
possibility that it was composed for the jig, two forms are given
here. Byrd's virginal arrangement, which appears in *Lady
Neville's Book* as "Lord Willobies Welcome Home" and in the
Fitzwilliam Book as "Rowland,"[1] is probably the earliest version
extant. It consists of the simple tune and two variations on it.
The air is as follows:

For the jig itself the most interesting of all the various forms
is "O Nachbaur, lieber Robert" in Hainhofer's lute book of
1603, since this is the only version accompanying a text of
"Rowland." I give the air from Bolte's transcription:[2]

Another German piece that might well have been an early
English jig is a singspiel published in *Engelische Comedien und*

[1] See *My Ladye Nevells Booke*, ed. Andrews, No. 33, and *Fitzwilliam Virginal Book*, ed. Maitland and Squire, No. CLX.

[2] For Hainhofer's and a number of other foreign versions, see *Singspiele*, pp. 167–69; *Jahrbuch des Vereins für nd. Sprachforsch.*, Vol. XIII, No. xxii*abc* in Musikbeilage at the end; *Deutscher Liederhort*, No. 488.

Tragedien under the title "Der Windelwäscher" (Text 30).
Here the popular farce motive of the shrewish wife found in
"Von den Männern" is developed much more broadly. The
singspiel is opened by the wife, who tells the audience about
taking her husband's hat from him when he came home too
drunk to know it, and about her plan to punish him for the loss.
Under a deluge of abuse and blows he is forced to wash swad-
dling clothes. A neighbor who enters pleads for him in vain.
Finally, as the day wears on for the weary husband, the neighbor departs to do his own wife's bidding lest he suffer a like fate.
The husband, taking up his burden, asks of the audience whether anyone wishes to be his yoke-fellow. Though the singspiel
was published in 1620, the material belongs to a farce type that
probably had its chief vogue in the sixteenth century, and the
brief ballad form and simple plot suggest an early jig. The main
incident is possibly borrowed from Ingelend's *Disobedient Child*,
in which the shrewish wife forces the husband to wash clothes.
This play was in turn based on Textor's school dialogue *Juvenis,
Pater, et Uxor*. A fragment of an earlier Prodigal Son play in
English, adapted from Textor, has been preserved,[1] but the
incident of the washing does not belong to the part that has
survived. In the Proclamation of Lyndsay's *Satire of the Three
Estates* a wife beats a husband and sends him home to do the
chores while she remains in the town.[2] The wife of John Heywood's *Johan Johan* assigns the husband various tasks which he
dares not neglect. But a wife's beating of her husband is perhaps the commonest motive of broad farce.

The three English jigs that fall within this chapter illustrate
as early as 1595 the process by which the type of farce jig already studied—simple in structure and conservative in the
modification of ballad conventions—expanded into operettas
with varied scenes and incidents. The ballad technique remains,
however, a characteristic feature of these earliest attempts at
elaboration, so that rather complex stories of a fabliau or novella
type are compressed into the limits of a broadside ballad.

So far as the dates can be established, the earliest of the more

[1] See *Malone Society Collections*, I, 27–30. The play was published about 1530.

[2] For a similar story in German folk song, see Erk and Böhme, *Deutscher Liederhort*,
No. 909.

elaborate farce jigs is found in Rawlinson Poet. MS 185, with the title "A proper new ballett, intituled Rowlands god sonne" (Text 20). In this jig Besse, in order to carry on an intrigue with her servant John, gives her husband an account of John's approaches to her and sends the husband disguised in her garments to meet and punish the presuming servant, while John is instructed to reproach the supposed wife for disloyalty and administer a beating. The husband is thus convinced of the honesty of both wife and man. This is the story of *Decameron*, VII, 7, widely used in the Renaissance in jests, tales, and plays.[1] Probably the author of the jig followed one of the versions found in English jestbooks, either that in *A Hundred Merry Tales*, No. ij, "Of the wyfe who lay with her prentys and caused him to beate her husbande disguised in her rayment," or that in *The Sackful of News*, No. 3, without title. These similar versions, like "Rowland's Godson," picture lowly life with realistic and commonplace details. The climax of both jest and jig is the husband's expression of his satisfaction with his wife and his servant. Two details of the jig are found in *The Sackful of News* but not in *A Hundred Merry Tales*—the use of the name John for the servant and the repetition of the husband's commendation. In *The Sackful of News* the husband says to John, "I have as good a servant of thee as a man can have, and I have as good a wife as the world affords," and then he makes almost the same statement to his wife. In the jig the husband says,

> o ioy out of measure
> to haue such a treasure
> of such a seruant and loue *and* loue;

and he expresses his joy in similar fashion at the end of the next stanza.

On the basis of the date assigned the manuscript,[2] the jig was composed by 1590. The only known allusions to it belong to 1592. On April 18 and 29 the two parts of "Rowlandes godson

---

[1] Clark, who printed the jig in *Shirburn Ballads*, has pointed out its relation to Boccaccio (p. 354). See Lee, *The Decameron. Its Sources and Analogues*, pp. 213–22, for various versions of the story. Some of the English plays using the motive are discussed on p. 220. In Ravenscroft's *London Cuckolds*, Act V, it is combined with several others that are also found in farce jigs.

[2] See p. 227 above.

moralized" were entered on the Stationers' Register to John Wolfe. In the Induction of Nashe's *Summer's Last Will and Testament*, probably written in 1592, Will Summer says: "Why, he hath made a *Prologue* longer then his Play: nay, 'tis no Play neyther, but a shewe. Ile be sworne, the Iigge of Rowlands God-sonne is a Gyant in comparison of it." There is no evidence that the jig was published except that the title as given in the manuscript suggests a copy of a printed ballad or of one prepared for entry on the Register. With its frequent refrain-like repetitions, "Rowland's Godson" has a more distinct suggestion of dance song than most of the farce jigs. The tune "Loth to depart" was popular at the end of the sixteenth century and throughout most of the seventeenth. The phrase evidently belonged to some parting song, and, like many other phrases connected with such songs, it became a stock expression before the end of the sixteenth century.[1]

In "Singing Simpkin" (Text 21) a woman hides one lover at the approach of another, and when her husband appears, makes the second depart threatening an enemy, so that neither the departing nor the hidden man, when he is disclosed, arouses the husband's suspicion. Of the forms of this tale, that in *Decameron*, VII, 6, was most frequently used in Renaissance stories and plays.[2] The chief features of Boccaccio's story are preserved in "Singing Simpkin," but, as is usual in jigs, the setting is changed to that of lowly life and the characters to stock comic ones—here the old man, his light wife, the clown, and the braggart soldier. Except in a jest of *Mery Tales and Quicke Answeres* (No. li) belonging to a different form, the one English version of the story early enough to be significant for the jig is "The Gentlewoman of Lyons" in *Tarltons Newes out of Purgatorie*. "The Gentlewoman of Lyons," based on Boccaccio, differs from the jig in setting and tone, however. Since *Tarltons Newes* is called in its title "Onelye such a jest as his Jigge, fit for Gentle-

---

[1] See Chappell-Wooldridge, *Old English Popular Music*, I, 102–3, for a "Loth to depart" taken from the *Fitzwilliam Virginal Book* (No. CCXXX) and for allusions to the song.

[2] See Lee, *The Decameron. Its Sources and Analogues*, pp. 203–12, for the versions, including a number of English plays. This is one of the stories combined in Ravenscroft's *London Cuckolds* with others that had a vogue in jigs. A similar combination with other farcical tales occurs in the comic plot of Beaumont and Fletcher's *Women Pleased*.

men to laugh at an houre," it is possible that, when the *Newes* was published in 1589, the story had already appeared in the jig, which passed from Tarlton's repertory to Kemp's.

The earliest extant text of "Singing Simpkin" in English is that in Robert Cox's *Actaeon and Diana*, published near the middle of the seventeenth century. Cox could not have written the jig nor even recast it radically, for the version in *Engelische Comedien und Tragedien* of 1620 corresponds usually line for line to Cox's version. This early Continental text shows four short expansions of the dialogue as given by Cox. On the other hand, two final stanzas of the English text which tell of the husband's eavesdropping with his servant, the discovery of the intrigue, and the beating of Simpkin are lacking in the various Continental versions. Cox may have added this discomfiture of the clown. In its essentials, however, the text as given in *Actaeon and Diana* probably goes back to the sixteenth century[1] when "Singing Simpkin" was apparently licensed for publication.

The best evidence for an early date is the entry to Thomas Gosson of "a ballad called Kemp*s newe Jygge* betwixt, a souldiour and a Miser and Sym the clown" on October 21, 1595. The soldier and Sim the clown suggest the identity of this ballad with "Singing Simpkin," but in the jig and the singspiel the old man is not called a miser. The loss or change of a single stanza in the transmission of the text, however, might easily have obscured the point. In *Tarltons Newes* the husband is rich, and in the stage adaptation in *Women Pleased* (II, vi), which like "Singing Simpkin" represents the soldier as the conventional swaggerer, the husband is a usurer. The one possible suggestion of the miser in the husband of the jig is found in his threat not to return Simpkin's pence after purchasing wine if the latter abuses his wife. In the German version, an additional stanza brings out with fuller comic effect the husband's attitude that this would be a sufficient penalty.

---

[1] The term roarer, applied to the soldier, suggests revision, for the word became popular after 1600 (see, however, *NED, s. v.*, for its use as early as 1586); but the typical sixteenth century term royster is also applied to him. The title "Monsieur" in "Monsieur *Simkin*" was, like "Cavaliero," conventionally used by clowns and was apparently affected by Kemp. A mock dedication of *An Almond for a Parrat* is addressed to him as "Caualeire Monsieur du Kempe."

There is also some slight evidence that "Singing Simpkin" was known in Germany before the end of the century. Ayrer was possibly influenced by "Singing Simpkin" in his fastnacht-spiel *Die zwen vereinigten Buler*, which has the same central incident of the wife's ruse to protect two lovers. In addition, details of Ayrer's farce found in the jig and not in Boccaccio are the sending of the husband for wine (at a different point in the plot, however) and his discovery of the wife's intrigue. But both motives are commonplace, and the last may have been added by Cox much later, so that the combination of motives may have been accidental with Ayrer. Again, as Bolte points out, the opening lines of "Singing Simpkin" were apparently sung to a tune used about 1592 for a broadside song printed at Basle, "Lied von den Falcken Euglein, auff Englische weiß gemacht." In meter and refrain the two are similar. The song opens,

> Ach Gott, wie schwer ist Liebespein, hey mein,
> Weil ich muß ohn mein Schätzigen sein, Falalala,

and the jig, "Blind *Cupid* hath made my heart for to bleed,/Fa la la," etc.—in the German version, "Mein Hertz ist betrübt biß in den Todt./Fa la la."

Neither of the two tunes used in the jig is named in the English, German, or Dutch versions—possibly an indication that they belonged distinctively to "Singing Simpkin." In "Der betrogene Freier" and "Droncke Goosen" there are passages with the same metrical form and refrain found in the first part of "Singing Simpkin," and these are sung to the tune of "D'Engelsche Fa la la." In a Dutch songbook of 1659 occurs a similar stanza and refrain to be sung to the tune "Pekelharing," Pickleherring being the clown in the foreign forms of "Singing Simpkin." Bolte conjectures that the air for these various similar stanzas and for the "Lied von den Falcken," cited above, is to be found in the songbook of Princess Louise Charlotte of Brandenburg, prepared under the direction of Walter Rowe in 1632. The air is accompanied by the lines,

> Delightles why sitzt thou soe, fa la la la la la la,
> Those foulded armes are signes of woe, fa la la la la la la.[1]

---

[1] For Bolte's discussion of the material, see *Singspiele*, pp. 18–19: for the tune, see *ibid.*, p. 169.

What seems to be a version of this song and tune is printed by Playford in *The Musical Companion*, Part II (1667).[1] Unless the opening tune of "Singing Simpkin" was composed for the jig, my surmise is that the first line—"Blind *Cupid* hath made my heart for to bleed"—was taken from an earlier love song and used here to indicate a borrowed air, as in the case of "Attowell's Jig" to be studied next. This cry against the arrows of Cupid seems out of keeping with the tone of the jig and unusual in the mouth of a woman, though it was conventional in the sixteenth century in the burlesque treatment of clownish love.[2] The "Fa la la" refrain was popular in sixteenth century madrigals, and Morley in his *Plaine and Easie Introduction to Practicall Musicke* of 1597 (p. 180) refers to a class of Italian ballets "commonly called *fa las* . . . . as I take it deuised to be danced to voices." Perhaps some English song with a dance tune modeled on these was used or imitated for the opening of "Singing Simpkin." Instances of the "Fa la" refrain in broadside ballads are not rare, and that and similar refrains were probably used freely in jigs. Part of "The Blackman" has a refrain of "Ho, ho, ho," and the piece closes with a stanza and a "Fa la" refrain like that in the opening part of "Singing Simpkin." D'Urfey's "Town Sharper and his Hostess," which I conjecture (p. 203) was based on an early jig, has the refrain "Fa, la, la" again.

Indication of the continued popularity and influence of a

---

[1] P. 128. The song opens:

> "Comly Swain, why sitt'st thou so? *Fa la la la la,* &c.
> Folded Arms are Signs of woe; *Fa la la la la,* &c.
>
> If thy Nymph no favour show,
> Chuse another, let her goe."

The words are suggestive of a pastoral dialogue noticed below (p. 254) in which a despairing lover is represented.

[2] Strumbo in *Locrine*, I, ii, and Onion in *The Case is Altered*, IV, iii, are melancholy and cry out against Cupid and the pangs of love. Compare Tophas in *Endimion*, V, ii, and Elderton's ballad "Pangs of Love." Bolte, *Das Danziger Theater*, pp. 175-76, gives the cry against the arrows of Cupid as a mark of the clown and lists other examples in *Tiberius und Anabella* (derived from Marston's *Fawne*), II, iii; Ayrer's *Phänicia*, near the beginning; the German *Phönix*; and Heywood's *Love's Mistress*, Act II. In these cases the clown appears pierced by the arrows. With the line near the beginning of "Singing Simpkin," "How is't Monsieur *Simkin*, why are you so sad?" compare the opening line of "Rowland's Godson"—"Tell me Jhon why art thow soe sade." Both recall Rowland's cry of woe.

successful jig is found in the history of "Singing Simpkin" even more than in that of "Rowland." Both in England and on the Continent "Singing Simpkin" had a vogue for something like a century. There is a remote possibility that Tarlton performed the jig, or even wrote it. Almost certainly it furnished one of Kemp's popular rôles. It is the one jig included in Cox's *Actaeon and Diana*, and was known as his when he was the chief performer of drolls and jigs in England. As late as 1673 Kirkman published it in his *Wits, or, Sport upon Sport*.[1] Bolte gives the details of the Continental vogue and prints the earliest German, Dutch, and Swedish texts.[2] In addition to the publication of a German form in 1620, which has already been mentioned, there are records from Saxony of the performance of some version in 1680 and again about 1730, the latter at the Saxon court. Toward the end of the seventeenth century the jig was imitated in Christian Weise's *Von dem dreyfachen Glücke*. In 1648 Isaac Vos's reworking of the German version of the English comedians was published at Amsterdam with the title "Pekelharing in de Kist," and seven other editions of his singspiel appeared in various cities of Holland by 1708. Vos's piece was translated into German in 1663. It also became the basis for more pretentious dramatic works—*De vrijer in de Kist*, performed by a fraternity in Amsterdam and published in 1678, and the Hamburg opera *Die Amours der Vespetta, oder Der Galan in der Kiste*, published in 1727. Finally, a free reworking of the singspiel was prepared in Sweden before 1691 and published at Stockholm in 1700.

The third elaborate jig surviving from the sixteenth century is "Attowell's Jig" (Text 22), in which a farmer's wife Besse, pursued by a gentleman, apparently consents to his wishes, but sends her husband for the gentleman's wife, who takes the place of Besse at the assignation and shames the errant husband. No direct source for this jig is known. The motive of the substitution of the wife occurs in the novel of the *Decameron* (III, 9) which served as a source for *All's Well that Ends Well*, and there

---

[1] Dryden's reference in *Mac Flecknoe* to "gentle Simkin" as still pleasing a taste that refuses Fletcher and Jonson may be to "Singing Simpkin" as Lawrence assumes (Herrig's *Archiv*, CXXXII, 312), but the epithet "gentle" seems against the identification. In Scott and Saintsbury's edition of Dryden (X, 448) the allusion is said to be to the "character of a cobbler in an interlude."

[2] See *Singspiele*, pp. 17–21, 50–82, 184–85.

are many variants.[1] A different story in Kirchhof's *Wendunmut*, I, 330, compared with the singspiel by Bolte,[2] is closer to the jig in setting and in some details like the gift of money, but the second husband does not appear. Shakespeare has used the motive also in *Measure for Measure*, and by virtue of the Duke's consultation with the two women involved, it furnishes one of the closest parallels to the jig. But if there was any borrowing, it was of course by Shakespeare. A story similar to that of the jig is told in a broadside licensed by Pocock (1685–88), "The Biter Bitten; Or, The Broker well-fitted by the Joyner and the Joyner's Wife,"[3] but there is no indication that this narrative ballad is much older than the date of licensing. In its mixture of comedy and romance the adaptation of the motive in the jig —like Shakespeare's two adaptations—reflects the tendencies of the age. "Attowell's Jig" is really a domestic romance idealizing the faithful wife, though a comic effect is sought in parts of the dialogue dealing with the intrigue. There is, too, a suggestion of an imitation of other jigs in phrases like "neighbour Richard" or in Besse's, "Your meaning I well vnderstand," like the reply of the woman in a similar situation of "A Spanish Gentleman and an English Gentlewoman"—"What your meanynge is sure I well vndrestand." But the portrayal of love between the country husband and wife is far removed from the burlesque of family ties usual in farce. Indeed, much of the jig is in the tone of the sentimental ballads and is formed of the conventional phrases that give charm and quaintness even to broadside balladry.

"Attowell's Jig" was licensed to Thomas Gosson on October 14, 1595, as "A pretie newe J[i]gge betwene ffrancis the gentleman Richard the farmer and theire wyves." It has survived in two English and one German version. A broadside form in two parts printed for I. W. is in the Pepys Collection (I, 226). This may be the original edition of 1595, as is suggested in Pollard's *Short-Title Catalogue*, but it may have been printed later— possibly for John Wright, a seller of ballads from 1605 to 1640. The name of George Attowell appears at the end. A manuscript version preserved at Shirburn Castle, with the title "Mr. *Attowel's* Jigge: betweene *Francis*, a Gentleman; *Richard*, a

[1] See Lee, *The Decameron. Its Sources and Analogues*, pp. 101–8.
[2] *Singspiele*, p. 27.   [3] *Roxburghe Ballads*, III, 445–48.

farmer; and their wives," is printed by Clark in *Shirburn Ballads*. The title seems to have been copied from a broadside, but the text varies from the extant broadside not only in the spelling of many words but in the reading of a few lines and in the omission of several stanzas. The German version, also preserved in manuscript, is printed here in connection with Text 22. Of the four scenes into which the jig is divided, the German text follows the English broadside in the first two except for the omission of one stanza and a few slight variations in the dialogue. The third section is considerably abbreviated. The last has been modified without changing the story. About half of the English stanzas in the section are retained in a somewhat different order, and the rest of the dialogue has been reworked.

George Attowell, to whom the jig is assigned in two of the varying titles and at the end of the broadside, may have been either the author or the chief performer of the jig, or both. There is no other evidence to show whether Attowell wrote ballads or not. He was an actor of some note, however. On December 27, 1590, and February 16, 1591, according to one set of accounts, he received payment on behalf of Strange's Men for plays performed at court by the combined Strange's and Admiral's Men and "for other feates of Activitye then also done by them." Greg has suggested that Strange's Men may have included members of the company of children under the patronage of Lord Strange who are heard of in the eighties as tumblers. Their feats of activity may have continued old rôles and included jigs. On June 1, 1595, however, a few months before the entry of the jig, Attowell witnessed a loan for Henslowe and was then no doubt a member of some company other than Strange's.[1]

Of the four tunes for "Attowell's Jig" the first and the last—"As I went to Walsingham" and "Go from my window" —are taken from old songs already traditional in the late sixteenth century and frequently mentioned or imitated far into the seventeenth.[2] The other two airs, "The Iewish dance" and

---

[1] See Greg, *Henslowe's Diary*, II, 71–72, 240, 336; Chambers in *Modern Language Review*, II, 10.

[2] See Chappell, *Popular Music*, I, 121–23, 140–42. Two arrangements of "Walsingham" (by Bull and Byrd) and two of "Go from my window" (by Morley and Munday) are found in *The Fitzwilliam Virginal Book*.

"Bugle Boe," apparently had less influence, at least under these names.[1] A recorder part for a "Jewes daunce" is preserved in Cambridge University MS Dd. V. 21, fol. 12, a manuscript dated about 1620; and an arrangement of "Buggle bowe" for the lute in Dd. II. 11, fol. 82, a manuscript almost contemporaneous with "Attowell's Jig." The title "Bugle Boe" suggests one of the folk games in which goblins appeared,[2] but the phrase may be a variant of "Bugle Blew," a name adopted by one of the riotous fellowships of the seventeenth century.[3] The practice of borrowing the opening lines of a jig from the song which furnished the tune has already been noticed. "Attowell's Jig" opens with the first five lines of "Walsingham," to which the actual dialogue is abruptly joined. The first words of the second scene, "Hey doune a doune," may have been associated with the air "The Iewish dance," but the refrain is a common one. Though no tunes are mentioned for the German version, it follows the English forms so closely in the use of different ballad measures as to suggest that the same tunes and dances were used.

Music for "Walsingham" is included in the manuscript text of "Attowell's Jig," and appears on the facsimile page which Clark prints opposite page 246 in *Shirburn Ballads*. Slightly modernized in form it reads:

[1] See Rollins, *Pepysian Garland*, p. 1. About 1685 "Bugle Bow" was listed among ballads of Thackeray (*Bagford Ballads*, I, lxxv).

[2] See "The Black Garland" (Brit. Mus. 11602. f. 4 [i]) for "The Meikle Black Deil or the Bogle-bo."

[3] See Graves in *Studies in Philology*, XX, 395–421.

The fact that this version of the old ballad tune actually accompanies the text gives it an authenticity for the English jig which no other piece of music possesses.

Three rather long singspiele of the ballad type, two of them from *Engelische Comedien und Tragedien* and one from *Liebeskampff*, remain to be considered here. There is no evidence in regard to their genesis beyond their inclusion in these volumes. The first, headed only by the names of the characters, is called by Bolte "Studentenglück" (Text 31). It is over three hundred lines long and is sung to one tune. "Studentenglück" deals with the wife of a tradesman who arranges for a schoolmaster to visit her one night in the absence of her husband. In the darkness the maid by mistake ushers to her mistress' chamber a student who appears at the door fleeing from a police officer. When he leaves, the wife gives him money. The next day, while the woman is marveling at the schoolmaster's refusal to admit that he has visited her, the student comes to buy cloth. She recognizes the money and gives him the cloth to keep silent. Pickleherring, who has attempted to win both wife and maid only to be mocked by them, and who utters throughout the singspiel the conventional series of comments and asides, forces the student to share his profit with him in a drinking bout.

Though stories of one man's intentionally taking the place of another at an assignation, as in the ballad "Glasgerion,"[1] are common in literature, no certain source for the singspiel is known. A somewhat similar motive is used in Middleton's *Phoenix* (1607). A jeweler's wife who is being bled by her lover, a knight, promises to have a large sum of money ready for him at a time agreed on. He is to "whirl the ring a' th' door once about" as a signal to the maid. Phoenix, giving the signal accidentally, is admitted by mistake and in the dark receives the purse. When the knight, who has been put under arrest on the complaint of his tailor, comes to the door with officers expecting to satisfy the claim with the promised money, admission is denied him. Later the wife is brought for judgment before Phoenix, who makes his identity known by showing her the purse. The intrigues of the wives of London tradesmen were a fruitful

---

[1] Child, *Popular Ballads*, No. 67. Compare the story of Shakespeare's replacing Burbage, given in Manningham's *Diary*, Camden Society, p. 39.

field for dramatists in the early part of the seventeenth century, Middleton in particular, and the jig may merely reflect the same interest. Middleton, however, may have taken this part of his plot from some early farce or jig, modifying a purely farcical treatment and conclusion in order to adapt the plot to the motive of the disguised prince spying out the evils of his land. A later variation of the jest is found in Ravenscroft's *London Cuckolds* (II, ii), where the maid brings the wrong man to the citizen's wife and the expected lover is locked out.[1]

The other singspiel from *Engelische Comedien und Tragedien*, to which Bolte has given the name "Der Pferdekauf des Edelmannes" (Text 32), is slightly longer and has three different verse forms, all of a ballad type. In the first scene a nobleman makes his servant Pickleherring prepare his equipment for riding, bring his horse, and follow him on foot. In the next, Pickleherring, having left his master rather than run on foot through the mire, takes service with a married woman. In the third scene, which forms a large part of the singspiel, the nobleman, seeing the wife, expresses, apparently in an aside, his willingness to give one hundred thalers to ride the "wacker schönes Pferdt." The wife overhears and sends Pickleherring to bring the nobleman to her. In the midst of their amorous dialogue the husband knocks on the door and is delayed until the lover is hidden in a backhouse. The husband will not allow her to put off retiring for the night. She then declares that she must go to the backhouse, and with difficulty prevents him from accompanying her to protect her. Finally he is persuaded to wait in the dark, rattling the keys to reassure her, while she joins the lover. When the husband on her return desires to visit the place himself, she again urges her emergency and returns to send the lover away.

In this common story of a wife's intrigue and of her wit in hiding it, the author deserves credit for originality chiefly in the coarseness of the device by which the wife outwits the hus-

---

[1] The motives of at least five jigs are combined in this famous satire of Ravenscroft on the worthies of London. Of these, the parallels to "Singing Simpkin" and "Rowland's Godson" have already been mentioned, and those to "Pückelherings Dill dill dill" and "Der Exorcist" will be mentioned later. In addition, the husband's descent upon the wife and her lover and her trick to enable the lover to escape (III, i) are paralleled in Ayrer's "Der Forster im Schmaltzkübel."

band. The husband's unexpected return and the locked door
are found in "Singing Simpkin" and in "Der Exorcist." Bolte
compares the love sickness of the nobleman healed by a kiss
with that of Simpkin, and the hiding of the lover with similar
parts of "Singing Simpkin" and "Studentenglück."[1] As the
pander of his mistress, Pickleherring has a somewhat fresh rôle,
in which he replaces the woman's maid in such singspiele as
"Studentenglück" and "Der Exorcist." Most of the features in
the characterization are usual, however. Scoffing and coarse
comment are fully represented in his speech. He shows the typical clownish itch for *trinkgelt*. In connection with his calling
himself "*monsoier domine* Herr Pickelhering," Bolte refers to
the titles Launcelot gives himself in *The Merchant of Venice* (II,
ii), but the series of terms that Nashe applies to Kemp[2] is more
suggestive. In his account of how he tried to ride behind his
master and was thrown into the mire, we have a characteristic
piece of mimus narration. The comparison of a woman to a
horse in "Der Pferdekauf des Edelmannes" is common, as in *The
Two Angry Women of Abingdon*, sc. i, ll. 156, 184, and sc. 2, ll.
40–95, in *Bartholomew Fair*, II, iii, v; III, ii; IV, iv, v (Knockem's
metaphors for three women), and in the song "Tie the mare, Tom
boy." It may have been influenced by the folk custom of ne-
gotiating for a bride by the pretended purchase of an animal,
such as a cow or a sheep.[3] Of the three airs used, the second,
"Runda dinella," which is named but not published with the
singspiel, is extant in German sources of 1611 and 1632.[4] The
other two seem not to be known elsewhere. Music for a "Cur-
ante" at the end probably indicates a closing dance.

The singspiel from *Liebeskampff*, called by Bolte "Der
Mönch im Sacke," depicts the amour of a monk (see Text 33).
Though the piece has a simple ballad form and is sung throughout to one tune, it is over six hundred lines long and falls into
a number of scenes suited for interact performance. If the
singspiel were performed as a series of intermeans, the one tune
would be far less monotonous. First there is a soliloquy of an

[1] *Singspiele*, pp. 25–26. He also refers to the beginning of Vos's *Klucht van Oene*.
[2] See p. 235 n. above.
[3] See *Folk-Lore*, VI, 94; Ford, *Vagabond Songs and Ballads of Scotland*, pp. 187–88.
[4] Bolte, *Singspiele*, pp. 25, 172–74.

old husband on the attentions of a monk to his young wife. He then discusses his troubles with the conventional neighbor but refuses to accept a mistress as consolation. His next step is to take his wife to task—without making any impression on her however. When he leaves home, the maid is sent at once to summon the monk. In the midst of their feasting, the husband returns and the monk is hidden under the table. They fail to dispose of his garments, and when the husband inquires about them, the wife boldly claims that they are her own. Finding the monk, the husband commands him to get into a sack. The monk, however, doesn't know how, and the old man finally agrees to show him. The monk ties him up, freeing him only in return for three hundred crowns and a promise that there shall be no more interference in the wife's affairs. A summoner who has been secretly watching the performance waylays the monk and by threat of exposure forces him to give up the booty. The witticisms and asides usual in the mouth of the clown are here uttered in much of the singspiel by the monk and at the end by the summoner.

"Der Mönch im Sacke" was composed before 1618 if Bolte is right in his conjecture that the *intermède* "de amoribus monachi et mulierculae senilis cuiuspiam uxoris" performed with Cramer's *Areteugenia* in that year was "Der Mönch im Sacke."[1] Probably from the beginning of the vogue there were jigs that dealt with the intrigues of churchmen. The motive was a common one in early Renaissance jest and farce, as in *Johan Johan.* Early in the seventeenth century Chapman in *May Day* (II, iv) says of "a friar's weed" that the "disguise is worn threadbare upon every stage, and so much villany committed under that habit that 'tis grown as suspicious as the vilest." About the time of the most sensational developments in the farce jig, it is reported that on one occasion the rabble at the Curtain insisted upon having the "Friars" performed.[2] Ayrer has used the motive in three of his singspiele. For the rest, "Der Mönch im Sacke," like many other song dramas, combines a number of popular motives. The talk of two neighbors about the evil wife of one, the pitting of husband and wife against each other, and

[1] *Singspiele*, pp. 13, 26.

[2] *Review of English Studies*, I, 186.

the treatment of the old man as a comic butt are noticed in other connections. The wife's bold denial of the monk's presence and of the identity of his monkish garb is similar to the jest of a very droll English ballad "Our Goodman," in which the wife brazenly explains away piece by piece the evidence of her lovers' visits.[1] In the unfriendly rivalry in rascality between monk and summoner there is a suggestion of Chaucer and Heywood. The sack incident is of a type conventional in farcical game[2] as well as in jest and farce.[3] Victim become victimizer furnishes the theme not only of ballads and farces[4] but of folk tales of many countries, as in the stories of Punch and Judy or the Fox and the Rabbit.

[1] Child, *Popular Ballads*, No. 274 B. Child points out parallels in "Clerk Saunders" (No. 69 F) and in a French ballad. There are a number of jests of a lover's leaving some garment behind, but with a different turn in that it is unwittingly worn by the husband or the woman involved. For a husband's appearing in garments of his wife's lover to his own amazement, see *Dumb Knight*, III, i; V, i; and "Debtford Frollick" in *Roxburghe Ballads*, IV, 30–32. See also Bolte, *Danziger Theater*, p. 222; *Decameron*, IX, 2; and variants cited by Lee in *The Decameron. Its Sources and Analogues*, pp. 274–77.

[2] See Byrd, *A Friendlie Dialogue betweene Paule and Demas*, fol. 15, for a reference to "seruing men in sackes" in folk games; Chambers, *Mediaeval Stage*, I, 268, n. 4, for Reiske's description of the revels of mummers in Germany in the eighteenth century, "cum saccis cursitantes, in quos abdere puerulos occursantes minitabantur." A passage in *A Curtaine Lecture* (1637), p. 206, indicates that such games were played by English adults on other than festival occasions. A motion is made that "they should go to a sport call'd *All-hid*, which is a meere childrens pastime." A wife persuades her husband to creep into a sack, and she and her gossips tie him up and beat him. For the sack in British games of pursuit and capture, see Gomme, *Traditional Games*, I, 215, and Maclagan, *Games of Argyleshire*, p. 122.

[3] See pp. 297, 298, 310, below; Bolte and Polívka, *Anmerkungen zu Grimm*, II, 7–10, 157–62; III, 188–92, 379–89 (in several cases someone contrives to get another into the sack in his place); Creizenach, *Geschichte des neueren Dramas*, III, 404, for a Brussels farce of the early sixteenth century; Smith, *Commedia dell'arte*, pp. 107–8 and note, for Trojano's farce of 1568 and other examples of the use of the sack.

[4] See pp. 313–14, 319–21, below.

CHAPTER VIII

RIVAL WOOERS IN FARCE JIGS

THE jigs that have just been studied are distinguished by an influence of literary *genres* like jest and novella and by a conformity to the technique of the ballads written by professional balladmongers. While a number of the remaining jigs might be grouped with these on account of their pure ballad form or their farcical character, the pieces discussed in this chapter are on the whole more strongly colored by the traditional element. "The Wooing of Nan," "Die streitenden Liebhaber," "Der alte und der junge Freier," and "Pückelherings Dill dill dill" form a natural group dealing with the wooing of rival suitors. In the three singspiele the farcical element becomes increasingly important, the wooing in one case being transformed into an intrigue. In "Der Narr als Reitpferd" and "The Blackman" the contest for a girl involves a conflict between the suitors. Traces of popular origin are found not only in the treatment of the wooing but also in some of the character types and in the frequent use of lyric rather than ballad measures for these song dramas. Much popular material was revived in pastimes and even in antic dances during the seventeenth century, and the more elaborate jigs, particularly "Der alte und der junge Freier," "Pückelherings Dill dill dill," and "The Blackman," seem to blend popular and sophisticated comic material. The vogue of antic and drollery probably influenced these three. The others are simpler and perhaps relatively early.

Forms of song and dance drama in which groups of rivals appear can be traced from the end of the Middle Ages, and various types evidently helped to create conventions of Elizabethan dances and jigs. In many singing games of children a group of boys as a unit woos either a group of girls or one girl of a group. Perhaps the oldest of these games is one that was current in Europe generally, with a characteristic English form opening

"Here come three Dukes." In some games where the two groups sing and dance together, as in the "Cushion Dance,"[1] there is a succession of leaders with individual choices. In the game that opens "Which of us all do you love best?"[2] each child in succession chooses a mate from the group. Among adults such games were replaced by dialogue songs and ballads representing a single wooer and girl, but in singing games of children and even in festival games of the folk the group often sang and danced with the individual wooer. These wooing games probably had their influence upon the dialogue songs of wooing groups introduced into drama. "Here come three Dukes" has already been compared with kindred songs found in the moralities (pp. 80–81); and during the seventeenth century, pantomime dances of wooing groups were frequently used as antic and comic dances in English plays and masques.[3]

From an early period the wooers also appear in various parts of Europe as a group of rivals contending for the favor of a single girl. Games of this type were used by adults in the chief seasonal festivals. In John Heywood's proverbs there is an allusion to rival wooers dancing for a rush ring,[4] and it is possi-

---

[1] See Gomme, *Traditional Games*, I, 87–94.

[2] *Ibid.*, II, 414–15.

[3] See Thomas Heywood's *Love's Mistress*, Act III, for "Love's Contrarieties" danced by a king and a beggar, a young man and an old woman, a lean man and a fat woman; Chapman's *Gentleman Usher*, II, i, for a dance in which a broom maid and a rush maid "rudely did their lovers scoff"; Jonson's *Lovers Made Men* for an antimasque danced by the "shades" of lovers (without women) "in severall gestures, as they liv'd in love," and his *Love's Triumph through Callipolis* for twelve "deprav'd Lovers," who leap forth, "a Mistresse leading them, and with antick gesticulation, and action, after the manner of the old *Pantomimi*, ... dance over a distracted *Comœdy* of *Love*, expressing their confus'd affections, in the Scenicall persons, and habits of the foure prime *European* Nations"; the second antimasque of Davenant's *Triumphs of the Prince d'Amour* for five bizarre lovers of different nations who in turn address their mistresses in balconies or windows. In several of these cases, as often in the games, the individual rôles are emphasized. An elaborate example of the tendency to separate the group wooing into individual acts is found in Motteux's "Musical Interlude" called *The Four Seasons or Love in every Age*, printed at the end of *The Island Princess* (1699) but said to have been "design'd for another Season, and another Occasion." For each season there is a wooing dialogue song of a conventional type, which is followed by a wooing dance in pantomime. To represent spring, for example, a young girl singing "Must I a Girl for ever be" is wooed by a youth, and then two sparks woo two girls in a dance. An early Continental specimen of the separate wooings within a group is found in Raber's "Von den 7 varben" of 1511 (Zingerle, *Sterzinger Spiele*, No. XIV).

[4] *Proverbs and Epigrams*, Spenser Society, p. 7. The use of the rush as symbolizing acceptance seems to be preserved in the refrain "Coll to me the russhes grene, Coll to

ble that Lodovico's statement in Chapman's *May Day* (I, i), "I have heard of wenches that have been won with singing and dancing," refers to such folk games. In the wooing song or dance, perhaps the most frequent symbol of favor was the garland, the importance of which in folk game is discussed later in connection with the singspiel "Die streitenden Liebhaber," where the choice between two rivals hinges upon the gift of the garland. Such contests would naturally belong primarily to the spring and summer games. But in a number of English mummers' plays representing chiefly the games of winter festivals also, the wooing of a single girl by two or more rivals is enacted, sometimes with song, sometimes with poetic dialogue all of which was probably sung in an early period.

Though the general tendency of these mummers' plays[1] is to emphasize two wooers, sometimes only a young and an old wooer, or the Old Man and the Fool, being present—probably as representatives of the old and new seasons in fertility rites—in most cases several rival wooers appear, and in some an old woman enters as a rival of the girl. The groups of three or more wooers probably represent old traditions of dance. That is, the secondary wooers may have served to make up the number conventional for the group dances. Blue Breeches, Pepper Breeches, and Ginger Breeches of the Revesby Play and the three "ribboners" of the Broughton Play suggest the type of costuming appropriate for dance. Such groups of three secondary wooers, however, may have been influenced by the conventional grouping by threes in popular games, dances, and tales. In most of the plays, the wooers have been individualized and made to reflect the organization of society, particularly phases of it significant for the folk. A seasonal lord and his eldest son and heir—sometimes the farmer's eldest son or merely the farmer's son—frequently appear, and the "Eldest

me," which evidently belonged to a song or group of songs well known in the sixteenth century. See Prologue of *The seuen sorowes that women haue when theyr husbandes be deade*, and *Laneham's Letter*, ed. Furnivall, p. clii. For "Green Grow the Rushes, O" in a children's game for the choice of mates, see Newell, *Games and Songs of American Children*, pp. 56, 272. For the same refrain in popular song, see Hecht, *Songs from Herd's Manuscripts*, pp. 118, 289.

[1] In *Modern Philology*, XXI, 225–72, I have discussed the nature, origin, and influence of the plays more fully and printed a number of the texts cited here.

Son" is a fairly constant figure among the rivals of the mummers' wooing plays. In the plays of the Lincolnshire region, which include the largest number of those surviving, the wooers of the "Lady," as she is called, represent various social classes and callings. An eldest son, a farming man, and a lawyer woo the lady of the Bassingham Play. The three ribboners of the Broughton Play are a knight, a lawyer, and the eldest son, to whom a husbandman is added to complete the secondary wooers. In one scene of the Revesby Play the characters are introduced as representatives of various estates—a lord, a knight or soldier, a beggar or "man of poor estate," and apparently a money-lender. Perhaps the most constant type is some representative of the farming class, as it is in the ballad dialogues of chapter vi, in which a scornful lady, like the one of the mummers' wooing plays, is wooed by a country clown, often as a rival of a member of a higher social class.

These mummers' wooing plays are clearly older than the jigs. Festival plays from the Balkans, especially from Thrace, with similar rival wooings and ritual acts but with choral song instead of dialogue, suggest a great age for the type of folk play. Machyn in his *Diary* (p. 33) describes a performance in connection with a procession of a London lord of misrule in 1553 which was clearly akin to the Revesby Play. The Broughton Play, one of the most elaborate of the extant specimens, may contain many parts of a play acted by the villagers from Broughton on New Year's Eve, 1524.[1] Apparently Shakespeare refers to some performance of the type, probably either a mummers' play of Warwickshire or an adaptation by strolling players, when the Lord in the Induction of *The Taming of the Shrew* says to an actor about the rôle of Soto, or the Fool,

> This fellow I remember
> Since once he play'd a farmer's eldest son.
> 'Twas where you woo'd the gentlewoman so well.[2]

Interrelations between folk games and other forms of popular drama and song probably began at an early period. The

---

[1] For the record, see *Hist. MSS Com., Middleton MSS*, p. 379.

[2] Possibly the "marriage of the son of a farmer" with the dance at his wedding acted by gentlemen before James I at Enfield and at Theobalds in 1618 (Sullivan, *Court Masques of James I*, pp. 107-8) was a burlesque of some kindred folk play.

framework of the mummers' wooing plays, for instance, had its basis in pagan rituals, but doubtless much of the dialogue and even some whole scenes resulted from the combination of this ritual with early wooing songs no longer extant, the whole being modified from time to time by new borrowings. There are numerous parallel passages in the wooing plays and ballads that seem to represent conventional phraseology, and it is often a question whether the plays themselves influenced the extant ballads or were influenced by earlier versions of the ballad dialogues in which a clown or farming man woos a scornful lady. From the latter part of the sixteenth century on, there is undoubted evidence that the folk plays borrowed from songs, jigs, and plays—probably as performed in feasts, wakes, and fairs. Thus the dialogue of the Broughton Play includes a large part of the Induction of *Wily Beguiled*; a Somersetshire wooing play has passages taken from Cox's pastoral droll *Diphilo and Granida*; the Swinderby Play contains a dialogue version of "Young Roger of the Vale" discussed in chapter vi; and in the various wooing plays fragments of songs and ballads occur.[1] Early farce must also have influenced the plays, for most of them are farcical. Whether Pickle Herring of the Revesby Play was taken from the rôles of the comedians or survived from old festival figures of the games is doubtful I think, but almost certainly parts of the comic prose patter of this and other plays show an influence of players of farces.

Before the rise of the jig the contest of rival wooers had been adapted for forms of farce.[2] Wooings similar to those in the mummers' plays, expanded and rendered farcical, are found in the German fastnachtspiele written for city dwellers who acted in the seasonal festival of Shrovetide. Like the renouveau described by Machyn in the spring festivities of a lord of misrule already cited, they were almost certainly adaptations of folk games. In England, Lyndsay treated farcically the contest of rival wooers in a scene of the Proclamation to his *Satire of the*

[1] See *Modern Philology*, XXI, 249, 251-52, 254, 255, 266, 270-71.

[2] For the evidence, see Creizenach, *Geschichte des neueren Dramas*, I, 412-15, and II, 173-79; *Modern Philology*, XXI, 229-40. See Erk and Böhme, *Deutscher Liederhort*, No. 848, for a traditional German dialogue—resembling the mummers' wooing plays—in which a girl scorns in turn five craftsmen and accepts a beggar (compare Nos. 841-47). For some German farce forms, see Keller, *Fastnachtspiele*, Nos. 15, 70, etc., and Zingerle, *Sterzinger Spiele*, Nos. XI, XV.

Three Estates, introducing it by a dance. The group and the handling, in which a courtier, a merchant, a clerk, and a fool woo an old man's wife, with the success of the fool, parallel the treatment in the Revesby Play.

From the point of view of traditional elements, the most interesting of the song dramas adapting the contest between rival wooers is the piece which I have named "The Wooing of Nan." The dialogue (Text 19) is found in a manuscript of Dulwich College probably belonging to the end of the sixteenth century.[1] Across the otherwise blank back page "Kitt Marlowe" is written in a different hand from that of the manuscript. Since this is probably a modern hand,[2] there is no good reason for believing that Marlowe was the author of the jig. The text was clearly written down from memory. The lines have been garbled, one line at least has been omitted, and it is possible that several stanzas are missing.

The opening of the jig depicts the rivalry between Rowland and Piers, the farmer's son, for the favor of Nan. The additional characters here are not wooers but are called friends and serve as advisers. Rowland complains that with gifts and skill in dancing Piers has stolen his love, but neither addresses Nan in wooing speeches. It is agreed that the best dancer shall win her, and a stage direction calls for dancing. Before the victor is proclaimed, a Gentleman enters to engage in the contest. He woos Nan with the conventional offers of gifts and is also evidently the winner in the dance contest. At the moment of his success, however, the Fool enters claiming Nan, and she immediately declares her preference for him. With the entrance of the Fool the measure changes to one of livelier lilt. There is no indication of a dance contest in the decision between the Gentleman and the Fool, though one may have taken place. The

---

[1] See Warner, *MSS and Muniments of Dulwich College*, p. 60. Collier made an incorrect transcript in *Alleyn Papers*, pp. 8–11, on which the reprints in editions of Marlowe's works are based. Dyce, in editing Marlowe, made the suggestion that the dialogue is a fragment of a play. On the basis of Dyce's statement and Collier's text, I once thought that the closing couplets in the printed copies might be garbled lines from a play (*PMLA*, XXXVII, 413). The manuscript, however, shows that these are clearly ballad lines. Further, they furnish a natural jig ending similar to a number already noted.

[2] Warner, *op. cit.*, p. 61.

Gentleman attempts to make good his claim to Nan but is flouted by her.

All the elements in this jig indicate adaptation of popular material skilfully woven into a consistent whole. The chief features are the simple contest in dance; the conventional wooing addresses; the rôle of the Gentleman, recalling that of the gentleman or knight of the pastourelles who pursues the sweetheart of the shepherd or clown;[1] and the triumph of the Fool over those of social standing, on the model of the medieval rivalry of knight and clerk. These elements of folk and medieval literary traditions are of course blended in various combinations in many of the folk plays and farces already mentioned here. In particular the group of rival wooers in the jig, which includes a gentleman, a farmer's son, and the successful Fool, suggests an adaptation of a mummers' play of the Lincolnshire type. I judge, however, that "The Wooing of Nan" is rather directly drawn from simpler forms of folk game, several of which are used in combination.[2] This conjecture is based partly on the tone and varying technique of the jig and partly on features of the dialogue.

In a number of its details "The Wooing of Nan" echoes different game songs. The opening dialogue preparing for the contest between Rowland and Piers seems to have been modeled on a type of folk game of which there are many traces. Rowland is pictured as standing aloof from the festival group and telling a friend that he is undone, his heart "will neer be as it was," because the farmer's son has stolen his love. Slightly later another friend enters and rebukes Rowland,

> fie lusty yonker what doe you heer,
>   that you are not all a daunsing on the greene to day.

---

[1] See the end of the chapter for the motive as used in Adam de la Halle's *Robin et Marion* and in "The Blackman."

[2] A clear example of the more elaborate folk game which has combined two simpler games of the same general class is found in the Revesby Play. In one scene the characters, announcing their estates, perform a sword dance before the lady. Driven out by the Fool, they enter again, announcing themselves as "a youth of jollitree," the "eldest son," etc., and dance a round after the entry of each character. Following the dance of entry, there is a contest of the wooers in love addresses to the lady. The wooing element is obscure in the first part, but, as in "The Wooing of Nan," two games, one a contest in dance and one a contest in wooing pleas, seem to be blended.

Numerous singing games of children represent an unchosen girl
or boy as sitting apart in sorrow until a wooer comes.[1] In games
of adults the rejected man or woman seems to have been com-
pelled to stand apart crowned with a willow garland.[2] Such a
game is reflected in Beatrice's remark in *Much Ado*, II, i, "I am
sun-burnt. I may sit in a corner and cry 'Heigh-ho for a husband!' " In a shepherds' game described in Browne's *Britannia's
Pastorals*, a dialogue "wooing song" opens with a passage similar
to that just quoted from "The Wooing of Nan":

> Fie, shepherd's swain, why sit'st thou all alone,
> Whilst other lads are sporting on the leys?[3]

The first lines of a song preserved in a German collection, perhaps with the same tune as "Singing Simpkin," were cited in
the preceding chapter (p. 236):

> Delightles why sitzt thou soe, fa la la la la la la,
> Those foulded armes are signes of woe, fa la la la la la la.

The friend and adviser of the disconsolate lover appears also
in some wooing dialogues of the English folk, as in "The Cushion Dance" and "My Man John." Rowland's friend encourages
him and insists that Nan shall not be taken from him. Rowland
is roused to defy his rival and declare that he himself will lie
with the bride. In the calling-on verses of a Scottish mummers'
play "Galations," edited by Maidment, the following lines
occur:

Sir Alexander.
> The first young man that I call in, he is the farmer's son,
> And he's afraid he lose his love because he is too young.

---

[1] See Gomme, *Traditional Games*, I, 204, 206, 248, 320–23; II, 47.

[2] See p. 21 above.

[3] Bk. I, Song 3, ll. 241–42. There is no preparation for a contest, and the "wooing
song" is merely a discussion of unrequited love full of conceits. Perhaps in this case,
as in Wyatt's "A Robyn Joly Robyn" and Deloney's "As I went to Walsingham," only
the opening of a popular old song was used. With the first line from Browne, compare
> "Here's a soldier left his lone,
> Wants a wife and can't get none,"
opening a traditional game (Gomme, I, 206; see also I, 371).

Farmer's Son.
Altho' I am too young sir, I've money for to rove,
And I will freely spend it before I lose my love.[1]

In another Scottish mummers' play the battle about which the
play centers is apparently fought for a girl.[2] After Rowland announces his determination not to lose Nan without a struggle,
one of the characters appeals to her to know why she has forsaken Rowland for a "newcome guest."[3] Rowland, she answers,
can have her "heart in hold" if he can dance as well as Piers.
Nan's expression is common in wooing songs and dialogues. It
can be traced as far back as Chaucer, in whose "Nonne Preestes
Tale" (l. 54) Pertelote is said to have Chauntecleer's "herte in
hold," a phrase drawn from the love song "My lief is faren in
londe."[4] The expression occurs in *The Marriage of Wit and Wisdom*,[5] *George a Greene* (l. 258), the sixteenth century ballad beginning "E. Hath my herte in holde,"[6] and the later ballads
"The Mercer's Son of Midhurst" and "The Repulsive Maid."[7]
The most significant use of it for the jig is in "A Wooing Song
of a Yeoman of Kent's Son," printed in Ravenscroft's *Melismata* (1611). In this burlesque of a conventional wooing address,
the clown, who calls himself "my vather's eldest zonne," has
the line "And eke thou hast my heart in hold."

[1] In calling-on songs for sword dancers which are not in dialogue, these verses are
usually spoken of a "squire's son." In some cases the second couplet is omitted. See
Balfour and Thomas, *Printed Folk-Lore concerning Northumberland, County Folk-Lore*,
IV, 81; Bell, *Early Ballads* (1885), p. 396; Henderson, *Folk-Lore of the Northern Counties*
(1879), pp. 67–70; etc.

[2] See MacTaggart, *Scottish Gallovidian Encyclopedia*, pp. 502–3.

[3] Dissimilar as all this is to the opening of "Rowland," the two jigs show a number
of common features which may come from the influence of the opening formula in some
type of wooing game. "My heart is full of woe," Rowland tells his friend Robert,
because Peggy loves the Sexton; and later it is said that she has long ago forsaken Rowland for her new love. The friend encourages Rowland and proposes to test her love
for the two rivals by the device of Rowland's feigned death.

[4] See Hinckley, *Notes on Chaucer*, p. 154. Wyatt uses several variations on the
phrase. See *Poems*, ed. Foxwell, I, 254, 286, 370.

[5] Shakespeare Society, p. 60.

[6] Crawford Collection, No. 331.

[7] See *Roxburghe Ballads*, II, 190: VI 210.

Parallels to the second part of "The Wooing of Nan" are perhaps more significant. The offer of rich possessions by the Gentleman in his wooing address,

> you [shall] haue both land & tower
> My love shall want nor gold nor fee,

is one of the most constant features of wooing pleas. The offer here is a poetic variation of "house and land" and "gold and silver" occurring in folk songs and the ballad dialogues discussed earlier. In Lyndsay's Proclamation the Merchant promises Bessy, "Ye sall of silk, haif kirtill, hude, and goun," and the Clerk promises her, "of fyne gold ye sall ressaif ane box." The endearing epithets uttered by the Fool and Nan are equally conventional and have been noticed (p. 196). These, as well as the entry of the Fool and his reception by Nan, are closely paralleled in Lyndsay's farce. This part of the jig opens:

> foole   & see you not nan to day my mothers mayde
> see you not my true love my pretty nany
> shes gon to the greene to day to seek her love they say
> but she will haue myn none self if she haue any
>
> wen[ch]   wellcom sweet hert & wellcom my tony
> wellcom my none true love wellcom my huny
> this is my love that my husband must be
> but when thou comst home boy as wellcom as he.

In Lyndsay's piece it is the husband seeking his wife who says:

> Quhair art thow, Bessy, my awin sweit thing,
> My hony, my hairt, my dayis darling?
> Is thair na man that saw my Bess,
> I trow scho be gane to the Mess.

To the Fool, who comes last in the group of wooers, Bessy says, "Now welcome to me aboif thame aw!"

Similar passages occur in wooing scenes of other pieces. In the Revesby Play, Pickle Herring approaches Cicely with the words "O, now, sweet Cis, I am come to thee!" and she replies,

> You are as wellcome as the rest,
> Wherein you brag so lustily.

Immediately afterward he offers "store of gold." In an Irish version of the game "King William," King William enters saying,

> The first girl that I loved so dear,
> Can it be she's gone from me?
>
> If she's not here when the night comes on,
> Will none of you tell me where she is gone?[1]

Both of these parallels to the jig may be accidental of course. It is less likely that accident accounts for the number of phrases from "The Wooing of Nan" that occur in the third stanza of a ballad "The Louers Lamentation to his loue Nanny, To the tune of Did you see Nan to day?"

> Did you see *Nan* to day my pretty *Nanny*,
> My heart, my Loue, my ioy, and mine owne Cunny?
> Banisht her company, I liue in misery,
> This is the life I lead for my sweet Hunny.[2]

Both the jig and the ballad may have borrowed from a lost ballad beginning "Did you see Nan today?" which furnished the tune of that name.[3] Since, however, the Fool's first words in the jig, "& see you not nan to day," are obviously incorrect, it is possible that his speech began, "Did you see Nan today?" and that the tune was the second air of the jig.[4]

A lost dialogue evidently related to "The Wooing of Nan" was entered to Thomas Nelson August 13, 1591, under the title "a ballad of *a newe northerne Dialogue betwene Will, Sone, and the warriner, and howe Reynold Peares gott faire Nannye to his Loue.*" Apparently, as in the Dulwich College jig, Piers and Nan were the central figures in a wooing contest which included a group of men and one girl. Possibly the dialogue had its basis in a game similar to the early part of "The Wooing of Nan," before the rivalry between the Gentleman and the Fool is introduced. The successful Piers of the ballad may represent the same tradition as Piers the farmer's son who succeeds in

---

[1] Newell, *Games and Songs of American Children*, p. 74.

[2] Pepys Collection, I, 332.

[3] The tune was used also for "A Pleasant New Song of Two Valentines and their Lovers" (see *Roxburghe Ballads*, VII, 114–15).

[4] Nan's words in parting from the Gentleman, "God give you good night," are a common formula often used mockingly. See *Mankind*, l. 156; *Jacob and Esau*, I, iv; *Jacke Jugeler*, l. 990; *Summer's Last Will and Testament*, l. 84; and the end of *Every Woman in her Humour*.

taking Nan from Rowland but is eliminated later by the addition of other rivals. The music of "Nanns Maske" preserved in Additional MS 10337, fol. 2v, may indicate the adaptation of some piece of the type for courtly entertainment.

Probably both "The Wooing of Nan" and "A New Northern Dialogue" were modeled on spring or summer games. The jig pictures a holiday group of young people centered about a dance contest on a village green. In the discussion of "Die streitenden Liebhaber" it is pointed out that dancing contests were frequently associated with garland customs. The wooing dances noticed in chapter i are chiefly connected with May game, morris, or pastoral festival belonging to summer. The possible influence of the pastourelle tradition in the jig has been noticed also. Perhaps the games that influenced the two wooing song dramas were current especially in the northern part of England. "A New Northern Dialogue" and the wooing song called "A New Northern Jig" were licensed the year in which ballads were first entered as jigs. As I have already suggested, the use of the word northern in titles was probably a fad of ballad writers. At the same time, the fact that a number of mummers' wooing plays of a distinct type have survived in Lincolnshire may indicate an especial vogue of wooing games in that region. The kinship of "The Wooing of Nan" to these Lincolnshire wooing plays has already been stressed. Further, the variety of song and the use of interspersed dance in the mummers' plays generally point toward a technique for the older folk game of the more formal sort which was similar to that found in "The Wooing of Nan." The changing of tunes becomes increasingly important in later song drama.

Of the German pieces that picture rival wooers, the one called by Bolte "Die streitenden Liebhaber" (Text 27) is most suggestive of festival practice. In this singspiel two rivals appeal to the jungfrau's mother, who refers them to the girl herself for a decision. When all have agreed to this solution, the girl gives her garland to one lover and takes the garland of the other for herself. The two women depart and the rivals engage in a dispute as to the girl's meaning, each claiming her favor. The lover whose garland she has worn boasts that his curled locks, his yellow beard, his fine limbs, and his great skill have turned the scale in his favor. The other mocks him, declaring that a basket, a symbol of rejection, is to be his portion and appealing to the audience to approve his own reasoning.

"Die streitenden Liebhaber" is based on a *demande d'amour* that was widely used in medieval and Renaissance literature.[1] Bolte traces the singspiel directly to Question I in Boccaccio's *Filocolo*, Book V, on the ground that the order of handling is the same, the mother occurs only in these two among the numerous treatments of the theme extant, and there are similarities of expression. The chief difference lies in the fact that, whereas Boccaccio's youths end with an argument as to the significance of giving as against receiving in matters of love, a comic turn in the singspiel comes from the boasting and jibing of the two wooers who are left in doubt. One is a courtly, the other a ballad treatment. There is no decision in either case. Filocolo, however, tells the story before the company over which Fiametta presides, and asks for her verdict. She gives it in favor of the lover on whom the girl bestows her garland, making subtle distinctions in love matters to reinforce her conclusions. Undoubtedly *Filocolo* was most influential in spreading the theme in the Renaissance. During the sixteenth century the work was translated and imitated in France, Germany, and England.

It seems to me more likely, however, that the author of a singspiel so early as "Die streitenden Liebhaber" was adapting an English jig using the theme than that he was drawing directly on Boccaccio. *Filocolo* had been current in England since 1567 in translation, and there were some sixteenth and seventeenth century English forms of the *demande d'amour* in question which have apparently escaped notice. About 1582 a letter was written to the Earl of Hertford by his chaplain containing what seem to be suggestions for an entertainment. These include the garland question from *Filocolo*:

If I misse the title of the boke of Questions, theise are some of theime. A lady loving two at a banquett she toke from one a garland and put

---

[1] For an account of the various versions and for the literature of the subject, see Bolte, *Vierteljahrschrift für Litteraturgeschichte*, II, 575–79, and Crane, *Italian Social Customs of the Sixteenth Century*, pp. 62–70. For a treatment of the broader theme of "The Contending Lovers," see an article by Farnham, *PMLA*, XXXV (1920), 247–323.

yt on her heade: to the other she gave a garland which before she had upon her head. The question ys, whether (of the two) she loved better.[1]

In a list of court pastimes given in Sloane MS 848 there is a group of five headed "Boccace his 13 questions," one of which reads (fol. 29v):

> Fiametta Lady off ye Game. Philocopo ye stranger. Philocopo^s question: 2 loving on woman ye one having a garland; ye other none, shee tooke y^t garland from her owne head, & put it on his had none: & tooke ye others & put on her head wch off them shee best Loved: Resol: him to whom shee gaue one

In Randolph's *Amyntas* a girl, urged to choose between two swains, repeatedly gives them answers showing equal favor, and they engage in subtle arguments about her meaning, each claiming her (I, vi; II, vii; III, i). In one case she gives her garland to one lover and takes the garland of the other (II, vii).[2] The record of Tarlton's taking part in what was apparently a *demande d'amour* (p. 98 above) indicates a possible interest of the comedians in the form.

Even if the immediate forerunner was *Filocolo* or some other courtly source, the material of the singspiel shows a marked influence of popular game. Filocolo states that the problem of the garlands arose at a festival in his native city, and it seems to me probable that Boccaccio was using a motive taken from festival practice. In England there are many references to garland customs in the games, the garland being used as a prize in dance, song, and other contests, as a symbol of a girl's choice of a mate in the May and summer games, and apparently as a symbol of the union of May lord and lady.[3] A thirteenth century French song in dialogue with garland dance, "Jeu du Chapelet," has

---

[1] See *Wiltshire Archaeological Magazine*, XV, 199.

[2] In *Der Jud von Venedig* (II, i), a play of English origin, Ancilletta, urged by her father to make a choice of two suitors who plead before her, finds their merits so equal that she asks a year for consideration (Meissner, *Die engl. Comödianten zur Zeit Shakespeares*, pp. 140–45).

[3] For some of these allusions, see Stowe, *Survey of London*, Everyman's Library, p. 87; Jeaffreson, *Middlesex County Records*, II, 185; 9 *N. and Q.*, VII, 45–46; D'Urfey, *Pills to Purge Melancholy*, IV, 147; Fellowes, *English Madrigal Verse*, pp. 211, 219; Browne, *Poems*, Muses' Library, II, 146, 158; *Faerie Queene*, VI, ix, 7–9; Cox, *Actaeon and Diana*, p. 6.

been published by Bédier.[1] In Germany, records of singing and dancing for a garland or of songs begging for the garland as a token of favor begin with the fourteenth century and are numerous in the sixteenth and seventeenth.[2] The only game known to me, however, which suggests the singspiel lacks the garland. It is a French dance in which a woman dancing with two men each of whom has a torch, takes the torch of one, gives it to the other, and embraces the first.[3] A detail of the singspiel not found in Boccaccio, one wooer's references to the basket as in store for his rival, points to the influence of folk tradition, for in the customs of folk betrothal a girl gave to the accepted suitor a symbol of acceptance and to an unsuccessful suitor a symbol of rejection, commonly a glove or a basket.[4]

A wooing contest purely farcical in treatment is found in the singspiel published in *Liebeskampff* to which Bolte gives the title "Der alte und der junge Freier" (see Text 34). It is a song drama of over three hundred and fifty lines in five scenes, each sung to a different tune. Possibly the piece was arranged for interact performance. In the first scene a rich old man expresses his hope of winning the merchant's young daughter Lucia, while his servant and a gallant mock him directly and in asides. The abuse of the old wooer, in fact, forms a large part of the text of the play; and the mocking asides of the clownish servant Schrämgen—many marked by stage directions as addressed *ad spectatores*—with their waggish mimicry of his master's imbecility, are the most characteristic feature of the technique. In the second scene the old man woos the girl with cries and probably grotesque capers, and as a climax falls helplessly from his seat. The third is a scene of love-making between the gallant

[1] *Revue des deux Mondes*, January, 1906, pp. 402–6.

[2] See Böhme, *Geschichte des Tanzes*, I, 52–54, 59; II, 9–10; Bolte, *Zeitschrift des Vereins für Volkskunde*, VII, 382–92.

[3] See Rolland, *Rimes et jeux de l'enfance*, p. 186, from *Les amusements du bel âge* (1816).

[4] See *NED* and *Eng. Dialect Dictionary*, under "mitten"; *Romania*, IX, 549 n. 2. Perhaps willow garlands were given at times as a symbol of rejection. A custom possibly related to that of giving a basket prevailed at one time in Scotland in connection with weddings. The young men in turn carried a basket containing stones until kissed by one of the young women present (Brand, *Popular Antiquities*, II, 98), or a young husband carried it until kissed by his bride (10 *N. and Q.*, VII, 186, 256–57, 296).

and Lucia with their plan to disgrace the old wooer. In it the pair sing a lively duet on the joys of marriage, with chorus and interspersed dances. In the fourth scene the old man comes to the door of the girl's home full of confidence in his success. Receiving no answer to Schrämgen's loud knocking, he leans against the door to wait, and as the door opens, falls into the house. The last scene represents the old man threatened by the gallant for his presence there, his wager of all he has on or about him that the girl will accept him, his receipt of the basket from her as a sign of dismissal, his being stripped by the gallant and the servant, and the return of his clothing at the girl's request. He departs crestfallen.

The old wooer in the singspiel has an obvious kinship to the pantaloon who appeared in early Italian farce, became popular in plays, and passed into the drama of many countries. This kinship may be due to earlier adaptations of the pantaloon, either English or German. In *Amantes amentes* (1609) Rollenhagen presents a rich old wooer Gratianus, a *Doctor Juris*—probably drawn from the Italian Dottor Gratiano—who is scorned for his age by the girl Lucretia.[1] A gallant and student wins her.[2] This play was adapted in the *Comoedia von Sidonia und Theagene*, published in *Engelische Comedien und Tragedien*. In *Unzeitiger Vorwitz*, which appeared in *Liebeskampff*, the rivalry of an old man and a young one and the giving of a bas-

---

[1] This is one of the three names by which the girl in "Der alte und der junge Freier" is called.

[2] See Gaedertz, *Gabriel Rollenhagen. Sein Leben und seine Werke*, pp. 19–33. There is also a clownish wooer, but the dramatist does not stress the rivalry, contenting himself with presenting in turn the lovers and the girl's attitude to them. The popular ballad rhyme in *Amantes amentes*,

"Ho Bawr lass mir die Röselein stahn,
Sie gehören für ein Edelman,"

appears in stanza 59 of "Der alte und der junge Freier" as,

"Alter last die Rößlein stahn/
Sie warten auff einen andern Mann/"

See Gaedertz, *op. cit.*, p. 40; Herrig's *Archiv*, LXXXVIII, 273 (in *Der pedantische Irrtum*); Erk and Böhme, *Deutscher Liederhort*, No. 459, "Nesselkranz." With the lines of stanza 55 in the singspiel,

"Wie wenn sie ein andern hett/
Der mit jhr künfftig solt gehn zu Bett/"

compare the lines of "The Wooing of Nan,"

"that if he think to haue the wench,
heer he stands shall lie wth the bride."

ket are used, but these motives were presumably borrowed from "Der alte und der junge Freier."[1]

Though parallels are not always found, the fact that in each important feature "Der alte und der junge Freier" resembles folk custom or popular ballad suggests to me the possibility that the elements of the piece had been combined in a game or farce from which they passed into an English original of the singspiel. The central motives—an old man's wooing of a sensual girl, the flouting of the old wooer, and the success of a lusty young one—are paralleled in the wooing scenes of the mummers' plays. In these points the singspiel shows an especially close kinship to the Revesby Play, in which the rich old Pickle Herring woos Cicely confidently, only to be jeered at by her and the young suitor whose vigor pleases her more than the other's gold. In a long song drama of another type, which was acted at the beginning of the nineteenth century in Yorkshire at Mell suppers, conventions of comic and romantic wooing ballads are combined with the motive of a girl's seeking employment. She mocks an old man who would engage her as a servant and possibly as a wife, and in a romantic wooing scene accepts a young squire.[2] Similar scenes were presented in the song and dance drama of the London stage at the end of the seventeenth century. In Motteux's operatic *Four Seasons*, published at the end of *The Island Princess* (1699), winter is symbolized by an Old Man and an Old Woman, who woo a girl and a boy but are scorned as the two youths turn to each other. In Vanbrugh's *Aesop* (1697) a young woman first shuns an old man in a dance and then rejects him in a song dialogue (V, i) in spite of his claim

[1] See Creizenach's introduction to the reprint of this play in *Schauspiele*, p. 257; and Richter, *Liebeskampf und Schaubühne*, pp. 35–36. Parts of the old wooer's rôle in the play which are lacking in the singspiel were borrowed from *Sidonia und Theagene*, so that apparently the author of *Unzeitiger Vorwitz* has combined two independent treatments of the old wooer found in dramatic pieces used by the English comedians.

[2] From an account by Blakeborough in Mrs. Gutch's *Printed Folk-Lore concerning the North Riding of Yorkshire, County Folk-Lore*, II, 259–65. In the first part the girl scorns not only the old man but an old woman who would employ her as well. The wooing scene with the squire shows a number of the conventions of traditional ballads and the ballad dialogues studied in chapter vi—the girl's rebuke of the London rake, her rejection of a plea for a kiss, her final recognition of the wooer as her long absent lover, and the offer of marriage, ease, and elegance made by a highborn lover to a humble maid.

THE ELIZABETHAN JIG

to vigor—like that of the old man in the singspiel. She next accepts a youth, calling the old man Winter and the young one Spring.

The rejection of an old man clearly had a long vogue as a motive in dance, game, and ballad. A tune in William Ballet's *Lessons for the Lute* in a manuscript of Trinity College, Dublin, belonging to the time of James I, has the interesting title "A Scotis gig, Ye owld Man."[1] Perhaps this jig was an adaptation of a traditional singing game of Scotland called "Old Glenae" or "The Silly Old Man."[2] It is known in several versions, in some of which it has been combined with other singing games.[3] The song represents the old wooer's eagerness. The girl's point of view is given in "Auld Rob Morris," published in Ramsay's *Tea-Table Miscellany* of 1724 as an old song. It is a pure dialogue between a mother and her daughter, the one recommending an old man of wealth and the other scornfully refusing him.[4] "The complaint of a widdow against an old man," beginning "Shall I wed an agèd man,"[5] was entered on the Stationers'

[1] D 1. 21, No. 408, p. 83. For this information I am indebted to Mr. W. J. Lawrence.

[2] This term is applied to the old wooer of the Revesby Play (l. 394; see also l. 367).

[3] See Chambers, *Works of Burns*, IV, 394; Cunningham, *Works of Burns*, IV, 5, and VIII, 88–90; Cromek, *Reliques of Burns*, pp. 253–54, and *Remains of Nithsdale and Galloway Song*, p. 101; Dick, *Notes on Scottish Song by Burns*, pp. 71, 78–79; Hecht, *Songs from Herd's Manuscripts*, pp. 119, 290–91; Gomme, *Traditional Games*, I, 371, and II, 196–99.

[4] Ed. of 1871, I, 59–60. See Dick, *Songs of Burns*, pp. 127, 398, for versions of the song and air. See Erk and Böhme, *Deutscher Liederhort*, No. 832, for a dialogue between mother and daughter, similar in content, which was published in 1609. See also Hecht, *op. cit.*, p. 139, for the advice "Never let an auld man kiss ye, Jean!"

[5] *Shirburn Ballads*, No. LXVI. Possibly the ballad entered December 4, 1559, "sende me your sonne go your waye," was of this type. Many ballads voicing the complaint of wives possibly reflect old *mal mariée* songs. See *Melismata*, No. 10, "I lay with an old man all the night"; *Roxburghe Ballads*, VIII, 197, "The Old Man's Complaint"; *ibid.*, VIII, 199, "The Complaining Maid"; *ibid.*, VIII, 244, Burns's fragment "What can a young lassie do wi' an old man?"; *ibid.*, IX, 678–81, "The Young Woman's Complaint," to the tune "What should a young Woman do with an old Man?"; Chambers, *Songs of Scotland*, pp. 239–40, "My Auld Man"; Dick, *Songs of Burns*, pp. 159, 411. Compare the "lamentation of an olde man for maryinge of a yonge mayde," entered in 1563–4 (Arber, *Transcript*, I, 232). See Playford's *Dancing Master* for the dance "An Old man a bed full of bones." The two songs, one early, in *Deutscher Liederhort*, No. 850, *a* and *b*, are warnings to a young girl against marrying an old man. Part of "Die Metamorphosis" is sung to the tune of a popular German song "Ein alter hat

Register September 4, 1564.[1] A later ballad, from the Douce Collection (I, 32a), "The Constant Maidens Resolution: Or Silver and Gold cant buy true Love," beginning "I am a young Damsel/that's plunged in Woe," has the appearance of being a debased dialogue. The young damsel of this ballad refuses to be dazzled by the gauds an old man offers. In "The Old Miser Slighted," beginning "My Mother duns me every day to marry with a Miser then," the girl desires to marry a brisk young gallant rather than the old miser with his diseases.[2] A series of kindred ballads, largely traditional and marked as folk songs by their repetitions and refrains, are even more suggestive of the singspiel. In one beginning "The carl he came o'er the croft," published in Ramsay's *Tea-Table Miscellany* of 1724,[3] the girl expresses her contempt for a rich old man favored by her father, declaring in the refrain,

> I winna hae him!
> For a' his beard new shav'n.

A traditional song, "There was an a'd man cam' over the lea," with a kindred refrain, belongs to the same type.[4] In another traditional song, "An old man came to see me," different from the preceding, the girl describes the old man of wealth with contempt and expresses her preference for a young man.[5] The ballad "There was an old man came over the sea," which used to be sung at the end of a Warwickshire mummers' play, has a refrain similar to that in Ramsay's song, but gives a girl's description of various mishaps to an old man chosen for her by her

---

nur Wort und Wind" (Bolte, *Singspiele*, p. 36), and a kindred song in "Der Exorcist" opens "Meine Zeit will ich jetzund" (pp. 15–16). No tune is indicated for the last (see p. 330 n. 1). In Wright and Halliwell's *Reliquiæ Antiquæ*, II, 210–12, there is a long fourteenth century monologue spoken by an old man on the decline of his powers.

[1] *Transcript*, I, 263.

[2] *Roxburghe Ballads*, VIII, 194–95. In a white-letter ballad called "A New Song," the old wooer is driven to suicide when a girl mocks him (*ibid.*, VIII, 198; IX, 814–15).

[3] Ed. of 1871, I, 121–22.

[4] Mason, *Nursery Rhymes*, p. 33. A similar opening, "The silly poor Man came o'er the Lee," is used in a seventeenth century broadside "The Gaberlunzie Man" (Crawford Collection, No. 1055).

[5] *Journal of American Folk-Lore*, XXIX, 188.

mother.[1] Like the old wooer in the singspiel, he both falls off
his "perch" and falls in when the door is opened.

Of the minor incidents and motives used in the development
of the singspiel, Schrämgen's[2] function in the early part as the
agent of the old wooer suggests both the adviser of folk song and
the agent who arranges marriages in the customs of many folk.[3]
The significance of the basket has just been discussed. In the
singspiel a number of references to the basket to be given to the
old lover prepare for the climax when the girl dismisses him
with one. Possibly the influence of ballad conventions and customs in pastimes was as decided in "Der alte und der junge
Freier" as in other pieces studied in this chapter.

In the next singspiel, "Pückelherings Dill dill dill," there is
rivalry for the favor of a wife, and the farce element has been developed further by the addition of a number of popular conventions. Derived apparently from a sixteenth century jig, this
singspiel is unusually interesting in both material and technique.
The clown Pickleherring, a miller, enters with his wife, whom
he instructs that if anyone comes while he is away at work, she
is straightway to answer "No" to everything. This will safe-
guard her against wooers. She gives her promise, and he leaves.
The "Gabilirer" now enters, singing to his servant:

> Don John of Barbary
> Spoke to his Lackey:
> Woo me this dainty miss
> And fetch her to me.
> Where this boor gives a kiss,
> I will give her three.
> Don John of Barbary
> Of kisses is quite free.

In a brief part that is spoken he asks the wife to take him into
her favor, and receives the answer, "No, no." The schoolmaster

[1] *Folk-Lore*, X, 186–94. Many traditional versions of the song have been collected
in England and in America. See Cox, *Folk-Songs of the South*, p. 489.

[2] A clown of this name appears also in *Aminta*, published in *Liebeskampff*, and a
Schramfritz in Hans Sachs's *Wiltbad* (Creizenach, *Schauspiele*, p. xcvii).

[3] See *Folk-Lore*, XVIII, 77–79, for a custom of the west of Ireland in which the
agent accompanied by the suitor negotiates with the parents of the girl.

Herr Jan, or in two versions Domine Johannes, next enters, capering and singing a song which begins:

> Hey, in comes Herr Jan lustily
> The beauteous maid to see.
> With a trip and a skip,
> With a flap and a snap,
> With a spring and a fling,
> Hey, merry will we be.

Resolved to try his fortune with the wife, he addresses her as little mouse and asks for her favor. When she answers his suit with her "No, no," he claims that two negatives make an affirmative and spouts the conventional Latin. After this prose part he "leaps around" and sings,

> I can spring,
> I can sing,
> I can dance, etc.

The Pedant and the Gabilirer now both give over their suits and leave. There is next a long song dialogue between the wife and a third wooer. He asks first that she stay with him a little while and then that she join in some merry-making tomorrow. To both she says, "No, no." His next step is to offer her presents, asking if she would scorn them.—"No, no."—"If you lacked a bed would you show me the door?"—"No, no."—"If I should desire kindly to take your husband's place would you treat it as an insult?"—"No, no." They retire.

Throughout the next scene there is an eight-line stanza with a lively refrain. The wife and the lover return, and Pickleherring comes back singing,

> Now homeward must I fare,
>   My work it wearies me.
> My wife the gayest clothes must wear
>   Although a clown I be.
> If someone's made my cogwheel go
>   Till till till till,
> Then he has spoiled for me even so
>   My very finest mill.

. . . .

> A miller by trade am I,
>   And swiftly can I grind,
> And make my mill go merrily,
>   If only I have wind, etc.

After the fourth stanza the wife and the wooer take part in the dialogue. The wife accepts a ring from him, and Pickleherring is convinced that another man has ground in his mill. To satisfy him the wooer offers to tell him a wonderful story. The three wooers come back with the clown in a new scene, and the wife conceals herself within hearing. The third wooer tells in song the story of an experience with a certain wife. At her first no's Pickleherring is full of joy, but as the tale proceeds he sees that he has been overreached. The third wooer now launches into coarse details reflecting on the wife, and Pickleherring contributes to them. She has all the while been protesting indignantly in asides, and she finally confronts them with their "lies." The third wooer saves the day by declaring that it was all a dream. Pickleherring is satisfied and begs her forgiveness on his knees. The most interesting feature of this last scene is its crescendo of *pfui* and *hinaus mit*. The wife cries out on the husband and the wooer; the husband and the wooers cry fie on the wife; all cry out on jealousy.[1]

Four versions of this singspiel are extant.[2] The first, called by Bolte "Die Müllerin und ihre drei Leibhaber," survives in an undated chapbook with the title "Das ander Engeländisch Possenspiel von Pückelherings Dill dill dill," etc. Text 28 is a reprint of the chapbook, and the account which I have given of the piece is based on this version. Bolte finds some indication of its date in the fact that Robert Reynolds, coming to Germany in 1618, supposedly introduced the name Pickleherring for the clown. In a later work, however, he points out that Reynolds was on the Continent in 1616.[3] Pickleherring is conventional for the clown in *Engelische Comedien und Tragedien* of 1620, and it is probable that many of the pieces in this collection were

---

[1] See Bolte, *Singspiele*, p. 34, for an allusion of 1699: "Da konte man auff singen, wie in den teütschen possenspiel. O Pfudian, hinauß, hinauß mit dir, pfui, pfui, o Pfudian hinauß undt all, die solche sein." See also p. 279 n. 3 below.

[2] Bolte, *Singspiele*, pp. 110–47, prints all four. For his discussion of them, see pp. 31–36.

[3] *Danziger Theater*, p. 47.

printed from forms much earlier than the date of publication. The second version was published at Amsterdam in 1658 with the title "Singende Klucht van Domine Johannes, ofte den jaloersen Pekelharing." This seems to be a translation of the preceding German version—for some German words are left in the text—but based on a more complete and careful text than that in the chapbook, which is far from satisfactory. The third version appeared in 1672 as an appendage to *Kunst über alle Künste Ein bös Weib gut zu machen*, a German adaptation of *The Taming of the Shrew*. It has the title "Singendes Possenspiel Die doppelt betrogene Eyfersucht Vorstellend." In the main the text is like that of the two preceding versions, but the schoolmaster's Latin has increased in quantity and his wife is added in an unimportant part. Having reason to believe that the compiler of *Kunst über alle Künste* used an earlier printed version for his play, Bolte conjectures that he had a printed source for the singspiel also. At any rate, he probably followed some earlier text even in the addition of the pedant's wife, for her name appeared in the playbill when German actors performed at Stockholm in 1733 what seems to have been a different adaptation of the singspiel.[1] The fourth version was published at Stockholm in 1691 as "Ett lustigt Nach-Speel, af 5 Personer agerat." Bolte calls it "Poudzdrumels Frau und ihre drei Liebhaber." In this Swedish adaptation a part of the story of "Singing Simpkin" seems to have been combined with a part of "Pückelherings Dill dill dill," and the stanza and tune of the Swedish "Singing Simpkin" are used throughout.

Though the title of the first German version identifies the piece as English, there is no trace of the jig in England. Bolte is convinced that it was performed at Danzig by English actors early enough to influence the comic scenes of Waimer's *Elisa*, published in 1591. In the play there are a rich pantaloon, a braggart, a jealous husband Zani, his wife Margretha, and her wooer Dominus Johannes, also called Pan Jan. Though the names of Pantalone and Zani point to Italian influence, Bolte regards Dominus Johannes as of English origin:

Vergleicht man aber Akt II, Sc. 3, wo Zani den D. Johannes aus dem Hause prügelt, weil er seine Frau Grete geherzt hat, und IV, 6,

[1] Bolte, *Singspiele*, p. 34.

wo Zani die vom Fischmarkte heimkehrende Frau ob ihres langen Ausbleibens schmält und dann ihr Gespräch mit dem Galan belauscht, um wiederum auf ihn loszufahren, vergleicht man, sage ich, diese Scenen mit dem anderwärts von mir in einer holländischen und zwei deutschen Übersetzungen mitgeteilten Singspiele vom Dominus Johannes, so wird man sich schwerlich der Schlussfolgerung entziehen können, dass Waimer jene englische Gesangsposse kannte und benutzte, ohne sich jedoch ihre leichtfertige Moral anzueignen.[1]

Perhaps, however, such features are too common in farce to be conclusive. If Bolte is right, it is probable that the jig was a popular one in Tarlton's day and formed part of the repertory of Leicester's men on the Continent, as I have conjectured that "Rowland" did. The long-lived popularity of "Pückelherings Dill dill dill" abroad is proved by records extending into the eighteenth century. A playbill of the second half of the seventeenth century announces the singspiel "nach der ersten Action" of the play; it was acted at Dresden in 1683; and a performance by German actors at Stockholm in 1733 has just been mentioned.[2]

The distinctive feature of the plot is the successful wooer's device of shifting his questions so that the no's of the wife become favorable answers. Bolte points out the use of this motive in "Nazario geloso con un'ordine, che lascia alla moglie, è causa ch'ella gli faccia le corna" from Costo's *Il Fuggilozio* of 1600 (p. 25) and also in some modern folk tales.[3] The simple jest of a woman's no's turned to consent has had a long career in English ballad and folk song. It was developed in three

---

[1] See Bolte, *Danziger Theater*, pp. 22–27, for his discussion. He also calls attention to the use of the English word gentleman by both Dominus Johannes and the braggart though he discounts this, and to the fact that evidence for an influence, direct or indirect, of Heywood's *Play of Love* (ll. 1294–1350) is found in a passage in which Zani cries "Fire, fire," and in answer to his wife's query declares that the fire is in the heart of the king.

[2] For evidence as to the vogue, see Bolte, *Singspiele*, pp. 33–34, 185; Richter, *Liebeskampf und Schaubühne*, p. 83 n. In the records of the three performances cited, the singspiel bears the title found in the Dutch version, "Domine Johannes."

[3] Imbriani, *La novellaja fiorentina* (1871), No. 26, "Il figliolo del pecoraio"; Pitrè, *Novelle popolari toscane* (1885), No. 16, "Il soldatino"; Pröhle, *Kinder- und Volksmärchen* (1853), No. 66, "Der listige Soldat." See *Singspiele*, pp. 33, 185. To these may be added Le Magnin de Rougemont, *Contes licencieux de l'Alsace* (1906), No. LX, "Dis toujours: Non!"

broadside ballads having *chanson d'aventure* openings and much reported dialogue. The first, written by Climsell about the middle of the seventeenth century, "A Warning for Maides" to a new tune "No, no, not I,"[1] turns on the sudden change in the significance of the girl's answer rather than on the wooer's skill in varying the questions. In a second part the man uses the refrain to mock the betrayed girl. The second broadside, "The Dumb Lady: Or, No, no, not I; I'le Answer," sold by Brooksby at the Golden Ball, emphasizes the wooer's varying the form of his questions to render favorable the lady's constant reply, "No, not I."[2] In the third ballad, "The Denying Lady: or, A Travellers Frolick with a Woman that Reply'd no to all Questions and Discourses put to her," to the tune "I marry and thank you too,"[3] the lover's report of his questions and of the girl's answers has some resemblance to the dialogue in "Pückelherings Dill dill dill." A dialogue form of the jest not unlike the corresponding part of the singspiel is found in "Consent at last," beginning "Ladys, why doth Love torment you?" which was published in D'Urfey's *Pills* (IV, 82–83). The lover asks a question in each stanza, and the lady merely repeats her no's. In a traditional dialogue of the English folk which is closely related to a number of the simple wooing dialogues discussed in other connections, the lady's constant reply is "O No, John! No, John, No, John! No!" but the wooer frames his questions so that he wins her consent to marriage. An adaptation has been used as a parlor song in England and America in the last half century and has possibly influenced a traditional version in America. Related songs have appeared as slip ballads and in songbooks in England and America since the eighteenth century. One of these had a great

[1] *Roxburghe Ballads*, III, 41–46, printed for "John Wright, the younger."

[2] *Ibid.*, IV, 349–54. Four ballads with similar refrains in which the woman answers no but without the shift in questions are "A Song" with the refrain "O nay, O nay not yet" in *Merry Drollery* (1661; reprinted in Ebsworth's *Choyce Drollery*, pp. 204–6); "Shall I? Shall I? No, No, No!" in *Roxburghe Ballads*, VI, 157–58; "Kind William, or, Constant Betty," *ibid.*, VII, 201; and "Tom and Doll. Or, The Modest Maid's Delight" in *Pills*, II, 26–28. See *Roxburghe Ballads*, I, 283, for the tune "Oh no, no, no, not yet," of the ballad "Death's Dance," and Chappell, *Popular Music*, I, 378, for its use in two ballads of the Pepys Collection.

[3] Pepys Collection, V, 248. This white-letter ballad was "Printed by and for A. Milbourn, at the *Stationers-Arms* in *Green-Arbor*."

popularity as a stage duet in America through a considerable part of the nineteenth century.[1]

The jest of a lover's telling the story of an intrigue to the husband of the woman involved is also found separately in a number of Continental stories. Bolte cites Straparola's *Notti* (1550), IV, 4; Agricola's *Sprichwörter* (1558), No. 624; and Hans Sachs's "Der Buler mit der rothen Thür."[2] In a sixteenth century English story drawn from Straparola, "The Tale of the Two Lovers of Pisa" in *Tarltons Newes*, the woman drops a ring into her lover's cup as he is telling her family of his adventures, and he protests that the incidents are "follies of mine owne braine."[3] The two motives of the woman's no's and the dream are combined in the story "Von einer neugetrauten Jungfraw" from *Das Kurtzweilige Leben von Clement Marott, Oder: Allerhand lustige Materi für die Kurtzweil-liebende Jugend* (1660).[4] Here the ring episode, omitted in the singspiel, appears also. Another combination of the two motives, which includes the ring incident but resembles the singspiel in some details of conversation, is found in IV, ii, and V, i, of Ravenscroft's *London Cuckolds* (1682).[5] The lover's statement that his experience was all a dream has been considerably embroidered. Ravenscroft evidently used a version that contained the ring incident, but the success of the jig probably determined his choice of material. Indeed the series of questions put by the lover is

[1] For "O, No, John" and related songs, see Sharp, *One Hundred English Folksongs*, pp. xxxv, 154–55, and Tolman and Kittredge in *The Journal of American Folk-Lore*, XXXV, 405–6.

[2] *Singspiele*, pp. 33, 185. He adds the modern example, Pröhle, *Kinder- und Volksmärchen*, No. 63, "Die Trommelschläger vom alten Fritz."

[3] Earlier the husband hunts for the hidden lover, claiming that he has had a dream of one's entering the house. In Middleton's *Roaring Girl*, IV, i, Moll sings snatches of two ballads telling of the tricks of women, and calls them her dreams.

[4] Bolte, *Singspiele*, pp. 31–33, analyzes the tale at some length on the ground that he has met no earlier form of the jest which seems to have been the source of the singspiel. The setting is French. According to the title of *Das Kurtzweilige Leben*, the book was translated from French into Dutch and thence into German. Bolte states that the Dutch version lacks this particular story, however.

[5] Ravenscroft's material is said to come largely from Sieur d'Ouville's *Contes aux heures perdues* (1644), but no source is given for this incident. See *Roxburghe Ballads*, IV, 354 n.; Summers, *Restoration Comedies*, pp. xxxv–xxxviii. In IV, ii, a husband repeatedly declares that a true tale of intrigue which his foolish wife is telling is a dream of hers. See p. 243 n. above for a list of the jig plots used in this play.

so much like that in the singspiel as to suggest that Ravenscroft knew some version of the jig and borrowed from it.

"Pückelherings Dill dill dill" departs farther from the form of pure ballad farce than any of the singspiele so far considered. In addition to parts in different ballad meters, there are choral passages and passages in irregular verse and in prose. Perhaps this modification came about under the influence of the operatic trend in the seventeenth century. But the new art was a revival of older traditions, and the singspiel as a whole may follow the model of older popular farce. It does not give the impression of unity, however. Most of the singspiel can be regarded as a story of the clown, his wife, and the successful wooer, written in regular ballad meters with elaborate refrains. Except for contributing to the chorus of fie's in the last scene, the other two wooers take part only in a small section near the beginning, which seems to form a distinct element, with spirited and irregular lyric portions set in prose. This may have been added from another source to introduce into an intrigue farce the popular motive of the group of rival wooers.[1] The schoolmaster and the "Gabilirer" are types. In the chapbook version, the successful wooer, on the other hand, is undistinguished by name or type, being merely "der Buler" or "der dritt Buler," though in the Dutch and the late German version he is the gentleman or cavalier who figures as wooer in several song dramas.

Herr Jan was clearly drawn from more formal drama. The pedant is a stock figure in neo-Latin, Italian, and English drama of the sixteenth century,[2] and is frequently a comic wooer or intriguer, as in *Pedantius*. In the singspiel, however, he evidently combines the rôle of schoolmaster with that of *premier danseur*, and this may account for the fact that a character so

---

[1] Similar groups were introduced into late sixteenth century plays of a popular type. In *Wily Beguiled* a student, a lawyer, and the clownish son of a rich farmer are rivals for Lelia; in *Grim the Collier*, the subplot represents the contest of a parson, a miller, and a collier for a country maid Joan; in Jonson's *Tale of a Tub*, a country girl is pursued by three rivals. See *Modern Philology*, XXIV, 423–28, for my discussion of these and other plays as in part possible adaptations of popular material.

[2] See Bond, *Early Plays from the Italian*, pp. xxix–xxx; Bolte, *Singspiele*, p. 33 n. 2. Bolte calls attention to a Scholar Johannes who appears as a wife's lover in a Brussels farce of 1549.

unimportant should have given the piece one of its titles. In his songs with their description of the dance movements and in the leaping dance called for by the description, he shows a kinship to the vices of the early moralities.[1] From the point of view of tradition, the most interesting figure in the group is Don Jansa of Barbary, whose rôle as wooer is least significant. His speech as he enters, with its narrative opening and its pictur-esque short lines, may well be the oldest element in the sing-spiel. It implies the presence of the conventional servant as agent of the wooer, but the servant does not appear.

Don Jansa represents the wanderer who comes wooing from strange lands. Such figures are conventional in early German forms of the wooing. In one of the garland songs already cited the wooer announces, "Ich kumm aus frembden landen her."[2] In nearly all of the English wooing games noticed at the begin-ning of this chapter, the fool seems to have taken the place of the wanderer, though the beggar, who represents one type of wan-derer in the German games,[3] is found in a group of the Revesby Play. Strange figures from foreign lands are popular, however, in English wooing songs, and I have no doubt that the Gabilirer "Don Jansa auß Barbaria" belongs to the same tradition, though the names may ultimately come from foreign sources.[4] Whether or not the term gabilirer is a variant of *cavaliero*[5]—and I do not believe that it is—there are traces in English song of a

[1] For the song and dance of Sensual Appetite in *The Four Elements* and the vice in *Like Will to Like*, see p. 84 above.

[2] See Böhme, *Geschichte des Tanzes*, II, 9. See Bolte, *Singspiele*, p. 47, for the statement "Er kombt aus frembden Landen" in a song which he regards as the basis of a late singspiel.

[3] Böhme, I, 57.

[4] The term gabilirer is used only twice—before the two speeches of the character in the chapbook version. Elsewhere in the German and the Dutch versions he is Don Jansa, or Jan, or Jean. The chapbook has no list of characters, however. A "King of the Barbarie" appears in one singing game of English children (Gomme, *Traditional Games*, I, 18–21). See Child, *English and Scottish Popular Ballads*, No. 100, for a ver-sion of "Willie o Winsbury" in which Johnny Barbary, "lately come from Spain," is a seducer. The name Don Jan is suggestive of the famous Spanish Don Juan. Don Jan's address to the wife in the German version of 1672 as "ein schwarzbraunes Mägdelein" smacks of the folk.

[5] Bolte, p. 33, calls attention to a reference to an English Pickleherring as a "Ju-bilirer" in 1621; to a German song printed in 1664, opening "Gabelier hinder der Thür"; and to the French word *gabeleur*, excise officer.

wandering wooer under similar names, whom a girl follows away.
What is probably the same term only slightly changed in trans-
mission occurs in a singing game from Yorkshire:

> Follow my gable 'oary man,
> Follow my gable 'oary man,
> I'll do all that ever I can
> To follow my gable 'oary man.

> We'll borrow a horse and steal a gig,
> And round the world we'll have a jig,
> And I'll do all that ever I can
> To follow my gable 'oary man.[1]

During the Puritan struggle use was made of a ballad called
"The North-country Maid's Resolution, and Love to her Sweetheart: To *a pleasant new Northern tune.*" The song opens:

> As from Newcastle I did pass,
> I heard a blithe and bonny lass
> That in the Scottish army was,
>   Say, "Prithee let me gang with thee, man."
> Unto a jolly Cavalier blade,
> As I suppose, her moan she made,
> For evermore these words she said,
>   "I'll follow my Cavalilly Man."

The refrain, which is repeated for each stanza, runs,

> "O my dainty Cavalilly man,
> My finnikin Cavalilly man,
> For God's cause and the Protestants,'
> I prithee le' me gang with thee, man."[2]

This ballad is apparently an adaptation or parody of an older
piece on a girl who would follow a wandering lover called by
a name close enough to "cavalier" to give point to "cavalilly."

The beggar is the vagabond wooer in the Scottish ballad
"The Gaberlunzie-Man," in which the girl is "aff with the

---

[1] Gomme, *Traditional Games*, I, 129–31.

[2] See Chappell, *Popular Music*, II, 440–41. Chappell calls attention to the popularity of the tune "Cavalilly Man." In *The Famous Historie of Fryer Bacon* one song
is to a "Northren tune: Of cam'st thou not from New-castle."

Gaberlunzie-Man."[1] A similar line, "She's awa' with the gypsie laddie," occurs in the ballad of the gipsy lover Johnny Faa, who wins the wife of a lord. Texts of this ballad are found in a seventeenth century broadside and in Ramsay's *Tea-Table Miscellany*, and variant traditional forms have been collected.[2] In the traditional folk song "The Wraggle Taggle Gipsies, O"[3] the lady follows three gipsies. A version of the singing game "Here come three Dukes" represents a gipsy from Spain as the wooer.[4] In "The Beggar-Laddie"[5] the beggar proves to be a lord. Among the ballad dialogues discussed in chapter vi there are many in which a girl follows a soldier, sailor, or outlaw. In some songs the lover comes from outlying parts of Great Britain, especially from the highlands of Scotland, as in "Lizie Lindsay," "Walter Lesly," "The Highland Laddie," and "The Blaeberry Courtship."[6] A number of similar wooing dialogues stress the invitation and the gift motives of the folk wooings. One, noted in chapter vi, with the lover's invitation to the "Bonny Lass" to wend to Liggan Water resembles the folk song "Bonie lassie, will ye go . . . . To the birks o' Abergeldie?" a song which influenced Burns.[7] In a singing game featuring the offer of gifts the lover invites the bonnie lassie, "Will you come to the Highland braes."[8]

Another interesting character type found in the singspiel is

[1] See Crawford Collection, No. 1055, for a seventeenth century broadside version; Ramsay, *Tea-Table Miscellany* (1724), ed. of 1871, I, 80–82; *Orpheus Caledonius* (1733), I, 95–98.

[2] See *Roxburghe Ballads*, VIII, 149–57; Child, *Popular Ballads*, No. 200.

[3] Sharp, *One Hundred English Folksongs*, pp. xix, 13–16.

[4] Gomme, *Traditional Games*, II, 455.

[5] Child, No. 280.

[6] See Child, Nos. 226 and 296; *Orpheus Caledonius*, I, 28–29; and *Journal of American Folk-Lore*, XXXV, 345–46.

[7] See Hecht, *Songs from Herd's Manuscripts*, pp. 153, 300–301; Dick, *Songs of Burns*, pp. 104, 389. See also Maidment, *Scotish Ballads and Songs* (1859), pp. 59–61, for a version from a broadside of the early eighteenth century.

[8] See Newell, *Games and Songs of American Children*, pp. 54–55. See Gomme, *Traditional Games*, I, 85, for the singing game with grotesque dance, "Will ye gang to the lea." Kindred dialogues are "Will ye gang o'er the ley-rigg," "Will ye go to the Flanders, my Mallie O?" and "Will ye gang to Fife, lassie?" (Hecht, *op. cit.*, pp. 100–101, 102, 182, 281–82).

the miller, who was a favorite in song, tale, and play. He was celebrated from the Middle Ages as a thieving and intriguing rascal, as in Chaucer's "Reves Tale" and its analogues.[1] In an old story told in *Greenes Newes both from Heauen and Hell* he is cuckolded through his own intrigue.[2] His unsuccessful intrigues, his wooing, and his thievery are frequent motives.[3] More suggestive of the situation in "Pückelherings Dill dill dill" is Skelton's reference in the *Garlande of Laurell* (ll. 1411–17) to a lost work of his dealing with a jealous miller and his "ioly make," a "wanton wenche" whom her husband could not guard.

Though the plot of the singspiel depicts Pickleherring as the victim of his own device, his song as he returns from his work reflects another tradition—that of the jolly miller who sings of his trade and his content with life. In the *Athenian Mercury* for December 1, 1691, it is said, "we require better bred Fools than our Forefathers were contented with, for a Merry Millar or *Cobler* wou'd make Excellent Sport at the *Red-Bull* or *Globe*." Just what the writer had in mind is not clear, but back of the few plays with millers and the jig discussed here, there were many popular songs that may have influenced stage song and dance. A ballad entered on the Stationers' Register on September 4, 1564, had the title "a myller I am,"[4] similar to Pickleherring's "Meins Handwercks ich ein Möllner bin," or "By trade a miller am I." In Ravenscroft's

---

[1] See especially "A Mery Jest of the Mylner of Abyngton."

[2] Ed. McKerrow, pp. 44–51. See also pp. 90–91, and *Wendunmut*, ed. Oesterley, I, 331, for earlier Continental versions. For ballad versions see *Roxburghe Ballads*, IX, clxvi*–clxviii*, "A Cuckold by Consent"; and *Bagford Ballads*, II, 527–33, "The Unfortunate Miller."

[3] For his intrigues see *Roxburghe Ballads*, VII, 426–27, "The Witty Maid of the West; Or, The Miller well thrash'd by *Robin* the Plowman"; IX, 626–28, "The Crafty Maid of the West; Or, The lusty brave Miller of the Western Parts finely Trapan'd"; IX, 623–24, "Ill-gotten Goods seldom Thrive." See also *ibid.*, IX, 625–26, "Roger the Miller's Present." For the miller as wooer, see *Grim the Collier; Shirburn Ballads*, No. XXIX, "A pleasant ballad of the mery miller's wooing of the Baker's daughter of *Manchester*"; *Works of Deloney*, ed. Mann, p. 413, the tune "The Miller would a woing ride"; Bolte, *Singspiele*, p. 34, illustrations from Continental farces and plays. For his thievery, see *Roxburghe Ballads*, IX, 611–12, "The Miller's Advice to his Three Sons, On taking of Toll," and variants cited there; *Journal of American Folk-Lore*, XXXV, 390–92; Newell, *Games and Songs of American Children*, pp. 102–4.

[4] See *Transcript*, I, 76, for a ballad called "a mylner."

Pammelia (1609) there is a catch which begins "A Miller, a miller, a miller would I be." The lines,

> The Mill a, the Mill a,
> So merily goes the mery Mill a,

presumably from some song of the miller, open a vigorous dancing and drinking song in *Tom Tyler*.[1] A song of one "that lives by his Mill" in D'Urfey's *Pills* (III, 125) has the refrain,

> His mill goes *Clack, clack, clack,*
> *How merrily, how merrily,*
> *His Mill goes* Clack.

"The Miller of Dee," beginning "There was a jolly miller once," was popular for several centuries.[2] Some of the songs of the miller have been preserved as singing games of children.[3]

Vulgar plays on terms connected with the miller's trade, which make up the refrain of Pickleherring's song, are common. In the story told in *Greenes Newes both from Heauen and Hell* the miller says, "wee Myllers are tyed to this custome, which is, when any young women dooth fortune thus to come to the Mill, wee vse as well to take toule of themselues, as of their sackes."[4] In *Grim the Collier*, Clack the Miller says to Joan,

---

[1] Ll. 256–57. The lines,
> "Dilla, my Doctor deare,
> sing dilla, dilla, dilla,"

used in Nashe's burlesque of Harvey near the end of *Saffron Walden*, and probably taken from some more popular old song, suggest Pickleherring's refrain "Dill, dill, dill, dill." Compare "Trilla, trilla, trillarie" in the spinning song of *Ralph Roister Doister*, I, iii.

[2] See Chappell, *Popular Music of the Olden Time*, II, 666–68; Hecht, *Songs from Herd's Manuscripts*, pp. 264–65, 331–32. See *Roxburghe Ballads*, IX, 613, for a similar song from Dodsley's *King and the Miller of Mansfield*. In an unpublished fragment of the Gothland and Egton Sword Dance collected by Cecil J. Sharp, there are two speeches of a miller, one beginning "I am the fusty Miller," and the other,
> "I am the brave Miller; I scorn to deny.
> I grind for both rich and for poor."

A part of his self-characterization is his boast of pleasing all women. See Chambers, *Songs of Scotland*, pp. 194–95, for the song
> "O, merry may the maid be
> That marries the miller!"

[3] See Gomme, *Traditional Games*, I, 289–93, "Jolly Miller"; Newell, *Games and Songs*, pp. 102–3, "Happy is the Miller"; Hecht, *Songs from Herd's Manuscripts*, pp. 204, 207, 316–17, 318–19.

[4] Ed. McKerrow, p. 44.

"there be as good Wenches as you be glad to pay me toll," and
Joan scornfully refers to him as "you that take toll of so many
Maids."[1] A ballad called "Maids, wives & widdows take heed
of the miller's tole dish" was licensed March 12, 1656. In "The
Jolly Miller," sung in D'Urfey's *Don Quixote* (Part III, III, ii),
toll is taken of three sisters; and in a related broadside, "The
Lusty Miller's Recreation,"[2] the mother also is included. Plays
on the grinding of the grist or turning of the wheel are more
frequent. "*A ballad Rebukinge the licencious livinge of Diverse
lewde personnes* Intituled *the grindinge in the myll*" was entered
on November 11, 1580. In Fletcher's *Maid in the Mill*, V, ii, the
supposed miller's daughter Florimel sings five vulgar songs of
invitation which all end with the idea of the mill's going round
though they vary in material. The first, to which she dances,
runs:

> Now having leisure, and a happy wind,
> Thou mayst at pleasure cause the stones to grind;
> Sails spread, and grist here ready to be ground;
> Fy,[3] stand not idly, but let the mill go round.[4]

[1] Ed. of 1662, p. 24.

[2] *Roxburghe Ballads*, IX, 618-21. D'Urfey's song is found also in *Pills*, I, 185-87.
Another song in *Pills* (I, 169), "The Willoughby Whim," is a dialogue of two sisters
with plays on "toll" and "grind." See Chappell, *Popular Music*, II, 587, for the air of
this song in ballad opera and in some editions of *The Dancing Master*, and II, 594, for a
short song from *The Jovial Crew* (1731), "There was a maid went to the mill."

[3] The second song ends,
> "Oh fy, oh fy, oh fy!
> Let the mill, let the mill go round!"
The repeated fie's found here and in the last scene of "Pückelherings Dill dill dill"
are common in Elizabethan ballads and plays. A coarse wooing ballad in *Shirburn
Ballads*, No. IV, "In the merry month of May," or "The lover's replye to the maiden's
fye fye," has a refrain with repeated fie's. "Fie, fie, fie" is the courtesan's constant
byword in *Blurt, Master Constable*. It is also used in *Merry Wives of Windsor* at the
end of II, ii. A children's singing game, "Wallflowers," has the refrain "Fie, fie, fie, for
shame" or variations on it (Gomme, *Traditional Games*, II, 330-40). In "Von den
Männern" Agnes says to Jan, "Ein Buhler pfui dich an."

[4] See Chappell, *Popular Music*, II, 589, for "Round and round, the mill goes
round" as the name of a tune. See Herrig's *Archiv*, CXIV, 337, for the spinning song
from Rawlinson Poet. MS 185, about 1590,
> "It was a maide of Islington,/and her wheell ran very rounde;
> and many a wanton web she spun,/and it cost her many a pound.
> Alas! said she, what hap had I,/run round, run round, my whele!
> I fere a mayden I shall die,/before my web I rele."

Among seventeenth century ballads of the type,[1] "Bonny Peggy
Ramsey," printed in D'Urfey's *Pills* (V, 139–40),[2] is conspicuous for its elaboration and vulgarity. Use is also made in these
songs of the double meaning in "cog" and "cogwheel" which
gives point to one line in the miller's song of the singspiel.
"The Mill, Mill—O," a coarse ballad of the early eighteenth
century with the usual plays on words, took its title from the
final refrain:

> O the Mill, Mill—O, and the Kill, Kill—O,
>   And the cogging of the Wheel—O;
> The Sack and the Sieve, a' that ye maun leave,
>   And round with a Sodger reel—O.

The song had an enormous vogue through the century.[3]
    It is possible that songs of the miller and his mill were dance
songs par excellence. The lilt and the refrain of many of them
suggest this as well as the mention of dance in several of the
cases already noted. Probably the song with the "Dill, dill,
dill, dill" refrain gave the clown his best chance for dancing in
"Pückelherings Dill dill dill." The miller's songs used as singing
games were of course accompanied by dance. In the October
Eclogue of *The Shepheardes Calender* Piers tells Cuddie,

> Of loue and lustihead tho mayst thou sing,
> And carrol lowde, and leade the Myllers rownde.

"The happy Miller" is found in *The Dancing Master* of 1696 and
1698,[4] and "The Dusty Miller" was a popular country dance

[1] See *Roxburghe Ballads*, IX, 622, for "Grist ground at Last; or, The Frolick in the
Mill" with a refrain "Sing hey ding ding, a ding ding"; *ibid.*, IX, 618–21, "The Lusty
Miller's Recreation"; *Bagford Ballads*, I, 34–36, "The Crafty Country Woman"; *Pills*,
II, 23–25, "Pretty Kate of Windsor." See Chappell, *Popular Music*, II, 750, for a
traditional song with the refrain "And the corn grinds well."

[2] See Dick, *Songs of Burns*, pp. 174, 416–17, for a different "Bonnie Peggie Ramsay"
used by Burns.

[3] See *Orpheus Caledonius* (1733), I, 40–41; Ramsay, *Tea-Table Miscellany* (1871),
I, 78–79; *Vocal Miscellany*, II, 188; *Merry Companion*, pp. 36–37; Hecht, *Songs from
Herd's Manuscripts*, pp. 115, 287; Dick, *Songs of Burns*, p. 455; etc. In the modified
traditional form the reference is to the miller's reel.

[4] Chappell, *Popular Music*, II, 589; the same tune as "Round and round, the mill
goes round."

tune in the eighteenth century.[1] The music of a "Miller's Jigg" is preserved in Add. MS 29371, fol. 46, in the British Museum,[2] a manuscript written in the first half of the eighteenth century. During 1710 "A Whimsical Dance between a Miller, his Wife, and a Town Miss" was specially advertised ten or twelve times in the *Daily Courant* as an interact performance at Drury Lane and Greenwich.[3]

The simplest of the extant farce jigs dealing with rival wooers is a piece of only seventy-six lines published in *Engelische Comedien und Tragedien*, which Bolte calls "Der Narr als Reitpferd" (see Text 29). Pickleherring opens the singspiel with the statement that he has come to Amsterdam to ease his pain and sorrow. He is looking for his sweetheart and approaches fearfully a stone house. The woman comes out, speaking of her unwilling visit to the city, of a chain given her by a merchant, and so on, while Pickleherring interjects slighting remarks. Then as he begins to tell her how "Cupido" has pierced his heart, each line of his wooing is countered by a scoffing remark of the woman's. A gallant who is her lover now enters, and during their love-making the clown stands aside expressing his fears. At the woman's suggestion that they must get rid of him, the gallant forces him to kneel while he is saddled and bridled for her to ride. After the pair have put Pickleherring through some of his paces, so to speak, he is set free. The chief interest of the singspiel must have lain in what could be made of the clown's rôle as horse.

Bolte points out that the woman's riding of Pickleherring in "Der Narr als Reitpferd" is a variation of the fable of Aristotle and Phyllis current in the Middle Ages.[4] In 1595, not far from

---

[1] See Chappell, *Popular Music*, II, 608. The song was collected by Herd (Hecht, *Songs from Herd's Manuscripts*, pp. 142, 297-98). See also Dick, *Songs of Burns*, pp. 161, 412. According to Dick, the tune has the name "Binny's jigg" in a manuscript of 1692.

[2] *Cat. MS Music*, II, 200.

[3] I am indebted to Professor Sherburn for this item. See Böhme, *Geschichte des Tanzes*, I, 58, and *Altdeutsches Liederbuch*, No. 44, for "Die schöne Müllerin," a popular dance song of Germany in the sixteenth century, in which a proud *müllerin* has a she-ass conveyed into the bed of an amorous canon who is pursuing her.

[4] *Singspiele*, p. 21. He cites Hagen, *Gesamtabenteuer*, No. 2; Keller, *Fastnachtspiele*, pp. 138, 150, 354, 1488, and *Nachlese*, p. 216; *Germania*, XVII, 306. Rolland, *Rimes et jeux de l'enfance*, p. 186, gives the title "Cheval d'Aristote" to a kindred French game in which a man is ridden by a girl who is kissed by the rest of the group.

the time when the jig was probably written, there appeared in London *The Brideling, Sadling and Ryding, of a rich Churle in Hampshire, by the subtill practice of one Iudeth Philips, a professed cunning woman, or Fortune teller. With a true discourse of her vnwomanly vsing of a Trypewife. . . . . For which fact, shee was . . . . whipped through the citie, the 14 of February, 1594.*[1] A woodcut pictures the old man bridled and saddled with Judith on his back. Whether or not the trick was suggested by some variant of the Aristotle story, the rôle of horse is by no means uncommon in English pastime and farce. A form of tilting with two men as horses is pictured in the Middle Ages, and survived among the courtiers of James I.[2] The doctor's horse figures in several mummers' plays and sometimes brings the doctor in.[3] A man performing equine tricks is ridden by a wooer in an Irish game.[4] At the end of *Like Will to Like*, Newfangle rides away on the Devil's back. In the *Trial of Treasure* there is an elaborate incident of the bridling of Inclination, the vice.[5] Probably the popular old farcical affair of one character's carrying another off on his back, especially the devil's carrying the vice off the stage, was the occasion for much comic horsemanship.[6] A seventeenth century play that makes passing use of the motive is Heywood's *Lancashire Witches*. In III, i, Mistress Generous enters with a bridle for a horse. When Robin, on

---

[1] The unique copy of this pamphlet is in the Huntington Library. Hazlitt has described it in his *Handbook* (p. 458). *A Quest of Enquirie* dealing with the incident of the tripewife has already been noticed as containing a jig. See pp. 72–73.

[2] Gomme, *Traditional Games*, I, 311–12; *Assheton's Journal*, Chetham Society, p. 47 n.

[3] See Baker, *Glossary of Northamptonshire Words and Phrases*, II, 430; Tiddy, *Mummers' Play*, pp. 164–65, 176, 220, 224, 230, 251.

[4] Kennedy, *Banks of the Boro* (1867), chap. xiv. See also Gomme, *Traditional Games*, I, 351–52; II, 147. For the ancient German festival at which girls were hitched to a plough, see Brand, *Popular Antiquities*, I, 97.

[5] Percy Society, pp. 20–22.

[6] See Bale, *King Johan*, ll. 791–96; *The Longer thou Livest*, G ii; *Inough is as good as a feast*, end; *Friar Bacon and Friar Bungay*, sc. 6; *Looking Glass for London and England*, IV, iv; *Histriomastix*, Act II; *Devil is an Ass*, V, vi; *Staple of News*, near end of I, ii, and intermean after Act II; Yorkshire play of 1628 (Chambers, *Elizabethan Stage*, I, 328 n. 3).

her husband's orders, refuses her the horse, she bridles him, saying,

> Horse, horse, see thou be,
> And where I point thee carry me.

"Exeunt Neighing" is the stage direction.

The single air and the short ballad form of the singspiel suggest an early date for the English original, and a number of details associate the piece with a group of jigs and ballads current in England about 1600. The entrance of Pickleherring looking for his lost love recalls the Fool's entrance in "The Wooing of Nan." In both "Der Narr als Reitpferd" and "Singing Simpkin" we find the clown's suffering as lover—the conventionality of which has already been noticed—a reference to Cupid, and a "Fa la" refrain. The opening line of the singspiel, "zu Ambsterdam bin ich gewesen," may have imitated a group of songs that included "As I went to Walsingham," "As from Newcastle I did pass," and "As I came from Tottingham."[1] Amsterdam would easily take the place of such town names in an English jig. The choice of Amsterdam perhaps points to an adaptation of the jig in the Low Countries before it passed to Germany.[2] The singspiel uses "Hum hu" and "Fa la" for the refrain of different lines in the stanza. Bolte finds an apparent imitation of it in a song from a collection published at Nuremberg in 1607:

> Einsmals kams mich gar gehling an, Ho, ho,
> Auch auff die löffeley zu gahn, Humm humm.[3]

In England "A balad intituled *Hum nun &c* Songe by Kendall" was licensed April 10, 1605. William Kendall was with the Admiral's Men in 1597–98, and he may have continued with

[1] See Chappell, *Popular Music*, I, 121–23, 219; II, 441.

[2] The tune was used in two Dutch singspiele—as "Ick ben tot Amsterdam gewesen, hu, hu" in Starter's "Betrogene Freier," and as "Mijn lief is met een ander op de been" in Fonteyn's adaptation of "The Blackman." The latter title was probably taken from some Dutch song written to the tune of the jig.

[3] See *Singspiele*, pp. 21–24, for a discussion of the use of the tune. Bolte quotes a German ballad printed about 1615, "Schön Anna, Hertzallerliebste mein! Ach Gott," as probably deriving its stanzaic form and air from "Der Narr als Reitpferd."

the organization as Prince Henry's Men when they occupied
the Fortune.[1] Fennor in his *Defence* of 1615 refers to having
"chaleng'd *Kendall* on the Fortune Stage."[2] It is quite possible
that "Hum nun" was a Fortune jig with a refrain that served
as title on the Register. If "Hum nun" is an error for "Hum
hum" or a variant of it, Kendall's song may be the jig with the
"Hum hum" refrain that was carried to the Continent and published without title in *Engelische Comedien*. There were probably imitations of the jig, however. What may be a fragment of
a related jig is sung by Bellafront in her brothel in I *Honest
Whore* (1604), II, i:

> Well met, pug, the pearl of beauty: umh, umh.
> How now, Sir Knave? you forget your duty, umh, umh.
> Marry muff, sir, are you grown so dainty; fa, la, la, leera, la.
> Is it you, sir? the worst of twenty, fa, la, la, leera, la.

The situation recalls Guilpin's allusion in Satire V of *Skialetheia*
to the chanting of Kemp's jig by whores and bawds. We have
here not only the refrains of the singspiel but the mockery with
rapid change of speakers, often in alternate lines. "Der Narr
als Reitpferd" goes much farther in coarseness, especially in its
many asides. Possibly it was the technique of such jigs or the
influence of them that Cartwright had in mind when he contrasted the wit of Fletcher with Shakespeare's "Old-fashion'd
wit" of the clown and lady's question that "walk'd from town
to town" and "made bawdry pass for comical."[3]

In "The Blackman" the central feature of the plot is the
capture of a clown's sweetheart by two gentlemen, and her final
rescue. The only extant English version was published by
Kirkman in 1673 in the second part of *The Wits, or, Sport upon
Sport* (see Text 23). A Dutch version by Fonteyn, "Monsieur
Sullemans Soete Vryagi," had appeared in 1633;[4] and apparently

---

[1] See Chambers, *Elizabethan Stage*, II, 190, 327. Thomas Kendall, the "Revels
patentee" of 1604 (*ibid.*, p. 327), is less likely to have sung the song.

[2] See Taylor's *Works* (1630), Nn 6*v*. Fennor states that Kendall did not meet him,
but that he himself extemporized on themes flung at him, a suggestion that Tarlton's
art of extemporizing continued into the seventeenth century.

[3] Beaumont and Fletcher, *Works*, ed. Dyce, I, xlv.

[4] This is discussed and reprinted along with "The Blackman" by Bolte, *Singspiele*,
pp. 28-30, 83-105.

there was a seventeenth century German form also, for as Bolte indicates, the farce "Mum" performed by Hamburg comedians in 1674 was presumably "The Blackman." Though Fonteyn has followed the material of the jig rather closely, his singspiel is more than twice as long, the gentlemen have become soldiers, and a rat-catcher and a mountebank are substituted for the brushman. It is possible, of course, that he had a longer original than the late seventeenth century form of "The Blackman," but more probably he adapted and expanded rather than translated. There is no record of the piece in England outside of its publication. I judge, however, that the jig was much older than the Dutch form of 1633. Though the comic characters and the various spirited verse forms are suggestive of seventeenth century drollery, the art is that of old comic figures and their songs. Further, the incidents of the jig represent old dramatic motives. Consequently, while the jig may be a seventeenth century expansion of an early piece, it does not seem to me probable that so many conventions of an earlier period would have been brought together *de novo* in the seventeenth century.

The motive of the capture of a girl apparently had some vogue in romantic drama, especially in the pastoral, and may have come upon the London stage in the sixteenth century with the triumph of a genuinely popular tradition.[1] In pastoral plays the captor is usually a savage or wild creature. An eclogue drama by Bentivoglio performed at Bologna in 1494 represents a giant as carrying off a shepherd's sweetheart and a group of shepherds as winning her back in a battle with the giant.[2] In a pastoral of 1513 by Cavassico a faun as captor is slain by the shepherd lover of the girl.[3] Creizenach regards these elements as belonging to old conventions. A pageant was presented at the English court on Twelfth Night, 1515, in which wild men captured four knights and their ladies, and other knights came to the rescue.[4] In *Mucedorus*, a play that has many marks of

[1] Popular English drama in the Renaissance probably utilized many conventions of an early romantic drama. In *Modern Philology*, XIV, 229–51, 467–512, and XXIV, 419–42, I have discussed at some length the possible extent of these conventions and their influence on English drama.

[2] Creizenach, *Geschichte des neueren Dramas*, II, 183.

[3] *Ibid.*, p. 184. A bear and a wild man appear here as in *Mucedorus*.

[4] *Modern Philology*, XIV, 476.

popular or traditional origin, a wild man carries off the princess and is slain by her lover, who has taken on the disguise of a shepherd. The motive of the capture is found with classical coloring in more formal literary pastorals, as in *The Faithful Shepherdess*. More suggestive of popular tradition is the capture of Earine by Maudlin and Lorel in *The Sad Shepherd*. Clearly, however, there is no direct influence of pastoral plays on "The Blackman."

To my mind, May games continuing pastourelle traditions in farcical form offer the most likely source for the combination of the capture theme with the rivalry between clown and gentleman which occurs in the jig. Though "The Blackman" is purely farcical, its main elements may have been derived ultimately from some dramatic form in which pastourelle conventions of the type found in Adam de la Halle's *Robin et Marion* survived. In the French piece a rustic girl with a clownish sweetheart encounters on the road a knight who covets her and makes two separate efforts to persuade her to go with him. In the jig the lovers meet two gentlemen who twice carry Susan off forcibly. In both cases the loutish lover makes a show of boldness to cover his cowardice. Robin and Marion were popular in French festivals long after Adam's time, and passed into English tradition.[1] The distinctly clownish traits of the shepherd group in *Robin et Marion* may well have led to farce rather than pastoral in folk plays.

In certain farcical devices and character types the jig resembles rather closely parts of the old morality *The Marriage of Wit and Wisdom*. After being driven off by the gentlemen the first time, the clown Thumpkin in "The Blackman" returns disguised as an old man, and takes Susan away while her captors fight over her. To prevent his interfering again, the gentlemen put him on a stool in a white sheet and command him to cry "Mum." The brushman calling his wares takes Thumpkin for a ghost and runs away. The clown then decides to change his "Mum, mum" to "Ho, ho." He discloses himself to the frightened blackman who has entered crying his black, and the two change places at Thumpkin's request. The gentlemen returning are put in a panic by the ghostly blackman with his

[1] See *Modern Philology*, XIV, 237-39.

"Ho, ho" and by his fellow, whom they take to be the devil. They deliver up their weapons and make off. In the morality, Idleness, the vice, after robbing Wit, disguises himself as a foreign doctor and cries his remedies. He is met by two rogues, who rob him and, to prevent his causing them trouble, wrap him in a sheet and command him to tell passers that he is mumming. Wit on entering takes him for a ghost but finally releases him. Afterward Idleness appears as a rat-catcher with his street cries. Besides the trade cries, both the morality and the jig contain much short, brisk verse of the general type belonging to vices.

Possibly "The Blackman" borrowed nothing directly from *The Marriage of Wit and Wisdom* but used incidents and figures conventional in farce and game. The device of setting one wrapped in a sheet to cry "Mum" was borrowed from the mumming of the folk in Christmas games. The disguises of Thumpkin and Idleness are similar to those of rogues in such plays as *Look about You*, *Blind-Beggar of Bednal-Green*, *Bartholomew Fair*, and *Winter's Tale*. A natural type of disguise in the sixteenth century would be that of a street vender or strolling representative of some trade—the tinker, rat-catcher, gelder, etc. The popularity of such figures in play, ballad, and jig is noticed later.[1] Possibly the blackman was a type similar to the collier. The black face of the collier may have been responsible for the conventional association of him with the devil, and it is probable that the fear which Thumpkin and the blackman inspire in the gentlemen is due to a black face as well as to the devil's cry of "Ho, ho, ho." The two Dutch singspiele dealt with in the next chapter suggest a popularity of devil disguises in farces and farce jigs.

Tunes for "The Blackman" are not specified. In the 1633 edition of Fonteyn's singspiel three of the tunes are named. "Enghelsche Fortuyn," or "Fortune my foe," is used for a passage at the end which is not found in "The Blackman"; and "Sir Edward Nowell's delight"[2] is used twice by the clown in passages that differ in meter from the corresponding parts of the

---

[1] Pp. 289–93. See "Turners dish of Lentten stuffe," stanza 13, for the blackman's cries (Rollins, *Pepysian Garland*, p. 34).

[2] See Chappell, *Popular Music*, I, 149–51, for this tune, which also went under several other names, and I, 162–64, for "Fortune my foe."

jig. The third, called by Fonteyn "Mijn lief is met een ander op de been," has been met as "Zu Ambsterdam bin ich gewesen, hu, hu" in connection with the preceding singspiel. Apparently the corresponding passage near the end of the jig could have been sung to this. In the 1643 edition of Fonteyn's piece, where all eight of the tunes used are printed,[1] the remaining five have Dutch titles. Some of the tunes in the singspiel may have been used in the jig first, but the two pieces differ considerably in metrical schemes, even in passages in which the English meter seems to have suggested the Dutch. At the end of the jig a passage with the refrain "Fa la la" was probably sung to the "Engelsche fa la" discussed in connection with "Singing Simpkin." In several other instances the wording of the jig may point to the tune. It is natural to suppose that the passage beginning "As ye came from Walsingham" was written to be sung to the tune of "Walsingham," and the words "Jog on," used twice by Thumpkin in his flight with Susan, suggest the tune "Jog on," or "Hanskin."[2] Stage directions carefully distinguish a large part of the verse in the singspiel as spoken, not sung. In the jig, probably the prose parts only were spoken. Though "The Cheaters Cheated" is longer and would require more tunes, "The Blackman" is the most interesting of the extant English jigs for complexity of form. Whether this is due chiefly to an elaboration that took place in late song drama or to the nature of the material is a question, as I have said.[3]

[1] Bolte, *Singspiele*, pp. 180–83, reprints all of them. See pp. 29–30 for his discussion of them.

[2] Chappell-Wooldridge, *Old English Popular Music*, I, 159–60.

[3] For a late German singspiel carrying on the conventions of the rivalry between gentleman and clown, see pp. 330–33 below.

CHAPTER IX

MISCELLANEOUS FARCE JIGS

THE material that remains for consideration consists of some titles of lost jigs not already taken into account, a dozen relatively early singspiele of foreign composition, a single English jig written after the stage vogue had passed, and several singspiele in late seventeenth century forms whose relation to the English jig cannot be established with certainty. The allusions to the lost jigs are few and too vague to be of much value, but the titles show the prevalence of certain interesting character types. The extant pieces frequently resemble those of the two preceding chapters in situations and motives—which after all are in the main the common property of all forms of farce. Yet they extend the range of droll incidents and also of odd comic characters. In spite of the small number of specimens left, these three chapters give, I believe, a fairly correct perspective of the farce jig.

A group of characters from humble life that evidently proved especially popular in the jig consists of the strolling chapmen who appear crying their wares in so many plays and ballads.[1] Of the jigs featuring these characters, however, only

[1] See, for example, the peddler of ballads and other wares in *Winter's Tale*, IV, iv, and Newcastle's *Triumphant Widow*, I, i; the ballad seller in *Three Lords and Three Ladies of London*, B4–C, and *Night Walker*, III, iii; the collier in *Westward Hoe*, III, iii; Irish costermongers in *Old Fortunatus*, IV, ii; etc. For the "pedlers Mask" of 1574–5 see Feuillerat, *Revels of Elizabeth*, pp. 238–40. Groups of such characters appear in *Bartholomew Fair*, Act II; *Beggar's Bush*, III, i; *Loyal Subject*, III, v; *London Chanticleers*; and *Britannia Triumphans*. See *Inigo Jones*, Shakespeare Society, Plate XIII, for Jones's sketch of the ballad singer in Davenant's masque, and Simpson and Bell, *Designs by Inigo Jones*, Plate XXXIV, for the kitchen maid and the crier of mousetraps. These figures are common also in plays and entertainments of the Restoration. For typical ballads, see "The Cries of Rome" printed at the end of Heywood's *Rape of Lucrece* as "added by the stranger that lately acted Valerius his part"; "Turners dish of Lentten stuffe" (Rollins, *Pepysian Garland*, pp. 30–38); "The famous Ratketcher" (*ibid.*, pp. 60–65); "The Pedlar opening of his Packe" (*ibid.*, pp. 116–20); "The Traders' Medly; or, the Crys of London" (*Bagford Ballads*, I, 115–16; second part in D'Urfey's *Pills*, VI, 124–27). A ballad called "pedler and his packe" was entered on the Register in 1568–9 (*Transcript*, I, 386; see also I, 436). See Chappell, *Popular Music*, I, 81, for versions of a song in *Deuteromelia*, "Who liveth so merry in all this land," with stanzas on the broom-man, the cobbler, etc. See also *Roxburghe Ballads*, VII, 46–58, 78.

"The Blackman" has survived. The broom-man and the kitchen-stuff woman furnished the titles for two of Kemp's lost jigs, and a garlic vender pretty certainly figured in "Garlic."[1]

On January 16, 1595, "a ballad intituled / *A plesant newe Jigge of the broome-man*" was licensed to Thomas Creede, with "Kempe*s*" written by the side of the entry. On May 2 of the same year "a ballad, of master Kempe*s Newe Jigge of the kitchen stuffe woman*" was entered to William Blackwall.[2] Nothing further is known of either jig. The titles indicate the presence of the hucksters and make probable the use of their street cries as in "The Blackman." Infidelitas as a broom-man hawks his wares in Bale's *Three Laws* (ll. 178–81). In *The Three Ladies of London* Conscience enters with brooms at her back,[3] and in Fletcher's *Loyal Subject* (III, v) an ancient enters in guise of a broom-man, both singing the cries of the trade. The brushman in "The Blackman" furnishes a variation on the figure. In "A sounge of the guise of London," a series of peddlers' cries with the refrain "Will you buy any Broome, Mistris?" broom is cried first and then brushes.[4] A ballad called "buy Bromes buye" was entered on the Register in 1563–4.[5] The title of Climsell's seventeenth century ballad "The Joviall Broome man"[6] suggests a rather unexpected conception of the character. The song is a series of boasts about marvelous and impossible exploits, but it seems to have no connection with the broom-man beyond the refrain "Hey jolly Broome-man," which may have come from an earlier ballad.[7]

[1] For the lost "Jig between a Tinker and a Clown" and "Jig between Jenkin the Collier and Nancy," see pp. 75, 190, above.

[2] Arber, *Transcript*, II, 669, 297.

[3] D iv. "Conscience Crye to all estates in sellinge of broom" was licensed July 25, 1592. Rollins, *Analytical Index*, p. 40, cites references to Conscience as a broom seller from Deloney (*Works*, ed. Mann, p. 31) and Greene (*Works*, ed. Grosart, XI, 238).

[4] Clark, *Shirburn Ballads*, pp. 335–36.

[5] See Arber, *Transcript*, I, 238. "The anotomy or particular description of a byrchen broome" found in Hall's *Court of Vertue*, fol. 125, was licensed in 1562–3 (*Transcript*, I, 200).

[6] *Roxburghe Ballads*, I, 499–503.

[7] A romantic treatment of a youthful broom-man is found in "The Jolly Broom-man: Or, the unhappy Boy turn'd Thrifty" of D'Urfey's *Pills* (VI, 100–102) and in a traditional version (*Journal of the Folk-Song Society*, I, 84–85).

Venders of food have received more attention, especially by
way of satire. The crying of kitchen-stuff forms part of "A
sounge of the guise of London" just mentioned. A picture of the
huckster is given in "Turners dish of Lentten stuffe," written
about 1613:

> The wench that cries the Kitchin stuffe,
>   I maruell what she ayles:
> She sings her note so merry,
>   but she has a dragle taile,
> An empty Car came running,
>   and hit her on the bum,
> Downe she threw her greasie tub,
>   and away that she did run.
>
> But she did giue a blessing,
>   to some but not to all:
> To beare a loade to Tyburne,
>   and there to let it fall.[1]

This may be an allusion to some actual incident, but its features
are conventional. The railing of kitchen-stuff women and others
who vend food is usual in ballad literature. In the ballad by
Ford printed as Text 17, a husband and a wife who is a kitchen-
stuff woman rail at each other.[2] A common trick at the expense
of venders was to overturn their wares, and an accident like that
described in the ballad would please the populace almost as
well. In a picture of Jenkin's truancy in *Jacke Jugeler* (ll. 152–
56) there is an account of his overthrowing the basket of a
"Freuteres wyfe." In *Bartholomew Fair* Busy upsets the
basket of the gingerbread woman in indignation at the images
as idols (III, i), and Nightingale trips the costermonger in order
to rob Cokes while he is scrambling for the pears (IV, 1). These
incidents may give a clue to the treatment of the kitchen-stuff
woman in the jig.

Any jig dealing with such a figure would probably make a
point of the coarseness, uncouthness, and filth associated in
jocular literature with those who handle food. The convention
goes back to the Middle Ages. Chaucer in the Prologue to *The*

---

[1] See Rollins, *Pepysian Garland*, p. 32.

[2] See also pp. 68–71, 172, above.

Canterbury Tales (l. 386) speaks of the diseased leg of the cook, and in *Cocke Lorelles Bote* the description of the butcher comes to a climax in "His hosen gresy" as a breeding place for maggots. Godfrey Gobelive's mother in Hawes's *Pastime of Pleasure* (chap. xxix) was "a gorgious baude," who "wyped her disshes wyth her dogges tayle." Thersites complains that his mother's nose drops as she prepares the food.[1] Later examples in drama are the cook in *Comedy of Errors* (III, ii) and Ursula in *Bartholomew Fair* (II, ii–v; IV, v). Nell is all grease. "Her rags and the tallow in them will burn a Poland winter." Her complexion is swart like Dromio's shoe, but her face is "nothing like so clean kept: for why, she sweats; a man may go over shoes in the grime of it." An ell and three-quarters "will not measure her from hip to hip." As one would expect from Jonson, Ursula, the abusive pig-woman and hawker of other viands, presents a thoroughgoing picture of size, greasiness, and filth. Jonson's play is made up of conventions of roguery and vagabondage, drawn in part, no doubt, from life, but probably from jocular literature chiefly; and in spite of his disdain of certain popular rôles, he may have borrowed his ironic realism largely from jigs and farces. A typical seventeenth century ballad is "The Old Pudding-pye Woman set forth in her Colours," which describes the old food vender as two yards about, with a long nose that often "doth drop" and hands that she washes "but twice or three times in a year."[2]

A passage in *This Worlds Folly* by I. H., printed in 1615, shows that a garlic vender played an important rôle in "Garlic" (B 2):

I will not particularize those *Blitea dramata* (as *Laberius* termes another sort) those *Fortune*-fatted fooles, and Times Ideots, whose garbe is the Tooth-ache of witte, the Plague-sore of Iudgement, the Common-sewer of Obscœnities, and the very Traine-powder that dischargeth the roaring *Meg* (not *Mol*) of all scurrile villanies vpon the Cities face; who are faine to produce blinde **Impudence* ["Gar-

---

[1] *Thersytes*, D iii.

[2] See *Roxburghe Ballads*, VII, 77; IX, 776–77. A ballad of "the kitchen boyes Songe" was licensed in 1570–1 (*Transcript*, I, 438) and another of "the oysters wifes songe" on November 29, 1614. For "kitchen-stuff" used as a term of contempt, see *Works of Nashe*, ed. McKerrow, I, 299; III, 125, 130; and *Works of Harvey*, ed. Grosart, II, 230.

licke" is here printed in the margin], to personate himselfe vpon their stage, behung with chaynes of Garlicke, as an Antidote against their owne infectious breaths, lest it should kill their Oyster-crying Audience.

In the figure behung with chains of garlic we probably have the typical huckster. A cry of a garlic seller is given in the first scene of Tailor's *Hog hath Lost his Pearl,* printed in 1614. When the jigmonger Haddit is interviewed by a player for whom he is composing a jig, two lines of the jig are sung by the player:

> And you that delight in trulls and minions,
> Come buy my four ropes of hard St Thomas's onions.

With the substitution of St. Omers for St. Thomas, the same two lines appear at the end of a song in *Choyce Drollery.*[1] In *Appius and Virginia* (1575) when a rope is offered to Haphazard, he replies (ll. 1119–20),

> Nay softe my maisters by saincte Thomas of trunions,[2]
> I am not disposed to by of your onions.

In Tailor's play Haddit also boasts in regard to his jig, "Garlic stinks to this; if it prove that you have not more whores than e'er garlic had, say I am a boaster of my own works, disgrace me on the open stage." The implication is that there was no lack of whores in "Garlic." The prominence of garlic and courtesans in both jigs is probably significant. According to an impoverished gentleman in *Ram-Alley* (1611),

> Your best retired life is an honest Punke
> In a thatcht house with Garlike [A 3].

The onion was connected with love and love divinations. Hill in *A Quatron of Reasons of Catholike Religion* (1600) attacks extravagant customs of Protestants, including "your Gallegascones, your Scabilonians, your *S. Thomas* Onions, your Ruffes, your Cuffes, and a thousand such new deuised Luciferian trinckets" (p. 86). In *A Dialogue Between Mistris Macquerella, a Suburb Bawd, Mr Scolopendra a noted Curtezan, and Mr Pimpinello an*

---

[1] Ed. Ebsworth, p. 100.

[2] For St. Trunion in England, see *Antiquary,* XXXI, 370–71.

Usher, Pittifully bemoaning the tenour of the Act (now in force) against Adultery and Fornication (1650), the old bawd says, "some convenient well scituated Stall (wherein to sit, and sell Time, Rue, and Rosemary, Apples, Garlike, and Saint *Thomas* Onyons) will be a fit Palace for me to practice pennance in" (p. 4). There is a series of instructions for divining a future husband in *Mother Bunch of the West* (1685) which includes dreaming on a St. Thomas onion.[1]

Taylor in *A Cast over the Water* (1615) declares that he will exhibit Fennor as "an old blind braue Baboone," and that

> for his action he eclipseth quite,
> The Iigge of Garlick, or the Punks delight.[2]

Taylor's jibe implies very vigorous dance action in both "Garlic" and "Punk's delight." Probably there was a romping group dance of the courtesans in the jig. On February 5, 1593, a "booke" was licensed with the title "A plesant fancie or merrie conceyt called 'the passionat morrys/daunst by a crue of Eight couple of w[h]ores, all meere Enimyes to love.'" Perhaps courtesans were associated with vigorous dancing; perhaps they fitted into the conception of antic dance. In one of the antimasques of Shirley's *Triumph of Peace*, a "Maquerelle, Wenches, Gentlemen, return, as from the tavern; they dance together; the Gallants are cheated; and left to dance in, with a drunken repentance." Shirley may have got suggestions for his drollery from earlier dances involving robberies (pp. 24, 138, above), from popular dances of courtesans such as would have been featured in "Garlic," and from performances like that of the drunken clown in the Dutch singspiele discussed later in this chapter.

In Dekker's *If it be not Good, the Diuel is in it* (1612), Scumbroth says:[3] "No, no, if Fortune fauourd me, I should be full,

---

[1] See Penny Merriments, Vol. II, in the Pepys Library. For divinations by onions, see Brand, *Popular Antiquities* (1849), III, 356–57. The passage from Hill and that from the Mistress Macquerella dialogue, quoted above from the originals, are also quoted by Brand. For early traces of some sort of game customs connected with garlic, see the London churchwardens' accounts published in *Journal of British Arch. Assn.*, XXIV, 266: in 1528, "It'm payd for brede ale & wyne a Sey't pet's daye Sett garlyke, viij*d*"; in 1534, "It'm payde for wyne brede and ale spente on saynte peters daye called Sette garlyk, viij*d*."

[2] Folio of 1630, Oo 4. "The Puncks Delight" is the name of a dance tune in Playford's *Dancing Master*.

[3] *Dramatic Works* (1873), III, 325.

but Fortune fauours no body but Garlicke, nor Garlike neither now, yet she has strong reason to loue it; for tho Garlicke made her smell abhominably in the nostrills of the gallants, yet she had smelt and stuncke worse but for garlike." Evidently "Garlic" was a great success with the rabble at the Fortune but met with hostility among gallants. If the attitude of the gallants was due to anything more than their better taste, it may mean that they were satirized or depicted in a poor light as in Shirley's anti-masque. Dekker's statement of 1612 that Fortune favored "nor Garlike neither now" seems to be another reference to the order of that year against afterpieces. In fact, the riotousness of audiences at "Garlic" may have occasioned the order.

Still another allusion to "Garlic" is found in Parrot's *Springs for Wood-cocks*, published in 1613 but said to have been finished "long since." Epigram 131, called "Theatrum licentia," reads:

> *Cotta's* become a Player, most men know,
> And will no longer take such toyling paines;
> For heer's the spring (saith he) whence pleasures flow,
> And brings them damnable excessiue gaines,
> That now are Cedars growne from shrubs and sprigs,
> Since *Greenes Tu-quoq;* and those Garlicke Iigs.

The use of the plural here suggests that there was a series of related jigs or imitations of "Garlic." If so, "Punk's Delight," which Taylor associates with "Garlic," may have been one of them. The fact that Haddit is modeling his jig on "Garlic" is perhaps a satire on the imitation of that famous piece. We have seen how the vogue of "Rowland" was capitalized in other jigs, and there is some indication also that a number of ballads were connected with the jig of "John for the King."

In *Saffron Walden* (1596) Nashe says of Thomas Deloney, "since *Candlemas* or his Iigge of *Iohn for the King*, not one merrie Dittie will come from him," and he alludes to the piece again in *Lenten Stuffe*, "strike wee vp Iohn for the King."[1] On October 24, 1603, Edward White entered on the Register "A new Ballet called '*John for the king*' To the tune of '*Hey Downe derrye*.'" This is presumably Deloney's jig. According to the clown in Heywood's *Rape of Lucrece*, however, John for the King was

[1] *Works*, ed. McKerrow, III, 84, 201.

the subject of many ballads, and these may have been typical jigs. In II, v, the clown sings:

> John for the king has been in many ballads,
>   John for the king down dino,
> John for the king has eaten many salads,
>   John for the king sings hey ho.

In Sharpham's *Fleire* (1607) Fleire says, "she euerie day sings *Iohn for the King*, and at *Vp tailes all*,[1] shees perfect"; and these are pronounced "farre better then your Scottish Iigges" (III, i, 169–73). As late as 1647 there is an allusion in *Mercurius Pragmaticus* to the singing of "John for the King."[2]

John fo de King is one of the characters in *Jack Drum's Entertainment,* and it is probable that the treatment of the character and at least some of the incidents in which he is involved were borrowed from the jigs or ballads dealing with him.[3] John, or Monsieur as he is called, is the lustful foreigner with a comic French-English jargon. His one concern is a wench or the money to procure one. Near the end of the first act when, burning with desire, he is finally allowed to follow Winifred off the stage, one of the characters says, "As the Iigge is cal'd for when the Play is done, euen so let *Mounsieur* goe." Though there may be a play here on the sexual connotation of the word, the passage would seem to designate as jig the amours and adventures of John fo de King which are to follow. He takes part in three distinct jests. In the first, in order to secure a wench he accepts money from Mamon to kill the latter's rival Pasquil. For fear of hanging, he decides to keep the money without slaying his man. Instead he reveals the plot to Pasquil and receives more money to announce its success to Mamon. Pasquil, feigning death, rises to beat Mamon, who believes his assailant is a ghost

---

[1] See Chappell, *Popular Music*, I, 196, for the tune.

[2] October 19–26, p. 48. Cited by Rollins, *Analytical Index*, p. 112.

[3] Possibly these borrowings reflect the tendency to the use of old material in comedy, which is attacked a number of times about this period. See *Warning for Faire Women*, Induction, l. 33 ("Some odd ends of old jests scrap'd up together"); *Histriomastix*, Act III, ll. 206–7 ("load the stage with stuff/ Rakt from the rotten imbers of stall jests"); and *Cynthia's Revels*, Induction ("promoters of other mens iests"). In *Jack Drum* itself (Act V, l. 112), the boys of Paul's are criticized for producing "mustie fopperies of antiquitie."

until Monsieur sings a derisive song. In the second, the maid Winifred, pursued by her lovers, arranges first with John fo de King that he is to carry her in a sack to a house where they can have privacy, and next with Jack Drum that he is to be brought to the house in a sack. As Monsieur comes along sweating under the load of the supposed Winifred, he is forced to open the sack, and the trick on both lovers is discovered. For a further jest at the expense of the lustful Monsieur, Brabant Senior offers to provide him a courtesan, and without explanation to his wife, takes the Frenchman to his own home and introduces the pair, assuming that she will prove immovable. This jest is turned against its contriver, however, for the wife yields readily enough and John innocently returns in exultation to thank the husband in the presence of his friends, who have been acquainted with the affair.

There is a fairly close relation between the treatment of John fo de King in the play and of Segnior Domegro in "A Spanish Gentleman and an English Gentlewoman," which I have argued was written with a view to dramatic presentation and was probably a definite jig of an early period.[1] Both are grossly lascivious foreigners with amusing dialect, bent on winning English women to their purposes. Two ideas recur over and over in the song—Domegro's insistence on the woman's coming to his "shaumbre" and his offer, with innuendo, to teach her to speak Spanish:

> make me your lovere & shewe me some playe
> me teache you parlere the fyne spaniolaye.

John fo de King begs Mistress Brabant, "Pree shew mee your bed-Chambre"; and she yields to him with, "Well, sir, if it please you to see my Chamber, 'tis at your seruice" (Act IV, ll. 232–52). In Act III he promises Twedle, "I, by my trott, ang you helpe me to a vench now, me teach you French, fiue towsand, towsand yeere," and a little later when Winifred, to lead him on, declares that she loves him infinitely, he answers, "By gor, mee teach you French foure towsand yeere dan!" (ll. 23–24, 51). At the end of the play he expresses his gratitude to Brabant Senior for helping him to a wench by saying, "By my

---

[1] See pp. 200–201 above and Text 14.

trote, me teche you French to t'end of the vorlde." The old dialogue may have influenced the play, but more likely material was incorporated into the play from a jig or jigs on John for the King which had followed the lines of treatment found in "A Spanish Gentleman and an English Gentlewoman."

Certainly the motives in the John fo de King episodes of the play would be appropriate for jigs. Several of them in quite different form are found in extant jigs—the feigned death, the beating by one supposedly dead, the belief that he is a ghost, the cuckolding of a husband through his own trick. A wily woman's playing her importunate lovers off against each other occurs in a number of forms in jocular literature and farce. In *Decameron*, IX, 1, one lover is sent to take the place of a corpse and the other to carry the corpse away.[1] The sack incident in *Jack Drum* is much nearer to the fifth story in Riche's *Farewell to Militarie profession*, where the woman sends after the dupes an accepted lover, who forces the opening of the sack in which one is carrying the other, and beats both of them.[2]

There is one other allusion to John for the King which may point to the type of incident associated with him in a jig. In Heywood's *Edward IV*, Part II (Sig. O), the Constable of France says to Burgundy, who has plotted with him and then, as he thinks, betrayed him,

> Haue not you plaide John for the king,
> To saue your selfe Sir?

This reference is probably not to the Frenchman's betrayal of Mamon's plot in *Jack Drum*—a play which is later than Heywood's or of approximately the same date—but to ballads or jigs that were old enough to furnish the basis for familiar allusion. An even more obscure reference to the figure comes from

---

[1] See Lee, *The Decameron. Its Sources and Analogues*, pp. 271–74, for parallels to this story, a number of them with three lovers.

[2] "The Foole of Essex" in *Jack of Dover, His Quest of Inquirie* is the story of how a widow in the same fashion tricks three suitors about arrangements for a secret marriage instead of an intrigue. The suitor sent to expose and beat the first two is also duped, for the woman marries a fourth man in the meanwhile. In Nabbes's *Tottenham Court*, Acts IV and V, a wanton wooer is hidden in a trunk at the approach of a second wooer, the second is led to carry the trunk off in the belief that the girl is in it, a third picks a quarrel with the second on the way, bringing about a disclosure of the girl's deception. She has accepted a fourth man as husband, however.

"The *Scene* interloping" in *A Tale of a Tub*, Act IV. Scriben says:

> Two words,
> *Cyning* and *Staple*, make a Constable:
> As wee'd say, A hold, or stay for the King,

and Clench replies, "All Constables are truly *Iohn's* for the King." These two allusions are probably to some incident well known in the period.

A possible inference from several of the passages cited is that John for the King was associated with songs having popular refrains. The ballad is entered as sung to the tune "Hey Downe derrye," and the clown of *The Rape of Lucrece* says that "John for the king sings hey ho." In the play he enters in Act II at line 240 singing "Grand sot Mamon, Pho, phy, phy, phy!"; in Act III he goes out at line 68 saying, "By gor mee sing la, liro, liro, la, lilo!"; and in Act IV (ll. 214–18) he sings a song with a "Ding, ding, ading" refrain. Such bits of song may have been characteristic of John for the King in jigs. They would serve well to accompany the dancing of a jig clown.

There is even less basis for conjecture about "Phillips *his gigg of the slyppers*," entered to Ralph Hancock on May 26, 1595.[1] The title probably refers to Augustine Phillips of Shakespeare's company, as Collier has pointed out.[2] It has been suggested that a clown's trick was the basis of the jig. Creizenach calls attention to what may have been a characteristic trick of stage clowns in their large, ill-fitting shoes: in *Every Man out of his Humour* (IV, v) Carlo says, "would I had one of *Kemps* shooes to throw after you," and Platter in 1599 gives an account of a play in which a servant threw a shoe at his master.[3] Chambers offers the theory that the incident had already found a place in Phillips's jig.[4] The piece might conceivably have been

---

[1] Arber, *Transcript*, II, 298.

[2] *Hist. Eng. Dram. Poetry* (1879), III, 323.

[3] *English Drama in the Age of Shakespeare* (London, 1916), p. 303.

[4] *Elizabethan Stage*, III, 362. In Greene's *James IV* a roguish clown who dances in a jig, a hornpipe, and an antic dance is called Slipper. See Smith, *Commedia dell'arte*, p. 14, for a "lazzo" of the slipper listed in 1699 by Perucci among the conventional jokes of the zanni.

a mere narrative ballad with pantomimic tricks, but since it was associated with a member of the Chamberlain's company and entered at the period when the farce jigs of comedians like Kemp and Attowell were being published, it was in all probability farcical in nature. One of the farcical situations in Ayrer's fastnachtspiel *Die zwen vereinigten Buler* hinges on a pair of slippers. The clown Jan Panser finds the slippers of his wife's lover under the bed and is told by her that their guest rested on the bed after a bath. It is pointed out earlier that Ayrer uses in this farce several situations found also in "Singing Simpkin," and he may have built the piece up largely out of jig motives, taking one from "The Jig of the Slippers." Among the various articles that the wife of "Our Goodman" has to explain to her husband are three pairs of boots, which she says are pudding bags.[1]

Two titles that may belong to lost jigs are "The Ship" and "Shankes Ordinary." In Field's *Amends for Ladies* (1611) one of the characters speaks of having "a great mind to see Long Meg and the Ship at the Fortune" (II, i). "The Ship" must have been either a jig or part of a double bill. If the former, this is the only evidence we have that the title of the jig to be performed was announced beforehand. Still Field's play was written near the time when the Fortune attained its great notoriety in connection with jigs, and it is not improbable that "The Ship" was a well-known jig of the period. A possibility that suggests itself for such a piece is that it was a series of satiric sketches modeled on the old device of the ship of fools or rogues;[2] but a more likely

---

[1] See p. 246 above. In connection with "The Jig of the Slippers" attention may be called to the use of slippers in games. See Gomme, *Traditional Games*, I, 241–42, for an English circle game in which the players represent cobblers and the owner searches for his slipper among them; Brand, *Popular Antiquities*, II, 9, for a mention of "lowp (*leap*) for slippers" among festival pastimes in 1686; Böhme, *Deutsches Kinderlied und Kinderspiel*, pp. 512–13, for an elaborate German wooing game, akin to "Here come three Dukes" but more dramatic, opening "Es chunnt en Hêr mit eim Pantoffel." Many customs involving shoes are connected with marriage.

[2] See p. 60 above for a passage from Fulwell's *Arte of Flatterie* which refers to the fool on the stage telling news of a shipload of the vicious; *Hyckescorner*, ll. 326–89, for Hyckescorner's news of ships loaded with the virtuous, all ironically drowned in the Irish Sea, and the ship Envy loaded with "good felawes," all rogues and rascals with allegorical names, who passed safely (see also ll. 820–43 for Freewill's description of the adventures of rogues in terms of steering a ship); Marston's *Fawne*, Act IV, with the fool's invitation to "al manner of fooles" to come aboard. See also Herford, *Literary Relations of England and Germany*, pp. 370–72.

motive for a jig would be, I think, the ancient one, still popular in the seventeenth century, of drunkards' imagining themselves on a rolling ship.[1] In Heywood's *English Traveller* (II, i) there is an account of how a group of tipsy revelers, believing that the room was a vessel and they were about to suffer shipwreck, tried to save themselves, partly by throwing the furnishings out of the window to lighten the load.[2] A similar description is found in Burton's *Anatomy of Melancholy*, taken from *Lectionum Antiquarum Lib. XXX* of Caelius, and in Molle's *Living Librarie* (1621), translated from *Operae Horarum Subcisiuarum siue Meditationes Historicae* (1602) of Camerarius.[3] Cowley developed the motive in a more dramatic form in his *Naufragium Joculare*. While a disard's narrative might have been used as a jig, the antic or medley dance of a drunken crew is of a type that had a vogue in the seventeenth century.

The fame of John Shank as a writer of jigs (p. 114 above) is the best reason for supposing that "*Shankes Ordinary*, written by Shankes himself" was a jig. On March 16, 1624, Herbert as Master of the Revels received one pound for licensing a piece with this title "For the king's company."[4] A pound was the usual fee for an old play, and it is not unlikely that the amount for the more dramatic jigs was the same. If the "Ordinary" was a farce jig, the fact of its being licensed for the King's Men presumably indicates the use of the more elaborate jigs at the Globe in 1624. Low comedy drew on many aspects of tavern life from the time of the mystery plays to Shakespeare's day, and the inns probably furnished the setting for other lost pieces with the hosts and hostesses as stock characters. At the end of his

[1] See Herford, *op. cit.*, p. 372 n. 1; Ward, *History of English Dramatic Literature*, II, 566 n. 3. In *Like Will to Like* (ed. Farmer, p. 26) the drunken Hance's dream that he was drowned in a barrel of beer which turned to a ship and sailed to France may reflect the motive. See D'Urfey, *Pills*, III, 304–6, for an elaborate drinking song (with a rousing refrain) beginning "All Hands up aloft," in which the toasts are woven into details of steering a ship and of a storm at sea.

[2] See also *Captives*, II, ii, 85–91, for a clown's accepting a report of a shipwreck as a matter of the sufferers' imagination, and Dekker's *If it be not Good, the Diuel is in it* (*Dramatic Works*, III, 293) for a seaman's cries and commands as if in a storm.

[3] See *Anatomy*, ed. Shilleto, I, 428–29; *Living Librarie*, pp. 376–77; and Bang and de Vocht, *Englische Studien*, XXXVI, 389–91, for a discussion of these forms and of Heywood's possible knowledge of them.

[4] See Adams, *Dramatic Records of Sir Henry Herbert*, p. 27. Collier in *Hist. Eng. Dram. Poetry*, III, 481, conjectured that the piece was a jig.

Nine Days' Wonder Kemp, telling of his search among ballad
writers for the "private Jigmonger of your jolly number" that
had written "abominable Ballets" on his morris dance, says of
one "penny Poet," "I heard, afterwards, his mother-in-law was
eye- and ear-witness of his father's abuse, by this blessed child,
on a public Stage, in 'a merry Host of an Inns' part.'" The
reference may be to a jig of the ballad maker's composition, for
he is not spoken of as a dramatist or an actor. Deloney, also
mentioned in Kemp's attack, made the hostess of an inn one of
the characters in his "Country Jig," and the character appeared
in the jig of "Cutting George and his Hostess." Both the Dutch
singspiele to be considered later have taverns as their settings
and tavern keepers as characters.

Naturally song drama written abroad by foreign authors
has less bearing on the English jig than that known to belong
at least to the canon of the English comedians. But in the ten
singspiele written by Jakob Ayrer[1] in professed imitation of the
English jig, we undoubtedly have a body of material that
throws light on the stage tricks of the clown, the range of droll
characters, and the variety of farcical situations used in English
song drama. According to Ayrer's own statement at the end of
"Von dreyen bösen Weibern," he was the first to write actual
German jigs:

> Das ist das erste Spil,
> Daß man bey vns hie singen thut.

All his singspiele were written early—six in 1598 and the rest
within a few years. Though they vary considerably in length,
all are simple in form, and each is sung to a single tune—five to
"Rowland" and a sixth to the tune of the related "Von den
Männern." Bolte speaks of the influence which the visits of
Browne's and Sackville's troupes to Nuremberg in 1593, 1596,
and 1597 must have had on Ayrer in this new venture.[2]

The question of the relation of Ayrer's singspiele to the English jig involves two problems, one as to his use of characters
with more or less stereotyped traits and tricks, and the other as
to his use of plots borrowed or adapted from jig prototypes. Of

[1] See Keller, *Ayrers Dramen*, Vol. V, Nos. 52, 58–66.

[2] *Singspiele*, p. 12.

Ayrer's extensive use of English clowns there is not the least doubt, though it is a question how far they were derived from jigs rather than from low comedy generally. "Der engelendische Jann Posset" figures in the title of one of his singspiele and two fastnachtspiele. In several other cases he describes his clowns as English, and in one makes of "English John" a class name.[1] Pretty clearly also he has preserved other characters that were popular in jigs but are not represented in the extant English specimens, though they do appear in the pieces carried abroad by the comedians. These are the old figures of the farce of village life—the intriguing monk; the bold, unscrupulous, and shrewish wife; the droll, abused husband; the neighbor. There is reason to believe that Ayrer's treatment of these various figures was not uninfluenced by their vogue in the farce jigs which he was frankly imitating, but the fact cannot be established because of their similarity to figures in European jocular literature generally. The group was of course international. The difficulty is the same in regard to plot. Some of the motives in Ayrer's singspiele were widely disseminated and thoroughly conventional. The material, however, was just of the type which the jigs must have exploited to a far greater extent than the surviving specimens indicate. Though only in a few cases are Ayrer's incidents clearly English in derivation, frequently analogues are to be found in English jest, farce, or ballad. In many cases a definite source or a probable one has been pointed out in German literature that was presumably known to Ayrer. Usually his singspiele depart from the supposedly direct source, however, especially in introducing features that were popular in ballads and jigs as well as in jocular literature generally. The situation is perhaps similar to that found in some of Ayrer's plays like *Phänicia*, which is known to be based in part on a German version of a Bandello story but was also probably influenced by an English play, a forerunner of Shakespeare's *Much Ado*.[2] Possibly in several cases Ayrer got his suggestion for a singspiel from an English jig, but used as a basis some variant of the theme known to him in German jocular literature.

Ayrer wrote three singspiele dealing with the favorite farci-

[1] See Creizenach, *Schauspiele*, p. xcvi.
[2] Wodick, *Jakob Ayrers Dramen*, pp. 62–64.

cal theme of the shrewish wife. In "Ein singets Spil, von dreyen
bösen Weibern, denen weder Gott noch jre Männer recht können
thun" (1598),[1] Wolfrum claims a pair of boots which Wilhelm
has long sought to give to one who is master in his own house.
The boots are taken from him, however, when he reveals his fear
of his wife Lisa on account of a soiled shirt. Then Lisa and
two neighbors quarrel and finally fight over the need of rain or
of sunshine. Next Wolfrum and a neighbor dispute and come to
blows over the shrewishness of their wives. On meeting his wife,
Wolfrum reproaches her because he has lost the boots through
her keeping him in subjection. Lisa is full of dreams of purchasing a cow. He rejoices at the thought of having butter and milk
every day, but she rails at him for being willing to take the milk
from the calf. He strikes her and the pair engage in a fight
which the husband calls off. The diverse motives of this singspiel were probably drawn from both German and English
sources. As Bolte points out, the incidents of the boots and of
the quarrel about an unpurchased cow follow closely *Wendunmut*, I, 363, 371. The quarrel about the cow recalls that of the
two shepherds in the Towneley "First Shepherds' Play" about
unpurchased sheep, a standard jest connected with the Wise
Men of Gotham.[2] The disputes of the two men and of the
women, with an approach to flyting in both cases, resemble the
various dialogues of neighbors and gossips discussed in chapter
vi. With the quarrel over the weather Bolte compares a story in
Wendunmut, V, 115, in which a farmer desires to control rain
and sunshine, and Pistl cites another in *Wendunmut*, I, 377, in
which two women are pleased with rain and a third is angry
with God;[3] but the incident in the singspiel is more like the
wrangling of two women in Heywood's *Play of the Wether* about
their respective desires for rain and sunshine.

The second of Ayrer's singspiele of the shrewish wife is "Ein
Fassnachtspil von dem engelendischen Jann Posset, wie er sich
in seinen Dinsten verhalten."[4] Though called a fastnachtspiel,

---

[1] Keller, *Ayrers Dramen*, V, 3051–62; Bolte, *Singspiele*, p. 12.

[2] See *A Hundred Merry Tales*, No. xxii, and *Mad Men of Gotham*, No. i.

[3] *Vierteljahrschrift für Litteraturgeschichte*, VI, 431.

[4] Keller, V, 2889–2905; Bolte, p. 14.

the piece is a pure song drama sung to the tune of "Rowland."[1] Jan Posset, leaving his parents—the father is called Rolandt—and mocking them as they rail at him, takes service with an old man. He insists on having his duties written down. When sent to bring writing materials, he clownishly misinterprets all commands and brings the wrong articles. He refuses to raise his master, who has fallen, because that duty is not in his list. When he is commanded to carry pears to a neighbor, he eats them. In a new section of the singspiel Jan, who has married Ela, is beaten and forced to carry the basket while she carries the keys and the purse. Two guardsmen, seeing them, tell her of the king's orders that wives must be submissive, and she has to exchange burdens with Jan. She cannot endure the rôle, however, and after subduing Jan, beats both him and the guards when they return.

The English origin of the part of the singspiel dealing with Ela has been recognized.[2] The same material is used in a comic scene of *Esther* (Act II), a play published in *Engelische Comedien und Tragedien*, and also in Ayrer's *Edward III* (Act III), drawn from English sources. The added feature of Ela's beating not only her clownish husband but the soldiers as well recalls Meretrix's conquest of the vice and two swaggering soldiers in *Cambises*. In "The Cobbler of Colchester" and in "Der Windelwäscher" the wife beats the husband and overawes his friends. Of more significance is the first part of the singspiel, depicting the clown, half knave and half fool, with many of the traits of the uninhibited simpleton or "natural" beloved of the folk in the Middle Ages and the Renaissance. The type owes a great deal to heroes of jestbooks like Howleglass and Scogan, but the tricks and conventions are of the sort already discussed as attributed to Tarlton and embodied in the English Johns of Julius and Ayrer. The clown's refusal to raise his old master has been traced to Pauli's *Schimpf und Ernst*, No. 139. The jest is widespread, however.[3] In Gifford's *Posie of Gilloflowers* (1580) there is a story "Of one that hyred a foolish seruaunt" made up

---

[1] It is, however, a variant of a fastnachtspiel with the same title. See Keller, V, 2869–88.

[2] See Bolte, *loc. cit.*

[3] See Bolte's edition of *Schimpf und Ernst*, II, 294–95.

of a series of jests showing the discomfiture of a master whose servant obeyed literally.[1] Jan Posset's eating the pears is a bit of clownish knavery conventional in jest and farce, but it may have been popularized by the English clowns. Ayrer has used similar incidents in a scene of *Der verlohren engellendisch Jahnn Posset*,[2] where Jan consumes the drink for which he has been sent, and in *Comedia von einem alten Buler vnnd Wucherer* (Act I), in which the servant Jan Grundo drinks the wine sent by his master to his sweetheart. In "Die Metamorphosis" Jan Pint drinks up the cobbler's beer. In spite of the conventionality of the tricks of clowns, it seems to me probable that Ayrer derived from the jigs of Sackville's company and Browne's, not only the name, but the art and much of the material for the depiction of clowns like Jan Posset.

The complementary motive of the taming of a shrew appears in Ayrer's "Ein schöns neus singets Spil von dem Knörren Cüntzlein."[3] In this, a husband, on the advice of a neighbor to whom he tells his troubles, consults a physician about his lazy and shrewish wife. The physician offers several burlesque prescriptions to be applied and well rubbed in with five fingers, a stout cudgel, and a broomstick. The husband's first effort to carry out the program is not a success. The wife is left in possession of the broom. In a second trial, however, he brings her to terms. Bolte traces the story to *Wendunmut*, I, 109. *A merry Ieste of a Shrewde and curste Wyfe lapped in Morrelles skin* and the traditional English ballad "The Wife Wrapt in Wether's

---

[1] Ed. Grosart, pp. 64–67. See Gomme, *Traditional Games*, I, 319, for a game of hiring servants, in which the terms of service, the duties, and the kinds of food are stipulated in rhyming formulas. These may have been used from the Middle Ages in engaging those who could not read.

[2] This farce (Keller, V, 2907–27), as the title suggests, may be from English sources. The chief incident is an adaptation of *Amphitruo* very similar to *Jacke Jugeler* and possibly influenced by it. Jan shows the same mixture of knavery and stupidity found in the singspiel. His several returns to repeat stupid queries when sent on an errand resemble the difficulties of Pickleherring when commissioned to deliver a letter in *Tugend- und Liebes-Streit* (III, ii), a German variant of *Twelfth Night*. In the fact that Jan is sent for wine in order that a lover may visit his mistress there is a similarity to Ayrer's *Die zwen vereinigten Buler*, in which the husband is made to go for wine at the approach of a lover. In *Johan Johan* the wife calls the husband back from his mission repeatedly. Ayrer, however, is not so close to this farce as to its source, *Pernet qui va au vin*. In the jig of "Singing Simpkin" the husband is sent out for wine.

[3] Keller, V, 3077–92; Bolte, p. 16.

Skin"[1] are like the singspiel in tone and details, though the device for curing a worthless wife is different.

In chapter vii something was said of the probability that the intrigues of churchmen illustrated in "Der Mönch im Sacke" were popular in jigs. Ayrer has dealt with the subject in three of his singspiele. "Ein schön singets Spil, der Forster im Schmaltzkübel"[2] (1598) dramatizes the first part of the famous Scholar of Paris story and adds other incidents, particularly one in which the student returns as the priest of the village and begins an intrigue with the wife. Finally surprised by a sudden return of the husband, the wife easily persuades him that he has a headache and places a tub of lard over his head while she exorcises the devil disturbing him. He recovers in time to see the devil leave and finds him so like the priest that his departure is a matter of especial rejoicing. Ayrer's sources are German. The story of *Wendunmut*, I, 138, is closely paralleled in the first part of the singspiel.[3] The incident of the exorcism is probably drawn from a fastnachtspiel of Peter Probst,[4] like Ayrer, a Nuremberg dramatist. The material was popular, however. The motive of a simple woman's being led to send presents to a former husband in paradise was widely used.[5] It appears as a ballad in Gifford's *Posie of Gilloflowers*,[6] where there is a fuller form of the Scholar of Paris story with the duping of the living husband added. A wife's meeting the discovery of an intrigue by a trick of exorcism is found in "The old wiues tale" of *The Cobler of Canterburie*. For a woman's aiding a lover to escape before her husband's eyes, Bolte cites *Gesta Romanorum*, Nos. 122 and 123.[7] In the Proclamation to Lyndsay's *Satire of the Three Estates* the wife throws a shirt over her husband's head. In *London Cuck-*

---

[1] See Hazlitt, *Early Popular Poetry of England*, IV, 179–226, and Child, *Popular Ballads*, No. 277.

[2] Keller, V, 3063–76; Bolte, p. 15.

[3] Pistl, *Vierteljahrschrift für Litteraturgeschichte*, VI, 431, cites also *Wendunmut*, I, 137, 148.

[4] See Wodick, *Jakob Ayrers Dramen*, pp. 16–17.

[5] See Bolte and Polívka, *Anmerkungen zu Grimm*, II, 440–51.

[6] Ed. Grosart, pp. 131–34.

[7] See also Bédier, *Les Fabliaux* (1895), pp. 320, 466–67.

olds, III, i, a wife hugs a husband so as to cover his face while a lover escapes from the room.

"Ein schön singets Spil, Der verlarft Franciscus mit der venedischen jungen Wittfrauen,"[1] sung to the tune of "Rowland," is a version of *Decameron*, IV, 2. A simple-minded widow goes to a friar with a story of having had visions of St. Francis, and he promises that the saint will visit her that night. When she talks of the honor to be paid her, a neighbor sees through the affair and, disguising himself as St. Peter, exposes the friar masquerading as St. Francis. Hönig in his review of Bolte's *Singspiele* suggested "The Tale of Friar Onyon" in *Tarltons Newes out of Purgatorie* as Ayrer's source.[2] Since then Bolte has pointed out a meisterlied of Ayrer's fellow-townsman Hager called "Sankt Franciscus und Sankt Petrus," which was written in 1588 and probably drawn from a French source.[3] In the poem the woman is a wife who tells her husband of the proposed visit and is saved by him in the same fashion. This version and both of Ayrer's differ from the others in the presence of St. Peter with his comic treatment of the friar, a dénouement much better suited to farce than the hounding of him by the mob in other versions. Boccaccio is followed closely in *Tarltons Newes*, but the woman is a widow as in the singspiel, not a wife with an absent husband as in the *Decameron*. The version in Whetstone's *Heptameron of Ciuill Discourses* (1582), Day 4, which is earlier than Hager's, departs more widely from Boccaccio than does "The Tale of Friar Onyon," but it does not noticeably resemble the singspiel except that the friar, who takes the form of the angel Gabriel in the *Decameron* and *Tarltons Newes*, here becomes St. Francis, as in the three German versions, because the tomb of that saint is in the vicinity. A popular version of the story using St. Francis may have been current in England before *Tarltons Newes*. If the *Newes* is made up of jig stuff, as the title implies, it is possible that the book was preceded by a jig closer to the singspiel than is "The Tale of Friar Onyon."

[1] Keller, V, 3025–38; Bolte, pp. 12–13. For a fastnachtspiel of Ayrer's with the same title and material, see Keller, V, 3001–23.

[2] *Anzeiger für deutsches Altertum*, XXII, 314.

[3] See *Alemannia*, XXII, 159–66. For other variants, see Lee, *The Decameron. Its Sources and Analogues*, pp. 123–35.

The author of the *Newes*, though taking suggestions for themes from jigs, might easily have returned to recognized literary sources for his treatment.

The third piece portraying the lustful monk is "Ein schöns neus singets Spil, ist genant der Münch im Keßkorb"[1] to the tune of "Rowland." It was written in 1598. A wife, weary of an old peasant husband, attracts the attention of a monk at confession. According to agreement the monk is summoned as the husband and servant go to their work in the woods, but the husband, returning unexpectedly, discovers him and warns him to keep away. Pretending to leave once more, the husband hides and reappears immediately upon a second arrival of the monk. He finds the monk covered over in a cheese basket, shuts him in, and sends for the abbot to exorcise a spirit. The indignant abbot takes the monk off to a stricter life, and the husband beats the wife, warning the audience in usual jig fashion against taking a wife of a different age. Bolte has indicated the source of the singspiel in Schumann's *Nachtbüchlein*.[2] Ayrer follows Schumann's story even in a number of minor details, but he has omitted the cutting of the rope by which the basket hangs and the dumping of the friar in the river Donau—a feature difficult from the point of view of presentation. On the other hand, he has added the servant and the first visit of the friar. One of the jests in the English *Frier Rush*, which is not found in the German original, is a version of the story in the singspiel.[3] Rush, having taken service with a farmer, returns to the house on various occasions to find a priest hidden once under a chest, again in a pile of straw, and finally in a cheese basket which hangs out of a window. On the first two occasions Rush rebukes him; but on the last he cuts the rope, dropping the priest in a pool of water, ties the basket to the tail of a horse, drags the priest through the water and then through the town, and finally releases him for a hundred pieces of gold, which he shares with his master. The incident in *The Merry Wives of Windsor* in which Falstaff is punished in his pursuit of Mistress Ford by being dumped into the river in a basket of clothes is

---

[1] Keller, V, 3093–3107; Bolte, p. 13.   [2] Ed. Bolte, pp. 63–67, 395–96.

[3] See the edition in Thoms, *Early Prose Romances*, pp. 33–40; Schumann, *Nachtbüchlein*, ed. Bolte, p. 386; Kittredge in *PMLA*, XV (1900), 415 n.

not found in any of the suggested sources of the play.¹ It seems possible that Shakespeare took the episode from some jig or farce, whether it was merely reported as in *Merry Wives* or actually enacted on the stage. The "Friar in the Well," recorded by Munday as a Robin Hood play, must have been built on some such motive.²

There is a decided kinship between these intrigues of churchmen and a jest found in *The Second Part of Tom Tram of the West* by "Humphery Crouch," printed for "J. Dacon," which in form suggests an adaptation of some dramatic song.³ Tom, seeing a parson enter the house of William of Wandsor, whose wife on pretext of illness has sent the husband five miles "to fetch her a bottle of water called the Water of Absalon," follows William and warns him. At Tom's suggestion William is carried back in a sack, which, with the wife's permission, is to be left in the chimney corner until morning. As Tom stands at the door, the wife and the parson, who are breakfasting together, begin to sing "the following song, in tune of, The Owl is the fairest, &c:

Woman.

William of Wandsor he is gone
To fetch some water of Absalon,
I'l make him a cuckold before he comes home,
Sing hey rro non ne, non ne, non ne.

Parson.

William of Wandsor, I know what I think
I'll eat of thy bread & drink of thy drink;
To end the strife, I'll lie with thy wife,
    Sing hey tro, &c.

¹ See *Merry Wives*, ed. Porter and Clarke, pp. 102–7.

² See pp. 26–27 above for Munday's allusion and for the use of the tune for dance.

³ A copy is preserved in Penny Merriments of the Pepys Collection. I quote from an eighteenth century copy with no fundamental variations. "Tom Tram of the West, sonne in law to Mother Winter, &c." was entered on the Register November 5, 1655. For an incomplete traditional version of the story, called "Little Dicky Milburn," see Williams, *Folk-Songs of the Upper Thames*, pp. 293–94; and for a complete variant collected in America, see *Journal of American Folk-Lore*, XXXVIII, 366–68. In a seventeenth century broadside, "The Witty Maid of the West; Or, The Miller well thrash'd by *Robin* the Plowman," a girl takes her lover to mill with her in a sack and calls him out when the miller is not to be put off (*Roxburghe Ballads*, VII, 426–27).

Tom comes in.
William of Wandsor, if thou be'st near,
Come out of the sack without any fear,
If any mishap I'll stand at thy back,
  Sing hey tro, &c.

William of Wandsor comes out of the
the Sack.
By your leave gentlemen all on a row,
Some of your secrets I very well know,
Sir John shall be gelded before he does go
  Sing hey tro, &c."

To save himself, the parson pays William and Tom five pounds apiece. Forms of this story have been collected from nearly every country in Europe, frequently with verse parts similar to those in *Tom Tram* spoken by the four corresponding characters.[1] Still the earliest records indicate that the jest circulated primarily as a farce or game in the sixteenth and seventeenth centuries. The oldest form known is a Dutch farce of the fifteenth century, *Van playerwater of van den man diet dwater haelde*. A painting dating from about 1550 pictures a dramatic presentation of the story at a church wake. The German version known as "Der alte Hildebrand" is recorded as a pastime at Königsberg in 1611, and Praetorius refers to it in 1666 as the typical puppet play.[2] Indications that the late seventeenth century English version retains parts of an older song drama on the subject are found in the stage directions, in the naming of the tune to be used, in the fact that the sung parts develop the plot, and in the address to an audience at the end, seemingly as "Cuckolds all a Row."[3]

The remaining singspiele of Ayrer call for only a brief notice. "Der Wittenbergisch Magister in der Narrenkappen"[4] is

---

[1] See Bolte and Polívka, *Anmerkungen zu Grimm*, II, 373–80. No English version is cited.

[2] *Ibid.*, pp. 376–77.

[3] Tom Tram suggests Trim Tram, used proverbially in connection with an odd pair. See *NED*, s. v. In Middleton's *Fair Quarrel* (1617) such a pair appear in Chough and his servant Trim Tram. A ballad "Trim Trym of ye golden world" was licensed August 19, 1579.

[4] Keller, V, 3109–24; Bolte, p. 15.

a droll jest of a pedant who, in order to appear disguised in a
Shrovetide mumming, engages a painter to paint his face instead
of wearing a mask. The painter merely wets his face with water,
and the victim in his fool's garb is recognized and mocked.
Bolte gives *Wendunmut*, I, 139, as the source. The same type
of mockery was represented on the English stage in *The Puritan
Widow*, IV, ii, where the gull Edmond is made to believe that a
conjurer has rendered him invisible.[1] Two other singspiele of
Ayrer's deal with heroes of German jestbooks. "Ein schöns
neus singents Spil von dem Eulenspigel mit dem Kauffmann
vnd Pfeiffenmacher"[2] is drawn from *Eulenspiegel*, Nos. 64 and
66. Eulenspiegel, engaged as a cook by the merchant, obeys so
literally that he leaves the roast uncooked and shames his master when guests come to dine. There is the usual beating, and
the wife and finally the guests take part in the fray that follows.
Offered service elsewhere, the clown proceeds to fulfil his new
master's ironic promise that he is to be the only guest. Eulenspiegel gets the wife out of the house by a ruse, takes possession,
and refuses to let the master and his wife in until he has eaten
his fill. He then offers to help her discipline the husband, and a
battle results. In spite of Eulenspiegel's droll literalness, he is
knavish rather than clownish. "Ein schöns neus singets Spil
von etlichen närrischen Reden des Claus Narrn vnd anderer,
zusammen colligirt,"[3] outside of the incident of a doctor's putting Claus and another clown in a bath to cure them, consists
of Claus's witticisms at the expense of a princely interlocutor,
and his proving to a hunter the costliness of the falcon hunt.
The singspiel "Von einem ungerechten Juristen, der ein Münch
worden"[4] is of an entirely different type from the rest. A judge's
acceptance of bribes leads to his wandering after death as a
ghost. As a result his son, also a judge, enters a monastery.
   The singspiele of foreign composition include two Dutch

[1] See Bolte, *Danziger Theater*, pp. 225–26, for farces on the stone that is supposed
to cause invisibility, in relation to "Ein lustig Pickelhärings-Spiel, darinnen er mit einem
Stein gar lustige Possen machet" of the English comedians.

[2] Keller, V, 3139–58; Bolte, *Singspiele*, pp. 13–14. See p. 75 n. 2 above.

[3] Keller, V, 3125–38. Bolte, *Singspiele*, pp. 14–15, points out as sources of the
different elements in the singspiel *Historien von Claus Narren* and *Wendunmut*, I, 425.

[4] Keller, V, 3039–50; Bolte, *Singspiele*, p. 16.

pieces that are closely related. The first is Jan Starter's long "Kluchtigh t'samen-Gesang Van dry Personagien," published in his *Boertigheden* and printed here as Text 35. Bolte calls the singspiel "Der betrogene Freier." Starter was born in London in 1594, lived in Holland, and died about 1628.[1] Not only his connection with England, but the general influence of the English comedians in Holland, would suggest that the singspiel may have been translated or adapted from an English jig. His great interest in English music at any rate is proved by the number of English tunes included in his *Friesche Lust-Hof*. Of the nine tunes used in "Der betrogene Freier," three at least might be regarded as the special property of the comedians—"Engelsche fa la la"; "Ick ben tot Amsterdam gewesen," used in "Der Narr als Reitpferd"; and "Pekelharings. Ofte, Pots hondert tausent Slapferment." The last, with the favorite exclamation of the English clown, is said to be the air found in Robinson's *School of Music* (1603) as "Walking in a Country Town."[2] The trick of fastening a rocket to the clown's breech, which will be noticed later, also speaks for a connection with the English actors. Bolte argues from Ayrer's repeated use of the device that it must have been conventional with the comedians from an early period, and he refers to the end of *The Merry Wives of Windsor*.

In a long passage at the beginning of the singspiel, Knelis tells of his failure to make any headway with Lysje and of his determination to seduce her. While he stands aside, Lysje moralizes on the evil ways of young men, but she leads him on in order to teach him a lesson. Hidden behind a door, she overhears his plan to take her to a tavern and ply her with wine in order to gain his desire. She falls in with the plan but sees to it that he drinks heavily while she merely sips the wine. By the time she has sung with him a vulgar wooing dialogue in anticipation of his pleasure, he is so drunk that sleep overcomes him and he lays his head on her lap. Lysje has the hostess bring her raw eggs in a dish and pours the stuff on his breech. Knelis wakes in amazement at his condition and realizes that she has made a butt of him. Drawing a circle, he conjures up a devil to bring him Lysje so that he may repay her. But she hangs

[1] Bolte, *Singspiele*, p. 27.

[2] *Ibid.*, pp. 27–28, 177–78; Chappell, *Popular Music*, I, 182.

squibs on him and sets them afire. He cries out wildly and flees. Left alone, Lysje closes this part of the singspiel with the proper warning to both young men and young women. Afterward there is a very coarse narrative ballad of the devil (Joosje) and a maid (Truytje), which is sung to a tune not used elsewhere in the piece and has no indication of the singer unless Lysje continues. Joosje tells his dam of his urgent passion and with her approval goes to seduce the maid, meeting with the same hardness of heart that put Knelis to rout. This mimus feature at the end is interesting because it illustrates the sort of material which I believe—merely on the general evidence of the clownish monologue—was frequently used for jigs.

The second of the Dutch pieces, Jan van Arp's "Singhende Klucht, Van Droncke Goosen," is much droller and more farcical. It was published at Amsterdam in 1639, and is reprinted as Text 36. When the singspiel opens, the host and hostess of a tavern have just dragged out Goosen, who snores in a drunken sleep. They blacken his face and hands, steal his money, knock him about to rouse him, and then go in. Goosen, waking, is surprised at his black hands and thoroughly frightened when he sees his face in a mirror which he takes from his sack. He isn't himself but doesn't know what he is, ghost or devil. On investigation he proves too substantial for a ghost. He understands that devils can fly, and he attempts it. Deciding finally to conjure the devil up and settle matters, he makes a circle and begins an incantation. When the hostess and, a moment later, the host come in, masquerading as the devil and his dam, Goosen is thrown into a panic. As in the preceding piece, the woman fastens a rocket on his breech and lights it. Goosen cries out in much the words of Knelis and to the same tune, running off in terror. The pair of devils are left to laugh at his plight and gloat over the purse. The close relation of this singspiel to "Der betrogene Freier" is evident. It extends even to tunes, all three of those used in van Arp's piece being among the tunes of Starter's.[1]

There are, I think, distinct indications that "Droncke Goosen" is English in origin outside of an apparent influence of

[1] See Bolte, *Singspiele*, p. 30, for the statement that "Janneman en Alemoer" is the same tune as "Pots hondert tausent."

English vocabulary. The opening suggests the early part of the Induction to *The Taming of the Shrew*.[1] The clown's apostrophe "O slaep, o slaep, o soete slaep" as he wakes from his drunken stupor may be a parody of the English sonnets on sleep, especially Sidney's "Come, Sleep! O Sleep, the certain knot of peace." When the host and hostess appear as devils and sing several stanzas in dialogue with the terrified Goosen, to the tune of the "Engelsche fa la," the situation and treatment recall the part of "The Blackman" with the same refrain, in which the gentlemen take Thumpkin and the blackman for devils. The blackened face was a device of popular game and farce which might have come from almost any source.[2] The incident of the purse bears some resemblance to a part of the *Prodigal Son*, a play of the English actors published in *Engelische Comedien und Tragedien*, but the treatment is too different for the parallel to have weight.[3] Conjurers, devils, and squibs had a vogue in low comedy of England, however, long before the period of these singspiele. In plays and pageants devils or wild men regularly carried wild fire and squibs or breathed fire.[4] To set fire on a clownish character was a recognized trick of the

---

[1] See *Puritan Widow*, I, iv, 208–11: "our Parson railes againe Plaiers mightily, I can tell you, because they brought him drunck vpp'oth Stage once,—as hee will bee horribly druncke."

[2] See Aubrey, *Remains*, p. 30, and *Assheton's Journal*, Chetham Society, p. 45 and note on p. 46, for a game called "Cap Justice," in which the judge who presides has his face blackened by those who plead before him. See Creizenach, *Geschichte des neueren Dramas*, I, 404, for a fourteenth century Dutch farce, *Buskenblaser*, in which an old husband who pays a quack to make him young and handsome for a young wife, has his face blackened instead. In the English farce "John Swabber," printed in Cox's *Actaeon and Diana*, the clown's face is blackened by a barber whom he employs to beautify him. Vos seems to have borrowed this incident from "John Swabber" for his farce *Oene* of 1642 (Bolte, *Danziger Theater*, pp. 229–30); and variations on it occur in a number of Continental dramatic pieces, including some written by imitators of the English comedians (see *ibid.*, p. 230 n. 3, for a list). It would be hazardous to try to connect "Droncke Goosen" with "the newe and most pleasant game of the goose" entered on the Register June 16, 1597.

[3] A host and hostess with the help of a daughter's wiles get the Prodigal so drunk at the tavern that they are able to steal his purse.

[4] See the diagram prefixed to *The Castle of Perseverance*; *King Darius*, l. 1155; *Play of Love*, l. 1293; *Prodigal Son* fragment (about 1530), l. 4; Machyn's *Diary*, Camden Society, p. 73 (for the year 1554); *Bugbears*, II, iv, IV, i, iii. An interesting seventeenth century example is found in the stage direction of Davenport's *A New Tricke to Cheat the Divell*, V, i: "*Ent.* DIVELLS *dauncing, with Fire wo[r]kes, and Crackers.*"

stage devil. In Redford's *Wit and Science*, line 363, Idleness utters the imprecation "The dyvyll set fyre one the." In *Doctor Faustus*, Robin the Ostler steals one of Faustus's books of magic and calls up the devil in order to play a trick on the Vintner. The stage direction in the quarto of 1604 reads here, "*Enter* Mephistophilis, *sets squibs at their backs, and then exit. They run about.*" This device was satirized by dramatists of the seventeenth century and apparently was not countenanced in the more reputable drama of the period. The Prologue to *The Two Merry Milke-maids* claims:

> 'Tis a fine Play:
> For we haue in't a Coniurer, a Deuill,
> And a Clowne too; but I feare the euill,
> In which perhaps vnwisely we may faile,
> Of wanting Squibs and Crackers at their taile.

In the Prologue to *The Doubtful Heir* which was "spoken at the Globe," Shirley describes his play as having "No bawdry, nor no ballads," "No clown, no squibs, no devil in't," and hence not likely to please the audiences of that house.[1] The comic elements of "Droncke Goosen" were evidently conventional in farcical scenes presented in the English theaters during the first half of the seventeenth century, and there is little doubt that the farce motives beloved of the masses were exploited in the jigs of the period. Though none of the allusions connect the popular interest in devils and squibs with the jig, I think it very probable that "Droncke Goosen," if not "Der betrogene Freier," was translated or adapted from an English jig.

The single extant English jig whose late date assigns it to this chapter is Thomas Jordan's "Cheaters Cheated. A Representation in four parts to be Sung, Nim, Filcher, Wat, and Moll, made for the Sheriffs of London." It was published in his *Royal Arbor of Loyal Poesie* of 1664, and the same edition was issued

---

[1] See also Prologue to *Every Man in his Humour; Hog hath Lost his Pearl*, II, i; the passage quoted on p. 117 above from *This Worlds Folly*, inveighing against those who "flash choaking squibbes of absurd vanities into the nosthrils of your spectators"; *Mercurius Politicus*, July 4–11, 1650, p. 72, "*Storms* and *Tempests*, which are tied ever like *Squibs*, at the breech of the *Family*." Mauermann ascribes to the influence of the English comedians the great vogue of such devices in Germany (*Bühnenanweisungen*, pp. 114–15). Fire was associated also with spirits or ghosts. See *Ayrers Dramen*, ed. Keller, V, 3393, and Creizenach, *Schauspiele*, p. 93.

in *A Nursery of Novelties* of 1665.[1] Text 24 is taken from *A Royal Arbor*. The date of performance is not given, but it probably did not long precede the date of publication, since Jordan's great activity as a pageant poet for the city began with the fall of the Commonwealth. In "The Cheaters Cheated" two hectors, in despair at the low state of their profession on account of the enforcement of law, rejoice to see Wat, a Somersetshire clown, appear and to hear him speak of the large sum of money he carries. By engaging Wat's attention with a glass through which he sees many colors, they pick his pockets. The rogues are chagrined to find that their booty is only nails, bread, and cheese. The next scene opens with Moll Medlar alone, carrying a basket. With the entrance of Wat, a livelier measure begins, and Moll introduces what is the only certain interlude of dance in the piece. The opening of her song, "I can dance, and I can sing," is like that of the pedant in "Pückelherings Dill dill dill" and of other characters whose song is primarily an accompaniment to dance. Wat offers to dance a spring with her, and relieves her of the basket. While both are dancing, she makes off, leaving him the basket, which contains a child. In another scene the rogues, again lamenting their state, see Wat carrying a trunk which he says is full of fine clothes. After a short resistance he gives it up to them, and they begin a battle over the division of the spoils. When Moll intervenes, they discover only the child. Moll convinces Filcher that it is his, they agree to marry, and all three renounce roguery for trade. Wat returns to sing a song of triumph and then a song on the twelve city companies.[2] The jig of over six hundred lines is entirely in verse and was evidently sung throughout. No tunes are mentioned. The use of the refrain "Which no body can deny" for the long section beginning with stanza 47 indicates that the tune was the one done to death in the satiric ballads of the time with that refrain. It was, however, an old air popular in the sixteenth century as "Greensleeves."[3] To judge from the verse forms, there was

[1] According to the *British Museum Catalogue* the *Nursery* is a "duplicate of pt. 1 of 'A Royal Arbor of loyal Poesie' except the titlepage and following leaf."

[2] See p. 121 above for Lupton's allusion in 1632 to a jig or dance of trades as commonly following a play.

[3] See Chappell, *Popular Music*, I, 227–33.

no such repetition of tunes as in some of the other long song dramas.

The occasional nature of "The Cheaters Cheated" as a performance at a great civic feast is reflected in some of its features. There are passing allusions to the dignitaries of the occasion, the present strict enforcement of law is held responsible for the hectors' distress, and a song in honor of the trades concludes the entertainment. In other respects this late song drama is made up of characteristic jig material. Two features that connect it directly with jig conventions of the late sixteenth century are the use of the country clown and the depiction of London coney-catchers.[1] The countryman who, like Wat, visits London and expresses his amazement at the marvels of the city is pictured in a number of songs and ballads.[2] Wat is the Somersetshire clown with a broad dialect. West country clowns, especially from Taunton Dean, have been noticed in connection with both the wooing and the political ballads of chapter vi.[3] "A West Country Song, made when the King was at Plymouth," beginning "A Riddle, a Riddle mee Neighbour *John*,"[4] is a clown's

---

[1] See pp. 94, 136-38, above.

[2] Tarlton's lost "Devise vpon this vnlooked for great snowe" (pp. 100-101 above) may have represented one form, but the clown's monologue on the wonders of London seems to have been usual. See "A Song," beginning "At *London* che've bin" (*Pills*, III, 267); "The Great Boobee," beginning "My Friend if you would understand" (*ibid.*, V, 94-97; *Roxburghe Ballads*, VII, 272-75); "Roger in Amaize or, The Countrey Mans Ramble through Bartholomew-Fair" to the tune of the "Dutch Womans Jigg," beginning "Adzooks Ches went the 'other day to *London* Town" (Pepys Collection, V, 428; *Pills*, III, 41-43; *Bagford Ballads*, I, 22-23); "The North-Country Man's Song," beginning "When Ize came first to *London Town*" (*Pills*, IV, 96-98; *Merry Drollery*, ed. Ebsworth, pp. 323-26). This last ballad may reflect a convention of sixteenth century "toys." Davies in Epigram No. 30 says in mockery of the poetaster Dacus,

"He first taught him that keeps the monuments
At Westminster, his formal tale to say."

Such a formal tale in ballad form appears in two drolleries (*Sportive Wit* [1656], and *Wit and Drollery* [1682], pp. 46-56), in *Pills*, V, 220-27, and in a broadside. See *Roxburghe Ballads*, VII, 268-72, for the broadside and a discussion of the forms. A preliminary description of the situation and the comments of the group of clowns who accompany the verger are omitted in the broadside.

[3] See also "A clown's journey to see London," beginning "At Taundeane lond I woz abore and a bred," in Ashmol. MS 36,37, No. 124. A late version is cited by Chappell in *Popular Music*, II, 671-72.

[4] See *Wit and Drollery* (1682), pp. 79-81; Rawlinson MS D. 398, No. 92; Ashmol. MS 36,37, No. 125; Dobell, *Poetical Works of William Strode*, pp. 114-18. Dobell prints a version from C.C.C. Oxford MS 325, with variant readings from C.C.C. MS

dialect song on the wonders of Plymouth, modeled on the news talk of neighbors. It was apparently used in an entertainment. Tom Hoyden of Taunton Dean figures in Brome's *Sparagus Garden;* and in the Epilogue of *The Court Beggar,* published in 1653, the country gentleman Swaynwit refers to *Antipodes* and *Tom Hoyden o' Tanton Deane* as jigs.[1] Possibly the comparison got its point from the existence of jigs dealing with similar material.

Jordan's treatment of the rogues is of a type conventional in prose pamphlets, but the best parallels to it are furnished by plays. In the relations of the two sharpers and the woman, for instance, in the quarrel of the two men, and in the interference of the woman, the jig resembles the opening scene of *The Alchemist.* Purse picking and a succession of robberies of a clown occur in a number of plays, including *The Winter's Tale* and *Bartholomew Fair,* often with two rogues as confederates.[2] "The Cheaters Cheated," however, reverses the situation of these early dramatic treatments and makes the clown rather than the rogue the crafty hero. This success of a clown in outwitting rogues is suggestive of the folk. A group of titles semi-proverbial in nature emphasizes the interest in stories of the type—"Wily Beguiled," "The Biter Bitten," "The Bilker Bilked," "The Deceiver Deceived," "The Cheater Cheated."[3] The last is the

---

328, and another version from Rawlinson Poet. MS 142. Worth, *West Country Garland,* p. 37, gives the date 1625 for the ballad. "The West-Country-man's Song at a Wedding," beginning "Uds hearty *wounds,* I'se not to *Plowing,* not I sir," was sung in the feast after Jordan's *Triumphs of London* (1683) and included in *A Choice Collection of 180 Loyal Songs* (1685), pp. 303–4, and in *Pills,* III, 277–79.

[1] The poet, he says, "has made prety merry Jigges that ha' pleas'd a many. As (le'me see) th'*Antipodes,* and (oh I shall never forget) *Tom Hoyden o' Tanton Deane.* Hee'l bring him hither very shortly in a new Motion, and in a new paire o' slops and new nether stocks as briske as a Body-lowse in a new Pasture." This epilogue, referring to *Sparagus Garden* of 1635 and *Antipodes* of 1638, seems to satirize the interest shown by men without taste in elements of plays that resembled jigs.

[2] For other examples, see *Modern Philology,* VI, 121–27.

[3] For the first, see early examples in Skeat, *Works of Chaucer,* V, 127, and *NED* under "wily"; the Oxford play of 1567, *Wylie Beguyly;* the extant *Wily Beguiled;* "A booke called *Wylie beguilde. &c*" entered November 12, 1606 (see also October 12, 1629); Cooper's *Wilie beguile ye, or the worldings gaine,* 1621; "wyly beguyly" entered March 8, 1636, and March 23, 1639; "The womans 'Wylly beguyly' " entered February 19, 1636; *Athenaeum,* September 4, 1875, p. 304; Nashe, *Works,* ed. McKerrow, III, 107. For "The Biter Bitten," see *Roxburghe Ballads,* III, 446–48. For "The Deceiver Deceived," see *ibid.,* IV, 34–37, and Mrs. Pix's comedy of that name. See *Henslowe's Diary,* ed. Greg, II, 199, for *'Tis no Deceit to Deceive the Deceiver.*

title given to a ballad in the Pepys Collection (IV, 279) and to a droll in Kirkman's *Wits* (1672) taken from the subplot of Marston's *Dutch Courtezan*. Among the various titles under which Marston's farce remained popular in the eighteenth century, *The Bilker Bilk'd, or, a Banquet of Wiles* is the one found in *The Strolers Pacquet Open'd* of 1742.

The central jest of the jig, that of palming off an unwanted child, is used in two forms. Moll manages by a ruse to leave the child on the hands of an overlusty wooer, and he in turn contrives to have it stolen from him. Both forms occur elsewhere. In Middleton's *Chaste Maid in Cheapside* (II, ii) two promoters who are taking meat from purchasers in Lent stop a country girl carrying a basket with meat on top and a child beneath. They take possession of the basket and receive the same shock that the rogues of the jig receive. The incident is handled similarly in the ballad called "The Country Girl's Policy; Or, the Cockney Outwitted." When two sharpers see the heads of geese hanging from the girl's basket, one offers to show her the Exchange while the other holds her basket. They make off with it.[1] In a late ballad of the Douce Collection, "Bite upon Bite; or, The Miser Outwitted by the Country Lass," a lustful miser pays a girl to go to an inn with him, stipulating that he is also to have everything in her baskets. When the fact that the booty includes a child comes out, she is haled before the mayor, who forces the miser to stand to his bargain.[2] Gayton in *Festivous Notes upon Don Quixot* (1654) tells the story (p. 34) of a gallant who straps two children to his back while he takes his pleasure with the mother. The woman robs him and then outruns him.[3]

[1] *Roxburghe Ballads*, VII, 286–87. See IX, 556–57, for "A Tryall of Skill; Perform'd by a poor decay'd Gentlewoman, who cheated a rich Grasier of Seven-score Pound, and left him a child to keep."

[2] III, 4. See also III, 33a, for "Fun in an Alley: or, The Footman Trapp'd," the story of how a footman carrying a pig in a basket to his master's betrothed stops in an alley with a courtesan, and a woman with a new-born bastard substitutes it for the pig. In the eighteenth century "Country-man's Garland" the first part, called "Country Johns Unfortunate Ramble to London" (Roxburghe Collection, III, 865; see *Roxburghe Ballads*, VIII, 183, and IX, 810–11), tells how a London woman manages to send the countryman on an errand with a basket containing her child, while she carries off his trunk and money.

[3] See *Roxburghe Ballads*, VII, 375, for Ebsworth's account of a ballad version of this jest, and pp. 375–79, 470–74, for a number of ballads with similar jests.

In a song called "Bung your Eye," which Logan prints from an early nineteenth century garland,[1] a girl leaves with a man whom she encounters, a basket supposedly full of gin, which turns out to be the usual child. A traditional song, "Eggs in her Basket,"[2] is the story of two sailors who, in preparation for a feast at an alehouse, carry off a girl's basket believing that it is filled with eggs. When they find out the truth, one of them offers fifty pounds to any woman willing to take the child. The offer is accepted by the girl herself, who has followed secretly. In one traditional French song an intriguing miller takes with him a girl who has a pannier, and is left with her child on his hands as she finds an excuse to slip away. In another—similar to the oldest form noticed here, that of *The Chaste Maid*—a town deputy, inspecting a girl's pannier, is duped in the same way.[3] Doubtless there are many versions of these jests that I have not met. It is not improbable that Jordan was imitating some form found in an earlier farce or ballad.

Three at least of the seven late singspiele listed by Bolte bear evidence of a connection with the tradition of the English jig. Of these, "Die Metamorphosis" and "Der Exorcist" are undoubtedly the work of the same anonymous adapter who is responsible for *Kunst über alle Künste* (a version of *The Taming of the Shrew*) and its afterpiece (a version of "Pückelherings Dill dill dill"), published in 1672. "Die Metamorphosis" was printed as an afterpiece with *Der pedantische Irrthum* in 1673, and "Der Exorcist" in the same way with *Alamodisch technologisches Interim* in 1675. All three publications were issued by the same man, Liebler, within a short time; and all are marked by the same peculiarities of style.[4]

"Die seltzame *Metamorphosis*, der Sutorischen/ in eine Magistrale, Person/ lustig/ In einem singenden Possen-Spiel/ fürgestellet" covers pages 261–301 of the volume taking its

[1] *Pedlar's Pack*, pp. 416-21. Logan compares the song with "The Cheaters Cheated."

[2] *Journal of the Folk-Song Society*, I, 46-47.

[3] See Tiersot, *Chansons populaires recueillies dans les Alpes françaises*, pp. 203-4, for these two songs.

[4] See Introduction to Köhler's edition of *Kunst über alle Künste*, and Ellinger in Herrig's *Archiv*, LXXXVIII, 272-84.

title from *Der pedantische Irrthum*, and through an error the numbers 270–79 are used twice. After a three-page Prologue by the ghost of Hans Sachs, the singspiel opens with an elaborate scene sung by a family of clowns. Hans Ungewaschen tells his idle, mocking, gormandizing son, Jan Pint, that he must seek a trade. Else Unflat, the mother, interferes as a result of the outcries of the son, and a railing contest follows, especially between Hans and Else. There is a free exchange of abusive epithets, coarse insults, and blows. In the next scene Jan, led by Hans, is attracted by the drinking song of Crispinus the shoemaker and consents to become an apprentice. Jan drinks the cobbler's beer during the negotiations and makes stipulations about his food. As soon as he is put to work, he runs away. In a new episode he wins the favor of a courtesan, Uttilie, as a result of his fine appearance in a cavalier's costume which he has just obtained. When Crispinus meets him, he recognizes Jan's stolen shoes. The two engage in a debate about the fulfilment of the cobbler's contract with his apprentice, and Jan refers the problem to Uttilie. Crispinus, declaring that Jan is his runaway apprentice and Uttilie a courtesan, would seize Jan; but Uttilie attacks him, and with the clown's help drives him away. In the next scene Jan seeks a position in the school of Magister Johannes Balhornius, who has taken a fancy to Uttilie, now apparently Jan's wife. As a test of his ability Jan is asked the question: "Noah had three sons, Shem, Ham, and Japhet; who was Japhet's father?" He once more lays his problem before Uttilie, making the clown's conventional blunders in attempting to repeat the proper names. She corrects him and gives him a homely parallel of the three sons of Thomas the Miller, which he understands. Jan returns to Johannes with the answer that Japhet's father is Thomas the Miller, and is dismissed with scorn. Uttilie next suggests that she become the mistress of Johannes in order to secure the position for Jan. He objects, but she tells him that it is the custom of the time and convinces him that he will lose nothing. Johannes now eagerly accepts Jan, introduces him to the pupils, assigns a Latin lesson, and hurries away to Uttilie. Jan sings a lament, to which his pupils sing a mocking chorus. When he attempts to chastise them, they beat him with their books, wrap his mantle around him, and leave him as he threatens vengeance.

There is no such definite evidence to connect "Die Metamorphosis" with the English comedians as in the case of the author's other two singspiele, but the indications are that he revised and expanded an early jig. About half of the singspiel is in prose, but a considerable part of the plot is carried on in the verse sections. These, I think, may survive from a form of the singspiel largely in verse. The adapter probably added the Prologue of Hans Sachs and modified and expanded the prose parts in particular. As in all of his adaptations, he has imparted a German color to the whole. Perhaps he contributed most in the burlesque jargon of the pedant. The pedant appears in several of the dramatic pieces with which he was concerned, and the same type of burlesque speech is prominent in all of them.[1] The adapter may be responsible also for speeches of the sort put in the mouth of Jan, who is in the main a stupid clown, but English dramatists also frequently give to the stupid clown subtle plays on words and pompous speeches. In "Die Metamorphosis" as in *Kunst über alle Künste* and "Der Exorcist," Latinized terms that may have been derived from English words occur, but they are less frequent than in "Der Exorcist."[2]

Characters, incidents, and some features of technique connect "Die Metamorphosis" with early song drama—first of all, with Ayrer's so-called fastnachtspiel "Von dem engelendischen Jann Posset," which, as I have said, is a typical early singspiel. The quarreling and railing of Jan Pint and his clownish parents, his gormandizing, his service under a master with whom he makes stipulations, his failure to stay with the master, and his marriage to a shrewish woman are all similar to incidents in Ayrer's singspiel and are handled in about the same order. Jan Pint's drinking the cobbler's beer, the debate of the two, and the courtesan's share in the beating of the cobbler are variants of incidents already discussed in connection with Ayrer. Like Bouset, or Posset, Pint may be one of the symbolic names used for the drinking and gluttonous clowns in English song drama. While the two clowns are, in the main, strikingly similar, details in the handling of Jan Pint give a fresh color to the conventional figure. His Gargantuan appetite, for instance, is especially stressed in the first scene. Here he seems to connect di-

---

[1] See the discussions of Ellinger and Köhler cited.

[2] See p. 329 below. There is more French than English in "Die Metamorphosis."

rectly with old farcical figures like Jack Pudding and Hans Wurst.[1] The English vogue of the gormandizing clown is illustrated also in jest, play, and farce by the eating scenes of Armin's *Nest of Ninnies*,[2] Lodge's *Looking Glass for London and England* (V, iv), and the droll published in Cox's *Actaeon and Diana* as "Simpleton the Smith." Pint's satiric remarks, especially his insulting asides, represent a convention of the English jig to which attention has already been called. Perhaps there is no more typical English clown in the surviving jigs and singspiele than Jan Pint.

In technique the cobbler and the pedant scenes differ from the scene of Pint's quarrel with his father, which is in verse of a pure ballad type except for two short passages. Possibly some old jig of a cobbler was the forerunner of the part of the singspiel dealing with the cobbler. Scenes in English plays, many of which were written at the end of the sixteenth century, feature the shoemaker and his trade; and the character was not infrequent in ballads, as in "The Cobbler of Colchester." Music for "The Cobbler's Jig" also has been preserved.[3] There can be little doubt, however, that the technique of the cobbler and the pedant scenes in "Die Metamorphosis," with their mixture of prose dialogue, sung dialogue, and interspersed special songs, was influenced by "Pückelherings Dill dill dill" or jigs of the same type. The drinking song and the trade song of the cobbler (pp. 272–73, 276–78) and the love lament of the pedant (pp. 282–83) are, like the miller's song in "Pückelherings Dill dill dill," of a sort conventionally associated with particular types.[4] The lament of Jan near the end, with the undersong of his pupils calling him a cuckold and employing the refrain "Kuk/kuk," has the same function as the final song in "Pückelherings

[1] For the first, see Chambers, *Mediaeval Stage*, I, 294; Morley, *Bartholomew Fair*, Index under "Jack Pudding" and "Merry Andrew"; and pp. 355, 368 n., below. For the second, see Creizenach, *Schauspiele*, p. xcvii.

[2] Shakespeare Society, pp. 12–14. See also Bolte, *Danziger Theater*, p. 176, for a similar feature of the clown in *Tiberius und Anabella*, *Jud von Venedig*, and *Tugend- und Liebes-Streit*—all plays of the comedians.

[3] Swaen, *Shakespeare Jahrbuch*, XLVI, 122–25; Chappell, *Popular Music*, I, 277–78.

[4] The drinking song of the cobbler and his journeyman calls for the air "Mein Hertzchen, mein Schätzgen"; and these are the opening words both of the same adapter's version of "Pückelherings Dill dill dill" and of Fonteyn's version of "The Blackman" (Bolte, *Singspiele*, pp. 84, 129, 180), a fact which suggests an earlier use of the tune among the English comedians.

Dill dill dill" sung chiefly by Pickleherring, with the chorus of "Pfui," etc., sung by the other characters.

Though the intriguing pedant may have been suggested by "Pückelherings Dill dill dill," I know no parallel for the clown's sale of his wife in "Die Metamorphosis." The central incident of this part of the singspiel, however—the pedant's question and Jan's answer—was apparently drawn from English jests. In *A Hundred Merry Tales*, No. lxxi, the jest is told of a young scholar, the son of a franklin, who seeks orders and, after his father has illustrated the point of the question about Japhet's father by means of his dogs, gives as his answer "Col my faders dog." In *Scoggins Jests*, No. x, the question put to the scholar concerns the sons of Isaac, and Scogan's instruction leads to the answer "Tom Miller." The jest probably passed into the original jig from some English variant that combined features of the two versions. The German parallels seem to have come from the singspiel; for in the numerous sixteenth and seventeenth century collections of jests preceding the publication of "Die Metamorphosis," no version has been traced, whereas a number dating from the period around 1700 have one suggestion or another of kinship with the singspiel.[1]

The general kinship of "Die Metamorphosis" to Ayrer's work would point to an early date for the original of the singspiel, though similar farce characters and conventions remained popular in song drama and droll through much of the seventeenth century. There is a recurrence of metrical forms in different parts of the singspiel[2] which suggests that the verse portion,

[1] Oesterley in his edition of *A Hundred Merry Tales* cites Memel's *Lustige Gesellschaft*, 1, and Gerlach's *Eutrapeliarum*, I, 665, for a version in which the miller figures in the answer. See Köhler, *op. cit.*, p. xxix n., for a tale by Balthasar Schupp in which a superintendent puts the question to a schoolmaster, who after appealing to his wife gives the answer "Laux der Müller." In a version cited by Bolte (*Singspiele*, p. 37) a cobbler, seeking to become a schoolmaster, fails to answer the test question of the village magistrate but is given the position upon his promise to mend the justice's shoes twice without charge ("in einer bisher unbeachteten, durch Reuters Schelmufsky angeregten Posse 'Der feige Prahler oder unhertzhaffte Auffschneider' [Des Politischen Bürstenbinders-Gesellen Lebens-Lauff 1705 S. 137–179. Berlin Yu 7991, 3]").

[2] For the use of the same simple quatrain, see the Prologue and pp. 269–71, 275, 270*–71*, 276*–77*, 278*, 283–84, 288–92, 298, 300. The air "Ein alter hat nur Wort und Wind &c. aus dem Seladon" is named only in the Prologue. An eight-line ballad stanza to the tune "More palatino" is used three times. Most of the tunes called for are found first about 1650 in German songbooks (Bolte, *Singspiele*, pp. 36–37), but they may have been derived from jigs or merely substituted for English airs without any change of metrical structure in the singspiel.

at least, does not differ greatly from the adapter's original. If "Die Metamorphosis" represents approximately the original jig, a late date of composition is to be inferred from the elaboration of form and the amount of prose, which is unusual even for game farce. But whatever the date of composition and whatever the changes which the piece may have undergone, the conventions as a whole speak strongly for its English origin.

"Der viesierliche *Exorcist*, Der die fleischlischen Geister/so den Mägden auffhockeln/ durch Kunst und Kurtzweil/ nicht *spiritualiter;* sondern fein *corporaliter* verjäget/ und außtreibet/ Lustig In einem/ redend und singend vermischtem/ Possenspiele fürgestellet" was published at the end of *Alamodisch technologisches Interim* with separate pagination (pp. 1–68). At the end of his list of dramatis personae the adapter comments as follows on his method of adaptation:

Mit diesem und vorigen Possenspiele/ Geehrter Leser/ gehet es/ wie mit der Kunst über alle Künste/ ein böß Weib gut zu machen: Ich habe sie von *Comœdianten*, auff dem Schauplatz fürgestellet/ gesehen/ wegen ihrer Artigkeit behalten/ und schreibe sie/ zu deiner nützlichen Belustigung/ hin/ wie sie mir/ nach Gutdüncken beyfallen. Ich mag meinen Kopff hierin nicht wegen neuer Erfindungen zerbrechen/ und hierüber Zeit verlieren/ welche ich besser in andern anwenden/ und hier nur *inventis addo:* Wer diese sonst gesehen/ oder gehöret/ wird den Unterscheid/ unter dem alten und neuen/ finden/ und daß ich in solchen Fratzen auch die Welt und ihre Eitelkeit zeige (welcher Ender- und Besserung ich/ mit unser aller/ hertzlich wünsche/ ersprießlich erkennen. . . . .

"Der Exorcist," then, was a version of some piece which the adapter had seen performed by the comedians, as was the case with the preceding possenspiel and with *Kunst über alle Künste*. I do not feel certain whether "vorigen Possenspiele" refers to "Die Metamorphosis," which had been published two years before, or to his version of "Pückelherings Dill dill dill," published slightly earlier still but with the adaptation of *The Taming of the Shrew* which is mentioned in the same sentence.

The story dramatized in "Der Exorcist" was current in Europe generally.[1] Characteristic forms are the fabliau *Le povre*

[1] See Ker in Bullen's edition of Davenport's *Works*, pp. 337–40; Bédier, *Les Fabliaux* (1895), pp. 453–54; Hart, *PMLA*, XXIII (1908), 343–74; Ellinger, Herrig's *Archiv*, LXXXVIII, 284–86; Bolte and Polívka, *Anmerkungen zu Grimm*, II, 1–18.

Clerc and Hans Sachs's fastnachtspiel *Der farendt Schuler mit dem Teuffelbannen*. Somewhat similar English versions are found in the section of *The Famous Historie of Fryer Bacon* "How Miles, Fryer Bacons man did coniure for meat, and got meat for himselfe and his hoast," and in Ravenscroft's *London Cuckolds*, II, ii, the last possibly derived from a French tale.[1] In these and the Continental forms known to me a person traveling alone, usually a crafty student, is the conjurer. In "Der Exorcist" the friar who does the conjuring has with him in his adventures an older friar. This form seems to be peculiar to Great Britain. It is first found in *The Freiris of Berwik*, a fabliau dubiously ascribed to Dunbar.[2] In 1639 it was dramatized by Davenport as a practically independent interlude in his *New Tricke to Cheat the Divell* (III, i). These two English versions and "Der Exorcist" are alike in all the essential incidents of the story: the journey of two friars late on a cold evening, the necessity of finding lodging for the night, the request for shelter from a wife whose husband is away from home, the wife's urging the danger to her reputation if she admits friars, the admission finally on the condition that they are to be isolated in a loft, the coming of the wife's lover, the preparation of a feast while the younger friar peeps through a hole, the husband's unexpected return, the wife's hiding of the lover and the food, the husband's desire for food and companionship, the noise or outcry of the young friar which leads to the husband's discovery of their presence and a summons to join him, the young friar's volunteering to conjure for food and bringing forth the wife's hidden feast, the desire of the husband to see the serving devil, the friar's calling for his spirit in the likeness of a human being and forcing the lover to come out of his hiding place, and the husband's chastisement of the departing spirit at the command of the friar.

Davenport's interlude and "Der Exorcist" have a close connection beyond their relation to *The Freiris of Berwik*. In both, the old and the young friar (called Allane and Robert in the fabliau) are named respectively Bernard (Bernardus) and John (Johannes), while Abbot John, the wife's lover in *The Freiris*,

---

[1] See Ker, *loc. cit.*, and Summers, *Restoration Comedies*, pp. xxxv–xxxvi.

[2] See Ker, *loc. cit.*; *PMLA*, XXIII, 360.

becomes the head constable in the play and the master of the watch in the German piece. In addition they agree in a score of minor details in which they depart from *The Freiris*, as in the fact that various dishes of the wife's banquet are found in succession hidden in different places instead of being brought all at once from the cupboard. Davenport apparently used the fabliau, retaining a few features not found in "Der Exorcist," like the lover's bringing bread and wine to the assignation and the extinguishing of a fire before the husband is admitted. In addition, the mention of the four religious orders at Berwick corresponds to Davenport's reference to the four kinds of friars in Islington. On the other hand, "Der Exorcist" is like *The Freiris* rather than the play in including the wife's maid, who aids the wife and her lover and brings the friars from the loft at the command of the husband, and in representing the lover as beaten with a stick, whereas he is kicked in the play. "Der Exorcist" also seems to connect with *The Freiris* rather than with Davenport in the emphasis on sensual details, the rascality of the young friar, and the elaboration of his conjuring. These rather general resemblances might result, however, from the farcical treatment of the story in the German piece even if it were borrowed from Davenport; while the maid could easily be an accidental restoration, for the maid is the assistant of an intriguing wife in other singspiele of the English comedians, as in "Studentenglück" and "Der Mönch im Sacke." It is possible then that the English original of "Der Exorcist" was borrowed from Davenport and expanded with or without reference to *The Freiris of Berwik*. Both Davenport's interlude and the original of "Der Exorcist," however, may be adaptations of a lost English piece closely related to *The Freiris*. At any rate, an English farce was probably translated into German and then adapted as "Der Exorcist" without material change of the main incidents taken from the English original.

The exact nature of this English original is something of a problem. In his version of "Pückelherings Dill dill dill" and *The Taming of the Shrew* the adapter followed the plot and language of his originals somewhat closely. His statement in regard to "Der Exorcist" and the relation of the piece to Davenport's play suggest the same sort of adaptation. Even the most

significant feature of his style, the insertion of Latin words and
derivatives, may have been characteristic of the group of dramatic pieces which he took from the repertory of the comedians,
though the amount of Latinized jargon is abnormal in all of
them and must have been due in part to expansion. Some at
least of the Latinized words in *Kunst über alle Künste* were derived from English words of *The Taming of the Shrew*.[1] Certainly much of the Latin in his version of "Pückelherings Dill dill
dill" was in the original. In "Die Metamorphosis," as I have
said, there is a similar intrusion of French terms as well as
Latin, whereas French phrases are rare in "Der Exorcist." No
doubt the Latin verse used in the conjuring of "Der Exorcist"
was drawn largely from the original, and many isolated Latin
or Latinized words suggest the survival of English words in the
adapter's original.[2] Although some of these may have resulted
from his partiality for French, enough that must have come
from English remain to indicate that the German text from
which "Der Exorcist" was drawn had retained from its original
a number of English words with Latin stems. There is reason
then to believe that on the whole "Der Exorcist" preserves
rather faithfully the farce from which it was adapted.

The German piece, called in the title a farce with mixed
speech and song, is different from the ordinary singspiel in that
the action is all carried by the prose dialogue, and the song element, which is very considerable, takes the form of interspersed
songs. The possenspiel resembles the sixteenth century farce
Tom Tyler, reprinted in 1661. Including the Latin stanzas of
the friar's conjuring, the songs of the singspiel are in ten different stanzaic forms, some of which recur. For eight of these,
including the two in Latin, the tunes are indicated, chiefly airs

---

[1] See Köhler, *op. cit.*, pp. xxii n., xxiv n. 2, xxv n. 2.

[2] *Beet*, rhyming with *recreet* in one song (p. 38), is probably an English term or
phrase misspelled because it was unknown. Among other possible survivals of English
words are *Exorcist* in the title, *vocal* (p. 7), *Credit* (p. 12), *influentz* (p. 17), *extra* (p. 21),
confortation (p. 22), *delicat* (pp. 22, 37, 43), Collation (p. 23), Appetit (pp. 23, 45),
Compan [*companion?*] (p. 25), *expedition* (p. 27), *scienz* und *sapienz* (p. 32), Register
euer *memori* (p. 33), *Secret* (p. 34), *supernatural* (p. 37), *miracul* (p. 38), *inclination* (p.
43), *mode* (pp. 46, 48, 60), *jalousie* (p. 47), *Director*, *quintessenz* (p. 48), and Organist
(p. 52). The italicized words are in roman type; the others in black-letter. On p. 45
roman is used for *appetit*.

found in German songbooks of the seventeenth century.[1] If the adapter adhered to his original as closely as the evidence would seem to indicate, there must have been an English piece dealing with the conjuring friar which was not a strict jig but a farce with much interspersed song. It is just possible that the English original of "Der Exorcist" was the "Friars," which, according to an account of Antimo Galli, the groundlings of the Curtain clamored for on an occasion between 1611 and 1615.[2]

A third late German piece, "Harlequins Hochzeit," which is printed by Bolte,[3] is a pure song drama with a clownish wooing as its theme. After Lisette has consented to the wish of her father Teneso that she accept a rich burgher's son named Levandin, the clown—now become a Harlequin—woos her, and Lisette mockingly encourages him. He swaggers about, boasting that he is a cavalier and that he will destroy anyone who approaches Lisette. Immediately Levandin kisses her before his eyes. Margodt, daughter of the broom-maker Rundum, now woos him, backed by her father; but he flouts them, and all three engage in a fist fight until driven out by Teneso. Harlequin meets Lisette again and continues his wooing, giving a list of his possessions as his equipment for marriage. Coming later with a ladder and musicians to serenade her, he climbs to her window and sings a song in which he begs for admittance. The ladder is taken away by Teneso and Rundum, and Harlequin is left hanging to the wall. Two officers arrest him and lodge him in jail. On condition that Harlequin marry her, Margodt and her father secure his release. He is hurried away to a justice, who marries the pair after much drollery resulting from

---

[1] See Bolte, *Singspiele*, p. 38. Bolte overlooks the tune "Eine reiche Magd hat Matz. Auß dem Voigtländer" on p. 16. I have not taken into consideration two bits of verse chanted as prayers (pp. 38, 60). On p. 7 the adapter adds a note before the second song: "Mercke; daß die Melodien/ welche in vorigen schon angezeiget seynd/ in diesen und folgenden nicht/ sondern nur/ was von neuem eingebracht/ angedeutet/ und beygesetzet wird." According to this, tunes are indicated when a song requiring one not already used is introduced. But this is misleading, since the two songs on pp. 8 and 15–18, both without tunes, do not conform to the stanza of any other songs in the piece.

[2] See Chambers in *Review of English Studies*, I, 186. See p. 107 above for the practice of calling for jigs.

[3] *Singspiele*, pp. 148–66. For his discussion, see pp. 38–42, 186–87.

his attempt to learn the names of the three louts. The bridal feast is announced, a hostess gets her tavern ready, and a group of guests, including Lisette and Levandin, gather to celebrate the bridal. As they enter for the feast, the company sing in chorus a special song which apparently accompanies a "Trapffen-Tantz" (l. 515), and the singspiel is brought to a close with a bridal dance. "Harlequins Hochzeit" has nearly six hundred lines, and in some editions boasts of seventeen scenes. Outside of the two special songs there are two stanzaic forms with frequent changes from one to the other. No tunes are mentioned.

The first trace of the singspiel is the edition of 1693, which Bolte reprints. The evidence for an enormous popularity in the period following close on this edition suggests that the piece was new, at least in its German form. Bolte records thirteen editions, various performances and allusions, two Continental continuations—one anonymous and one by Reuter—and a translation into Danish (along with Reuter's continuation) published in 1730. There is no external evidence to connect the singspiel with the English comedians, and most of its conventions are common in European farce and wooing drama. Some features associate it, however, with the group of song dramas treated in chapter viii, and others are best paralleled in English comedy. "Harlequin's Hochzeit" may, after all, be a late reworking or expansion of an earlier jig.[1]

The motive of a clown's aspiring to a lady and seeing her carried off by a lover of higher station has been noticed in "Der Narr als Reitpferd." The complementary motive of his being claimed at the same time by an uncouth mate does not appear in the extant song dramas but is frequently met in wooing plays, as in Raber's *Rex Viole*, Rollenhagen's *Amantes amentes*, and *Sidonia und Theagene*, a play of the English comedians adapted from *Amantes amentes*. In *Tiberius und Anabella*, a comedy in German which seems to have been acted by English comedians as early as 1604, a peasant and his daughter Greta force the

---

[1] Bolte points out a number of details which indicate that the edition of 1693 was published at Hamburg. Reynolds's troupe played at Hamburg for nine weeks in the autumn of 1648 (Herz, *Englische Schauspieler*, p. 56).

clown Hans to consent to marriage with the girl (I, iii).[1] He afterward falls in love with the highborn lady. The important part played by the father of one or both of the women in all of these instances, as in "Harlequins Hochzeit," is one of the strongest indications of the conventionality of the whole wooing plot in this form. The scene in *Tiberius und Anabella* (I, ii) in which the clown is subdued is akin to one in *Locrine* (III, iii) in which the shrewish Margerie with the help of her father compels Strumbo to marry her,[2] and both are similar to the corresponding part of "Harlequins Hochzeit." The abusive epithets that Margerie hurls at Strumbo resemble those that Harlequin showers on Margodt, and the beating administered to Strumbo parallels the fight in the singspiel. An old trick of the English clowns is used by both Hans and Harlequin when they call themselves cavaliers and boast of their quality.[3] All three of these clowns have the traits and tricks that mark the extremely droll type developed by the English actors and so much beloved in Germany, as in Ayrer's Jan Posset. Many of the details in the portrayal, however, are common in both English and Continental comedy. A feature of the singspiel that has already been noticed as a convention of wooing game, ballad, and farce is the clown's comic inventory of his property.[4] The portrayal in ballad and farce of the sensual girl frankly eager for marriage has also been discussed.[5] The serenade might have come from

[1] The play is printed from a manuscript and discussed by Bolte in *Das Danziger Theater*, pp. 171–218. It is based on Marston's *Fawne*, but the scene in question is not in the original. In the notes to his edition of "Harlequins Hochzeit" (based partly on the earlier notes of Ellinger) and in his discussion of the affiliations of the comic plot in *Tiberius und Anabella* (*Danziger Theater*, pp. 175–76), Bolte has pointed out a number of parallels to the clown's forced marriage and other features of the singspiel. Most of these are drawn from Continental drama. He calls attention, however, to *Locrine* and to the Shakespeare parallels mentioned in the next note.

[2] Strumbo (I, ii) and Hans (II, iii) cry out on the arrows of Cupid and indulge in love letters. Hans also has a monologue with his stick (III, iii) like Launce's in *The Two Gentlemen of Verona*, and a scene with his father (V, iii) like Launcelot's in *The Merchant of Venice*.

[3] See p. 201 above; *Tiberius und Anabella*, III, iii; IV, v; V, iii; and "Harlequins Hochzeit," ll. 63, 411–16. Hans three times calls himself "Monsieur Signior Cavagliere."

[4] See pp. 192–97 above. Bolte in *Singspiele*, p. 153 n., cites a number of German examples.

[5] See pp. 205–7 above.

the customs of any European folk.[1] In *Monsieur Thomas* there is a scene (III, iii) which, in spirit at least, is rather close to the incident in the singspiel. Thomas, who comes to the window of his inamorata with a song pleading for admission, attempts to climb up, is frightened, and falls. Bits of song belonging to the night visit of a lover[2] are used akin to one stanza of Harlequin's song. In the allegorical *Fucus Histriomastix* (1623) the clown Villanus is represented as coming with musicians to sing and dance for Ballada.[3] The jest of leaving Harlequin hanging from the wall is like the trick of a suitor's being kept suspended in a basket in *Englishmen for my Money* (ll. 2090 ff.), an incident drawn from the folk book *Vergilius*. The device of bringing drama to a close with dance by means of a wedding celebration is a natural one that had found favor with English dramatists earlier (p. 86). It is of course possible that "Harlequins Hochzeit" was written in Germany in the latter part of the seventeenth century and made up of native material. But it also seems to me possible that its basis was an old jig in which the clown fell from his pretensions to a lady and became the victim of his own amour with a shrewish slattern, their comic affair serving as a foil to the love-making of a more courtly pair.

I have not seen the still later song dramas of which Bolte gives an account.[4] According to Bolte, in the anonymous continuation of "Harlequins Hochzeit," written in the same two stanzas, news is brought to Harlequin of the birth of a son twenty weeks after his marriage; he is sent to summon Lisette, Levandin, and the justice as godparents; and a christening feast is held, with much merriment at the expense of the clown, though the justice has explained to Harlequin's satisfaction that twenty weeks of marriage for him and twenty for his wife make three quarters of a year. Reuter's continuation dealing

[1] Bolte, *Singspiele*, p. 155 n., refers to the first *intermède* of Molière's *Malade imaginaire* (1673), in which Polichinelle stages a serenade on the street at night and is taken by the watch, and also to Weise's *Lustspiel von dem dreyfachen Glücke*, in which the fool is driven off when he attempts a serenade.

[2] See pp. 198–200 above; *PMLA*, XXXVI, 565–614.

[3] Ed. G. C. Moore Smith, I, iv; II, v; etc. According to stage directions the tunes of a number of popular ballads are used for the Latin songs.

[4] *Singspiele*, pp. 42–48.

with the birth and christening of Harlequin's child is described as independent of the preceding, and inferior. "Lustige Nacht-Comoedia," also said to be modeled on the verse form of "Harlequins Hochzeit," seems to be concerned with an intrigue in which Hans the miller is frightened by a character who plays the ghost. In "Harlequin, Der ungedultig, hernach aber mit Gewalt gedultig gemachte Hahnrey," published in 1743, there is satire on political conditions of the period; but the singspiel is built on the typical farcical situation of a wife's outwitting a clownish husband in order to carry on an intrigue, this time with two French lovers. Finally, "Der Offizier im Nonnenkloster" tells of a discharged officer who gains access to the room of a prioress by passing himself off as her kinsman. Bolte assigns it to the end of the eighteenth century and points out its kinship with a ballad probably a century older, "Von Closter-Frauen," which has three speakers but is not a pure dialogue.

CHAPTER X

THE BACKGROUND OF DANCE

THE stage jig combined three arts in which the Elizabethans delighted and excelled—drama, music, and dance. This study is undertaken from the point of view of drama and is concerned primarily with the "librettos" of the jigs. But dance was the distinctive feature of the jig and evidently the one that made the greatest appeal. The material bearing directly on dance in the stage jig has been discussed. It is small in amount but leads, I think, naturally to the conclusion that, if a complete study of stage practice could be made, it might easily involve the whole range of dance in the late sixteenth and early seventeenth centuries. In origin and background also, the stage jig is intimately connected with the general field of dance. For these reasons some understanding of the state of contemporary dance in England seems to me of no little importance for a study of the jig. Anything so ambitious as a technical account of Elizabethan dance is out of the question, especially in view of the fact that contemporary English treatises are lacking. I hope merely to give some general idea incidentally of the chief types in vogue but particularly of the trends in dance out of which the popularity of the jig seems to have grown.

No doubt the dance developed in great complexity in England during the Middle Ages. Dancing is one of the accomplishments of the gay Absolon in "The Miller's Tale" (ll. 142–44):

> In twenty manere coude he trippe and daunce
> After the scole of Oxenforde tho,
> And with his legges casten to and fro.

The author of *Colkelbie Sow*, ascribed to the fifteenth century, names a host of dances attempted by the peasants in their merrymaking, and mocks their bungling of the courtly base dance (l. 301). After the coming of the Tudors, there are many records of courtly festivities with the masquers' dances and the social dances of the accompanying revels. At the same time the increasing mass of literature shows the importance of dancing in the social life of the people. During the reign of Elizabeth dance felt the same quickening that gave new life to the other arts, and in the last quarter of the century England from courtier to country clown seems to have been dance mad.

It is from the attacks of the satirists and the moralists that we get the best conception both of the passion for dance and of the general type that was in favor toward the end of the sixteenth century. Northbrooke about 1577 declares that it would grieve chaste ears to hear what "newe kinde of daunces, and newe deuised gestures the people haue deuised, and daylye doe deuise." Of grave women he says, "it is a worlde to see, nay, a hell to see, howe they will swing, leape, and turne when the pypers and crowders begin to play." Northbrooke contrasts the religious dancing of the ancients with "our hoppings, and leapings, and interminglings men with women, &c. (dauncing euery one for his part)," and he declares that David did not dance "leaping and turning of his bodie with playerlyke mouings and gestures."[1] In *A Friendlie Dialogue betweene Paule and Demas* (1580) Byrd speaks of the turning on the toe, the capers, and other tricks of the young man who dances (fol. 38*v*). According to Stubbes, dancers of his day sometimes crippled themselves. "Some haue broke their legs with skipping, leaping, turning, and vawting," he says.[2] Gascoigne, making a general attack on dance in the Fourth Song of his *Grief of Joy* (1576), speaks in stanzas 29–30 of "oure tossings and oure turnes,/Owre frysks, oure flyngs,"

> the movings wch we make,
> As forward, backward, lefte hande turne, and right/
> Upwards, and downewards, tyll owre hartes do quake/
> And last of all, (to shew owre selves owtright)
> A turne on toe, must grace owre giddy spright,
> Untyll sometymes, we stoomble in the same,
> And fall downeright, to geve the gazers game./

[1] *Treatise against Dicing, Dancing*, etc., Shakespeare Society, pp. 150, 151, 176, 177.

[2] *Anatomy of Abuses* (1583), New Shakspere Society, Part I, p. 156. Lodge in *Wits Miserie* (1596) reminds his readers of the fate of "Lewis Archbishop of Magdenburghe) who in treading his lauolas and corrantos with his mistresse, in trying the horsetrick broke his necke" (p. 34).

In Satire XI of *The Scourge of Villanie* Marston satirizes in
the person of Curio the absorption of the gallant in dancing
and the type of dancing which he affects:

> Who ever heard spruce skipping Curio
> Ere prate of ought but of the whirle on toe,
> The turne about ground, Robrus sprauling kicks,
> Fabius caper, Harries tossing tricks?
> Did ever any eare ere heare him speake
> Unlesse his tongue of crosse-points did intreat?
> His teeth doe caper whilst he eates his meat,
> His heeles doe caper whilst he takes his seate;
> His very soule, his intellectuall
> Is nothing but a mincing capreall.
> He dreames of toe-turnes; each gallant he doth meete
> He fronts him with a traverse in the streete.
> Praise but Orchestra, and the skipping art,
> You shall commaund him, faith you have his hart
> Even capring in your fist.[1]

Allowance must be made for the fact that to the Puritan all
dance was anathema and that exaggeration is a necessary weap-
on of the satirist. Even so, the type of dance pictured is virile,
even acrobatic, calling for vigor and agility rather than dignity,[2] and, according to Northbrooke, often combined with
gesture and dramatic action.

The changing fashion in late sixteenth century dance can be
traced more easily among the courtly than among the folk.
Naturally the records are fuller for the upper classes,[3] and as
the courtly dances with one probable exception were imported
from the Continent, various foreign treatises offer a basis for a
study of courtly dance in England. The most important of these

[1] *Works of Marston*, ed. Halliwell, III, 300–301.

[2] See also Marston's satire on Curio in *Pigmalions Image and Certaine Satyres*,
near the end of Satire I; Sir Andrew Aguecheek's boast in *Twelfth Night* near the end of
I, iii; the practice of the "crosspoynt back caper" in *Returne from Parnassus*, Part II,
II, vi; *Old Law*, III, ii; *Every Woman in her Humour*, H 4; etc. For early examples, see
the loutish dance in *John the Reeve* (Laing, *Early Popular Poetry of Scotland*, ed. Hazlitt,
I, 270–71); *Four Elements*, ll. 964–68, 1253–57.

[3] Reyher, *Les Masques Anglais*, chap. viii, has collected a large number of the
more interesting English allusions to the various types of dance, since between the set
dances of the masque the masquers joined with the spectators in the ordinary social
dances, which were on these occasions called the revels.

treatises is the *Orchesographie* of Arbeau (or Tabourot), which was published in 1588, just at a time to make it significant for the period in English dance with which we are concerned.[1]

In the dancing that represents the older courtly tradition of the sixteenth century there is a distinct impression of the schematic. On formal occasions the program of social dancing opened with the slow and stately court dances and proceeded with court and country dances that were progressively livelier and more informal.[2] Selden says in *Table-Talk* that in the time of Elizabeth at "a solemn Dancing, first you had the grave Measures, then the Corrantoes and the Galliards, and this is kept up with Ceremony, at length to *French*-more [Trenchmore], and the Cushion-Dance, and then all the Company Dance, Lord and Groom, Lady and Kitchin-Maid, no distinction."[3] The dances in vogue changed, but the principle remained until well into the seventeenth century. It was also conventional for a single "number" to consist of a suite of dances with a lively finale—two base dances followed by a tordion, or two pavans by a galliard, or a series of almains or brawls or other courtly dances, usually three, performed with increasing speed.[4] This progression seems natural enough except for its fixity. As for the dance itself, courtly dance apparently lost its natural accompaniment of song much earlier than folk dance, and by the sixteenth century seems to have become rather rigid and monotonous. This was perhaps due partly to the medieval passion for elaborate and rigid systems. Morley tells us that the galliard following the pavans *en suite* was "a kind of musicke made out of the other," and with the same number of strains, but set to triple instead of quadruple time.[5] According to Arbeau, the

---

[1] References are by folio to the facsimile of the original edition with an Introduction by Fonta. A translation by C. W. Beaumont appeared in 1925. See also Böhme, *Geschichte des Tanzes in Deutschland*, Vol. I, chap. ix, for comment on the dances arranged alphabetically. See *Musical Times*, LVII, 142–45, 489–92, for two valuable short articles by Mrs. Dolmetsch dealing with a number of the courtly dances partly on the basis of treatises by Negri and Caroso.

[2] See Reyher, *Les Masques Anglais*, p. 447.   [3] Ed. Arber, p. 62.

[4] See Arbeau, 26, 28, 67, 69, 74, etc.; Fonta's Introduction to Arbeau, pp. xviii–xix.

[5] *Plaine and Easie Introduction*, p. 181. For some examples in the *Fitzwilliam Virginal Book*, see Naylor, *An Elizabethan Virginal Book*, pp. 14, 21, 114–15.

base dance to be regular required a "chanson" with an opening of sixteen measures repeated, a "médiation" of sixteen, and a
close of sixteen repeated (24v). In his notation of certain base
dances (translated from the French) Copland designates their
measures as "perfect" or "imperfect" according to the number
of movements in each part.[1] Ravenscroft, in a passage from his
Briefe Discourse which will be quoted later in this chapter, crit-
icises the dancing both of the revels and of the masque because
of its bondage to "particular *Rules* and *Numbers*" and recommends the antic dance as a corrective.

Ravenscroft's protest belongs to a movement away from
formalism in the dance which set in long before the end of the
sixteenth century. This movement was evidently widespread.
The conservative Arbeau complains repeatedly of the changing
times in France, and it is in the *Orchesographie* that the newer
tendencies can be most definitely traced. Except on formal occasions, the slow and stately dance fell into relative disuse.
Emphasis was placed more and more on a rapid and vigorous
type of dance which demanded agility and cleverness in the
individual dancer. The leaping or hopping step gained favor
generally over the step "par terre," and the caper became the
touchstone of the dance. There was also a strong drift toward
eclecticism that is especially significant for the seventeenth
century and will be noticed at the end of the chapter.

The old tradition of the slow and stately type of dance with
its step "bas" is represented in the base dance and the pavan,
the one in triple and the other in duple time. According to the
Orchesographie, these dances are seemly for honorable personages, chiefly the ladies (29). The pavan, Arbeau adds, is suitable
for the ceremonious court function or for the triumphal entry
of gods and goddesses or royal personages in a masque. In both
dances the movements by which the dancers progress are the
elementary "simples" (in English "singles") and "doubles." To
make two simples, says Arbeau, you step with the left foot for
the first measure, bring the right foot to join it for the second,
advance the right foot for the third, and join the two feet for
the fourth. The double calls simply for three steps for the first

---

[1] See *Laneham's Letter*, ed. Furnivall, pp. clxi–clxii.

three measures, with the feet brought together for the fourth.[1]
In the pavan the dancers make two simples and a double forward and the same backward, unless they prefer to go forward
always (28v). Arbeau records that the base dance has been out
of fashion in France for forty or fifty years (24v), and he regrets
that such wholesome dances as this and the pavan should be
displaced by the dances "lasciues & deshontées" which have
been introduced to the regret of the wise and modest (29v). The
appeal of these dances as Arbeau describes them would lie in the
grace and dignity and precision of the movements. The pavan,
however, as he shows later, was modified to meet the taste of
the time.

Apparently by the beginning of Elizabeth's reign the base
dance had been superseded in England by the measures, for
according to Selden it was the measures that conventionally
opened the dancing on formal occasions in her day. In *Much
Ado*, II, i, however, Beatrice describes the measures as "full of
state and ancientry," and various references to the "old measures" imply that by the end of the century the dance was out of
fashion except on state occasions.[2] Its formal use among the
courtly is particularly interesting, as the dance seems to have
been a native development. For the same reason a satisfactory
account of it is lacking. The mass of rather vague and confusing
evidence as to the nature of the measures—confusing largely
because the word was used in so many senses in connection with
dance—cannot be assembled here. That the movements called
for precision is to be inferred from Riche's statement in the
first Preface to his *Farewell to Militarie profession* that he could
never tread the measures aright "although I desired to performe
all thynges by line and by leavell, what so ever I tooke in
hande." But the measures did not represent a rigid or monotonous type. In the *Masque of Queens* Jonson says that after the
masquers' second dance "they tooke out the men, and daunc'd
the *Measures*, entertayning the time, almost to the space of an

---

[1] See 26–28. Of the other three movements in the base dance, the *reverence* is the
movement of courtesy with which the dance opens; the *branle* (not to be confused with
the dance called the "branle," or in English the "brawl") seems to be a slight swaying
movement first to one side and then to the other without moving the feet, and suggests
the *congé*; the *reprise*, says Arbeau, requires a slight movement of the knees or feet
or toes as if the feet trembled.

[2] See Reyher, pp. 447–48.

hower, with singular variety." The same quality comes out in
our fullest description of the measures—by Davies in *Orchestra*
(stanzas 65–66). This dance, he says, is "full of change and rare
varieties," although always spondaic, solemn, grave, and slow,
and is marked by "fair order and proportion true" and by "cor-
respondence every way the same." These passages suggest to
me a formal and stately type of dance based, like the "figure"
dances of the folk, on the idea of maneuvers.[1] A geometric conception of the dance is seen among the courtly in Vander Noodt's
flattery of Elizabeth as expert in song, skilled in the use of musical instruments, and "according to the exact proportions of
geometrie exquisite in the measures of the daunce."[2] In
Browne's *Britannia's Pastorals* (Book I, Song 3, ll. 409–18) shepherds and shepherdesses dance first a "crooked measure," then
measures which bring them to rest in the form of an I and a Y,
and finally a round. The principle is of course found at its
most elaborate in the evolutions of the masques.

In the era of the pavan and the base dance the typical lively
dances of the courtly were the galliard and the tordion, which
regularly followed these two *en suite*. They are both in triple
time. In the galliard the unit of action is the cinquepace, corresponding to six beats of the music. The cinquepace, according
to Arbeau's account, consists of four movements of the feet followed by a "cadence," which is made up of a leap ("sault majeur") and a final "posture." Arbeau devotes a number of
generously illustrated pages to describing the various steps of
the galliard and their combination in recognized ways in the
cinquepace (38–49). The dancer, for example, raises one foot
in front or behind or across the other, and so on. At the same
time, with the foot which bears the weight he makes a "petit
sault." This gives the characteristic hopping motion of the
galliard. Such a dance calls for considerable strength and dexterity. Arbeau describes it as a dance for young men (40r). The
tordion is characterized as a kind of galliard but danced "par
terre," and with the "sault majeur" softened to a "sault moy-
en." Its movements are more rapid but lighter and less violent
than those of the galliard (39v, 49v).

[1] But see *Musical Times*, LVII, 145.

[2] See the Dedication to his *Theatre for Voluptuous Worldlings* (1569) in Corser's
Collectanea Anglo-Poetica, Part 10, p. 314.

Our best single source of information about the courtly dance of Elizabethan England is the poetic *Orchestra* of Davies (1594). When Davies takes up specific dances, he seems to be following out his conception of the development of dance in England (stanzas 64–70). Love, he says, first taught men to tread rounds and heys—that is, country dances. As men more civil grew, Love framed the measures, which moved the eye with sober wondering and sweet delight. "But for more divers and more pleasing show" the galliard was invented, a gallant dance, with a "spirit and a virtue masculine." Then Davies describes the courant and rises to a climax in the volte. The last two belong to the newer tradition in dance. The same might be said of the galliard except in point of time. A galliard was danced in the early *Wit and Science*.[1] But the dance belonged to a type that grew in favor, and it readily lent itself to modification. While the base dance, the measures, and to a less extent the pavan were becoming antiquated, the galliard took on new life.

At the time of his writing, that is about 1588, Arbeau declares that the galliard was likely to be danced in the towns of France, not with the same discretion as of old, but "tumultuously," some passages without "disposition," the dancers being content to come in on the cadence (38v). But the cadence of the galliard could be omitted until the eleventh or seventeenth or corresponding beat (48v),[2] and the passages substituted for the cadence gave further chance for variation. One note might also be broken up into two of half the value, with a correspondingly larger number of faster movements. Arbeau shows how easy it was for the dancer to vary the number of movements preceding the cadence and to introduce embellishments at will. For the "sault majeur" the more agile dancers also substituted an exaggerated leap called the "capriole."[3]

[1] At l. 332. Reyher (p. 450) cites a passage from Elyot's *Castel of Helthe* (1539) in which the dancing of galliards is mentioned among exercises both violent and swift.

[2] This accounts for the "tricke of XVII. in a sinkapace" mentioned in Harington's *Apologie for Ajax* (A 2), and the same idea underlies the tricks of twenty and of other numbers (see *Dutch Courtezan*, III, i; *Malcontent*, IV, ii; *City Wit*, IV, i).

[3] See Mrs. Dolmetsch in *Musical Times*, LVII, 490, for the capriole: "One must jump as high as possible, during which time the feet should pass and repass one another in a straight line, from four to six times." She refers also to the interlaced caper and to a "cut caper" in which the legs are beaten together in the air—this being one of ten different "cut capers" described by Negri.

The English galliard could hardly have fallen behind that of the Continent in its variations and exaggerations. Davies mentions the uncertain passages of the galliard to and fro and its lofty turns and caprioles in the air. In the Preface which has already been cited several times, Riche declares,

Our galliardes are so curious, that thei are not for my daunsyng, for thei are so full of trickes and tournes, that he whiche hath no more but the plaine sinquepace, is no better accoumpted of then a verie bongler; and for my part thei might assone teache me to make a capricornus, as a capre in the right kinde that it should bee.

In the Address to the Reader prefixed to *Penelope's Complaint* (1596) the writer figuratively describes himself as "desiring rather to teach the simple their uniforme cinque pace, then effect Courtiers in their lofty galliards, which alter every day with new devises." One of the marvels of London described by Piers Plowman in *Newes from the North* (1585) by "T. F." is the performance of a galliard dancer in a dancing school (E iii): "at our entring hee was beginning a trick as I remember of sixteens or seuenteens, I do not very wel remember but wunderfully hee leaped, flung and took on." One of the party who was deaf and had seen the dancer without hearing the music "thought verily that hee had been stark mad and out of his wit." The extravagances of the galliard are satirized by Rowlands in "My fine Dauncer" from *Looke to it: for, Ile Stabbe ye* (1604). After describing how the dancer turns nimbly about and hops up and down in his galliard, Rowlands concludes:

> You nimble skipiacke, turning on the toe,
> As though you had Gun-pouder in your tayle:
> You that do leape about and caper soe,
> Esteeming our old Country Daunces stale.
> You that do liue by shaking of the heele,
> By hopping, and by turning like a wheele.

The galliard had all the elements that made for popularity in its day, and it is safe to say that no other dance is mentioned so often in English literature at the close of the sixteenth century.

According to the *Orchesographie* (63–65), the volte is a species of galliard in which the leap is preceded by two steps instead of four. With each movement the dancers turn their bodies sharply so that they whirl round and round. The man encircles his partner with one arm and holds her so that, as she springs for the leap, he lifts her high in the air. Arbeau strongly disapproves of this dance on the ground that it is unseemly for young girls, and produces a vertigo as well. A woman often shows her bare knees, says the old dancing master, unless she holds her dress down with her hands (45.) Davies, on the other hand, speaks enthusiastically of the volte as the most delightful kind of dance,

> A lofty jumping, or a leaping round,
> When, arm in arm, two dancers are entwined,
> And whirl themselves, with strict embracements bound.

Reyher (pp. 451–53) cites passages showing the extreme popularity of the dance both on the Continent and in England, and also its extreme violence. So great a perspiration did the volte induce that ladies of the French court were forced to change their linen during the court festivities.

The courant as Arbeau describes it (65–67) is in duple time and consists of simples and doubles danced forward, to the side, or backward, with a jumping step. In his youth, he says, it was used in a form of "jeu" and "ballet" in which three young men wooed three young women in pantomime. After each in turn had advanced to his lady, had sued for favor by gestures, and had been refused, all three advanced together and, kneeling, begged for pity with clasped hands; whereupon the ladies surrendered themselves to their lovers' arms, and all danced the courant pell-mell. The steps are still the same, Arbeau continues, but now young men who do not know the meaning of simples and doubles dance the courant according to their own notions, turning the body and making other innovations. Fonta in the Introduction to the *Orchesographie* points out that the Italian version of the courant was adopted in France early in the seventeenth century. This was a very different dance, in triple measure, with a gliding step suitable for making all sorts of turns and for moving in every direction. It was danced, according to Fonta, with short movements to and fro and had a very pliant motion of the knee, recalling that of the fish when he plunges lightly and returns immediately to the surface of

the water. The English courant seems to have come from
Italy. It is pictured in *Orchestra* as running on a triple dactyl
foot "Close by the ground, with sliding passages,"

> Wherein that dancer greatest praise hath won,
> Which with best order can all orders shun;
> For everywhere he wantonly must range,
> And turn, and wind, with unexpected change.

The courant was distinguished not by "lofty turns" but by
speed and fluidity. "Lavoltas high and swift corantos" taught
in the English dancing schools are mentioned in *Henry V* (III,
v), and Morley describes the volte as danced "rising and leaping," the courant "trauising and running."[1] Yet in *The Young
Gallant's Whirligig*, printed in 1629, the gallant is represented as
"Capring Corantoes." Possibly the passion for high dancing
affected the courant also.

The almain, according to the *Orchesographie* (67–68), is a
rather simple and grave dance in which the dancers, one couple
behind the other, move forward or backward, making three
steps and then raising one foot, with or without a leap. The
third part of the conventional suite was danced in a much more
lively fashion with "petits saults." Morley characterizes the
dance as "(fitlie representing the nature of the people, whose
name it carieth) so that no extraordinarie motions are vsed in
dauncing of it."[2] But in England at least the almain was distinguished by a particular caper of some kind. Nashe in his
Preface to *Astrophel and Stella* speaks of his style as "heauie-
gated," his prose without skill to imitate the "Almond leape
verse"; and in Jonson's *Devil is an Ass* (I, i) it is said that the
vice of the old school might, at the end of a sheriff's dinner,
"Skip with a rime o' the Table" and "take his *Almaine*-leape
into a custard."[3]

At the opposite pole is the canaries, a dance that is made a

---

[1] *Plaine and Easie Introduction*, p. 181.

[2] *Ibid.*

[3] Cotgrave defines *Trois pas, & vn saut* as "The Almond, or Alman, leap," and gives
under "leap," "The Almond leape, Trois pas & un saut." Florio defines *chiaranzana* as
"a kind of leape, or hopping or dauncing, as the Alman leape."

symbol for what is vigorous when Lafeu in *All's Well* (II, i)
offers the king a medicine

> That's able to breathe life into a stone,
> Quicken a rock, and make you dance canary
> With spritely fire and motion.

The steps of the canaries, according to Arbeau (95v–96), are
lively but strange and bizarre. You may learn them from those
who know them, or you may simply invent new ones for yourself. The version which he gives is marked by stamping and a
heel-and-toe movement. It is danced by a man and a woman
who stand some distance apart facing each other. When the
man has advanced to his partner and retreated to the original
position, the woman goes through the same movements. This
alternate dancing, noticed again later in the modern step dance
and the morris jig, was probably very common and is admirably
suited to accompany dialogue singing where the stanzas, as is
often the case, are sung by the performers in turn.

It is in connection with this dance that Arbeau takes up the
Spanish pavan (96v–97), which he says has been in use for a
short time in France. His explanation probably illustrates the
way in which the soberer dances kept up with the march of the
times, and it helps one to understand the breaking down of
sharp distinctions and the confusion of terms in late sixteenth
century dance. By way of moderating the gravity of the pavan,
he says, some dancers after the two simples break up the four
notes of the double into eight half notes or sixteen quarter notes
with more rapid movements. The result is the Spanish pavan
with a certain kinship to the canaries (33r). In substituting for
the double a variety of steps similar to those of the galliard,
especially active dancers sometimes double or triple the leaps,
the occasional penalty being a tumble which makes them objects of ridicule (63r). The Spanish pavan was popular in England as well as in France.[1]

[1] See Chappell, *Popular Music*, I, 240–41, for allusions to the dance and for a tune
called "The Spanish Pavan" (different from Arbeau's) which was used for ballads and
appeared in English virginal and lute books, and II, 776, for a version included in the
Dutch *Friesche Lust-Hof* of 1621 as "Engelsche indraeyende Dans Londesteyn." I have
not attempted to deal with several dances of Spanish origin which, so far as the English
records go, belong to the seventeenth century. The most important of these is the sara-

A far more interesting dance is the brawl. In his Introduction to Arbeau, Fonta remarks on the ancient tradition to which the brawl belongs. It is performed, says Arbeau, by a number of couples either in line or in ring formation. He declares that the brawl should offer no difficulties to one who can dance the base dance or the pavan, as it consists of simples and doubles but made always to the side instead of forward or backward (68*v*). Yet he goes on to name and describe almost a score of distinct forms, some in triple, some in duple time, with features that seem to range from galliard to country dance. Even in the most dignified form, the "Branle Double," it is permissible to introduce the position "pied en l'air," and agile young men make other modifications at their pleasure, though of such laxity Arbeau does not approve (71*r*). The "Branle Gay," says his pupil, must have got its name because one foot is always in the air. The "Branle du Hault Barrois," which calls for movements of the shoulders and arms, is danced in a light and rapid measure with "petits saults" for alternate steps. "Petits saults" appear in other brawls, and the "sault majeur" or the capriole in several.[1] The "Branle de l'Official" ends with a leap like that of the volte. The "Branle de la Montarde" and the "Branle de la Haye" introduce the interweaving movement of the hey, and the latter opens, says Arbeau, like a courant. The gavotte is described as only a composite of "Branles Doubles" (93), with the dancers substituting galliard features for the doubles. Perhaps the directions given for a brawl in *The Malcontent*, IV, ii, are less of a burlesque than they may at first appear: "Why, 'tis but two singles on the left, two on the right, three doubles forward, a traverse of six round: do this twice, three singles side, galliard

band, though little is known of its nature. See Böhme, *Geschichte des Tanzes*, I, 139–40. It is mentioned by Jonson in *The Devil is an Ass*, IV, iv. See Chappell, *Popular Music*, II, 497–98, for a saraband tune reprinted from *The Dancing Master* and for the dancing of a saraband to castanets in Davenant's *Law against Lovers*. See Crowne's *Country Wit*, IV, i, and John Playford's title *Musick's Delight on the Cithren . . . . being the Choicest of our late new Ayres, Corants, Sarabands, Tunes, and Jiggs* (1666) for the association of sarabands with jigs and courants. The *NED* cites an allusion late in the century to "a Saraband-Step, two steps forward and three backwards." The fact that one of the tunes for Starter's "Der betrogene Freier" is a "Courante Serbande" has already been mentioned. See *NED* for the rigadoon and chaconne, dances whose vogue was later still than that of the saraband.

[1] See, 77*v*, 81*r*, 84, 89*r*, 91*v*.

tricke of twentie, curranto pace; a figure of eight, three singles broken downe, come up, meete two doubles, fall backe, and then honour."

The brawl as described by Arbeau is particularly rich in mimetic and dramatic features. The "Branle du Hault Barrois," he says, was danced by valets and chambermaids, and sometimes by young men and women when they took part in masquerades disguised as peasants and shepherds. A large number of the brawls are classified as "branles morguez," which are danced "auec mines, morgues, & gesticulations" (82). The "Branle des Lavandieres," the "Branle des Hermites," and the "Branle des Chevaulx" are all mimetic. In the "Branle du Chandelier" a dancer with a lighted torch chooses a partner to whom he delivers it after they have danced together. She, in turn, makes her choice and passes the torch on. An adaptation of the "Branle des Sabots," says Arbeau, was danced in a masquerade in the town of Lengres by a "mère folie" and her three sons, the "fols" repeating the movements after the mother. But from the point of view of the organized folk game the most interesting record of the brawls in dramatic or festival dancing is found in connection with the gavotte. In the midst of the performance one couple will be left to dance alone, after which the man may kiss the women in the group of dancers and his partner the men. But sometimes the prerogative of the kiss is given only to the festival leader and the lady of his choice. She finally presents a chaplet or bouquet to the dancer who is to be chief of the next assembly, and the prerogative passes to him.[1]

The brawl was danced in England long before the Elizabethan era, as the examples given in the *New English Dictionary* go to show. Cotgrave, like Arbeau, defines it as a dance "wherein many (men, and women) holding by the hands sometimes in a ring, and otherwhiles at length, moue altogether." Its variety of form is implied by Davies, who says in *Orchestra* that of the seven motions found in nature—upward and downward, forth and back, to this side and that, and turning round—Love compounds a thousand brawls.[2] Song to accompany the brawl

[1] See also Fonta's Introduction, pp. xxxi–xxxii.

[2] Stanza 62. See the early ballad "Good Fellowes must go learne to daunce," *Ancient Ballads and Broadsides*, Philobiblon Society, pp. 327–29, for references to the different dancers in a brawl as leaping, hopping, turning, and bouncing like a top. The ballad was entered on the Register in 1567–8 (*Transcript*, I, 362).

seems to have been especially common, even late in the sixteenth century. Spenser, as I have shown, uses the term brawl for love song in *The Faerie Queene* (III, x, 8). In *Love's Labour's Lost* (III, i) Moth, after asking, "Master, will you win your love with a French brawl?" goes on to describe the dance as very dramatically rendered with love song to accompany it:

to jig off a tune at the tongue's end, canary to it with your feet, humour it with turning up your eyelids, sigh a note and sing a note, sometime through the throat, as if you swallowed love with singing love, sometime through the nose, as if you snuff'd up love by smelling love; with your hat penthouse-like o'er the shop of your eyes; with your arms crossed on your thin-belly doublet like a rabbit on a spit; or your hands in your pocket like a man after the old painting; and keep not too long in one tune, but a snip and away.

The pastorals described at the end of Book I of Sidney's *Arcadia* include a dance to responsive singing by two groups of shepherds, "as it were in a braule." In England, as well as in France, the brawl seems to bear the marks of an origin in festival use among the people.

Our earliest detailed knowledge of any type of English folk dance comes from *The Dancing Master* of John Playford, first published in 1651, which gives directions for performing a large number of country dances. The general art of the "figure" dances of the folk—the sword dance, morris, and country dance —is familiar to most readers through the modern revival of folk dancing based largely on tradition; and Cecil J. Sharp has dealt with their technique at length in his *Sword Dances of Northern England, Morris Book*, and *Country Dance Book*. The sword dance and the morris are ritual dances performed by men on special occasions, and showing in their tone and in a number of features the direct influence of their ritual origin. The country dance is a social dance of men and women. Yet the three have in common the use of figures in which the dancers interact. Sharp has emphasized their kinship in the matter of figures and evolutions. "Almost every representative figure of the Country-dance," he says, "can be traced to its origin in the Morris- or Sword-dance. This seems to indicate that the Country-dance has been derived from the more ancient religious dances, the figures of which have been simplified and adapted to the re-

quirements of the amateur social dance of the country people."[1]
The hey, for example, which Sharp defines as "the rhythmical
interlacing in serpentine fashion of two groups of dancers, moving in single file and in opposite directions,"[2] whether in a circle
or a straight line, is found in all three of these dances and is
mentioned innumerable times in the sixteenth century. Davies,
we have seen, seems to make the hey and the round stand for
early popular dance.

For several decades before the publication of *The Dancing
Master*[3] country dance had been the fad of the courtly, and we
may be pretty sure of its having undergone considerable sophistication. But even in the forms as given by Playford, the country dance is marked not only by variety but by spontaneity and
dramatic quality. The dances call for kissing, shaking hands,
clapping, stamping, snapping the fingers, peeping, wiping the
eyes ("Putney Ferry"). In "Sweet Kate" the dancers are instructed: "Set your right foot to your womans, then your left,
Clap your woman on her right hand, then on the left, Wind
your hands and hold up your finger, wind your hands again and
hold up another finger of the other hand." The somewhat formal "General Set," or longways formation for an indefinite
number of couples, in which the dancers stand in two parallel
lines facing each other, has supplanted other formations in the
modern country dance; but in Playford's time it shared honors
with the longways for four, six, or eight, the square for eight,
and the round for six, eight, or "as many as will." The round,
which lends itself to a rollicking type of action, was a favorite
formation in Elizabethan times, to judge from the great number
of references to dancing in a round. Again, the figures of *The
Dancing Master* are numerous, and, while varied in type and
complexity, they are in general shorter than those of modern
times. This gives a chance for a well-nigh endless variety of

[1] *Morris Book*, Part I, p. 17. See also *Country Dance Book*, Part II, pp. 16–18.
Sharp excepts the movements of courtesy, which naturally belong to the social dance,
and the progressive movement, which he regards as distinctive of the modern country
dance.

[2] *Country Dance Book*, Part II, p. 41.

[3] In Parts II–IV of the *Country Dance Book* Sharp has deciphered the notations for
a number of Playford's dances in the light of usage among modern folk dancers, and he
gives in each part a succinct account of the steps and figures of the country dance.

combinations. For, as Sharp points out, the series of figures for a given dance was arbitrarily chosen to fit the tune, and only rarely became stereotyped.[1] Thus the leader of the dance seems to have been free to "call" whatever figures he chose, provided he brought the dance to an appropriate close with the end of the music. Playford pictures, in a word, a group of dancers kaleidoscopically advancing and retreating, swinging each other about, crossing from one side to the other, moving up or down inside the lines or outside, weaving in and out, passing under an arch of hands, sometimes only the men being involved in the movement, sometimes only the women, sometimes only one couple, sometimes the whole group. Playford does not explain the matter of steps, perhaps, as Sharp surmises, because they could be taken for granted with the public which he was addressing,[2] but perhaps also because considerable eclecticism prevailed. Much is made of individual variations in steps in a passage from Breton which may be worth quoting as an early general description of country dancing.

After a banquet, says Breton, youth would dance:

> First, *galliards;* then *larousse;* and *heidegy;*
> 'Old lusty gallant;' 'all flow'rs of the bloom;'
> And then a hall! for dancers must have room.
>
> And to it then; with set, and turn about,
>   Change sides, and cross, and mince it like a hawk;
> Backwards and forwards, take hands then, in and out;
>   And, now and then, a little wholesome talk,
> That none could hear, close rowned in the ear.

After declaring that dancers may claim a kiss of right after the dance and before, but that it "goes sore" when kiss upon kiss is taken, the account continues:

[1] *Country Dance Book,* Part I, p. 26; Part II, pp. 7–8.

[2] Part II, pp. 13, 20–21. Sharp regards the walking, running, and skipping steps, the double hop, and the "slip" of Playford (a sideways movement) as the characteristic country dance steps. On the ground that they show the contamination of country dance by courtly dance, Sharp rejects the gavotte and the bourrée steps which John Essex in his *Treatise on Chorography* (1710) includes in the five most ordinary steps of the country dance. I have no doubt, however, that country dancers used all five of the steps accepted by Sharp, and others taken both from courtly dance and from folk dance.

But to behold the graces of each dame!
   How some would dance as though they did but walk;
And some would trip, as though one leg were lame;
   And some would mince it like a sparrow-hawk;
And some would dance upright as any bolt;
And some would leap and skip like a young colt!

And some would fidge, as though she had the itch;
   And some would bow half crooked in the joints;
And some would have a trick; and some a twitch;
   Some shook their arms, as they had hung up points;
With thousands more that were too long to tell,
But made me laugh my heart sore, I wot well.[1]

For any comprehensive idea of the ritual dances we are dependent largely on tradition. In the Introduction to his *Sword Dances of Northern England*, Part I, Sharp has compared the sword dance as described on the Continent and later in England with the modern traditional dance, and concludes that "the sword-dance has altered little in the last four hundred years" (p. 25). The figures are much more intricate than those of the country dance, the most significant being the locking of the swords together for the ritual slaying. The dancers are linked together by their swords, each usually holding his own by the hilt and his neighbor's by the point as they execute their figures. No point seems to be made of the steps. Sharp mentions a walking step, an easy running step, a tramp, a skipping or springing step in different localities.

So far as Elizabethan allusions to the morris go, they indicate that this dance also has remained much the same. Six seems to have been the usual number of dancers in the sixteenth century as at the present time. Laneham describes the morris dance performed before Elizabeth at Kenilworth in 1575 as "a liuely morisdauns, according too the auncient manner, six daunserz, Mawdmarion, and the fool."[2] The movements of the hands, which are a striking feature of the modern dance, are responsible for the Renaissance definition of *chironomus* as "he that daunc-

---

[1] See *Works of Breton*, ed. Grosart, end of Vol. I, where, under the title "Gleanings," parts of *Workes of a young Wyt* are reprinted from George Ellis's *Specimens of Early English Poets*, 3d ed. (1803), II, 270–78.

[2] See *Laneham's Letter*, ed. Furnivall, pp. 22–23.

eth with gesture of the handes in a morys" and of *chironomia* as "the morrice dance."[1] These movements were emphasized in the sixteenth century by morris "napkins" or by scarfs attached to the sleeves,[2] as they are by the handkerchiefs held in the hands of the modern dancers. In the same way, movements of the feet are emphasized by the bells worn on the legs in Elizabethan as well as in modern times. There is no indication as to the figures characteristic of the ancient dance. The typical step in the traditional morris is a very characteristic jerk. The dancer, says Sharp, "must keep the knees straight, and bring each foot *forward* alternately in a sharp swing (almost a jerk) of some fifteen to eighteen inches."[3] That is, the swing is made from the hips. Frequently every alternate or every fourth step is a hop. In the "jump" the dancer with his legs straight springs off both feet as high as possible, sometimes turning as he springs. The caper is described as "an exaggerated Morris step . . . . emphasised by a vigorous jump made by the supporting foot,"[4] some dancers at the same time shaking the free leg. The steps are varied but extremely vigorous. In the sixteenth century also, the typical morris step seems to have been a jerk. "Let us jerk it over the greene," says the leader of the morris dancers in *John a Kent and John a Cumber* (Act IV), and the bumpkins who dance the morris of Jonson's *Entertainment at Althorpe* are told,

> Not a jerke you have shall make
> Any Ladie here in love.

In II *Henry VI*, III, i, 365, occurs the comparison "caper upright like a wild Morisco," and morris men in *Old Meg of Herefordshire* are spoken of as "fetching loftie trickes."[5] *Moulinet*

---

[1] See Cooper, *Bibliotheca Eliotae*, s.v., and Junius-Higgins, *Nomenclator*, pp. 299, 521.

[2] See Brand, *Popular Antiquities* (1849), I, 251. In the *Nine Days' Wonder* Kemp records that the Chelmsford maid who danced with him an hour insisted on the "old Fashion" of a napkin on the arm. See also Weelkes, *Airs or Fantastic Spirits*, No. xviii. Scarfs are pictured in the case of two dancers in the fifteenth century window at Betley and in a cut of Kemp from *Nine Days' Wonder*, both reproduced by Sharp. See also Browne, *Britannia's Pastorals*, Book II, Song 4, l. 368.

[3] *Morris Book*, Part I, p. 50.

[4] *Ibid.*, Part III, p. 21.   [5] *Miscellanea Antiqua Anglicana*, p. 6.

is defined by Cotgrave as "a Morisdauncers Gamboll." The Lambeth Library contains a copy of *A Treatise of Daunses*, published in 1581, which describes a so-called morris:

> When the lusty and fyne man should holde a young damosel, or a woman by the hand, and keeping his measures he shal remoue him-selfe, whirle, & shake his legges aloft (which the daunsers call crosse capring) for pleasure, doth not she in ye meane while make a good threede, playing at the Moris on her behalfe [B 7].

Cotgrave's definition of *moulinet* and the reference from II *Henry VI* apply to a single performer—though he may be conceived merely as one of a group. The passage from *A Treatise of Daunses*, however, deals with a pair of dancers, a man and a woman. In his *Nine Days' Wonder* Kemp celebrates his morris dance from London to Norwich, performed alone except as a chance Maid Marian joined him. In fact, the morris as de-scribed in the *Orchesographie* of Arbeau (fols. 94–95) is a solo performance. Apparently individuals or small groups from the morris troupe commonly performed special dances which were recognized as belonging to the morris, but it is impossible to say whether they were regularly of the true morris type or whether they represented various types which at an earlier period had been featured in the organized folk game along with the morris. At any rate, they seem to me to offer an interesting glimpse into the general field of folk practice from which I conjecture that the jig was drawn.

With the decay of the May game, in which the ritual morris was commonly performed, its leaders and at least some of their attendants attached themselves to the morris, and to the pres-ent day they have remained with it, even when the dance was independently performed.[1] The contamination of the morris by the Robin Hood play, another outstanding feature of the May game, is seen in the appearance of Maid Marian and even the Friar with the morris in the sixteenth century. The most con-

---

[1] For these various figures and the different parts they have played, see Douce, *Illustrations of Shakespeare* (1807), II, 431–82; Brand, *Popular Antiquities* (1849), I, 253–70; Chambers, *Mediaeval Stage*, I, 195–98; Sharp, *Morris Book*, Part I, pp. 27–29. Parallel figures, presumably relics of the winter games, belong to the various modern sword dances. See *Sword Dances*, Part I, p. 27, and the general accounts of the separate sword dances described by Sharp.

ventional of the supernumeraries were the May lord and lady
(the latter often Maid Marian), the fool (sometimes the leader
of the game), and the hobbyhorse. But figures of the vice or
goblin type, which always appealed to the folk, may have been
common in the May game and not infrequent with the early sixteenth century morris. Giants, devils, soldans, Moors, and similar grotesques at least went in the London May game.[1] The
blackening of the morris dancer's face would represent a similar
tradition.[2]

In the sixteenth and early seventeenth century some, at
least, of the morris supernumeraries performed special dances
or comic tricks. The hobbyhorse in the period of his glory was
a famous prancer and dancer, performing often when no morris
is recorded.[3] The fool was conventionally the cleverest dancer.
Nashe refers in the Preface to *Astrophel and Stella* to the lively
dancing of shepherds who had been fools in the morris. In
Brathwaite's *Strappado for the Devil* (1615) when Jug and Tib
are pictured as visiting the May games of Wakefield to "see
Tom-liuely turne vpon the toe,"[4] there is more than probably a
reference to the solo dance of the morris fool. Gayton in *Festivous Notes upon Don Quixot* speaks of Sancho's leaping "above
the rise of Jack-pudding in a Morrice dance."[5] The fool has
kept his pre-eminence to the present day. The stock joke of the
fool accompanying the traditional morris, says Sharp, is " 'Here

---

[1] See Machyn, *Diary*, Camden Society, pp. 20, 89, 137, 201, 230. For Fetherston's
apparent reference to a devil in a May game, see Douce, *Illustrations*, II, 444; for a picture of a Turk in a May game at Plymouth, 1580–81, see Worth, *Plymouth Municipal
Records*, p. 124; for a definition of *manducus* as "A Giant or Turke, such as they vsed
in maygames & shewes, made of brown paper," see Junius-Higgins, *Nomenclator*, p. 314.

[2] See Chambers, *Mediaeval Stage*, I, 197, 199. The morris dancer described in
Arbeau's *Orchesographie* (fol. 94) has his face blackened.

[3] See Garry, *Churchwardens' Accounts, St. Mary's, Reading*, p. 28; Richardson,
Extracts from the Municipal Accounts of Newcastle-upon-Tyne, p. 16, under the year
1566; Stevenson, *Records of the Borough of Nottingham*, IV, 132; Murray, *English
Dramatic Companies*, II, 335, 372, 383.

[4] Ed. Ebsworth, p. 203.

[5] Ed. of 1654, p. 186. The leather pudding is mentioned in *The Returne of Pasquill*
(*Works of Nashe*, ed. McKerrow, I, 83) as part of the morris fool's equipment. The
expression to "play the Pudding in a May-day farce" occurs in Egerton MS 2623, fol.
87. "Jack Pudding, or (Merry Andrew.)" is one of the dance tunes in Playford's
Dancing Master.

we be, masters! six fools and'—pointing to himself—'one dancer.' "[1] In the sixteenth century the fool, sometimes at least,
danced with the lady. Breton alludes to this custom in his
Poste with a Packet of Mad Letters: "for your steeple tire, it is
like the gaud of a Maid-Marion, so that had you a foole by the
hand, you might walke where you would in a Moris-dance."[2]
Earlier Nashe pictures the morris fool as dancing around Maid
Marian to "court" her.[3] Here we probably have a remnant of
the wooing dance so prevalent in the folk festival. Besides the
regular morris which is introduced near the beginning of
Summer's Last Will and Testament, the hobbyhorse cavorts and
dances, being warned, "goe not too fast, for feare of wearing out
my Lords tyle-stones with your hob-nayles," and Ver, with the
promise "we'le haue variety," brings on three clowns and three
maids, who dance to their own singing. Vinckenboom's picture
of morris dancers (about 1625), which is reproduced by Douce,[4]
seems indeed to represent not so much the regular morris as
special features by the morris troupe. The fool is shown passing
his ladle, and the hobbyhorse dancing alone. Maid Marian
dances with one of the morris men, who faces her, holding both
her hands.

If on the basis of these indications we attempt to reconstruct
the dancing of the May game, the picture seems to be that of a
variety of dance acts by the performers singly or in different
combinations, in addition to the ritual morris. The use of wooing dance and of solo dances by game figures like the hobbyhorse
and the disard is clearly indicated. These may have been performed before the festival lord and lady in connection with different elements in the May game, but as dance they tended in
survival to attach themselves to the morris, which was the central dance feature. I have found no cases at an early period in
which the dances of individuals or small groups in the May game
or morris are definitely spoken of as jigs, though the use of the
term jig in a general way for May game and morris dancing is
common.[5] The modern morris, on the other hand, shows a

[1] See *Morris Book,* Part I, p. 28. A "Fool's Dance" is noticed below.

[2] Bk. II, Letter 28.

[3] *Works,* ed. McKerrow, I, 83.   [4] *Illustrations of Shakespeare,* II, 469–70.

[5] See pp. 363–64 below. The music of the solo morris as given by Arbeau is said
by Danckert (*Geschichte der Gigue,* p. 21) to be related to one of the distinct types which
he finds running through the early jigs.

rather full development of dances which are called jigs. One of them described by Sharp is the "Fool's Dance," designed to "enable the fool, who is usually a very clever dancer, to show his prowess." Though the modern morris jig is primarily a solo dance, it is frequently performed by two dancing in turn, sometimes by three or four, and usually by the regular morris men, with music, steps, and hand movements typical of the morris.[1] The quaint "Bacca Pipes," which is said to be known to all morris men, is danced to "Greensleeves," a favorite dance tune in the sixteenth century. Perhaps the use of the word jig in connection with the morris represents as old a tradition as some other features that can be traced back more successfully. It may easily, I think, be reminiscent of jig dances performed along with the morris in the sixteenth century May game.

The chief step dances of the folk in the sixteenth century were the jig and the hornpipe, to judge from their importance in the allusions of the period. Though we are at a loss for any technical description of the jig, its general nature is plain. The jig was a lusty and rapid dance, marked by leaping and whirling. Riche's "heeles are too heavie" for the jig. Marston in Satire IX of *The Scourge of Villanie* refers to "wanton jiggin skips." In *The Two Noble Kinsmen* (V, ii) occurs the passage,

> He daunces very finely, very comely,
> And for a Iigge, come cut and long taile to him,
> He turnes ye like a Top.

Lupton says of the dancers in the dancing school, "But in the next Jigge you shall bee sure to haue them turne like Globes all round."[2] A seventeenth century ballad called "Jockie's Lamentation" contains the lines,

> Our Enemies to *Starling-bridge*
> (Like a whirlegig, did dance a jig).[3]

---

[1] For these various points, see *Morris Book*, Part I, p. 48; Part II, pp. 6, 23–24; Part III, pp. 66–68. For the particular jigs mentioned, consult the Index to the *Morris Book*. See Tiddy, *Mummers' Play*, p. 253, for a dance called a jig at the end of a Gloucestershire mummers' play.

[2] *London and the Countrey Carbonadoed*, Aungervyle Society, p. 28.

[3] *Bagford Ballads*, I, 333.

In *The Knight of the Burning Pestle*, the Citizen's Wife at the end of Act III orders a boy to dance "Fa-ding,"[1] which she assures the audience is a fine jig, and she apparently follows the progress of his dance with, "Now 'a capers, sweetheart!— Now a turn o' the toe, and then tumble! cannot you tumble, youth?" Probably the Scottish jig was especially spectacular, for Beatrice in *Much Ado* (II, i) describes wooing as "hot and hasty, like a Scotch jig, and full as fantastical," and Florio in defining *chiarantana* uses the comparison "full of leapings like a Scotish gigge."

A number of references to the jig show that it was used as a social dance for the general group of young men and women. In the opening scenes of *A Woman Killed with Kindness* the "mad lads" and "country-lasses" are pictured as dancing "all their country measures, rounds, and jigs." According to a seventeenth century ballad of the Pepys Collection (III, 47), "The Young-Man's Ramble,"

> *Priscilla* did dance a jig with *Tom*
> which made her buttocks quake like a Custard;

and according to another ballad, "The merry Countrey Maids Answer To the Countrey Lovers Conquest," in the Wood Collection (E. 25, No. 124),

> He was such a fellow,
>   when he danc'd a Jig
> He kis't like *Punchanello*
>   or a sucking pig.

John Cleveland's poem "The Mixed Assembly" satirizing the Puritans represents their leaders as advancing in couples to dance a jig. Whirling is again shown as characteristic, for

> *Wharton* wheels about, till *Mumping Liddy*
> Like the full moon, hath made his Lordship giddy.

---

[1] An Irish dance. See *NED* and Grattan Flood, "Notes on the Irish Jig," *Musical Opinion*, February, 1914. For allusions and for the use of the word as a refrain, see Chappell, *Popular Music*, I, 234–36, and the commentators on *The Winter's Tale*, IV, iv, 194–95. In Jonson's *Irish Masque* twelve Irishmen dance "Fa-ding," and in his Epigram XCVII "the old *Fa-ding*" is mentioned as if it were a well-known form of entertainment. See Fairholt, *Civic Garland*, Percy Society, pp. 38–41, for a song beginning "Let's drink and droll, and dance and sing," which was sung at the Lord Mayor's feast in 1672 to the tune "With a fading."

Thomas Morley, who deals chiefly with courtly dances in the discussion of dance music in his *Plaine and Easie Introduction*, fails to describe the jig musically, though he mentions it (p. 181). He implies, however, that the Scottish jig had a very simple form: "And I dare boldly affirme, that looke which is hee who thinketh himselfe the best descanter of all his neighbors, enioyne him to make but a scottish Iygge, he will grossely erre in the true nature and qualitie of it" (p. 182). One of the very earliest references to the jig of the north ridicules its musical character. In his *Discourse of English Poetrie* (1586) Webbe speaks of the alehouse song "hobbling vppon some tune of a Northern Iygge."[1] The growing popularity of the jig among the upper classes caused it to be represented in some early musical collections along with pavans, galliards, courants, and other courtly dances; but in passing through the hands of such trained musicians as Byrd, Bull, and the Farnabys, the jig may have suffered considerable sophistication of form. The earliest example seems to be Byrd's "A Galliards Gygge" in *Lady Neville's Virginal Book* of 1591, where already in the combination of "galliard" with "jig" we see the influence of courtly dance. Danckert concerns himself with the jig as a musical form in *Die Geschichte der Gigue* (1924), the most recent and extended treatment of the subject. In the first chapter, given to the English jig, he concludes that the jig had its origin in Great Britain from dances of the folk accompanying their songs, and he emphasizes the folk character of the music—its simplicity and unity of structure and its vigor—outside of the specimens elaborated by the professional composers of the time. The well-known extant jigs of the Elizabethan period are printed by Danckert, classified into three types on the basis of form.[2]

Even less is known about the early hornpipe than the jig. In *James IV* Slipper and "a companion, boy or wench," dance a hornpipe at the end of Act II, and antics apparently dance a hornpipe with Slipper at the end of IV, iii. As they depart, Slipper says, "Nay, but, my friends, one hornpipe further! a refluence backe, and two doubles forward! What! not one crosse-

---

[1] See Gregory Smith, *Elizabethan Critical Essays*, I, 246.

[2] See also *Proceedings of the Musical Association*, XL, 78-82, for Pulver's discussion of the musical form of the early jigs.

point against Sundayes?" and when he discovers that he has been robbed, he threatens to teach them to caper in a halter. Like the jig, the hornpipe seems to have been used by groups of men and women somewhat in the manner of country dance. An early ballad, "Our Jockye sale have our Jenny," gives an account of a hornpipe at a wedding, the like of which was never seen "I trowe, in all the nothe lande." All are urged to dance for company, and the first to break the stroke must pay the piper a penny. The dance proceeds with the leader's calls of "Halfe torne, Jone, haffe now, Jocke!"—"In with fut, Robsone! owt with fut, Byllynge!"—"Torn rownde, Robyne! kepe trace, Wylkyne!"—"Mak churchye pege behynde"—"Set fut to fut a pas"—"Abowt with howghe let us wynde"—"Kepe in, Sandar, hold owte, Syme." As is frequent in sixteenth century dancing, the end is climactic:

> "A gambold," quod Jocky, "stand asyde;
> Let ylke man play his parte.
> Mak rom, my mastars; stand mor wyde;
> I pray youe with all my harte."[1]

Spelman in 1609 compares the dancing of American Indians to "our darbysher Hornepipe, a man first and then a woman, and so through them all, hanging all in a round";[2] and there are many other allusions to the hornpipe as a dance for a number of participants, especially as a round dance.[3]

It would be interesting to know what were the steps of the jig and the hornpipe even as late as the middle of the eighteenth century. In 1752 the Scottish dancing master John McGill wrote out for the benefit of his pupils instructions for dancing hornpipes, jigs, and certain country dances. An early correspondent to *Notes and Queries*, who owned one of McGill's manuscripts, writes in regard to it:

I do not know that the dancing instructions for sixteen steps in the hornpipe, and fourteen in the gigg, would be very intelligible now-

---

[1] *Songs and Ballads*, ed. Wright, Roxburghe Club, pp. 123–24. Cotgrave translates *gambader*, "to turn heeles ouer head, make many gambols, fetch many friskes, shew tumbling trickes."

[2] See *Antiquary*, XII, 252.

[3] See Chappell, *Popular Music of the Olden Time*, II, 545.

a-days; seeing that in the former, the second, third, and fourth steps are "slips and shuffle forwards," "spleet and floorish (?florish) backwards," "Hyland step forwards;" and there are elsewhere directions [these presumably for the jig] to "heel and toe forwards," "single and double round step," "slaps across forward," "twist round backward," "cross strocks aside and sink forward," "short shifts," "back hops," and finally, "happ forward and backward" to conclude the gigg with *éclat*.[1]

According to Thomas Ratcliffe, writing to *Notes and Queries* in 1907,

> There were many men step-dancers, and a few women ones, well into the later half of the nineteenth century in most villages, and step-dancing displays were usual incidents at feasts and wakes. On Saturday nights also "stepping" would suddenly break out at village ale-houses, when two or three men would pit themselves against each other in short spells, hardly of the nature of contests. When a lad I saw many such steppings, and step-dancers are by no means dead, though gone out of village life, maybe. A good dancer was one capable of taking any step music, or without any music whatever. Many of the dancers used stepping shoes or light clogs—the latter preferred in the clog-wearing localities. Nimbleness and clatter were essentials, with a good "crowdy" to give the music. There were a number of men who were good "crowdies" = fiddlers, playing from ear the tunes to which the dancers stepped. The dancing was always on wood—a floor or large table: the latter preferred, as the steppings and beats could be seen to the better advantage. . . . . Sometimes there would be a couple of dancers on the table. When one had gone through an arranged number of steps, he stopped, the other taking his place; and this was done so deftly that there was no break in the music whilst the change was made.[2]

It is highly probable that these dances kept the characteristic features of the old jig dance and that the same is true of the breakdowns, cakewalks, and other dances current formerly among the American negroes. Danckert, at least, finds that the music for these "pseudo-negro" dances is fundamentally akin to that of the Elizabethan jigs, and he argues that it was brought to America from Great Britain in the nineteenth century (p. 26).

[1] Ser. 1, XII, 159.
[2] Ser. 10, VII, 378-79. See also p. 269.

One of the greatest difficulties in dealing with English dance in the Renaissance comes from the fact that allusions to dance are often confusing—even apparently contradictory at times—a fact which seems to indicate a general lack of hard and fast distinctions. References to "Masks & morrishes" or to "disguisings and morisks" and to "divers Sortes of Morisks"[1] in accounts of court festivities during the earlier Tudor period suggest that "morris" stood for folk dance serving as a kind of antimasque. The essential unity of the sword dance and the morris as ritual is argued by both Chambers and Sharp.[2] Mercurialis mentions the use of the name *morisca* for the sword dance on the Continent,[3] and the same identification was made in England. Cotgrave translates *danser les buffons*,[4] "To daunce a morris," and Malevole in *The Malcontent* (I, iii) speaks of a knight who can "do the sword-dance with any morris-dancer in Christendome." The sixteenth century country dance also seems to shade into the morris more completely than the modern dance. In *The Two Noble Kinsmen* (III, v) a number of men and women, apparently six couples, perform a dance which is called a morris and includes typical characters taken from the May game, but its tone is that of the country dance rather than the morris. The Schoolmaster, for example, admonishes the women, "carry it sweetly. . . . . And now and then a fauour, and a friske." On the other hand, the very popular country dance "Trenchmore" was distinguished by its stamping step and its capers, and Taylor in *A Navy of Land Ships* associates it with the morris when he speaks of capering a "Morrisca or Trenchmore of forty miles long."[5] Sharp remarks

[1] For examples see Withington, *English Pageantry*, I, 113, 114; Reyher, *Masques Anglais*, p. 172; Hall, *Henry VIII* (1548), fol. cliv.

[2] Chambers, *Mediaeval Stage*, I, 195, 199–201; Sharp, Introduction to *Morris Book*, Part I, and to *Sword Dances*, Part I.

[3] *De arte gymnastica* (1572), Bk. II, chap. vi, p. 98: "Pyrrhichias autem nostris temporibus aemulantur illa pugnarum genera, quas Morescas populari uocabulo appellant."

[4] See p. 79 n. 1 above.

[5] Folio of 1630, Sig. Iv. Deloney in *The Gentle Craft* (*Works*, ed. Mann, p. 154) says, "like one dauncing the trench more he stampt vp and downe the yard, holding his hips in his hands." "Tricks above Trenchmore" are mentioned in *Wit of a Woman*, Sig. C, and in Breton's *Wits Trenchmour*, ed. Grosart, p. 20.

that Playford's "longways-for-six" are especially interesting because they have the morris formation and many of the movements and figures are identical with those of the morris.[1] This formation is found in "Jack a Lent," in "Jack Pudding"—both named for grotesques of the games—and in "Woodycock, or the Green man," the last part of the title suggesting a similar origin.[2] Hybrid forms occur occasionally in the modern morris.[3]

The kinship in figures would easily account for the overlapping in the figure dances, but there is a similar confusion between the figure dances and the step dances of the folk. With large groups of men and women dancing jigs and hornpipes, as well as country dances, in the social gatherings of the people, a confusion of types is natural. Another natural link for these dances is to be found in the May game, which included a great deal of what might be called semi-social dancing around the May pole or about the arbor of the May lady. The terms morris, hornpipe, and jig all occur in connection with such dancing. In an Elizabethan tract, *Plaine Percevall the Peace-maker of England*, cited by Brand,[4] a stranger is represented as seeing "a quintessence (beside the Foole and the Maid Marian) of all the picked youth, strained out of a whole endship, footing the Morris about a May-pole." In Barnfield's *Shepheards Content* (1594) it is said that the shepherd "leads his Wench a Country Horn-pipe Round,/ About a May-pole on a Holy-day." A song from Weelkes's *Airs or Fantastic Spirits* associates both "mor-

[1] *Country Dance Book*, Part II, p. 16.

[2] This title of Playford's has a number of interesting associations. There was pretty certainly a sixteenth century morris called "Woodycock" (see Breton, *Pasquils Fooles-Cap*, ed. Grosart, pp. 20, 22). For "Gigg-a-gogge, or Woddycocke" as a ballad tune, see *Shirburn Ballads*, ed. Clark, p. 189. The tune "Wooddy-Cock" was included in *The Fitzwilliam Virginal Book* (No. CXLI). It was carried to the Low Countries, not improbably by the English comedians, and was published by Valerius in a collection of 1626 (see Bolte, *Singspiele*, p. 4). For Woody, or Woody Garius, as one of the grotesques in a modern sword dance, see Sharp, *Sword Dances*, Part III, pp. 19, 24.

[3] See Sharp, *Morris Book*, Part I, pp. 8–9; Part III, pp. 12, 94–100. In the Abbots Bromley Horn Dance, which is described both in the seventeenth century and in modern times, we have a ritual dance in which the performers are said to dance heys and other country dances. See Sharp, *Sword Dances*, Part I, pp. 33–34, 105–12, for Plot's account in the seventeenth century and for the modern dance.

[4] *Popular Antiquities* (1849), I, 250.

ris" and "jigging" with a dance around the May pole,[1] and a
ballad printed in *Westminster Drollery* tells of a May pole dance
in which

> *Jonny* has got his *Jone,*
> To jigg it, jigg it, jigg it, jigg it,
> Jigg it up and down.[2]

The use of the term morris for any sort of dance in the May
game is explicable enough, and in the seventeenth century "jigging" seems to have been applied to any dancing with marked
rhythm and vigorous step.[3]

To some extent a lack of distinction is found also between
folk and courtly dances. This is naturally most noticeable in
the types that especially illustrate the taste of the times. The
same features, for example, are often stressed in the morris, the
jig, and the galliard, and these dances probably influenced each
other strongly. The galliard in particular seems to have crossed
with the dance of the folk. In *Misogonus* (II, iv, 260–83) where
country dances are called for and several are named—for
their double meaning—the priest is told to keep his cinquepace and is especially commended for his vigorous dancing.
Perhaps a galliard was danced, first one of the men and then the
other acting as Melissa's partner, but the presumption is that
galliard terms were used with country dance. Breton in *Wits
Trenchmour* has the expression "among a number of these
Countrey daunces, I did light on such a Galiard, as had a trick
aboue Trenchmour."[4] The ballad called "The West-Country
Jigg; Or, a Trenchmore Galliard" (Text 12) tells of a roistering
dance. In the jig described in Cleveland's "Mixed Assembly" a
couple are said to tread cinquepace.[5]

---

[1] No. xviii. See Fellowes, *English Madrigal Verse*, p. 229.

[2] Part II (1672), ed. Ebsworth, pp. 80–82.

[3] See D'Urfey, *Pills to Purge Melancholy*, IV, 100 ("We Jig the Morris upon the *Green*" in a song with the refrain "With a Fadding, &c."), 124, 125; Halliwell, *Notices of Fugitive Tracts*, Percy Society, pp. 92–93 ("we'll jigg and caper,/Cuckolds all arow"). For a later example, see Dixon, *Ancient Poems, Ballads, and Songs*, Percy Society, p. 193 ("They jig it o'er the green," in a "Haymakers' Song").

[4] Ed. Grosart, p. 20.

[5] The difference between jig and galliard remained striking enough, however, to give point to Beatrice's contrast when she likens wooing to a hot and hasty Scotch jig, and repentance with his bad legs to a galliard. Mrs. Dolmetsch (*Musical Times*, LVII, 143) attributes the comparison to the "limping hop" of the galliard.

There is a bewildering confusion in the use of dance terms around 1600, which points to a lack of distinction in types and to the freest transference of features from one type to another. Brome seems to be satirizing the general state of dance when he represents one of the characters in *The City Wit* (IV, i) as saying, "I can my Cinquepace friend. But I prithee teach me some tricks," and the friend as replying, "Ha! Tricks of twenty: Your traverses, Slidings, Falling back, Jumps, Closings, Openings, Shorts, Turns, Pacings, Gracings—As for—Corantoes, Levoltoes, Jigs, Measures, Pavins, Brawls, Galliards, or Canaries." The best dancers apparently followed their own devices in the interest of variety and novelty. Morley may have had this eclecticism in mind when he wrote in 1597 that the art of dancing had "come to that perfection that euerie reasonable dauncer wil make measure of no measure, so that it is no great matter of what number you make your strayne."[1] The standard dances of the sixteenth century undoubtedly laid the foundation for the art of the seventeenth, but an exaggeration of the trends that have been mentioned led to what were virtually new phases of both social and professional dancing—in antic and mimetic dances, in drollery, and in related romping, confused, and medley dances of groups.

As I have said, in less formal pastimes the dances of the folk came into general use with the cultured. The passion for country dancing finds expression in Playford's *Dancing Master*, brought out in 1651, which ran into sixteen editions by 1716. The craze for the dancing of jigs seems to have been equally as great. There are many references to it before 1640.[2] Apparently along with the vogue of northern and Scottish song came a corresponding vogue of jig dancing. In the book of conduct called *Mysteries of Love & Eloquence*, published in 1658, the statement occurs under the heading "Mode of Balls" (p. 9):

---

[1] *Plaine and Easie Introduction*, p. 181.

[2] Fitzgeoffrey in his "Notes from Black-Fryers" included in *Certain Elegies, Done by Sundrie Excellent Wits. With Satyrs and Epigrams* (1620) refers to the puppet—"yon *French Sincopace* . . . . with a *Coranto* grace"—whom the ladies solicit to dance "A *Galliard* or a *Iigg*." See also Shirley, *Hyde Park*, II, ii, for footing "chamber jigs"; Lupton, *London and the Countrey Carbonadoed*, p. 28, for the readiness of those in dancing schools to turn like globes in the next jig; Prynne, *Histrio-Mastix*, p. 252, for comment on "artificiall *curious Galliards, Iigs, or Carontoes*, learned with much paines and practise at a Dancing-Schoole, as ours are."

"*Sarah* shall dance a North countrey Jigg before 'um too; I warrant it will please the Ladies better then all your French whisks and frisks; I had rather see one freak of jolly Milkmaids, then all the story that will be here to night." In satire on the taste of the age in Shadwell's *Sullen Lovers* there are references to the dancing of jigs as one of the qualifications of a gentleman (Act II)[1] and to ladies who love beaux for "dancing of a Jigge, or singing of a Stanza of fashionable Non-sence" (Act III). The spirit of all this folk dancing is no doubt revealed in Selden's strictures on the romping element in country dance. After speaking of the old custom at court revels of passing from courtly dance to country dance in which all joined—lords and servants without distinction—he says: "So in our Court in Queen *Elizabeth*'s time Gravity and State were kept up. In King *James*'s time things were pretty well. But in King *Charles*'s time, there has been nothing but *French*-more and the Cushion Dance, *omnium gatherum*, tolly, polly, hoite come toite."[2] In fact, Selden fitly characterizes here much of the dance of the period.

I have already compared the masque with the stage jig as a minor dramatic type of the sixteenth century in which song and dance were the dominant features. Reyher, in dealing with the dances of the masque, conjectures that in its early history the masquers danced the ordinary base dances and rounds, and that the distinction between the dances of the masquers and the "intermixed" dances of the revels developed gradually during the course of the sixteenth century.[3] But at least when the records become definite, we find that the ingenuity of experts was taxed to devise the three or four special dances which the masquers presented on each occasion. Elaborate evolutions ending in geometric figures or significant letters were affected. In describing the third dance in the *Masque of Queens*, Jonson says that

a more *numerous* composition could not be seene: *graphically* dispos'd into *letters*, and honouring the name of the sweete and ingenious

---

[1] In this act a gallant commends one house for its devil and "Fat Fryer" and "t'other house" for its "Play, with a Jigg in't." See Halliwell, *Works of Shakespeare*, VII, 289–90, for the passage from Healy's *Characters*, "Hee is not ashamed, being sober, in coole bloud to dance country dances and matachines, as a zanie or pantaloon."

[2] *Table-Talk*, ed. Arber, p. 62.   [3] *Les Masques Anglais*, pp. 441–46.

Prince, Charles, Duke of Yorke, wherin, beside that principall grace of perspicuity, the motions were so even and apt, and theyr expression so just, as if *Mathematicians* had lost *proportion,* they might there have found it.

In Jonson's *Hymenaei* again one of the dances is characterized as full of "Subtility *and* Device." Letters signifying the name of the bridegroom were formed, and the dance "ended in manner of a chaine." It is evident that the limit to the real effectiveness of such dancing is soon reached. As Bacon says in his essay "Of Masques and Triumphs," "Turning dances into figure is a childish curiosity." The reaction was expressed in the growing emphasis on the antimasque with the fresh appeal of its dancing through the spirited, odd, or dramatic action appropriate to its characters.

The antic dance, like the jig, was of popular provenience, as I have indicated. Its figures seem to have been a development out of the animal figures and other grotesques of the folk game. Frequently the dancers performed the ordinary dances of the folk. In Marlowe's *Edward II* (I, i) one of Gaveston's plans to please the king is to have men like satyrs dance the "antic hay" with their goat feet. I suspect that in Jonson's *Masque of Owls* the six owls introduced by Captain Cox accoutered as a hobbyhorse were antics who danced a morris. The same author's *Golden Age Restored* contains an antimasque by a group of evils who present a "*Pyrrhic* dance" to "two Drums, Trumpets, and a confusion of Martiall Musick." This may have been a form of sword dance.[1] Naturally the dance of comic human types as antics would often follow the same principle. A gipsy dance in the *Metamorphosed Gipsies* is compared with the morris.

It was characteristic of the antic dance, however, that it should express the nature of the dancers—animals, supernatural beings, or grotesques of any kind. Ravenscroft in the Preface to his *Briefe Discourse* (1614) recommends dancing as a recreation, but

with some difference from the common *Exercise* now a daies of it, in our *Maskes* and *Reuells:* As not grounded on the *Dauncing* of *Meas-*

[1] See Reyher, pp. 457–58. In the eighteenth century, morris and sword dances of countrymen were sometimes called antic dances. See *Journal of American Folk-Lore,* XXII, 394; Balfour and Thomas, *Printed Folk-Lore concerning Northumberland, County Folk-Lore,* IV, 86.

ures, and accordingly bound to some particular *Rules* and *Numbers,* proper to the *Nature* of that *Daunce* onely, which then is afoot: But fashioned like those *Antique Daunces,* which the *Poets* would haue vs beleeue, the *Fayries,* and the *Satyres,* and those other *Rurall Natures* frequented, and hauing in them, much more *variety* and *change* then any other *Composition* [A 3].

The prancing hobbyhorse was an antic dancer. Fairies tripped and skipped in their rounds. "Cry mercy, sir," says the gentleman usher in Chapman's *Widow's Tears* (III, i), "here's a whole chorus of Sylvans at hand, curveting and tripping ath' toe, as the ground they trod on were too hot for their feet." Their dances are called "winding hays" and "active and antic dances." Of the twelve herdsmen in *Winter's Tale* (IV, iv) who, according to the servant, "have made themselves all men of hair" and "call themselves Saltiers," it is said that their dance is a "gallimaufry of gambols" and that not the worst of three "but jumps twelve foot and a half by the squire."

The conception of antic runs through various related forms of comic dance with a few recurrent terms. In city pageants there were mimetic types of dance called drollery. Heywood says in *Londini Speculum* of 1637: "The third Pageant or Show meerly consisteth of Anticke gesticulations, dances, and other Mimicke postures, devised onely for the vulgar, who are better delighted with that which pleaseth the eye, than contenteth the eare, in which we imitate *Custome.*" Jordan has many drolls in his pageants, sometimes with song. A characteristic example is the fourth pageant in *London's Triumphs* (1677), in which "Rusticks, and Shepherd-like persons, Pipe, Dance, and exercise the activity of their limbs, in Gambolling, Tumbling and Capering, with divers mimical motions and ridiculous actions." According to the song for the masque of the Seven Deadly Sins in Randolph's *Muses' Looking-Glass* (I, iv),

> Disorder is the masque we bring,
> And discords are the tunes we sing.[1]

[1] An interesting term suggestive of confused action is "vagary," used often in connection with Jack Pudding. The *Figure of Nine* mentions "Jack puddings fegaries" among "pretty sports." In the ballad the "Young-Man's Ramble: Or, The Horse can Trot, and the Mare can Amble" (Pepys Collection, III, 47), it is said that Tib danced "Salingers round" and the "French Canaries" in a way that "passed Jack

The principle of variety and change commended by Ravenscroft was clearly carried to the point of extravagance in much of the professional dancing of the seventeenth century, and it is easy to see how a strong interest in comic and antic dance helped to bring about the decline of the stage jig. Emphasis on acrobatic and pantomimic features of dance drew attention away from dialogue and plot and made the extensive use of them impossible. Not until the beginning of the eighteenth century did the vagaries of song and dance yield again to principles of organization, individual acts being welded together in the plots of ballad opera and in the organized pantomimes of Harlequin.

---

pudding and all his fegaries." The ballad called "Jack Pudding's Fegary" (*ibid.*, IV, 266) was inspired by a Jack Pudding rôle at Bartholomew Fair. For earlier uses of the word, see *Spanish Gipsy*, I, v; Shirley, *Love Tricks*, III, v, and V, i; "A light heart's a jewell" to the tune of "Jacke Pudding's vagary" with a refrain "to have mine own vagary" (*Roxburghe Ballads*, II, 18–23); Climsell, "Love's Lunacie; Or, Mad Bessie's Fegary . . . . To the tune of *The Mad man's morris*" (*ibid.*, II, 6–11). The tunes "The New Vegarie" and "Chestnut (or Doves Figary)" are included in *The Dancing Master*.

PART II
TEXTS

THE TEXTS

In the texts which follow I have kept the original spelling, punctuation, capitalization, and even as many indications of mechanical arrangement as proved feasible, though these often have no significance. Speakers' names are supplied when needed, stanzaic forms are restored where they have been obscured in a few of the originals, and, for the English texts, obvious errors are corrected. These changes are noted in connection with the individual pieces however. Where stanzas are not numbered in the original I have added marginal numbers for the lines, but in No. 22, the stanzas are numbered instead, in order to facilitate comparison of the two texts. The pages or the folios of texts printed from books, pamphlets, and manuscripts have been indicated, but not the columns of broadsides, except in the case of No. 5, where the form of the original is retained. The originals of Nos. 4, 5, 6, 7, and 17, all in two parts, are printed on two sheets in double columns. No. 12 is similar except that the second sheet is not called a second part. No. 22 has three columns on the first sheet and two on the second. Nos. 2, 9, and 13 are printed on single sheets with double columns, No. 9 having a cut in the middle of the sheet as well as at the head. In No. 16, a single broad sheet with three columns headed by cuts, the title extends across the first two columns. Nos. 8, 10, and 11 are printed on single sheets with two pages on the same side of the sheet, each having double columns. No. 3 is the second of two ballads on a similar sheet. Except as indicated in the notes, the indentation and alignment of all the originals are followed with comparative accuracy in both titles and texts. The relative spacing between stanzas has not always been preserved however. The problem of indicating the variety of type found in the originals has proved somewhat awkward. I have used roman as the basis of all the texts. With incidental use of italic, this has sufficed for Nos. 14, 19, and 20, taken from manuscripts; Nos. 1 and 27, reprinted from modern editions; and Nos. 13, 15, 18, 21, 22, 23, and 24, originally printed in roman. The basis of the other originals is black letter. With roman type substituted for black letter, the roman found in the originals has been changed to italic, and the occasional italic to cloister. An exception is the titles and colophons of the English broadsides and the two Dutch pieces (Nos. 35 and 36). The basis of these is roman in the originals, and they have been left unchanged. I have made no note of broken and inverted characters or of punctuation marks in a style differing from that of the preceding word. Initial capitals of the texts (usually in roman), which vary greatly in size, have been made uniform. Of the special characters occurring in the originals, I have not used the long s, ligatures not common in roman (except the German ß), or the *oo* and *ee* found in some English broadsides either as ligatures or with an accent over the first letter. In the German and Dutch pieces, capital I and J, not differentiated in the original black letter, are distinguished, and the various forms of umlaut have been normalized, except that the superior *o* found in No. 26 has been retained. The music printed with a number of the German pieces is here given in facsimile. All of the texts except Nos. 1, 20, 21, 23, and 27, have been either printed from rotographs or checked by them. Variant readings in other old forms or in modern editions are cited for a few of the more important texts and for a few others found in forms differing widely enough to suggest both popularity and oral transmission. But in general, variants have not been recorded. For the discussion of the individual pieces printed here, consult the Index under the separate titles.

1

A Iigge for the Ballad-mongers to sing fresh and
fasting, next their hearts euerie morning, insted
of a new hunts-vp, to giue a good morrow to the
Tripe-wife.[1]

O Neighbour Tripewife,
  my heart is full of woe:
That cousning Doll the Iugler,
  should iumble with you so.

I that am your poore neighbour,
  had rather spent a crowne:
Then haue ye thus defamed
  by boyes about the towne.

Abroad in euerie corner,
  the Ballads doo report: 10
That you were trimd vnwomanly,
  and in most shameful sort:

By standing on a Triuet.
  to heare what she could say: P. 11
She lopt ye of[f] a louers locke,
  and caried it away.

Alas were you so simple,
  to suffer such a thing:
Your owne maids sit and mocke ye,
  and euerie where doth ring,   20
The trimming of the Tripe wife:
  it makes me in a rage,
And doubt least that the players
  will sing it on the Stage.

I am sorrie for your husband,
  alacke good honest man;
He walkes about, yet mends not,
  but looketh pale and wan:

¹ Printed from the edition of *A Quest of Enquirie*, pp. 10–12, in Grosart's *Elizabethan England in Gentle and Simple Life*, Occasional Issues, 1881. The piece is there
printed in italic.

That where before he vaunted,
    the conquest he hath got: 30
He sits now in a mammering,
    as one that mindes it not.

A number doo imagine,
    that he repents his marriage,
And gladly to the shambles,
    would send ye with your carriage;
For all the carts of houshold stuffe,
    that came to London bridge,
Nere pleasd him so, as this one greefe
    doth rub him on the ridge.   40

If gold bring such a hart-breake,   P. 12
    Ile none I thanke ye I:
Tis shame it should be spoken,
    and if it be a lie.
But would he be aduisde by me,
    if it be true or no:
I would turne her to her Tripes againe,
    and let all matters go.

FINIS.   I. K.

2

A new Northeren Iigge, called,
Daintie come thou to me.[1]

[CUT]

[*Lady.*] WIlt thou forsake mee thus,
    and leaue me in misery?
And I gaue my hand to thee,
    onely with thee to die:
Cast no care to thy heart,
    from thee I will not flee,
Let them all say what they will,
    Dainty come thou to me.

[*Lover.*] VVere my state good or ill,
    rich, or in misery,   10
Yet would I loue thee still,
    prooue me and thou shalt see.
Cast no care, &c.

[*Lady.*] VVere you rich, were you poore,
    were you in miserie,
I will[2] beg from doore to doore,
    all for to maintaine thee:
Cast no care, &c.

[*Lover.*] VVere I Lord, were I Knight,
    came I of high degree,   20
All my Lands should be thine,
    try me and thou shalt see.
Cast no care, &c.

[*Lady.*] If the Indie Gold were mine,
    and all the wealth of Spaine
All that it should be thine,
    prooue me yet once againe:
Cast no care, &c.

---

[1] Printed from Roxburghe Collection, I, 204. Chappell in *Roxburghe Ballads*, I, 628-31, printed the ballad from the same source.

[2] Chappell has *I'd.*

[*Lover.*]   Thy beauty doth excell,
                aboue all I loue thee,   30
             VVith thee I meane to dwell,
                try me and thou shalt see:
             Cast no care, &c.

[*Lady.*]   I promise for thy sake,
                all other to forsake,
             And onely thee to take,
                trye mee and thou shalt see:
             Cast no care, &c.

[*Lover.*]   Let me thy loue obtaine,
                or else I am but slaine,   40
             Reuiue me once againe,
                sweet I desire[1] thee.
             Cast no care, &c.

[*Lady.*]   If Friends doe frowne and fret,
                and Parents angry be,
             And Brothers griefe is great,
                yet I loue none but thee.
             Cast no care, &c.

[*Lover.*]   Heres my hand and my heart,
                faith and troth vnto thee,   50
             From thee I will not start,
                try mee and thou shalt see.
             Cast no care, &c.

[*Lady.*]   Thus my Friends I forsake,
                with thee my life to spend,
             Refusing no paines to take,
                vntill my life doth end:
             Cast no care, &c.

[*Lover.*]   Farewell my trusty Loue,
                true as the Turtle-doue.   60
             I will as constant proue,
                till we two meet againe.[2]
             Cast no care, &c.

                                              Finis.

Printed by the Assignes of
Thomas Symcocke.

[1] Chappell inserts *but*.   [2] Chappell substitutes *above*.

3

The Souldiers Farewel to his love.
Being a Dialogue betwixt *Thomas* and *Margaret*.[1]

To a pleasant new Tune.

[CUT]

Thomas.[2]

MArgaret my sweetest, Margaret *I* must go,
        Margaret.
Most dear to me, that never may be so:
T. Ah, Fortune wills it, *I*[3] cannot it deny,
M. then know my love your Margaret must dye.[4]

T. Not for the gold my Love that *Cræsus* had,[5]
Would I once see thy sweetest looks so sad,[6]
M. Nor for all that the which my eye did see,
Would I depart my sweetest Love from thee.[7]

T. The King commands, & I must to the wars
M. Ther's others more enough may end the jars   10
T. But I for one commanded am to go,
And for my life I dare not once say no.[8]

---

[1] Printed from the Pepys Collection of Broadsides, IV, 42 (also printed by Rollins in *A Pepysian Garland*, pp. 173–75). The jig is the second of two ballads on one broadside, the other being "A Pleasant Song made by a Souldier." What seems to be another edition by the same publishers is listed in the *Catalogue* of the Crawford Collection, No. 793, and dated 1655–60. A version in the *Percy Folio Manuscript* (ed. Hales and Furnivall, II, 334–37) has the title "A Iigge." In it the speakers are not indicated. The variations of this text from that printed here are given in the notes. Both versions are corrupt in some places, and both may be late texts transmitted orally.

[2] At the head of each column the speakers' names are given in full in black letter.

[3] as ffortune willes, I.

[4]   then know thy loue, thy Margarett, shee must dye.

[5] gold *that* euer Crœssus hadd.   [6] fade.

[7]   nor ffor all *that* my eyes did euer see,
        wold I once *p*art thy sweetest loue from mee.

[8]   ". . . . enow to end those cares."
      "but I am one appointed ffor to goe,
      & I dare not ffor my liffe once say noe."

379

M. Ah[1] marry me, and you shall[2] stay at home,
Full thirty weeks you know that I have[3] gone,
T. There's time enough another for to take[4]
He l love thee well, and not thy child forsake.

M. And have I doted on[5] thy sweetest face?
and dost infringe that which thou suedst in chase[6]
Thy faith I mean but I will wend with thee,
T. It is too far for Peg to go with me.   20

M. I'le go with thee my Love both night and day
I'le bear thy sword, i'le run and lead the way.[7]
T. But we must ride, how[8] will you follow then,
Amongst a Troop of us that s Armed men?

M. I le bear the Lance, i le guide[9] thy stirrop too,
Ile rub the[10] horse, and more then that i le do,
T. But Margarets fingers they are[11] all too fine,
To wait on me, when she doth see me dine.[12]

Margaret.
Ile see you dine, ile[13] wait still at your back,
Ile give you wine, or any thing you lack.   30
Thomas.
But you l repine when you shall see me have
A dainty wench that is both fine and brave.

M. *I* le love your[14] wench, my sweetest, *I* do vow,[15]
I'le watch time[16] when she may pleasure you.
T. But you will grieve to see me sleep[17] in bed,
And you must wait[18] still in anothers stead.

M. *I*'le watch my love to see you sleep in rest,[19]
And when you sleep then *I* shall[20] think me blest.
T. The time will come you must delivered be,[21]
If[22] in the Camp it[23] will discredit me.   40

[1] O.   [2] may.   [3] am.   [4] another ffather take.   [5] ouer.
[6]   & dost infring the things I haue in chase.
[7]   & I will beare thy sword like lakyney; Lead the way!
[8] &.   [9] Ile beare thy Lance, & grinde.   [10] thy.   [11] be.
[12]   to stand & waite when shee shall see mee dine.   [13] &.
[14] thy.   [15] my sweetest loue, I vow.   [16] watch the time.
[17] see vs lye.   [18] watch.   [19] you take your rest.
[20] shall I.   [21] deliuered you must bee.   [22] then.   [23] you.

M. *I* le go from you[1] before the[2] time shall be,
When all is well my love again i le see.
T. All will not serve for Margaret must[3] not go,
Then do resolve my Love, what else to do.

M. *If* nought wil serve why then[4] sweet love adieu
I needs must die, and[5] yet in dying true.
T. Nay stay my love, for *I* love Margaret well,[6]
And here *I* vow with Margaret to[7] dwell.

M. Give me your[8] hand, your[8] Margaret livs again
T. Here is[9] my hand, i le never breed thy[10] pain.   50
M. *I'*le[11] kiss my Love in token it[12] is so.
T. We will be wed, come Margaret let us go.

FINIS.

London, Printed for F. Coles, T. Vere, and
J. Wright.

---

[1] thee.   [2] *that*.   [3] may.   [4] Must I not goe? why then.
[5] needs must I dye, but.   [6] a! stay my loue! I loue my Margarett well.
[7] still to.   [8] thy.   [9] heeres.   [10] thee.   [11] I.   [12] *that*.

4

A Country new Iigge betweene *Simon* and *Susan*, to be sung
in merry pastime by Bachelors and Maydes.   To the
tune of I can, nor will no longer lye alone:
Or, Falero lero lo.[1]

[TWO CUTS]

Simon.

O Mine owne sweet heart,
   and when wilt thou be true:
Or when will the time come,
   that I shall marry you.
That I may giue you kisses,
   one, two, or three,
More sweeter then the hunny,
   that comes from the Bee.

Susan.

My Father is vnwilling,
   that I should marry thee: 10
Yet *I* could wish in heart,
   that so the same might be.
For now me thinkes thou seemest,
   more louely vnto me:
And fresher then the Blossomes,
   that bloomes vpon the Tree.

Simon.

Thy mother is most willing,
   and will consent I know,
Then let vs to thy Father
   now both together goe: 20
Where if he giue vs his good will,
   and to our match agree:
T'will be sweeter then the honny,
   that comes from the Bee.

[1] Printed from Pepys Collection, I, 278, 279. The copy in Pepys Collection, I,
260, 261, printed in Rollins's *Pepysian Garland*, pp. 132–38, has numerous insignificant
variations in spelling, capitalization, etc., not noted here. The title of the text printed
here covers only three lines in the broadside.

Susan.

Come goe, for *I* am willing,
   good fortune be our guide:
From that which I haue promised,
   deare heart ile neuer slide.
If that he doe but smile,
   and I the same may see: 30
Tis sweeter then the blossomes,
   that bloomes vpon the Tree.

Simon.

But stay heere comes my[1] mother,
   weele talke with her a word,
I doubt not but some comfort,
   to vs she may afford:
If comfort she will giue vs,
   that we the same m[a]y see,
Twill be sweeter then the honny,
   that comes from the Bee.   40

Susan.

O Mother wee are going
   my Father for to pray:
That he will giue me his good will,
   for long I cannot stay.
A young man I haue chosen,
   a fitting match for me:
More fayrer then the blossomes,
   that bloomes vpon the Tree.

Mother.

Daughter thou art old enough,
   to be a wedded wife,   50
You Maydens are desirous
   to lead a married life.
Then my consent good Daughter,
   shall to thy wishes be:
For young thou art as blossomes,
   that bloome vpon the Tree.

[1] *my* in both versions.

Simon.

Then Mother you are willing,
    your Daughter I should haue:
And *Susan* thou art welcome,
    ile keepe thee fine and braue.   60
And haue those wished blessings
    bestowed vpon thee,
More sweeter then the honny,
    that comes from the Bee.

Susan.

Yet *Simon I* am minded
    to lead a merry life:
And be as well maintained,
    as any Citty wife:
And liue a gallant Mistresse
    of Maydens that shall bee   70
More fayrer then the blossomes,
    that bloome vpon the Tree.

The second part,   to the same tune.
[TWO CUTS]

Simon.

THou shalt haue thy Caudles,
    before thou dost arise:
For churlishnesse breeds sicknes
    and dainger therein lies,
Young Lasses must be cheerisht,
    with sweets that daynty be,
Farre sweeter then the honny,
    that commeth from the Bee.   80

Mother.

Well said good son and Daughter,
    this is the onely dyet:
To please a dainty young wife,
    and keepe the house in quiet:
But stay, heere comes your Father
    his words *I* hope will be:
More sweeter then the blossomes,
    that bloome vpon the Tree.

Father.

Why how now Daughter *Susan*,
   doe you intend to marry?
Maydens in the old time,
   did twenty winters tarry:
Now in the teenes no sooner,
   but you a wife will bee:
And loose the sweetest blossomes,
   that bloomes vp on the Tree.

90

Susan.

It is for my preferment,
   good Father say not nay:
For I haue found a Husband kind,
   and louing euery way:
That still vnto my fancy
   will euermore agree:
Which is more sweet then honny,
   that comes from the Bee.

100

Mother.

Hinder not your Daughter,
   good Husband, least you bring
Her loues consuming sicknes,
   or else a worser thing:
Maydens youngly married
   louing wiues will bee.
And sweet as is the honny,
   which comes from the Bee.

110

Simon.

Good Father be not cruell,
   your Daughter is mine owne:
Her mother hath consented,
   and is to liking growne.
And if your selfe will giue then,
   her gentle hand to me,
Twill sweeter be then honny,
   that comes from the Bee.

120

Father.

God giue thee ioy deare Daughter,
    there is no reason I,
Should hinder thy proceeding,
    and thou a Mayden dye:
And after to lead Apes in hell,
    as Maydens doomed be:
That fayrer are then blossomes,
    that bloome vpon the Tree.

Simon.

Then let's to the Parson,
    and Clarke to say Amen: 130
    Susan.
With all my heart good *Simon*,
    we are concluded then:
My Father and Mother both,
    doe willingly agree:
My *Simon's* sweet as honny,
    That comes from the Bee.

All together sing.

You Maydens and Batchelors,
    we hope will loose no time:
Which learne it by experience,
    That youth is in their prime,   140
And dayly in their hearts desire,
    Young married folkes to be;
More sweeter then the blossomes,
    that bloome from the Tree.

FINIS.

Printed at London by W I.

A mery nevv Iigge.

Or, the pleasant wooing
betwixt *Kit* and *Pegge*.[1]

To the tune of Strawberry leaues make Maidens faire.

[TWO CUTS]

M. WEll met faire Maid,
my chiefest ioy.
W. Alas blinde foole,
deceiu'd art thou.
M. I prethee sweet *Peg*
be not so coy.
W. I scorne to fancy
such a Cow.

M. Thy beauty sweet *Peg*,
hath won my heart.
W. For shame leaue off
thy flattery.
M. From thee I neuer
meane to part.
W. Good lacke how thou
canst cog and lie!

M. For *Peggies* loue
poore *Kit* will dye.
W. In faith what colour
then shall it be?   10
M. In time my constant
heart will try.
W. Then pluck it out,
that I may see.

M. My life I will spend
to doe thee good:
W. Alas good sir,
that shall not need.
M. For thee I will
not spare my blood.
W. God send your Goslings
well to speed.

M. Yet faine would I be
thy wedded mate.
W. Alas good sir I am
already sped.
M. What lucke had I
to come so late?
W. Because thou broughtst
a calfe from bed.   20

M. O pitty me,
sweet *Peg* I thee pray.
W. So I haue done
long time God wot.
M. Why dost thou then
my loue denay?
W. Because I see
thou art a sot.

Printed at London for H. Gosson.

[1] Printed from Pepys Collection, I, 258, 259. The text in *Roxburghe Ballads*, II, 100–104, is from another edition issued by Gosson.

Now here doth follow a pleasant new Song
Betweene two young Louers that lasted not long.

OR,

The second part,   To the same tune.

[CUT OF A MAN AND A WOMAN]

M. WHy Ich haue wealth
　　　and treasure store.
W. And wit as small,
　　　as small may be.
M. A chaine of Gold
　　　I might haue worne.
W. A Cocks-combe fitter had
　　　it beene for thee.

M. Thou lou'st the Miller
　　　of the Glen.
W. What if I doe,
　　　what is that to thee?　30
M. I will bang the Millers
　　　loue from him.
And therefore wend,
　　　and gang with me.

W. Great boast small roast
　　　such brags will make:
But if *Tom Miller*
　　　he were nie.
He would bang thee well
　　　for *Peggies* sake,
And like a Puppy
　　　make thee cry.

M. Yet kisse me now
　　　for my good will,
And if my life
　　　thou meanst to saue.

W. To giue a kisse,
　　　I thinke it best,
To rid me from
　　　a prating knaue.　　40

Be packing hence
　　　you Rusticke clowne.
M. No haste but good
　　　I hope there be.
W. Take heed lest that
　　　I cracke your crowne
For bussing *Pegge*
　　　so sawcily.

M. Nay in friendly sort
　　　now let vs part,
I pray thee sweet Loue
　　　so let it be.
W. Adue kind *Kit*
　　　with all my heart,
I am glad I am rid
　　　of thy company.

M. All you young men
　　　take heed by me,
That vnto women
　　　set your minde.　　50
See that your Louers
　　　constant be,
Lest you be serued
　　　in like kinde.

Written by Valentine Hamdultun.

6

Clods Carroll: or, A proper new Iigg, to be sung Dialogue wise, of a man and a woman that would needs be married.[1]

To a pleasant new Tune.

[TWO CUTS]

Man.   NOw in the Garden
           are we well met,
To craue our promise,
     for promise is a debt.
Wom Come sit thee down all by my side,
     and when that thou art set,
         say what thou wilt vnto mee.

M.   Shew me vnfaignedly,
     and tell me thy mind,
For one may haue a yong wench   10
     that is not ouer-kind.
W.   Seeke all the world for such a one,
     then hardly shall you find
         a Loue of such perfection.

M.   This single life is wearisome,
     faine would I marry:
But feare of ill chusing
     makes me to tarry:
Some sayes that flesh is flexible,
     and quickly it will vary.   20
W.   It's very true, God mend them.

M.   Why speak'st thou ill of women,
     sith thou thy selfe art one?
W.   Would all the rest were constant
     saue I my selfe alone.
M.   Faith, good or bad, or howsoe're,
     I cannot liue alone,
         but needs I must bee married.

[1] Printed from Roxburghe Collection, I, 64, 65 (also printed in *Roxburghe Ballads*, I, 201–6).

389

W. To marry with a yong wench,
    shee'l make thee poore with pride: 30
To marry with one of middle age,
    perhaps she hath beene try'd:
To marry with an old one,
    to freeze by fire side;
        both old and young are faulty.

M. Ile marry with a yong wench,
    of beauty and of wit.
W. It is better tame a yong Colt,
    without a curbing bit.
M. But she will throw her rider downe.   40
    W. I true, he cannot sit.
        when Fillies fall a wighing.

M. Ile marry one of middle age,
    for she will loue me well.
W. But if her middle much be vs'd,
    by heauen and by hell;
Thou shalt find more griefes
    than thousand tongues can tell:
        Ah, silly man, God helpe thee.

M. Ile marry with an old wench,   50
    that knowes not good from bad.
W. But once within a fortnight
    shee'l make her husband mad.
M. Beshrew thee for thy counsell,
    for thou hast made me sad:
        but needs I must be married.

W. To marry with a young wench,
    me thinkes it were a blisse:
To marry one of middle age,
    it were not much amisse.   60
I'de marry one of old age,
    and match where money is;
        there's none are bad in chusing.

M. Then thou for all thy saying,
    commendst the single life.
W. I, freedome is a popish
    banishment of strife.

M. Hold thy tongue fond woman,
    for I must haue a wife.
W. A Cuckold in reuersion.   70

When you are once married
    all one whole yeare,
Tell me of your fortune,
    and meet with mee here:
To thinke vpon my counsell
    thou wilt shed many a teare;
      till which time I will leaue thee.

M. Were I but assured,
    and of a Beggars lot,
Still to liue in misery,   80
    and neuer worth a groat,
To haue my head well furnished
    as any horned Goat;
      for all this would I marry.

Farewell you lusty Batchelors,
    to marriage I am bent:
When I haue try'd what marriage is,
    Ile tell you the euent;
And tell the cause, if cause there be,
    wherein I doe repent,   90
      that euer I did marry.   *FINIS.*

The second part,   To the same tune.

[TWO CUTS]

W. **G**ood-morrow to thee new married
    how doest thou fare?   (man,
M. As one quite marr'd with marriage,
    consum'd and kill'd with care:
Would I had tane thy counsell.
    W. But thou wouldst not beware.
M. Alas, it was my fortune.

W.   What griefe doth most oppresse thee?
   may I request to know?   100
M.   That I haue got a wanton.
   W.   But is she not a shrow?
M.   Shee's any thing that euill is,
   but I must not say so.
W.   For feare that I should flout thee.

M.   Indeed to mocke at misery,
   would adde vnto my griefe.
W.   But I will not torment thee,
   but rather lend reliefe:
And therefore in thy marriage,   110
   tell me what woes are chiefe;
      good counsell yet may cure thee.

W.   Is not thy huswife testy,
   too churlish and too sowre?
M.   The deuill is not so waspish,
   shee's neuer pleas'd an hower.
W.   Canst thou not tame a deuill?
   lies it not in thy power?
M.   Alas I cannot coniure.

W.   What, goeth she not a gossiping,   120
   to spend away thy store?
M.   Doe what I can, I promise you,
   shee's euer out of dore;
That were I nere so thrifty,
   yet she would make me poore:
      woes me I cannot mend it.

W.   How goeth shee in apparell?
   delights she not in pride?
M.   No more than Birds doe bushes,
   or harts the riuer side.   130
Witnesse to that, her looking-glasse,
   where shee hath stood in pride
      a whole fore-noone together.

W.   How thinkst thou? was she honest,
   and loyall to thy bed?

M.   I thinke her legs doe fall away,
    for spring time keeping head.
And were not hornes inuisible,
    I warrant you I were sped
        with broad browed Panthers.   140

W.   Thy griefe is past recouery,
    no salue will help but this:
To take thy fortune patiently,
    and brooke her what she is.
Yet many things amended are,
    that haue beene long amisse;
        and so in time may she be.

M.   I cannot stay here longer,
    my wife or this doth stay:
And he thats bound as I am bound,   150
    perforce must needs obey.
VV.   Then farewell to thee new married
    since you will needs away;   (man,
        I can but grieue thy fortune.

M.   All you that be at libertie,
    and would be void of strife:
I speake it on experience,
    ne're venture on a wife.
For if you match, you will be matcht
    to such a weary life,   160
        that you will all repent you.

        FINIS.

London, Printed by *A. M.* for
    Henry Gosson.

7

The Souldiers delight in the North[1]
OR,

A New North-countrey Jigge betwixt a Man and his Wife,
Who were in a kinde of conjugall strife:
She finding his fancie to grow dull and moody,
Thus stil cals upon him, Come cudle me Codie.

To the Tune of the Northerne Diddle, or Raged and torne, &[c.][2]

[LARGE CUT]

Peggie.

C*Vdie* and *Peggie* together
   did meet in an euening late,
And pleasant like the weather,
   sweet Peggie began to prate.
Now is it a Moone-shine night
   the season doth require,
That we should take delight
   and blow up Cupid's fire.
Canst thou not cudle me Cudie
   And canst thou not cudle me now?   10
I pray thee come cudle me Cudie,
   as thou hadst wont to doe.

Cudie.

Then Cudie began to say,
   sweet P[egg]ie I pray thee be whiet,
And both [by] night and by day
   my S[weet I']ll allow thee diet:
My B [   ]yeeld thee drink,
   [   ]he Parish,
[   ]euer shrink,
   [   ]ue and cherish.   20
[*Then hold thee*] *contented Peggie*
   [*and take what I*] *am able;*
[*I'le neuer forsake m*]*y Meggie*
   [*while I haue a Na*]*g in my stable.*

---

[1] Printed from the Manchester Free Reference Library Collection, II, 32. A jagged tear in the lower left-hand corner of the first sheet and two in the second—one along the margin, and one in the middle with the edges overlapping—account for the gaps. I have supplied the bracketed words and letters.

[2] Torn at the margin.

[Peg]gie.

[   ],
  [   ] kinde,[1]
And therefore I need not studie,
    nor vainly trouble my minde.
But one thing I do want
    whereof I had once enough: 30
Before I'le of that be scant,
    I'le sell both Cart and Plough.
Then canst thou not, &c.

Cudie.

O Peggie dost think the Moone
    will alwayes be at the full,
I cannot do as I haue done,
    now age my courage doth pull.
Then Peggie be content,
    to take what I can giue,
When all our meanes is spent   40
    so well as we can we must liue.
Then hold thee, &c.

Peggie.

Alas my Duck my Doue,
    why art thou growne faint-hearted?
Long time we increased in loue,
    and smoke's to flams conuerted.
The Calfe will grow to a Bull,
    and the Lambe will be a Tup,
But thou being growne to the full
    falst down when thou shouldst rise vp.   50
Then canst thou not, &c.

The second Part to the same Tune.

[CUT]

Cudie.

The Mickle deuil's in the woman,
    what would'st thou haue me to do,
But wealth and wit I do summon
    if I can please thee so.

[1] End of the first column.

And yet thou lokest for meare
   then I haue to bestow.
But I pray thee[1] my loue forbeare,
   for in troth my state grows low.
Then hold thee contented Peggie,   60
   and take what I am able;
I'le neuer forsake my Meggie
   while I haue a Nag in my Stable.

Peggie.

Nay Cudie if thou art distasted
   at that which I haue said,
My time in vaine I haue wasted,
   would I were againe a Maid.
Then would I take a Lad
   should giue me better content,
When we were first wed, I had   70
   a time of merryment.
[The]n canst thou not cudle me Cudie,
   [And] canst thou not cudle me now,
[I pra]y thee come cudle me Cudie
   [as th]ou wert wont to doe.

Cudie.

[M]y Peggie I took by the middle,
   and I laid her upon her ridge,
[A]nd I bad her lie still bonny Lasse,
   and I'le play her the other Jigge.
For shee l haue a Lad with a lock,   80
   whatsoeuer else betide;
Shall play her a Jigge in her smock,
   before that shee'l be his Bride.
Then hold thee, &c.

Meggie.

[Now] thou hast cudl'd me once,
   [and] thou hast cudl'd me twice,
And if thou hast cudl d me once again,
   then thou hast cudled me thrice.
I pray thee rock the Babe,
   the cradle runs on wheeles,   90
When my Host goes drunk to bed,
   up flies my Hostesses heeles.
Then canst thou [not], &c.

---

[1] *pray thee* torn and blurred.

[*Cudie.*]

My Peggie I pr[ay t]hee be ciuill,
    and speak no m[o]re then's fit,
I hope thou hast g[ot] no euill
    by me, therefor[e] learne more wit.
And do not thy foll[y] bewray,
    in such an unseemly manner,
I'le please thee as well as I may,
    then do not thy Sex dishonour.
Then hold thee, &c.   100

Peggie.

Sweet Cuddie be better appeased,
    thy Peggie speaks but in iest,
With what thou art able I'me pleased,
    and so let the quarrell rest.
Yet still I can neuer chuse,
    but say in a louin[g] sort,
To a Wife it is he[i]nous newes,
    of her [lo]ue to be kept short.
Then can[s]t thou not, &c.   110

Cudie.

Well Peggie I am contented,
    with this thy modest excuse,
My anger is well preuented,
    and nothing is tane in abuse.
I'le be thy louing mate,
    and thoust be my loyall spouse,
Then learne to liue after the rate,
    that thy honest *Cudie* allowes.
Then hold thee, &c.   120

FINIS

8

The New Scotch-Jigg:[1]

OR,

The Bonny Cravat.

Johnny wooed *Jenny* to tye his Cravat;
But *Jenny* perceiving what he would be at,
With delayes put him off, till she found out his mind;
And then afterwards she proved more kind:
At length, both Parties were well agreed,
And went to the Kirk to be Wed with all speed.

Tune of, *Jenny come tye my*, &c.

[TWO CUTS]

[*Johnny.*]　　AS *Johnny* met *Jenny* a going to play,
　　　　　　　Quoth *Johnny* to *Jenny*, I prithee love stay:
Since thou art my honey, my joy, and delight,
I'le love thee all day, & I'le please thee at night.
　　　　Jenny *come tye my*, **Jenny** *come tye my*,
　　　　Jenny *come tye my bonny Cravat.*
[*Jenny.*]　　*I have tyed it behind, and I've tyed it before,*
　　　　　　I've ty'd it so often, I'le tye it no more.

[*Johnny.*]　　O say not so *Jenny*, nor do me not scorn,
For better poor *Johnny* had never been born:　　　　10
O kill not my *H*eart with being unkind,
I'le ever endeavour to pleasure thy mind.
　　　　Jenny *come tye my*, **&c.**[2]

[*Jenny.*]　　But *Johnny* I ken it, altho to my grief,
When you stole my heart away like a sly thief,
*Y*ou promis'd me Marriage, with many things
Which yet is not wiped out off the old score, (more
[*Johnny.*]　　**Jenny** *come tye my*, **&c.**

---

[1] Printed from Douce Collection, II, 164. The ballad has been printed in *Roxburghe Ballads*, VIII, 466–67, from a copy in the Pepys Collection.

[2] The omission of the refrains obscures to a certain extent the alternation of the speakers.

398

[*Johnny.*] O *Jenny*, let none of this trouble thy mind,
For now thou shalt see, I'le be loving and kind: 20
A little forgetful I was, I confess,
But all shall be mended that now is amiss.
Jenny *come tye my*, etc.[1]

[CUT]

[*Johnny.*] I Le buy thee a Gown, and a Scarf, & a Hood:
If thou wilt believe me, I'le ever be good:
For Rings, & for Ribbonds, ne'r matter for that,
If thou art but willing to tye my Cravat.
Jenny *come tye my*, etc.

[*Jenny.*] All this you did promise me often before,
If I would but tye it one time, or two more; 30
But yet you were never so good as your word,
Therefore for to tye it I cannot afford.
[*Johnny.*] **Jenny** *come tye my*, &c.

[*Johnny.*] My *Jenny* if thou wilt be ruled by me,
It shall not be long ere we wedded will be:
For I have got Mony, & House, & good Land,
Which all shall be ready at *Jenny's* Command.
Jenny *come tye my*, &c.

[*Johnny.*] Besides, on the Common I have got a Cow
To give us some Milk, and bonny black Yow; 40
I likewise at Heam have a Dog and a Cat,
Then prithee good *Jenny* come tye my Cravat.
Jenny *come tye my*, &c.

[*Jenny.*] Your House, I believe, is not often repair'd;
And as for your Land, it lies in the Church-yard:
Your Money, if any such thing you may have,
With it keep you honest, & prove not a Knave.
[*Johnny.*] **Jenny** *come tye my*, &c.

[*Jenny.*] Your Cow on the Common that grazes you say,
May wheadle another your will to obey: 50
Then prithee make much of your dog & your Cat,
For I am not willing to tye your Cravat.
[*Johnny.*] **Jenny** *come tye my*, &c.

[1] In the broadside the refrain is given in full for this stanza and the next, probably because the stanzas come at the end of one page and the beginning of the next.

[*Johnny.*]   O *Jenny*, why art thou so hard of belief?
I fear thou art minded to kill me with grief:
Before thee I'le open my Heart to the life
I tell thee I mean for to make thee my Wife.
    Jenny[1] *come tye my*, etc.

[*Johnny.*]   Then do not thou flout me, but freely comply,
Nothing shall be wanting for *Jenny* and I: 60
Then give me my *Jenny*, thy heart & thy hand,
For I will be ever at *Jenny's* command.
    Jenny come tye, &c.

[*Jenny.*]   O *Johnny!* I fear thou dost flatter me now,
Or else I could love thee, J swear and *I* vow:
But with fair delusions I may be undone,
Therefore from thy *Jenny* good *Johnny* begone.
[*Johnny.*]   *Jenny come tye, &c.*

[*Jenny.*]   A Maid by her choice she may soon be destroy'd
And left in the lurch, when she hath bin injoy'd:
But if you be honest, declare it in brief,   71
And let me not languish in sorrow and grief.
[*Johnny.*]   *Jenny come tye, &c.*

[*Johnny.*]   My *Jenny*, then prithe take one word for all,
I never will leave thee what ever befall:
In Sickness and Health *I* will for thee provide,
And at the next Kirk, *I* will make thee my bride.
    Jenny come tye, &c.

[*Jenny.*]   Then *Johnny I* love thee as dear as my Life,
And *I* am contented for to be thy Wife: 80
And we will be marryed to both our content,
I hope we shall never have cause to repent.
[*Johnny.*]   *Jenny come tye my, Jenny come tye my,*
    Jenny come tye my bonny Cravat.
[*Jenny.*]   *I have ty'd it behind, and I've ty'd it before,*
    And now J will tye it a hundred times more.

London, Printed for *W. Thackeray, T. Passenger,* and *W. Whitwood.*

[1] *nn* is blurred in the word. The refrain is given in full for this stanza, which stands at the head of the second column of the page.

9

The Second Part of the new Scotch Jigg:[1]
OR,
JENNY'S Reply, To *JOHNNY'S* Cravat.

The Case [i]s alter'd now; *Jenny* Wooes *Johnny*
To tye her Kirtle, and shee'l be his Honey;
Which *Johnny* took so kindly sitting by her,
That for his heart, he could not well deny her,
At length they did agree, so plain and pat,
That he her Kirtle ty'd; She his Cravat.

Tune of, *Jenny* come tye my, &c.

[CUT]

[*Jenny*.] AS *Jenny* sate under a Siccomore Tree
She spi'd her love *Johnny* come over the Lee;
O welcome my *Johnny!* now welcome my dear!
I prithy my honey, come sit thee down here.
Johnny come tye my, Johnny come tye my,
Johnny come tye my Kirtle so gay.
[*Johnny*.] *I've ty'd it so often, and ty'd it in vain;*
Yet if thou wilt love me, I'le tye it again.

[*Jenny*.] I prithy my *Johnny*, ne're doubt of my Love;
For *I* am constrained by *Cupid* above,   10
To love thee as dear, as the blood in my heart;
Then do not thou fear, that we ever will part.
Johnny come tye my, etc.[2]

[*Jenny*.] O *Johnny*, my honey, thou know'st it is true
How scornful thou was[t] when *I* did thee first woe,
[*Johnny*.] And when *I* begg'd of thee to tye my Cravat;
You said, that *I* wanted a bit for my Cat.[3]
[*Jenny*.] *Johnny come tye my*, etc.

[1] Printed from Roxburghe Collection, II, 420 (also in *Roxburghe Ballads*, VIII, 468–70).

[2] The identical refrains are printed in full for each stanza in the broadside.

[3] A clear allusion to the related ballad "The Scotch Currant; Or, The Tying of Johnny's Cravant." See *Roxburghe Ballads*, VIII, 469, 463.

[*Jenny.*]   My *Johnny*, *I* love the as dear as my Life,
And could be contented for to be thy Wife,   20
Although *I* was fickle, and seem'd to be Coy:
Yet now *I*'le be constant, my Love and my joy.
    Johnny *come tye my*, etc.

[CUT]

[*Johnny.*]   BUt *Jenny*, if that I thy Kirtle should tye,
Come tell[1] me my Honey, and tell me no lye;
If thou wilt be willing my Love to requite,
[*Jenny.*]   O *Johnny* I'le please thee by day, and by night.
    Johnny *come tye my*, etc.

[*Jenny.*]   I'le buy for my Love, a Cravat that is new,
If thou wilt be constant, and ever be true;   30
And ty't with a Ribbond of Popinjay green,
The like in the Parish there shall not be seen.
    Johnny *come tye my*, etc.

[*Jenny.*]   But *Johnny* now tell me, if that *I* consent,
Shall I never have any cause to repent?
To gain a bad Bargain, may make me to rue,
Then prithee resolve to be faithful and true.
    Johnny *come tye my*, etc.

[*Jenny.*]   As true as the Steel I'me resolved to be;
And all that I have, is my *Johnny*, for thee;   40
Thou kens, that my Portion I have for to take,
And how I have kept it so long for thy sake.
    Johnny *come tye my*, etc.

[*Johnny.*]   My *Jenny*, I joy for to see thee so kind
To tell thee my love, it rejoyces my mind;
Thy looks are so Bonny and blith, for to see:
Of all the brave Lasses, my *Jenny* for me.
[*Jenny.*]   **Johnny** *come tye my*, etc.

[*Jenny.*]   O *Johnny!* I sware by the Lace of my Gown,
I love thee above the Lads in the Town: 50
And for to gang with thee, what ever befall;
I'le leave both my Daddy, and Mammy, and all,
    Johnny *come tye my*, etc.

[1] *well* in the original.

[*Johnny.*]   My *Jenny*, I'me willing thy Kirtle to tye,
           Since thou art so loving, I cannot deny:
           And ever hereafter my own thou shalt be;
           Then prithee my *H*oney, be loving to me.

[*Jenny.*]   **𝔍𝔬𝔥𝔫𝔫𝔭** *come tye my*, etc.

[*Jenny.*]   Now *Johnny*, since I ken what you would be at,
           I likewise am willing to tye thy Cravat: 60
           And by this same Kiss, *I* will ever be true;
           My *Johnny* shall never have cause for to rue.
              𝔍𝔬𝔥𝔫𝔫𝔭 *come tye my*, **𝔍𝔬𝔥𝔫𝔫𝔭** *come tye my*,
              𝔍𝔬𝔥𝔫𝔫𝔭 *come tye my Kirtle so gay.*

[*Johnny.*]   *I've ty'd it so often, and ty'd it in vain;*
             But now I will tye it again and again.

London. Printed for *W*. *Thackeray*, *T*. *Passenger*, and *W*. *Whitwood*.[1]

[1] Printed *Whoditwo* on the broadside.

10

A

Pleasant JIGG

Betwixt

Jack and his Mistress:[1]

Or, The Young Carman's Courage cool'd by the
suddain approach, of his Master, who found him too kind to his
Mistress.

Tune of *Mary Live Long.*   *Licensed according to Order.*

[TWO CUTS]

A Carman of late,
⠀⠀VVho liv'd in the City,
⠀⠀A sorrowful Dity,
His wife was too great
⠀⠀with their Prentice Boy,
But a swinging young Spark
At a wench in the dark;
⠀⠀Now this his Dame knew,
And therefore stout *Johnny*,
And therefore stout *Johnny*,⠀⠀⠀⠀⠀⠀⠀⠀10
⠀⠀Must tickle her to.

It happen'd one day,
⠀⠀His Mistriss came to him,
⠀⠀No question she knew him,
To be e[v]'ry way,
⠀⠀a Lad for her turn;
Where's your Master, she cry'd?
With a friend, he reply'd;
⠀⠀She then void of shame,
Said *Johnny* come kiss me,⠀⠀⠀⠀⠀⠀⠀⠀20
Sweet *Johnny* come kiss me,
⠀⠀Make much of thy Dame.

---

[1] Printed from Douce Collection, II, 182*b*. In *Roxburghe Ballads*, IX, 703–4, the
ballad is printed from Roxburghe Collection, II, 258.

[TWO CUTS]

Sweet Mistress I fear,
  A woful disaster,
   The wrath of me Master,
If once he should hear,
  I play'd with your Lute,
He would liquor my hide,
You're a fool, she reply'd,
  Take courage for shame,   30
O fear not your Master,
Boy fear not your Master,
  But pleasure your Dame.

I count it no crime,
  To dally in pleasure,
   We'll Toy out of measure,
'Tis not the first time,
  Nor sha'n't be the last,
Therefore come on my Boy,
Let us Pleasure enjoy,   40
  Take Courage for shame,
'Tis sweet Recreation,
'Tis sweet Recreation,
  To pleasure thy Dame.

Thy Master, I'll swear,
  If once he should Cavel,
   We'll send to dig Gravel,
With Friends to *Horn-Fair*,
  He dare not say no,
But at home we will stay,   50
Then in order to play,
  The Frolicksome Game,
Boy do not deny me,
John do not deny me,
  But pleasure thy Dame,

Thy Corral and Bells,
  And Whistle I know it,
   If thou wilt bestow it
For pleasures excells,
  The best[1] in the Town,   60

[1] *lest* in the original.

Thou art *L*usty and strong
And can lay me along,
   Take Courage for shame,
Thou here in the Stable,
Thou here in the Stable,
   Shall pleasure thy Dame.

His master by chance,
   Then being near them.
   Did soon over-hear them,
And strait did advance,   70
   With fury and Rage,
Like a Fellow Horn-mad,
He fell on the Lad,
   His shoulders he paid,
'Cause *John* in his Pasture,
'Cause *John* in his Pasture,
   a Tresspass had made.

Ah! what hast thou done,
   So sad a vexation,
   Was ne'r in the nation,   80
Horn-mad I shall run,
   Without all dispute,
Oh ye villain said he,
I will not make you Free,
   But bring you to shame,
Because you have wrong'd me,
Because you have wrong'd me,
   and play'd with your Dame.

Printed for J. *Deacon*, at the *Angel* in *Guilt-spur-street* without *New-Gate*.

11

𝕿𝖍𝖊 𝖂𝖊𝖘𝖙-𝕮𝖔𝖚𝖓𝖙𝖗𝖞 𝕵𝖎𝖌𝖌:

OR,

Love in Due Season.[1]

A Longing Maid which had a mind to marry,	And liking of her well, resolv'd to try her:
Complaining was, that she so long should tarry;	And courting her, and vowing to be constant,
At length a brisk young Lad did chance to spy her,	They there clapt up a bargain in an instant.

To a pleasant New Tune, called, New Exeter.   *With Allowance.*

[TWO CUTS]

WHen *Soll* with his Beams,
   Had guilded the Streams,
And Nymphs, and Young Shepherds
   awakt from their Dreams:
I heard a Sad Moan
In a Neighbouring Grove
   from a Voice all alone.

A Languishing Maid,
   By *Cupid* Betray'd;
Was Sighing, and Sobbing,   10
   And often she said:
Love! Cruel to me:
When shall I be Eas'd
   Of my Misery.

'Tis known I am Fair,
   And Brisk as the Air;
Not one in a thousand
   With Me can Compare:
Yet ne'r a Young-man
Will ease me of Sadness,   20
   to help me! that can.

My time I do spend,
   Yet want I a Friend

---

[1] Printed from Douce Collection, II, 245. The text in *Roxburghe Ballads*, VII,
250-51, is printed from Roxburghe Collection, II, 506.

To Rally, and Dally,
   And please me toth' End:
   Which makes me to say,
O *Cupid!* Great *Cupid!*
   I love no Delay.

[TWO CUTS]

ALL Night in my Bed,
   With Cares in my Head,   30
And weeping, and wailing,
   I wish I were Wedd:
   And yet no Relief
I find in the Morning
   For all my sad Grief.

How happy's the Birds
   Which Mate in the Woods?
Enjoying most freely,
   Their Love without words;
   Whilst I do complain   40
Of Young-mens Unkindness
   And Cruel Disdain.

A Young-man hard by,
   This Maid did Espy;
Admiring her Beauty,
   He to her did hye:
   Quoth he, pritty Saint,
It grieves my Heart for
   to hear your Complaint.

What think you of me?   50
   I'm active and free;
And willing to serve you
   In every Degree:
   And by this sweet Kiss,
To proffer my Service
   It is not amiss.

The Bonny Young Maid
   was nothing afraid;
But modestly Blushing,
   unto him, she said: 60

Since you are so free,
If you will be Constant,
We two may agree.

Quoth he, thou shalt find
Me Loyal, and Kind,
And Ready, and willing,
To pleasure thy Mind:
then do you not fear
But I will be Constant
My Joy and my Dear.   70

this made her Rejoyce,
And with Cheerful Voice,
Quoth she, mine own Dearest,
thou shalt be my Choice:
take Heart and take Hand,
I always will be at
thy will and Command.

then did they retire,
With Longing Desire;
Expecting, and waiting   80
For quenching Loves fire:
And now lives most free,
Although a Quick Bargain
was made as you see.

FINIS.

Printed for *P. Brooksby*, at the Golden-ball, near the *Hospital-gate* in *West-smithfield.*[1]

---

[1] The colophon is printed as one line in the broadside.

12

The West=Country Jigg:

OR, A Trenchmore Galliard.[1]

See how the Lads and *Lasses* flock together,
A Merry makeing, like Birds of a Feather;
Here's *Sam*, and *Sawny*, gentle James and jonny,
With Moll and Moggy, and those Girls so bonny:
Where they had store of Mirth, and mickle laughter:
Therefore observe it for the best comes after.
To a Merry Scotch Tune, Or, *Up with Aley Aley, &c.*

[TWO CUTS]

Ack's a naughty Boy
   for calling his Mother Wh . . .
I'le tell you the reason why,
   because she was one before:
Then up with Aley, Aley,
   up with Frank so free,
In came wanton Willy,
   and smuggl'd them hansomely.

Four and twenty Lasses
   went over *Trenchmore* Lee,   10
And all of them were Mow'd,
   unless it were two or three
Then up with Aley, Aley,
   up with jumping Joan,
In came wanton Willy,
   and then the game went on.

Jonny he plaid with *Jenny,*
   and *Jenny* she plaid with *Jock;*
And he pull'd out a Guinney,
   to buy her a Holland Smock: 20

[1] Printed from Roxburghe Collection, II, 502, 503 (also in *Roxburghe Ballads*, VII, 342–44).

Then up with Aley, Aley,
*   up with Sue, and Siss,*
And in came wanton Willy,
*   and then they Mump and Kiss.*

Willy he teuk up *Moggy,*
    and askt if she would Dance,
But oh! how she did Simper,
    with many a wink, and glance:
Then up with Aley, Aley,
*   up with Bess so Brown;*
In came wanton Willy,
*   and tumbl'd them upside down.*   30

[CUT]

The Piper he struck up,
    and Merrily he did play,
The shakeing of the sheets,
    and eke the Irish hay:
Then up with Aley, Aley,
*   up with Priss and Prue;*
In came wanton Willy,
*   amongst the Jovial crew.*   40

The Awd wife she came up.
    and she began to Mutter,
I think you'r all grown
    you make so great a clutter:
Then up with Aley, Aley,
*   up with Doll, and Jane.*
In came wonton Willy,
*   and Kist them over again.*

The Coague of Ale went round,
    and each one drank a Health,   50
Their sorrows for to drown'd,
    they took no care for wealth:
Then up with Aley, Aley,
*   up with mincing Nan:*
In came wanton Willy,
*   and prov'd himself a Man.*

The Parson of the Parish,
    he left the Kirk in haste,
For at this merry meeting,
    he would not be the last: 60

Then up with **Aley, Aley,**
   up with **Kate,** *and* **Joyce;**
In came wanton **VVilly,**
   and there he took his choice.

And thus with nappy Liquor,
   their senses they did warm,
It made their wits the quicker,
   they thought not any harm;
Then up with **Aley, Aley,**
   with Boozy **Bridget** *too;*   70
In came wanton **VVilly,**
   and he began to Wooe.

Deale faw my lugs, quo *Jammy,*
   My Friends I pray now hark
Let us conclude a Wedding,
   to make the Parson wark:
Then up with **Aley, Aley,**
   up with **Sarah,** *and* **pegg:**
In came wanton **VVilly,**
   and there he danc't a Jigg.   80

The bargain was agreed,
   that *Billy,* he should have **Bess,**
And so they sent out *Harry,*
   for to invite the Guess:
Then up with **Aley, Aley,**
   up with **Gillian** *fair:*
In came wanton **VVilly,**
   and them twa made a pair.

Now with this jovial Wedding,
   I do conclude my Song,   90
And wish that *Trenchmore* Lasses,
   they may live merry and long:
Then up with **Aley, Aley,**
   up with all the train:
We will all be merry,
   if e're we meet again.

                    With Allowance.

Printed for P. Brooksby, at the Golden Ball, West Smithf[ield.][1]

[1] The colophon is supplied in script on the broadside.

13

THE

Soldiers CATCH:

OR,

𝕿𝖍𝖊 𝕾𝖆𝖑𝖎𝖘𝖇𝖚𝖗𝖞 𝕵𝖎𝖌𝖌,[1]

Lately Sung at COURT.

Licensed according to Order.

To the Tune of, *Let the Soldiers Rejoyce.*

1

ROom boys, room, room boys, room;
For from[2] *Ireland* we com:
We have mawl'd the Original *Tories;*
We have baffled the League
Between *Monsieur* and *Teague,*
And eclips'd the *Grand Lewis* his Glories.

2

They all fly in the Field,
Their best Garrisons yield,   (Passes.
They stand trembling, while we take their
Our brave King at our Head,
We fear no Steel, nor Lead,
But laugh at their Beads and their Masses.

3

If some Bloud we have spilt.
To compound for the Guilt,
In *Love*'s Camp *we* will do double Duty;
Mankind *we* will repair,
With the *Leave* of the Fair,
And pay our *Arrears* to *true Beauty.*

[1] Printed from Pepys Collection, V, 68, a white-letter ballad.
[2] *form* in the original.

413

4

Our worst *Noise* in the Pit,
Shall pass all for good Wit,
While the *City* and the *Bumkins* adore us.
We will pay the *Rogues* well,
Their *Wives Bellies* shall *swell*,
And the Cuckolds at random shall score us.

5

The next Summer for *France*.
We will boldly *advance*,
Our *Noble Redeemer* shall *lead* us:
We will *break* the *Slaves* Chains,
And drink off their *Champains*,
To the *Health* of that *Heroe* that *freed* us.

6

He hates *Lewis-le-Grand*,
Like a *true English* Man,
And ne'er will consent to a Treaty,
Till each *Neighbouring Crown*
Have what's justly their own,
And *the French strike Sail when they meet ye.*

7

Since *Elizabeth*'s Reign,
No *Protestant Queen*,
We have had, but the present, *God bless her*
Since our *Edward* the Fourth,
No *brave Prince* of such worth,
But *William*, his Valiant *Successor*.

8

With a *Queen* so *devout*,
And a *People* so stout;
A *Parliament* that will supply *'em*,
A *Cause* that is Right,
And a *King* that will fight,
Our *Enemies* all *we defie 'em*.

Printed for *S. Smith*, 1691.

14

[A SPANISH GENTLEMAN AND AN
ENGLISH GENTLEWOMAN]¹

[*Man.*] Maddame dangloyse me tell you verye true
    me be verye muche Enamored wythe youe
    me loue you muche bettro then I cane well saye
    no queris hablario hyspanyolaye

[*Woman.*] Segnior Domegro me loue you twyse so well
    but what your meaninge is sure that cane I not tell
    for lacke of your languayge I knowe not what to saye
    because I cannot parle youre spanyolaye

[*Man.*] Ladye mattresso knowe you notynge what
    me praye you what call you me tyttye poure tatt   10
    make me your lovere & shewe me some playe
    me teache you parlere the fyne spaniolaye.

[*Woman.*] Par moyfoye monseure you bene a merrye man
    what your meanynge is sure I well vndrestand
    you seme suche a wanton I swere by my faye
    that I dare not lerne of you to speake spaniolaye

[*Man.*] Counta my goutt ladye my shaumbre to come bye
    me make you de velcome as velcome as I
    the grand pettye tynge me geue you by my faye
    Coutte for to lerne you to speake spaniolaye   20

[*Woman.*] your spanyolaye hyt is all so trymme
    thatt hyt for to lerne I wold fayne begyne
    ffor teachynge of me your spanyolaye
    you shall haue a kysse of me once euerye daye

[*Man.*] Gotte a mercye goutte maddame gott a mercye for tys
    twentye gramercyes me geue you for one kys
    you be de goutte ladye you do as you saye
    me warrant you quiecklye the best spanyolaye

¹ Printed from Rawl. Poet. MS 108, fol. 12. See p. 201 for the title. In the manuscript *u* in *you* and *r* in *segnior* are regularly written above the *o*, *ll* is crossed, and
certain words, expanded here as indicated, are abbreviated.

[*Woman.*]   but tell me my segnior where your chaumbre ys
                  that when I come to you I nede not to mys   30
                  and I wyll not lett to do as I saye
                  to come to your chaumbre once euerye daye

[*Man.*]   Ladye prettye ladye praye gotte me neuer see
                  but tatte you make muche comfort to[1] me
                  my hart dothe leape quycke within my bellye
                  oh my swette maystres you make me so merrye

                  my shaumbre hard by the signe of the pye
                  make axe for domegro the segnior where he lye
                  the lane you call abshurche by lumbar strete
                  me knowe when you com me there you wyll mete   40

[*Woman.*]   I wold not come when[2] you haue companye   [fol. 12v]
                  I wyll send word before that no man me see
                  you be so iolye so prettye and neette
                  that you & me els some folke wyll suspecte

[*Man.*]   You come torre a backe dore my payge lett you in
                  me make all tyngz for you so gaye and so tryme
                  you no sonner come aboue in my shaumbre
                  but you smell the swette muske & de fyne aumbre

[*Woman.*]   ffare well then segnior a dewe for this tyme
                  provyde you good cheare somme sugere & wyne   50
                  I loue verye well the thynges that be lyckeryshe
                  marche payne & quince pye I care for no stockfyshe

[*Man.*]   Bezeles maynes oh you my faire ladye
                  me lacke[3] no tynge datte me maye get dayntye
                  take you my shane here & make your gorg gaye
                  no man in the world tat haue so muche shoye.

                                        ffinis

[1] *for* is crossed out before *to* in the manuscript.
[2] *when* is inserted above the line.   [3] After *lacke* a word has been crossed out.

15

[THE MERRY WOOING OF ROBIN AND JOAN.][1]

To the Tune of The beginning of the
World. R. P. Delight.

[*Robin.*]   O Mother, chave bin a batchelour,
        This twelve and twanty yeare;
  And I'ze have often beene a wowing,
    And yet cham never the neare:
  Ione Gromball chee'l ha' non s'[2] mee,
    Ize look so like a lowt;
  But I vaith, cham as propper a man as zhe
    Zhee need not be zo stout.

  She zaies if ize, cond[3] daunce and zing,
    As *Thomas Miller* con,   10
  Or cut a cauper, as litle *Iack Taylor:*
    O how chee'd love mee thon.
  But zoft and faire, chil none of that,
    I vaith cham not zo nimble;
  The Tailor hath nought to trouble his thought
    But his needel and his thimble,

[*Mother.*] O zon, th'art of a lawfull age,
    And a jolly tidy boy,
  Ide have thee try her once a gaine,
    She can but say thee nay: 20
[*Robin.*] Then O Gramarcy mother,   P. 169
    Chill zet a good vace o' the matter,
  Chill dresse up my zon[4] as fine as a dog
    And chill have a fresh bout at her.

---

[1] Printed from *Wit Restored* (1658), pp. 168–71. A version, here called W, is found in *Wit and Drollery* (1682), pp. 90–93, with the title "The West-Country Batchelors Complaint," and another, here called B, in the Roxburghe Collection, II, 343 (*Roxburghe Ballads*, VII, 307–11), with the title "The Merry Wooing of Robin & Joan The West-Country Lovers. To the tune of, *The beginning of the World*, Or, *Sellengers Round*, Or, *Great Boobe*." There are numerous variations in the three versions, especially in the spelling of the dialect words. Only a few are cited. In these B and W agree.

[2] *none a* in W.   [3] *cou'd* in W.   [4] *Zell* in W.

	And first chill put on my zunday parrell
	That's lac't about the quarters;
	With a paire of buckram slopps,
	And a vlanting paire of garters.
	With my sword tide vast to my zide,
	And my grandvathers dug'en and dagger 30
	And a Peacocks veather in my capp
	Then oh how I'ch shall swagger.
[*Mother.*]	Nay tak thee a lockrum napkin son,
	To wipe thy snotty nose,
[*Robin.*]	T's noe matter vor that, chill snort it out,
	And vlurt it athart my cloths:
[*Mother.*]	Ods, bodikins nay fy away,
	I prethee son do not so:
	Be mannerly son till thou canst tell,
	Whether sheele ha' thee or noe, 40
[*Robin.*]	But zirrah Mother harke a while
	Whoes that that comes so near?
[*Mother.*]	Tis *Ione Grumball*, hold thy peace,
	For feare that she doe heare.
[*Robin.*]	Nay on't be she, chill dresse my words
	In zuch a scholards grace,
	But virst of all chall take my honds,
	And lay them athwart her vace.
	Good morrow my honey my sugger-candy, P. 170
	My litle pretty mouse, 50
	Cha hopes thy vather and mother be well,
	At home at thine own house.
	I'ch am zhame vac't to show my mind,
	Cham zure thou knowst my arrant:
	Zum zen, Jug, that I mun a thee.[1]
[*Joan.*]	At leasure Sir I warrant.
	You must (Sir Clowne) is for the King,
	And not for such a mome,
	You might have said, by leave[2] faire maid,
	And let your (must) alone. 60

[1] In W the line reads, "Zome zain, *Jugg*, that I mun ha thee."
[2] *by're leave* in W.

[*Robin.*]   Ich am noe more¹ nor clowne thats vlat,
        Cham in my zunday parrell,
        I'ch came vor love and I pray so tak't,
        Che hopes che will not quarrell.

[*Joan.*]²   O *Robbin* dost thou love me so well?
[*Robin.*]²   Ivaith, abommination,
[*Joan.*]   Why then you should have fram'd your words
        Into a finer fashion.
[*Robin.*]   Vine vashions and vine speeches too
        As schollards volks con utter,   70
        Chad wrather speak but twa words plaine
        Thon haulfe a score and stutter.

        Chave³ land, chave houss, chave twa vat beasts,
        Thats better thon vine speeches;
[*Joan.*]²   T's a signe that Fortune favours fooles
        She lets them have such riches.
[*Robin.*]²   Hark how she comes upon mee now,   P. 171
        I'd wish it be a good zine,
[*Joan.*]²   He that will steale any wit from thee
        Had need to rise betime.⁴   80

¹ *mome* is probably the correct reading. W, doubtless following this text, changes the line to "Ich am no more a Clown, that's vlat."

² The name of the speaker is given in B.

³ B has *Robin.* before this line.

⁴ There is the following addition in B:

    [*Robin.*]   Ise, Vaith Ise am no vool Ise Zay
                Ise think you Zud know better:
                Dost thou think Ise not know I pray,
                Good speech and manners better:
    [*Joan.*]   'Tis sure you know not if you did
                You'd nee'r have been a Lover.
    [*Robin.*]   Nay nay, my Dear, nay nay udzlid
                Why mun not I discover.

                What long in secret i'se ha kept
                And woud ha longer done it
                Had not my Passion been Zo heap'd
                Ise had no more Room for it.
    [*Joan.*]   And are you in Love as you Zay.
    [*Robin.*]   Yes Vaith and Troth Ise Zware it
    [*Joan.*]   Then prithee *Robin* set the day
                And wees ee'n both be Married.

16

The North Country lovers:

Or: The plain Downright wooing between *John* and *Joan*.

A Pleasant new Song as it was sung before the Court at *Windsor*.

Johney Addresses to his **Joan** most dear
And on her Piggsneys casteth many a lear,
Telling her how he wealth and love had got

The which so far transports the subtel slut,
That unto **Venus** sport she drew him in
And in her mortrice fastened straight his pin.

To a New tune. Quoth **John** *to* **Joan**.[1]

[TWO CUTS]

John.

QUoth **John** to **Joan** what wilt thou have me,
  I prithee now do and i'le marry with thee,
My Cow and Calf my house and Rents
And all my Lands and Tenments.
Say my Joan, *say my* Joan *will not this do,*
I connot I connot come every every day to woe.

I have Corn and Hay in the Barn hard by
And three fat Hoggs pend up in sty,
I have a mare and she is cole black
I ride on her Taile instead of her back   10
Say my Joan, *say my* Joan *what wilt thou do,*
I connot I connot come every every day to woe.

I have a Cheese upon the shelf
[I'se cannot eat it awe my self:]
[I have three Mark ty'd up in a Ragg,][2]
In the Nook of a Chimney instead of a Bag.
Say my Joan, *say my* Joan *will not this do,*
I connot I connot come every every day to woe.

To marry I would have thy consent
But I faith I cannot complement,   20

[1] Printed from Pepys Collection, IV, 24.

[2] Cut off at the foot of the first column; supplied from the corresponding stanza of "The Country-man's Delight," Roxburghe Collection, II, 74 (see *Roxburghe Ballads*, III, 594).

I connot court but hey gee who
Such as I say at Cart or Plow,
Say my Joan, *say my* Joan *what wilt thou do*
I connot nounds I connot come every every day to
                                        (*woe.*

Joan.

What i'st my **John** that thou wouldst ha
A milking I must and cannot stay,
Ise hear mine Kine begin to mooe,
And ise must dable in the dew.   (*do*
Then say me John *say me* John *what wouldst thou*
[*Since you connot*, &c.][1]   30

[SMALL CUT AT THE HEAD OF THE THIRD COLUMN]

Come shall we gang to yonder hedge
To see if **Margery** be fledge,
Or ise to morrow gang to kirk
And i'le provide for thee a Sirk,
Say my John *say my* John *what wouldst thou do*
Since you connot, &c.

John.

Udsbobs i se like it wondrous well
But think'st thou that the hedge wont tell
For if it should by these new shoone
Ise in revenge would cut it down,   40
Then say my Joan *say my* Joan *wilt thou do*
I connot I connot, &c.

Joan.

Ise under yond broad Oak will lye
Upon mine back to see the Skye,
But first you shall swear on my paile
That you to morrow will not fail.
Say my John *say my* John *what wilt thou do*
Since you connot, &c.

John.

Now we are come unto the place
Let me my pretty Pig embrace,   50
To morrow for the marriage day
And then the Priest will bid us play.
Say my Joan *say my* Joan *shall I do*
I connot, &c.

[1] Cut off at the foot of the second column; supplied from the next stanza.

Joan.

But after this now we must part
Which grieves poor *Joan* unto the heart,
But till to morrow we divide
And then Ise shall be *Johney's* bride
Say my John *say my* John *when must we do*
Since you connot, &c.   60

John.

I marry shat thou and have all
That thy *Johney* his own can call
Farwell then till to morrow day
And then wee'l freely sport and play
Say my Joan *say my* Joan *is not this true*
Seeing I connot I connot come every every day to
                                          (*woe.*[1]

---

[1] The seller's name has apparently been cut away. A few dots indicate the tops of some letters. The ballad was probably printed some time after the Restoration. The cut of a woman at the head of the second column appears also in "The Loyal Soldiers Courtship" printed for P. Brooksby, J. Deacon, J. Blare, and J. Back (Pepys Collection, IV, 207).

17

. . . . ¹

OR

A merry discourse, twixt him and his *Ioane*,
That sometimes did live as never did none,
But now at the last she proves very kinde,
And doth what heed have her, as here you may finde.

To three severall tunes, called, But I know what I know, Captaine
Ward, and Gilty Coate Peggy.

[CUTS OF A MAN AND OF A WOMAN]

The Tune, but I know, &c.

Man.

[C] Ome *Joane* by thy owne deerest husband sit downe
And cast away from thee this impudent frowne,
[You] know I doe love thee as deere as I doe,
[Bear]e² with a Taylor³ that's honest and true.

Woman.

[Awa]y thou dissembling varlot a way,
[And] leave this thy prating and cogging, I say,
[For] whilst like a drunkard thou thus dost remaine
[I ne]ver shall love thee, I tell thee againe.

¹ Printed from the unique broadside in the Roxburghe Collection, I, 82, 83 (also
by Chappell in *Roxburghe Ballads*, I, 248–53). The first line of the title has been cut
away, and the text cut into on the left of the first sheet and the right of the second.
Words in brackets, unless otherwise indicated, are supplied by Chappell (C). A few
marks of punctuation have probably been cut away without injuring the text. A number of letters and marks of punctuation are blurred, but I have not indicated them.

² C reads [*Forbear*]e, but only three or four letters are missing.

³ C emends to *Tinker*, pointing out the fact that the ballad deals with a tinker.

423

[Tune,]¹ *Captaine Ward.*

Man.

[Now]² wife what would'st thou have me doe
   [m]ore³ then I now have done,   10
[Did] not I pawne my cloathes for thee,
   [an]d likewise sould my shune,
[Pu]t my shirt in lavender,
   [my] cloake is like wise sould:
[And d]ost⁴ thou *Joane* for all this love,
   [be]gin with *Jacke* to scould.

Woman.

Why, thou deboist and drunken sot,
   did'st doe all this for me,
Or for the love you alwayes bare,
   to evill company?   20
And therefore hold thy selfe content,
   and leave this idle prate,
Or as I am thy honest wife,
   Ile lay thee o're the pate.

[Tune,] *Gilty Coate Peggy.*⁵

Man.

Come chucke no more of this, but sit thee downe by me,
And then what is amisse, Ile mend in verity,
My money I will save out of the Cup and Can,
And keepe thee fine and brave, as I am an honest man:
Then chide no more my deere, but all my faults remit,
And then as I am here, Ile mend my drunken fit.   30

Woman.

How many times hast thou this promised unto me,
And yet hast broke thy vow the more's the shame for thee
And therefore Ile be wise, and take your word no more,
But scratch out both your eyes if you goe out of dore;
And therefore sit you still and stirre not for your life,
I once will have my will, although I am your wife.

¹ I follow Chappell in supplying the word *Tune* here and later.
² C has [*Oh,*]. The rounded edge of a last letter remains.
³ C capitalizes the words supplied by him for these indented lines.
⁴ C reads [*Why d*]*ost.*
⁵ Chappell has the note, "The lines to this tune rhyme in the middle throughout the ballad. So, virtually, two lines are printed as one."

The second part, to the same tunes.

[Tune,] *But I know what, &c.*

Man.

WEll, do what thou wilt, I am thine at command,
  But let not my neighbours of this understand;
For that if thou dost, I know it will be
A shame to thy selfe, disgrace unto me.   40

Woman.

No matter for that, Ile make you to know,
What 'tis for to iniure a loving wife so,
In pawning her goods, and making her be,
A scorne to her neighbours, and all long of thee.

[Tune,] *Captaine, &c.*

Man.

Come *Joane*, be satisfied I pray,
  forgive me what is past,
And I will thee never[1] offend,
  whilst life and breath doth last:
My pots and my Tobacco too,
  Ile turne, for to be briefe,   50
Into a dainty house-hold loafe,
  and lusty powder-beefe.

Woman.

Well, if I thought all this were true,
  and that thou didst intend
To doe as thou relates to me,
  I then should be thy friend;
But I am *Jacke* so fearefull growne,
  of thy relaps againe,
That I can little credite give,
  to what you now maintaine.   60

[Tune,] *Gilty Coate Peggy, &c.*

Man.

Here's my hand sweet Ducke, what I have said to thee,
Ile keepe, if I have lucke, till such time that I dye,

---

[1] C emends to *never thee.*

And fore that I am dead my love I will unfold
To helpe thee in thy need, if that thou wilt not scould,
I will not cossened be, I tell thee gentle *Joane*,
But I will bring to thee my sheete, and Ile have none.

Woman.

Why then sweet-heart forgive the words that I have said,
For surely while I live, Ile never thee upbraid,
I will not scould nor brawle, but keepe my clapper still
And come when thou dost call do all things to thy will,   70
Then *Jacke*, forgive thy *Joane*, that is to thee so kinde,
Or else as hard as stone I surely shall thee finde.

[Tune,] *But I know, &c.*

Man.[1]

Why, here is my hand, I am pacified *Joane*,
And as I will live with thee never lived none,
Then be but as kind as I carefull to thee,
And then none new married shall better agree,

For thou with thy Kitchin-stuffe, I with my toyes,
My Hammer and Kittle, will make such a noyse,
That all that does heare me shall tell it for true,
I mend well their worke and pleasure um too.   80

[Tune,] *Captaine, &c.*

Woman.

Then *Jacke* take up thy budget straight,
    thy kettles brasse enough,
And I will follow thee and cry,
    Maides have you any Kitchin-stuffe;
And then the neighbours seeing us
    so friendly for to goe
Will say that they are loving growne,
    who thought it would be so.

---

[1] This speech is printed as one eight-line stanza in the original.

[Tune,] *Gilty Coate, &c.*

Man.

Then to the Ale-house we will go with mighty speed
And seale up presently what we have now decreed,   90
A full pot of the best, a crust, and so away,
And then we will protest we can no longer stay:
This is a thriving course, if I do not mistake,
I am sure I have done worse but now amends Ile m[ake.]

Woman.

Well say no more, sweet-heart but let us both away
For friends you know must part, though ne're so long[1] [they stay;]
Go thou through Canon-street, Ile take the laines a[nd Row,]
And then at night we'le meet at home for ought we kn[ow:]
But if I be not *Jacke*, at home so soone as you,
It shall but little lacke: and so sweet-heart adieu.   100

[Tune,] *But I know, &c.*

[Man?]

And thus you have heard an end of my song,
Which I would be loath that any should wrong,
But if that you do, I tell you but so,
I little will say, but I know what I know.

FINIS.

Ed. Ford.

Printed at London for F. Coules.

[1] Only a small part of *g* remains.

18

[A DROLL

BY THOMAS JORDAN][1]

This Song being sung and applauded, a chearful and temperate
Cup of Wine goes about; in the mean time the Consort of Musick
play two or three sutes of Airs; which being ended, they make provision for a piece of Drollery to be sung in Parts, and Shapes by
these three, *viz.*

Hoyden, the Country-man of the West. *Freeman*, the Citizen.
Billet the Souldier.

Enter Hoyden.

Hoyd.   FRom how-d'ye calt Town in what call y'um zhere,
       To *Lungean* cham come, Lord what vine volks are here;
Zure thick is the place Ich zmell the good cheer:
Chil knock at the gate then—what ho! God be here.   [*Knocks.*

Enter the Citizen.

Freem. What are you Sir?
Hoyd. A West-Country mon Sir. (*Free.*) Good Bumkin forbear,
Such Hobnails as you are do seldom come here.
Hoyd. Uds zooks here s a vellow would make a man zwear;
Ich come to speak Sir with Mr. Lord Mayor:
Free. What to do Sir?   10
Hoyd. To zee his vine Doublet, his Chain, and his Ruff,
His Beaver, his Gown, and zuch vinical stuff:
Free. And what do you think of a kick or a cuff ?

---

[1] Printed from *London's Resurrection to Joy and Triumph* (1671); also printed in
Fairholt's *Lord Mayors' Pageants*, II, 123–27. The early version of this droll in *Merry
Drollerie* (1661), pp. 171–75 (D), called "The new Medley" lacks the names of the
speakers and the stage directions. It has a number of variations of spelling and even
of text, some of which are recorded in the notes. It opens:

> From what-you-call't town, in what-call-you't shire
> To *London* Cham come, what fine Volk are here!
> Sure thick is the place, itch smell the good chear,
> Che'le knock at the Yate, then what ho God be here.
>   What are you Sir?
> Cham a West Country man Zur.
> Good Bumkin forbear, etc.

428

Hoyd. If my whip will but hold vaith[1] chill give thee enough;
And well laid on. [*Whips him.*
    Free. Hold hold prethee Country-man be not so hot.
    Hoyd. Chave a great[2] mind to lay a long lace on thy Coat.
    Free. Prethe tell me thy name, and my Lord Mayor shall know't?
    Hoyd. My name is *Tom Hoyden,* what zayst thou to that?
    Free. Tom Hoyden? 20

The Tune alters. P. 9

Then *Tom Hoyden,* pack hence to *Croyden;*
    The Country s fitter for thee.
    Hoyden. Though you abhor us, and care not vor us,
        Without us you can no[3] be.
    Free. We can live without you, and your rural rout.[4]
    Hoyd. Did we not vittle your house
        My Lady Mayress with all her Fairies[5]
        Would zhit as small as a Mouse.[6]
    Free. We have mony. (*Hoyd.*) And we have honey.
    Free. We have the Silver and Gold. 30
    Hoyd. We have fuel. (*Free*) And we have Jewel.
    Hoyd. And we have zheep in the vold.
    Free. We have Silk enough. (*Hoyd.*) We have milk enough.
    Free. We have treasure untold.
We have means and ease. (*Hoyd.*) We have Beans and Pease,
    Bacon hold belly hold.
    Free. We have forces.[7] (*Hoyd.*) And we have horses.
    Free. And we have powder and shot.
    Hoyd. We have Pullets. (*Free.*) And we have Bullets.
    Hoyd. And we have spirits as whot. 40
    Free. We have Honours. (*Hoyd.*) And we have Mannors.
    Free. And we are wall'd about.
    Hoyd. But when we begin to keep our Cattel in
        Vaith you'l quickly come out.
    Free. We have Gallies. (*Hoyd.*) And we have Vallies.
    Free. And we have Cannons of brass:
        We have Feathers. (*Hoyd.*) And we have Weathers
        On Mountains matted with grass.
    Free. We have Wine and Spice, Sugar, Fruit, and Rice.

[1] D *but last, ifaith.*
[2] D *Che have a huge.*   [4] D *rustick coat.*   [6] D *Lowse.*
[3] D *cannot.*   [5] D *Baries.*   [7] D *Purses.*

Hoyd. We have good Barley and Wheat,   50
And were we put to t, better can live without
    Money than you without meat.

Chorus of both Voices.

Both.   *Then since 'tis so that we cannot be*
       Without one another, let us two agree;
       Let the Country prove fruitful, and City be free.
       No Climat in Europe *so happy as we.* [They stand aside.

      Enter Billet *the Souldier. The Tune changeth.*   P. 10
Bill. He that would be made by a Soldiers Trade,
    Let him be encourag'd by me:
    For never did any man gain by the Blade   60
      As we have in[1] Forty three.
Hoyd. What Gallant[2] is that? (*Free.*) It seems a Soldat.
Bill. Good morrow. (*Hoyd.*) Good morrow to thee.
Bill. Why how now, good Friends, what, all for your ends
    Will you make up a Peace without me?
    You know in a word the Power of the Sword.
Free. A Cannon can conquer a King.
Bill. A sharp Sword will make a City[3] to shake.
Hoyd. Vaith you have the World in a Zling.
Bill Compare the whole Land to the Parts of a Man.   70
Hoyd. The Countrey's the Legs and the Toes.
Free. And, without a Riddle, the City's the Middle.
Bill. The Soldier's the Head. (*Hoyd.*) And the *Nose.*
Bill. Though now we wear Blades, we once were of Trades,
    And shall be whilst Trading endures:
    Our Officers are, although Men of War,
      Some Goldsmiths, some Drapers. (*Hoyd.*) And Brewers.
Bill. They fortunate are, and valiant in War.
Free. They were so. (*Hoyd.*) Che very well knew 'um.
Bill. Some of them were Lords. (*Hoyd.*) Some of 'em wore Cords,
    And went up to *Hangum tuum.*[4]   81
Bill. Do you get encrease, we'll guard you with Peace,
    The Sword shall not come where the Ax is:
    We ll take off your Cares, we ll take off your Fears.
Hoyd. I but when will you take off our Taxes?

---

[1] D *since.*   [2] D *Fellow.*   [3] D *Scepter.*
[4] The four lines ending with *tuum* are omitted in D.

Bill. We keep Nations[1] from ye, that would overcome ye,
    Whilst you do Plow, Harrow, and Thresh:
    The *Frenchman's* our own. (*Hoyd.*) Faith, What's bred in the
    Will hardly get out of the Flesh.[2]
    (Bone

The Tune changeth.

Free. Then, Sir, the City still shall fit ye   90
    With what you deserve.
Hoyd. The Countrey Cow-man, and the Plow-man
    Will not let thee starve.
Free. With Buff and Bever we will ever   P. 11
    Bless thy Back and Head.
Hoyd. We'll give thee yearly Wheat and Barley,
    For thy Beer and Bread.[3]
Free. I will give thee Silver, and enough good Ammunition.[4]
    I seal to this Condition.
Hoyd. And so do I, introth.   100
Bill. I will spend my Blood, Sir.
Free. And I will waste[5] my Treasure,
Hoyd. To do the Soldier pleasure.
Bill. Why now I thank ye both.

Chorus *of all Three.*

Let the City, the Countrey, the Camp, and the Court,
Be the Places of Pleasure, and Royal Resort:
And let us observe, in the midst of our Sport,
That Fidelity makes us as firm as a Fort:
A Union well-grounded no Malice can hurt.   [Exeunt.

At the Conclusion of this Droll the Second Course comes in. . . .

[1] D *Spaniards.*

[2] In D the following two stanzas appear here:

    We quarter in Villages, Cities, and Towns,
    And sometimes we lie in the Fields.
    But if from your Coulours you offer to run,
    Then you must be laid neck and heels.

    Through Countries we march, & for enemies search,
    And command all things in Bravadoes.
    But oh, my good friend, if you do offend,
    I'm sure you must have the Strappadoes.

[3] D lacks this and the preceding line.

[4] D *We will give thee money enough, and Amunition.*   [5] D *spend.*

19

[THE WOOING OF NAN[1]]

[*Rowland*][2]   Seest thou not[3] yon farmers sonn
         he hath stolne my love frome me alas
      what shall I doe I am vndonn
         my hart will neer be as it was [4]

      oh but[5] he gives her gay gold rings.
         & tufted gloves to were vppon a[6] holly day/
      and many other goodly things,
         that hath stolne my love away/[7]

frend   Lett him give her gaie gold rings.
         or stufted[8] gloves were they nere so sweete my boy.[9] 10
      or were her lovers lords or kings
         they should not cary the wench away

---

[1] I print from a rotograph of Dulwich College MSS, Vol. I. fol. 272 (No. 139). The text is in English script; and most of the stage directions and speakers' names are in Italian script. The punctuation seems to indicate the end of verses, though it is irregular and disappears early. W indicates Warner's readings in the *MSS and Muniments of Dulwich College*, pp. 60–61; C those of Collier in the *Alleyn Papers*, pp. 8–11. I have not given all of the minor variations of Collier's text where Warner's readings support mine. Many of his changes are designed to correct the meter. He omits all stage directions. The first half he prints in eight-line stanzas, assigning each to one speaker. Warner's changes in punctuation and capitalization are not indicated in my notes.

[2] C supplies *Jack;* W gives the names of speakers only when they are in the manuscript.

[3] *that* has been deleted after *not*.

[4] Possibly a stanza spoken by the Friend has been omitted here.

[5] *but* is inserted above the line.

[6] For *to were vppon a* C substitutes [*for*].

[7] *lett* has been deleted after *away*. The scribe began a new line with the next word, "frend." Preceding each speech for which the name of the speaker is given, a light straight line from an inch to two inches in length separates parts of the text. The speakers' names are written in the margin.

[8] C reads *tufted*.

[9] For *sweete my boy* C has [*gay*].

[*Rowland*]¹   Oh² but a daunces wondrous³ well
    & wth his daunce⁴ stolne away⁵ her love from me.
   yett she was⁶ wont to say I bore away⁶ the bell
    for daunsing & for Courtisie. /*daunsing*⁷

*Jack*⁸   fie lusty yonker⁹ what doe you heer,
    that you are not all a¹⁰ daunsing on the greene to day.
   we feare¹¹ perce the farmers¹² sonn
    is lik to carry your¹³ wench away,   20

[*Rowland*]¹   good dick bid them all¹⁴ com hether
    & tell perce from me beside,
   that if he think to haue the wench,
    heer he stands shall lie wth the bride/¹⁵

W[*ench's*] *fre*[*nd*].¹⁶
   Fy nan fie willt thou¹⁷ forsake thie¹⁸ olde lover¹⁹
    for any other²⁰ newcom guest
   thou l[ong]²¹ time his love did know.
    & whie shouldst thou now vse him so²²

¹ C does not indicate a new speaker.

² Lines in the MS above and to the left of *Oh* are probably intended to indicate a new speech. C omits *Oh*.

³ The reading is doubtful. W reads *wondrers*; C, *wonders*.

⁴ C reads *daunces*. An *s* may have been obliterated on the margin of the MS.

⁵ For *stolne away* C reads *stole*. After *away* a deletion has been made.

⁶ Omitted by C.

⁷ Written in English script.

⁸ *Jack* has been written above a deleted word, possibly *entr*. *Jack* is probably an error for *Dick*.

⁹ *Iack fie will* has been deleted and *lusty yonker* written above.

¹⁰ C omits *that you are* and *all a*.

¹¹ C inserts *For* in place of *we feare* and puts *I feare* at the end of the line to supply the rhyme.

¹² W reads *farmer's*, probably through an oversight.

¹³ *your* has been written above a deleted *the*.

¹⁴ After *all* some words have been deleted at the end of a line of the MS. The letters *to g* are legible.

¹⁵ The curved mark here comes at the end of a line and section of the MS.

¹⁶ W has *W*[*ench*] *Fre*[*nd*]. Dick seems to be the character speaking.

¹⁷ W reads *then*; the word does not differ from other *thou's* in the MS.

¹⁸ W reads *thee*; the *i* is clear.

¹⁹ For this line C has: *Fy, Nan! why use thy old lover soe.*

²⁰ *other* is inserted above the line.

²¹ The rotograph indicates a hole in the MS; both C and W read *long*.

²² W reads *soe*; only *o* is legible on the blurred margin. C omits *&* at the beginning of the verse and substitutes for the last four words *not use him best*.

[*Wench*][1]   Whie bony dicky[2] I will no[t][3] forsake
         my bony rowland for any gold   30
        if he can daunce as well as[4] perce
        he shall haue[5] my hart in hold[6]

per[ce]   why then my harts letts to this geer
        & by dauncing I may wonn
        my nan whose love I hold so[7] deere
        as any creatur[8] vnder sonn

They[9] *daunce*

Entr gent.[10]   [Good][11] speed frende[12] may I[13] be so bold to daunce
        a turne[14] or to w[th]out offence
        for as[15] I was walking[16] by chaunce
        I was told you[17] daunst to gain a [wench][18]   40

[1] C does not indicate a new speaker.

[2] For *Whie bony dicky* C has *Bonny Dick*.

[3] W reads *not*; a hole renders *t* illegible.

[4] The *s* of this *as* and a *well* following it have been scored through.

[5] W and C read *have*.

[6] W reads *hold*; the *d* on the margin is almost illegible. The transcript of W ends here.

[7] C reads *soe*; a small hole has obliterated all of the *e* except possibly the beginning of the stroke.

[8] C reads *realme* and inserts *the* after *vnder*.

[9] *y* has apparently been written over an *n*.

[10] C substitutes for the speaker and the first line:
        Frend.   Then, gentles, ere I speed from hence,
             I will be so bold to daunce
His five-line stanza does not conform to the metrical scheme, and his distribution of the speeches obscures the situation.

[11] Some blurred ink marks and a hole render the word illegible. I judge that originally there were at least four letters.

[12] The last symbol, somewhat blurred, might possibly be that for *es*, but it is not used elsewhere in the MS. The Gentleman probably addresses Dick, Nan's friend, as the others are still dancing.

[13] *may* is blurred; two letters are illegible after *I* and apparently deleted. A fold of the MS here accounts for the many difficulties.

[14] *a turne* has been written above a deleted word.

[15] There is a blank space after *as*, and the next word begins beyond a tear in the paper, suggesting that the tear was present when the jig was written down.

[16] After *walking* C inserts *along*.

[17] After *you* C substitutes for the rest of the line *did agree*.

[18] The scribe, coming to the margin, wrote this word above the line; *wench* is probably the reading, but only fragments of the letters remain.

[*Frend*]¹ Tis true good sir & this is shee²
　　　　　I hope³ yoʳ worshipp comes not to craue her
　　　　　for she hath lovers to or three
　　　　　　& he that daunces best must have her

gen[*t*] how say you sweete hart⁴ will you daunce wᵗʰ me.
　　　　　　& you [shall]⁵ haue both land & tower⁶
　　　　　My love shall want⁷ nor gold nor fee
　　　　　. . . . .

We[*nch*]⁸ I thank you sir for yoʳ good wil[l]⁹
　　　　　　But one of thes¹⁰ my love must be.
　　　　　I ham¹¹ but a homly countrie maid¹²　　　　50
　　　　　　& farr vnfitt¹³ for yoʳ degree

fre[*nd*] Take her good sir by the hande
　　　　　as she is fairest if she were¹⁴ fairer
　　　　　&¹⁵ by this daunce you shall well¹⁵ vnderstand
　　　　　　that¹⁵ he that can win her¹⁶ is lik to were¹⁷ her, /*daunce*
　　　　　　*.againe.*¹⁸

foole [*enters. The tune changes.*]
　　　　　& see you not nan to day my mothers mayde
　　　　　see you not my true love my prety nany
　　　　　shes gon to the greene to day to seek her love they say
　　　　　but she¹⁹ will haue myn none self if she haue any

---

¹ C does not indicate a new speaker.　　　² C has *she.*

³ For *I hope* C has *Hopes.* A heavy upright line after *e* may cover a deleted *s.*

⁴ For *sweete hart* C has *sweet.*　　　⁵ Omitted in the MS; supplied by C.

⁶ The reading is somewhat doubtful; the word has been written above the line at the margin. C substituted [*hill;*] to rhyme with *will* of the next stanza and added a line at the end of that stanza to furnish a rhyme for *maid*, printing the two stanzas as one eight-line stanza. The fact that each speaker has a four-line stanza indicates his error and shows that the last line of this stanza, probably with some rhyme word like *bower*, is missing.

⁷ This is C's reading; possibly the spelling is *woont.*

⁸ Omitted by C. The letters *We* have been written under a deletion in the midst of a line, with a straight mark before them.

⁹ C reads *will* ; only the *wi* and a stroke of the first *l* are now legible on the margin.

¹⁰ C reads *these.*　　　¹¹ C has *I'm.*

¹² C reads *maide*; the *e* may have been lost at the margin.

¹³ C reads *farre unfitt.*　　　¹⁴ For *if she were* C has *were she.*　　　¹⁵ Omitted by C.

¹⁶ After this word, a deleted one at the end of a line began *shu.*

¹⁷ C reads *like to ware.*

¹⁸ Verses indicating the Gentleman's victory may have been omitted. In the next two stanzas C reworked the text considerably to give six lines to each. His readings are not given, since none seem significant for a construction of the correct text.

¹⁹ *shell* in the original. *will* is inserted above the line with a caret.

wen[*ch*][1]   wellcom sweet hert & wellcom my tony[2]   60
                  wellcom my none[3] true love wellcom my huny[4]
                  this is my love that my husband must be
                  but when thou comst home boy as wellcom as he.

gen[*t*]   whie[5] how now sweet nany[6] I hope you doe[7] Iest
we[*nch*]   no by my troth sir[7] I love the foole[8] best
                  & if you be Ielous god give[9] you god[10] night
                  I feare you are[11] a gelding you caper so light   *Exnt.*

gen[*t*]   I thought she had but[7] Iested & ment but to[12] fable
                  but now I doe[13] see she hath play[d][14] wth his bable
                  I wishe all my frends by me to take heed[15]   70
                  that a foole com not neere you when[16] you mene to
                      spee[d][17]

[1] From this point on the names of the speakers are in old English script. I have italicized them in conformity with the rest of the MS.

[2] The first two lines of this stanza are blurred as the result of an old fold in the MS. This is the only word that seems to me doubtful. The *y* is clear. A straight line at the beginning is apparently part of a *t*. The other letters seem to be *o* and *n*, possibly *m*. The rhyme indicates *tony* rather than *tomy*, which is a more usual name for the fool. In a related passage of "The Louers Lamentation to his loue Nanny" (see p. 257) *Cunny* and *Hunny* rhyme, but the first letter here could hardly be *c*.

[3] This word begins with what looks like a *t* crossed out, the scribe probably having begun the next word *true*. It is possibly a blurred *l*.

[4] The scribe, coming to the margin, wrote *my huny* above the line.

[5] C reads *Why*.

[6] C reads *Nan*.

[7] Omitted by C.

[8] After *foole* C inserts *the*.

[9] C reads *giue*.

[10] C reads *good*.

[11] For *you are* C has *you're*.

[12] C has *a*.

[13] C changes *I doe* to *doe I*.

[14] *th* in *hath* is blurred; C supplies the *d* of *play*[*d*] omitted in the MS.

[15] C reads *heede*.

[16] Inserted above a deletion.

[17] The corner of the MS is torn away. C reads *speede*.

20

A proper new ballett, intituled Rowlands god sonne,
To the tune of loth to departe.[1]

Besse   Tell me Jhon why art thow soe sade.
        tell me Jhon, tell me Jhon,
        what iste will make thee glade.
        thow knowest thy misteries loues thee well.
        soe dearely as I shune to tell.
          Tell me I praye thee,
          lett nothinge dismaye thee.[2]
        but lett mee inioye thy loue thy loue.

Jhon   O misteris myne I cannot be merrye.
Bes   Tell mee Jhon, tell me Jhon,   10
        why lookes thow soe heauylye.
Jhon   my master carries a Jealous eie
        and warnes me ffrom your companie.
Bes.[3]   Heauens fforfend it.
Jo   you maist amende it,
        or ells fare well to our loue our loue

Be   Why Jhon, thy master mistrustes not thee
Jo   wo[4] is me wo is me,
        much he mistrus[t]eth[5] me.

---

[1] Printed from Rawlinson Poet. MS 185, fols. 15*v*–19*r*. The jig has been printed by Bolle in Herrig's *Archiv*, CXIV (1905), 348–51, and by Clark in *Shirburn Ballads*, pp. 354–60. I follow Clark in dividing the stanzas into eight lines. In the manuscript there are six, lines 2 and 3 of Clark's arrangement and usually 7 and 8 being written as one. Sometimes, however, lines 6 and 7 are written together (instead of 7 and 8) when the two lines belong to the same speech. Bolle invariably prints as one not only lines 2 and 3 but also 6 and 7 of Clark's form. There is no indentation in the manuscript. The title and speakers' names are in Italian script and the text in English. In the Italian, *I* is used for *J*. In the text a long capital is used for both *I* and *J*. After stanza 4 this is always crossed. I follow Bolle and Clark in normalizing these characters and in expanding contractions like *y^e* and *w^t*. I have not always indicated the divergent readings of Bolle and Clark in the transcription of the manuscript. Clark divides the ballad into scenes and adds a number of appropriate stage directions.

[2] Lines 6 and 7 are one in the manuscript.

[3] A small circle around the period is printed by Bolle as *o*.

[4] Written *who* with *h* scored through.

[5] Bolle reads *mistrustes*; Clark, *mistrusteth*.

| | and sayes he sawe me kisse your lippes | 20 |
| | suspectinge other secrete slippes |

Be   I will excuse thee.
Jo   I will refuse thee
    except you excuse our loue[, our loue.]

Be   Why tell me Jacke and be not afrade
        Tell me Jacke tell me Jacke,
        haste thow not hard it saied
    That weomen in loue haue witt at will
Jo   I praye you misteries shew your skill
        heare comes your husband.   30
Be   Hid thee my leaman,
    and I will goe plead ffor our loue our loue

Hu.[1]   How now sweete wiffe what all amorte.   [fol. 16]
Be.   I my deare I my deare
        I haue no lust to sporte
    although I was tempted very late
    to abuse yo*u*r bed and my mariage state.
        yet in my tryall
        I made a denyall.[2]
Hu.   how happie am I in my loue my loue.   40

    But tell me Wyffe who tempted[3] thee.
Be.   John your man John yo*u*r man
        vrginge me shamfully
    and had I not graunted to meete him at length
    he would haue forst me with his strength.
Hu.   out one him villaine
Be.   not for a millaine
    of gould, would I loose my loue my loue.

Hu.   O Besse the knaue is growne to proude
        take him downe take him downe   50
        such twiges must need*es* be bound.
Be.   but in *th*e Orcharde where I should meete him
    there in my apparell yo*u*r selfe shall greete him.
        gett thee a coudgell.
Hu.   Ile pay the young lossell
    for offering to tempt my loue my loue.

---

[1] Possibly a new hand begins here. A different pen at least was used. There is also a slightly different system of punctuation and abbreviation.

[2] On account of the division of the speeches in this stanza, line 7 is written as one with 6 instead of with 8 as usual.

[3] There is a curved mark over *m* in the manuscript.

	Thou didst appoynte to meete him there	
Be.	out alas out alas	
	I did it all for feare.	
Hu.	how didst thow say thow wouldst come attired.	60
Be	In my blacke silke gowne for soe he desired. [fol. 16*v*]	
Hu.	that will I put on	
Be.	looke to thy selffe John.[1]	
Hu.	Ile course him for tempting my loue my loue.	

	But where did he point this sporte should bee.	
Be.	all alone all alone	
	vnder the holly tree.	
Hu.	then of that tree Ile get a wande	
Be.	I would you had a stronger hande.	
	to chastise the treacher.	70
Hu.	out one him leacher	
	*tha*t would haue defieled my loue &c.	

	O what a wiffe haue I of thee.	
Be.	praise thy god praise thy god	
	tis he hath blessed thee.	
Hus.	would all my neighbors were so sped	
	with such a trew loue in their bed.	
Be	good wives are daintie	
Hus.	not one amongest twentie	
	so constant as thow in thy loue &c.	80

	Vppon what howre did you agree.	
Hus.	Vppon what howre did you agree.	
Be.	By and by [by] and by	
	after the stroke of three.	
Hus.	then it is tyme that I were gone	
Be.	I if you meane to meete *wi*th John.	
	lay him one sowndlye.	
Hus.	Ile beat him *p*rofoundly	
	for offeringe to tempte my loue &c.	

	But hide yo*u*r bearde in any case.	[fol. 17]
Be.	But hide yo*u*r bearde in any case.	
Hus	hould thy peace hould thy peace	90
	a moufler shall hide my face.	
	and when he comes and thinkes to settle.	
	his flowre shall prowfe a stinkinge nettle.	

. . . .[2]

[1] Line 7 with speaker's name is on the same line with 6.

[2] Space is left in the manuscript for two omitted lines, and a light stroke indicates where each of the two lines should begin.

Be	Then goe and make you readie straight
Hus.	now I goe now I goe
	for John to lie in waight
	the goose is betraide vnto *the* fox
Be.	the ase will prowfe himselfe an ox.
Hus.	what sayest thow my sweetinge.
Be.	I say in yo*ur* meettinge 100
	you will course him for tempting yo*ur* loue [&c].

Thus doe the weed*es* overgroe the corne
   alunseene alunseene
   wi*th* laughing and great scorne.
Ist not a world to heare vs speake
then doe yo*ur* vessels soonest leake
   men are importune
   then blame not o*ur* fortune
o*ur* sex were ordained to loue to loue.

Jo.—	Say m*ist*ris which waie[1] blowes the winde	[fol. 17*v*]
Be—	towardes the cost towardes the cost	111
	whi*ch* we too strive to finde	
Jo.—	oh that I could *tha*t cost descerne	
Be.—	playe thow the pylot at the stearne	
	and feare not aryving	
	no winde is dryvinge[2]	
	to hinder vs of our loue o*ur* loue.	

Jo.[3]—	What sayes my m*aste*r to this geare	
Be.—	Now *the* mouse now *the* mouse	
	sleepes in *the* catt*es* eare.	120
Jo.—	but tell me m*ist*ris what doth hee say	
Be.—	that he will wincke while we two playe	
Jo—	Is all this veritie	
Be.[4]	I of my honestye.	
Jo—	but tell me[5] how my loue my loue.	

---

[1] An *s* has apparently been marked out at the end of the word.

[2] This line is combined with line 6.

[3] From this point the *o* in *Jo.* is a capital in speakers' names.

[4] Line 7 was combined with line 6 and *Be.* was crowded in afterward.

[5] *my* was written first and *e* inserted above the canceled *y*.

Be—	O John I haue complayned of thee.
	Blamynge thee blaminge thee
	all for thy leachery.
Jo—	out alas why did you soe
Be—	thow knowest not how the winde doth blowe 130
	It was my pollicye
Jo.	to kyll his Jelowsie[1]
Be—	onely for that my loue my loue.

Jo—	I stande accused in this case [fol. 18]
Be—	be content be content
	Ile keepe thee from abuse.
	within the orchard looke thow staye.
	and when thy master comes this waye
	In my apparell.
Jo—	will he not quarrell 140
	with me about our loue our loue.

Be—	Thow must suppose him to be me.
	raile one me[2] raile one me
	blame my dysloyaltie.
	and to make his loue to roote the faster.
	. . . .[3]
	and in your talkinge
	let blowes be walkinge
	and call him a whore in his loue his loue.

Jo—	The finest device that euer I harde
	That so soone that so soone 150
	my loue hath got a bearde
	therefore mistris get you awaye
Be—	looke in the orcharde see you staye
Jo—	I do conceyte you
Be—	I will a waight you
	and see how you handle our loue our loue.

Hus—	Now John we will pay the score.
Jo—	fye one thee fye one thee
	thou art an arrant whore.

---

[1] Lines 6 and 7 are one in the manuscript.

[2] *me* has been inserted above the line.

[3] There is no indication in the manuscript of the omitted line. Clark suggests that it might have been "something like—'fail not to protest thou dost honour thy master.'"

Hus.—	John I know thou doest but iest	[fol. 18*v*]
Jo—	I know thou art a filthie beast	161
	to fawne one a leaman	
	and leaue thy good husbande[1]	
Hus—	o John it is for loue for loue.	

Jo—	The devill in hell take such a wiffe	
	hearest thou me hearest thou me	
	tys pittie of thy liffe	
Hus.—	Why wilt thou wound and giue no plaster.	
Jo—	Why wilt thou haue me wroung my master.	
Hus—	thou saidst thou didst loue me	170
Jo	I did it to proue thee	
	and therefore take this for thy loue thy l[oue].	

Be.	Be advised and hould thy hand	
	seest thou not seest thou not	
	where thy m*aste*r doth stand.	
Jo—	What makes my m*aste*r in you*r* weede	
Be—	he came to rate thy filthy deed.	
Hus.—	o John I loue thee	
	for now I haue proved thee.[1]	
	thou wilt not fleet in thy loue. thy loue.	180

Be—	O husband you will not take it soe.	
Hus.—	yes my loue yes my loue	
	and ioy in euery blowe	
Jo—	m*aste*r my m*istr*is is very light	
Hus.—	no John my wiffe is pure and right	
	now I haue tryde ye.	[fol. 19]
Be—	knaue I defie thee	
	for callinge me light in my loue my lo[ue].	

Hus.	O John thou art my seruant trew.	
	and my loue and my loue	190
	Ile change the for no new.	
Jo—	a seruan*tes* dewtie prict me one	
Hus—	now Jesus blese thee gentle John.	
	o ioy out of measure	
	to haue such a treasure[1]	
	of such a seruant and loue *and* loue.	

[1] Lines 6 and 7 are one in the manuscript.

Goe wiffe goe make vs merrie cheare
  of the best of the best
  let nothinge be to deare
Be— I will seeth you will haue it soe   200
Jo— about you*r* busines I will goe
Hus—   doe soe good John
  how happie I am[1]
that haue such a seruant and loue *and* loue.

Finis

[1] Lines 6 and 7 are one in the manuscript.

21

Singing Simpkin.[1]

The Names of the Persons.

Simpkin, a Clown.
Bluster, a Roarer.
An old Man.
His Wife.
A Servant.

Enter the wife, Simpking following

Wife. **B**Lind *Cupid* hath made my heart for to bleed,
   Fa la, la, la, la, la, la, la, la.
Simp. But I know a man can help you at need,
  With a fa la, la, la, la, fa, la, la, la, la, la.

Wife. My husband he often a hunting goes out,
  Fa la, la, &c.
Simp. And brings home a great pair of horns there's no doubt;
  with a fa la, la, la, &c.

VVife. How is't Monsieur *Simkin*, why are you so sad?   P. 12
  Fa la, la, la, &c.   10
Simp. I am up to the ears in love, and it makes me stark mad,
  with a fa la, la, la, &c.

I am vext, I am tortur'd, and troubled at heart,
  Fa la, la, &c.
VVife. But Ile try my skill to take off your smart,
  With a fa la, la &c.

And on that condition I give you a kiss,
  Fa la, la, &c.
Simp. But what says your husband when he hears of this?
  with a fa la, la, &c.   20

---

  [1] Printed from Cox's *Actaeon and Diana*, pp. 11–17. In the original there is no indication of stanzas, and some of the speeches are printed as prose. See pp. 235, 238, for the various editions and versions of the jig.

VVife. You know my affection, & no one knows more,
 With a fa la, la, &c.   *Knock within.*
Simp. 'Uds niggers noggers who knocks at the door?
 with a fa la, la, &c.

    Enter Servant. *The tune alters.*

 Serv. There is a Royster at the door,
  he seems a Fellow stout.
 Sim. I beseech you worthy friend,
  which is the back way out?
 Serv. He swears and tears he will come in,
  And nothing shal him hinder.   *Exit Servant.*
 Simp. I fear hee'l strip me out my skin.   31
  And burn it into tinder.

 VVife. I have consider'd of a way,
  and twill be sure the best.
 Simp. What may it be my dearest Dear?
  VVife. Creep into this same Chest.   *A chest set out.*
 And though he roar, speak you no word,
  If you'l preserve my favour.
 Simp. Shut to the chest, I pray, with speed,
  For something has some savour.   *Enter Bluster.*

 Blust. I never shal be quiet   P. 13
  if she use me in this fashion.   42
 Wife. I am here to bid you welcom;
  what mean you by this passion?
 Blust. With some young sweet-fac'd fellow
  I thought gone out you were.
 Simp. in the chest. No sooth, the sweet-fac'd fellow
  is kept a prisoner here.

 Blust. Where is the foole thy husband?
  Say, whither is he gone?   50
 Wife. The Wittall is a hunting.
  Blust. Then we two are alone:
 But should he come And find me here,
  what might the Cuckold think?
 Perhaps hee'd call the neighbours in,
  Simp. And beat you till you stink.

Blust. Yet in the bloody war full oft,
　My courage I did try.
Wife. I know you have kild many a man.
　Simp. You lie, you slut, you lie.　　　　　　　　60
Blust. I never came before a foe,
　By night nor yet by day,
But that I stoutly rouz'd my self,
　Simp. And nimbly ran away.

Blust. Within this chest Ile hide my self,
　If it chance he should come.
Wife. O no my love, that cannot be,
　Simp. I have bespoke the room.
Wife. I have a place behind here,
　Which yet is known to no man.　　　　　　　　70
Simp. She has a place before too,
　But that is all to common.　　　　　　*Old man within.*

Old man. Wife, wherefore is the door thus bar'd?
　what mean you pray by this?
Wife. Alas! it is my husband.
　Sim. I laugh now till I piss.　　　　　　　　P. 14
Blust. Open the chest, Ile into it,
　My life else it may cost.
Wife Alas I cannot open it.
　Simp. I beleeve the key is lost.　　　　　　　80

Wife. I have bethought my self
　upon a dainty trick.
Blust. What may it be my dearest love?
　I prethee now be quick.
Wife. You must say that your enemy
　Into this house is fled,
And that your heart can take no rest,
　Untill that he be dead.

Draw quickly out your furious blade,
　And seem to make a strife.　　　　　　　　90
Swear all th'excuses can be made,
　Shall not preserve his life.

Say that the Rogue is fled in here,
  That stole away your coin,
And if Ile not deliver him,
  You'l have as much of mine.

Blust. Here's no man but my self,
  On whom shall I complain?
Wife. This great fool does not understand,
  This thing you must but faign.   100
My husband thus must be deceiv'd,
  and afterwards wee'l laugh.   *Enter old man.*
Old man. Wife, since you will not ope the door,
  Ile break't ope with my staff.

Blust. Good woman shew me to the slave,
  His limbs I strait wil tear.
Wife. By all the honesty I have,
  Theres no man came in here.
Blust. When I have fought to purchase wealth,
  And with my blood did win it,   P. 15
This Rogue has got my purse by stealth.   111
  Simp. But never a peny in it.

Old man. She's big with child, therefore take heed
  you do not fright my wife.
Blust. But know you who the Father is?
  Simp. The Roarer on my life.
Old man. She knows not of your enemy,
  then get you gone you were best.
Wife. Peace husband, peace, I tell you true,
  I have hid him in the chest.   120

Old man. I am glad on't at my heart,
  but doe not tell him so.
VVife. I would not for a thousand pound
  the Roarer should it know.
Blust. When next we meet his life is gone,
  no other must he hope;
Ile kill him whatsoere comes on't,
  Simp. Pray think upon a rope.

Old man. What kind of person is it
  that in the chest does lie?   130

VVife. A goodly hansome sweet young man,
  as ere was seen with eye.
Old man. Then let us both entreat of him—
  Pray put us not in fear:
we do beseech you go from hence.
  Blust. But to morrow Ile be here.   *Exit Blust.*

Old man. Wife, run with all the speed you can,
  and quickly shut the dore,
I would not that the roaring man
  should come in any more.   140
Mean time I wil release the youth,
  and tell him how we have sped.—
Be comforted my honest friend.   *Simpkin* comes
  Simp. Alas, *I* am almost dead.   forth.

my heart is tortur'd in my breast
  with sorrow, fear and pain.
Old man. Ile fetch some *Aqua vitæ*,
  to comfort you again.
Simp. And cause *I* will requite you,   P . 16 :
  VVhose love doth so excell,   150
Ile graft a pair of horns on your head,
  That may defend it well.

VVife. Good husband, let the man stay here,
  'Tis dang'rous in the street.
Old man. *I* would not for a crown of gold,
  The Roarer should him meet.
For should he come by any harm,
  They'd say the fault were mine.
VVife to Simpkin. There's half a crown, pray send him out
  to fetch a quart of wine.   160

Simp. There's money for you Sir,—
  Pray fetch a quart of Sack.
Old man. 'Tis well, 'tis well, my honest friend,
  Ile see you shall not lack.
VVife. But if he should dishonest me,
  For there are such slipp'ry men.
Old man. Then he gets not of his half crown
  One peny back agen.   *Exit.*

Simp. Thy husband being gone my love,
   VVee'l sing, wee'l dance, and laugh,   170
I am sure he is a good fellow,
   And takes delight to quaff.
VVife. I'le fold thee in my arms my love,
   No matter for his listning.
       The Old man and his servant listen.
Simp. Gentlemen, some forty weeks hence
   You may come to a Christning.

Old man. O sirrah, have *I* caught you,
   Now do the best you can,
Your Schoolmaster nere taught you
   To wrong an honest man.   180
Sim. Good sir, *I* never went to Schole,   P. 17
   Then why am *I* abused?
The truth is, *I* am but a foole,
   And like a fool am used.

Old man. Yet sirrah you had wit enough
   to think to Cuckold me.
VVife. I jested with him, husband,
   his knavery to see.
Simp. But now you talk of knaverie,
   I pray where is my Sack?   190
Old man. You shall want it in your belly, Sir,
   And have it on your back.
       They beat him off.   *Exeunt.*

22

Frauncis new Iigge, betweene Frauncis a Gentleman, and Richard a Farmer. To the tune of *Walsingham.*[1]

[TWO CUTS]

Besse.[2]

1. **A**S I went to Walsingham,
 to the shrine with speed,
Met I with a iolly Palmer,
 in a Pilgrims weede.   *[Enter Frauncis]*
Now God you[3] saue you iolly Palmer.
Fran. Welcome Lady gay,
Oft haue I sued to thee for loue.
B.[4] Oft haue I said you nay.

[DIE TUGENDHAFTE BÄURIN.]

Ain Engellendische Comedia mit vieren Personnen.

Edlman: Paur: Peurin: Frau vom Adl:

1. *Edlman:*	Einsmaß spaciert ich über felt, in ain Wißen war Grüen,
	Begegnet mir ain schönes Bilt Barfueß ohne Schuch.
	Gott grüeß euch Edles Schones Bilt:
Peurin:	Willkhomb Junkher Schön,
Edlman:	Wiewoll ich offt eur Lieb verhofft
[Peurin:]	Aber jch sieh woll Nein

---

[1] Printed from a broadside in the Pepys Collection, I, 226 (also printed by Rollins in *Pepysian Garland*, pp. 1–10). The title covers a single line reaching across the top of the first sheet. I have made some changes in form, indicated by notes or brackets, to bring out better the dramatic nature and the verse forms of the ballad. In the notes important variants of the manuscript version in *Shirburn Ballads*, pp. 244–54 (S), as printed by Clark, are cited. At the foot of the text the German adaptation of the jig is printed from the edition in *Archiv für Litteraturgeschichte*, VI (1877), 48–52, presumably edited by Franz Schnorr von Carolsfeld. The text is printed there as prose, but paragraphing and punctuation seem designed in part to indicate stanzas and lines. I have attempted to restore verse forms—evidently those of "Attowell's Jig"—leaving, however, long lines suggested by the punctuation in the first two parts. Speakers' names are supplied in the first four stanzas, and italics are used instead of capitals for speakers' names. I have made no emendations. The stanzas are not numbered in the original English and German texts. For the title "Attowell's Jig" see pp. 239, 457 n. 1.

[2] S omits. Clark supplies "*Besse, Richard's* wife" at line 5.   [3] S omits.

[4] S *Besse.* S usually has *Fr.* where the broadside has *F.* There are other slight variations in abbreviations of speakers' names.

2. *F.* My loue is fixed. *B.* And so is mine,
  but not on you:
For to my husband whilst I liue,
  I will euer be true.
F. Ile giue thee gold and rich array.
B. Which I shall buy too deare.
F. Nought shalt thou want: then say not nay.
B. Naught would you make mee I feare.

3. What though you be a Gentleman,
  and haue lands great[1] store?
I will be chaste doe what you can,
  though I liue ne're[2] so poore.
F. Thy beauty rare hath wounded mee,
  and pierst my heart.
B. Your foolish loue doth trouble mee,
  pray you Sir depart.

4. *F.* Then tel mee sweet wilt thou consent
  vnto my desire:
B. And if I should, then tel me sir,
  what is it you require?
F. For to inioy thee as my loue.
B. Sir you haue a wife:

2. [*Edlman:*] Mein Lieb jst wahr[3]
Peurin: vnd so ists [ichs] mein, Aber nicht zue Euch,
    Mein Haußwiert weill ich Lebe, Beweiß ich jm Lieb
    vnnd Treu.
Edlman: Goldt vnd Khlaider geb ich euch
[*Peurin:*]   jch werde sie khauffen zue Theur,
[*Edlman:*] dz soll doch gar khain mangl haben,
Peurin: Ich beger nicht eurer Steur:

3.   Ob jhr gleich Hoch vom Adl seith vnd habt Gnueg
    zuuerzern,
    Betriegt ihr mich nicht durch eur gab vnd zieht mich
    nicht zue vnehrn.
Edlman: Eur grosße Schönheit zwinget mich vnd Krenkhet mier
    mein Herz:
Peurin: Eur vnkheuschheit betriebt mich sehr, vnd bringt mier
    grosßen Schmerz:

---

[1] S *haue land and good.* [2] S *never.* [3] Part of next speech in original.

Therefore let your sute haue an end.
F. First will I lose my life.

5. All that I haue thou shalt commaund.
B. Then my loue you haue.
F. Your meaning I well[1] vnderstand.
B. I yeeld to what you craue.
F. But tel mee sweet when shall I enioy
        my hearts delight.
I prethee[2] sweete heart be not coy,
B.[3] euen soone at night.

6. My husband is rid ten miles from
        money to receiue: (home,
In the euening see you come.
F. Til then I take my leaue. (*Exit:*
B. Thus haue I rid my hands[4] full
        of my amorous loue,   (well
And my sweet husband wil I tell,
        how hee doth me moue.

4. *Edlman:*	Alß was ich Hab dz gib ich euch,
[*Peurin?*]	dorzue eur Puel will sein,
[*Edlman:*]	Darauf habt jhr mein hertz vnnd handt,
Peurin:	des gleichen jhr auch mein.
Edlman:	Ach sagt mir aber Wan solt ich dan meiner Lieb genies-ßen.
Peurin:	heut zur nacht drauf worth so Lang, vnd Losst euchs nicht verdriesßen.

5.	Mein mon jst vber Feldt verreisst, vber Perg vnd Thall,
	vnd khombt heut wider nicht zue Hauß, den er thuet schult einholln.
Edlman:	So nimb ich vrlob von eur Lieb,
Peurin:	Khombt bei rechter Zeit,
Edlman:	Vnd wann ich khomb so lasst mich ein,
Peurin:	eur Pedt jst schan bereith.

Jetzt Redt *Die Peurin* mit jhr selbst:

Jetzt will ichs meim man alß offenbarn, was er zu mier
    Hot gesagt,
Jch Hoff sein Lieb, durch meine Lieb, werdt vmb sonst
    sein gemacht.

---

[1] S *well I.*   [2] S *praye the.*
[3] Placed before the preceding line in both S and the broadside.   [4] S *husband.*

*Enter Richard Besses husband. To
the tune of the Iewish dance.*

7. *Rich.* Hey doune a doune,
    hey doune, a doune a doune,
There is neuer a lusty Farmer,
    in all our towne:
That hath more cause,
    to lead a merry life,
Then I that am married
    to an honest faithfull[1] wife.
  B. I thanke you gentle husband,
    you praise mee to my face.
  R. I cry thee mercy, Bessee,[2]
    I knew thee not in place.

8. *B.* Beleeue me gentle husband,
    if you knew as much as I,
The words that you haue spoken,
    you quickly would deny:
For since you went from home,
    A sutor I haue had,
Who is so farre in loue with mee,
    that he is almost madde.

Jetzund Khombt *Der Paur* haimb vnd redt mit ihm selbst.

6.   Es hot khain Paur im dorff khain Pesßer Lebm,
        den ich allain, vnd wos mein frau thuet gebm,
        sie jst schön, Kheusch vber die maß,
        Jhr Lieb zue mir sie nimermehr verloßt.

Peurin: Jch sag euch dankh mein Lieber Hannß jhr preißet mich
        zue sehr,

Paur: Verzeih miers drein habs nicht vermeint dz du werst
        jtzundt hier.

7. *Peurin:* Wan ihr wüsßet vnd wos jch weiß,
        jhr wuert mich nicht so sehr Loben vnd preißen,
        dieweill ihr auß Hobt euren weg genomen,
        Hob ich derweill ain reichen Puel bekhomen,

---

[1] S omits.   [2] S *Besse.*

Heele giue me gold and siluer[1] store,
    and money for to spend,
And I haue promis'd him therefore,
    to be his louing friend.

9. *R.* Beleeue me, gentle wife,
    but this makes mee to frowne,
There is no gentleman nor[2] knight,
    nor Lord of high renowne:
That shall enioy thy loue, gyrle,
    though he were ne're so good:
Before he wrong my Bessee[3] so,
Ile spend on him my blood.
And therefore tell me who it is
    that doth desire thy loue.
    B. Our neighbour master Francis,[4]
    that often did me moue.

10. To whom I gaue consent,
    his mind for to fulfill,
And promis'd him this night,
    that he should haue his will:
Nay doe not frowne, good Dickie,
    but heare me speake my minde:
For thou shalt see Ile warrant thee,
    Ile vse him in his kind.

    er jst gegn mier so sehr verliebt, er weiß nicht wer[5] nicht
        wos er thuet,
    dz macht dz ich jhn wider Lieb er Gibt mier Gelt vnd
        Guet:

8. *Paur:*   Warlich mein drein dz thuet mier nicht gefallen
    Dein worth thuen mier in meine ohren erschallen
    es jst khain junckher in dißem Ganczen Landt,
    der mier mein drein solt nemen auß mein Handt,
    Drumb sag miers Drein vnd wer er jst, vnd wer er noch
        so Khlueg,
    Dein Ehre zue bedekhen, wog jch mein junges Bluet:

9. *Peurin:*   Es jst junkher Franciscus, der wohnt alhie jm Schloß,
    Dem hab ich Geßtern zuegesagt zue schlaffen in seinem
        Schoß,
    Aber seit nuer zuefriden vnd Lasst den Zoren Stillen,

---

[1] S *Jewels.*   [2] S *or.*   [3] S *Besse.*   [4] S adds *'tis.*
[5] Omit *nicht wer* ? Ed. says that reading *wer* is doubtful.

For vnto thee I will be true,
   so long as I doe liue,
Ile neuer change thee for a new,
   nor once my mind so giue.

11. Goe you to mistrisse Frauncis,
   and this to her declare:
And will her with all speed,
   to my house to repaire:
Where shee and ile deuise
   some pretty knauish wile:
For I haue layd the plot,
   her husband to beguile.
Make hast I pray and[1] tarry not,
   for long he will not stay.
R. Feare not, ile tell her such a tale,
   shall make her come away. [*Exit*]

12. *B.* Now Besse bethinke thee,[2]
   what thou hast to doe.
Thy louer will come presently,
   and hardly will he woo:

	so wert ihr woll erfaren wie ich jhm will bezallen.
Paur:	wie khan dz sein herzliebe drein,
Peurin:	Gor woll mit weniger müeh,
Paur:	So sag mirs drein so will ich auch mein Roth geben dorzue:

10. *Peurin:*   So soltu jezt zue seiner Hausfrau Gehn,
   vnnd sogen sie solt khomen zu mier allain,
   da wöllen wier guet roth zuesamen schaffen,
   vnd jhn belohnen dz ihr daruon wert lachen,
   drumb Lauff geschwindt mein Liebe[r] drein, sonst möchts
     der Junkher erfahren,

Paur: Jezt Lauf jch hin mein Liebe drein, mein fleiß will jch
   nicht sparen.

Jetzt redt die *Peurin* mit jhr selbst.

11. *Peurin:*   Jezt mueß jch all mein wüz zusamen suechen,
   sonst wuert der junkher mein Arbeit thuen fluechen,

[1] S *yow.*

[2] In S this line reads "Make hast sweet *Francis.*" *B.* is omitted and Clark supplies
Bess.

I will teach my Gentleman,
    a tricke that he may know,
I am too craftie and[1] too wise,
    to be ore-reached so:
But heere he comes now: not a word,
    but fall to worke againe.   *she sowes [as Frauncis enters]*
F. How now sweetheart, at worke so hard:
B. I sir, I must take paine.[2]

13. F. But say, my louely sweeting,
    thy promise wilt thou keepe?
Shall I enioy thy loue,
    this night with me to sleepe?
B. My husband rid[3] from home,
    heere safely may you[4] stay.
F. And I haue made my wife beleeue,
    I rid another way.
B. Goe in good sir, what ere betide,
    this night and lodge with mee.
F. The happiest night that euer I had,
    thy friend still will I bee. [*Exit*]

        es schadt doch nichts, mein Treu will ich beweißen
        [. . . . .]
        sieh wie er khombt noch meinem wuntsch, jezt ist dz
            anfang,
Edlman: wie stets mein schaz.
Peurin: gar woll mein herr, jch wort eur mit verlangen.

12. *Edlman:*   So khomb mein Schaz vnd Loß vns gehn Hinein,
            mich thuet verlangen, bei euch zue sein allein.
Peurin: gehet ihr nuer Hin ich hab noch was zue erberben,
            damit mein man nicht khombt darzue vnß baider will
              verderbet:
Edlman: Jch sag euch dankh füer eure Sorg, jch bitt khombt balt
            zue mier.
Peurin: hob du khain zweifel an meiner Lieb jch will balt sein
            bei dier:

---

[1] *aud* in original.   [3] S *is rid.*

[2] Reading of S; *paines* in the broadside.   [4] S *yow may.*

*Enter Mistris Frauncis with Richard. To
the tune of* 𝕭𝖚𝖌𝖑𝖊 𝕭𝖔𝖊.[1]

14. *W* **I** Thanke you neighbour Richard,
      for bringing me this newes:
   R. Nay, thanke my wife that loues me so,[2]
      and will not you[3] abuse.

15. *W.* But see whereas shee stands,
      and waiteth our return.
   R. You must goe coole your husbands heate,
      that so in loue doth burne.

16. *B.* Now Dickie welcome home,
      and Mistris welcome hither:
   Grieue not although you finde
      your husband and I together.

17. For you shall haue your right,
      nor will I wrong you so:
   Then change apparrell with me straight,[2]
      and vnto him doe goe.

18. *W.* For this your kind goodwill,
      a thousand thankes I giue:
   And make account I will requite
      this kindnesse, if I liue.

19. *B.* I hope it shall not need,
      Dick will not serue me so:
   I know he loues me not so ill,
      a ranging for to goe.[4]

Jetzt Wexelt die *Peurin* mit der *Frau Vom Adl* Khlaider.

13. *Peurin:*   So wexel die Khlaider mit mier Bolt
                  vnd gehe zu jm Hinein,
   Frau Vom Adl: Von Herzen gehrn Drein Hülff mier nuer
                  jch will bolt bei jm sein:

---

[1] *Bugle Boe* is in italics in the original. This stage direction comes at the end of the first part and is followed by the colophon "Imprinted at London for I.W." The heading of the second sheet reads, "The Second part of *Attowels* new Iigge. To the tune of as I went to *Walsingham*." There is no division into stanzas in the section sung to the tune of "Bugle Boe."

[2] S omits.   [3] S *me*.   [4] S omits stanzas 18 and 19.

20. *R.* No faith, my louely Besse,[1]
    first will I[2] lose my life:
    Before Ile[3] breake my wedlock bonds,
        or[4] seeke to wrong my wife.   [*Exit Mistress Frauncis*]

21. Now thinks good Master Frauncis,
    he hath thee in his bed:
    And makes account he is grafting
    of hornes vpon my head.

22. But softly stand aside,
    now shall wee know his minde,
    And how hee would haue vsed thee,
    if thou hadst beene so kind.

*Enter Master Francis with his owne wife,
hauing a maske before her face, supposing
her to be Besse.*

To the tune of goe from my window.

23. *F.* Farewell my ioy and hearts delight,[5]
    til next we meete againe:

14. *Peurin:*   Wos denkhstu jetzt mein Lieber Hanß
                         vber mein Argen Lüsst:
    Paur: Die Schönste vnd die Khluegste frau
                         in vnßerm dorff du Bist,

15.   Jezt maint junkher Francisce,
                         er lag bei dier im Bett,
                       Ehe dz solt sein wolt ich Lieber
                         dz ich khain Leben Het.

16. *Peurin:*   Ich Lieb dich mein Hannß vber die welt,
                         Dein Armuet macht mich reich,
                       Hunger vnd Durst Leit ich mit dier
                         es gilt mier alles gleich.

Jetzt nimbt der *Edlman* von seiner *Frauen* so er die Peurin zu sein
geweßen vermaint vrlab.

17. *Edlman:*   Ade mein Schaz mein Ainiger Trosst,
                       Ich will dein Gunsst belohnen,

---

[1] S *Bessee.*   [2] S *I will.*   [3] S *I.*   [4] S *to.*

[5] Probably to save space, the third and fourth lines of the stanzas in this section
are printed as one in the broadside, the end of the long line being inserted in the space

Thy kindnes to requite,
for lodging me al night,
   heeres ten pound for thy paine:

24. And more to shew my loue to thee,
   weare this ring for my sake.
W. Without your gold or fee
you shal haue more of mee.
F. No doubt of that I make.

25. *W.* Then let your loue continue still.
   F. It shall[1] til life doth end.
   W. Your wife I greatly feare.
   F. for her thou needst not care
     so I remaine thy freind.[2]

26. *W.* But youle suspect me without cause,
   that I am false to you:
And then youle cast mee off,
and make mee but a scoffe,
   since that I proue vntrue.

       deine bewüßen Liebe,
       Loß dich nicht betrüebn,
     da hostue ain Hundert Cronen.

18.   Vnd alß ain Zaichen meiner Lieb,
       nimb du den Ring von mier,
        Deine Lieb vnd Holt,
        Acht jch für rottes Golt,
       mein schoz dz Khlog jch dier:

19.   Ich hob euch Altzeit Gliebt:
Frau: Ach Gott es mag so sein, jch fürchte eures weibs,
       eur weib jst weiß vnd Khlueg,
        sie mags erfohren thuen
       Alß don ists mit mir verlohrn.

---

after the next line when necessary. I have broken this long line of each stanza in two.
Clark has the same arrangement of lines but combines them in ten-line stanzas. Stanzas
23 to 26 of the text as printed here are printed solid in the broadside, stanzas 27 to
40 as seven eight-line stanzas. This leaves one four-line stanza at the end. Seven of
the first lines have extra stresses. Clark suggests emendations for two of those that
appear in S also. See Chappell, *Popular Music*, I, 140–42, and *PMLA*, XXXVI (1921),
581–83, 588–89, for songs presumably sung to the air "Go from my window," which
are printed sometimes in four-line stanzas, sometimes in five-line, and show some
metrical irregularities.

  [1] S *shall be.*   [2] S omits this line.

27. *F.* Then neuer trust man for my sake,
      if I proue so vnkind:
   [*W.*]¹ So often haue you sworn,
   sir, since that you² were borne,
      and soone haue³ changde your minde.

28. [*F.*]¹ Nor wife nor life, nor goods nor lands,
      shall make me leaue my loue,
   Nor any worldly treasure
   make me forgoe⁴ my pleasure,
      nor once my mind remoue.

29. *W.* But soft a while, who is yonder? doe you see
   my husband? out alasse.

20. *Edlman:*   Mein Weib, mein Leib, mein Lanndt mein Guett,
                 vnd alles wos jch hob,
                     solt mich nicht dohin maßen
                     eur schönheit zuuerlaßen
                 es solt sein Biß in den Todt.

21.   Ehe ich mein Lieb obwenden thue,
                 ehe wüntsch jch mir den Todt,
   Frau: Ihr hobt mirs offt geschworen
                     es jst doch alß verlohren,
                 jhr wert mich noch bringen in Nott.

22.   So lasst eur Lieb StandtHofftig sein.
   Edlman: Es soll sein biß Todt:
   Frau: Ich fürchte eures weib,
   Edlman: Wen ich eur freundt nuer bleib,
                 mit ihr hots gor khain nott.

   Jetzt Khombt der *Paur* mit seinem *Weib* so der vom Adl Khlaider
     an hot,

23. *Frau:*   Ach wehe vnd Angst, wer khombt alda
                 Behüet Gott es jst mein man,

---

¹ In S, but not in the broadside.   ³ S *haue soone.*

² S *thow.*   ⁴ S *forget*, probably the correct reading.

F. And yonder is my wife,
now shall we haue a life[1]
　　how commeth this to passe?

30. *R.* Com hither gentle Besse I charge thee do confesse
　　what makes Master Francis heere.
[*W*].[2] Good husband pardon me,
Ile tel the troth to thee.
R. Then speake and doe not feare.

31. *F.*[3] Nay, neighbour Richard harke to mee,
　　Ile tel the troth to you.
[*B*].[4] Nay tell it vnto me,
good sir, that I may see,[5]
　　what you haue here to doe.

32. But you can make no scuse to colour this abuse,
　　this wrong is too too great.
R. Good sir I take great scorne
you should profer me the horne
W. Now must I coole this[6] heate.

Edlman:　　　　vnd mein frau dorneben,
　　　　　　　　Ich wolt vill Golts drumb geben
　　　　　　　　zu wüßen was sie wolten han.

24. *Paur:*　　　Khomb her mein Drein, vnd sog es mier,
　　　　　　　　wos macht der Junkher bei dier,
　Frau:　　　　Ich will euch alles sagen,
　　　　　　　　Wen ihr mich nicht wolt schlagen,
　[*Paur:*]　　　khomb her, vnd sog es mier.

25. *Frau:*　　　Warumb jst eur angesicht Bedekht:
　Edlman:　　　Ich schamb mich meiner Thatt,
　Frau:　　　　Warumb seit ihr so rott,
　Edlman:　　　Ich wolt dz ich wehr Todt,
　Frau:　　　　eur Angst khombt vill zu spott.

---

[1] In the broadside *a life* is printed as one word.

[2] *B.* in the broadside and in S.

[3] Omitted in S. Clark supplies *Francis.*

[4] *W.* in the broadside; obviously Bess disguised as the Wife speaks. No speaker is indicated in S, and Clark supplies *Richard*, probably because the first line of the next stanza has *B.* before it in S.

[5] In S the line reads, *that I may quickly see.*　　　　[6] S *his.*

33. Nay[1] neighbour Richard be content,
    thou hast no wrong at all:
Thy wife hath done thee right,
and pleasurde me this night.
F.[2] This frets mee to the gall.

34. Good wife forgiue me this offence,
    I doe repent mine[3] ill.
W.[4] I thank you with mine[3] hart,
for playing this kind part,
    though sore against your[5] will.

35. Nay gentle husband frowne not so,
    for you haue made amends:
I thinke it is good gaine,
to haue ten pound for my paine:[6]
    then let vs both be friends.

36. *F.*[2] Ashamed I am and know not what to say,
    good wife forgiue this crime:[7]
Alasse I doe repent.
W. Tut I could be content,
    to be serued so many a time.

26. *Edlman:*   Ach wehe vnd Angst es jst mein Weib
              wie bin jch jetzt betrogn:
   Frau: es jst euch recht geschehen
                eur Hauß jst euch zue Khlein
            jr seit nicht mehr meiner Lieb gewogn.

27. *Edlman:*   Ach Liebe Frau vergebt mier dz
              es solt nicht mehr geschehen,
   Frau: Ich bin des woll zue friden,
              wen jhr die Zeit eurs Leben
           ain solche Buesße thuet.

---

[1] In the broadside *F.* stands at the beginning of this line.

[2] Omitted in S. Clark supplies *Francis.*   [3] S *my.*

[4] S also has *W.* here. Clark, probably on account of the pronoun used by the speaker (see the next note), omits it and supplies *Wife* for stanza 35.

[5] S *my.*   [6] S *paynes.*

[7] S *forgiue me, this tyme.*

37. *F.*[1] Good neighbour Richard be content,
     ile woo thy wife no more:
     I haue enough of this.
     W.[2] Then all forgiuen is.
     I thanke thee Dick therefore.

38. And to thy wife ile giue this gold,
     I hope youle not say no:
     Since I haue had the pleasure,
     let her enioy the treasure.
     F.[1] Good wife[3] let it be so.[4]

39. *B.* I thank you gentle Mistris. *R.* Faith & so do I.
     sir, learne your owne wife to know:
     And shoote not in the darke,
     for feare you mis the marke.
     B. He hath paid for this I trow.

40. All women learn of me. *F.* All men by me take heed
     how you a woman trust.
     W. Nay women trust no men.
     F. And if they do: how then?
     W. Ther's few of them prooue iust.

28.   Aber Nochtber Hannß nimb du dz Gelt von mier,
             du hosts verdient gegn mier,
                damit du vnd dein weib,
                mögt Leben in grosßen freuden
             Du hets verdiennet mehr dorzu:

29. *Paur:*   Junkher Francischee hört mier zue,
             jch will euch etwos sagn,
                es thuet aim Haußmon wehe,
                wen ainr bricht die Ehe,
             Khain grösßere schandt jst auf Erdt.

[1] S omits. Clark supplies *Francis*.

[2] So in S also. Possibly the line was spoken by Richard and the Wife began with
the next line.

[3] S *wise*, obviously an error.   [4] S ends here.

41. Farewell neighbour Richard, farewell honest Besse
    I hope wee are all friends.
    W.[1] And if you stay at home,
    and vse not thus to rome,
    heere all our quarrell ends.

               𝕱𝕴𝕹𝕴𝕾.   George Attowell.[2]

At London Printed for I. W.

30.   Aber khombt Herein, wier wollen frölich sein,
                       mein weib thuet mier gefollen,
                          Guet freundtschofft wöllen Wier Hobn,
                          All Zorn soll sein begraben,
                       Ade zu gueter nocht.

[1] Probably repeated because the Wife now addresses her husband.
[2] At the end of the column. The colophon is centered at the bottom of the sheet.

23

The Black Man[1]

The Actors Names.

Black Man.
Thumpkin.
Two Gentlemen.
Brush.
Susan.

Enter Thumpkin *and* Susan.

Thump. SWeet *Susan* remember the words I have said.
        Sus. I'le rest on my *Thumpkin*, I'le do as I may.
Thump. Then soon in the night I will come to thy Bed,
   And spend the whole time in sweet pleasure and play.
I'le chace thee.
        Sus. I'le embrace thee, my Love and delight.
Thump. And spend the whole time in sweet sports of the night.

Sus. But what if you afterwards should me mislike;
   And not be contented to make me your Wife.
Thump. Ne're fear, I will stand to it if I do strike,
   Although, *Sue*, it cost poor *Thumpkin* his Life.   10
I will love thee.
        Sus. I will prove thee, who-ever says no.
Thump. Jog on then, my pretty *Susan*; come, *Sue*, let us go.

Enter two Gentlemen.   P. 2

1. *Gent.* Y'are well over-taken, Sir; whither so fast?
2. *Gent.* H'as got him a pretty Companion beside.
Thump. I'm jogging hard by, Sir.

---

[1] Printed from Kirkman's *Wits, or, Sport upon Sport*, Part II (1673), pp. 1–9. The cries are printed as prose, and in some other cases two or more lines of the verse are run together. There is no spacing to indicate stanzas and no consistent system of indentation. See p. 284 for the Dutch version.

1. *Gent.* Pray make not such haste.
Are you the Groom, Sir, and this your fair Bride?
Thump. Why I, Sir.
      2. *Gent.* You lye, Sir.
              Thump. What a pox mean you by this?
1. *Gent.* Then see, Sir, we'l fee, Sir, your Lass with a kiss.

Thump. I thought your chaps water'd: Come, *Sue*, let us go,
    W'ave paid for our passage, and now we are free.   20
2. *Gent.* Nay, soft, Sir, a while, it must not be so,
    You may go if you please, but your Lass stays with me.
Thump. Alas, Sir.
      1. *Gent.* No pass, Sir, by this hand I protest;
I speak now in earnest, I mean not in Jest.

Thump. In Jest, or in Earnest, I care not a pin;
    'Tis not you bravado's shall bear her away.
2. *Gent.* Now soft, Brother *Roger*, pray what doth he mean?
    1. *Gent.* Perhaps in his Valour shew some bloody Fray.
Thump. O no, Sir.
      2. *Gent.* Why so, Sir?
              Thump. I mean not to fight.
1. *Gent.* Then pack, Sir; your back, Sir; get out of our sight.   30
                              [*Exit* Thumpkin.

2. *Gent.* Come, Sweet-heart, look not so sadly,
    All for the loss of a Countrey Clown;
Prethee look merrily, Prethee look chearily,
    Cast away cares, and sorrow down.   P. 3

Sus. How can I look merrily? How can I look chearily?
    All in the absence of my Dear:
I cannot look merrily, No, nor chearily,
    Since my true Love is not hear.

1. *Gent.* Hold thee contented, thou shalt have thy liking;
    We but for kindness put in for a share: 40
Thou shalt get no harm by our striking,
    We'l play fair, and stake fair, and play ware for ware.

                Enter Thumpkin.

Thump. As ye came from *Walsingham*
    saw ye not my Dear?
2. *Gent.* Truly Aged Father, no.
    Thump. Ye lye, ye Rogues, she's here.   [*Aside.*

She was as fair as fair might be,
   and of a comely hue.
1. *Gent.* Oh, such a Lass for my money.
   Thump. More Whoring Rogue are you.   *[Aside.*

2. *Gent.* Prethee sweet, give me thy hand;   51
   Say, Dearest, wilt be mine?
1. *Gent.* Nay, soft, my Friend, that must not be;
   I will not yield her thine.

2. *Gent.* Sweet, by this Old Man stand thou then,
   Whilst he and I do try
Which shall bear the prize away.
   Thump. And that I hope shall I.   *[Aside.*
                             [They fight.

And art thou here my own sweet heart?
   Sus. Who is this I see?   60
Thump. I am thy *Thumpkin* stiff and stout,
   Who hath fool'd them bravely.

Sus. Nimbly then let us be gone,   P. 4
   Without all delay;
Thump. Whilst they are fighting for the Bone,
   I will bear the prize away.   *[Exeunt.*

1. *Gent.* But soft, my Friend, why do we fight?
   S'death, where is the VVench?
2. *Gent.* This Leacherous gray-beard hath us beguil'd,
   And away hath born her hence.   70

1. *Gent.* Then let's like Lightning him pursue,
   And for this Treacherous part,
VVe'l give the gray-beard Rogue his due,
   S'death, I am vext at heart.   *[Exeunt, losing the Wench.*

       Enter Thumpkin *and* Susan.

Thump. Jog on, my pretty *Susan;*
   How lik'st thou my device?
I think I over-reach'd the Rogues,
   And gull'd them in a trice.

Sus. Thy wit has got my Liberty,
   And freed me from all woe.   80
Thump. Jog on, Jog on, my pretty *Sue;*
   Come, *Susan,* let us go.

Enter two Gentlemen.

1. *Gent.* You are well over-taken, Sir.
   I'm glad I've found you out.
Thump. O woe is me, O woe is me;
   They'l hang me out of doubt.

Look how my back-side trembles, and
   See how my buttocks quake: P. 5
O woe is me, O woe is me,
   VVhat Excuse shall I make?   90

2, *Gent.* None at all, Sir; here's part of a Mornings purchase for
you, get up.

   [*They set him on a stool with a sheet about him, like a Ghost.*

1. *Gent.* In this same plight, Sir, thus disguis'd,
   A mumming you must go.
Thump. I never got a VVench with Child,
   VVhy should you use me so?

1. *Gent.* No matter for your Wenching, Sir,
   if any body come,
Remember 'tis our will, that still
   you answer all with mum.   100

Thump. But how if any Body, Sir,
   Should ask me what's a Clock?
1. *Gent.* Then answer them with mum, you Slave.
   Thump. Then they will think I mock.

2. *Gent.* No matter for their thinking, Sir,
   If any body come;
Remember still, it is our will,
   You answer all with mum.

Thump. Mum, mum; *Sue*, *Sue*, mum.
1. *Gent.* Mum, you Slave.   [*Exeunt two Gentlemen.*

Enter Brush.

Brush. Come buy a Brush—   111
   Buy a Brush for your Cloaths,
To keep them from the dust and Moths;
   Handsill I will not forsake,
Lucky money I would take.

Come buy a Brush, or[1] Table-Book,
will ye buy a Brush—
                    Thump. Mum—
Brush. VVhat is this I do behold?   P. 6
All my Joynts do quake with cold;
'Tis the Spirit of some lewd Knave,   120
Newly risen from his Grave:
And wandring from his home, doth fright
Those that walk i'th' dead of Night.
Gentle Spirit, tell to some
The cause of thy appearance—
                    Thump. Mum.
Brush. 'Tis a gentle Ghost I see,
He and I shall soon agree;
I'le Barter all the ware *I*'ve here
For Bottle Ale, and double Beer.
Come, come, come,   130
to the next Red Lettice let us—
                    Thump. Mum.

Brush. VVhat, nothing but mum: Mum by your self, and be
hang'd if you will.   [*Exit running.*

Thump. O woe is me, was ever Man thus crost?
In this poor plight my wits *I*'ve almost lost.
    My pretty *Sue*
    I bid adieu:
And here like one that's dumb;
    In this sad plight,
    Much like a spright,   140
Must answer all with mum.

But 'tis no matter————

I'le turn my mum to ho, ho, ho;
And fright the next doth come or go.

                    Enter Black Man.   P. 7

        Black. Black do I cry,
        Will you any of me buy?

---

[1] *on* in original.

Look on my Wares,
and view them well;
Cloaths I do want,
and my money it is scant,   150
and my Trade, pox on't,
is but poor and bare.
Buy black, buy my black Ware.
Maidens if you will
come and try your skill;
I have black, buy my black,
the best you e're did lack;
come, a swop, a swop;
be it old Boots, or Shooes,
handsil not refuse.   160
Come buy my black Tinder-box;
what is't you lack?
How long shall I
call and cry,
e're handsil I take:
Maidens buy, buy, buy;
but ah to me,
what's this I see?
My mirth and glee
is turn'd to grief.   170
Thump. Ho, ho, ho, ho.
Black. Oh, gentle spright,
thy ghastly sight
does me affright,
what shall I do?————

Thump. Man, forbear this place,
    For none to hurt I seek;
Let not my shadow chace
    Thy countenance from thy cheek.

Then Man forbear,   180
this Garment wear,
to all that comes or goes,
to thy best skill,
perform my will,
by answering all with Oh,
oh, oh, oh, oh, oh.

Who's that, Old House?

Black. What *Thumpkin?*[1] Old House do's call me? If I had been an Old House thou hadst shaken me to pieces e're this; I'm sure the Gable end of my House began to open in the Joice. But why did you fright me so, *Thumpkin?*   191

Thump. Ah, Old House, I have had the worst luck. Didst thou not know my Sweet-heart?

Black. What, *Sue*, at the Church stile? ⟨P. 8⟩

Thump. I, the same; a couple of Cony-catching Rascals have stoln her from me.

Black. What, were they Butchers, or Rabbet-men.

Thump. They might be Butchers by their slippery tricks, but I take them to be Gentlemen, Cony-catchers, Smell-smocks, Tear-plackets. Now, Old House, if thou wilt help me to get her again, thou shalt have her Maiden-head, if thou canst get it.   201

Black. Sayst thou so? Well, a match if it stand. But what must I do?

Thump. Why, do you take this Sheet, and do as I did.

Black. I, but who shall cry my Black?

Thump. Why, that will I; now hear.

> Come buy my black,
> dilicate black,
> who buys my black,
> dainty fine white black,   210
> come buy my black.   [*Exit.*

Enter Gentlemen.

1. *Gent.* Our Sentinel keeps well his standing.
   Black. Ho, ho, ho, ho.
2. *Gent.* But has not done to our commanding.
   Black. Ho, ho, ho, ho.

1. *Gent.* Wherefore did he leave his mumming?
   Black. Ho, ho, ho.
2. *Gent.* The reason was of our not coming.
   Black. Ho, ho, ho, ho.

1. *Gent.* This House is haunted surely, Brother.   220
   Black. Ho, ho, ho.

[1] *Thumpkin* in the original.

2. *Gent.* See, here comes just such another.

[*Enter* Thumpkin.

  Black.   Ho, ho, ho, ho.

1. *Gent.* Brother, I think it is the Devil.   P.9
  Black.   Ho, ho, ho.
2. *Gent.* He's come to plague us for our evil.
  Black.   Ho, ho, ho, ho, ho.   [*Jumps off the Stool.*

A kind Young Man you have abused, fa la, fa la.
T*hump.* And in troth his Love mis-used, fa la, la.

Black. Your furious Weapons straight deliver, fa, la, la.   230
T*hump.* See how the Rascals quake and quiver, fa, la, la.

Both. We do, we do, here, pray Sirs, take e'm, fa, la, la.
Black. Our looks do like an Ague shake e'm, fa, la, la.

Both. It does, it does, pray leave your roaring, fa, la, la.
T*hump.* Be gone, and say y'ave scapt a scouring, fa, la, la.

[*Exeunt.*

24

The Cheaters Cheated.[1]

A Representation in four parts to be Sung, Nim. Filcher, Wat, *and* Moll, *made for the Sheriffs of*
London.

Enter Nim. *a Cheat at one door, and* Filcher *his
fellow at the other.*

[1.]

Nim. GOod morrow fellow *Filcher*,
  What, do we sink or swim?
Thou look'st so like a Pilcher?
 Filch. Good morrow fellow *Nim*,
The Devil's in our destiny,
 I cannot get a pluck.
Nim. No, surely if the Devil were in't
 We should have better luck.

2.

Fil. What Star is my director,
 I am in such a state?
Nim. Nay, prethe brother *Hector*
 Do not fall out with Fate;
For we are fortunes Minions,
 And fight under her banner,
'Tis she is Queen of all the world.
 Fil. A mischief light upon her.

3.

No money is reveal'd yet,
 I wonder where it lingers?
Nim. The Souldier hath conceal'd it,
 'Tis fast in iron fingers;

P. 35

---

[1] Printed from Jordan's *Royal Arbor of Loyal Poesie* (1664), pp. 34–55. Collier reprinted *A Royal Arbor* in his *Illustrations of Old English Literature*, Vol. III. Fairholt printed the jig from *A Nursery of Novelties* (see pp. 316–17 above) in his *Lord Mayors' Pageants*, II, 214–36.

From whence if we could get it
    By fury or by fraud:
We had as good attempt to pick
    The Pocket of a *Baud*,

4.

Filch. Your roaring *Cavalier*
    Who when he had the Chink,
Would bravely domineer
    In diceing, drabs and drink:
Go ask him now for money
    And he hath none at all,
But cryes 'tis in my Compting-house
    In *Haberdashers-Hall*.

5.

Nim. Our sly Trappanning trade
    Maintain'd with so much fury,
Is openly bewray'd
    Both by the Judge and Jury;
For Lawyers have so many quirks,
    And are such curious skanners,
That they grow cunninger then we,
    And do trappan Trappanners.

6.

Fil. Our dyceing Trade is down too,
    For when we do begin
By drilling wayes to draw   P. 36
    A yonger Brother in
The Souldier falls upon us
    And proves the best Projector.
Nim. Faith every Red-coat now can make
    A puppy of a Hector.

7.

Enter Wat, *a West Countrey-man.*
Fil. Stay prethe who comes here,
    Nim. A gaping Countrey Clown.
Fil. Look how the slave doth stare;
    Nim. He's newly come to town.

Filch. He gazeth in the air as if
    The sky were full of Rockets;
Let's fleece him. (*Nim.*) But how shall we get
    His hands out of his pockets?

8.

Fil. Let me alone for that:
    I lately bought a glass,[1]
Wherein all several colours may
    Be seen that ever was,
If held up thus with both hands.
    Nim. A pretty new design,
This trick will fetch his fingers out;
    Filch. And hey then in go mine.

9.   *Tune changeth.*

Wat. Our *Taunton den* is a dungeon,
    And yvaith cham glad cham here,
This vamous zitty of *Lungeon*
    Is worth all *Zomerzet-zhere:*
In Wagons, in Carts, and in Coaches   P. 37
    Che never did yet zee more horse,
The Wenches do zhine like Roches,
    And as proud as my fathers vore horse.

10.

Che never zince che was able
    To keep my vathers voulds,
Did ever zee such a stable
    As thick a thing called *Powls:*
A Mezle in a red Jacket
    Had like to have knack me down,
Because che'd undertake it
    Held all the beast in the Town

11.

Ch'am come to zee my Lord Major,
    And thick as do hang the Thieves,
Ch've forgot what vine neames they are;
    (A meazle on them) the zhreeves,

[1] The first two lines are printed as one in the original.

They zay they wear Chains and Scarlets,
    And vollow'd by many Guardiants,
Ch'ave lost the neams of the Varlets,
    A mischief on them, the Serjeants.

12.

And now chill walk my stations
    To every place in Town,
Che mean to buy new vashons,
    Iche have above fifty pound;
Che took't away from vather
    When he was gon a vield:
Cham come away the rather   P. 38
    'Cause ch'ave got a wench with childe.

13.

Filch. The Rainbow never knew   *Tune change.*
    Such Colours as are here,   Filcher *and*
Nim. Here's Purple, Green and Blew, Nim. *looking*
    Wat. Zooks what have they got there. *in the glass.*
Good morrow Master, what d'ye cal't,
    Filch. Good morrow good man clot.
Wat. Nay vaith vine Gallant there y'are out
    My Neame is honest *Wat.*

14.

Fil. I'le shew thee such a slight that
    Thou ne're saw'st honest *Wat,*
Neither by day nor night yet.
    Wat. Yvaith ch'ud laugh at that.
Fil. Here take this glass into thy hand
    And hold it to thy eyes,
Thou there wilt see more colours than
    A Dyar can devise.

15.

Wat. I cannot zee a colour yet,
Nim. Thou dost not hold it high,
Wat. Che hav't, che ha't, ch'av got it now,
    Nim. Ifaith and so have I.   (green,   *Picks his*
Wat. Here's black, and blew, and gray, and   *Pocket.*
    And orange-tauny, white;
And now Ich ave lost all agen.   Filch. *picks*
    Fil. In troth y'are in the right,   *tother Pocket.*

16.

Now prethe tell me honest *Wat*,
  How do'st thou like my glass
Wat. It is the vittest veat yvaith
  That e're was brought to pass
And if that thou wilt spare it
  Chill give thee money down.
Fil. I will have nothing for it   *feels in's*
  [*Wat*.]¹ Chill give thee half a Crown.   *pocket*.

17.

Yvaith cham very willing.
  Nim. You shall not do it now,
[*Wat*.]¹ To give thee vour zhilling,
  Filch. 'Tis more then you can do.   *Aside*.
Nim. Farewel good *Wat*, thou shalt not pay,
  Good morrow Gentlemen;
Wat. Chill get me gone vor vear that they
  Zhould get my glass agen.   *Exit* Wat.

18.   *Tune change.*

Fil. Quick let us share
  For fear of apprehension.
Nim. *Gusman* could ne're
  Compare with this invention.
Fil. That rustick Clown
  Hath brought a happy harvest.
Nim. Lay your Money down.
  Fil. My purse is at your service
Crown for Crown.

19.   P. 40

Nim. Open the Purse,
  Our Ship of Fortune sail's in't.   *Open it.*
Fil. O heavy curse
  It hath nothing but nails in't.
Nim. Ne're men till now
  Were gull'd by such a Costard;
Fil. If we meet I vow
  Wee'l bang the bacon bastard
    black and blew.

¹ Written in the margin in the copy in the British Museum.

20.   *Open the*
                                            other.
Unlock that font
    Let's enter by degrees in't.
Nim. A pox upon't,
    There's nought but bread and cheese in't.
Fil. Come let's depart
    And drink a Saxon Rumkin.
Nim. I am vext at heart,
    But if I spare the *Bomkin*,
Hang me for't.   *Exeunt.*

Enter Mol Medlar Sola, *with a Basket.*

Tune changeth.

[21.]¹

Souldiers fight and Hectors rant on
    Whilst poor Wenches go to rack,
Who would be a wicked wanton
    Onely for Suppers, Songs, and Sack,
To endure the alteration
    Of these times that are so dead;
Thus to lead a long vacation   P. 41
    Without Money, Beer, or Bread.

22.

Farewel *Bloomsberry* and *Sodom*,
    Lukeners-lane and *Turnbull-street*,
Woe was me when first I trod 'em
    With my wilde unwary feet.
I was bred a Gentlewoman,
    But our family did fall
When the Gentry's coin grew common,
    And the Souldiers shar'd it all.

23.

I was sure unto a Hector
    Who hath basely broke his vow,
Would I had a good projector
    That would well support me now.

¹ Not in the original. The numbering of the stanzas proceeds correctly, however, after the omission here and at 33 and 56.

Who comes here? what simple Thumkin,   *Ent.* Wat.
　　Oh! I guess him by his coat,
This is sure some Countrey Bumkin,
　　Now 'tis time to change my note.

24.

I can dance, and I can sing   *Tune chang-*
　　I am good at either,   *eth, she sing-*
And I can do the tother thing   *eth and dan-*
　　When we get together.   *ceth.*

25.

I have lately lost my dear,
　　'Twas a holy Brother;
If he do not meet me here
　　I faith I'le get another.

26.

P. 42

I can nimbly come above,
　　I can tumble under,
And If I do but like my *Love*,
　　Wat. What *Vary's* that is yonder?

27.

'Tis a dainty dancing Girle,
　　Zhee would make me gladder,
Her vace doth zyne like mother of Pearl,
　　chould chuse no more and chad her.

28.

Mol. A Dutch-man loves his Pipe and Can,
　　A Jew doth like a Turk well,
But I could hug a *Countrey-Man*,
　　For he will do his work well.

29.

Citizens are full of slight,
　　They will cog and flatter;
But a Countrey-man will do me right.
　　Wat. Che long now to be at her.

30.

Good morrow Mistris Trip and goe,
   Mol. My *Countrey-man* I take it,
I love you Sir, (*Wat*) Chill love thee to,
   And vayth chil veze thy Jacket.

31.

Mol. What's thy name, come tell me that
   Thou shalt be my Jewel?
Wat. Why zom vorzooth do call me *Wat*,
   But my neame is *Water-Gruel*.

32.

Prethe zay, and ben't avrayd,
   Art not thou a Pedlar?
Mol. I live close by in Tickle Yard,
   My name is *Mary Medlar*.

P. 43

33.

Wat. Then zweet *Mol* come buss thy *Wat*,
   Let us twain be merry:
Mol. I could nimbly dance, but that
   My Basket makes me[1] weary.

[34.][2]

Wat. Give it me, chill dance a Spring,
   Che have no veaver Lurden?
Mol. If thou wilt dance, then I will sing,
   And thou shalt bear the Burden.

*He takes
her Bas-
ket.*

35.

Wat. A match, a match, it's well a vine,
   We both zhall make some ztuff on't.
Mol. Unless thy feet keep pace with mine
   Thoul't quickly have ynough on't.

*Both dance
to their
own sing-
ing*

36.

Wat. Well don *Moll*, (*Moll*) 'tis well done *Wat*,
   Wat. Chill do it to a tittle,
Mol. But I have too much strain'd my throat,
   I prethe sing a little,

She doth

---

[1] *we* in the original.

[2] Stanzas 33 and 34 are printed as one eight-line stanza.

dance off.

37.

Wat. Fa la la la liera lo
    This is pretty prancing,
We will go to Tickle Yard
    When we have done dancing.

38. P. 44

Now che think ch'av vetcht it up
    Zing a little *Mary,*
We will gulge a merry zup,
    Zhuggar and *Canary.*

39.

Thou dost dance and make no noise   *Turns about*
    Zhall I turn and kiss thee?   *and misseth*
Prethe let me hear thy voice.   *her.*
    Hoop where the Devil is she?

40.

Zhe hath left me all alone
    Here to mum and mask it,
But yvaith if zhe be gon
    Ich chill keep her Basket.

41.

Here's good vortune come to me
    In a merry minuit,
Now chill puttne down and zee
    What zhee have gotten in it.

42.   *Tune changeth, he*

Oh! wo, wo, what zhall chee do,   *sets down the Bas-*
Che con no know which way to go   *ket and looks in it.*
With thick whore here and her vyne zong,
Che have a bore her burden too long;
Che may curse the occasion that e're che came here,
Would che were agen in *Zomerzet-zhere.*

43.   *Pulls a Childe*

O! Lungeon Ich cham undone   *out of the*
Ch'ave a brungeon a daughter or a zon,   *Basket.*

Thick a jewel hath me beguil'd,   P. 45
Water Gruel must now veed the childe,
Ich chud never be zorry, but vind it a place
If che had now but good store of Larzhant;
It looks Tory rory, and zmells zo of Mace,
That a zure it was got by zome zarzhant.   *Hushes it,*
                                                            carries it
                        44.   *to the men,*

Goodman zhreeve ze, look on the vace   *then to the*
Vor a believe me it may be your own case,   *women.*
Honest vree men Ich cham basely begeld,
Good a woman hold but the cheld,
Chil but step here hard by, 'tis but home to *Taunden*,
And chill bring ye zom gold in a Casket,
Thick all are hard hearted both women and men,
Che must march with my youth in a Basket,   *Puts it in*
                                               agen to the
                        45.   *Basket*
                                               and Exit.
                Enter Filcher *and* Nim.   *Tune change.*

Fil. We shall ne're have lucky minuit,
    None of our designs will hit;
Nim. Some ill Planet sure is in it,
    Fortune makes a fool of wit:
            All our feats
            Are simple cheats,
                And destiny will have it so.
            Fil. There's nothing hits
            But with those wits
                That cheat *Cum Privilegio*.
            Nim. The holy drum   P. 46
            And godly gun
                Are now the onely Engines that
            Make Pimp and Whore
            And Hector poor,
                And wise men do they know not what.

                        46.

Fil. All our joyful dayes do leave us,
    Nim. Never were such times as these,
Fil. Every Bumkin can deceive us   (cheese.
    Nim. With hob-nails (*Fil.*) and with bread and

Fil.[1] Though we mist it
He confest it
   That he brought up fifty pound,
Nim. Where he did it
How he hid it.
   Is the plot that may be found.
Filch. If we meet him
We will fit him.
   Nim. Hark I here one coming in
Very pleasant   *They retreat to*
'Tis the Peasant   *several corners.*
   Filch. Now let's to our guards agen.

                       Tune changeth.

Enter Wat *with a little Trunck on a stick hanging at
his back.*

47.

Now farawel Lungeon Iche may zing,
Chill no more here until the next spring,
Chave put in security vor the thing,   P. 47
       Which no body can deny.

48.

Che did a veat in *Zomerzet-Zhere*
Which vorst me at virst to zee vashons here,
Ich cham out of the vrying pan into the vere,
       Che either must burn or vrye.

49.

In plush and in zatten a vynely wrought,
Ich chave laid out forty pound every groat.
Fil. I want a silk Wastcoat, (*Nim.*) I lack a plush Coat,
     Wat. Ch'have puttne all in the Trunk.

50.

Here's zilk and gold, and zilver strings,   {*Fil. comes a-
Here's Gloves, silk Hozen, Points, and Rings.   {*lone to* Wat.
Fil. Stand (*Wat.*) what are you (*Fil.*) Lay down your
   things.
     [*Wat.*] Why zure the Meazle is drunk.

[1] *Nil.* in the original.

51.

What would ye do to a poor Countrey man,
Nim. First lay down your Trunk, you shall know
    more anon:
Wat. And a very vine way to have my Trunk gone:
        Filch. Do so or I'le knock thee down.

52.   (it man

Wat. Nay vaith good man Gentle since ch'have zeen
Chill lay it down there, and if che can win it
Thou zhalt have my Trunk and all that is in it:
        'Twill cost above vorty pound.

53.   P. 48

Fil. I'l have as much blood as thy heart   *Filch. draws*
    can afford.   *and fights.*
Wat. Thou cowardly knave, wilt thou vight with a
    zword;
But since 'tis but one, Ich che care not a Twoord,
    [*Nim.*] And what do you think of another.   *Nim. draws.*

54.

Nim. This Rapier I thorow thy body will run,
Wat. Ud zooks there's no vighting with two   *Exit.*
    agen one,   *Wat.*
Ich che rather will trust to my legs and be gon.
    Fil. Why now gramercy brother.

55.

Nim. The rascal already is run out of sight,
Fil. His hands are vile heavy. (*Nim.*) His legs are as
    light,
The Plush for a Jacket, I claim as my right,
    Fil. Which really I deny.

[56.]

For was it not I that prov'd the Projector. (tector,
Nim. But if this good sword had not been your Pro-
The clown would have made you a pittiful Hector,
    And beaten you. (*Fil.*) Sirra ye lye.

57.

My force hath been try'd against Castles and Towers,
The prize as it lies is equally ours,
Let victory make it out mine or yours,
    Nim. I grant it with all my heart.

They fight,
Enter Moll.

P. 49

58.

Mol. What mad men are these! pray what do you
    mean,
I never did see such a sorrowful scene;
Nay sweet Mr. *Filcher* (*Fi.*) stand further ye Quean,
    I'le make the proud Rascal smart.

59.   (out?

Mol. You always were friends, what makes ye fall
Pray tell me true, what is the quarrel about;
Nim. This duel will suddenly end all the doubt:
    Mol. I'le suffer between your swords.

*They make
passes.*

Moll *is
between.*

60.

E're such a kind couple of Hectors as yee
Shall squabble and quarrel for *Paddington-tree.*
Jack Filcher, Tom Nim, be counsel'd by me,
    Deliver your Cause in words,

61.

You know that the Law against Duels is high:
Nim. That *Rodomontado* there gave me the lye,
Mol. Pray do but consider that *Tyburn* is nigh;
    Nim. That very word cools my wrath.

62.

For my own part I onely would live by my Trade,
Fil. The Bargain betwixt us must end by the blade;
Mol. Pray let me but know the conditions ye made,
    I'le judge it between ye both.

63.

Fil. Ile tell you then how the quarrel did rise,
This fellow and I have took a rich prize,
Nim. And now he denies me my share in't. (*Fil.*) he lies,
    We agreed that the sword should decide it.

P. 50

64

This Trunk is well furnished as e're it can hold,
With silk and with velvet, with silver and gold.
Mol. Turn't all into money, and when it is sold,
    You equally may divide it.

65.

But first what assurance have you when you win it,
'Tis worth all this danger (*Nim.*) We yet have not seen [it.]
[*Mol.*] Why then let us open't and see what is in it,
    That ev'ry thing may be shown.

66.

Nim. A match, let her break the Trunk open and see.
Mol. It may be by this means you'l sooner agree.
Fil. Faith open't or shut it 'tis all one to me,
    I vow I'le have all or none.

{ Mol *opens*
{ *The trunk.*

67.

Mol. Then look on your bargain, you both are be-
    guil'd,
Pray tell me if this be the velvet three pil'd,
Is this figur'd satten? (*Nim.*) I vow 'tis a child.
    You swore you'd have all or none.

Mol *takes*
out the
childe.

68.

Fil. I'le stand to my bargain, for I will have none.
Nim. What? can you so suddenly alter your tone.
Mol. Come kiss it and love it, for faith 'tis your own.
    Remember when we were alone.

69.

For this pretty Babe I have shed many showers,
And suffer'd a thousand disconsolate hours,
As sure as 'tis mine, I'm certain its yours,
    I never knew Man but you.

P. 51

70.

Fil. These Projects to me are Riddles and Charms,
How came the child hither? (*Mol.*) For fear of worse
    harms,
I left it even now in a Countreymans's arms,
    A fellow that I never knew.

71.

'Twas left to be lost though the plot would not hit,
I never could see you to tell you of it,
A Countrey-man brought it. (*Fil.*) A pox of his wit,
    I would I were rid of my life.

72.

Mol. Before I knew *Filcher*, I was a pure Maid,
Pray do but Remember the Contract we made;
You said you would wed me, and live by your trade.
    Fil. I'le presently make thee My Wife.

73.

Mol. For all the worlds wealth I will ne're be a whore.
Fil. I'le purchase new Credit upon an old score.
Nim. Ile deal in these damnable courses no more.
    All. We every one will mend.

74.

Fil. I never will quarrel, or swagger and roar,
Nim. Then make the poor *Simpletons* pay all the score,
Mol. I never will do as I have done before.
    All. We every one will mend.

Enter Wat Solus.

Exeunt.
P. 52

75.

Tune change.

Ch'have overcome my voes,
    And *Watty* now is vree;
It is no zin to couzen those,
    That would have cheated me:

76.

Had che but met with one,
    Che had not been o'remaster'd;
Ich che wonder what they thought upon,
    when they did vind the Bastard.

77.

Did ever vellow vinde
    Zuch zimple zots as these,
To leave my fifty pounds behinde,
    And steal my Bread and Cheese:

78.

Theise zitty theeves are fool'd,
    That meant to do me hurt,
The Meazles could not vind my gold,
    che knittne in my zhurt;

79.

Ich che cannot chuse but zmile,
    That men who can talk lattin,
Zhould be zuch fools to take a Child
    Vor velvet, zilk, and zatten:

80.

But Pride will have a vall,
    The Proverb zaith as much;
Now how do you my Measters all,   P. 53
    Ich cham com to laugh a touch.

81.

God bless my Lady Zhreeve,
    And all that noble pack;
Ch'am almost dead with grief,
    Che want a cup a zack.

82.

God zave my measter too,
    And zend him to live long;
Vayth now ch'a nothing else to do,
    Chill zing a merry zong.

A Song on the twelve Companies.

83.

THe other day among many papers,
    Che vown'd a vine zong of the Merchants and
  Drapers,   (ners,
The Grocers, the Goldsmiths, the Taylors and Skin-
And many zuch vinical zinners.

1 *Mercers*. 84.

The *Mercer* virst a vine dapper blade is,
He zells yee zoft zattin, and very well paid is;
He makes his Commodity cover the Ladies,
Zo zoft and zweet his Trade is.

2. *Grocers*. 85.

The *Grocer* layes his zhuggered baits,
He loves to have his zhip zail in the Straits;
He deals for sweet Almonds, Prunello's, and Dates,
With Ladies as light as his weights.

3. *Drapers*. 86.

The *Drapers* next in my fancy doth hover.
It is the best Trade betwixt *Barwick* and *Dover;*
But when his zhort Yard the women discover,
They will have a handful over.

P. 54

4. *Fishmongers*. 87.

And now have at the *Fishmongers* jacket,
It proves a good trade as the Taverns do make it:
But of all the vish in the zea chil undertake it,
He'd rather have a virgin naked.

5. *Goldsmiths*. 88.

The *Goldsmiths* stall will make me to stop,
For *Goldsmiths-Hall* hath been a great prop;
Of all the rich mysteries this is the top,
The Tower was a *Goldsmith's* zhop.

6. *Merchant-Taylors*. 89.

The *Merchant-Taylors* may not be outed,
His Calling hath been e're zince *Adam* was routed:
A zuit makes a Gallants wealth not to be doubted,
That is but a Beggar without it.

7. *Skinners*. 90.

The *Skinners* hate Ich che must not incurr,
He covers the Corps of your Worshipful Zur,
And cleaves to your Aldermans back like a bur,
Whose lineing is Voxes vur.

8. *Haberdashers.* 91.

Your *Haberdashers* Art che may call,
The onely fine trade that doth cover us all;
But woe to the *Cavalier* that did vall
Into *Haberdashers-Hall.*

9. *Salters.* 92.

P. 55

The *Zalters* trade we zhall not omit,
The *Scholars* zay Zalt is an Emblem of Wit;
But vaith I believe they love a vresh bit,
When *Mutton* and *Capers* meet.

10. *Iron-mongers.* 93.

The fame of *Iron-mongers* do ring,
The strength of the Mettle can conquer a King;
The *Helmet, Musket,* and *Gauntlet* can bring
A *Scepter* out of a *Sling.*

11. *Vintners.* 94.

The *Vintner's* Art but vew men do know,
Vor it is a zience too zuttle to zhow;
The Devil and he a Conjuring go,
When both are a brewing below.

12. *Cloth-workers.* 95.

The *Cloth-workers* trade is a very vine thing,
And of all the Trades may be counted the King;
But yet he will merrily tipple and zing,
'Till his wits go a Wool-gathering.

96.

And now Ic che hope no Tradesman will take
Exzeptions at me vor my merriment sake;   (niest,
Their Trades are all good, but the *Vintner's* the bon-
God bless them and make them all honest.

97.

Ic che now will go home to *Zomerzetzheere,*
And tell all the Countrey what vine things are here;
Chil jog to my *Jug,* and zee what God hath zent her,
And chil come here agen next Winter.

End of the Representations.

25

Roland genandt.[1]

Ein Fewr new

Lied/der Engellendisch Tantz

genandt / zugebrauchen auff allerley Instrumenten/&c. Gar kurtzweilig
zusingen vnd zu Dantzen: In seiner eignen Melodey.

[CUT]

1599.

[1]

[*Roland.*]	O Nachbar Robert/ mein hertz ist voller Pein:	[A j*v*]
Robert.	O Nachbar Roland/ warumb soll das so sein?	
Roland.	Johan Küster liebt meine Greten/ vnd das bringt mir ein schmertz.	
Robert.	Sey zu friden guter Rolandt/ es ist noch wol ein schertz.	

2.

Rolandt.	Sie sind mit einander auffm Kirchhoff/	
Robert.	O weh vnd was schadt aber das?	
Roland.	Sie schertzen da/ ich förcht mich/ sie thun ich weiß nicht was.	
Robert.	Sey zu friden guter Rolandt/ vnd thu nach meim gebott/	
Roland.	Sih/ wo sie kommen zusamen/ so ist mein hertz schier Todt.	A ij

[1] Printed from Berlin Library Ye 726, a pamphlet of eight small pages, the last
blank. The text is in black letter, as are also the speakers' names, which are printed
in a smaller type above the speeches. In a few cases speeches of more than one line are
printed as verse. Usually they are printed as prose, the punctuation in most cases
indicating the verse division. See pp. 219–20 for the various texts. Speakers' names
omitted from the original are supplied in brackets from the version in "Zwey Schone
newe Lieder/ genanndt der Rolandt."

491

3.

Robert.	Lig nider vnd verstecke dich/ vnnd hör nur was sie sagen.
Roland.	Nein/ so wil ich auffstehn/ vnd wil sie hinweg jagen.
Robert.	So verlaß ich dich guter Roland/
Roland.	O Robert wie bistu gesindt?
Robert.	Mein klugheyt sol dir helffen/
[*Roland.*]	ich schlag den Küster blind.

4.

[*Küster.*]	Was mangelt meiner Margreta/ das sie mich so fremd ansicht.	
Margreta.	Ich glaub das du mich nicht Liebest/ so wol als ich thu dich.	
Küster.	Hastu verlassen Roland?	[A ij*v*]
Margreta	Das ist schon lang geschehen.	
Küster.	So wil ich dich nun haben:	
Roland.	Aber hie ligt einer/ spricht nein.	

5.

Robert.	Gott grüß euch liebe Margreta/ ich bring nichts guts News:
Margreta.	Vnd was ist das gut Robert/ du machst mich nicht fast weiß.
Robert.	Ewer Roland ist gestorben/
Margreta.	Ach Robert hastus gesehn?
Robert.	Drumb das jhr liebt den Küster/
Küster.⟨A iij⟩	Ey last jhn vmmer gehn.

6.

Margreta.	O vnbarmhertzig Margreta/ hastu jhn bracht vmbs Leben?
Küster.	Süsse Lieb verlasse jhn/
[*Roland.*]	Ich wil dir stösse geben/
[*Margreta.*]	O Robert es gerewet mich/
Robert.	Vnd das ist dir ein spott.
Küster.	Ker vmb zu mir/ vnd liebe mich/
Roland.	Ich schlag den Küster Todt.

7.

Robert. Sihe/ wo Er liget/
    der dich wolt ausserweln.
Margreta. Vergib mir gutter Rolandt/
    mein schmertzen kan keine erzehln.
Küster. [A iijv] Vmb sonst ist all diß trawren/
    komm Margret geh mit mir.
Margreta. Trän können Roland nicht helffen/
    komm Küster ich gang mit dir.

8.

Küster. Jetzunder soll mein Hochzeit sein/
Margreta. Mein willen hastu berait.
Roland. Aber hört zu Nachbar Kister
    ein wort/ eh jhr hingeht.
Margreta. Lebt noch mein lieber Roland/
Küster. Das ist mir ein hertzlaid vnd[1] pein.
Roland. Geh in die Kirch leut die Glocken/
    Heut sol mein Hochzeit sein.

9.

Margreta. [A iv] Ich lieb kein andern/ als Roland/
Robert. Du Küster geh hinwegk/
Küster. Wil Margret mich verlassen?
Margreta. Du bist ein Närrischer Geck.
Küster. Leichtfertigen Jungkfrawen traw ich nicht.
Roland.[2] Geh mach dem Küstners Grab:
Nun ist Margreta Rolands/
    darumb geh du Narr bist schabab.

ENDE.

[1] vn in the text.
[2] Rob. in "Zwey Schone newe Lieder/ genanndt der Rolandt."

26

Zwey Schone

newe Lieder/genanndt der
Rolandt/von der Männer
vnd Weyber vn-
trew.

[CUT]

Das erste.
Von den Männern/&c.[1]

1. Agnes.

E In weyl last vns beysamen bleybn/
Ir dörfft nicht so baldt heime eyln/
Cl. Mein Mann ich weyß der wart zu hauß
Vnd wunder das ich bleybe auß.
2. Cat. Habt grossen danck ach liebe Agnes/
Vor alles gûts vnd ewre Speyß/
Jetzund kan es nicht anders sein/
Ich mûß zu Hauß zum Lieblein mein.
3. Clar. Mein Mann/ ich weyß/ der warte meinr/
Car. Vnd meiner auch so wol als deinr/
Clar. Mein Mann liebt mich vber die massn/
Cat. Vnd meiner will mich nicht verlassen.
4. Ag. Ach schweiget doch was saget jhr/
Mein Mann der geht dem ewren für/
Seins gleichen nicht vnderm Himmel ist.
Clar. Vor falscher Lieb vnd arge lüst.
5. Ag. Mein Mann hat mich zu mahlen lieb/
Clar. Wenn er bey dir alleine blieb/
Ag. Er liebet doch kein andere als mich/
Clar. Er hat ein andere lieber als dich.

[1] Printed from Berlin Library Yd 7850,17, a pamphlet of eight pages with the last blank. This singspiel is closely printed in the four pages immediately following the title-page and is followed by a version of "Rowland." It has been reprinted in Keller's *Fastnachtspiele*, II, 1021–25, and by Kopp in Herrig's *Archiv*, CXVII, 8–10. I have preserved the form of the original.

6. Ag. Ach weh ist mir.
Cat.   Was mangelt euch.
Ag. Mein Hertz ist wehe
Clar.   Sie wirdt gar bleich:
Cat. Ach seydt zu friden vnd förcht euch nit/
Wer weyß obs euch zu Glauben steht/
7. Clar. Versuch sein Lieb vnd sey getrew/
Denn wirst erfaren was er sey.
Ag. Das will ich thůn dir zu gefallen/   A ij
Aber Jan/ liebt mich vber alln.
8. Clar. Fraw Agnes seht da kompt ewr Mann/
Den jr seht für den getrewsten an/
Ligt nider da als werd jr Todt/
So will ich euch helffen auß der noth/
9. O Nachbar Jan/
Jan/   Was saget jr.
Clar. Ewer Fraw ist todt.
Jan/   O weh ist mir.
Clar. Ach seydt zu friden vnd habt gedult/
Jan. Lieber will ich sterben vmb jr huld.
10. Ich will mich selber vmbbringen/
Clar. Nein Jan/ das soll euch nicht gelingn.
Ag. Ach liebe Clar nun wartet seinr.
Clar. Er wirdts nicht thůn gedencket meinr.
11. Jan. O weh/ O weh mein liebes Weyb/
Hat der Todt berürt deinen Leyb/
So sey es zu gesaget dich/
Kein ander Weyb will nemen ich.
12. Ag. Ach du aller getrewester Jan/
Clar. Still/jetzt wirdts hören jederman/
Wie getrew das er zu euch ist/
Gebt vns doch noch ein wenig frist.
13. Cat. Gůt Nacht/ gůt Nacht O lieber Jan/
Ag. Mein einger allerliebster Mann/
Cat. Gůt Nacht/
Jan. Auch euch/ aber bleybt jhr hie/
Clar. Das will ich gern/ was wolt jr mir?
14. Jan. Ach liebe Clar was saget jr/
Ich hab euch lieb/ das glaubet mir.
Clar. Köndt jr ewr Fraw so bald vergessn.
Das hett ich euch nit zugemessn.   [A ij*v*]

15. Jan. Ach schweigt doch mein Fraw ist todt/
Wolt jr mir helffen auß der noth/
Seht da nembt alles von jr hin/
Wo ich euch anderst der liebste bin:

16. Hie nimb die Schlüssel denn als ist dein/
Clar. Ach lieber Jan wilt du mein sein/
Jan. Ja liebe Clar denn kusset mich/
Ag. O du vngetrewer Bößwicht.

17. Jan [.] hie nimb die Ring von jhrer Handt/
Die geb ich dir nun all zum Pfandt/
Sie ist nun Todt wer fragt nach jr.
Ag. Das hab[1] ich nit zu getrawet dir.

18. Jan. Kom*m* laß vns gehn/ wer fragt nach jhr/
Ich will ein Schuffkarrn schicken hier/
Der sie nach Kirchhoff führen kan/
Sie stincket schon auff disem Plan.

19. Ag. O du böser Schelm will dich bezahln/
Wilt du einen Schuffkarrn lassen holn/
Jan. Kom*m* laß vns von hinnen gehn/
Ag. Aber ich bin hie/ vnd sage nein.

20. Jan. Ach halt nun still ich bitt dich/
Ag. Kanst du die Ring nemen von mich/
Gib du mir wider alle ding/
Vnd auch darzu die Gûlden Ring.

21. Cla. Gibs wider zu deiner Frawen Gaist/
Jan. Nein es ist der Teüffel das ich wol weyß/
Ein Gaist nit so hart schlagen kan/
Ag. Ich laß dich nit du vntrew Mann.

22. Jan. Ach halt nur still vmb Gottes willn/
Vnd laß doch deinen zoren stillen/
Ag. Du sagst du wolst mich lassen schuffn/
Jan. O liebes Weyb/ peccaui ich rûffe/

A [iij][2]

23. Ag. Ein Buhler pfui dich an/
Mein Mann der ist der gemeste Han/
Jan. Ach lieb Nachbarn euch bitte ich/
Ihr sagt sie solt vergeben mich.

24. Cat. Das wöllen wir thûn O lieber Jan/
Cla. Vergebt doch jetzund ewrem Mann/
Ag. Das will ich thûn auff dein zusagn/
Jan. Was ist es dann ich will es wagn.

---

[1] *hah* in the original.   [2] "A v" in the original.

25. Ag. Heb auff zwen Fingr/ vnd schwere hier
Daß du gehorssam leistest mir/
Vnd haltest mich für deinen Herrn/
Vnd diene mir in grossen Ehrn.
26. Jan. Das will ich thůn.
Ag.   Den folge mir.
Jan. Ich will gehorsam sein zu dir/
Nun seh ich was ich offt hab gehört/
Die grawen Mern sind dbesten Pferdt.
27. Cla. Nun liebe Nachbarn lobet mich/
Die Frawen hann gewunn den Sieg/
Cat. Laß alle Frawen lernen weyt vnd breyt/
Zu wissen jrer Männer Schalckheit.

[DIE STREITENDEN LIEBHABER][1]

Ein neuw Liedt mit vier Personen
auff die Melodei: Ach nachbar Roland.

A. Der Erste buhler tregt einen krantz auffem Heubt,
B. Der ander buhler stehet mit blossem Heubtt,
C. Die Jungfrauw tregt ein krentzelein,
D. Der Jungfrauwen mutter.

1.

A. Jungfreulein, mein Jungess Hertz
    hastu vorwundet sehr,
    von deinet wegen leid ich smertz;
    dein Hertze zu mir ker,
    lass mich der lieb geniessen,
    verlass mich nimmermer;
    thue für mir nit zuschliessen
    dein Hertz, ist mein beger.

2.

B. Gleicher mas, Jungfrauw zardt,
    durch ewre schon gestalt
    bin ich mit lieb verwundet hart,
    vorwirret mannigfalt.
    Wolt godt, ihr kont ermessen,
    wie ich euch liebe so sehr,
    Eur Hertze sol vorgessen
    meiner auch nimmermer.

3.

Eur Diener will ich stetes sein,
gebt mir nur ewre gunst,
damit nicht muge das Hertze mein
gemartert sein vmsonst,

---

[1] The text is that printed by Johannes Bolte, "Die streitenden Liebhaber, eine Gesangsposse aus dem 17. Jahrhundert," *Vierteljahrschrift für Litteraturgeschichte*, I, 111–16, from a manuscript songbook in the Königliche Bibliothek of Copenhagen, written by Petrus Fabricius at Rostock in the years 1605–8. The bracketed titles among the singspiele have been supplied by Bolte.

den lieben kostet leben
vnd bringet in grosse nodt,
euch hab ich mich ergeben,
errettet mich auss dem todt.

4.

Ach liebe mutter tugentsam,
vernemt, was ich beger:
Ewr tochter mocht ich gerne hahn
zum weib.   A. Das sey Ja ferr!
Dan mir must ihr sie geben,
das kan nicht anders sein.
Wer wil mich widerstreben?
B. Ach bruder, ich sag nein.

5.

D. Ich danck euch beiden seuberlig
wegen der tochter mein,
mit bit, wolt ihr fein zuchtiglich
anhórn, was ich rate drein.
Ich will euch nit verleiten,
sonder in kurtzer zeidt
thun von einander scheiden,
behend ohn allen streidt.

6.

Mein tochter soll erwehlen,
dan ess billich geschicht;
den wil ich ihr vormehlen,
den sie am liebsten sicht;
man muss bei solchen sachen
Jetzundt in der welt
vernufft vnd Rahtt gebrauchen.
A.B. Der anschlag vns gefelt.

7.

D. Nun Tochter, thue du weisen
mit einem zeichen schnell,
welcher sei von den beiden
dein hertzliebster gesell.

C. Wolt ihr dan damit friedlich sein,[1]
   so saget es mir frey.
A. B. Schons megdelein, gewislich,
   es soll nicht anders sein.

8.

B. Zu wahrer trew vnd sicherung
   geb ich euch meine handt.
A. Zu gewisser verpflichtung
   sol dis auch sein mein pfandt.
A. B. Wir bitten aber fleissig,
   Ihr wolt ohn lang anfaht[2]
   Erlösen vns.   C. Gantz hofflich
   sol das geschehen baldt.

9.

Ach schoner knab, mit diesem schmuck
   soltu gezieret sein,
   von meinetwegen vnverruckt
   lass dirs befolen sein.
B. Ich sage euch danck von Hertzen.
C. Das dorfft ihr warlich nicht.
A. Das bringt mir grosse schmertzen.
B. Die gab erfreuwet mich.

10.

C. Ach Jungelein, ach Jungelein,
   gib mir das krenzlein her.
A. Euch soll es nit vorsaget sein,
   wens auch von perlen wer,
   Ich frew mich aus der massen
   von wegen solcher Ehr.
B. Solt ich den sein vorlassen?
   das hoff ich nummermer.

11.

C.D. Hiemit gehn wir von hinnen,
   Ade zu guter nacht.
A. Mein hertz fertt vort zu brinnen
   in meinem leib mit macht.

---

[1] Bolte conjectures *Wolt ihr sein damit friedlich.*
[2] Bolte emends to *aufhalt.*

B. Wie schon vnd auch wie lieblich
   Ist doch das krentzelein!
A. Die Jungfrauwe gantz hoflich
   nam hin die gabe mein.

12.

Ich hoff vnd achte, das ich sey
   der liebste. B. Nein, ich bins.
A. Wir wollen baldt zusamen frey
   leben— B. Das denck nicht eins!
A. In lusten vnd in freuden
   vnd aller fröligkeit.
B. Du must sie warlich meiden,
   wers dir auch immer leidt.

13.

A. Sie setzt mein krentzlein auff den kopff,
   zu zeigen deutlich an,
   das ich solt— B. Ey du grober tropff!
A. Gewisslich sein ihr man.
B. Ja hinter sich! A. vnd herschen,
   wie mir das wolgefelt.
B. Mich dunckt, man wirt euch gecken,
   der korb ist schon bestelt.

14.

A. Kein grosser freud auff dieser Erd
   mir kondt ietz widerfaren,
   den das ich heut ein megdlein werdt
   beynah von aczein Jaren
   Erlangt. B. Lass doch dein rumen,
   vergeblich ist dein sin,
   du mochtest dich wol betruben;
   den ich sie nemme hin.

15.

A. Das hat gemacht mein krauses Har —
B. O tropff! A. Vnd gelber bardt —
B. Du bist ein narre, das ist wahr.
A. Dazu mein glieder zardt,
   mein grosse kunst — B. Hans Hase!

A. Verlest mich nit in nodt,
 setzt mich — B. Dreck auff die nase.
A. Das megdlein in den schoss.

16.

 Ach Bruder, lass dich raten!
B. Dir selber raht entbricht.
A. Weich ab von solchen thaten,
 dass megdlein — B. kreigstu nicht.
A. Tregt mein krantz — B. Vnd ich ihren.
A. Zum zeichen warer treuw,
B. Sie thutt dich recht vexieren.
A. Das ich mich ser erfreuw.

17.

 Was mir Godt hadt bescheret,
 das wirstu mir wol lahn.
B. Ein korb ist dir vorehret,
 den machstu sicher han.
A. Ich mus man gan vnd kauffen
 zur Hochzeit alles ein,
B. Du machst wol sachte lauffen,
 die Braudt ist doch woll mein.

18.

 Ach gnedig Hern vnd freulein,
 weil ihr gesehen habt,
 wie mir ist heutt das krentzelein
 verehr[1] zu einer gab,
 Ich bit, ihr wolt erkennen,
 wer doch der liebste sey,
 vnd ihnen deuttlich nennen;
 dass sol euch stehen frey.

19.

 Hiemit wil ich von hinnen gehn,
 dess vrtheils gwertich sein.
A. Ich hoff, das megdlein werd ich sehn
 baldt in mein kemmerlein.
B. Im kuhstall lass dich warmen,
 dass du so gar verblendt,
 des muss ich mich erbarmen.
 Solchs schenck ich euch behend.

---

[1] Bolte emends to *verehrt.*

Das ander Engeländisch Possenspiel von Pückelherings

Dill dill dill╱so hat

er mir verdorben╱mein al-
lerschönste Möhl.[1]

Gantz lustig mit fünff Personen

zu agirn╱darbey zu mercken╱was

mit kleiner Schrifft gedruckt╱
nicht gesungen wird.

[TWO CUTS]

Im Thon: Wie vielen╱so er zu öfftern
agirn gehört╱bewust.

Ein lustigs Possenspiel╱ gesangsweiß   [p. 2]
mit fünff Personen zu agieren.

Pückelhering sampt sein Weib treten ein (Pückelhering singt:

1.

MEin liebes Weib╱ wenn ich außgeh╱
heut in die Arbeit mein╱
vnd so etwan einer kompt zu dir╱

[1] Printed from Berlin Library Yq 9101, a pamphlet of eight pages without pagination or signatures. The piece is printed as prose. The general scheme followed is that
of giving a paragraph to each stanza and numbering the paragraphs. In a few cases,
however, the division fails to correspond with the correct stanzaic division. A prose
section, if short, is usually run into the paragraph with the preceding stanza, occasionally into a separate paragraph. The one long prose passage is broken into several un-
numbered paragraphs. Practically all the stage directions, speakers' names when combined with stage directions, and some passages that are properly prose are printed in
small black-letter type. The use of small type is very inconsistent however. Many of
the long stage directions, especially those at the beginning of stanzas, are centered on
the page. Bolte reprinted this text in *Singspiele*, pp. 110–28, with that of the Dutch

vnd will dein Buler seyn/[1]
so sprich Nein/ es kan nicht seyn/
vnd jhn bald schaffe ab/
denn es ist ein schlupfferich Zeit
(*Weib*)   Seydt jhr zu fried/
euch nicht bemüht/
wider euch ich nimmer streit.

2.

(*Pückelhering*) Dann wann ein Puler kompt zu dir/
Pulschafft auff dich zu dringen/
alsbald sprich Nein/ so solt du sehen/
daß keiner dich wird zwingen/
(*Weib*)   Nein Nein nein nein/
Ich will jhn weg schicken alsbald/
daß er sich meiner enthalt/
gebt euch jetzundt zu ruh/
(*Pückelhering*)   Ader[2] mein Adelische Zier/
(*Weib*)   Danck hab Hertz lieber Mann/
komm bald wider zu mir.

Pückelhering geht ab vnd sagt zu seinem Weib/ hör Weib/ wann einer
zu dir kompt/ so vergiß daß nein nicht.)

3.

(*Gabilirer tritt ein vnd singt zu seim Lackey*)
Don Jansa auß Barbaria/
sprach zu seinem Lackey/
Bule mir diese Cortisan/
vnd bring sie bald herbey/
wo der Bawr jhr gibt ein Kuß
will ich jhr geben drey/
von Janha[3] auß Barbaria/
der ist jetzt kusses frey.

"Domine Johannes" of 1658 (D) opposite and the text of the late German version,
"Die doppelt betrogene Eifersucht" (G), following (pp. 129–37). He changed the form
and repunctuated. I have followed the original as closely as possible except for the re-
arrangement in stanzas. Bolte's text has been of great service, but I have made a
different arrangement of much of the verse. For this the other two versions, which
follow the same basic text in spite of much supplementary material, have been valuable.
A few passages have been cited from them indicating the nature of the problems connected with the text.

[1] A line corresponding to the one "Mit nein, nein, nein, nein," which follows in D
and G, has probably dropped out here.

[2] Bolte corrects this to *Ade*.   [3] Bolte substitutes *Don Jansa*.

(Geht drauff zu dem Weib vnd spricht/ schönes Fräwlein wolt jhr mich
nit in ewer lieb annehme*n*/
sie sagt Nein Nein/)
Der Buler sagt auch/ Nein Nein.

4.

(Herr Jan tritt ein vnd thut ein Sprung vnd singt)

> Hey lustig tritt herein/ herr Jan/
> die schön Jungfraw zu sehen/
> mit dem tritt/ vnnd dem trat/
> mit dem Schnip auff den Schnap/
> mit dem Sprung/ wie ein Jung/
> hey lustig wolln wir seyn.

5.   [p. 3]

(Herr Jan)   Sein Schenckel mit Capriol/
> sein Jugend mit widerholt/
> mit eim Trunck/ guten Wein/
> zu eim Sprung/ muß es seyn/
> will ich jhr frisch bezahlen/
> harr doch/ merck noch/ diß anligen/
> macht Fewer vnd flacks stets begegnen/
> weg/ weg/ weg/ weg/
> diesen Pfadt ich gern wolt wandern.

6.

(Herr Jan singt weitter)

> Soll ich mich vnterstehen/
> hinan zu gehen/
> soll ich es thun wagen/
> es ist ein anmuhten/
> ich wills versuchen/
> daß ergst ist mein[1] zu sagen.

(Herr Jan geht auff sie zu/ redt mit folgenden Worten an. Ach mein
schönstes Hertz allerliebstes missicken/[2] schönes vnd Adeliches
Fräwlein/ freundlich in jhrem Angesicht/ lieblich in jhren
Aügelein/ vnd warumb auch nicht barmhertzig/ schönes Fräw-
lein/ wolt jhr mich nicht zu lieb annehmen.
(Weib) Nein/Nein/

[1] Bolte makes the correction to *nein.*
[2] Bolte has the note, "wohl = Müseken, Mäuschen."

Herr Jan sagt Nein Nein/ zwey Nein/ seyndt so viel als ja/ **nam duae negationes faciunt affirmationem,** Nein nein **sunt duae negationes, ergo affirmas.**

Daß Weib vexiert Herrn Jahn: sprechent: Herr Jahn woher habt jhr die grosse Witz vnnd Geschickligkeit bekommen/

drauff wirfft er noch mehr mit Latein vmb sich: **Amicus certus in re incerta cernitur/**

spricht drauff zu jhr: Schönes Fräwlein/ wist jhr nicht/ daß ich ewer erster **praeceptor** war vnd schriebe euch für/ erstlich/ das A.B.C. vnnd dann das a b/ ab/ daß ich aber so begierig bin/ darzu treibt mich die strenge Lieb/ wolt jhr mich nicht zu Lieb annemen/ (*Fraw*) Nein:

7.

(*Herr Jan springt herumb vnd singt*)

> Ich kan springen/
> ich kan singen/
> ich kan tantzen/
> ich kan auch frisch vnd [p. 4] lustig seyn/
> kans wagen auff die Schantzen/
> beweist mir Lieb für Lieb

(*Weib*)   Nein nein/
> ich sag schulpfaff back dich von hier/
> dein Gunst thue ich abschlagen/

(*Herr Jan*)   So bleib stets keutsch/[1] ich verheiß dir/
> nimmer so nach zu sagen.[2]

8.

(*Gabilierer tritt zu jhr vnd singt*)

> Ade mein gewin
> ist hin/[3]
> Cupido soll mich nicht treffen/
> seht euch wol für/
> schließt zu die thür/
> denn ich wills nimmer öffnen/ (*geht drauff ab.*)

---

[1] Bolte corrects to *keusch*.   [2] Bolte changes this to *fragen*.

[3] This speech opens in D:

> Dan hadieu, mijn bemindt,
> Het is schoon hindt,
> Kupido, etc.,

and in G:

> Wohlan weil es nicht seyn kan, mus es bleiben.
> *Adieu* mein Gewin,   ich scheid dahin.
> Cupid, etc.

Der dritt Buler kompt vnd singt.

9.

Gott grüß euch Jungfraw oder Magd/
wend euch doch nicht von mir/
ich bitt Hertzlieb seydt nicht verzagt/
ein wenig bleibt allhier

(*Weib*)   Nein nein nein nein/
denn ich hab hoch geschworen/
mein Mann wirdt es thun zorn/
wo er sein Willen nicht fünd.[1]

10.

(*Buler*)   Morgen werden wir lustig seyn/
beym Meth vnd kühlen Wein/
mit musiciern vnd tantzen/
vnd werd jhr nicht da seyn?

(*Weib*)   Nein nein nein nein/
deß dings acht ich nicht viel/
es ist nur Kinderspiel/
es ist kein Speiß für mich

(*Das Weib will abgehn/ der Buler singt*)

Verzieht ein weil/
nit so sehr eylt/

(*Fr.*)   Allein zu seyn/ lieb ich allein.

11.

(*Buler*)   Jahrmarckt hab ich gekaufft ohn Schertz/
für dich Gürtel Handschuch vnd Ring/
vnd wolt dann dein vnfreundlich Hertz/
verachten solche Ding/

(*Weib*)   Nein nein nein nein/
wie wol es nicht weiß mein Mann/
nemb ichs zu gfallen an.[2]

[1] This stanza continues in D:
      J. Karel. Verstocktes harts,   erlost mijn smarts!
      Vrou.   Die liefde is gaer blint;
but in G it has the form found here.

[2] A line is apparently missing here and another at the beginning of the next stanza.
The lines at the end of this stanza and the beginning of the next in D read:
      Vrou.   Nein, nein, nein, nein,
              Golt alle ding bekracht.
              Ein vrouwen hart spricht nein,
              Das geschenck zy nicht veracht.

12.[1] (*Buler*)   Ich befindt hierinn/
                                   eins Weibes Sinn/
                                   Geschenck alles bewegt/

                                   ein frag ich euch jetzt lege für/
                                   sagt mangelt euch dann red/[2]
                                   wolt jhr mir weisen die Thür/
(*Weib*)   Nein nein nein nein
                                   ein Red[2] hab ich so sanfft/
                                   wo Cupido gekempfft.
13. (*Puler*)   Der Kampff bringt lust vnd frewd/   [p. 5]
(*Weib*)   mein Mann ist hin/
                                   sein eyfferig Sinn/
                                   vervrsacht solchs allzeit/

(*Buler*)   Aber wann ich solte begeren/
                                   euers Mannes Stell mit glimpff/
                                   wolt jhr mich dann nicht gewehren/
                                   vnd beweisen ein Schimpff.
14. (*Weib*)   Nein nein nein [nein]/
                                   Eyfer ich nicht leyden kan/
                                   ich hab euch lieber dann mein Mann/
                                   drumb folget meinem Rath/

J. Karel.   Hier door 'k bevin   de vrou er sin,
                        Door 't golt daer toe gebracht.
                  4. Iet sonder gelt ein wedt
                        Ein vraeg ich dy leg veur:
                        Oft mier gebrecht ein bedt,
                        Wolt ier my weisen de deur?
Vrou.   Nein, nein, nein, nein.
In G the passage reads:
Frau.   Nein, nein, nein, nein,
                        Geschenck' ich nicht veracht:
                        Ein Frauen Hertz spricht nein,
                        Geschenck' es doch betracht.
Cavalier. 3. Ich find' hierin der Weiber Sinn,
                        So durchs Gold wird bewegt.
                        Wann ich jetz hätt Lust zu dem Bett,
                        Wurd' auch nein eingelegt?
Frau.   Nein, nein, nein, nein.

---

[1] The numerals 12, 13, 14, 20, and 22, which in the original are so placed as to come in the middle of stanzas, have been transferred from the center of the page to the margin in this reprint. Two of the numbers are superfluous according to my arrangement of the stanzas.

[2] Bolte has the note, "lies Bett statt Red."

(Sie beyde gehn beseyd vnd singen)

> Wir habens versehn/
> last vns bald gehn/
> es wird vns sonst zu spat : *gehn ab:*

Bleiben ein weil außn kommen wider sampt dem
Bückelhering/ welcher singt.

15.

> Zu Houß mouß ich hinein/
>   mein Orbeit wird mir sower/
> mein Woib wol kleyd soll seyn/
>   ob ich gleich bin ein Boer/
> Ob man mir hat gemacht mein Kamrath gehn/
>   Till till till till
> so hat man mir verdorben/
>   mein aller beste Mühl.

16.

> Jetz da ich von meiner Orbeit
>   thu gehn/ hab ich so bald
> gesehen/ mein nochbar
>   bey meiner Frowen stehn/[1]
> wo der hat gemacht mein Kamrath gehn/
>   Dill dill dill dill/
> so hat er mir verdorben/
>   Mein aller schönste Möhl.

17.

> Meins Handwercks ich ein Möllner bin/
>   kan doch mahlen gesch[w]ind[2]
> vnd mach mein Möhll fein lostig gehn/
>   wann ich nur hab got Wind/
>   Dill dill dill dill/[3]
> so hat er mir verdorben/
>   mein aller schönste Möhl.

[1] The rhymes and the bars indicate that either the first four lines of this stanza were translated as three lines or a line has been lost. The stanza is not in D and G.

[2] Corrected by Bolte.

[3] The first line of the refrain has been omitted.

18.

Ich hab heut lang georbeit schon/
vnd ist mir worden heiß/
vnd der ist bey meiner Frowen schon/
welchs mich dann sehr verdreust.
O er hat gemacht mein Kamrath gehn/
Dill dill dill dill/
so hat er mir verderben/[1]
mein allerschönste Möhl.

19.   [p. 6]

(*Daß Weib vnd Buler geben einander die Händ vnd singen.*)
    (*Weib*)   Ade mein Herr
    (*Buler*)   habt danck mit Ehr/[2]
                        nembt den Ring ehe ich geh.
20. *Pü:*   Mein Weib das macht mich kranck/
                 mein Haupt/ daß thut mir weh
(*deut auff den Buler singt*)
                 O der hat gemacht mein Kamrath &c.

21.

(*Der Buler redt Pückelhering an.*)
                 Mein Freund wie so allein/
(*Pückelhering singt*) du machst mirs leyden sawer/
                 vmb dich mag ich nicht seyn/
                 ob ich schon bin ein Boer/
                 O du hast gemacht mein Kamrath gehn/
                 Dill dill dill dill/
   : *Weib:*[3]   vnd warumb solt ein ander Mann/
                 mahlen auff meiner Mühl.

(*Der Buler redt jhn ferrner an.*)
                 Gut Freund wie gehts wie stehts/
                 geht jhr auch diesen Weg.
22. (*Pückelhering*)
                 Ich förcht er hab spatziert/
                 auff meiner Frowen steg/
                 wo er hat gemacht mein Kamrath &c.

---

[1] Bolte corrects to *verdorben.*

[2] Bolte has the note, "Streiche: mit Ehr."

[3] Bolte omits *Weib*, an obvious correction.

23.

Der Buler redt jhn weiter an:

vnnd ich will euch erzelen
ein wunderlich Geschicht.[1]

(Pückelhering wend sich ab vnd sagt.)

Es wird mir doch gefallen nicht/
wo er hat gmacht mein Kamrath &c.

24.

*Sie gehen beyde ab/ vnd kommen die drey Buler vnd Pückelhe-
ring/ vnd die Fraw verbirgt sich an heimlichs Ort:*

Der dritt Buler fragt/ soll ichs sagen oder singen?

(Sie sagen/ sings)

Er singts?	Ich sprach sie an vmb jhre Lieb/
	Nein sprach sie
(Pü:)	O es ist mein Weib/ wie fein/
(Dritt Buler)	Morgen [p. 7] sind wir beym Wein/
	werd jhr da nicht seyn:
	Sie sprach: Nein/
(Pückelhering)	O es ist jmmer fein/
[Dritt Buler][2]	ich hab jr kauffen thon/
	Stiffel vnnd Beutel schon/
	werd ihrs verachten thon:
	Sie sprach: Nein/
(Pückelhering)	Wie ist das/
[Dritt Buler][2]	ich hab jhr kauffen thon/
	Stiffel vnnd Beutel schon/
	werd jhrs verachten thon:
	Sie sprach: Nein.[3]

[1] Apparently the third line of the stanza is missing.   [2] Supplied by Bolte.

[3] For this passage G has:

Cavalier.	Ich sprach sie an um ihre Lieb.
	Nein, nein, sprach sie.
Peckelhering.	Ach ehrlich Weib.
Cavalier.	Ich fragt', ob Sie wollt gehn zum Wein?
	Nein, nein, sprach sie.
Peckelhering.	Ey, das war fein.
Cavalier.	Wann ich mit macht euch zieh' hinein.
	Seyd ihr dann bös? Sie sprach: ach nein.
Peckelhering.	Sprach sie nein?
Cavalier.	Wann ich hier bleib, wers euch zu wieder?
	Nein, nein, sprach sie, da lagen wir nieder.
Peckelhering.	Laget ihr nieder?

D is similar.

25.

Pückelhering singt.

O es ist mein Weib/ die lose Hur/
die Hur die scheisset fettel/
zwar die stinckt gleich wie ein Ose/
wann jhrs nun sehet zwar/
ey pfuy dich an hinauß/

(*Fraw*)   hinauß mit dir bey weit/
(*Die Buler*)   ey pfuy dich an hinauß/
vnd alle solche Säw.

26.

(*Pückelhering*) Vnd wann sie sich nur nider legt/
rumpump geht ab jhr Geschoß/
daß ich mit grossem erschrecken/
darvon erwachen moß/
ey pfuy die an hinauß/

(*Fr:*)   hinauß mit dir beij weit/
[*Buler*   ey pfuy dich an hinauß][1]
vnd alle solche Säw.

27.

(*Pückelhering*) Vnd wann sie sich nur nider duckt/[2]
etwas zu heben auff/
so bricht jr dann mit gantzem gwalt/
jhr hinders Schloß bald auff/
ey pfuy die an hinauß/

(*Fraw*)   hinauß mit dir bey weit/
: *Buler:*   ey pfuy die an hinauß/
vnd alle solche Säw.

28.

(*Pückelhering:* Vnd wann sie sich nur nider legt/
zu schnarchen fängt sie an/
daß man sie auch gar leichtlich/
über drey viertel Meil hören kan/
ey pfui die an hinauß/

Fraw: hinauß mit dir beij weit/
: *Buler:*   eij pfui die an hinauß/
vnd alle solche Säw.

[1] Supplied by Bolte.   [2] Bolte has *buckt.*

29.

Die Fraw geht hinzu vnd singt:

Hör loser vnd verlogner Mann/
was thust bezüchten mich/
allhie vor diesen Leuten:

Pückelhering: Liebs Weib ich mein dich nicht/
      eij pfui dich an hinauß/

:Fraw: hinauß [p. 8] mit dir beij weit/

:Buler: eij pfui die an hinauß/
      vnd alle solche Säw.

30.

[Pückelhering][1] Dieser mich deß berichtet hat/
      dem glaube ich fürwar/
      wie könnt ers so erdencken/
      wann es nicht gwesen war/
      eij pfui dich an hinauß

: Fraw: hinauß mit dir beij weit/

Die drey Buler: [ei pfui dich an hinauß][1]
      vnd alle solche Säw.

31.

Fraw: Hör du loser verlogner Mann/
      wie kanst bezeugen diß/

er saget daß ein Traum allein gewesen ist/[2]

---

[1] Supplied by Bolte.

[2] Bolte prints the whole line as a stage direction, possibly correctly. In G the section corresponding to stanzas 29–31 reads:

Peckelh. Frau.	Wer ist, der mich so lobt?
Peckelhering.	Mein schatz, ich mein dich nicht.
Frau.	Ich kenn dich Schelmen wohl mit deinem Diebs-Gedicht.
Alle.	O pfuy dich an etc.
Frau.	Beweiß mir nur den Mann, der etwas sagen kan Von mir, so sol er bald ein neu Lied fangen an.
Peckelhering.	Alhier steht er.
Frau.	Mein Herr, den Anfang bringt zu end.
Cavalier.	Jetzt meinen Witz ich spitz zu schlichten dis behend.
Alle.	O pfuy dich an etc.
Cavalier.	Als wir nun lagen sanfft, begunte meine Freud. Ach weh, als ich erwacht, war Freud verkehrt in Leid.
Alle.	O pfuy dich an etc.
Peckelhering.	War dieses nur ein Traum?

D has somewhat similar passages.

:*Fraw:*	ey pfui die an hinauß/
:*Pückelhering?*	hinauß mit dir beij weit
:*Puler:*	eij pfui die an hinauß/
	vnd alle solche Säw.

32.

Pückelhering tritt zu dem Mann vnd singt?

	War denn das nur ein Traum:
(*Mann*)	Nichts anders war es nun/
:*Fraw:*	so bist du ein verlogner Mann/
	daß ich bezeugen kan/
	eij pfui die an hinauß/
:*Pückelhering:*	hinauß mit dir beij weit
: *Puler*)	eij pfui dich an hinauß/
	vnd deine falsche Trew.

33.

Pückelhering fällt auff die Knie/ vnd bittets der Frawen ab:

	O liebes Weib vmb Gottes willen/
	laß deinen Zorn fahren/
	all Gut will ich anwenden/
	vnd kein Wolthat nicht sparen:
Fraw?	O pfui dich an hinauß/
:*Pückelhering:*	hinauß mit mir beij weit:
Buler)	O pfui den Eifer an
	vnd alle falsche Trew.

34.

Pückelhering?	Das Lied hab ich erdacht/[1]
	vnd habs allhie gesungen/
	zu tausend guter Nacht:
Fraw:	eij pfui dich an hinauß/
Pückelhering:	hinauß mit mir beij weit:
Buler:	O pfui den Eifer an
	vnd alle falsche Trew.

Pückelhering kehrt sich zu dem Volck vnd singt.

> Ihr lieben Männer schlagts
> nicht so gäh in [den][2] Wind/
> thut ewre Weiber nicht verachten/
> jedoch seijdt drumb nicht blind/
> daß das Lied gar lang hat gewehrt/
> drumb jhr euch nicht dran kehrt/
> eij pfui die an hinauß &c.

---

[1] Apparently the first line of the stanza is missing.   [2] Supplied by **Bolte**.

29

Aliud.

[DER NARR ALS REITPFERD]¹

Perſonen: 1. Narr. 2. Fraw. 3. Junckcr.

1.

Pickelhering² zu Ambsterdam bin ich gewesen/
Mein Pein vnd Schmertz allzumassen/ hum hu
Aber mein Lieb find ich nicht durchaus/
Ich glaub sie sey in dem Steinhaus/ fa la:

2.

Klopff ich denn an vnd frag vmb sie/
Der Hencker kam vnd finge mir/ hum hu/
Ich kam vngern in das Steinhaus/   Zz iij
Aber sach dort kömpt mein Lieb heraus/ fa la.

3.

F. Zu Ambsterdam kan ich nicht genesen/ hum/
N. In dem Steinhauß ist sie gewesen/
F. Ich kam vngern in diese Stadt/
N. Ich fürcht der Bittel acht auff sie hat/ fa la.

---

¹ Printed from a copy of *Engelische Comedien und Tragedien* (1620) in the British
Museum. I have not reprinted the first of the singspiele in the volume, a version of
"Singing Simpkin" (see p. 235 above). "Der Narr als Reitpferd" is the second, with
the simple heading *Aliud* above the music and the names of the speakers arranged
as in the facsimile.

² Obviously the name of the speaker.

4.

F. Ich nehm die Goltketten von mein Halß/
N. Die Ketten ist Kupffer vnd jhr seid falsch/
F. Ein Kauffman gab mirs zu grosser Beut/
N. Der Ketten seyd jhr viel zu leicht.

5.

F. Diß groß Vnrecht kan ich nicht vertragen/
N. Der Scholtz kömpt sie aus der Stadt zuja-
Von einer Armuth schweig ich still/   (gen/
Sie hat Beut rund vmb Wassermühl.

6.

Fürwar ich bin ein grosser Pengel/
F. Von Weißheit hastu grossen mangel.
N. O Catharina gedenck/ gedenck an mir/
F. Geh zu Hauß du solst dein nicht verliern.

7.

N. *Cupido* hat mein Hertz geschlagen/
F. Weiß mir die Wunden so wil ichs glauben/
N. Von Hertzen gern ich bins zu frieden.
F. Nessel zu/ nessel zu/ solches kan ich nicht
    leiden.

8.

N. Sie hat darin ein grossen Verstandt/   [Zz iij*v*]
F. Pfuy/pfuy/ es ist eine grewliche schandt/
N. Ich bitt jhr Lieb lasts also seyn.
F. Dein Wund ist nicht so groß als die mein.

9.

Jun. Wie stehts mein Schatz/wie so betrübt/
F.   In euch bin ich so sehr verliebt/
J.   Alle betrübnis last jetzund versagen/
N.   Potz schlapperment er wird mich schlagen.

10.

J. Mein Schatz/ jetzt sind wir gar allein/
N. Wolt Gott ich wer wieder daheim/
F. Von meinem Leib zweiffel nicht durch aus/
N. Wolt Gott ich were wieder zu Hauß.

11.

J. Mein Schatz jetzt haben wir gute Sachen/
N. Sie werden mich gewiß zum Kupler machen/
F. Den groben Narren mustu erst verjagn/
J. Mit meiner Mehr wil ich jhn zerschlagn.

12.

J. Du grober Narr was machstu hie/ hum hu
J. Geschwind du Narr verantwort mir/ hum hu
J. Der Narr ist geschnitten er kan nicht reden/
F. Betriegerey kan ich nicht leiden.

13.

J. Jetzt wil jhn all seins Gelts berauben/
N. Das ist gar leichtlich wol zu glauben/
F. Gib her den Sattel/ den ich wil reiten/   Zz 4
N. Das groß Vnrecht kan ich nicht leiden.

14.

J. Nu Narr leg dich nieder also bald/
N. Pickelhering ist jetzt in ewer Gewalt/
J. Der schwere Last bistu wol würdig/
N. Potz schlapperment sie ist leichtfertig.

15.

F. Gebt Habber her für diß mein Pferdt/
J. Der Esel ist das Futters nicht werth/
  Stich dapffer zu mit deinem Sporn/
N. Der Teuffel hol alle falsche Hurn.

16.

J. Jetzundt wil ich mich an dir rechen.
N. Wolt Gott du möchst den Halß zerbrechn/
J. Gehe fort du Narr/oder ich wil dir sagen/
F. Der Narr ist geschnitten/ er kan nicht tragn.

17.

N. Ihr habt mich noch nicht angerührt/
Ich hab alls was eim Mann gebührt/
Ists anders/ so wolt ich mich selbst verfluchen/
Wolt jhrs nicht glauben jhr möchts versuchen.

18.

J. Gute Nacht mein Tochter/ es ist Zeit zu essen/
Wenn jhr auffn Abend reit/ so last mich wissen/
Das Pferdt hat schon den Sattel an/
Ich wil jhn dienen so viel ich kan.

19.   [Zz 4v]

N. *Bon jour monseur* gegenwertig hier/
Wenn jhr reit auff Abend/ so gleubt mir/
Mein Jung frisch Pferdt ist genandt/
Vnd kömpst nicht zu Hauß/ wie meines Va-
    ters Hund/ fa la la.

30

Den Windelwäscher[1] zu
agiren mit drey Personen.

Mann. Fraw. Nachbawr.

1. [Weib.]

MEin Mann ist nächten voll heim kom-
Den hab ich seinen Hut genom*m*en/(me*n*/
Davon er nichts drumb wissen thut/
Drumb wird er seyn gantz vngemuth.

2.

So bald er aber stehet auff/
Wil ich jhn den erinnern drauff/
Vnd jhn den Hut auffsetzen fein.
Davon er nicht gar froh wird seyn.

3.

Sich da da kömpt der volle Tropff/
Wie zuricht ist er vmb sein Kopff/
Wie zeuchstu her du erbar Mann/
Alß einer der kaum gehen kan.

4.

Das macht alles dein schrecklichs sauffn/
Ich glaub du seyst dem Henckr entlauffn/
Zeuchts her ohn Hut du lumpen Mann/
Sag wo du jhn hast hingethan.

5. Mann.

O Gott du fromms gezognes Weib/
Wo mein Hut bliebn bey meinem Leib/
Weiß ich nicht. (Weib) so wil ichs sagn dir/
Wann du die Stöß empfangn von mir.

Zz v

[1] From *Engelische Comedien und Tragedien.*

6. Weib.

Auff der Gassen du volle Saw/
Hast jhn verlohren/ darumb schaw/
Zur Straff solstu aus vnserm Hauß/
Die Wäsche tragen selber rauß.

7. Mann.

Wils gern thun/ hör nur auff mein Grett
Zu schlagen/ zu murren/ zu kurren stett/
Vnd dir die Wäsch tragen herbey/
Damit du nur zu frieden sey.

8. Weib.

Geh hin/ wann du sie bracht hieher/
Mustu mir büssen noch viel mehr/
Darauff du wol wirst dencken nicht.
(Mann) hier bring ich die Wäsch:
        (Weib) halt bleib Bösewicht.

9.   [Zz vᵥ]

Du must dein Haut besser streckn dran/
Weil dein Maul wol waschen kan/
So sollen dein heilose Händ/
Mir mein Wäsch aus waschen geschwind.

10.

Greiff an laß dichs nicht lenger heissn/
Sonst ich dich auff die Guschen schmeissn/
Vnd jetzo fang zu waschen an/
Dieweil es anders nicht seyn kan.

11. [Mann.]

Wie vnflätig ist meine Wäsch/
So schwartz besudelt als mein Tasch/
(Weib) So schlag du desto besser drauff/
Machs rein odr mir gar entlauff.

12. Nachbar.

Ey Nachbarin das ist nicht fein/
Maß ewer Mann der Wäscher seyn.
(Weib) Ja daß ist er : Wert jhr mein Mann/
Ihr müst solches auch gleichfals thun.

13. Nachbar.

Mein Fritz wie hastu das verschuldt/
(Mann) Ich muß es tragen mit Gedult/
[Nachb.] Ey Nachbar mein das Gott erbarm/
(Mann) Wie weh thun mir doch meine Arm.

14. Nachbar.

Was schadts du gibst ein Wäscher steiff/
W. Ey daß man dem Eßl nicht darzu pfeiff.
Machs fort/ thues geschwind vnd wasche weg/   [Zz vj]
M. Wil doch nicht aus den Windln der Dreck.

15. Weib.

So stippl/ so schüttl/ so halt fest an/
Denn ich wil mit dir anderst dran/
(Nachb.) Last jhn doch ein mal hören auff/
(Weib) Nein/ nein/ mach fort/ schlag besser
          drauff.

16. Nachbar.

Mein Fritz ich wolt dir helffen gern/
Du siehsts sie wil michs nicht gewehrn/
(Mann) Ach weh wer ein solch böß Weib hat/
(Weib) Du könnest es wol haben nicht.

17.

Thetstu daheim bey deim Weibe bleibn/
Thetst jhr bißweiln die Zeit vertreibn/
Daß wer dir bessr/ dann du lieffst rumb/
Als wie die Hirsch in Brunsten thun.

18.

Du thust täglich wie ein Kuh sauffn/
Von einer Fettl zur andern lauffn/
(Nachb.) Ey beschembt jhn doch nicht so sehr/
(Mann) Ja sie meynt es sey jhr ein Ehr.

19.

Ach wie feyren mir meine Händ/
Mein Puckl/ mein Achßl/ mein Rück/mein
          Lend/
Seynd bald halb todt/(Nachbar.) du armer
Laß jhn doch einmal feyrabend han. (Mann/

20. Weib.　　　　　　　　　　[Zz vj*v*]

Nein/nein/ du must noch besser dran?
Es ist noch nicht genug mein Mann/
Zum Wassr mustu mein Wäsch tragn naus/
Vnd sie alle fein schweffen aus.

21.

Alßdenn so bring sie wieder heim/
Vnd thu sie hencken auff allein/
Fein sauber/ daß sie trucken wol/　　　(toll.
(Mann) Ey Greth du machst mich schier halb

22. Weib.

Es hilfft nichts für/ es muß so seyn.
(Nachb.) Verrichts nur vollends Nachbarin.
(Weib) Darauff wird dir das Essn schmeckn
Ein andermal verlier mehr den Hut.　(gut/

23. Nachbar.

Ich muß gehn vnd mich alßbald schickn/
Vnd meiner Frawen den Peltz flickn/
Ade jhr Herrn ich muß davon/
Sonsten bekom ich auch den Lohn.

24. Weib.

Faß auff vnd gehe zum Wasser fort/
Es hilfft nichts/ drumb sag nur kein wort/
(Mann) So muß man die Männr geduldig
Wenn sie nicht jhrer Weiber achtn. (machn/

25.

So faß ich nun mein Creutze auff/
Damit ich zu dem Wasser lauff/
Seht daß es euch wie mir nicht geht/　　　[Zz vij]
Wenn jhr auff ewren Hut nicht sehtt.

26.

Wenn einer vntern Hauffen wer/
Der mein Gespan/ derselb kom her/

Vnd helff mir die Wäsch tragen hier/
Ein guten Morgen/ ey wie gehts mir.

31

[STUDENTENGLÜCK][1]

F. Fraw/   P. Pickelhering/
M. Magd/   M. *Magister*,
S. *Studiosus.*

[Zz vij*v*]

[1] From *Engelische Comedien und Tragedien.* In stanzas 8–15, 33–34, M. is an abbreviation for *Magister*, and in 3, 23, 26–28, for Magd.

1. Fraw.

WEil mein Mann ist hinweg gezogen/
 Findt sich groß Trawrigkeit/
Denn er aus meinem Hertzn entflohn/
 Ein andr im Sinn mir leidt/
Bey dem zu seyn einig in still/
 Ich stetigs sorge trage/
P. Ich merck wol was sie haben wil/
 Ich sol heut bey jhr schlaffen.

2.

Fr. Mein Magd sol jetzund zu jhm gehn/
 Denn es bald wird seyn Zeit/
P. Ach nein/ mein Mädgen bleib nur stehn/
 Hier bin ich schon bereit.
Fr. Pack dich hinweg/ du böser Geck/
 Odr ich wil dir Füsse schaffen/
P. Ja wol die kleinest Zehe nicht/
 Könt jhr mir daran machen.

3.

Fr. Hör zu Magd was ich sage dir/
 Zum Herrn Magister gehe/
 Sag zu jhm daß er komm zu mir/
P. So bleib der Teuffl hie stehen/
M. Ich wil es bald habn außgericht/
 Wil jhn selbst führen her/
P. Vmb Pickelherings willen nicht/
 Denn er sieht es nicht gern.

4.

Fr. Er würd erfüllen mein begehrn/
 So bald ers wird erfahren.
P. Ich wil es thun von Hertzen gern/
 So dörfft jhr nicht lang harren/
Fr. Sieh da Picklhering was machstu hier?
 Wie thustu so trawrig stehen?
P. Gläub wol er ist schon vor der Thür/
 Picklhering muß weg gehen.

5.

Fr. Wie so trawrig/ sag doch/ laß dich ein we-
      nig ansehen.
P. Ja jetzt kom vnd blaß mir ins Loch/
      Zuvor solt ich weg gehen.
Fr. Sag mirs/ denn ich trag sorg für dich/
      Weil ich dich hab sehr lieb.
P. Ja ich gleub fein wol hinter sich/
      Wie süsse Wort sie giebt.

6.

P. Vor wart jhr zornig vber mich/
      Jetzt seyd jhr sehr verliebet.
Fr. Ach ja mein Schatz das klag mir nicht/
      Drumb bin ich so betrübt/
P. Denn werdt jhr mir ja gebn ein Schmatz/
      Weil ichs wol bin werth.
Fr. Freylich/ warumb nicht meinem Schatz/
      So bald ers nur begehrt.

7.

P. Ich hab es allbereit im Sinn/
      Thut es nur bald zu handen.
Fr. Nein Pickelhering halt ein wenig inn/
      Du hast mich nicht recht verstanden/
      Ich sagt mein Schatz/ meynt dich abr
          Dort thut derselb hergehen.   (nicht/
P. Da schlag Bley drein/ zu solchn Gedicht/
Fr.   Laß dich bey Leib nicht sehen.

8.

M. Hie kom ich schon bereit gegangn/ Fraw
      Sehet hier ewer begehr.
Fr. Nach euch trag ich gar groß verlangn/
      Mein Schatz kompt zu mir her.
      Ich wil euch etwas erzehlen/
          Recht verstehet mich/
      Zum Buhlen ich euch erwehle/
P.   Awe wo bleib denn ich?

9.

Fr. Mein Mann ist hinweg gegangen/
  Mein Hertz ist sehr betrübt/
P. Vnd ich bin hier gefangen/
Fr. In euch bin ich verliebt
M. Mein Schatz/ ich bin auch deßgleichen/
  Von Lieb sehr matt vnd schwach/
P. Drumb thut er also herein schleichen/
  Das gantze Hauß erkracht.

10.

Fr. Wormit wird denn geholffen mir/
  Von meiner Trawrigkeit.
M Vnd mir matten vnd schwachen/
P. Mit eim Kuß alle beyd:
M. Also wil ich jetzt abwenden/
  Ewr Noth vnd Trawrigkeit.
Fr. Vnd so wil ich euch thun stärcken:
P. Das sagt ich vor bey Zeit/

11.

[Aaa j*v*]

Fr. Diese gantze Nacht wir alle beyd/
  Wollen beysammen bleiben/
  In Kurtzweil vnd auch in Frewden/
  Die lange Zeit vertreiben/
P. Awe so merck ich wol/ ich hab
  Hier nichts im Spiel/
M. Ach ja mein Schatz es geschehen sol/
P. Zur Magd ich gehen wil.

12.

M. Wann aber ewer Mann heim kem/
  Was wolten wir anfangen/
P. Die Frage war so gar bequem/
  Am Galgen mustu hangen/
Fr. Ach mein Schatz last solches fahren/
  Denn ich noch hab ein fund/
  Darin ich euch wil verwahren/
P. Weiß nicht es ist *numero* eins.

13.

Fr. Vnd wenn er denn heimkommen thut/
    Thut er nichts als nur schlaffen/
    Darumb ich jhn bald weiß zu Bett/
    Thet mich widr zu euch machen/
    Weil er doch nichts als schlaffen kan/
P.   Vnd euch nicht *contendirt.*
Fr. Muß er solchs wol geschehen lan/
P.   Weil er nichts dran verliert.

14.

M.   Weil dem so ist/ so bleibs darbey/
    So lebn wir heint in Frewden/
    Weil wir dann sind allr Sorgen frey/
    Ich wil ein weil abscheiden/
Fr. Jetzund ichs euch vergönnen wil/
    Vmb 9. Vhr thut euch herfügen/
P   Ich wolt dieweil anfangn das Spiel/
    Wann sie mich nur nicht schlügen.

15.

M.   Ade mein Schatz nunmehr ich scheid/
P.   Ein Schelm der wieder kömpt.
Fr. An euch allein mein Hoffnung leit/
P.   Das hab ich jetzt vernommen/
    Jetzt hab ich wiedr den Platz allein/
    Wil mich hin zu jhr machen/
    Gebt acht/ wie wird sie doch so fein/
    Vnd freundlich mich anlachen.

16.

F.   Mein Picklhering gefelt der dir/
P.   Wie solt er mir gefallen/
    Ich wolt er kem nimmermehr her/
    So liebt jhr mich für allen/
Fr. Wie so zweiffelstu denn hieran/
    Das kan ich nicht verstehen/
P.   Ja wol ichs nicht verstehen kan/
    Denn ich habs jetzt gesehen.

17.

Fr. Kom her hör was ich sage dir/
    Ich wil mich legen zu Bette.
Bleib du hie stehen an der Thür/
    Die Sachen recht vertrete/
Dann du weist wol was geschehen soll/
    Heimlich heint in der stille.
P. Nemt mich doch ein klein wenig mit/
    Vmb des Magisters willen.

18.

Fr. Ja wol bleib nur ein wenig hier/
    Wenn d'Zeit wird seyn verhanden/
Wil ich ein Boten schickn nach dir.
    Hastu mich recht verstanden?
P. Ach ja mein Schatz/ das nur gescheh/
    Von hinnen wil ich nicht scheiden/
Fr. Gar gewiß voran ich gehe/
    Daß ich den Weg bereit.

19.

St. Potz schlapperment was steh ich hier?
    Seynd das nicht tolle Possen/
Ich bin erschrocken/ weiß nicht wie/
P.   Das Hertz liegt jhm in Hosen/
St. Ihr Schelm vnd Dieb kommpt jmmer her/
    Daß euch der Teuffel hole/
Ihr losen Häscher allzumal/
P.   Haha doch nicht so toll.

20.

St. Sie seynd hinweg gelauffen all/
    Vnd lassen mich im stich.
P. Ein Narr der bleibt in diesem Fall/
    Sie werden bald fahen dich.
St. Potz schlapperment sie kommen her/
    Wo sol ich nun hingehen/
P. Ha ha ha seht alle her/
    Wie tapffer thut er stehen.

21.

St. Sol ich denn gehen hier hinein/
   Ich steh in grossen zweiffel.
P. Ja ja/ du wirst gar willkommen seyn/
   Pack dich du armer Teuffel.
St. Es ist doch bessr/ ich wags hinein/
   Als daß ich werd gefangen.
Magd. Potz Herr Magister kompt herein/
   Mein Fraw wart mit verlangen.

22.

St. Potz schlapperment was sol das seyn/
   Wofür thun sie mich ansehen?
P. Der Teuffel kömpt auch hinein/
   Ich muß allein haussen stehen.
St. Ich merck jetzund wol was es ist/
   Was gilts es wird sich schicken.
P. Wann du auch nur die Schliche wüst/
   Küntstu sie leichtlich drücken.

23.   [Aaa iij*v*]

M. Mein Fraw hat sich zu Bett gelegt/
   Wo seyd jhr so lang blieben?
St. Ich hab mich da ein wenig verspät/
   Vnd so die Zeit vertreiben.
M. Nun nun kompt jetzt mit mir herauff/
   Ich wil euch zu jhr weisen/
St. Fürwar es ist ein guter Kauff/
   Wil mich nicht lang drum reissen.

24.

Fr. Seht her M. kompt jetzt jhr/
   Ich hab gewart mit schmertzen.
St. Ich weiß nicht was jhr thut allhier?
   Ob ich also sol hertzen?
P. Ich wusts wol wenn es nicht angieng/
Fr. Nun thut euch zu mir machen.
P. Mit stillschweigen ich es auch anfieng/
   Des Possen muß ich lachen.

25.

Fr. Potz Herr Magistr wisset jhr auch/
    Ihr seyd gewiß was truncken/
P. Stillschweigen ist das best vor dich/
    Nach meinem gut bedüncken/
Fr. Nun nun was thut jhr lang hier stahn/
    Thut doch ein mal rein kommen/
P. Jetzund wil ich zur Magd hingahn/
    Der hat das Spiel gewonnen.

26.

P. Ach Hertzgen mein Schätzgen/ wie geht es
    Thut mir ein Schnäutzel geben/   (dir/
M. Wil dich niemands habn/ so kom zu mir
    Sol ich deinr Gnade leben/
P. Ach nicht so zornig/ bitt ich dich/
    Thu dich doch meinr erbarmen/
M. Ich hab gantz vnd gar nichts vor dich/
    Thu nur hinweg dein Arme.

27.

P. Ach hertziger Schatz sey nicht so wildt/
    Mein Hertz thue ich dir schencken/
M. Deins Hertzens ich gar nicht bedarff/
    Es seynd viel in Fleischbäncken/
P. Mein einiger Auffenthalt vnd Schildt/
    Thu dich doch zu mir wenden/
M. Pack dich hinweg du loses Wildt/
    Mit deim tölpischen Händen.

28.

P. Ich merck wol es ist nun mehr aus/
    Mit vnser beyder Liebe/
M. Gar reichlich hier in diesem Hauß/
    Gleich wie mit jungen Weibern/
P. So wil ich auch hinweg thun gehn/
    Vnd mir ein andre suchen/
M. Deßwegen ich nicht sawer sehe/
    Wil dir auch nicht drumb fluchen.

29.

P. Ich weiß nicht was für ein Planet/
 Jetzt diese Stundt regieret/
 Da ich mich bey der einen hembd hett/
 Hat sie mich angeführt/
 Daß ich der andern worden loß/
 Zahlt mich mit gleichen Sorten/
 Haha was ist das für ein Poß/
 Die seynd schon fertig worden.

30.

Fr. Bhüt Gott/ warumb thut jhr so eilen/
 Bleibt noch ein weil allhier/
P. Er hat jetzund gar nicht der weile/
 Man mög sonst schmeckn das Bier.
Fr. Hier habt jhr zehen Thalr zum Schmaus/
 Thut morgen wieder kommen.
Weil mein Mann noch nicht kömpt zu Hauß/
 Vffn Abend wie jhr vernommen.

31.

St. Das war gut Glück das ich jetzt hab
 So geschwind zehn Thalr bekommen/
 Vnd noch weil ich zu dieser Gab/
 Mein *oculos* mitgenommen/
 Aber potz hundert schlapperment/
 Das Hauß hab ich vergessen/
 Weiß auch nicht zu finden das End/
 Da ich erst bin gewesen.

32.

Aaa 5

 Nun zum Gedächtnis wil ich mir/
 Tuch zu einem Kleid thun kauffen/
P. Warlich das thu/ das rath ich dir/
 Weil du das Gelt erlauffen.
St. Ich wil nun wieder gehn zu Handt/
 Wol in die Grimmisch Gassen/
 Vnd wil mir Tuch außnehmen thun/
 Zu Mantel/ Wams vnd Hosen.

33.

M. Guten Morgen Jungfr: wie stehts mit euch/
    Wie habt jhr heint geschlaffen.
Fr. Gar wol Gott lob/ hab ich vor mich/
    Warumb thut jhr aber fragen/
  Werdet jhr auch halten ewer verheiß.
    Wie jhr mir heut versprochen.
M. Wie so/ ich darvon nichts nicht weiß/
    Daß ich ein Wort könt sprechen.

34.

Fr. Ach ja stelt euch mir gewaltig frembd/
    Ihr werdet mich nicht betriegen/
M. Ich weiß von nichts beym schlapperment/
    Meynt jhr/ ich wolt euch lügen.
Fr. Das ist mir gar ein schönes Spiel/
    Daß er nichts darvon wil wissen/
  Weiß nicht/ warumb er stets schweigt still/
    Wann ich doch were betrogen.

35. [Aaa 5v]

St. Ein guten Morgen geb euch Gott/
Fr.   Habt danck mein lieber Herr/
  Der Herr sag mir ohn allen Spott/
    Was ist des Herrn begehren/
St. Ich wolt gern habn was gelts von Tuch/
    Ob ichs hier könt bekommen/
Fr. Gar wol/ denn ich hab dessen genug/
    Thut nur herein kommen.

36.

St. Wie thewr die Elln von diesem Stück/
    Sagt mir den nechsten Kauff/
Fr. Vmb 2. Reichsthaler ohn Betrug/
    Das ist der gemeine Lauff/
St. Zweene Gülden wil ich euch fürgeben/
    Kompt her vnd nehmt Gelt/
  Den Thaler zu Sieben dreyssig Groschen/
    Wie sie jetzunder gelten.

37.

Fr. Mein Herr wo habt jhr das Gelt bekom*m*en/
St.   Wie so/ warumb thut jhr fragen/
Fr. Vmb etzlicher gewisser Vrsach willen/
     Ich bitt jhr wolt mirs sagen/
St. Ich habs von einer Fraw bekommen/
     Bey der ich nächten gewesen/
Fr. Ach weh/ daß sind mein Thaler gewiß/
     Er ist derselb gewesen.

38.   [Aaa vj]

Fr. Vmb hundert Gotts Willn ich bitt/
     Thuts doch kein Menschen sagen.
     Ach daß mein Magd an kom der Ritt/
     Wem sol ich solches klagen/
     Seht da/ nehmt diese Thaler wieder/
     Thuts aber bey Leib nicht sagen/
     Zu Lohn das Tuch/ daß jhr begehrt/
     Solt jhr davon auch tragen.

39.

St. Ewren Willen ich gern folgen wil/
     Thu mich höchlich bedancken/
     Bey mir bleibt es wol in der still/
     Habt nur kein andere Gedancken.
P.   Ists war/ mag es wol müglich seyn/
     Weil du die Braut bekommen/
     Das mag mir wol ein Posse seyn/
     Als ich mein Tag vernommen.

40.

St. Was Glück mag ich jetzund wol sagen/
     Hat mich hieher geführt/
P.   Halb Beut wil ich auch davon tragn/
     Wenn er heraus gehen wird/
St. Die Häscher ich jetzt loben muß/
     Die mich her thun jagen/
P.   Dagegen ists jhr ein schwere Buß/
     Das mag ich kühnlich sagen.

41.

St. Wolan nunmehr ich bin bereit/
    Jetzund wil ich heim gehen/
P. Holla mein Gesell gib mir halb Beut/
    Weiß wol was ich gesehen.
St. Siehe du Pickelhering kom mit mir/
    Wir wollen zum Keller gehn/
Vnd vns zu sauffen in Wein vnd Bier/
    Daß keiner mehr kan stehen.

42.

P. Mein Seel/ das würd gar wol angehen/
    Dann mich gewaltig dürstet/
St. Hastu die *Action* gesehen/
P.   Für lachen ich schier zubörstet/
St. Es hat hier trefflich guten Lufft/
    Daß ich mich drüber verwundert/
P. Den bring ich dir von Hertzen das pufft/
    So dencken die Bawren es donnert.

F I N I S .

32

[DER PFERDEKAUF DES EDELMANNES.][1]

Action 4. Person.

E. Edelmann/ *P.* Pickelhering/
F. Fraw/ *M.* Mann.

I. Melodia.

E. Picke[h]ering kom geschwind herzu/ ꝛc.

I.

E. Pickelhering kom geschwind herzu/
    Ich wil morgen außreiten/
    Putz mir die Stieffeln vnd die Schue/   [Aaa vij*v*]
    Hastu kein Schwertz nimb Kreiden.
P. Warlich ich hab jetzt gar viel Kreiden/
    Sinds aber die Stieffeln auch werth/
    Holla mein Herr/ jhr wolt wol reiten/
    Wo aber ist das Pferdt.

[1] From *Engelische Comedien und Tragedien.*

2.

E. Da trag du gar kein sorg dafür/
    Es ist schon wol bestellet.
P. Mein Seel/ es geht nicht an die Thür/
    Viel weniger vber die Schwelle.
Ich wil ihn lassen Sorgen dafür/
    Vnd wil die Stieffeln putzen/
Mein Herr gibt ein weisen Cavallier/
    Er wird außbündig stutzen.

3.

Seht da Herr sind sie recht geputzet/
    Ich hab viel Kreide verschmieret/
E. Wie hastu mir die Stieffeln vernützet/
P.   Mein Herr mich nicht vexiret/
Ich hab es trefflich wol gemacht/
    Wolt jhr es besser haben/
So nehmets selbr vnd macht mirs nach/wo
    So wil ich euch außschaben.   (nit/

4.

E. Warumb hastu mirs mit Kreiden beschmirt/
    Wil dirs bald vmb Kopff schmeissen/
P. Mein Seel/ es hat sich wol vexiret/   [Aaa viij]
    Ihr habt michs ja geheissen/
E. Nun laß jetztund die Possen bleiben/
    Hol mir geschwind das Pferdt.
P. Mein Herr jhr könt es doch nicht reiten/
    Vnd ist des Gangs nicht werth.

5.

E.Ich bin ein Herr in meinem Hauß/
    Vnd thue ich was befehlen.
So heist mein Herr/ richts selber aus/
    So weistu daß es geschehe/
Die Zeit zu reiten laufft dabey/
    Biß ich mich hab gestieffelt.
Wann ich meyn/ alles verrichtet sey/
    Ists mit einem Quarck versiegelt.

6.

P. Das Pferd ist da/ kompt nun bald her/
　　Es ist aber nur eins.
E. Sihe da worzu bedarff ich mehr/
P. 　　Ja Herr/ wo bleibt denn meins.
E. So war es nur vmb dich zu thun/
　　Nim du des Schusters Rappen.
P. Warlich mein Herr/ nembt jhr dasselb/
　　Es thut gar wacker trappen.

7.

P. Eylet / eilet mein Herr/
　　Das Pferdt wird müde/
　　Wenn es so lang sol stehn/
E. Sich Narr wird es von stehen müd.　　[Aaa viij*v*]
　　Wie würd es denn fortgehen.
P. Mein Herr gewaltig lang machet jhr/
　　Fein hurtig seyd wie ich/
E. Nun nun kom her vnd folge mir/
　　Ich wil versuchen dich.

Die andere Melodey/geht wie
das *Runda dinella*.

8.

P. Wist jhr warumb ich so bald wiederkom/
　　rund.
　　Ihr werdet ein theil schon haben vernom*m*n/
　　runda dinella.
　　Wolt jhr es wissen ich wils euch sagn.
　　Wann jhr es könt behalten/
　　Könt jhr nicht alles in Hosen tragen/
　　So steckt es zwischen den Falten.

9.

P. Warlich ich kan nicht lenger/
　　Bey mein Herrn bleiben/
　　Ich sol zu Fuß in Dreck gehen/
　　Er wil alleine reiten/

Da ich jetzt war mit heraus kommen/
Vnd wolt mit auffs Pferdt sitzen/
Da sprang er mit den Pferdt herumb/
Vnd ich fiel in die Pfützen.

10.

P. Biß daß ich wieder thet auffkommen/*rund.*
  Hat mir der Herr schon Pferdt genommen/
    rund.
  Er ritt hinweg/ ich solt nachlauffen/
  Warlich es dünckt mich schwere/
  Ich muß sehen/ ob ich nicht kan draussen/
  Zu jhm kom ich nicht mehr.

11.

P. Habters gehört/ habt danck ich muß nun
    gehen/ *rund. &c.*
  Vnd nach einen andern Herrn vmbsehen/
    rund.
  Potz schlapperment/ da wer gut dienen/
  Ich thet es gar vmbsonst/
  Wil mich ein wenig zu jhr finden/
  Wil brauchen alle mein Kunst.

12.

  Guten Abend Ehrenveste Jungfraw/ *rund.*
Fr.Sihe dein Begehren mir vertrawe/
P. *runda rund.*
  Hört jhr ich muß euch etwas sagen/
  Ihr hat ein Lieblein zarte/
  Wolt jhr mich zu einen Diener halten/
  Tag vnd Nacht wil ich auffwarten.

13.

Fr.Es gescheh/ sag mir dein Namen geschwind/
P.   *runda dinella.*
  Ich hieß *monsoier domine.*
    Herr Pickelhering *runda dinella.*
Fr.Wolan wiltu mir fleissig dienen/
  So sag es mir behend/
P. Kein mangel sol an erscheinen/
  Aber potz schlapperment.

14.

E: Das ist ein wacker schönes Pferdt/
       Da wer gut auff reiten/
Der Ritt wer 100. Thaler werth/
       Wenn sie mich wolte leiden/
Fr. Vmb solchs Gelt könts wol geschehn/   Bbb ij
       Wenn Worten wer zu trawen/
P.   Vmb Gottes Willen last jhn gehn/
       Ich kan jhn nicht anschawen/

15.

Fr. Pickelhering hastu die Wort vernommen/
P.   Ich hab sie wol gehört.
Fr. Jetzund wil ich dein Trewe versuchn/
       Gehe sihe/ wo er einkehrt/
Sag du zu jhm/ wenn er begehrt
       Zu halten was er geredt/
Sey jhm darzu mein Leib beschert/
       Heut auff den Abend spat.

16.

P.   Wann ich es aber hab außgericht/
       Sol ich ein Tranckgelt haben/
Fr. Ja/ doch geh fort verseum es nicht/
       Thu wacker jhm nachtraben/

    Die hundert Thaler weren gut/
      Sie sind doch bald verdient/
    Solch reiten kan ich leiden wol/
      Weil es mir nichts benimbt.

17.

E. Nun feiner Gesell kömpstu wieder/
    Wo warstu hin geloffen/
P. Mein Herr ich hab ein außbündig Pferdt/
    Jetzunder angetroffen.
E. Du solt reden was mir gefelt/
    Gedenck vnd thu mirs sagen.
P. Hört jhr nicht ich hab ein Pferdt bestellt/   [Bbb ij*v*]
   Was thut jhr mich viel fragen.

18.

E. Was sagstu mir lang von den Pferdt/
    Hörst wol das frag ich nicht/
P. Mein Herr/ jhr habt ja begehrt 100. Tha-
   ler vor ein Ritt.
E. Was Phantasirstu mir jetzt viel daher/
    Ich weiß nicht was dir ist/
    Ich glaub du wilst zum Narren werden/
    Odr ob du schon einer bist.

19.

P. Das ist ein wunder seltzam Ding/
    Daß euch schon ist vergessen/
    Ich bin kein Narr/ Hans Pickelhering/
    Wolt jhr heut mit mir essen/
    So kompt mit mir geschwind zu Hauß/
    Nehmet 100. Thaler mit.
E. Was ist dir doch/ sags recht heraus/
    Sonst verstehe ich dich nit.

20.

P. Versteht jhr kein Amadisisch deutsch/
    Das nimpt mich leiden Wunder/
    Nun wil ichs euch auff gut Bäwrisch/
    Sagen den gantzen Blunder/
    Wist jhr daß jhr ein schönes Weib/
    Dieselb ist mein Fraw/
    Begehrt vor einer kleinen Zeit/
    Jetzund thut er sich krawen.

21.

P. Versteht jhrs nun/ hab ich jetzt recht/
E. Ja ich hab schon vernommen/
   Fürwar du bist ein wacker Knecht/
   Wie sol ich sie bekommen.
P. Wann jhr das ander auch wolt haben/
   So kompt jetzunder mit/
   So viel jhr nach ewren Willen wollet/
   Vnd vollführen ewren Ritt.

22.

E. Ja ja führ mich nur balden dahin/
P. Holla es leit mir was in Sinn/
E. Was ists warumb bleibstu stehen/
P. Wann ich euch hab dahin geführt.
   Ein Trinckgelt muß ich haben.
E. Ja ja/ freylich/ wie sichs gebührt/
   Laß vns jmmer fort traben.

23.

P. Herr/ stehet da/ daß ist das Hauß/
   Da möget jhr gehen hinein/
   Aber dort kömpt sie selbst heraus/
   Ihr werdet jetzt willkommen seyn/
   Fein gravitetisch thut euch stellen/
   Also müst jhr es machen.
E. Ja ja/ vertritt du nur dein Stell/
   Thu dich vmb mich nichts plagen.

24.

E Ein guten Abend mein schönes Lieb.
F.   Der Herr sey nur willkommn/   [Bbb iij*v*]
P. Hört jhr/ kompt jhr ein wenig herbey[1]/
     Ich hab jetzt was vernommen/
   Ihr wisset wol was jhr zugesagt.
E.   Was essen/ was wiltu haben/
P. Mein Tranckgelt muß ich fordern bey Zeit/
     Ihr möcht sonst davon traben.

---

[1] *herhey* in the original.

25.

E. Mein Schatz gegen euch mit Lieb/
  Mein Hertz gar sehr verwundet ist/
  Drumb ich mich euch gantz ergeb/
  Jetzund zu dieser Frist/
Fr. Gar gern ich euch auffnehmen thu/
  Wil heilen ewre Wunden/
  Zu ewer Kranckheit ein *Medicum,*
  Habt jhr an mir jetzt funden.

26.

E. Last mich versuchen ewer *medicin*
  Erquickt mich mit einem Kusse/
Fr. Ewer Kranckheit *curir* ich nicht so ge-
  schwindt/
  Ich muß sie vor recht wissen/
E. Hertzliebste nicht lang warten thut/
  Sonst werd ich gar verderben.
Fr. Ach nein mein Schatz die Farb ist gut/
  Ihr werdet so bald nicht sterben.

27.   Bbb iiij

Fr. Langt mir doch Herr jetzt ewer Händ/
  Den Pulß muß ich begreiffen/
  Fürwar der Pulß schlägt gar behend/
E.   Groß Hitz thu ich erleiden/
Fr. Wo aber muß dieselbig seyn/
  Gewiß ist sie am Hertzen/
Ed. Ach ja dasselb leidt grosse Pein/
Fr.   Ists wahr ohn alles schertzen.

28.

Fr. Dieselbig thut sich nach dem brauch/
  Schlagen zu allen Gliedern/
  Drumb muß ich es versuchen auch/
E.   Es ist mir nicht zu wieder/
Fr. Denn ich es alles wissen muß/
  Ehe ich euch kan Curiren/
E. Danck habt mein Schatz vor diesen Kuß/
  Ich mich schon besser spüre.

29.

E. Groß krafft befind ich/ weil ich mehr
    Bekom/ als ich begehrte/
Fr. Ja ja/ rümht euch noch nicht so sehr/
    Wer weiß was noch draus werde/
    Diß Fiebr vergehet nicht so leicht/
    Es schlägt bald wieder vmb.
E. Darumb mein Schatz ich bitte euch/
    Denselben bald vorkompt.

30.   [Bbb iiij*v*]

F. Ach ja mein Schatz es sol geschehn/
    Folgt jhr nur meinem Rath/
E. Von hertzen gern wil ichs thun/
    Awe wer klopfft so starck/
Fr. Holla Pickelhering wo bistu/
    Geh sich wer klopfft an.
P. Ja ja was sols/ hie bin ich nun/
    Ich forcht es sey ewer Mann.

31.

P. Wer da/ wer klopfft an die Thür/
    (Mann) Ich bins laß mich hinein/
P. Ja wart/ es ist kein Schlüssel hie/
    Ich wil gehen holen einen/
    Potz schlapperment es ist der Herr/
    Was wollen wir anfangen.
E. Ach mein Schatz helffet jetzund mir/
    Daß ich an jhn nicht gelange.

32.

Man) Mach auff was lest mich lang hier stehe*n*/
P. Ich kan kein Sch[l]üssel finden/
Fr. Mein Schatz/ thut flugs mit mir hingehen/
    Ich wil euch führen dahinden/
    Damit jhr seyd verwahret recht/
    Von Herrn werdet jhr nicht vernommen/
    Wenn ich jhn werd haben bracht zu Bett/
    Wil ich wieder zu euch kommen.

33.

Fr. Pickelhering mach nun jmmer auff/
    Es hat nichts mehr zu bedeuten/
P. Warlich mein Herr wird jetzt ein Gauch/
    Darff darzu kein Geleute/
Man. Sieh da machstu nun auff ein mal/
    Wo hastu denn Schlüssl nun funden/
P. Er war mir aus dem Sack gefallen/
    Da trugen jhn die Hunde.

34.

Fr. Ach hertziger Herr/ wie leid ists mir/
    Daß jhr so lang müssen stehen/
    Das Gsind gibt auff nichts achtung hier/
    Wir sind gar vbl versehen/
Man. Es ist also/ was sol man machn/
Fr.   Ach Herr legt euch zu Bette/
P Des Possens muß ich warlich lachen/
Fr.   Denn es ist zimlich späte.

35.

Man. Es hat kein Noth mein liebes Weib/
    Ich kan nicht gar wol warten/
    So lang biß du bist auch bereit/
P.   Das dient nicht in jhrn Garten/
Fr. O hertzigr Herr/ das thut ja nicht/
    Es wird euch gar zu lang.
Man. Ich mag nicht gehn/ du gehst denn mit/
P.   Jetzt wird jhr erst recht bang.

36.

Fr. Wolan mein Herr/ weil jhr nicht wolt/
    Allein zu Bette gehen/
    Wil ich mit euch gehn also bald/
    Mein Sachen lassen stehen.
M. Das thu/ was wiltu lang außbleibn/
    Morgen kömpt auch ein Tag.
P. Es ist einr hier der wolt gern reitn/
    Das ist die gröste klag.

37.

Fr. Nun kompt/ ach wie wird mir so weh/
M.   Was ist dir liebes Weib/
Fr. Es kömpt mich an/ ich muß flugs gehn/
     Ich hab groß reissn im Leib/
M. Ich wil mitgehn/ wiltu es habn/
     Daß dir kein Leid gescheh/
Fr. Nein Herr/ die Kälte möcht euch schadn/
     Ich wil allein hingehn.

38.

M. Ich laß dich doch nicht gehn allein/
     Es möcht dich was erschrecken/
Fr. O nein mein Herr/last es nur seyn/
P.   Der Alb der wird sie decken/
Fr. Ihr solt euch solchs nicht thun zu leid/
     Es wird euch gar zu lange/
M. O nein es ist noch als gut Zeit/
Fr.   Warlich mir ist recht bange.

39.

[Bbb vj]

Fr. Nun weil jhr dann ja wolt mitgehn/
     Vnd haltets vor bequem/
     So bleibt doch auff den Gang mit stehn/
     Denn ich mich sonsten schem/
M. Hier wil ich bleiben an der Treppn/
P.   Der Narr lest sich bethören/
Fr. Thut dieweil mit ewren Schlüsseln klepprn/
     Damit ich euch nur höre.

40.

F.d. Mein Hertzen Schatz thut jhr widrkommn/
     Ich hab gewiß vermeynet/
     Vnsr Lieb die hette ein End genommn/
     Jetzund ists erst recht Zeit.
Fr. O nein Hertzallerliebster mein/
     Die Frewd wolln wir anfangen/
     Denn wir beyde jetzt sind allein/
     Mein Mann mag warten lange.

41.

Fr. Kompt her mein Schatz/ mein Mann hat
    Lang gnug herumb getrieben/ (mich
    Biß daß zu euch bin kommen ich/
E.   So ists ewr Mann zu frieden/
Fr. Wie sol ers nicht zo frieden seyn/
    Vnd thut ein Ständgen machen/
E. Was hör ich/ ist das ewer Mann/
    So muß ich warlich lachen.

42.   [Bbb vj*v*]

Fr. Darzu hab ich jhn bstellet her/
    Der Narr ist bessers nicht werth/
Ed. Ihr seyd fürwar gar viel geschwindr/
    Als heutiges Tages mein Pferdt/
Fr. Last euch ein weil begnügen/
    Denn ich muß jetzt wieder gehn/
    Vnd zu meim Mann verfügen thun/
    Ihm wird zu lang das stehen.

43.

Ed. Gar wol ich es zu frieden bin/
    Macht das ich kom hinweg/
Fr. Das sol alles geschehen fein/
    Wenn er wird seyn zu Bett/
    Last euch die Zeit nicht werden lang/
    Ihr dürfft euch nichts besorgen/
    Ich wil nun gehen auff den Gang/
Ed.   So bleib ich hier verborgen.

44.

Fr. Ach mein Herr thut jhr noch hier stehn/
M.   Kömpstu mein liebes Weib/
    Ich wil ein wenig auch hingehn/
    Es ist mit mir auch Zeit/
P. Warlich er hat ein guten Sinn/
    Das Zäpffgen ist noch dahinden.
Fr. Ach weh Herr ich muß widr dahin/
    Mein Schmertzen ich befinde.

45.

Fr. Ach wie ist mir wieder so weh/
P.　　　Das ist fürwar erlogen/
Fr. Ach mein Herr last mich flugs hingehn/
P.　　　Der Narr wird doch betrogen/
M. Wolan so geh du hin auff diß/
　　　Ich wil hinauff thun gehen/
P. Warlich hettstu gewartet biß
　　　Jetzt ist es schon geschehen.

46.

Fr. Kompt her mein Schatz/jetzund ists zeit/
　　　Daß jhr von hinnen scheidet/
Ed. Ewr Mann wird ja zu frieden seyn/
Fr.　　　An jhm mir gar nichts leit/
Ed. Ich bitt mein Schatz nempt meinr in acht/
Fr.　　　Anders verseht euch nichts/
Ed. Ade mein Schatz zu guter Nacht/
P.　　　Ich wil nicht gehen mit.

FINIS.

Curante.

F I N I S.

33

Nun folgen etliche newe
Singe Comœdien/so zur
Lust wol agiret werden
können.

[DER MÖNCH IM SACKE][1]

Cantus   6. *Person.*

1. *A.*   Alter.
2. *N.*   Nachtbar.
3. *F.*   Fraw.
4. M.   Magd.
5. *M.*[2]   Münch.
6. *L.*   Landsknecht.

[1] This and the following piece are printed from a copy of *Liebeskampff Oder Ander Theil Der Engelischen Comoedien und Tragoedien* (1630) in the British Museum.

[2] This letter is distinguished from the one above it by the use of Roman instead of black letter type. I have used italics throughout to indicate the Roman type of the original.

1.

A. Höret was mich außgetrieben hat [Cc viij*v*]
Weil ich herkom auffm Abend spat/
Daheim hab ich ein junges Weib
Fraw Elßlein zart vnd schön von Leib/
Die hab ich lieb im Hertzen.

2.

Allein sie helt sich nach mir nicht
Fast andere Buler ins Gesicht
Weiß nicht ob ich jhr bin zu alt
Zu heßlich oder vngestalt?
Ein Freund möcht jetzt wol klagen.

3.

Schaw kompt nicht dort mein Nachbar für/
N. Ein guten Abend: Was mächt jhr hier
Mein lieber Herr vnd Nachbar gut
Mich dünckt euch sey nicht wol zu Muth/
A. Ihr habts warlich errathen.

4.

N. Was mangelt euch/ was ligt euch an/
Ist kein Artzt der euch helffen kan?
A. Ach mein schönes Weib ach Nachbar hört/
Ist in der Lieb so betört/
N. Das hab ich mich lan duncken.

5.

Wer ist der Knab mit dem sie bullt/
A. Ich habe daran keine Schuld/
N. Mein lieber Herr mich recht versteht
Wist jhr wer jhr in Lieb nachgeht
A. Ein Münch auß einem Kloster.

6.

Dd [j]

N. Was ist für Ordens derselbe Mann?
A. Ein Augustiner Capelan/
N. Er wird kal vmb den Schnabel seyn/
A. Er ist viel hurtiger als wir zwein/
N. Daß kan ich wol gedencken.

7.

Vielleicht ist es nicht böß gemeint?
A. Ach schweigt ich bin jhm Spinne feind/
N. Mein lieber Herr vrtheilt nicht bald/
Erkündigt euch vor aller Gestalt/
A. Es ist mir vngelegen.

8

Ein Weib hab ich genommen mir/
Vnd halt sie keinem München für:
N. Habt jhr sie dann ergriffen beyd?
A. Ach schweiget still/es wer mir leyd/
Ich wolt dem München erschiessen.

9.

So viel Nachrichtung hab ich wol/
Mein Fraw mich nicht bekriegen soll/
Kan ich den Vogel [e]inmal erschnapn/
Streiffen wil ich jhm seine Kapn/
Das buhlen jhm erwehren.

10.

N. Mein Herr ein Rath wil ich euch geben/
Was hilffs euch? brecht jhn vmbs Leben/
Ihr kompt sampt ewewrem[1] Weib zu Spott/
A. Solt ich das leyden? Behüt mich Gott/
N. So thut mein Rath anhören.

11.   [Dd j*v*]

F. Wo muß nur seyn mein alter Herr?
N. Ich bitt mein Herr/ hört ohn Beschwer/
Die Katz die lest das Mausen nicht/
F. Da hört doch nur was jener spricht?
N. Mir ists auch also gangen.

12.

Derhalben rath ich euch zu letzt/
Daß jhrs auffs euserts Mittel setzt/
Nehmet auch einen Bulen an/
A. Vergebs euch Gott/ Ich alter Mann/
Kan nicht die eine bewahren.

[1] The first two letters should probably be omitted as a case of dittography.

13.

N. Also wird sie bezahlet par/
F. Schaw steht dort nicht mein alter Narr/
Wer ich sein loß so wer ich fro/
A. Nachtbar rath jhr ein andern so/
Ihr brecht mich vmb das Leben.

14.

N. Wie so mein Herr? wenn sie ersicht/
Daß jhr euch darumb kümmert nicht/
Sondern stellt euch so frölich gantz/
Bey ewer Bulschafft/vnd den Tantz/
Es wird die Sach sie rewen.

15.

Daß sie jhr Huld eim andern gibt/
Vnd nicht jhrn Herrn vorm Mönche liebt/
Daheim hab ich ein schöne Dirn/
Die will ich euch noch heut zuführn/
F. Ey das sehe ich gar gerne.

16.

Dd ij

A. Was meinet jhr mit solchem sagen/
Wolt jhr mich in mein alten Tagn
Bereden/daß ich brech die Ehe/
Das soll geschehen nimmermeh?
F. Es müst ein nach dir lüsten.

17.

A. Ich hab die Zeit des Lebens mein/
Verhalten mich stets keusch vnd rein/
F. Darbey bin ich gewesen nicht.
A. Hab mich zu sterben keusch verpflicht/
F. Wolt Gott es wer geschehen.

18.

N. Mein Herr/ weil jhr wolt folgen nicht/
So steht jhr euch selbst vor dem Liecht/
Ich wolt der Mönch hett sie allzeit/
F. So wer der Alt ja wol geheit:
A. Das sol jhm noch wol fehlen.

19.

Nun will ich schleunig gehen hin/
Nach meinem eigen Kopff vnd Sinn/
Mein Elßelein besuchn zu Hauß/
Find ich den Mönch ich schlag jhn nauß/
F.　Kein Narren hastus gesaget.

20.

M.　Fraw Elßlein kompt alsbald mit mir/
F.　Schweig Magd/ denn vnser Herr ist hier/
M.　Der Mönch mit grossm verlangn wart/
F.　Es muß noch lenger sein gespart/
　　Dort kömpt der Herr gegangen.

21.　　　　　　　　　　　　　　[Dd ij*v*]

Wo her mein allerliebster Schatz?
Vor Lieb muß ich[1] euch gebn ein Schmatz/
A.　Pack dich Elßlein/ Ich hör du hast
　　Ein andern Buhln an dich gefast/
F.　Das wird niemand beweisen.

22.

A.　Es weis davon die Stadt zu sagen/
F.　Mein edler Herr/ wenn ich solt klagn/
　　Wie offt man euch nur gibt die Schuld/
　　Als wenn kein Mann in der Stadt so bult/
　　Ich thus darumb nicht glauben.

23.

Wann ich auch so argdencklich wer/
Als eben jhr mein liebster Herr/
So müst ich euch zu keiner Stund/
Vergönnen meinen rothen Mund/
Darumb thut mich loß zehlen.

24.

A.　Desto lieber solt mir fort seyn/
　　Befleisse dich der Keuschheit rein/
M.　Wie mein rechter vnd lincker Schuch
　　So thustu deinen Ehren gnug/
F.　Das soll jmmer geschehen.

---

[1] *ist* in the original.

25.[1]

Zart edler Herr wo wolt jhr hin?
A. Weit vber Feldt da steht mein Sinn/
    Ein Sach hab ich zu richten auß/
    Vnd kom auch heut nicht wider zu Hauß/
M. Das sehn wir alle gerne.

26.

Dd iij

F. Wolt jhr nicht bey der Malzeit bleiben/
    Mein Edler Herr vnd kurzweil treibn/
    Denn ich hab einkaufft auffs best/
    Gleichsam als solt jhr haben Gäst/
M Der Münch wirds wol verzehren.

27.

A. Nein/mein Hertzallerliebste Fraw
    Elßlein/ich bitt hab acht vnd schaw/
    Daß vnser Hauß werd vol verwacht
    Ade ich scheid/ein gute Nacht/
M. Wol in dem nechsten Graben.

28.

F Herr? wann werd jhr wider kommn
A. Warumb fragst du/
F.   Wann ichs vernommn/
    So wil ich euch mit höchstem Fleiß
    Entgegen gehen auff der Reiß/
A. Fraw es ist vnvonnöthen.

29.

F. Mein lieber Herr behüt euch Gott
M. O lieber Herr/werd jhr schon todt/
F. Damit euch widerfahr kein Leyd
A. Dir auch mein Elßlein allezeit/
F. So ziehet hin ohn alls Trauren.

30.

Magd lauff vnd hol den Münche bald
Eh vns die Braten werden kalt/
M. Ich wil jhn holen schleunig eben
    Vielleicht wird mir auch was darneben
    Schawt/ schawt/wer kompt dort gangen.

---

[1] "26" has been crossed out and "25" written in.

31.

F. Mich dünckt es sey mein Bul gewiß/
M. Mein liebes Elßlein *Bonus dies,*
   Kom ich auch jetzt zu rechter Zeit/
F. Ach liebster Herr seyd hoch erfrewd/
   Mein Mann ist außgefahren.

32.

M. So kom ich zur glückseligen Stund/
F. Seyd mir wilkom frisch vnd gesund/
M. Wie secht jhr so bleich im Gesicht.
F. Herr mein Mann ist der Sach bericht/
M. Was hör ich newes sagen?

33.

   Wer hat das alles jhm vertrawt?
F. Vielleicht hat er vns zu geschawt/
   Wie wir vns gehalst vnd geküst/
   Gar offtmals/wie jhr dann wol wüst/
M. Was thet jhr darzu sagen?

34.

F. Dem Altn thet ich schwern vnd laugnen/
   Nam jhm den Argwohn auß den Augen/
   Bezwang jhn mit freundlichen Wort/
   Daß er von dieser Sachn auffhort/
M. Das Spiel haben wir gewonnen.

35.

   Billig zieh ich mein Kutten ab/
   Weil ich darzu gut Vrsach hab/
   Vnd henck sie an die Wand hinan/
   Hie hengt der Mönch/hie steht der Mann/
   Was wolt jhr ferner haben?

36.   Dd iiij

F. Setzt euch mein Herr wol zu dem Tisch/
   Allhier stehn schon gut Vogl vnd Fisch/
M. Fraw Elßlein setzt euch auch herbey/
   Daß ich mit euch recht lustig sey/
F. Magd hol vns auch zu trincken.

37.

M. Das will ich thun von Hertzen gern/
    Das best Bier/vnd Wein holn dem Herrn
Denn ich wol weiß die rechten Faß/
    Weil ich darvon sehr offt einlaß/
M. Mein Dirn das glaub ich gerne.

38.

F. Mein Herr/ wie sitzt so trawrig jhr/
    Rückt doch ein wenig her zu mir/
    Habt jhr mich dann nicht mehr so lieb/
M Ach liebster Schatz achtung ich gieb/
    Auff ewre hohe Schue.

39.

Denn mich bedünckt in meinem Sinn/
Als seß ich bey einer Königin/
Wie könt jhr doch dem alten Mann/
So freundlich offtmals lachen an/
F. Herr das will ich euch sagen.

40.

Mein Alter hat der Kronen viel/
Nach diesen schieß ich zu dem Ziel/
Biß ich dieselben all bekom/
M. Fraw Elßlein ich bitt euch darumb/
    Thut ja nicht mehr auffhören.

41.   [Dd iiij*v*]

F. Magd daß dich alles Vnglück rühr
    Wie bleibstu so l[a]ng[1] mit dem Bier/
M. Ich ließ das Bier Sanct Velten han
    Der Wein der macht ein starcken Mann/
    Hier ist beydes vorhanden.

42.

F. Mein Herr habt jhr kein Messer nicht/
M. An diesem mir gar nicht gebricht/
F. So ziehet es auß legt mir vor/
M. Ja warlich ich bin gleich wie ein Thor/
    Hett bald das best vergessen.

---

[1] There is space for *a*.

43.

Doch lest sichs vbel essn vnd schlingn
Wenn man nicht thut hoffirn vnd singn/
Mein liebes Mensch/ was könt jhr guts/
M. Ja Herr es soll geschehen jetzt/
Das Korn das thut schon reiffen.

44.

M. Fraw Elßlein dieser Becher mit Wein
In einem Trunck euch bracht sol seyn/
F. Gesegns euch Gott mein lieber Herr
Ich wolt daß es bald gar auß wer/
M. Das glaub ich warlich gerne.

45.

M. Fraw Elßlein/ Ich/jhr kent jhn wol
F. Herr jhr auch wenn ichs sagen sol/
M. Singen mein ich/
F.   Daß ich auch mein
Wol nach der rechten Music fein/
M. Bitt last euch nicht verdriessen.

46.   Dd v

F. Ach liebster Herr/ warumb solt ich
Bey euch nicht sein billig frölich/
Zu Ehrn vnd Gefallen allein/
Wil ich nun singn ein Liedelein/
M. Darauff so wil ich mercken.

> Hier muß Fraw Elßlein
> ein LöffelLiedlein sin-
> gen.

47.

F. Wie ists mein Herr/ wolt jhr einschlaffn/
M. Das thut das schöne Liedlein schaffn.
F. Schlafft wann jhr in dem Kloster seyd/
M. Ach liebster Schatz/ mein höchste Frewd/
Ich muß euch einmal halsen.

48.

F. Darzu muß ich euch geben ein Schmatz/
M Vnd ich euch auch mein liebster Schatz
    Ein fein hurtigs Hertzlein trücken/
M. Darzu kan sich mein Fraw wol schicken/
M. Das giebt Krafft meinem Hertzen.

49.

    Ich muß auch ewer Mündlein Küssn/
F. Vnd ich auch Herr/daß solt jhr wissn.
M. Wie ist doch ewer Näselein
    So schön vnd hüpsch wie Helffenbein/
M. Wirds bald an mich auch kommen.

50.   [Dd v*v*]

M. Potz tausent sieben Schlapperment/
    Wie wers ein sach/ wenn jetzt behend
    Ewer Alter kem/ Fraw Elselein/
    Vnd schlüg mir entzwey Arm vnd Bein/
    So hett ich wol gefischet.

51.

F. Mein Herr seyd aller Sorgen loß/
M. Hilff Gott was ist daß für ein Stoß/
    Der so geschwindt ans Hauß geschicht?
M. Vor Angst mir fast daß Hertz zerbricht/
    Daß wer ein schöner Handel.

52.

F. Seidt vnverzagt Herr vberall/
    Es seynd die Pferd vnten im Stall/
M. Wann daß were/ so giengs wol hin/
    Mich dünckt aber vnd ist zu Sinn/
    Als sey Jemandt vorm Hause.

53.

    Hört wie es noch einmal so knalt/
F. Erschreckt nicht vnterm Tisch nicht falt/
    Magd hör wer klopfft so sehr anß Hauß/
    Geh/ mach nicht auff/ schaw nur hinauß/
M. Fraw es ist vnser Herre.

54.

F. Führt jhm der Hencker jetzo her/
   Ich wolt lieber es kem ein Beer/
M. Versteckt den Münch/ geschwind behendt/
   Damit der Herr jhn nicht erkent/
   Ich muß die Thür auffmachen.

55.   [Dd vj]

M. Potz Lufft/ potz Floh wo werd ich hin/
   Schönß Lieb/ wird mich ewer Alter in/
   Sterben muß ich/da hilffet nicht/
   Kein Entschuldigung Flehn vnd bitt/
F. Euch wil ich wol verbergen.

56.

Mein Herr kriecht jhr hinter den Tisch/
Seyd nur behertzt dapffer vnd frisch/
Bringen sol es[1] euch kein Gefahr/
M. Das wolte Gott/ ich förcht mich sehr/
   Wer ich davor im Kloster.

57.

M. Wie kompt so schleunig vnser Herr/
   Vnd thut so eilendt lauffen sehr/
A. Wie kompt das man das Hauß verspert/
   Gleichsam ob jhr daheim nicht wert/
   Das ich so lang muß warten.

58.

F. Seydt mir wilkommn/ wie geht es zu/
   Das ich so bald euch sehen thu/
   Mein edler Herr/ dieweil ich dacht/
   Ihr würdt nicht kommen diese Nacht/
   Ist es nicht wol gelungen

59.

A. Fraw jetzt erkenn ich dein Vntrew/
   Die du mir hast erwiesen new/
M. Ey was sagt jhr mein lieber Herr/
   Daß sey von meiner Frawen fern/
A Pack du dich in die Küchen.

---

[1] Only a faint and scarcely legible impression of *e* remains.

60.

F. Mein edler Herr/ was ant euch doch/
Daß jhr euch so betrübet hoch/
Ich weiß von keiner Vntrew nicht/
A. Der Alte hie viel anders spricht/
M. Awe wie wirds nur gehen.

61.

A. Was hastu denn für frembde Gäst/
Daß du das Hauß verschliessen lest/
F. Herr ich habs zum besten gethan/
Das kein Frembder sol einher gahn/
A. Das ist alles erlogen.

62.

Bin ich doch kommen kaum ins Hauß/
Bey vnsern Nachbar gesehen rauß/
Alda ich deine Bubenstück
Geschawet an mit Seufftzen dick/
Also muß ichs erfahren.

63.

Du meinst ich wer schon vber Feldt/
Darumb hast dir dein Münch bestelt/
Den Possn hab ich vorlengst gemerckt/
Mich wundert wer dich drauff verstèrckt/
F. Ich weiß von keinem Mönche.

64.

Hilff lieber Vater/ wo denckt jhr hin/
Was thut jhr euch ziehen zu Sinn/
M. Ich glaub das vnser alter Herr/
Vielleicht etwan gehabt daß pler/
F. Ach Schatz thut euch besinnen.

65.   [Dd vij]

Kompt legt euch nieder zu der Ruh/
A. Pack dich/ ich hab dir gesehn zu/
F. Kompt her last euch ewer Hertzlein trückn.
A. Fraw es wird sich wol anders schickn/
M. Ich wolt alle S. Velten.

66.

A. Ich sag dir Fraw/ denck nur geschwind/
Schaff mir den Mönch ich bin nicht blind/
Der zu dir in das Hauß spatziert/
M. Hat mich der Hencker hergefürt/
A. Ich wil jhm sonst selbst suchen.

67.

F. Mein edler Herr kein Mensch ist hier/
Habt jhrs doch sonst gethan noch nie/
A. Das glaub ich gern falsch Fräwelein.
Du schwürst mirß aus dem Sinne mein/
M. Ach Fraw thut mich nicht melden.

68.

A. Derhalben gib den Mönch herfür/
F Mein Schatz es ist ja niemand hier/
A. Wem ist das Gewand an dieser statt/
F. Mein edler Herr es ist mein Wandt/
M. Erst bin ich recht im Sacke.

69.

A. Schaw Fraw ist daß dein Mäntelein?
M. Erbarm es Gott es ist der mein/
A. Wie sicht es doch dem Mönch so gleich/
F. Mein edler Herr hoch bitt ich euch/
Thut kein arges gedencken.

70. [Dd vij*v*]

Der gute Herr kam hint herein/
Meint jhr würd noch daheime sein/
Wolt euch auff den Weg gebn den Segn/
Wie er zuvor thet allewegn/
M. Ja wenn er es wolt gleuben.

71.

A. O Weib dein List vnd Trug ist groß/
Warumb sitzt er bey dir so bloß/
Das ziembt ja nicht dem Orden sein/
F. Mein Schatz weil wir waren allein/
Zu Gast wolt ich jhn bitten.

72.

Damit jhm würdt gelohnet ebn/
Weil er euch wol den Segen gebn/
A. So sol er dafür segnen dich/
M O weh es geht als vber mich/
A. Dafür wil ich jhm dancken.

73.

Zeig mir jhm bald zu dieser frist/
So lieb dir Leib vnd Leben ist/
Wo ist der Mönch/ an welchen orth/
F. Zart edler Herr da er euch hort/
Zum Fenster er außsprange.

74

A. Was kattert dann so vnterm Tisch/
M. Wie sawr werden mir Vogl vnd Fisch/
M. Wie wird der Herr nun thun rumorn/
M. Wolt Gott ich wer bey dir davorn/
F. Es ist niemand darunter.

75.   [Dd viij]

A. Wiltu mir nicht in guten sagn/
So wil ich dir die Haut voll schlagn.
F. Mein edler Herr schlagt nicht so risch/
Der Mönch der steckt vnter dem Tisch/
M. Ach das muß Gott erbarmen.

76.

A. Mönch kreuch herfür daß sag ich dir/
M. Was wolt jhr mit mir machen hier/
Mein edler Herr es wer ein Schandt/
An einm Geistlichn zu legn die Handt/
A. Daß soltu wol erfahren.

77.

L. Was vor ein Gschrey thu ich erhörn/
Schaw einer zu den alten Herrn/
Was gilts er hat den Mönch erschnapt/
Vnd jhn bey seinem Weib erdapt/
Daß end muß ich erwarten.

78.

A. Schaw seyd jhr der Geistlose Mann/
Der die Jungen Frawn trösten kan/
Mit glatten Worten beschorner Kopff/
Heut mustu sterben du loser Tropff/
M. Ach Herr frist mir mein Leben.

79.

Was hilffs euch wenn jhr mirs genommn/
Ach ich wil nimmer wieder kommn/
Vorrede ewer gantzes Hauß/
Ach Herr last mich nur jetzo nauß/
A Nein Münch heut mustu bezahln.

80.   [Dd viij*v*]

Knie nieder ich wil dich erstechn/
M. Erst wil mir gleich mein Hertz zerbrechen/
Ach Herr das Stechen thut so weh/
Ich wolt mich lieber hencken eh/
A. Wolan ich bin zu frieden.

81.

Dieweil du tregst das Recht bey dir
Ein Strick vmb dich der gehöret dir/
Entblöß dein Halß ohn alle Sorgen/
So kanstu dann alsbald erworgen/
F. Ach Herr erzeigt jhm Gnade.

82.

M. Ich weiß nicht wie ich mich sol hengen/
Ich bin nicht viel vmbgangn mit Strengn/
Lieber wolt ich ins Wasser lauffn/
Darinnen könt ich bald ersauffn/
A. Mein Mönch bleib du hierinnen.

83.

Zum Wasser lauffen wird zu lang/
Du möchst mir gehn ein ander Gang/
Ein Brunnen hab ich in mein Hauß/
Darinnen soltu baden auß/
Daß dir das Buhln vergehe.

84.

Magd hole mir ein grossen Sack/
Das ich den Buben hinein pack/
Vnd vber jhm den binde zu/
Daß er in Brunnen ersauffn thu/
M. Ach thut euch mein erbarmen.

85.

M. Wie tawret mich der gute Herr/
    Wolt Gott daß er vorm Hause wer/
M. Dafür geb ich der Gülden roth
    Zweyhundert oder helff mir Gott/
A. Kein zappeln hilfft vorn Galgen.

86.

M. Vnd muß es dann gestorben sein/
    So geb ich mich gar willig drein/
M. Herr da bring ich den Sack behendt/
    Machts mit dem Herrn nur bald ein end/
M. Darumb thu ich auch bitten.

87.

A. So kreuch bald in den Sack hinein.
    Magd greiffe zu/ vnd halt jhm fein/
    Eil fort vnd machs nicht gar zu lang/
M. Ach Herr ich bin schon sterbe kranck/
A. Es wird noch besser werden.

88.

M. Ach Herr schont meiner Jugendt doch/
    Das ich manch Messe schmiede noch/
    Die euch zum besten dienen kan/
A. Vnd sols auch mein Fräwlein angahn/
    Die Messen sind geschmiedet.

89.

Wie stelstu dich? du loser Tropff/
Kreuch erstlich nein mit deinem Kopff/
Die Füsse kommen wol hernach/
M. Der Todt ringt mit mir allgemach/
    Ich kan euch nicht verstehen.

90.

Ach thut mir zeigen mein lieber Herr/
Weil ich doch gern zu sterbn begehr/
Ich seh vnd hör vor Zagn mehr nicht/
A. So gib acht drauff du Bösewicht/
M. Der Mönch wird euch geheyen.

91.

A. Also must dich in Sack nein schmügn/
L. Alter der Münch wird dich betriegn/
A. Biß vber deinem Gürtel rab/
M. Den Alten ich gefangen hab/
F. Herr daß thu ich mich frewen.

92.

M. Den Sack bin ich nun billig zu/
Vnd mit zum Brunnen wandern thu/
A. Ach hertzes Weib/ vnd liebe Magd/
L. Daß hab ich wol zuvor gesagt/
A. Thut mich vom Münch erretten.

93.

M. Mein lieber Herr so war lebt Gott/
Du hast dich selbst gesteckt in Noth/
Helfft nur den Sack heben empor/
In Brunn mustu da hilfft nichts vor/
F. So walt es alle Götter.

94.

A. Ach lieber Münch/last jhr mich lebn/
In ewre Straff wil ich mich gebn/
Vnd wil drey hundert euch zu Lohn/
Geben gut alte Sonnen Kronn/
Last mich nur auß dem Sacke.

95.   Ee ij

M. So fall im Sack auff deine Knie/
Schwer vns ein trewen Eyd allhie/
Daß du zu keiner Zeit vnd Stundt/
Solches von vns wolst machen kundt/
A. Ich wil es angeloben.

96.

M. Wo nicht so wil ich mich gleich rechn/
Dich mit dein eigen Schwerdt erstechn/
Vnd werffen dort in Brunn hinein/
So könn wir für dir sicher sein/
A. Ach nein/ich wil gehorchen.

97.

M So fern wil ich zu frieden sein/
Wenn dein zart edles Fräwelein/
In Burgschafft wil für dich bestahn/
Wo nicht so mustu Hare lahn/
L. Groß Wunder thu ich schawen.

98.

A. Ach liebstes Hertz wie denckstu doch/
Lest du mich steckn in diesem Loch/
F. Ey Herr last doch mein Alten rauß/
M. Ja wol da wird je nichts darauß/
Biß er im Sack thut schweren.

99.

A. Ich schwer im Sack ein thewren Eydt/
Das ich mein Fraw vnschuldig heut
Loß zehle von allen bösen wahn/
Will sein forthin jhr lieber Mann/
M. Noch mehr mustu auffpfeiffen.

100.   [Ee ij*v*]

A. Auch wil ich jhr zu keiner Zeit/
Vmb ewrer willn an thun ein Leid/
Sondern kompt offt vnd mit jhr est/
Vnd dieses Handels als vergest/
F. Ey ja es sol geschehen.

101.

A. Zu dienen bin ich euch bereit/
Darzu mein Elßlein allezeit/
Kein Argwohn wil ich haben mehr/
Macht auff den Sack mein lieber Herr/
M. So haben wir gewonnen.

102.

M. So kreuch heraus vnd denck daran/
    Was Hoffnung hat ein gfangner Mann.
    Zehle auff das Gelt laß mich gehn/
L. Ich wil dir fleissig nachsehen/
A. Ich wils gar willig geben.

103.

Nembt hin mein Herr den Seckel wol/
Der ist der gülden Kronen voll/
Drey hundert/vnd habt danck darnebn/
L. Was gilts der Mönch muß sie mir gebn/
M. Ihr dörfft darfür nicht dancken.

104.

Ihr Herren macht vns einen Tantz/
Darmit werd vnser Frewde gantz/
Fraw Elßlein kompt jhr her zu mir/
Die Köchin/Herr Alter/nembt jhr/
So sind wir abgetheilet.[1]

105.   Ee iij

Nun folget vnd habt kein beschwer/
Mit ewr Köchin mein lieber Herr/
Weil ich den Streit gewonnen hab/
So tantz ich mit Fraw Elßlein ab/
A. Halt Münch ich thu es nicht gestatten.

106.

L. Heist das nicht den Alten betrogn/
   Vnd bey der Nasn herumb gezogn/
   Ein Grube ward dem Münch gegrabn/
   Darein der Alt must selber falln/
   Des Possen muß ich lachen.

107.

Schreckt noch darzu den alten Mann/
Als hab er sehr vnrecht gethan/
Daß er noch eine Rantzion/
Den Mönch darfür muß gebn zu Lohn/
Es sol den Mönch nicht drücken.

---

[1] Apparently there is a dance of the four persons.

108.

Schaw dort kömpt gleich der glatte Knecht/
Der die Fräwlein kan trösten recht/
Frolocket vnd sich lustig macht/
Weil er den Altn vmbs Gelt gebracht/
Er sol es nicht lang haben.

109.

M. Heut muß das gantze Firmament/
All Planeten/ odr wie mans nent/
In rechten guten Zeichen stehn/
Weil mein Sachen so glücklich gehn/
Bey meinem schönen Bulen.

110.   [Ee iij*v*]

So gehts wenn sich die alten Narrn/
Wolln setzen auff Fraw Venus Karrn/
Vnd wollen junge Weibr freyen/
So thun dieselben sie geheyen/
Wie diesem alten Geschehen.

111.

L. Wie kompt daß jhr so spat vmbgeht/
M Freundt *Bonus Vesper* mich vorsteht/
L. Ich glaub jhr geht jungn Weibrn nach/
M. Behüt mich Gott denckt was jhr sagt/
Es ist mein Orden zuwieder.   .

112.

Zu Gaste bin ich heut gewesn/
L. Den Frawen die *horas* gelesn/
M. Mein lieber Herr seht mich recht an/
Denn ich bin nicht ein weltlich Mann/
Die ding sind mir verborgen.

113.

L. Wie daß jhr dann geht ohne Licht/
M Auß bösen solches nicht geschicht/
L. Ihr wist daß jhr bey tages Schein/
Sollet stets wieder im Kloster sein/
M. Es kan nicht gleich zugehen.

114.

L. Ich kenn dich wol in dein Gesicht/
Welchs mehr Weltlich/ denn Geistlich ist/
Ein rechter Buhlr bist in der Haut/
Wenn man in Kloster zur Mettn leuth/
Soltu noch anheim kommen.

115.   Ee iiij

Ein Kleid tregst in der Geistligkeit/
Ein rechter Schalck darunter leidt/
Du gehörst in die Gottloß Rott/
M. Nein ich dien/ Tag vnd Nacht mein Gott/
L. Ja wol bey schönen Frawen.

116.

Derhalben so bin ich bestelt/
Du magst sagen was dir gefelt/
Zu führen dich an sonders Orth/
Dein Buhlen hab ich wol gehört/
Daß kanstu mir nicht laugnen.

117.

Derhalben so für ich dich hin/
Vnd wil dir eine hübsche Zin/
M. Ihr seht mich nicht vorn rechten an/
Darumb last mich mein Strasse gahn/
L. Bey mir solstu bleiben.

118.

Ins Narren Heusel gehörest du/
Damit wol auff dem morgen früh/
Ein Jedermann dein Heiligkeit/
Darin du lebest Jederzeit/
Offentlich thut erkennen.

119.

M. Ach mein ich bitt erbarmbt euch mein/
Ich wil ewer Gefangener sein/
Ins Narrenheusel mag ich nicht/
Man wirfft mich mit Kott ins Gesicht/
L. Darumb ist angefangen.

120.

Darzu wil ich viel Buben ruffn/
Die dich mit Steinen redlich buffn/
Vnd trencken ein dein Büberey/
Damit der Alt gerochen sey/
Den du auch stets betrogen.

121.

M. Ach thut mich des Spots vberhebn/
    Wil euch drey hundert Cronen gebn/
L. Was sagt ich vor/ gehts nicht also?
M. Ich hab sie auch schon bey mir do/
L. Das kompt mir gleich zu rechte.

122.

M. Was sol ich thun/ ich denck im Sinn/
    Wie es herkompt/ so geht es hin/
L. Gib her das Gelt vnd denck daran/
    Daß dir must gebn der alte Mann/
M. Erst bin ich recht betrogen.

123.

Hat dich der Henckr hieher geführt/
Daß du mich heunt hast ausgespürt/
Nim hin das Gelt vnd laß mich gehn/
Die Metten die wird bald angehn/
Lauff hin an lichten Galgen.

124.

[*L.*] Also sols allen Buhlern gehn/
     Die andern nach den Weibern stehn/
     Das Gelt kömpt mir eben zu recht/
     Der Mönch den grossen schaden tregt/
     Ade es muß sein verzehrt. *Finis*

34

[DER ALTE UND DER JUNGE FREIER]

Ein andere [Cantus] mit 4. Person.[1]

1. *A.* Alter.
2. *L.* Jungfraw.
3. *S.* Stutzer.
4. *Z.* Schrämgen.

I.

A. Wann ich betracht meinr Liebsten Gestalt/
Ihr Leben vnd Wandel mannigfalt/
So gefellt sie mir allein/   [Ee vv]
Z. Von Hertzen ich sie mein/
S. Sie soll mein eigen seyn/
A. Vor andern Jungfräwlein.

[1] From *Liebeskampff.*

2.

Ihr Hertz gegn mir in Lieb ist entbrandt/
S. Ich glaub es wol ohn allen Tand/
A. Sie hatt mich hertzlich lieb/
Z. Du leugst du alter Dieb/
A. Vor Frewde ich hüpff gar/
   Gott sie vnd mich bewahr.

3.

Ich wolt daß sie jetzt were bey mir/
S. Ein warme Suppen gönt ich dir/
A. Mein Lust mit jhr zu büssn/
Z. Ein Esel solstu küssn.
A. Ich wolt diß wagen dran/
Z. Sie nimbt gern geschencke an.

4.

A. Wenn doch Schremgen bald käme zu mir/
   Ich wolt jhn hinschicken zu jhr/
   Aber sie eben recht/
Z. Herr hier steht ewer Knecht/
   Was soll ich euch gebietn/
   Wolt jhr euch widerumb vermietn.

5.

Auff die Bullschafft werd jhr wollen gahn/
Daß jhr euch so schön angethan/
A. Wer hat dirs angedeut/
Z. Auff der Gassen alle Leut/   [Ee vj]
   Die wissn von ewrn Possn/
   Daß jhr so grewlich seyd gschossn.

6.

Wo habt jhr ewren Sinn hingewand/
Ist es hier oder vber Land/
A. Kenstu Luciliam.
Z. Des Kauffmans Tochter da/
A. Die ists/   Z. Wunder sachen/
   Ich muß ewer Thorheit lachn.

7.

Ad spectatores.

Ihr Geselschaffter in Hahnreyen Geschlecht/
Ewren Orden wird er zieren recht.
Ich bitt nehmet jhn auff/
Er wird gern tragen drauff/
Hörner auff seinen Grind/
Wie pflegt des Hahnreyß Gsind.

8.

A. Meynstu daß es sey vbel gethan/
Z. Ihr seyd ein feiner alter Mann/
Fürwar ich riethe euch/
Ihr bliebt bey ewers gleich/
Jung bey Jung/ Alt bey Alt/
Das giebt die aller best Gestalt.

9.

Ein harte Nuß ein stumpffen Zahn/
Ein junges Weib ein alter Mann/
Schicken sich gar nicht woll/
Zusammen jeder soll/
Seins gleichen frewen fein/   [Ee vj*v*]
Dann wird rechte Liebe seyn.

10.

A. Ob ich gleich bin ein sehr alter Mann/
So kompt mirs doch zu zeiten an/
Z. Ihr werd das Husten meinn/
A. Ich will ein junge freyen/
Ich bin genung staffirt/
Wie ein freyers Man gebürt.

11.

Gehe du zu jhr vnd rede sie an/
Ich will dich brauchn zum Freyersmann/
Z. Soll ich ewr Kupler seyn/
A. Das hörestu.   *Z.* O nein/   *Adspectat.*
Ich hett dich selber gern/
Euch kan ich nicht gewehrn/   zum Alten

12.

Es sey denn daß jhr wollet zusagn/
Meint wegn ein breiten Hut zu tragn/
Vnd daß ich soll zuvorn/
Ihr verstehet mich wol/
Vnd dann so offt ich will/
A. Du begehrest gar zu viel.

13.

Doch will ich dir eins theils nach lahn/
Z. Ich nehm es alls zu Danck an/
Ihr solt mein Zeugen seyn/   *Adspectat.*
A. Nun geh zu jhr hinein/
Frag ob sie mir sey hold/
Z. Wo nicht euch doch ewer Gelt.

14.   [Ee vij]

Wann sie mein suchn kein Glaubn will gebn/
Was soll ich machn?   *A.* Mercke mich ebn/
Diß alles zum *præsent*,
Solt an jhr Halß vnd Händ
Hencken/ vnd jhr verehrn/
Sagn ich begehre sie in Ehrn.

15.

Z. Ich will nun stracks Fuß hin zu jhr lauffn/
Ein par Hörner soll sie jhm kauffn/   *Adspectat.*
Ich wills jhm setzen auff/
A. Was stehestu lange lauff/
Z. Soll ich mich kehren vmb/
Wann ich dann so wider komb.

16.

A. Gehe fort.   *Z.* Wie verlangt jhn nach eim Korb/
            Adspectatores.

A. Er wirds wol halten fein verborgen/
Daß es niemand erfahr/
Biß daß der Kauff ist war/
Ich dürfft bald hinnach schleichen/
So thut sie mich erweichen.

17.

Hiermit zu tausent malen jhr Mund/
Geküsset[1] sey zu dieser Stund/
Daß sie der Teuffel hett/
Vnd führt sie in mein Bett/
    Hier kompt Lucia vnd Schremgen.[2]
Z. Er muß sich fein helffen lahn.

18.   [Ee vij*v*]

L. Was bild sich in Sinn der alte Geck/
    Sein Nasen solt er steckn in Dreck/
Z. Er hat aber viel Gelt/
L. Solchs mir gar nicht gefellt/
    Ein junger *Caualier,*
      Kan viel besser Trappeliern.

Die ander Melodey

19.

A. Ey da kömpt sie eben her gegangn/
    Nach der m[e]in[3] Hertz trägt groß verlangn/
    Juch/Juch/ Hoscha/
    Mein Lieb ist da/
Z. Sehet dort das verliebte Hertz stahn.

---

[1] *Geüksset* in original.
[2] Line of text apparently printed as a stage direction.   [3] There is space for the *e.*

20.

A. Grüß euch Gott mein aller schönste Zier/
   Nach euch trage ich ein groß Begiehr/
   Ey mein Lieblein/
Z. Ey mein Schätzlein/
A. Keine als jhr mein eigen soll seyn.

21.

L. Danck euch Gott mein guter alter Herr/
   Schremgen bringt für wunderliche Mehr/
A. Glaubts mein Mäußlein/
Z. Glaubts mein Täublein/
A. Was er gesagt soll alles ja sein/

22.

A. Verzeiht mir ewern roten Mund zu küssen/
L Haltet in/   *A* Last mich doch geniessen/
   Mein tausend schön/
Z. Mein Frewd vnd Wohn/
A. Ich will euch alles vermachen lahn.

23.

Kan es sein so bitt ich euch von Hertzen/
Last vns nieder sitzen gehn vnd schertzen/
L. Wie wolt das stehn/
A. Last es geschehn/
Z. Ich will weggehn vnd gar nicht zu sehn.

24.

Hier schicken sie sich zum nieder
sitzen.

A. Setzt euch nieder mein künfftiges Bettschelm-
   lein/
   Ich will küssen ewer Zucker Mündlein/
L. Ho was hör ich/
A. Ach gewehr mich/
Z. Wenn ich es wehr so glaub ichs.

25.

A. Habt jhr mich auch lieb thut mir es sagen/
L. Je warumb nicht warumb thut jhr fragen/
A. Ach ach halt mich/

Hie fellt er.

Z. Alter fallt nicht/
L. Je wie leyd ist mir/   *Z.* Ich glaub es nicht.

26.

L. Je wie thut mich ewer Fall bewegen/
Z. Mich auch/   *A.* Ich kan mich kaum regen/
O schönste Zier/
Ihr köndt helffen mir/
L. Bin ich kein Artz/   *Z.* Nehmet warm Bier.

27.

A. Ein Artzney thut jhr im Munde tragen/
Wenn jhr sprecht/   *Z.* Wolt jhm zum Schosse
haben/
A. Denn wird ich gesund/
L. Mein Schoß alle Stund/
Will ich euch nenn auß Hertzen Grund.

28.

A. Nun drauff will ich euch dieses schencken
L. Mein Schoß seyd jhr/   *Z.* Seiner zugeden-
cken/
L. Mein Schoß allzeit/
A. Ade Trawrigkeit/
Diese Wort bringen Fröligkeit.

29.   Ff [j]

L. Behüt euch Gott mein Schoß/ ich muß heim-
gehen/
A. Ich bitt freundlich bleibt noch etwas stehen/
L. Ach mein Schoß nein/
Z. Nembt vns mit heim/
A. Heut will ich wider bey euch seyn.

Tertia Melodia.

30.

S. Nach euch mein Frewd vnd Wonne/
L.   O mein Krone/
S. Hat mich verlanget gar/
L. Ich glaubs für war/
S. Hier mit ewren roten Mund will ich schöns Lieb
   eins küssen/
L. Wann es gleich noch offter wer/ so soll michs
   doch nicht verdriessen.

[Beyde zugleich.

Hertzen, vnd schertzen frölich in Ehren/ Frölich :/:
:/: :/: frölich in Ehren/ soll zweyen Verliebten
niemand wehren.][1]

[1] The bracketed parts of stanzas 30 and 33 are printed with the music as in the
facsimiles. I have given the facsimile of the text here as well as of the music in order
to indicate more clearly the arrangement.

Ff ij

Herzen, vnd scherzen frouch in Ehren/Frölich :/:
:/: :/: fröllch in Ehren / soll zwinen Verliebten
niemand wehren.

31.

S. Ich muß euch eins erzehlen/
L.   Ich wills hören.
S. Was mir im Schlaff fiel ein/
L.   Was mags wol sein/

S. Mich traumet wie ein alter Mann/ Euch mir
    wol gantz entziehen/
L. Diß thut euch nicht nehmen an/ Es wird lang-
    sam geschehen.

Beyde zugleich.

Hertzen vnd schertzen/ &c.

32.

S. Vnd als er nun im Willen/
L.   Schweiget stille/
S. Mit euch zu gehn ins Bett/
L.   O spart die Redt/
S. Da thet man jhm einen Korb/ Meint wegen
    *praesenti*ren/
L. Für war das ist nicht halb recht/
S.   Drob thet ich jubiliren.
Hertzen vnd schertzen/ &c.

33.

[Ff ijv]

L. Ich will ewern Traum außdeuten/
S.   Ich kans leiden/
L. Theils ist er schon erfüllt/
S.   Was hör ich schöns Bild/
L. Kent jhr Tiltap Nimmerfro den alten Win-
    ckelfechter/
S. Gar wol.
L.   Der will mich bethörn durch Bey-
    stand seines knechtes.
[S. Wird es jhm dann gehen an/
L. Der Alt soll zu rück stahn/

Beyde zugleich.

In Ehelicher Liebe/ wollen wir beyde zu Bette
    gahn.]

S. Wird es jhm dann gehen an/

L. Der Ak soll zu rück stahn/
Beyde zugleich.

I.

In Ehelicher Liebe/ wollen wir beyde zu Bett
gahn.

34·

L. Er war zimlich geschossen/
S.   Wunder Possen/
L. Sein Bart wolt jmmer hertzen/
S. Kondt er so fein schertzen/
L. Darmit ich jhm solt sein holt/ thet er mir diß an-
      hencken/
S. Das ist viel/   Z. Ihr bleibt mein Schatz/ Euch
      thu ichs wider schencken/
L. Wolt jhr den habn zum Mann/
S. Nein er soll hinden nach gahn.

Beyde zugleich.

In Ehelicher Liebe/ wol.

35·

L. Er will mich heunt besuchen/
S.   Ich werd fluchen/
L. Eiffert hierüber nicht/
S.   Wann Schad mir geschicht/

L. Wird er weiter halten an/ So soll er ein Korb
kriegen/
S. Ich kan es geschehen lahn/
L.   Ich will jhn wol betriegen/
S. Last vns wider gehen heim/
L. In Ehrn wolln wir lustig seyn/

Beyde zugleich.

Wann kompt rechte Zeit/ Wollen wir beyde zu
Bette gahn.

[Ff 3v]

Quarta Melodia.

36.

A. Abschied will ich halten eben/
Vnd mich hin zu jhr begebn/
Ich werd sehr willkommen seyn/
Z. Wie im Juden Hauß die Schwein.

37.

A. Geh Schremgen vnd k[l]opffe an/
Schaff das bald werd auffgethan/
Z. Was mein Herr die hinder Pfort/
A. Pfui dich/ weistu sonst kein Ort.

38.

Z. Zürnet nicht Herr Senior/
    Ihr Hauß hat für war zwey Thor/
    Eins vorn für die junge Leut/
    Eins hindn da die Altn durchreitn.[1]

39.

A. Ey was sagts von hinder Thor/
    Gehe du hin vnd klopffe vorn/
Z. In Schimpff werd jhr gewiß gerathen/
    Denn ich rieche schon den Bratn.

40.

    Wie wenn sie nicht wolt auffthun/
A. Zweiffelstu du Galgenhuhn/
    Wird sie auff zumachn versagn/
    Denn hastu darüber zu klagn.

41

Z. Freylich thu ich zweiffeln sehr/
    Denn ich weiß daß sie vielmehr/
    Liebn thut ein jungen Knabn/
    Der bey Tag vnd Nacht kan trabn.

42.

    Warlich jhr seyd jhr zu alt/
    An allen Gliedern zu kalt/
    Noch wolt jhr ein junge freyn/
    Stattlich wird sie euch geheyn.

43.

A. Schweig nur still/ bekümmer dich nicht/
    Ich hab mir lassen zurichtn/
    Sterckmorseln/die solln sein gut/
    Zu erwecken frisch Geblüt.

44.

Z. Weh euch Altn wenns kompt dahin/
    Daß jhr euch ziehet in Sinn/
    Durch solch Mittel zu erlangn/
    Was der Natur ist entgangen.

Ff iiij

---

[1] *duechreitn* in the original.

45.

Wolt jhrs Korbs gefreyet seyn/
So gehet heute wider heim/
Vnd fangt ewer Sach klüger an
A. Gehe[1] klopfft biß wird auffgethan/

46.

Z. Nun es muß ein Anfang seyn/
Holla ho ist niemand heim?
Ist der Korb bald zugericht?
A. Schlag sterker an/ sie hörets nicht.

47.

Sie ist schamhafft vber die massn/
Daß sie mich nicht will einlassn/
Oeffnet mir doch ewer Hauß/
Z. Oder gebt den Korb herauß.

48.

A. Seht was ich euch schencken will/

Guckt durch die Thür.

Z. Es ist alles finster vnd still/
A. Ich will etwas bleiben stehn/
Vielleicht bekom ich sie zu sehn.

S. Macht die Thür auff/ da fellt der
Alte in Hauß.

Ff v

Quinta Melodia.

---

[1] *Gege* in the original.

49.

S. Das mag wol ein Bawer sein/
    Der da felt mit der Thür herein/
    Gib Antwort/ (stelt als wol er schlagen/
A.   Ach strafft nicht fort/
    Ich will sagn das begehren mein.

50.

S. Welcher Teuffel führt dich her/
Z. Narr sacht/ ich habs gethan mein Herr/
S. Zu was endt/   *A* eylt nicht so bhendt/
    Ihr seyd ja mein bester Förderer.

51.

S. Förderer hin vnd Förderer her/
    Sag fort eh ich schlag/ was ist dein bgehr/
A. Die groß Lieb/ Mich hieher trieb/
    Anzusprechn mein liebste Jungfraw.

52.   [Ff v*v*]

S. Was thustu von Jungfrawn sagn
    Hastu ein?   *A.* Freylich thut nicht fragn/
    In diesm Hauß/   *Z.* Dort kuckt sie rauß/
    Seht Herr/   *A.* Die mich zum Mann wil han.

53.

    Ach mein allerliebster Schatz/
    Kompt heraus ich wil euch gebn ein Schmatz/
S. Warumb nicht? Sag was dir gebricht/
Z. Ich wil mit dir nicht theiln das *Deograts*.

54.

S. Bistu dann mit jhr bekant/
A. Ja ja/ jhre Gunst hab ich zum Pfandt/
    Daß sie mein/ Schatz wil stets sein/
Z. Glaubts nicht es ist ein lauter Tant.   *Ad sp.*

55.

S. Wie wenn sie ein andern hett/
    Der mit jhr künfftig solt gehn zu Bett/
    Gfiel es dir.   *A.* Ey glaubet mir/
    Sie liebt mich allein/ Ich wolt drauff wettn.

56.

Was wilstu verlohren han/
Wann dirs feilt/   *A.* Alls was ich vmb vnd an/
Trag bey mir/ Mein edle Zier
Wird mich gewiß nicht verspieln lan.

57.

S. Alter wie gefelt euch die/   kömpt *L.*
Z. Daß wer ein stück Fleisch in seine Brüh/
A. Wol wol wol/ drumb ich auch sol/
Hingehn vnd freundtlich reden mit jhr.

58.   [Ff vj]

A. Schatz ich stell mich wieder ein/
Z. Ich auch/   *L.* Was sol ewr bhehrn sein/
A. Ewren Mundt/ wolt ich jtzund/
Küssen gern/ vnd mit euch schertzen fein.

Greifft nach den Brüsten.

59.

L. Alter last die Rößlein stahn/
Sie warten auff einen andern Mann/
Der sie wol/ abbrechen soll/
Wenn die rechte Zeit kompt heran.

60.

A. Wie thut jhr so eckel sein/
Seyd jhr doch mein liebs Schätzelein/
L. Wer sagts mehr/   *S.* Nun alter Herr/
Gehts wol ab/ *Z.* so hin/ *A.* Mengt euch nit drein.

61.

Hiermit wil ich euch vorehrn/
L. Behaltet jhrs/   *A.* Thut euch nicht wehrn/
L. Traun hiermit/ werd jhr mich nicht/
Das ich euch vor mein Schatz hielt/ bethörn.

62.

A. Habt jhr mirs doch zugesagt/
L. Was denn/   *Z.* Alls was jhm wolbehagt.
A. Daß jhr mein/ Schatz wollet sein/
L. Diß hab ich nicht gthan sondern mein Magd.

63.

A. Ihr nahmt ja Geschencke drauff/
Z. Ihm zu setzen ein par Hörner auff/   *Ad sp.*
L. Ist diß war/   *A.* Traun/ traun/ fürwar/   [Ff vjʋ]
L. Ich habs vergessn/   *A.* Besint euch drauff.

64

L Nun damit ich danckbar bin/
So ward hie/ ich wil bald gehen hin/
Vnd herbring/ was dient zum dingn/
Daß jhr seht wie hold ich euch bin.

65.

S. Alter du verspielet hast/
A. Was denn? *S.* Alles was du an dir tregst
A. Nein noch nicht/ *Z.* Ihm recht geschicht.   *Ad sp.*
S. Gib her/ *Z.* Wer wol klagen den Fantast.   *Ad sp.*

Lucretia/bringt einen
Korb.

66.

L. Weil jhr nicht vorstehen wolt/
Das mein Sinn nicht ist euch zu sein holt/
So nembt hir/ den Korb von mir/
Vnd enthalt euch meinr freyt wo jhr wolt.

67.

An mich dürfft jhr gar nicht denckn/
A. Besind euch bessr/   *Z* Behalt ewr Geschenck/
S. Sagt ichs nicht?   *A.* Thut vor mich bittn/
S. Schwerlich wirds gschehn/   *A.* Wie thut michs
(krenckn.

68.

Z. Hab ich euch gewarnet doch/
A. Es ist wahr/   *Z.* Auch diese Stunde noch/
Drumb behalt/ den Korb/   *S.* Alsbald/
Zieh dich auß auß ich was mehres versuch.

69.   [Ff vij]

A. Ach verschonet mich hiemit/
S. Zieh alls aus/ *A.* Ach schont/ *S.* Du hast verspielt/
Z. Das ist fein/ Soll alls mein sein/
So will ich wacker ausziehen mit.

Ziehen jhn auß.

70.

L. Last den alten Jecken stahn/
Kompt mein Lieb/ wir wolln nach Hause gahn/
Gebt jhm wiedr/all seine Kleidr/
A. Ach da bitt ich vmb/   *S.* Ich loß geschehn.

71.

Nim hin all deinen Vorrath/
Z. Herr wir wollens theilen/   *A.* Ey danck habt/
S. Geh trag heim/ den Korb allein/
L. Ade.   *S.* Ade.   *A.* Gott vergelt die That.

72.

Z. Ey wie schön werdet jhr prangn/
Wan jhr diesn Korb an Halß thut hangn/
A. Thu nicht spottn/ mich armen Troppn/
Z. Seyd jhr doch offt darnach gegangn.

73.

Geht nach Hauß eh jemands kompt/
A. Ich wils thun/   *Z.* Vnd diese Sach vernimbt/
A. Nimmermehr/ komb ich hieher/
Z. Ich rahts selber weils euch nichts frombt.

Alter gehet abe.

74.   [Ff vijᵥ]

Z. Merckts jhr alten Eselsköpff/
Last euch nicht gfalln die schönen Zöpff/
Sie werdn sonst/ mit gleicher Kunst/
Meisterlich bethörn/ Ewr grawen Köpff.

75.

Ich wil selbst meins gleichen Freyen/
Der Hoffnung es wird mich nicht gerewn/
Wenn ich dann/ euch werde lan/
Zur Hochzeit bitten so stelt euch ein.[1]

[1] Music headed "Satyri Tantz" follows.

35

[JAN STARTER,
DER BETROGENE FREIER][1]

Kluchtigh t'samen=Gesang
Van dry Personagien.

Knelis Ioosten, een half-backen Vrijer.
Lysje Flepkovs, syn Vryster, een deur-
trapt Meysje.
Griet Kaecks, een Waerdinne.

Stemme:

Pekelharings. Ofte, Pots hondert tausent Slapferment.

KNELIS   IAE wel het moet sint felten doen/dat ick niet aen
      de Meyd
Ken raecken/daer myn hart/myn sin/myn siel/
     myn lyf op leyd/
Ick hebse nu gevryd wel thien of twalef dagen/
En sy en wil geen ia noch seggen tot myn vragen.
    En is dat niet de plaegh? Ick vraeght iou allegaer/
Wy gingen gister avongd uyt-kuijeren met melkaer/
Ick vraeghden of sy wou my tot haer man verkiesen?
Neen/ sey sy/ Vaer: ick sou daer aen te veul verliesen.
    Dus meugh jy na een aere Meyd (verstaeje dat wel)
     gaen/
Want siet; ick seg iou eens voor al/ jy staet my gans
     niet aen/   10
Jy bent een kalen Duyvel/ iou goed is door de billen/
Dus al wou ick iou schoon/myn Moer en sou niet willen.
    Wel (seyden ick) myn soete kynd/ hoe spreeck jy doch
     dus fel?

---

[1] Printed from a copy of Starter's *Boertigheden* in the British Museum (bound at
the end of his *Friesche Lust-Hof* [1621]) with signatures A, etc., and no pagination. A
part (B 4*v*, C [1], the first half of C 1*v*, the second half of C 2, and C 2*v*) is printed in
double columns. In the small capitals of the name Lysje as a speaker, *J* is regularly
printed as a heavy *j*. The long lines of verse sung to the tune "Pots hondert tausent
Slapferment" are not broken in the original after line 6. Most of the stage directions
are in smaller type than the body of the piece.

Een duysend gulden/ of een ding/ sal my geworden wel/
Wanneer ick maer een reys aen 't Hylicken kan komen:
Dus/ o myn soete schaep! wilt daer niet eens van dromen.
Jae wel/ summi summarum/ sy gaffer al niet om/   B 3
En nochtans moet ick maken dat ick weer by haer kom/
En of ick dan al schoon by haer eens kom te raken/ 19
So seyd sy: wegh Jan Hen/ jy meught my niet vermaken.
  Jae wel/ wat dunckt iou kijeren/ en soumen niet wel
    sot
Haest worden alsmen so van 't Meysken word bespot?
En siet/ ick kan 't niet laten/ ick moetse nochtans vrijen/
Al sou ick schoon om haer thien duysend dooden lijen.
  Want s' is so kraftigh mooy/ so mooy/ dat 't niet en
    lyckt/
O kijeren saegh jy eens hoe dat haer backus pryckt!
En gaet sy over straet/ haer lieve leden trillen/
Och denck ick dan/maer moer/wat hebje een mooije elle-
    boogh!
  En dan begin ick my inwendigh te verblijen/
En denck/ hoe sullen wy noch eens te samen vlijen! 30
Lysjen uyt   Wat staen ick lang te praten: ick wil voort nae haer
    gaen/
Maer beyd/ wat hoor ick ginder? beget daer komt sy aen.
  Hoe siet sy dus bedroeft? wat of haer vreughd bed-
    wingt?
Ick wed sy ons terstond een treurigh Liedtjen singt/
Ick wil my hier soo lang wat voegen gaen in 't duyster/
En singt sy dan wat aerdigs/ick wed ick dat beluyster.

Stem: Courante Serbande, fol: s 9.

Lysjen   *G*Een liefde, geen trouwe, geen deughde nochte eer,
    Vindmen nu by de loose Iongmans meer,
  Sy seggen veel wonders, sy klagen van groote smart,
  Sy noemen ons Meesterssen van haer hart,
  Sy noemen ons al haer geneughd,   40
  Iae de Voedsterssen van haer Ieughd,
  Sy noemen ons haer leven: maer
  Och! och! sy dencken 't niet een hayr.

  2 Sy prysen, sy loven ons tot den Hemel toe,   [B 3v]
  Wy syn so schoon, sy weten 't selfs nau hoe.
  Ons oogen syn helder, ons voorhoofd hoogh en wit,
  Ons hayr is geel al is 't so swart als git,

Sy noemen ons al te gelyck
Gratieus, eerbaer, en deughden-ryck,   50
Iae duysend dingen meer daer by,
Maer ach! 't is al flickflooijery.

3 *Ick heb een Vrijer die Knelis Ioosten hiet:*
Hy vryd my vaeck so hittigh dat hy swiet,
Het is een Iongman, soo treftigh van gelaet
Dat hy de rest al veer te boven gaet:
Syn wesen staet soo stemmigh staegh,
Gelyck een Dorp-sot alle daegh,
Het vrijen weet hy op syn duym,
En hy sou niet lachen om een pruym.   60

4 *Hy sal hier wel komen dewyl ick noch wander hier,*
Want dat plach soo te wesen syn manier:
Hy schynd my te minnen, maer ick acht hy met my spot,
En ach! ick ben al heel op hem versot,
Syn bruyn oogen, syn mooije mond
Heeft myn ionck hart al heel doorwond.
O Knelis Ioosten! lieve Vaer!
Had ick iou in myn armen maer.

𝖲temme: [B 4]

Pots honderd tausent slapferment, &c.

KNELIS	Hoe nu myn soete Suyckermond? hoe benje dus bedruckt?
LYSJEN	Om dat myn saeck in 't minste my niet nae myn sin geluckt. 70
KNELIS	Tut/ tut/ nu laet iou schreijen/ kom/ kom myn soete dier/
	Laet ons eens gaen nae buyten/ wat doen wy langer hier?
	Daer sulle wy om soete melck/ en room met suycker dincken/
	En daer de klare koele wyn uyt groote roemers drincken.
	Ha/ ha/ wat dunckt u daer af? dat sal verseker wesen
	Sock in iou lieve borsten/ en dat sal iou genesen.
LYSJEN	Hoe soud' ick met u uytgaen/ ick ben doch niet gekleed?
	Ick heb geen kraegh/ geen schorteldoeck/ geen huyf/ noch niet een beet: 78
	En sagen dat de Meysjes/ sy souwen met my gecken/

	Maer wilje na myn wachten/ ick salse aen gaen trecken.
KNELIS	Och ia myn eygen hartjen/ al duerden 't noch so lang.
LYSJEN	Wel aen dan Knelis Joosten/ siet daer myn Vaer dat 's gang:
KNELIS	Neen/ neen myn lief/ also niet/ wy moesten so niet scheijen.
LYSJEN	Wat wilje van myn hebben? *KNELIS*. Een kus most iou geleijen.
LYSJEN	Een kus/ dat 's een kleyn principael/ al waerter acht of thien
KNELIS	Wel aen myn hart/ myn ingewant/ myn lyf het sal geschie'n/

Och! och! hoe smaeckt my dat! och ick moet noch een reys.

Lysjen in, *doch blyft* *after de deur* *staen luyste-* *ren.*	Nu mallert / nu adieu / adieu. *KNELIS*. Wat het sy blancker vleys! Hoe sal ick (hoop ick) daer noch eens op sitten pruyssen! Maer beyd/ hoe sal ick dat doch met een abelheytjen kuyssen?

                                                                        90
Ick moet my eens bedencken: ha! 'k heb my al bedacht/
Wy gane flus na buyten toe/ dan is sy in myn macht.
  Daer sal ick dan een kanne wyn met suycker doen bereijen/
En dan sal ick haer na de mond soo soet weten te vleijen
Dat sy my sal bescheyd doen op 't geen ick haer toe drinck/
Ick wed sy kryght haer korntje vol al eer sy daer op dinckt.

𝕾temme: [B 4*v*]

D'Engelsche fa la la, la la la, &c.

*W*Ant suyckerde wyn loopt soetjes in/
  Fa la la/ la la/ la la la leyne/
En dat is de Meysjes recht na haer sin/
Fa la la/ la la/ la la la leyne.   100

LYSJE singt achter de deur staende.

LYSJE.	Hy meend my te loeren met de wyn/

Fa la la/ etc.
Maer ick wed hy sal self eerst droncken syn/
Fa la la/ etc.

Die andere iaeghd/ staet selve niet stil/
Fa la la/etc.
Dat sal hy bemercken/ doch niet met syn wil/
Lysj: uyt   Fa la la/ etc.

Stemme:

Ick ben tot Amsterdam gewesen, hu, hu.

KNEL: *W*EL soete hartje/ benje daer weerom?
         Laet ons gaen kuijeren met melkaer/·
            kom/ kom/   110
Ick sal u brengen op een goeden oort
      Daer wy vrolick sinne.
LYSJE.   Wel aen myn Vaer/kom gane wy dan voort/
KNEL: Hier woond de Waerdinne.

Hou/ hou/ Griet Kaecks/ komt voort hier
      veur en doet op.   (klop:
GRIET.   Wel wie raest so voor myn deuren? *KN:* Ick
GRIET.   Neen: ick most iou naem eerst weten
      Eer ick u laet inne.
KNEL: Knelis Joosten ben ick geheeten.
         'k Wed wy komen binne.   120

GRIET.   Wel Knelis Joosten/ benje daer? welkom/
Wat hadje garen lieve vaer? *KN.* Goe Mom/
Suyckerde wyn en leckere bancketten/
      Fa la la/ etc.
Griet in: Wel ick sal 't hier datelyck gaen setten/
      Fa la la/ etc.

LYSJE.   Nu Knelis maeckt het niet te grof/stil/stil/
KNEL: Hoe? macher niet een soentjen of met wil?
O jy bent sucken soeten soeten sackje!
      Fa la la/etc.   130
LYSJE.   Knelis/ my dunkt iou schort maer een quackje/
      Fa la la/ etc.

GRIET.   Knelis Joosten/ als 't iou gelieft sit an/
Ick heb iou nou na lust gerieft: *KN:* Wel dan
Hartje Barents/ soete Butterdoosje/
      Fa la la/etc.
Sit wat by/ komt eet en drinckt een poosje /
      Fa la la/ etc.

Stem: *La Picarde, &c.*

KNEL: *M*Yn toeverlaet, myn vreughd,
    Myn troost en myn geneughd,   140
Die alleen my helpen meught:
    Toond u wat bly,
    Dit breng ick dy
Tot aenden grond,
Met een kusjen voor u mond.

LYSJEN. Om u te doen bescheyd   C [1]
Met alle billickheyd,
Daer toe ben ick wel bereyd:
    Keerd het maer om,
    't Sal wellekom   150
My wesen weer.
KNEL: Wel siet daer, wat wilje meer?

LYSJEN. So ghy myn wil en wens
Voldoen wilt, lieve mens!
Lapt het noch eens in iou pens.
KNEL: Twee tegen een,
    Dat 's tegen re'en:
Maer Liefste, siet
Ick sal het doen; wyl ghy 't gebied.

    Dat 's uyt, komt hier Waerdin   160
En schenckter weer wat in,
So 't geweest is, meer noch min:
    Drollige meyd,
    Doet my bescheyd,
En drinckt het uyt,
Lapt het schoontjes in iou huyt.

LYSJEN. O Vrijer! dit 's te veel,
En meerder als myn deel,
't Moet nochtans al door de keel.
    Dan sult ghy   170
    Twee glasen my
Bescheyd doen weer.
KNEL: Iae by Gort, al waer het meer.

LYS*JE*.   *Het valt my veel te bang.*
KNEL: *Ghy leppert al te lang,*
              Wat, sa lustigh, gaet u gang.
                    Drinckt het leegh
                    Met een veegh.
              Wat dat is wel.
LYS*JE*.   *Doet my twee bescheyd.* KN: *Ick sel.*   180

              O Lief! al waerter thien,
              Als icker dy me dien,
              So sal 't dadelyck geschie'n.
                    Dit gelter nae toe,
                    Siet wat ick doe.
LYS*JE*.   *Wel gaet dan voort,*
              Drinckt, so doet ghy als ghy hoort.

              KNELIS *droncken synde, singt uyt het Vleysboeck,*
                    Op de wyse:

                    Als ghy dan komt inden Hage, &c.

KNEL: M Eysje met iou blancke billen
              En iou blond gekruyfde hayr/
              Soud jy niet een reysje willen   190
              Met een landsknecht hier of daer?
              Tirittum fa sol la. Tirittum fa sol la.

LYS*JE*.   Wel/ hoe spreeckt ghy doch dus paerdigh
              Knelis Joosten? lieve man
              Soud' ick so strax wesen vaerdigh/
              Als ghy maer gaet singen van
              Tirittum fa sol la? etc.

              Nu/ nu/ dat mach ick niet velen/   [C 1*v*]
              Tierd iou wyslick/ houd u stil/
              Meent ghy so terstond te spelen   200
              Met my/ naer u wensch en wil
              Tirittum fa sol la/etc.

KNEL: Hebt ghy 't wel oyt ondervonden?
              't Is een soete nering/ kom
              Lieve Lam! de domme honden
              Byten vaeck malkand'ren om/
              Tirittum fa sol la/etc.

LYSJE.
> Wat/ die woorden syn te glandigh/
> Benje dol? of benje mal?
> Drinckt die glaesjens uyt knaphandigh/   210
> Wie weet of ick dan niet sal
> Tirittum fa sol la/ etc.

KNEL:
> Als ick iou daer me kan dienen/
> Kom/ ick lapse in myn gat.

LYSJE.
> So/ so/ nu heeft hy stroo-bienen/
> Hy is wel te degen sat/
> Tirittum fa sol la/etc.

Stemme: *Pots honderd tausend slapferment, &c.*

LYSJE.
> Kom/ lust iou wat te slapen/ so leght u hier wat neer?

KNEL:
> Ja/ een kleyn hallef uurken/ het hoofd doet my so seer/
> Myn suyckertje/myn waerde/ ey laet my met myn hoot
> Een weynigh rusten doch in u gebenedyde schoot.   221

LYSJE.
> Kom/ kom myn Knelis Joosten/myn eygen soete
> Vaer/
> Leght hier iou hoofd in mynen schoot/ en legt iou
> lichaem daer/
> En slaept dat het iou gaet aen 't hart/ so soetjes as jy
> meught/
> Wie weet hoe dat dy noch beslaet dyn voorgenomen
> vreughd?
> Waerdinneken so 't u gelieft/ haeld my een weynigh
> hier
> Een tinne schuttel/ en daer by een rauw ey drie of vier/
> Ick sal u moeyten wel seer eerelyck betalen.

GRIET.
> Wel blyft een weynigh hier/ ick sal 't iou strax gaen
> halen.

LYSJE.
> Wel nu leght daer en slaept ghy rechte droncken
> snuyt/   230
> Ick wed ick sal u nu wel lustigh strycken uyt/
> Tot spiegel van all' andere Jongmans/ die garen souwen
> Bedriegen dus met list die eerbare Juffrouwen.

GRIET.
> Daer syn de rauwe eijeren en 't schuttelken daer by.

LYSJE.
> Hier sal ick nu gaen maken van een excellente bry.
> Wilt ghy dan ondertusschen het tafel-goed wegh dragen.
> Nu/ nu/ my dunckt de Eijers syn bekans genoegh
> geslagen.

Sy giet hem d'Eijers inde boxen. C 2

Nu/ dat dan in syn boxen behendighlyck gesmeten/
So meent hy/ als hy wacker word/ dat hy hem heeft
    bescheten.
Siet so/ leght daer myn soete man/ so moeten sy al
    varen   240
Die Dochters met bedriegery tot oneer brochten garen. *in.*

Daer word gespeeld terwyl hy slaept, ten lesten wacker
synde, singt hy.

KNEL: Daer heb ick nu een soete slaep in myn Liefs schoot
    gehadt.
Ja wel/ wat droes is dit? hoe ben ick hier so nat?
Wat toovery is hier? ick kan 't by Gort niet weten.
Maer; nae dat ick hier voelen kan/ my dunckt ick ben
    bescheten.
De pocken hael de Meyd/ dat haer sint felten schen/
Nu merck ick eerst te recht dat ick verraden ben/
Want hoe ick 't meer en meer beruyck/ so merck ick
    lieve keijeren
Dat ick my niet bescheten heb/ maer dit syn rauwe
    eijeren   249
Die my die loose hoer heeft in de broeck gegoten/
Daer voor sal haer de droes het lyf aen stucken stoten.
Ick will de droes besweeren dat hy haer brengt by my/
Ick wed moer/ ick vergeld dy noch dyn loose boevery.

Hy maeckt een Circkel met eenige Characteren, ende singht
op de wyse vande Engelsche fa la la, doch die fa la la
syn hier met woorden uytgedruckt:

N̄V Duyvel, siet, ick besweere dy voort,
    By Starren, by Locht, by Hemel, by Aerd,
By Zee, by Hel, by Zuyd en by Noord,
Dat ghy u hier met de Meyd openbaerd.

De loose Hoer heeft my bedrogen,
Daerom besweer ick dy thienmael meer:
Kom brengtse hier datelyck voor myn oogen,   260
Ick sal het haer wel vergelden weer.

Sy hanght een clap-busse met nat bosse-kruyt aen syn aers,
en steeckt dat in brand, hy verbaest synde, singt al
loopende op de wyse:

Wy twee syn hier alleen, &c.

*W*At drommel voel ick hier?
    My dunckt ick ben vol vyer.
O myn aers is in brand!
O myn aers is in brand!
O myn aers is in brand!
O myn aers! o myn aers!
Gort schen de Duyvel en die loose flaers.   in.

LYSJEN alleen uyt, singt   [C 2v]
Op de wyse:
De Mey die ons de groente geeft, &c.

G Hy Jongmans die uyt vrijen gaet/
   De eere houd voor oogen/   270
Want quaed beloond syn Heer met quaed/
In 't end word ghy bedrogen.
   Die door des droncks arglistigheyd/
Of and're lapperijen/
Een Maeghd van 't padt der eeren leyd/
Sal nimmermeer bedijen.
   So ghy een Dochter eerlyck mind/
Laet haer dat eerlyck weten:
Maer soo ghy sulcx schandlyck begind/
In 't end word ghy bescheten.   280
   Want soo ghy doet/ sal u geschie'n/
Dat spreeckwoord kan niet liegen:
Dus wilt dit als een spiegel sien/
En wacht u voor 't bedriegen.

Stem: 't Schaep dat voer naer Alckmoer.

F Lus was ongse Truy so mooy/
   Sy setten heur mongtjen inde plooy/
En dat bekoorden Joosje.
Och! (docht hy) had ick iou nou int hooy
Ick soende iou wel een poosje.

2 Joosje teegh syn Moertjen aen/ 290
Myn pols (seyd hy) begind te slaen.
Och! och! het is te byster/
Ick moet terstond uyt vrijen gaen/
En soecken my een Vryster.

3 Dus Moertje geeft my doch een wyf/
Of neemt de broeck strax van myn lyf/
En brengtse by de snijer/
Want siet/ myn leden worden styf/
Dus moet de broeck wat wijer.

4 Maer dat ick een reys nae Truytjen teegh/ 300
Ich wed / ich kreegse met een veegh/
En maeckten haer myn Bruydtje/
Doet so (seyd sy) dat is te deegh/
Loopt al iou best nae Truytje.

5 Hy ging iou duwen aen de wynd/
Och Truytjen (seyden hy) lieve kynd
Wat benje een mooije Meysje!
Ick wedmen in al de Stad niet vynd
Suck e' eler blancker vleysje.

6 Jy bent waerte-eert/ e-groet/ 310
Want siet/ jy bent soo suyckerigh soet/
Ick sou iou wel schier licken.
Staet stil (seyd sy) jy malle bloed/
Of ick sla iou de kop an sticken.

7 Hoe nu myn soete butterdoos?
Hoe benje doch soo kraftigh boos
Dat jy myn vel wild touwen?
Jy weet wel dat ick iou verkoos
Veer boven and're Vrouwen.

8 En weyger jy my noch een soen? 320
Wie sou toch dat van iou vermoen?
Ick meende dat jy myn lief hadt.
Neen/ neen/ 'k heb met iou niet te doen/
Want ick iou voor een brief schat.

9 Dus pack iou hier terstond van daen/
Of 'k sal iou de kop aen flarden slaen
En dat met dese schoenen.
Neen/ neen/ so wil ick liever gaen/
Wegh met die harde soenen.

EYNDE.

36

[JAN VAN ARP,]

SINGHENDE

KLUCHT,

Van

DRONCKE GOOSEN.[1]

Op de Regel,

**Selden raecktmen inde ly/
Of men isser selver by.**

[DESIGN]

t'AMSTELREDAM,

Voor *Dirck Cornelisz Hout-haeck*, Boeckverkooper
op de Nieuwe zijds Kolck, Anno 1639.

PERSONAGIEN, [A 1*v*]

Droncke GOOSEN.
De WAERDT.
Een WAERDIN.

Tot den berisper.

Momist een anders werck niet laeckt,
Of siet dat ghy het beter maeckt.

Droncke Goosen wort al singhende op een A 2
Stoel ghedraghen, Op de Wijse: Van
Janneman, en Alemoer.

Waerdin. HOe swaer valt my dit draghen nu?
　　　　　Ick word' werentich moe.
Waerdt.　Swijgt Wijf/ of ik geef jou een duw'
　　　　　Of hout jou backus toe.

---

[1] Printed from a copy in the British Museum. The singspiel is also printed by
Bolte, *Singspiele*, pp. 106–10. The speakers' names and the stage directions in the
margin are in a much smaller type than that of the text.

Wat Duyvel ofje nou weer schort?
Ick loof niet je bint dol.

Waerdin.   Ey Man hoe leghje soo en knort?
Den Dronckaert die is vol.

Waerdt.   2 Nou set den armen Duyvel neer/
Want hy is veer ghenogh.   10

Waerdin.   Wat duncktje nou van desen Heer/
En lijckt hy niet een sogh?

Waerdt.   Ick sweer haest dattet hem berout
Dat hy oyt droncke was.

Waerdin.   Want kosten sal het hem sijn Gout/
Vyt sijn ghespeckte tas.

Waerdt.   3 Siet hoe den snorkart leyt en ronckt/
En suysebolt/ en knickt:
Ras strijckt hem 't swarsel om sijn monckt
Hoe staje soo en mickt: 20
Want soo hy weet wie 't heeft ghedaen
Gans bloedt ten was niet goedt.

Waerdin.   Soo swart ghelijck een Moeriaen
Maeckt
hem   Maeck ick dees droncken bloedt.
swart.

Waerdt.   4 O elementen wat ick sien
Hy lijckt de Duyvel wel/
De Kinders sou hy haest doen vlien/
Vervaert voor sulcken spel:
Het lijckt gheen mensch maer bulleback/
Of eenich hels ghespoock/   30
Ras haelt sijn handen uyt sijn sack   [A 2*v*]
En maecktse swart als roock.

Waerdin.   5 Kom krijgh' wy 't gheldt nu uyt zijn broeck
Eer dat hy wacker wordt.

Waerdt.   Hier ist niet wijf/ of isset soeck?
Tast diep maeckt gheen ghehordt.

Waerdin.   Het is ghevonden/ 'k heb het vast/
Ten sal mijn niet ongaen.

Waerdt.   Hey! nou ghesoopen en ghebrast
De Vasten die komt aen.   40

Waerdin.   6 Hy sluymert noch al even stijf/
Hy weet noch nerghens van.

Waerdt.   Kom stooten wy hem op het lijf.

Waerdin. Ey sacht mijn lieve Man:
Ick sal wel maecken dat het raeck
Soo stijf sal ick hem slaen/
Hy lustich dat is voor sijn kaeck/
Nu hier niet langh ghestaen.

Sy loopen binnen.

*Goosen ontwaeckt, en Singht op de
selfde Wijs.*

O Slaep/ o slaep/ o soete slaep
  Je bint mijn aenghenaem: 50
Gans felten hoe staen ick en gaep
En geeuw' dat ick mijn schaem.
O bloet/ wel wat mach dit doch zijn
Ick ken mijn selver niet?
Of ist de Nicker in mijn schijn
Ick loof het is gheschiet.

  2 Hoe sien mijn handen als een Mol
Wel is het spoockery?
Gans felten ben ick nou gheen Kol
Of is het Toovery: A 3

Hy haelt
een Spie-
ghel uyt
sijn sack.

Ick wilt besien hier in dit glas   61
Nou lustich als een Man:
Och dat ick nou een Duyvel was
Wat raedt soo gingh mijn an.

Hy kijckt
in de spie-
ghel.

  3 Och is het niet ghelijck ick segh
Och! och och ick ben soo angh
Ick loop schier van mijn selfs e wech
Mijn hart is mijn soo bangh/
Dat ick schier uyt mijn schoenen springh/
Ben ick gheen mensch gheweest/   70
Of ben ick eenich ander dingh?
O bloedt ick ben een Gheest.

  4 Een Geest/ een Geest/ dat kan niet zijn
Want ick ben vleys en bien:

Hy wijckt
ter zyen.

Siet daer mannen ick verdwijn/
Seght kanje mijn noch sien?
Soo is de Kaert valsch/ of ick bin
Wat anders als ick schijn/
Ben ick Duyvel? of Duyvellin
Siet daer mee ick 't bevijn.   80

5 Ick heb voor desen wel ghehoort
Dat Duyvels vlieghen veer:
Hy springt Ick wilt beproeven rechtevoort
op als of By 't Vaghevyer ick sweer
hy vliegt. Ben ick gheen Duyvel heb ick macht;
Ick roep de Nickers hier/
Ghelijckmen in voortijden placht
Beneen uyt 't Helsche vyer.

Hy maeckt een Circkel, ende eeni-
ghe Caracteren.

6 Voor eerst moet zijn een ronde kringh   [A 3*v*]
Op dat ick ben bewaert/   90
Voor eenich spoock of ander dingh
Waer voor 'k mocht zijn vervaert:
Vier Cruysjes elck aen eenen hoeck/
Een streep/ en hier een strick;
'k Legh schier een neghel in mijn broeck
Ick beef/ ick tril/ ick schrick.

7 Ick sweer by gort/ by bockemeel/
By carremelck en huy:
By grutten/ en oock by men keel
En voort by al den bruy/   100
Dat yemant stijghe uyt de hel
Van *Lucifers* ghebiedt/
Op dat hy daed'lick my vertel
Wat dat mijn is gheschiet.

Waerdin   8 O lijde waer verbergh ick mijn
vermomt   Ick hoor het naer ghemor;
uyt.   Wat heb ick nou gheen hart ick schijn
              Vervaert voor sulck gheknor:
              Verwis het lijckt de Duyvel wel
              Een backus als een grijns.   110
Waerdin.   Voort/ voort/ je moet me nae de hel/
Goosen.   Ick hoor hy is goedt mijns.

De Waerdt, en Waerdin in Duyvels kleeren,
Singhen op de Wijs: Van d'Engelsche
Fa, La, La.

Waerdt.   D E Duyvel mach de Duyvel halen/ hu/hu/hu.
Goosen.   Hy sou mijn kop an stucken malen/ hu/hu/
              Wat raedt soo ginck mijn dan weer an/fa/ la/la
              Maer wat soo binje voor een Man/fa/la/la.

Waerdt.	2 De liefste van *Plutoos* ghesellen/hu/hu.
Goosen.	Och 't is de Nicker uyt der Hellen/ hu/hu.
Waerdin.	En ick ben selfs de Duyvels Moer/ fa/la/la. [A 4]
Goosen.	Wat doeje hier jou ouwe Hoer? fa/la/la. 120
Waerdt.	3 Wy komen hier om jouwent wille/ hu/ hu.
Goosen.	Och hoe dat mijn leden trille/hu/hu/
	Ick bin soo bangh ick weet niet hoe/fa/la/
	Dat ick mijn eyeren schier uyt broe/fa/la/la.
Waerdt.	4 Voort je moet met ons gaen heenen/hu/hu/
	Of ick neemje by de beenen/hu/hu.
Goosen.	Och broer ick bidt toch laet mijn gaen/fa/la.
Waerdt.	Voort hier langh ghenoegh ghestaen/fa/la/ la.

De Waerdin hanght een klap-bos met nat
Bosse-kruyt aen sijn Broeck, en steect in brant: Hy
verbaest zijnde, singht al loopende, op de Wijse:

Wy twee zijn hier alleen.

Goosen.	WAt voel ick aen mijn naers
	Och 't is een barrende kaers/ 130
	O mijn Broeck is vol vier/
	O mijn Broeck is vol vier/
	O mijn/ wat pijn/
	Ghevoel ick aen mijn naers het doet soo sier.

Goose loopt binnen.

De Waerdt en Waerdin lacchen, en Sin-
ghen voort op de wijs van Ianneman.

Waerdt.	1 Ick lach schier dat ick barst van een
	En scheur schier van malkaer:
	Daer loopt den dronckert angstich heen
	En weet waer heen/ of waer:
	O bloedt/ och! och ick lach mijn doot/
	Mijn buyck splijt schier van een/ 140
	Wijf/ wijf/ wy hebben nou gheen noot
	De Beurs is ons ghemeen.
Waerdin.	2 Hey! vrolijck Man ten is gheen tijdt [A 4v]
	Om hier nou langh te staen:
	De Beurs vol geldt/ ten is gheen mijt
	De Vasten die komt aen.
Waerdt.	En suypen/ brassen/ dat het klinckt/
	Vastelavondts manier/
	Verteeren 't gheldt op dat 't niet stinckt
	Aen Wijn en lecker Bier. 150

De Tijdt Leert.

INDEX

INDEX

CATALOGUE OF DOVER BOOKS

Music

A GENERAL HISTORY OF MUSIC, Charles Burney. A detailed coverage of music from the Greeks up to 1789, with full information on all types of music: sacred and secular, vocal and instrumental, operatic and symphonic. Theory, notation, forms, instruments, innovators, composers, performers, typical and important works, and much more in an easy, entertaining style. Burney covered much of Europe and spoke with hundreds of authorities and composers so that this work is more than a compilation of records . . . it is a living work of careful and first-hand scholarship. Its account of thoroughbass (18th century) Italian music is probably still the best introduction on the subject. A recent NEW YORK TIMES review said, "Surprisingly few of Burney's statements have been invalidated by modern research . . . still of great value." Edited and corrected by Frank Mercer. 35 figures. Indices. 1915pp. 5⅜ x 8. 2 volumes. T36 The Set, Clothbound **$12.50**

A DICTIONARY OF HYMNOLOGY, John Julian. This exhaustive and scholarly work has become known as an invaluable source of hundreds of thousands of important and often difficult to obtain facts on the history and use of hymns in the western world. Everyone interested in hymns will be fascinated by the accounts of famous hymns and hymn writers and amazed by the amount of practical information he will find. More than 30,000 entries on individual hymns, giving authorship, date and circumstances of composition, publication, textual variations, translations, denominational and ritual usage, etc. Biographies of more than 9,000 hymn writers, and essays on important topics such as Christmas carols and children's hymns, and much other unusual and valuable information. A 200 page double-columned index of first lines — the largest in print. Total of 1786 pages in two reinforced clothbound volumes. 6¼ x 9¼. The set, T333 Clothbound **$15.00**

MUSIC IN MEDIEVAL BRITAIN, F. Ll. Harrison. The most thorough, up-to-date, and accurate treatment of the subject ever published, beautifully illustrated. Complete account of institutions and choirs; carols, masses, and motets; liturgy and plainsong; and polyphonic music from the Norman Conquest to the Reformation. Discusses the various schools of music and their reciprocal influences; the origin and development of new ritual forms; development and use of instruments; and new evidence on many problems of the period. Reproductions of scores, over 200 excerpts from medieval melodies. Rules of harmony and dissonance; influence of Continental styles; great composers (Dunstable, Cornysh, Fairfax, etc.); and much more. Register and index of more than 400 musicians. Index of titles. General Index. 225-item bibliography. 6 Appendices. xix + 491pp. 5⅝ x 8¾. T705 Clothbound **$10.00**

THE MUSIC OF SPAIN, Gilbert Chase. Only book in English to give concise, comprehensive account of Iberian music; new Chapter covers music since 1941. Victoria, Albéniz, Cabezón, Pedrell, Turina, hundreds of other composers; popular and folk music; the Gypsies; the guitar; dance, theatre, opera, with only extensive discussion in English of the Zarzuela; virtuosi such as Casals; much more. "Distinguished . . . readable," Saturday Review. 400-item bibliography. Index. 27 photos. 383pp. 5⅜ x 8. T549 Paperbound **$2.00**

ON STUDYING SINGING, Sergius Kagen. An intelligent method of voice-training, which leads you around pitfalls that waste your time, money, and effort. Exposes rigid, mechanical systems, baseless theories, deleterious exercises. "Logical, clear, convincing . . . dead right," Virgil Thomson, N.Y. Herald Tribune. "I recommend this volume highly," Maggie Teyte, Saturday Review. 119pp. 5⅜ x 8. T622 Paperbound **$1.25**

WILLIAM LAWES, M. Lefkowitz. This is the definitive work on Lawes, the versatile, prolific, and highly original "King's musician" of 17th century England. His life is reconstructed from original documents, and nearly every piece he ever wrote is examined and evaluated: his fantasias, pavans, violin "sonatas," lyra viol and bass viol suites, and music for harp and theorbo; and his songs, masques, and theater music to words by Herrick ("Gather Ye Rosebuds"), Jonson, Suckling, Shirley, and others. The author shows the innovations of dissonance, augmented triad, and other Italian influences Lawes helped introduce to England. List of Lawes' complete works and several complete scores by this major precursor of Purcell and the 18th century developments. Index. 5 Appendices. 52 musical excerpts, many never before in print. Bibliography. x + 320pp. 5⅜ x 8. T706 Clothbound **$10.00**

THE FUGUE IN BEETHOVEN'S PIANO MUSIC, J. V. Cockshoot. The first study of a neglected aspect of Beethoven's genius: his ability as a writer of fugues. Analyses of early studies and published works demonstrate his original and powerful contributions to composition. 34 works are examined, with 143 musical excerpts. For all pianists, teachers, students, and music-minded readers with a serious interest in Beethoven. Index. 93-item bibliography. Illustration of original score for "Fugue in C." xv + 212pp. 5⅝ x 8⅜. T704 Clothbound **$6.00**

CATALOGUE OF DOVER BOOKS

JOHANN SEBASTIAN BACH, Philipp Spitta. The complete and unabridged text of the definitive study of Bach. Written some 70 years ago, it is still unsurpassed for its coverage of nearly all aspects of Bach's life and work. There could hardly be a finer non-technical introduction to Bach's music than the detailed, lucid analyses which Spitta provides for hundreds of individual pieces. 26 solid pages are devoted to the B minor mass, for example, and 30 pages to the glorious St. Matthew Passion. This monumental set also includes a major analysis of the music of the 18th century: Buxtehude, Pachelbel, etc. "Unchallenged as the last word on one of the supreme geniuses of music," John Barkham, SATURDAY REVIEW SYNDICATE. Total of 1819pp. 2 volumes. Heavy cloth binding. 5⅜ x 8. T252 The set, Clothbound **$12.50**

THE LIFE OF MOZART, O. Jahn. Probably the largest amount of material on Mozart's life and works ever gathered together in one book! Its 1350 authoritative and readable pages cover every event in his life, and contain a full critique of almost every piece he ever wrote, including sketches and intimate works. There is a full historical-cultural background, and vast research into musical and literary history, sources of librettos, prior treatments of Don Juan legend, etc. This is the complete and unaltered text of the definitive Townsend translation, with foreword by Grove. 5 engraved portraits from Salzburg archives. 4 facsimiles in Mozart's hand. 226 musical examples. 4 Appendixes, including complete list of Mozart's compositions, with Köchel numbers (fragmentary works included). Total of xxviii + 1352pp. Three volume set. 5⅜ x 8.
T85 Vol. I Clothbound **$5.00**
T86 Vol. II Clothbound **$5.00**
The set **$10.00**

BEETHOVEN'S QUARTETS, J. de Marliave. The most complete and authoritative study ever written, enjoyable for scholar and layman alike. The 16 quartets and Grand Fugue are all analyzed bar by bar and theme by theme, not over-technically, but concentrating on mood and effects. Complete background material for each composition: influences, first reviews, etc. Preface by Gabriel Fauré. Introduction and notes by J. Escarra. Translated by Hilda Andrews. 321 musical examples. xxiii + 379pp. 5⅜ x 8. T694 Paperbound **$1.85**

STRUCTURAL HEARING: TONAL COHERENCE IN MUSIC, Felix Salzer. Written by a pupil of the late Heinrich Schenker, this is not only the most thorough exposition in English of the Schenker method but also extends the Schenker approach to include modern music, the middle ages, and renaissance music. It explores the phenomenon of tonal organization by means of a detailed analysis and discussion of more than 500 musical pieces. It casts new light for the reader acquainted with harmony upon the understanding of musical compositions, problems of musical coherence, and connection between theory and composition. "Has been the foundation on which all teaching in music theory has been based at this college," Leopold Mannes, President of The Mannes College of Music. 2 volumes. Total of 658pp. 6½ x 9¼. The set, T418 Clothbound **$8.00**

ANTONIO STRADIVARI: HIS LIFE AND WORK (1644-1737), W. Henry Hill, Arthur F. Hill, and Alfred E. Hill. Still the only book that really delves into life and art of the incomparable Italian craftsman, maker of the finest musical instruments in the world today. The authors, expert violin-makers themselves, discuss Stradivari's ancestry, his construction and finishing techniques, distinguished characteristics of many of his instruments and their locations. Included, too, is story of introduction of his instruments into France, England, first revelation of their supreme merit, and information on his labels, number of instruments made, prices, mystery of ingredients of his varnish, tone of pre-1684 Stradivari violin and changes between 1684 and 1690. An extremely interesting, informative account for all music lovers, from craftsman to concert-goer. Republication of original (1902) edition. New introduction by Sydney Beck, Head of Rare Book and Manuscript Collections, Music Division, New York Public Library. Analytical index by Rembert Wurlitzer. Appendixes. 68 illustrations. 30 full-page plates. 4 in color. xxvi + 315pp. 5⅜ x 8½. T425 Paperbound **$2.25**

THREE CLASSICS IN THE AESTHETIC OF MUSIC, Claude Debussy, Ferrucio Busoni, and Charles Ives. Three very different points of view by three top-ranking modern composers. "M. Croche, the Dilettante-Hater" consists of twenty-five brief articles written by Debussy between the years 1901 and 1905, a sparkling collection of personal commentary on a wide range of topics. Busoni's "Toward a New Aesthetic of Music" considers the nature of absolute music in an attempt to suggest answers to the question, What are the aims of music?, and discusses modern systems of tonality and harmony, the concept of unity of keys, etc. Ives's "Essays Before a Sonata," a literary complement to the movements of the author's "Concord, 1845" piano sonata, contains his most mature analysis of his art. Stimulating reading for musicians, music lovers, and philosophers of the arts. iv + 188pp. 5⅜ x 8½.
T320 Paperbound **$1.45**

Dover Classical Records

Now available directly to the public exclusively from Dover: top-quality recordings of fine classical music for only $2 per record! Almost all were released by major record companies to sell for $5 and $6. These recordings were issued under our imprint only after they had passed a severe critical test. We insisted upon:

> First-rate music that is enjoyable, musically important and culturally significant.

> First-rate performances, where the artists have carried out the composer's intentions, in which the music is alive, vigorous, played with understanding and sensitivity.

> First-rate sound—clear, sonorous, fully balanced, crackle-free, whir-free.

Have in your home music by major composers, performed by such gifted musicians as Elsner, Gitlis, Wührer, Beveridge Webster, the Barchet Quartet, Gimpel, etc. Enthusiastically received when first released, many of these performances are definitive. The records are not seconds or remainders, but brand new pressings made on pure vinyl from carefully chosen master tapes. "All purpose" 12" monaural 33⅓ rpm records, they play equally well on hi-fi and stereo equipment. Fine music for discriminating music lovers, superlatively played, flawlessly recorded: there is no better way to build your library of recorded classical music at remarkable savings. There are no strings; this is not a come-on, not a club, forcing you to buy records you may not want in order to get a few at a lower price. Buy whatever records you want in any quantity, and never pay more than $2 each. Your obligation ends with your first purchase. And that's when ours begins. Dover's money-back guarantee allows you to return any record for any reason, even if you don't like the music, for a full, immediate refund—no questions asked.

MOZART: STRING QUARTETS: IN A (K. 464) AND C ("DISSONANT") (K. 465), Barchet Quartet. The final two of the famous Haydn Quartets, high-points in the history of music. The A Major was accepted with delight by Mozart's contemporaries, but the C Major, with its dissonant opening, aroused strong protest. Today, of course, the remarkable resolutions of the dissonances are recognized as major musical achievements. "Beautiful warm playing," MUSICAL AMERICA. "Two of Mozart's loveliest quartets in a distinguished performance," REV. OF RECORDED MUSIC. (Playing time 58 mins.)   HCR 5200 **$2.00**

MOZART: STRING QUARTETS: IN G (K. 80), D (K. 156), and C (K. 157), Barchet Quartet. The early chamber music of Mozart receives unfortunately little attention. First-rate music of the Italian school, it contains all the lightness and charm that belongs only to the youthful Mozart. This is currently the only separate source for the composer's work of this period. "Excellent," HIGH FIDELITY. "Filled with sunshine and youthful joy; played with verve, recorded sound live and brilliant," CHRISTIAN SCI. MONITOR. (playing time 51 mins.)   HCR 5201 **$2.00**

MOZART: SERENADES: #9 IN D ("POSTHORN") (K. 320), #6 IN D ("SERENATA NOTTURNA") (K. 239), Pro Musica Orch. of Stuttgart, under Edouard van Remoortel. For Mozart, the serenade was a highly effective form, since he could bring to it the immediacy and intimacy of chamber music as well as the free fantasy of larger group music. Both these serenades are distinguished by a playful, mischievous quality, a spirit perfectly captured in this fine performance. "A triumph, polished playing from the orchestra," HI FI MUSIC AT HOME. "Sound is rich and resonant, fidelity is wonderful," REV. OF RECORDED MUSIC. (Playing time 51 mins.)   HCR 5202 **$2.00**

MOZART: DIVERTIMENTO FOR VIOLIN, VIOLA AND CELLO IN E FLAT (K. 563); ADAGIO AND FUGUE IN F MINOR (K. 404a), Kehr Trio. The divertimento is one of Mozart's most beloved pieces, called by Einstein "the finest and most perfect trio ever heard." It is difficult to imagine a music lover who will not be delighted by it. This is the only recording of the lesser known Adagio and Fugue, written in 1782 and influenced by Bach's Well-Tempered Clavichord. "Extremely beautiful recording, strongly recommended," THE OBSERVER. "Superior to rival editions," HIGH FIDELITY. (Playing time 51 mins.)   HCR 5203 **$2.00**

SCHUMANN: KREISLERIANA (OPUS 16) AND FANTASIA IN C (OPUS 17), Vlado Perlemuter, Piano. The vigorous Romantic imagination and the remarkable emotional qualities of Schumann's piano music raise it to a special eminence in 19th-century creativity. Both these pieces are rooted to the composer's tortuous romance with his future wife, Clara, and both receive brilliant treatment at the hands of Vlado Perlemuter, Paris Conservatory, proclaimed by Alfred Cortot "not only a great virtuoso but also a great musician." "The best Kreisleriana to date," BILLBOARD. (Playing time 55 mins.)   HCR 5204 **$2.00**

CATALOGUE OF DOVER BOOKS

SCHUMANN: TRIOS #1 IN D MINOR (OPUS 63) AND #3 IN G MINOR (OPUS 110), Trio di Bolzano. The fiery, romantic, melodic Trio #1 and the dramatic, seldom heard Trio #3 are both movingly played by a fine chamber ensemble. No one personified Romanticism to the general public of the 1840's more than did Robert Schumann, and among his most romantic works are these trios for cello, violin and piano. "Ensemble and overall interpretation leave little to be desired," HIGH FIDELITY. "An especially understanding performance," REV. OF RECORDED MUSIC. (Playing time 54 mins.)   HCR 5205 **$2.00**

SCHUBERT: QUINTET IN A ("TROUT") (OPUS 114), AND NOCTURNE IN E FLAT (OPUS 148), Friedrich Wührer, Piano and Barchet Quartet. If there is a single piece of chamber music that is a universal favorite, it is probably Schubert's "Trout" Quintet. Delightful melody, harmonic resources, musical exuberance are its characteristics. The Nocturne (played by Wührer, Barchet, and Reimann) is an exquisite piece with a deceptively simple theme and harmony. "The best Trout on the market—Wührer is a fine Viennese-style Schubertian, and his spirit infects the Barchets," ATLANTIC MONTHLY. "Exquisitely recorded," ETUDE. (Playing time 44 mins.)   HCR 5206 **$2.00**

SCHUBERT: PIANO SONATAS IN C MINOR AND B (OPUS 147), Friedrich Wührer. Schubert's sonatas retain the structure of the classical form, but delight listeners with romantic freedom and a special melodic richness. The C Minor, one of the Three Grand Sonatas, is a product of the composer's maturity. The B Major was not published until 15 years after his death. "Remarkable interpretation, reproduction of the first rank," DISQUES. "A superb pianist for music like this, musicianship, sweep, power, and an ability to integrate Schubert's measures such as few pianists have had since Schnabel," Harold Schonberg. (Playing time 49 mins.)   HCR 5207 **$2.00**

STRAVINSKY: VIOLIN CONCERTO IN D, Ivry Gitlis, Cologne Orchestra; DUO CONCERTANTE, Ivry Gitlis, Violin, Charlotte Zelka, Piano, Cologne Orchestra; JEU DE CARTES, Bamberg Symphony, under Hollreiser. Igor Stravinsky is probably the most important composer of this century, and these three works are among the most significant of his neoclassical period of the 30's. The Violin Concerto is one of the few modern classics. Jeu de Cartes, a ballet score, bubbles with gaiety, color and melodiousness. "Imaginatively played and beautifully recorded," E. T. Canby, HARPERS MAGAZINE. "Gitlis is excellent, Hollreiser beautifully worked out," HIGH FIDELITY. (Playing time 55 mins.)   HCR 5208 **$2.00**

GEMINIANI: SIX CONCERTI GROSSI, OPUS 3, Helma Elsner, Harpsichord, Barchet Quartet, Pro Musica Orch. of Stuttgart, under Reinhardt. Francesco Geminiani (1687-1762) has been rediscovered in the same musical exploration that revealed Scarlatti, Vivaldi, and Corelli. In form he is more sophisticated than the earlier Italians, but his music delights modern listeners with its combination of contrapuntal techniques and the full harmonies and rich melodies charcteristic of Italian music. This is the only recording of the six 1733 concerti: D Major, B Flat Minor, E Minor, G Minor, E Minor (bis), and D Minor. "I warmly recommend it, spacious, magnificent, I enjoyed every bar," C. Cudworth, RECORD NEWS. "Works of real charm, recorded with understanding and style," ETUDE. (Playing time 52 mins.)
                                                                HCR 5209 **$2.00**

MODERN PIANO SONATAS: BARTOK: SONATA FOR PIANO; BLOCH: SONATA FOR PIANO (1935); PROKOFIEV, PIANO SONATA #7 IN B FLAT ("STALINGRAD"); STRAVINSKY: PIANO SONATA (1924), István Nádas, Piano. Shows some of the major forces and directions in modern piano music: Stravinsky's crisp austerity; Bartok's fusion of Hungarian folk motives; incisive diverse rhythms, and driving power; Bloch's distinctive emotional vigor; Prokofiev's brilliance and melodic beauty couched in pre-Romantic forms. "A most interesting documentation of the contemporary piano sonata. Nadas is a very good pianist." HIGH FIDELITY. (Playing time 59 mins.)   HCR 5215 **$2.00**

VIVALDI: CONCERTI FOR FLUTE, VIOLIN, BASSOON, AND HARPSICHORD: #8 IN G MINOR, #21 IN F, #27 IN D, #7 IN D; SONATA #1 IN A MINOR, Gastone Tassinari, Renato Giangrandi, Giorgio Semprini, Arlette Eggmann. More than any other Baroque composer, Vivaldi moved the concerto grosso closer to the solo concert we deem standard today. In these concerti he wrote virtuosi music for the solo instruments, allowing each to introduce new material or expand on musical ideas, creating tone colors unusual even for Vivaldi. As a result, this record displays a new area of his genius, offering some of his most brilliant music. Performed by a top-rank European group. (Playing time 45 mins.)   HCR 5216 **$2.00**

LÜBECK: CANTATAS: HILF DEINEM VOLK; GOTT, WIE DEIN NAME, Stuttgart Choral Society, Swabian Symphony Orch.; PRELUDES AND FUGUES IN C MINOR AND IN E, Eva Hölderlin, Organ. Vincent Lübeck (1654-1740), contemporary of Bach and Buxtehude, was one of the great figures of the 18th-century North German school. These examples of Lübeck's few surviving works indicate his power and brilliance. Voice and instrument lines in the cantatas are strongly reminiscent of the organ: the preludes and fugues show the influence of Bach and Buxtehude. This is the only recording of the superb cantatas. Text and translation included. "Outstanding record," E. T. Canby, SAT. REVIEW. "Hölderlin's playing is exceptional," AM. RECORD REVIEW. "Will make [Lübeck] many new friends," Philip Miller. (Playing time 37 mins.)   HCR 5217 **$2.00**

DONIZETTI, BETLY (LA CAPANNA SVIZZERA), Soloists of Compagnia del Teatro dell'Opera Comica di Roma, Societa del Quartetto, Rome, Chorus and Orch. Betly, a delightful one-act opera written in 1836, is similar in style and story to one of Donizetti's better-known operas, L'Elisir. Betly is lighthearted and farcical, with bright melodies and a freshness characteristic of the best of Donizetti. Libretto (English and Italian) included. "The chief honors go to Angela Tuccari who sings the title role, and the record is worth having for her alone," M. Rayment, GRAMOPHONE REC. REVIEW. "The interpretation . . . is excellent . . . This is a charming record which we recommend to lovers of little-known works," DISQUES.
HCR 5218 **$2.00**

ROSSINI: L'OCCASIONE FA IL LADRO (IL CAMBIO DELLA VALIGIA), Soloists of Compagnia del Teatro dell'Opera Comica di Roma, Societa del Quartetto, Rome, Chorus and Orch. A charming one-act opera buffa, this is one of the first works of Rossini's maturity, and it is filled with the wit, gaiety and sparkle that make his comic operas second only to Mozart's. Like other Rossini works, L'Occasione makes use of the theme of impersonation and attendant amusing confusions. This is the only recording of this important buffa. Full libretto (English and Italian) included. "A major rebirth, a stylish performance . . . the Roman recording engineers have outdone themselves," H. Weinstock, SAT. REVIEW. (Playing time 53 mins.)
HCR 5219 **$2.00**

DOWLAND: "FIRST BOOKE OF AYRES," Pro Musica Antiqua of Brussels, Safford Cape, Director. This is the first recording to include all 22 of the songs of this great collection, written by John Dowland, one of the most important writers of songs of 16th and 17th century England. The participation of the Brussels Pro Musica under Safford Cape insures scholarly accuracy and musical artistry. "Powerfully expressive and very beautiful," B. Haggin. "The musicianly singers . . . never fall below an impressive standard," Philip Miller. Text included. (Playing time 51 mins.)
HCR 5220 **$2.00**

FRENCH CHANSONS AND DANCES OF THE 16TH CENTURY, Pro Musica Antiqua of Brussels, Safford Cape, Director. A remarkable selection of 26 three- or four-part chansons and delightful dances from the French Golden Age—by such composers as Orlando Lasso, Crecquillon, Claude Gervaise, etc. Text and translation included. "Delightful, well-varied with respect to mood and to vocal and instrumental color," HIGH FIDELITY. "Performed with . . . discrimination and musical taste, full of melodic distinction and harmonic resource," Irving Kolodin. (Playing time 39 mins.)
HCR 5221 **$2.00**

GALUPPI: CONCERTI A QUATRO: #1 IN G MINOR, #2 IN G, #3 IN D, #4 IN C MINOR, #5 IN E FLAT, AND #6 IN B FLAT, Biffoli Quartet. During Baldassare Galuppi's lifetime, his instrumental music was widely renowned, and his contemporaries Mozart and Haydn thought highly of his work. These 6 concerti reflect his great ability; and they are among the most interesting compositions of the period. They are remarkable for their unusual combinations of timbres and for emotional elements that were only then beginning to be introduced into music. Performed by the well-known Biffoli Quartet, this is the only record devoted exclusively to Galuppi. (Playing time 47 mins.)
HCR 5222 **$2.00**

HAYDN: DIVERTIMENTI FOR WIND BAND, IN C; IN F; DIVERTIMENTO A NOVE STROMENTI IN C FOR STRINGS AND WIND INSTRUMENTS, reconstructed by H. C. Robbins Landon, performed by members of Vienna State Opera Orch.; MOZART DIVERTIMENTI IN C, III (K. 187) AND IV (K. 188), Salzburg Wind Ensemble. Robbins Landon discovered Haydn manuscripts in a Benedictine monastery in Lower Austria, edited them and restored their original instrumentation The result is this magnificent record. Two little-known divertimenti by Mozart—of great charm and appeal—are also included. None of this music is available elsewhere (Playing time 58 mins.)
HCR 5223 **$2.00**

PURCELL: TRIO SONATAS FROM "SONATAS OF FOUR PARTS" (1697): #9 IN F ("GOLDEN"), #7 IN C, #1 IN B MINOR, #10 IN D, #4 IN D MINOR, #2 IN E FLAT, AND #8 IN G MINOR, Giorgio Ciompi, and Werner Torkanowsky, Violins, Geo. Koutzen, Cello, and Herman Chessid, Harpsichord. These posthumously-published sonatas show Purcell at his most advanced and mature. They are certainly among the finest musical examples of pre-modern chamber music. Those not familiar with his instrumental music are well-advised to hear these outstanding pieces. "Performance sounds excellent," Harold Schonberg. "Some of the most noble and touching music known to anyone," AMERICAN RECORD GUIDE. (Playing time 58 mins.)
HCR 5224 **$2.00**

BARTOK: VIOLIN CONCERTO; SONATA FOR UNACCOMPANIED VIOLIN, Ivry Gitlis, Pro Musica of Vienna, under Hornstein. Both these works are outstanding examples of Bartok's final period, and they show his powers at their fullest. The Violin Concerto is, in the opinion of many authorities, Bartok's finest work, and the Sonata, his last work, is "a masterpiece" (F. Sackville West). "Wonderful, finest performance of both Bartok works I have ever heard," GRAMOPHONE. "Gitlis makes such potent and musical sense out of these works that I suspect many general music lovers (not otherwise in sympathy with modern music) will discover to their amazement that they like it. Exceptionally good sound," AUDITOR. (Playing time 54 mins.)
HCR 5211 **$2.00**

Literature, History of Literature

ARISTOTLE'S THEORY OF POETRY AND THE FINE ARTS, edited by S. H. Butcher. The celebrated Butcher translation of this great classic faced, page by page, with the complete Greek text. A 300 page introduction discussing Aristotle's ideas and their influence in the history of thought and literature, and covering art and nature, imitation as an aesthetic form, poetic truth, art and morality, tragedy, comedy, and similar topics. Modern Aristotelian criticism discussed by John Gassner. lxxvi + 421pp. 5⅜ x 8.
T42 Paperbound **$2.00**

INTRODUCTIONS TO ENGLISH LITERATURE, edited by B. Dobrée. Goes far beyond ordinary histories, ranging from the 7th century up to 1914 (to the 1940's in some cases.) The first half of each volume is a specific detailed study of historical and economic background of the period and a general survey of poetry and prose, including trends of thought, influences, etc. The second and larger half is devoted to a detailed study of more than 5000 poets, novelists, dramatists; also economists, historians, biographers, religious writers, philosophers, travellers, and scientists of literary stature, with dates, lists of major works and their dates, keypoint critical bibliography, and evaluating comments. The most compendious bibliographic and literary aid within its price range.

Vol. I. THE BEGINNINGS OF ENGLISH LITERATURE TO SKELTON, (1509), W. L. Renwick, H. Orton. 450pp. 5⅛ x 7⅞.
T75 Clothbound **$4.50**

Vol. II. THE ENGLISH RENAISSANCE, 1510-1688, V. de Sola Pinto. 381pp. 5⅛ x 7⅞.
T76 Clothbound **$4.50**

Vol. III. AUGUSTANS AND ROMANTICS, 1689-1830, H. Dyson, J. Butt. 320pp. 5⅛ x 7⅞.
T77 Clothbound **$4.50**

Vol. IV. THE VICTORIANS AND AFTER, 1830-1940's, E. Batho, B. Dobrée. 360pp. 5⅛ x 7⅞.
T78 Clothbound **$4.50**

EPIC AND ROMANCE, W. P. Ker. Written by one of the foremost authorities on medieval literature, this is the standard survey of medieval epic and romance. It covers Teutonic epics, Icelandic sagas, Beowulf, French chansons de geste, the Roman de Troie, and many other important works of literature. It is an excellent account for a body of literature whose beauty and value has only recently come to be recognized. Index. xxiv + 398pp. 5⅜ x 8.
T355 Paperbound **$2.00**

THE POPULAR BALLAD, F. B. Gummere. Most useful factual introduction; fund of descriptive material; quotes, cites over 260 ballads. Examines, from folkloristic view, structure; choral, ritual elements; meter, diction, fusion; effects of tradition, editors; almost every other aspect of border, riddle, kinship, sea, ribald, supernatural, etc., ballads. Bibliography. 2 indexes. 374pp. 5⅜ x 8.
T548 Paperbound **$1.85**

MASTERS OF THE DRAMA, John Gassner. The most comprehensive history of the drama in print, covering drama in every important tradition from the Greeks to the Near East, China, Japan, Medieval Europe, England, Russia, Italy, Spain, Germany, and dozens of other drama producing nations. This unsurpassed reading and reference work encompasses more than 800 dramatists and over 2000 plays, with biographical material, plot summaries, theatre history, etc. "Has no competitors in its field," THEATRE ARTS. "Best of its kind in English," NEW REPUBLIC. Exhaustive 35 page bibliography. 77 photographs and drawings. Deluxe edition with reinforced cloth binding, headbands, stained top. xxii + 890pp. 5⅜ x 8.
T100 Clothbound **$6.95**

THE DEVELOPMENT OF DRAMATIC ART, D. C. Stuart. The basic work on the growth of Western drama from primitive beginnings to Eugene O'Neill, covering over 2500 years. Not a mere listing or survey, but a thorough analysis of changes, origins of style, and influences in each period; dramatic conventions, social pressures, choice of material, plot devices, stock situations, etc.; secular and religious works of all nations and epochs. "Generous and thoroughly documented researches," Outlook. "Solid studies of influences and playwrights and periods," London Times. Index. Bibliography. xi + 679pp. 5⅜ x 8.
T693 Paperbound **$2.75**

A SOURCE BOOK IN THEATRICAL HISTORY (SOURCES OF THEATRICAL HISTORY), A. M. Nagler. Over 2000 years of actors, directors, designers, critics, and spectators speak for themselves in this potpourri of writings selected from the great and formative periods of western drama. On-the-spot descriptions of masks, costumes, makeup, rehearsals, special effects, acting methods, backstage squabbles, theatres, etc. Contemporary glimpses of Molière rehearsing his company, an exhortation to a Roman audience to buy refreshments and keep quiet, Goethe's rules for actors, Belasco telling of $6500 he spent building a river, Restoration actors being told to avoid "lewd, obscene, or indecent postures," and much more. Each selection has an introduction by Prof. Nagler. This extraordinary, lively collection is ideal as a source of otherwise difficult to obtain material, as well as a fine book for browsing. Over 80 illustrations. 10 diagrams. xxiii + 611pp. 5⅜ x 8.
T515 Paperbound **$3.00**

WORLD DRAMA, B. H. Clark. The dramatic creativity of a score of ages and eras — all in two handy compact volumes. Over ⅓ of this material is unavailable in any other current edition! 46 plays from Ancient Greece, Rome, Medieval Europe, France, Germany, Italy, England, Russia, Scandinavia, India, China, Japan, etc. — including classic authors like Aeschylus, Sophocles, Euripides, Aristophanes, Plautus, Marlowe, Jonson, Farquhar, Goldsmith, Cervantes, Molière, Dumas, Goethe, Schiller, Ibsen, and many others. This creative collection avoids hackneyed material and includes only completely first-rate works which are relatively little known or difficult to obtain. "The most comprehensive collection of important plays from all literature available in English," SAT. REV. OF LITERATURE. Introduction. Reading lists. 2 volumes. 1364pp. 5⅜ x 8.
Vol. 1, T57 Paperbound **$2.25**
Vol. 2, T59 Paperbound **$2.50**

MASTERPIECES OF THE RUSSIAN DRAMA, edited with introduction by G. R. Noyes. This only comprehensive anthology of Russian drama ever published in English offers complete texts, in 1st-rate modern translations, of 12 plays covering 200 years. Vol. 1: "The Young Hopeful," Fonvisin; "Wit Works Woe," Griboyedov; "The Inspector General," Gogol; "A Month in the Country," Turgenev; "The Poor Bride," Ostrovsky; "A Bitter Fate," Pisemsky. Vol. 2: "The Death of Ivan the Terrible," Alexey Tolstoy "The Power of Darkness," Lev Tolstoy; "The Lower Depths," Gorky; "The Cherry Orchard," Chekhov; "Professor Storitsyn," Andreyev; "Mystery Bouffe," Mayakovsky. Bibliography. Total of 902pp. 5⅜ x 8.
Vol. 1 T647 Paperbound **$2.00**
Vol. 2 T648 Paperbound **$2.00**

EUGENE O'NEILL: THE MAN AND HIS PLAYS, B. H. Clark. Introduction to O'Neill's life and work. Clark analyzes each play from the early THE WEB to the recently produced MOON FOR THE MISBEGOTTEN and THE ICEMAN COMETH revealing the environmental and dramatic influences necessary for a complete understanding of these important works. Bibliography. Appendices. Index. ix + 182pp. 5⅜ x 8.
T379 Paperbound **$1.35**

THE HEART OF THOREAU'S JOURNALS, edited by O. Shepard. The best general selection from Thoreau's voluminous (and rare) journals. This intimate record of thoughts and observations reveals the full Thoreau and his intellectual development more accurately than any of his published works: self-conflict between the scientific observer and the poet, reflections on transcendental philosophy, involvement in the tragedies of neighbors and national causes, etc. New preface, notes, introductions. xii + 228pp. 5⅜ x 8.
T741 Paperbound **$1.50**

H. D. THOREAU: A WRITER'S JOURNAL, edited by L. Stapleton. A unique new selection from the Journals concentrating on Thoreau's growth as a conscious literary artist, the ideals and purposes of his art. Most of the material has never before appeared outside of the complete 14-volume edition. Contains vital insights on Thoreau's projected book on Concord, thoughts on the nature of men and government, indignation with slavery, sources of inspiration, goals in life. Index. xxxiii + 234pp. 5⅜ x 8.
T678 Paperbound **$1.65**

THE HEART OF EMERSON'S JOURNALS, edited by Bliss Perry. Best of these revealing Journals, originally 10 volumes, presented in a one volume edition. Talks with Channing, Hawthorne, Thoreau, and Bronson Alcott; impressions of Webster, Everett, John Brown, and Lincoln; records of moments of sudden understanding, vision, and solitary ecstasy. "The essays do not reveal the power of Emerson's mind . . . as do these hasty and informal writings," N.Y. Times. Preface by Bliss Perry. Index. xiii + 357pp. 5⅜ x 8.
T477 Paperbound **$1.85**

FOUNDERS OF THE MIDDLE AGES, E. K. Rand. This is the best non-technical discussion of the transformation of Latin pagan culture into medieval civilization. Covering such figures as Tertullian, Gregory, Jerome, Boethius, Augustine, the Neoplatonists, and many other literary men, educators, classicists, and humanists, this book is a storehouse of information presented clearly and simply for the intelligent non-specialist. "Thoughtful, beautifully written," AMERICAN HISTORICAL REVIEW. "Extraordinarily accurate," Richard McKeon, THE NATION. ix + 365pp. 5⅜ x 8.
T369 Paperbound **$2.00**

PLAY-MAKING: A MANUAL OF CRAFTSMANSHIP, William Archer. With an extensive, new introduction by John Gassner, Yale Univ. The permanently essential requirements of solid play construction are set down in clear, practical language: theme, exposition, foreshadowing, tension, obligatory scene, peripety, dialogue, character, psychology, other topics. This book has been one of the most influential elements in the modern theatre, and almost everything said on the subject since is contained explicitly or implicitly within its covers. Bibliography. Index. xliii + 277pp. 5⅜ x 8.
T651 Paperbound **$1.75**

HAMBURG DRAMATURGY, G. E. Lessing. One of the most brilliant of German playwrights of the eighteenth-century age of criticism analyzes the complex of theory and tradition that constitutes the world of theater. These 104 essays on aesthetic theory helped demolish the regime of French classicism, opening the door to psychological and social realism, romanticism. Subjects include the original functions of tragedy; drama as the rational world; the meaning of pity and fear, pity and fear as means for purgation and other Aristotelian concepts; genius and creative force; interdependence of poet's language and actor's interpretation; truth and authenticity; etc. A basic and enlightening study for anyone interested in aesthetics and ideas, from the philosopher to the theatergoer. Introduction by Prof. Victor Lange. xxii + 265pp. 4½ x 6⅜.
T32 Paperbound **$1.45**

Language Books and Records

GERMAN: HOW TO SPEAK AND WRITE IT. AN INFORMAL CONVERSATIONAL METHOD FOR SELF STUDY, Joseph Rosenberg. Eminently useful for self study because of concentration on elementary stages of learning. Also provides teachers with remarkable variety of aids: 28 full- and double-page sketches with pertinent items numbered and identified in German and English; German proverbs, jokes; grammar, idiom studies; extensive practice exercises. The most interesting introduction to German available, full of amusing illustrations, photographs of cities and landmarks in German-speaking cities, cultural information subtly woven into conversational material. Includes summary of grammar, guide to letter writing, study guide to German literature by Dr. Richard Friedenthal. Index. 400 illustrations. 384pp. 5⅜ x 8½.
T271 Paperbound **$2.00**

FRENCH: HOW TO SPEAK AND WRITE IT. AN INFORMAL CONVERSATIONAL METHOD FOR SELF STUDY, Joseph Lemaitre. Even the absolute beginner can acquire a solid foundation for further study from this delightful elementary course. Photographs, sketches and drawings, sparkling colloquial conversations on a wide variety of topics (including French culture and custom), French sayings and quips, are some of aids used to demonstrate rather than merely describe the language. Thorough yet surprisingly entertaining approach, excellent for teaching and for self study. Comprehensive analysis of pronunciation, practice exercises and appendices of verb tables, additional vocabulary, other useful material. Index. Appendix. 400 illustrations. 416pp. 5⅜ x 8½.
T268 Paperbound **$2.00**

DICTIONARY OF SPOKEN SPANISH, Spanish-English, English-Spanish. Compiled from spoken Spanish, emphasizing idiom and colloquial usage in both Castilian and Latin-American. More than 16,000 entries containing over 25,000 idioms—the largest list of idiomatic constructions ever published. Complete sentences given, indexed under single words—language in immediately useable form, for travellers, businessmen, students, etc. 25 page introduction provides rapid survey of sounds, grammar, syntax, with full consideration of irregular verbs. Especially apt in modern treatment of phrases and structure. 17 page glossary gives translations of geographical names, money values, numbers, national holidays, important street signs, useful expressions of high frequency, plus unique 7 page glossary of Spanish and Spanish-American foods and dishes. Originally published as War Department Technical Manual TM 30-900. iv + 513pp. 5⅜ x 8.
T495 Paperbound **$1.75**

SPEAK MY LANGUAGE: SPANISH FOR YOUNG BEGINNERS, M. Ahlman, Z. Gilbert. Records provide one of the best, and most entertaining, methods of introducing a foreign language to children. Within the framework of a train trip from Portugal to Spain, an English-speaking child is introduced to Spanish by a native companion. (Adapted from a successful radio program of the N. Y. State Educational Department.) Though a continuous story, there are a dozen specific categories of expressions, including greetings, numbers, time, weather, food, clothes, family members, etc. Drill is combined with poetry and contextual use. Authentic background music is heard. An accompanying book enables a reader to follow the records, and includes a vocabulary of over 350 recorded expressions. Two 10″ 33⅓ records, total of 40 minutes. Book. 40 illustrations. 69pp. 5¼ x 10½.
T890 The set **$4.95**

AN ENGLISH-FRENCH-GERMAN-SPANISH WORD FREQUENCY DICTIONARY, H. S. Eaton. An indispensable language study aid, this is a semantic frequency list of the 6000 most frequently used words in 4 languages—24,000 words in all. The lists, based on concepts rather than words alone, and containing all modern, exact, and idiomatic vocabulary, are arranged side by side to form a unique 4-language dictionary. A simple key indicates the importance of the individual words within each language. Over 200 pages of separate indexes for each language enable you to locate individual words at a glance. Will help language teachers and students, authors of textbooks, grammars, and language tests to compare concepts in the various languages and to concentrate on basic vocabulary, avoiding uncommon and obsolete words. 2 Appendixes. xxi + 441pp. 6½ x 9¼.
T738 Paperbound **$2.45**

NEW RUSSIAN-ENGLISH AND ENGLISH-RUSSIAN DICTIONARY, M. A. O'Brien. Over 70,000 entries in the new orthography! Many idiomatic uses and colloquialisms which form the basis of actual speech. Irregular verbs, perfective and imperfective aspects, regular and irregular sound changes, and other features. One of the few dictionaries where accent changes within the conjugation of verbs and the declension of nouns are fully indicated. "One of the best," Prof. E. J. Simmons, Cornell. First names, geographical terms, bibliography, etc. 738pp. 4½ x 6¼.
T208 Paperbound **$2.00**

96 MOST USEFUL PHRASES FOR TOURISTS AND STUDENTS in English, French, Spanish, German, Italian. A handy folder you'll want to carry with you. How to say "Excuse me," "How much is it?", "Write it down, please," etc., in four foreign languages. Copies limited, no more than 1 to a customer.
FREE

Teach Yourself

These British books are the most effective series of home study books on the market! With no outside help they will teach you as much as is necessary to have a good background in each subject, in many cases offering as much material as a similar high school or college course. They are carefully planned, written by foremost British educators, and amply provided with test questions and problems for you to check your progress; the mathematics books are especially rich in examples and problems. Do not confuse them with skimpy outlines or ordinary school texts or vague generalized popularizations; each book is complete in itself, full without being overdetailed, and designed to give you an easily-acquired branch of knowledge.

TEACH YOURSELF ALGEBRA, P. Abbott. The equivalent of a thorough high school course, up through logarithms. 52 illus. 307pp. 4¼ x 7. T680 Clothbound **$2.00**

TEACH YOURSELF GEOMETRY, P. Abbott. Plane and solid geometry, covering about a year of plane and six months of solid. 268 illus. 344pp. 4½ x 7. T681 Clothbound **$2.00**

TEACH YOURSELF TRIGONOMETRY, P. Abbott. Background of algebra and geometry will enable you to get equivalent of elementary college course. Tables. 102 illus. 204pp. 4½ x 7. T682 Clothbound **$2.00**

TEACH YOURSELF THE CALCULUS, P. Abbott. With algebra and trigonometry you will be able to acquire a good working knowledge of elementary integral calculus and differential calculus. Excellent supplement to any course textbook. 380pp. 4¼ x 7. T683 Clothbound **$2.00**

TEACH YOURSELF THE SLIDE RULE, B. Snodgrass. Basic principles clearly explained, with many applications in engineering, business, general figuring, will enable you to pick up very useful skill. 10 illus. 207pp. 4¼ x 7. T684 Clothbound **$2.00**

TEACH YOURSELF MECHANICS, P. Abbott. Equivalent of part course on elementary college level, with lever, parallelogram of force, friction, laws of motion, gases, etc. Fine introduction before more advanced course. 163 illus. 271pp. 4½ x 7. T685 Clothbound **$2.00**

TEACH YOURSELF ELECTRICITY, C. W. Wilman. Current, resistance, voltage, Ohm's law, circuits, generators, motors, transformers, etc. Non-mathematical as much as possible. 115 illus. 184pp. 4¼ x 7. T230 Clothbound **$2.00**

TEACH YOURSELF HEAT ENGINES E. DeVille. Steam and internal combustion engines; non-mathematical introduction for student, for layman wishing background, refresher for advanced student. 76 illus. 217pp. 4¼ x 7. T237 Clothbound **$2.00**

TEACH YOURSELF TO PLAY THE PIANO, King Palmer. Companion and supplement to lessons or self study. Handy reference, too. Nature of instrument, elementary musical theory, technique of playing, interpretation, etc. 60 illus. 144pp. 4¼ x 7. T959 Clothbound **$2.00**

TEACH YOURSELF HERALDRY AND GENEALOGY, L. G. Pine. Modern work, avoiding romantic and overpopular misconceptions. Editor of new Burke presents detailed information and commentary down to present. Best general survey. 50 illus. glossary; 129pp. 4¼ x 7. T962 Clothbound **$2.00**

TEACH YOURSELF HANDWRITING, John L. Dumpleton. Basic Chancery cursive style is popular and easy to learn. Many diagrams. 114 illus. 192pp. 4¼ x 7. T960 Clothbound **$2.00**

TEACH YOURSELF CARD GAMES FOR TWO, Kenneth Konstam. Many first-rate games, including old favorites like cribbage and gin and canasta as well as new lesser-known games. Extremely interesting for cards enthusiast. 60 illus. 150pp. 4¼ x 7. T963 Clothbound **$2.00**

TEACH YOURSELF GUIDEBOOK TO THE DRAMA, Luis Vargas. Clear, rapid survey of changing fashions and forms from Aeschylus to Tennessee Williams, in all major European traditions. Plot summaries, critical comments, etc. Equivalent of a college drama course; fine cultural background 224pp. 4¼ x 7. T961 Clothbound **$2.00**

TEACH YOURSELF THE ORGAN, Francis Routh. Excellent compendium of background material for everyone interested in organ music, whether as listener or player. 27 musical illus. 158pp. 4¼ x 7. T977 Clothbound **$2.00**

TEACH YOURSELF TO STUDY SCULPTURE, William Gaunt. Noted British cultural historian surveys culture from Greeks, primitive world, to moderns. Equivalent of college survey course. 23 figures, 40 photos. 158pp. 4¼ x 7. T976 Clothbound **$2.00**

Miscellaneous

THE COMPLETE KANO JIU-JITSU (JUDO), H. I. Hancock and K. Higashi. Most comprehensive guide to judo, referred to as outstanding work by Encyclopaedia Britannica. Complete authentic Japanese system of 160 holds and throws, including the most spectacular, fully illustrated with 487 photos. Full text explains leverage, weight centers, pressure points, special tricks, etc.; shows how to protect yourself from almost any manner of attack though your attacker may have the initial advantage of strength and surprise. This authentic Kano system should not be confused with the many American imitations. xii + 500pp. 5⅜ x 8.
T639 Paperbound **$2.00**

THE MEMOIRS OF JACQUES CASANOVA. Splendid self-revelation by history's most engaging scoundrel—utterly dishonest with women and money, yet highly intelligent and observant. Here are all the famous duels, amours, banishments, thefts, treacheries, and imprisonments all over Europe: a life lived to the fullest and recounted with gusto in one of the greatest autobiographies of all time. What is more, these Memoirs are also one of the most trustworthy and valuable documents we have on the society and culture of the extravagant 18th century. Here are Voltaire, Louis XV, Catherine the Great, cardinals, castrati, pimps, and pawnbrokers—an entire glittering civilization unfolding before you with an unparalleled sense of actuality. Translated by Arthur Machen. Edited by F. A. Blossom. Introduction by Arthur Symons. Illustrated by Rockwell Kent. Total of xlviii + 2216pp. 5⅜ x 8.
T338 Vol I   Paperbound **$2.00**
T339 Vol II Paperbound **$2.00**
T340 Vol III Paperbound **$2.00**
The set **$6.00**

BARNUM'S OWN STORY, P. T. Barnum. The astonishingly frank and gratifyingly well-written autobiography of the master showman and pioneer publicity man reveals the truth about his early career, his famous hoaxes (such as the Fejee Mermaid and the Woolly Horse), his amazing commercial ventures, his fling in politics, his feuds and friendships, his failures and surprising comebacks. A vast panorama of 19th century America's mores, amusements, and vitality. 66 new illustrations in this edition. xii + 500pp. 5⅜ x 8.
T764 Paperbound **$1.65**

THE STORY OF THE TITANIC AS TOLD BY ITS SURVIVORS, ed. by Jack Winocour. Most significant accounts of most overpowering naval disaster of modern times: all 4 authors were survivors. Includes 2 full-length, unabridged books: "The Loss of the S.S. Titanic," by Laurence Beesley, "The Truth about the Titanic," by Col. Archibald Gracie; 6 pertinent chapters from "Titanic and Other Ships," autobiography of only officer to survive, Second Officer Charles Lightoller; and a short, dramatic account by the Titanic's wireless operator, Harold Bride. 26 illus. 368pp. 5⅜ x 8. T610 Paperbound **$1.50**

THE PHYSIOLOGY OF TASTE, Jean Anthelme Brillat-Savarin. Humorous, satirical, witty, and personal classic on joys of food and drink by 18th century French politician, litterateur. Treats the science of gastronomy, erotic value of truffles, Parisian restaurants, drinking contests; gives recipes for tunny omelette, pheasant, Swiss fondue, etc. Only modern translation of original French edition. Introduction. 41 illus. 346pp. 5⅝ x 8⅜.
T591 Paperbound **$1.50**

THE ART OF THE STORY-TELLER, M. L. Shedlock. This classic in the field of effective storytelling is regarded by librarians, story-tellers, and educators as the finest and most lucid book on the subject. The author considers the nature of the story, the difficulties of communicating stories to children, the artifices used in story-telling, how to obtain and maintain the effect of the story, and, of extreme importance, the elements to seek and those to avoid in selecting material. A 99-page selection of Miss Shedlock's most effective stories and an extensive bibliography of further material by Eulalie Steinmetz enhance the book's usefulness. xxi + 320pp. 5⅜ x 8. T635 Paperbound **$1.50**

CREATIVE POWER: THE EDUCATION OF YOUTH IN THE CREATIVE ARTS, Hughes Mearns. In first printing considered revolutionary in its dynamic, progressive approach to teaching the creative arts; now accepted as one of the most effective and valuable approaches yet formulated. Based on the belief that every child has something to contribute, it provides in a stimulating manner invaluable and inspired teaching insights, to stimulate children's latent powers of creative expression in drama, poetry, music, writing, etc. Mearns's methods were developed in his famous experimental classes in creative education at the Lincoln School of Teachers College, Columbia Univ. Named one of the 20 foremost books on education in recent times by National Education Association. New enlarged revised 2nd edition. Introduction. 272pp. 5⅜ x 8. T490 Paperbound **$1.75**

FREE AND INEXPENSIVE EDUCATIONAL AIDS, T. J. Pepe, Superintendent of Schools, Southbury, Connecticut. An up-to-date listing of over 1500 booklets, films, charts, etc. 5% costs less than 25¢; 1% costs more; 94% is yours for the asking. Use this material privately, or in schools from elementary to college, for discussion, vocational guidance, projects. 59 categories include health, trucking, textiles, language, weather, the blood, office practice, wild life, atomic energy, other important topics. Each item described according to contents, number of pages or running time, level. All material is educationally sound, and without political or company bias. 1st publication. Second, revised edition. Index. 244pp. 5⅜ x 8.
T663 Paperbound **$1.50**

THE ROMANCE OF WORDS, E. Weekley. An entertaining collection of unusual word-histories that tracks down for the general reader the origins of more than 2000 common words and phrases in English (including British and American slang): discoveries often surprising, often humorous, that help trace vast chains of commerce in products and ideas. There are Arabic trade words, cowboy words, origins of family names, phonetic accidents, curious wanderings, folk-etymologies, etc. Index. xiii + 210pp. 5⅜ x 8. **T710 Paperbound $1.25**

PHRASE AND WORD ORIGINS: A STUDY OF FAMILIAR EXPRESSIONS, A. H. Holt. One of the most entertaining books on the unexpected origins and colorful histories of words and phrases, based on sound scholarship, but written primarily for the layman. Over 1200 phrases and 1000 separate words are covered, with many quotations, and the results of the most modern linguistic and historical researches. "A right jolly book Mr. Holt has made," N. Y. Times. v + 254pp. 5⅜ x 8. **T758 Paperbound $1.35**

AMATEUR WINE MAKING, S. M. Tritton. Now, with only modest equipment and no prior knowledge, you can make your own fine table wines. A practical handbook, this covers every type of grape wine, as well as fruit, flower, herb, vegetable, and cereal wines, and many kinds of mead, cider, and beer. Every question you might have is answered, and there is a valuable discussion of what can go wrong at various stages along the way. Special supplement of yeasts and American sources of supply. 13 tables. 32 illustrations. Glossary. Index. 239pp. 5½ x 8½. **T514 Clothbound $4.00**

SAILING ALONE AROUND THE WORLD. Captain Joshua Slocum. A great modern classic in a convenient inexpensive edition. Captain Slocum's account of his single-handed voyage around the world in a 34 foot boat which he rebuilt himself. A nearly unparalleled feat of seamanship told with vigor, wit, imagination, and great descriptive power. "A nautical equivalent of Thoreau's account," Van Wyck Brooks. 67 illustrations. 308pp. 5⅜ x 8. **T326 Paperbound $1.00**

FARES, PLEASE! by J. A. Miller. Authoritative, comprehensive, and entertaining history of local public transit from its inception to its most recent developments: trolleys, horsecars, streetcars, buses, elevateds, subways, along with monorails, "road-railers," and a host of other extraordinary vehicles. Here are all the flamboyant personalities involved, the vehement arguments, the unusual information, and all the nostalgia. "Interesting facts brought into especially vivid life," N. Y. Times. New preface. 152 illustrations, 4 new. Bibliography. xix + 204pp. 5⅜ x 8. **T671 Paperbound $1.50**

HOAXES, C. D. MacDougall. Shows how art, science, history, journalism can be perverted for private purposes. Hours of delightful entertainment and a work of scholarly value, this often shocking book tells of the deliberate creation of nonsense news, the Cardiff giant, Shakespeare forgeries, the Loch Ness monster, Biblical frauds, political schemes, literary hoaxers like Chatterton, Ossian, the disumbrationist school of painting, the lady in black at Valentino's tomb, and over 250 others. It will probably reveal the truth about a few things you've believed, and help you spot more readily the editorial "gander" and planted publicity release. "A stupendous colleotion . . . and shrewd analysis." New Yorker. New revised edition. 54 photographs. Index. 320pp. 5⅜ x 8. **T465 Paperbound $1.75**

A HISTORY OF THE WARFARE OF SCIENCE WITH THEOLOGY IN CHRISTENDOM, A. D. White. Most thorough account ever written of the great religious-scientific battles shows gradual victory of science over ignorant, harmful beliefs. Attacks on theory of evolution; attacks on Galileo; great medieval plagues caused by belief in devil-origin of disease; attacks on Franklin's experiments with electricity; the witches of Salem; scores more that will amaze you. Author, co-founder and first president of Cornell U., writes with vast scholarly background, but in clear, readable prose. Acclaimed as classic effort in America to do away with superstition. Index. Total of 928pp. 5⅜ x 8. **T608 Vol I Paperbound $1.85**
T609 Vol II Paperbound $1.85

THE SHIP OF FOOLS, Sebastian Brant. First printed in 1494 in Basel, this amusing book swept Europe, was translated into almost every important language, and was a best-seller for centuries. That it is still living and vital is shown by recent developments in publishing. This is the only English translation of this work, and it recaptures in lively, modern verse all the wit and insights of the original, in satirizations of foibles and vices: greed, adultery, envy, hatred, sloth, profiteering, etc. This will long remain the definitive English edition, for Professor Zeydel has provided biography of Brant, bibliography, publishing history, influences, etc. Complete reprint of 1944 edition. Translated by Professor E. Zeydel, University of Cincinnati. All 114 original woodcut illustrations. viii + 399pp. 5½ x 8⅝. **T266 Paperbound $2.00**

ERASMUS, A STUDY OF HIS LIFE, IDEALS AND PLACE IN HISTORY, Preserved Smith. This is the standard English biography and evaluation of the great Netherlands humanist Desiderius Erasmus. Written by one of the foremost American historians it covers all aspects of Erasmus's life, his influence in the religious quarrels of the Reformation, his overwhelming role in the field of letters, and his importance in the emergence of the new world view of the Northern Renaissance. This is not only a work of great scholarship, it is also an extremely interesting, vital portrait of a great man. 8 illustrations. xiv + 479pp. 5⅝ x 8½. **T331 Paperbound $2.00**

New Books

101 PATCHWORK PATTERNS, Ruby Short McKim. With no more ability than the fundamentals of ordinary sewing, you will learn to make over 100 beautiful quilts: flowers, rainbows, Irish chains, fish and bird designs, leaf designs, unusual geometric patterns, many others. Cutting designs carefully diagrammed and described, suggestions for materials, yardage estimates, step-by-step instructions, plus entertaining stories of origins of quilt names, other folklore. Revised 1962. 101 full-sized patterns. 140 illustrations. Index. 128pp. 7⅞ x 10¾.
T773 Paperbound **$1.85**

ESSENTIAL GRAMMAR SERIES
By concentrating on the essential core of material that constitutes the semantically most important forms and areas of a language and by stressing explanation (often bringing parallel English forms into the discussion) rather than rote memory, this new series of grammar books is among the handiest language aids ever devised. Designed by linguists and teachers for adults with limited learning objectives and learning time, these books omit nothing important, yet they teach more usable language material and do it more quickly and permanently than any other self-study material. Clear and rigidly economical, they concentrate upon immediately usable language material, logically organized so that related material is always presented together. Any reader of typical capability can use them to refresh his grasp of language, to supplement self-study language records or conventional grammars used in schools, or to begin language study on his own. Now available:

ESSENTIAL GERMAN GRAMMAR, Dr. Guy Stern & E. F. Bleiler. Index. Glossary of terms. 128pp. 5⅜ x 8.
T422 Paperbound **$1.00**

ESSENTIAL FRENCH GRAMMAR, Dr. Seymour Resnick. Index. Cognate list. Glossary. 159pp. 5⅜ x 8.
T419 Paperbound **$1.00**

ESSENTIAL ITALIAN GRAMMAR, Dr. Olga Ragusa. Index. Glossary. 111pp. 5⅜ x 8.
T779 Paperbound **$1.00**

ESSENTIAL SPANISH GRAMMAR, Dr. Seymour Resnick. Index. 50-page cognate list. Glossary. 138pp. 5⅜ x 8.
T780 Paperbound **$1.00**

PHILOSOPHIES OF MUSIC HISTORY: A Study of General Histories of Music, 1600-1960, Warren D. Allen. Unquestionably one of the most significant documents yet to appear in musicology, this thorough survey covers the entire field of historical research in music. An influential masterpiece of scholarship, it includes early music histories; theories on the ethos of music; lexicons, dictionaries and encyclopedias of music; musical historiography through the centuries; philosophies of music history; scores of related topics. Copiously documented. New preface brings work up to 1960. Index. 317-item bibliography. 9 illustrations; 3 full-page plates. 5⅜ x 8½. xxxiv + 382pp.
T282 Paperbound **$2.00**

MR. DOOLEY ON IVRYTHING AND IVRYBODY, Finley Peter Dunne. The largest collection in print of hilarious utterances by the irrepressible Irishman of Archey Street, one of the most vital characters in American fiction. Gathered from the half dozen books that appeared during the height of Mr. Dooley's popularity, these 102 pieces are all unaltered and uncut, and they are all remarkably fresh and pertinent even today. Selected and edited by Robert Hutchinson. 5⅜ x 8½. xii + 244p.
T626 Paperbound **$1.00**

TREATISE ON PHYSIOLOGICAL OPTICS, Hermann von Helmholtz. Despite new investigations, this important work will probably remain preeminent. Contains everything known about physiological optics up to 1925, covering scores of topics under the general headings of dioptrics of the eye, sensations of vision, and perecptions of vision. Von Helmholtz's voluminous data are all included, as are extensive supplementary matter incorporated into the third German edition, new material prepared for 1925 English edition, and copious textual annotations by J. P. C. Southall. The most exhaustive treatise ever prepared on the subject, it has behind it a list of contributors that will never again be duplicated. Translated and edited by J. P. C. Southall. Bibliography. Indexes. 312 illustrations. 3 volumes bound as 2. Total of 1749pp. 5⅜ x 8.
S15-16 Two volume set, Clothbound **$15.00**

THE ARTISTIC ANATOMY OF TREES, Rex Vicat Cole. Even the novice with but an elementary knowledge of drawing and none of the structure of trees can learn to draw, paint trees from this systematic, lucid instruction book. Copiously illustrated with the author's own sketches, diagrams, and 50 paintings from the early Renaissance to today, it covers composition; structure of twigs, boughs, buds, branch systems; outline forms of major species; how leaf is set on twig; flowers and fruit and their arrangement; etc. 500 illustrations. Bibliography. Indexes. 347pp. 5⅜ x 8.
T1016 Clothbound **$4.50**

CHANCE, LUCK AND STATISTICS, H. C. Levinson. The theory of chance, or probability, and the science of statistics presented in simple, non-technical language. Covers fundamentals by analyzing games of chance, then applies those fundamentals to immigration and birth rates, operations research, stock speculation, insurance rates, advertising, and other fields. Excellent course supplement and a delightful introduction for non-mathematicians. Formerly "The Science of Chance." Index. xiv + 356pp. 5⅜ x 8. T1007 Paperbound **$1.85**

THROUGH THE ALIMENTARY CANAL WITH GUN AND CAMERA: A Fascinating Trip to the Interior, George S. Chappell. An intrepid explorer, better known as a major American humorist, accompanied by imaginary camera-man and botanist, conducts this unforgettably hilarious journey to the human interior. Wildly imaginative, his account satirizes academic pomposity, parodies cliché-ridden travel literature, and cleverly uses facts of physiology for comic purposes. All the original line drawings by Otto Soglow are included to add to the merriment. Preface by Robert Benchley. 17 illustrations. xii + 116pp. 5⅜ x 8½. T376 Paperbound **$1.00**

TALKS TO TEACHERS ON PSYCHOLOGY and to Students on Some of Life's Ideals, William James. America's greatest psychologist invests these lectures with immense personal charm, invaluable insights, and superb literary style. 15 Harvard lectures, 3 lectures delivered to students in New England touch upon psychology and the teaching of art, stream of consciousness, the child as a behaving organism, education and behavior, association of ideas, the gospel of relaxation, what makes life significant, and other related topics. Interesting, and still vital pedagogy. x + 146pp. 5⅜ x 8½. T261 Paperbound **$1.00**

A WHIMSEY ANTHOLOGY, collected by Carolyn Wells. Delightful verse on the lighter side: logical whimsies, poems shaped like decanters and flagons, lipograms and acrostics, alliterative verse, enigmas and charades, anagrams, linguistic and dialectic verse, tongue twisters, limericks, travesties, and just about very other kind of whimsical poetry ever written. Works by Edward Lear, Gelett Burgess, Poe, Lewis Carroll, Henley, Robert Herrick, Christina Rossetti, scores of other poets will entertain and amuse you for hours. Index. xiv + 221pp. 5⅜ x 8½. T1020 Paperbound **$1.25**

LANDSCAPE PAINTING, R. O. Dunlop. A distinguished modern artist is a perfect guide to the aspiring landscape painter. This practical book imparts to even the uninitiated valuable methods and techniques. Useful advice is interwoven throughout a fascinating illustrated history of landscape painting, from Ma Yüan to Picasso. 60 half-tone reproductions of works by Giotto, Giovanni Bellini, Piero della Francesca, Tintoretto, Giorgione, Raphael, Van Ruisdael, Poussin, Gainsborough, Monet, Cezanne, Seurat, Picasso, many others. Total of 71 illustrations, 4 in color. Index. 192pp. 7⅜ x 10. T1018 Clothbound **$6.00**

PRACTICAL LANDSCAPE PAINTING, Adrian Stokes. A complete course in landscape painting that trains the senses to perceive as well as the hand to apply the principles underlying the pictorial aspect of nature. Author fully explains tools, value and nature of various colors, and instructs beginners in clear, simple terms how to apply them. Places strong emphasis on drawing and composition, foundations often neglected in painting texts. Includes pictorial-textual survey of the art from Ancient China to the present, with helpful critical comments and numerous diagrams illustrating every stage. 93 illustrations. Index. 256pp. 5⅜ x 8. T1017 Clothbound **$3.75**

PELLUCIDAR, THREE NOVELS: AT THE EARTH'S CORE, PELLUCIDAR, TANAR OF PELLUCIDAR, Edgar Rice Burroughs. The first three novels of adventure in the thrill-filled world within the hollow interior of the earth. David Innes's mechanical mole drills through the outer crust and precipitates him into an astonishing world. Among Burroughs's most popular work. Illustrations by J. Allan St. John. 5⅜ x 8½. T1051 Paperbound **$2.00**
T1050 Clothbound **$3.75**

JOE MILLER'S JESTS OR, THE WITS VADE-MECUM. Facsimile of the first edition of famous 18th century collection of repartees, bons mots, puns and jokes, the father of the humor anthology. A first-hand look at the taste of fashionable London in the Age of Pope. 247 entertaining anecdotes, many involving well-known personages such as Colley Cibber, Sir Thomas More, Rabelais, rich in humor, historic interest. New introduction contains biographical information on Joe Miller, fascinating history of his enduring collection, bibliographical information on collections of comic material. Introduction by Robert Hutchinson. 96pp. 5⅜ x 8½. Paperbound **$1.00**

THE HUMOROUS WORLD OF JEROME K. JEROME. Complete essays and extensive passages from nine out-of-print books ("Three Men on Wheels," "Novel Notes," "Told After Supper," "Sketches in Lavender, Blue and Green," "American Wives and Others," 4 more) by a highly original humorist, author of the novel "Three Men in a Boat." Human nature is JKJ's subject: the problems of husbands, of wives, of tourists, of the human animal trapped in the drawing room. His sympathetic acceptance of the shortcomings of his race and his ability to see humor in almost any situation make this a treasure for those who know his work and a pleasant surprise for those who don't. Edited and with an introduction by Robert Hutchinson. xii + 260pp. 5⅜ x 8½. T58 Paperbound **$1.00**

CATALOGUE OF DOVER BOOKS

GEOMETRY OF FOUR DIMENSIONS, H. P. Manning. Unique in English as a clear, concise introduction to this fascinating subject. Treatment is primarily synthetic and Euclidean, although hyperplanes and hyperspheres at infinity are considered by non-Euclidean forms. Historical introduction and foundations of 4-dimensional geometry; perpendicularity; simple angles; angles of planes; higher order; symmetry; order, motion; hyperpyramids, hypercones, hyperspheres; figures with parallel elements; volume, hypervolume in space; regular polyhedroids. Glossary of terms. 74 illustrations. ix + 348pp. 5⅜ x 8.   **S182 Paperbound $2.00**

PAPER FOLDING FOR BEGINNERS, W. D. Murray and F. J. Rigney. A delightful introduction to the varied and entertaining Japanese art of origami (paper folding), with a full, crystal-clear text that anticipates every difficulty; over 275 clearly labeled diagrams of all important stages in creation. You get results at each stage, since complex figures are logically developed from simpler ones. 43 different pieces are explained: sailboats, frogs, roosters, etc. 6 photographic plates. 279 diagrams. 95pp. 5⅝ x 8⅜.   **T713 Paperbound $1.00**

SATELLITES AND SCIENTIFIC RESEARCH, D. King-Hele. An up-to-the-minute non-technical account of the man-made satellites and the discoveries they have yielded up to September of 1961. Brings together information hitherto published only in hard-to-get scientific journals. Includes the life history of a typical satellite, methods of tracking, new information on the shape of the earth, zones of radiation, etc. Over 60 diagrams and 6 photographs. Mathematical appendix. Bibliography of over 100 items. Index. xii + 180pp. 5⅜ x 8½.   **T703 Paperbound $2.00**

LOUIS PASTEUR, S. J. Holmes. A brief, very clear, and warmly understanding biography of the great French scientist by a former Professor of Zoology in the University of California. Traces his home life, the fortunate effects of his education, his early researches and first theses, and his constant struggle with superstition and institutionalism in his work on microorganisms, fermentation, anthrax, rabies, etc. New preface by the author. 159pp. 5⅜ x 8.   **T197 Paperbound $1.00**

THE ENJOYMENT OF CHESS PROBLEMS, K. S. Howard. A classic treatise on this minor art by an internationally recognized authority that gives a basic knowledge of terms and themes for the everyday chess player as well as the problem fan: 7 chapters on the two-mover; 7 more on 3- and 4-move problems; a chapter on selfmates; and much more. "The most important one-volume contribution originating solely in the U.S.A.," Alain White. 200 diagrams. Index. Solutions, viii + 212pp. 5⅜ x 8.   **T742 Paperbound $1.25**

SAM LOYD AND HIS CHESS PROBLEMS, Alain C. White. Loyd was (for all practical purposes) the father of the American chess problem and his protégé and successor presents here the diamonds of his production, chess problems embodying a whimsy and bizarre fancy entirely unique. More than 725 in all, ranging from two-move to extremely elaborate five-movers, including Loyd's contributions to chess oddities—problems in which pieces are arranged to form initials, figures, other by-paths of chess problem found nowhere else. Classified according to major concept, with full text analyzing problems, containing selections from Loyd's own writings. A classic to challenge your ingenuity, increase your skill. Corrected republication of 1913 edition. Over 750 diagrams and illustrations. 744 problems with solutions. 471pp. 5⅜ x 8½.   **T928 Paperbound $2.00**

FABLES IN SLANG & MORE FABLES IN SLANG, George Ade. 2 complete books of major American humorist in pungent colloquial tradition of Twain, Billings. 1st reprinting in over 30 years includes "The Two Mandolin Players and the Willing Performer," "The Base Ball Fan Who Took the Only Known Cure," "The Slim Girl Who Tried to Keep a Date that was Never Made," 42 other tales of eccentric, perverse, but always funny characters. "Touch of genius," H. L. Mencken. New introduction by E. F. Bleiler. 86 illus. 208pp. 5⅜ x 8.   **T533 Paperbound $1.00**

Prices subject to change without notice.

Dover publishes books on art, music, philosophy, literature, languages, history, social sciences, psychology, handcrafts, orientalia, puzzles and entertainments, chess, pets and gardens, books explaining science, intermediate and higher mathematics, mathematical physics, engineering, biological sciences, earth sciences, classics of science, etc. Write to:

Dept. catrr.
Dover Publications, Inc.
180 Varick Street, N.Y. 14, N.Y.

1834

DATE DUE

MAY 29 '70			